About Island Press

Since 1984, the nonprofit organization Island Press has been stimulating, shaping, and communicating ideas that are essential for solving environmental problems worldwide. With more than 1,000 titles in print and some 30 new releases each year, we are the nation's leading publisher on environmental issues. We identify innovative thinkers and emerging trends in the environmental field. We work with world-renowned experts and authors to develop cross-disciplinary solutions to environmental challenges.

Island Press designs and executes educational campaigns, in conjunction with our authors, to communicate their critical messages in print, in person, and online using the latest technologies, innovative programs, and the media. Our goal is to reach targeted audiences—scientists, policy makers, environmental advocates, urban planners, the media, and concerned citizens—with information that can be used to create the framework for long-term ecological health and human well-being.

Island Press gratefully acknowledges major support from The Bobolink Foundation, The Curtis and Edith Munson Foundation, The Forrest C. and Frances H. Lattner Foundation, The JPB Foundation, The Kresge Foundation, The Summit Charitable Foundation, Inc., and many other generous organizations and individuals.

The opinions expressed in this book are those of the author(s) and do not necessarily reflect the views of our supporters.

Sustainable Landscape Construction
A Guide to Green Building Outdoors

Third Edition

Sustainable Landscape Construction

A Guide to Green Building Outdoors

Third Edition

Kim Sorvig with J. William Thompson

with drawings by Craig D. Farnsworth, ASLA

Washington | Covelo | London

ISLAND PRESS is a trademark of The Center for Resource Economics.

Keywords: Bio-based products, Biophilic design, Climate change, Ecosystem management, Efficiency, Energy use, Erosion, Graywater, Green infrastructure, Integrated pest management, Irrigation, Landscape architecture, LEED, Life-cycle assessment, Lighting, Machinery, Maintenance, Materials selection, Nontoxic building materials, Paving, Permaculture, Phytoremediation, Recycled materials, Renewable energy, Resilience, Restoration, Site assessment, Soil, Solar, Stormwater, Sustainable Sites Initiative

Library of Congress Control Number: 2017948523

All Island Press books are printed on environmentally responsible materials.

Manufactured in the United States of America
10 9 8 7 6 5 4 3 2

The Fine Print

This book reports information from designers, contractors, manufacturers, academic researchers, and many others. The author has attempted to ensure that all the information herein is credible but has performed no independent testing of these reports. Reporting such information does not constitute endorsement of any product or method. Exclusion of products or methods does not imply a negative evaluation. All trademarks remain property of their respective owners. The author and publisher specifically disclaim any and all liability purported to result from inclusion or exclusion of a product or method in this book.

Variations among regions and sites result in very different performance from the same products and methods, and no assurance can be given that any information reported herein is suitable for any given site. The information reported herein may contain errors and omissions, and even where complete and accurate it is not a substitute for local expertise and professional judgment. Illustrations are not intended as ready-to-build, step-by-step instructions, but rather to depict concepts and processes. The author and publisher specifically disclaim any and all liability for any situation resulting from use or attempted use of this information.

Contents

List of Figures

For location, project, image source, and design firm information, see full captions and main text.

List of Tables

Preface to the Third Edition

Between the release of the first edition of *Sustainable Landscape Construction* in 2000, the second in 2007, and this third edition, the world has changed. Both the environment in which green builders operate and green building itself have gradually changed over nearly two decades. The principles around which this book is organized, however, have not changed, nor have the *main* issues that the landscape professions face in trying to achieve sustainability. Much of what was said in the preface to the second edition remains true today, for better and for worse.

For context, in 2000, Y2K had fizzled, and 9/11 hadn't happened. Hybrid cars were experimental, GPS a clumsy novelty. Al Gore hadn't made a film, let alone won an Oscar. By 2007, the first iPod had been released, as had the last Harry Potter book, and the housing bubble was in the process of bursting, taking so much of the economy, and especially the construction sector, with it.

When Bill Thompson and I first decided to write a book treating landscape construction as a value-driven activity, we weren't quite crying in the rapidly shrinking wilderness. Neither were the streets overrun with like-minded professionals. It took hard work to find some hundred firms whose mission and focus revolved around sustainable design and construction.

As of 2017 there are too many sustainability-driven planning, design, construction, maintenance, and even engineering firms to count accurately. In general this is welcome. The bandwagon has room to carry widely varied degrees of commitment. That, too, makes it difficult to count who's involved.

For better and for worse, sustainability is part of the 2017 mainstream in design and construction. Today's internal debates are about what works best and how to prove it, not about whether it's even worth trying these methods.

The backdrop for sustainable construction has clearly changed economically and politically. First, lingering effects of the housing bubble and recession mean construction money is still tight, and sustainability is now evaluated on its cost-saving capacities as much as on any ecological benefit. Second, the current administration is apparently dedicated to anti-environmentalism, sworn to create an Environment Prevention Agency, roll back renewable incentives, remove protections and funding for clean air and water, deny climate change, and in general stir public sentiment against ecological thinking of any sort. I promise not to linger on these concerns, but clearly, if environmental regulations are scapegoated for all the world's troubles, it will affect business for landscape professionals. Whether there is funding for "green" work, and whether that funding is federal, local, or private, remain to be seen.

It would be easier not to write this book right now.

However, there is still potential for positive results, and the landscape professions still have great (and too often unrealized) potential to impact those results. Membership and donations for progressive causes, including the environment, have soared since the election; the increases are sustained, not one-time. During the past decades, momentum for green building has multiplied fast, and has remained surprisingly independent of political tides. It is worth remembering that energy conservation, clean air and water, and pollution prevention got their biggest boost under Nixon. Momentum for sustainability wasn't stopped by ripping solar panels off the White House; it survived James Watt, Gale Norton, Dick Cheney, and other malign administrators. In fact, spending for green building grew steadily, from $10 billion to nearly $200 billion annually, under *both* George W. Bush and Barack Obama and, allowing for the recession, at fairly similar rates.[1] Each time the federal government has withdrawn policy support, states have stepped up their efforts to create sustainable and resilient communities and to adapt to effects of climate change that are already destroying property.

Green building in general, and renewable energy in specific, are *growing* at rates well above conventional construction and conventional energy. As such, free-market economics itself is likely to continue to drive sustainable projects, even without federal support. The fossil-fuel industries, which are heavily implicated in all anti-environmental policy, may yet be ousted from dominance, not by policy, but by price.

The environmental movement, says a friend of mine, has had a "success disaster," coming so far so fast that backlash is simply evolutionary. Thus this book has an unexpected message: don't give up. Sustainability—whatever that means exactly—is about the long term, about resilience, adaptability, durability, and true cost-effectiveness. The same applies to professional survival and resilience in times when the social climate fluctuates like extreme weather. To work for sustainability is to invest in the long term.

Authorship Changes

Responsibility for this edition reflects a happy change for one of the authors, a bit less so for the other. Bill Thompson, after years of toiling in the ASLA vineyards, has retired. His input continues to influence this edition but from a much loftier position as, essentially, editorial reviewer. As this preface is being written, he has just released a compelling book titled *From Memory to Memorial: Shanksville, America, and Flight 93*, detailing the creation of the Flight 93 National Memorial.

This leaves me, Kim Sorvig, to blame for all content, omissions, errors, and odd bits of humor in this book. As in earlier editions, sustainability is explicitly about *values*, and so it remains important to present opinion clearly as such. Many of the points of opinion in this edition are ones that Bill and I reached together in writing the previous editions. However, for readability (and at Bill's urging), I have rather reluctantly rewritten all references to "the authors" or "us" as if they were my solo opinions. (If readers or reviewers take issue with any of these judgments, I will of course immediately give my coauthor full responsibility.)

Why a New Edition?

Diffusion of innovation, such as the gradual mainstreaming of sustainable building concepts, follows patterns regular enough that it has become a niche discipline in academic circles. Although it is easier to study the spread of a single new product than the social acceptance of a cluster of techniques and strate-

gies of building, there are some recognizable signs of maturation in green building. In particular, what was once a small market with a few pioneering products and services has seen proliferation of both, followed by what economists like to call "market corrections." This process has been conspicuous with some products (wood preservatives, strawboard, LEDs, for example) and even more so in competing green certification programs. Historians and ecologists recognize this pattern of rapid growth followed by consolidation.

Positive social trends have continued to reshape sustainability itself. These include:

- Surprisingly, today's major drivers of sustainability may prove to be ones with little relationship to environmental ideals as such. These drivers include the fact that young potential home-buyers strongly prefer walkable, economically and socially diverse communities; that such communities are energy efficient, especially in drastic cuts to driving frequency; and that a tipping-point in price and desirability has been achieved, at long last, by photovoltaic and wind power.
- Protracted federal inaction under G. W. Bush spurred surprisingly proactive *local* initiatives, which intensified under the generally favorable policies of the Obama administration.
- Active support for sustainability has spread to new groups, including some industrialists and conservatives.
- "Green business" has become a recognized model for profitable enterprises across the economic spectrum.
- Coverage of green topics has spread to mainstream media.
- Several major national and local conventions on green building are held annually.
- Research centers and school curricula are reflecting sustainability.

All of these are well established and are likely to survive and even strengthen under repression.

New landscape-specific developments include:

- Public and press have recognized that changes in land use and vegetative cover play a major role in climate change. Recognition that climate change is a clear and present danger has become more widespread among citizens than among politicians.

- The expectation that *performance* of "green" design be monitored and meet specific goals indicates real maturation of the discipline. Certification programs have proliferated, competed, and merged, including the landscape-focused Sustainable Sites Initiative, now known as SITES.

- Surveying, mapping, sampling, and monitoring technologies are improving individually, and becoming better integrated, with sophisticated data and what-if calculators making it easier to understand specific landscapes dynamically in real time.

- Official highway standards recognize "context sensitivity," traffic calming, and improved stormwater management, decreasing damage done by overpaving, as well as designing for wildlife protection. Designers should work to ensure that the recently promised trillion-dollar infrastructure project incorporates these standards and employs green professionals.

- Landscape publications are covering work that goes well beyond the old limits of the field, such as restoring the Colorado River, or advocating for landscape-scale planning to avoid damage from extractive industries. Even the *Wall Street Journal* has covered sustainable landscaping.

- Landscape lighting has continued to improve in efficiency, design flexibility, and appropriateness for "dark-sky" protection.

What's New in This Edition?

This section discusses *criteria* used in updating this edition, and lists major *subject-matter* revisions, for the convenience of practitioners, educators, and students who have used the first or second edition.

Although "what's new?" is the focus of much design writing, this book is explicitly driven by principles, and in the field of sustainability, newness is not the dominant virtue.

Thus, if an existing project example (or product or resource) still illustrates an important idea, it hasn't been replaced simply for the sake of novelty. Pioneering examples from the previous editions are still in-cluded unless truly out of date; new examples have been added if they clearly show new approaches or significantly improved performance. In the third edition, there has been little need to add projects just to demonstrate one technique; rather, the most noteworthy new projects seem to share one characteristic: *integration* of green techniques into full-fledged systems. Of necessity, I have been selective about including projects and photos; there are many that deserve to be included but could not be. Including every worthy project would now require an encyclopedia, and in fact, online resources are the only medium that could provide a representative catalog of sustainable *projects*, as opposed to strategies.

Still an Evolving Effort

It would be tempting to try to produce a sort of best practices manual for sustainable landscapes, but sustainability remains far from standardization. Any formulaic instructions for sustainability outdoors must always be adjusted for regional reasons, if no other. This difficulty has plagued certification efforts, especially where landscapes rather than buildings are the focus. In this book, detailed how-to information has seemed appropriate for only a few materials and techniques; more often, it seemed more honest to give a description, some principles, and references for following tomorrow's evolution. I considered changing the book's subtitle to "A *Strategic* Guide to Green Building Outdoors," but it was verbose enough already. Sustainable landscape practices have grown, but not truly normalized.

For standard information, this book will not replace basic texts filled with details of retaining walls and decks, or formulas for grading and drainage. An understanding of these conventional construction skills will be required as long as landscapes are built. This book offers tools and ideas for *adapting* these conventions to new conditions, new materials, new regulations, and new client demands, all driven by environmental concerns.

Future landscape construction will need to be more sophisticated, not only in technique, but in careful consideration of *why* we build and *what* is appropriate. This sophistication must grow from a combination of innovation, convention, and rediscovered tradition, not from new technologies alone. The most sustainable landscapes, arguably, are indigenous and folk creations, many of which have lasted millennia, often in the face of deliberate attempts to plow them under.

The original edition took what was then an unusual tack, treating landscape construction not as a functional, value-free topic, but as a step toward *applying* environmental ethics. That approach, which felt right to us as authors, clearly resonated with readers and reviewers, and continues in this third edition.

Overview of Updates, by Chapter

This edition covers topics from the first two editions (sometimes more succinctly), *with the following updates, additions, and changes*:

- The introductory chapter, "'Sustainability' in Context," retains its focus on big-picture issues. The chapter's resource list includes the reading list for the graduate seminar that I give at the University of New Mexico School of Architecture and Planning, based on this book. The books on that list offer context on the history of green building and planning; comparative concepts of how a society "owns" land; and the relatively new concept of world history and economics researched through a green lens. The section on climate change has, unfortunately, needed expansion, recalling the proverb that crisis is also opportunity. New practices in what is called integrative design have been added. The explosion of competing certification schemes, including one devoted to landscapes specifically, has been moved to the new "Principle 11: Demonstrate Performance, Learn from Failure."

- The main updates in Principle 1 involve drone-based surveying and recent site-visualization software.

- Principle 2 proposes that site restoration may be the future of the landscape professions for many years to come, and discusses several projects that exemplify new business and funding strategies alongside innovative involvement in revegetating the land.

- Principle 3 adds some new information on green-roofs, and new concerns about artificial turf. It also

covers new street-tree planting aids that outperform structural soil mixes on every metric except cost.

- Principle 4 reflects new stormwater products and concepts, and reports on progress in "smart" irrigation and outdoor water conservation policies.

- Principle 5 notes a number of pavement-related updates, and studies on the positive effects of reducing and repurposing pavement.

- Principle 6 adds new sources of material evaluation, yet seems stuck in a time-warp: recurrent controversies about sustainable certification of wood, polyvinyl chloride (PVC), and wood preservatives have persisted for the past decade, and came close to dividing LEED and the green building community.

- Principle 7 notes a few new tools that impact the environment, and revisits alternative energy generation, which has come of age but is fighting for market share. Some new tools for estimating energy, carbon, water, and other impacts, and combining them into life-cycle footprints, are also discussed in this chapter. My own tables on embodied energy, now dated, have been archived but are available via Island Press's website: see "Visit and Contribute to the Website," p. xxv.

- Principle 8 notes new research on light pollution and its interactions with other pollutants. The ascendancy of LED lighting continues, with a few minor concerns, while OLED technology, on the horizon, suggests further revolution.

- Principle 9 is largely unchanged; no major new strategies for outdoor mitigation of noise appear to have developed.

- Principle 10 is also relatively unchanged. Some new products and a few Integrated Pest Management strategies have been added, along with improvements in efficiency of maintenance tools, including solar power for cordless ones.

- Principle 11 is new to this edition. It details three interlinked issues: performance monitoring, certification of products and projects, and recognition that failure is part of the evolution of sustainability. A very young trend in landscape circles, the analysis of failures is well under way in architecture, where efficiency goals have occasionally gone unmet, sometimes for complex reasons. The difficulties that design professionals have in acknowledging failure, and thus in learning from it, are also noted.

- The conclusions reflect my current thoughts on landscape sustainability.

Resource Lists for Further Information

Extensive *Resource Lists*, providing links to organizations, suppliers, experts, websites, and publications have been *posted online*. (See the following section.) The lists from previous editions have been expanded where appropriate, and will be updated periodically online.

In many cases, resources can provide real-time updates on recent developments. Others provide specialized detail about techniques and materials, which this book describes more broadly. Be sure to check closely related chapters for resources *indirectly* related to your topic.

Since the first edition, broader acceptance of sustainable practices has made information on the field far more widespread. There are many new publications about green building, as the resource lists reflect. When updating the lists, information quality and relevance has been the criterion—somewhat subjective and definitely selective.

In addition, a selection of keywords or search terms that are helpful in locating current information are included at the end of each chapter. (See "Finding Landscapes Along the Information Highway," below.) The explosion of green building publications, and especially websites, means that a comprehensive catalog is essentially impossible.

Periodicals that represent the landscape professions have greatly increased their coverage of and seriousness about sustainable practices. Bill and I are happy to take some of the credit (and blame) for this. This change, however, has been occurring throughout the design world, and credit for that goes to the professions themselves.

The *most general* resources, such as organizations, consultants, and suppliers, are perhaps your most valuable resources followed by books, periodicals, and websites. If your questions are broad or a bit fuzzy, human resources are generally best. If your question is fairly specific, there may be published information or a website that exactly meets your needs.

Manufacturers and suppliers of specific products have kindly provided information on many topics. There is no way to list all of them as resources, nor is endorsing individual products appropriate. Supplier information is included to promote broader awareness of sustainable construction, rather than to advertise particular wares.

For these reasons, suppliers are listed in resources if (1) they have been helpful as sources of *general* information, and (2) their product is either typical or not yet well-known. Where a dozen manufacturers of roughly the same product exist, they are not all listed; more likely, a magazine that regularly carries ads from most of them would be a resource on that topic. Associations are similarly general resources and can often help in locating consultants or manufacturers.

The endnotes also serve as information sources for particular questions. In this book, endnotes are not just citations; they comment and expand on the main text.

Visit and Contribute to the Website

While this edition is at the printer, some lists and tables will be posted on a dedicated page of Island Press's website, http://islandpress.org/sustainable-landscape-construction. The second edition stated the intent of doing this, but unfortunately, life intervened, and a website for this book (like many American infrastructure projects) never materialized.

- The major new posting is the **resource lists**, one per principle. In order to make these lists most useful to readers, they will be posted with live links to information sources where possible, and may be downloaded for personal use.
- The **embodied energy tables**, originating in the first edition of this book, will also be posted. They are somewhat outdated, although they remain unusual in focusing on landscape-specific materials. I am posting them nonetheless for those who wish to compare estimates—use at your own discretion. The University of Bath study discussed in Principle 7 is the most up-to-date source for embodied

energy figures; it includes, but does not specifically flag, many "raw" landscape materials.

- Other tables of information may be posted.
- A **study guide** based on the second edition will be posted, subject to my finding time to update it.
- Island Press's Web page will, with any luck, also be able to accept **corrections** specific to this book, and **suggestions** of worthy strategies, projects, and products to be added to the resource lists. If it cannot accept a submission you would like to make, please see "Contacting the Author," below.

To use the posted resources, please visit the URL listed at the beginning of this section.

Who Should Use This Book?

Sustainable Landscape Construction is still intended for three main audiences:

- professionals in private- and public-sector landscape architecture, construction, and maintenance, and their suppliers. Some architects, planners, engineers, and developers have also found the book useful.
- students in landscape construction and design courses, as well as some who study architecture, planning, project management, and engineering.
- landowners and others concerned with the health of specific sites, ranging from individuals and businesses to neighborhood associations and conservation groups.

This edition continues a proud tradition of writing that is accessible to people with various levels of experience. Professionals will please excuse the basic definitions that help students and other readers. Accessibility also means that concepts of environmentalism and development rub shoulders; I have attempted to keep these interactions positive and understandable from various perspectives.

There is value in understanding the development of our discipline, sustainable planning, design, and construction. Throughout this edition, there are occasional "historical" notes to demonstrate how, and how quickly, sustainable approaches to landscape have grown between 2000 (the first edition), 2007 (the second), and today, in 2017.

How to Use This Book

Use this book to develop or improve your ability to conceptualize sustainable materials or methods. Then adapt these concepts to site-specific conditions, referring to local consultants and the resources listed for further expertise and detail.

The chapters of this book can be read in almost any order. Each focuses on a central issue, such as sustainable use of water, and on construction related to that issue.

The introduction considers larger, contextual questions. These political, social, and ethical issues are critically important; *please* don't just read the technical chapters. More than ever, landscape architectural practice must deal with such global matters as fires, drought, floods, extreme storms, drilling and mining, material scarcity, and climate change. Environmental justice is also percolating into professional awareness, and must become part of the new standard. Discussion of these connections has become a necessity for putting site-scale sustainability into context. Conversely, the *landscape perspective*, looking at the living surface of the world as an open interconnected system, is badly needed in decisions about energy generation, infrastructure development and maintenance, and resource conservation. The approaches used by engineers have their place, but frequently create unintended consequences "downstream," where (as the saying goes) we all live.

Principle-focused Organization

This book is organized by *principle* rather than by technique or material. Principles are *values that people act on*. Sustainability itself is a principle. Each chapter focuses on one overarching idea that *can and should* be implemented in the landscape. These principles, in various forms, have guided the landscape professionals whose work is reported here and should[2] guide anyone who makes, modifies, or manages a landscape. Subsections of each chapter offer specific methods to accomplish the principle.

Many of these methods can be used in concert with each other. It is not unusual, however, to find two methods of achieving the same goal, which, if used simultaneously, would cancel each other. A commonly encountered example is that both porous paving and water harvesting are techniques for sustainably managing stormwater, but porous paving may reduce water available for harvesting, while harvesting water often decreases the need for porous pavement. Some methods or materials also work best, or only, in certain climates. Please read each chapter as a whole, then choose from the range of techniques based on local experience.

The "principled" approach gives a clear picture of interrelationships in living landscapes. Where principles overlap or complement each other (which is frequent because the landscape is a web of interacting influences), cross-references are provided for easy access to techniques or materials covered in other sections.

Abbreviations

In general, any abbreviated term is explained when first used. However, a few agencies and publications crop up so often that defining them every time is truly tedious. These are:

- DOT for department of transportation, often combined with the abbreviation for a state (MNDOT for Minnesota DOT). FHWA is the US DOT.
- "Caltrans" for California's DOT.
- AASHTO for American Association of State Highway and Transportation Officials.
- DER or DEP for Department of Environmental Resources or Protection.
- EPA for Environmental Protection Agency; unless specified, this is federal.
- ADA for Americans with Disabilities Act, which increasingly affects sustainable design by demanding excess paving, reconstruction of buildings, and even avoidance of planting.

- *EBN* for *Environmental Building News*, the incomparably useful newsletter from BuildingGreen, now in its twenty-sixth year. Its name officially changed, as of January 2017, to *The BuildingGreen Report*. For convenience, at least until the *fourth* edition, citations here will use the old abbreviation.
- *LAM* for *Landscape Architecture Magazine*.
- ASLA for American Society of Landscape Architects and ALCA for Associated Landscape Contractors of America. Both have regional chapters.
- NAHB for National Association of Home Builders, which has gone from resisting green building to promoting green standards of its own.

Finally, US states are abbreviated when they serve as part of a city name, using the standard two-letter postal abbreviations. Anyone unfamiliar with these abbreviations (I'm happy to say that I know of readers in nearly two dozen foreign countries) can find a list at www.stateabbreviations.us/ and a map on that site's subpage, /states.htm. Other place-names are spelled out.

Individuals and Firms Mentioned in This Book

People quoted are introduced *only* the first time they are mentioned (some are mentioned in several chapters). If information comes from a person's published work, an endnote cites this. People quoted *without* endnotes gave information in interviews. Job titles and locations are those *current at the time* of the interview or of the project described. Names of individuals and firms are in **boldface** in the index. Because of the ease of locating people and firms with any search engine, detailed contact information is seldom given, except (online) if an individual or firm is also a resource.

Exemplary Landscapes

This book would not exist if many people had not put sustainable principles into landscape practice already. A few of the ideas discussed here are still just that—ideas. Most, however, have actually been implemented; where appropriate, real-world examples are described and illustrated. Projects and place-names are

Finding Landscapes Along the Information Highway

Because "landscape" is both a broad subject and a term often misappropriated, searching for land-scape information can be awkward. It is often the only way, however, to find comprehensive, up-to-the-minute detail and *locally* adapted products or expertise.

Thus, you, gentle reader, *must* develop the skill of searching for landscape information. Here are a few suggestions.

Search capabilities and the volume of information posted online have grown massively between the first and third editions of this book. Because of this, I have pared down the detail given here, for example, about locating firms, individuals, and even some publications, because with little more than a name you can find them online. It is in fact sometimes *more* frustrating to have detailed URLs and other contact information, because these may have changed. I have tried to strike a balance between simplicity and detail. In addition, as noted above, the resource lists will be posted online rather than printed. This will allow me to provide extra detail, and to include more resources, than I could in print.

Use the search terms provided in this book's resource lists. These are keywords, combined in the strange and often unlovely grammar of search engines, that will unearth a *reasonably* high percentage of relevant hits. They are the same terms used to track down much of the information in this book, and have been further tested by diligent UNM graduate assistants Allison Wait, Satya Rakurty, and Samuel Fantaye.

Search engines are literal-minded things. Most offer the ability to set conditions and relations between the **search terms**: With All the Words, With the Exact Phrase, With At Least One of the Words, and Without the Words. The following written conventions describe searches of these types. *All-the-words*: no punctuation; *"Exact Phrase"*: in quotes; *At-Least-One*: OR between terms; *Without*: minus (dash) before term. Therefore, *Geology Topography (erosion OR river OR glacier) —wind —"glacial deposition"* could be a search for landforms caused only by water or ice erosion. You may need to translate my shorthand into the preferred notation of your favorite search engine.

Know the most specific name(s) for your topic. Search for "landscape" or "environment" and you will get "Political Landscape," "Landscape of Ideas," and "Environment (computer systems)," to name only a few. Try more-specific terms from geology, soil science, horticulture, or architecture. When in doubt, ask an expert, teacher, or research librarian what the accepted term(s) would be. For products, local suppliers may help you identify the generic name for That Widget That Goes Between the Whosit and the Whatsit.

One source of semi-standardized search terms is the Library of Congress Subject Headings (LCSH). See http://id.loc.gov/authorities/subjects.html for a searchable list of major topics. Searching for "landscape" results in sixteen pages containing over 300 headings (not documents) with "landscape" in their names. LCSH are also published in book form, available in most libraries. Many databases and university or local libraries follow LCSH definitions.

The Gale Encyclopedia of Associations lists *groups* for every imaginable subject, by name or topic. Most libraries subscribe to these directories, in print or online.

Search engines return mixed information, opinion, irrelevancies, and, of late, "alternative facts" and "fake news." Partisan denial and exaggerated commercial claims are surprisingly common when the built environment is the topic. Always compare different sources. Ask yourself, "Who is this source?" and "What is their motive for publishing this?" Another way to winnow wheat from chaff is to "follow the money": whose dollars are pushing this information into public awareness? Google's linkage-rating system helps screen out some, but not all, irrelevant hits, and has improved over the years—a topic that generated 50,000 hits in 2007 may produce only 2,500 ten years later, but the relevance of the results is usually much better. Yahoo! is sometimes better for suppliers and products. Google's option to display what it considers to be "similar sites" (the down arrow by the URL of each listed search result) is occasionally very useful.

Websites disappear without warning. If information is valuable, save the HTML file for offline viewing, convert it to PDF, or cut and paste text into a word-processor file. Copy the Web address and insert the date for a permanent record in case the site crashes or gets pulled.

Governmental agencies like the Natural Resources Conservation Service (formerly Soil Conservation Service) and the National Oceanic and Atmospheric Administration—NRCS and NOAA, respectively—maintain websites that bring together a wealth of disparate information related to central concepts like soils and climate. Sites specific to green building have proliferated. Be on the lookout for new ones. Send them to me if you like.

Remember that some governmental sites suffer from political editing.[3] There are also many sites and organizations whose names look environmental, but on closer inspection turn out to be property-rights groups whose true agenda is *eliminating* environmental regulation, under the guise of cost-effectiveness or "wise use." Searching for an organization's or person's name plus the word "controversy" or "lawsuit" can often reveal their politics and funding.

Google Earth (see p. 59) could be invaluable as a central repository for site-specific information, or at least links to that information. However, postings still seem to be dominated by casual uses, like tourist photos. A new visual search engine, GeoVisual Search from Descartes Labs, finds *visually* similar features anywhere on Earth. Click on a windmill, solar farm, or center-pivot irrigation system to find other examples, often by the thousand. This search cannot be done verbally, and it does not rely (like Google Earth and others) on someone's having previously categorized the object with tags. Though limited to objects that are graphically striking and consistent, thus mostly built by humans (clicking on a volcanic caldera, for instance, returned nothing useful), this is a tool with amazing potential for land-related searches.

The globalization of knowledge has begun to change the boundaries of most fields, including the landscape professions. A few decades ago, a book like this would have been a compilation of what other landscape folk were doing, and very little else. The ability to search the Web has expanded the landscape profession's tendency to borrow wherever we can—to retread concepts from architecture and the arts, but also to commandeer ideas from agriculture, high-tech manufacturing, and far-flung disciplines in the sciences. This is all to the good, but makes critical thinking essential: it is easy to gather just enough information to misunderstand and misapply. With ecosystem health and social sustainability in the balance, landscape theory and practice cannot afford to be based on "truthiness" and hearsay, so the responsibility for honest and intelligent use of the Web's astonishing resources is greater than ever.

italicized in the index. Like names of individuals and firms, general project information, such as location, is given only when a project is first mentioned. Firm names are usually the one(s) most closely connected with *landscape* aspects of the project. Inevitably, some names have been omitted, especially on larger projects where the roster of names would be a chapter in itself.

In a few cases, it was impossible to determine who did the project. Factual corrections are welcome.

I hope this third edition of *Sustainable Landscape Construction* will help the landscape professions continue to mature, to prosper in what will almost certainly be difficult times ahead, and to keep fighting for a livable and beautiful environment.

Acknowledgments

A first-edition grant from the Graham Foundation for Advanced Studies in the Fine Arts, Chicago, and the many donations that support our publisher, the Center for Resource Economics / Island Press, are gratefully acknowledged.

Books, like ecosystems, evolve through a web of interactions. Thanks to everyone who responded generously to information and image requests, including those whose projects, pictures, or words *aren't* included for lack of space, time, or computer compatibility.

Special thanks to:

Meg Calkins for her book *Materials for Sustainable Sites*, and good advice; Bruce Ferguson; Leslie Sauer; Fritz Steiner; Bill Wenk; and Christian Gabriel for information and suggestions; Alex Wilson and the researchers and writers at *Environmental Building News* without whose reporting I could never keep up to date. Tom Ryan, Bob Pine, Duke Bitsko, and Stephen Apfelbaum for their work on landscape forensics, and for agreeing to interviews. Alf Simon of UNM for making research assistance available. My students at UNM for trying to keep me honest, and ferreting out surprises.

Special thanks to the good people of Island Press: Courtney Lix, my editor, for encouragement and insight; Elizabeth Farry, her assistant, who converted files, took on photo permissions, and did so many organizational tasks with great generosity; Sharis Simonian, production editor who deservedly has acknowledg-

ments in more books than many people read in a lifetime; Pat Harris, copy editor (who can pick the appropriate nits and still make an author feel valued); and Heather Boyer, whose guidance and patience shaped *both* the first two editions.

The first edition would never have happened without John Lyle and Ian McHarg for inspiration, J. B. Jackson for computer help, and The Nine Readers of the Manuscript.

Thanks to Bill Thompson for starting this epic; to him and his wife, Anne Herzog, for friendship; and to my wife, Mary Sorvig, for kind and clear-headed support of this and all my projects.

Contacting the Author

To send corrections or suggestions, please visit the Island Press Web page, http://islandpress.org/sustainable-landscape-construction. This is intended as a repository of matters concerning the next edition of *Sustainable Landscape Construction*—in other words, I don't expect to correspond about items posted there. To contact me for questions, speaking engagements, or other discussion, try ksorvig@unm.edu. I can't guarantee a response, and I deliberately check messages only every few days, as a matter of discipline and productivity.

Thank you!

Basic Principles: "Sustainability" in Context

If we put our minds to it, can we gardeners, with our centuries of practical experience, help rescue species from the brink of extinction?
—*Janet Marinelli,* Stalking the Wild Amaranth: Gardening in the Age of Extinction

Concern for the health of outdoor places is a central theme in landscape architecture and landscape contracting, and has been since long before "sustainability" was a word. "Stewardship" is almost the mantra of the American Society of Landscape Architects. It is a concern shared by many members of related disciplines like architecture, planning, public-lands administration, and horticulture, as well as by private gardeners. Yet in translating this concern to the materials and methods of *making* landscapes, there frequently seems to be a disconnect between ethical intentions and practical actions.

Several landscape theorists have suggested that landscape architecture and construction (as opposed to land-use planning at the larger scale) have nothing to contribute to a sustainable future.[1] Many practitioners feel that landscapes are (or even should be) merely decorative. Others have simply declared landscape architecture dead.[2] While sympathizing strongly with the perception that landscape architecture *as conventionally practiced* is dead to current realities and has next to nothing to contribute to them, I hold with those who see *changes* in landscape-making as serious and essential parts of a livable future (for humans and nonhuman species). More proactive writers have identified ways to improve environmental practice and education.[3] (See p. 414.)

Those who believe that sustainability is essential in the landscape, and vice versa, must address these concerns. One way to start is by looking at the context in which the landscape professions exist and operate—the definitions and conventions, policies and politics that surround sustainable practice.

Designers are used to focusing within their project boundaries. Thinking outside this box, more and more landscape professionals approach each project as part of an *open regional system of natural and cultural elements*. Although this way of thinking has ancient roots, it began to acquire modern momentum in the 1960s and '70s, with books like *Silent Spring, The Limits to Growth,* and *Design with Nature.* The questions raised by those books are still critical, the answers still evolving. What are the relationships between human technology and nature? What concepts can best guide people to live within our ecological means?

For landscape professionals, the central question is: how can people make environmentally responsible choices in the process of conceiving and constructing landscapes? In a book of technical strategies, such questions are of real importance. Without considering the big picture, it is nearly impossible to make good decisions on a project-by-project, site-by-site scale.

At the national scale, urban and suburban development reshapes millions of acres of previously undeveloped land each year—at the peak of the housing bubble in Colorado alone, ten acres *per hour* by one estimate.[4] While worries about development usually focus on structures—tract homes, commercial strips, and industrial buildings—the constructed *landscapes* that accompany these buildings also contribute to widespread environmental change, and sometimes damage. When self-sustaining ecosystems are converted to built landscapes, the hidden costs may include soil loss, degradation of water, toxic and nonrenewable materials, and unsustainable energy use. These costs are unacceptable, but also largely avoidable.

Figure 0.1   The Phipps Center for Sustainable Landscapes integrates on-site energy production, water harvesting, and stormwater and wastewater management, making the research and education site net-zero for multiple resources. (*Project:* Andropogon. *Photo:* Paul G. Wiegman.)

Compare an ordinary quarter-acre landscaped lot with a two-thousand-square-foot house, each a mainstay of the American Dream. The landscape directly affects an area of environment five and a half times as large as the house. More important, if the landscape introduces toxic materials and invasive plants or diseases, they are free to spread; inside the house, such problems might be contained or controlled by walls, filters, or mechanical systems. In addition, many landscape practices are "nonpoint" sources of pollution, crossing ownership and jurisdictional lines.

Historically, some of the green of the garden has been lost in the broader battle to "control" nature. Social expectations of appearance, style, and conformity bring heavy doses of industrial-strength technology into the landscape. To pretend the technology is not there is to continue the myth that gardens are 100 percent natural. This myth, ironically, plays into the hands of those who would happily accept all landscape technology as equally wholesome, and let constructed environments replace natural ones everywhere.

If a new generation of designers and a new era in design is to contribute meaningfully to sustainability, it is critical to think carefully about context, values, and goals. Sustainability is a framework, a systematic way of linking ourselves with the natural systems that support us. Without that framework, individual green buildings and restored landscapes will not *add up* to what is really wanted: a worldwide network of healthy places that sustain people and sustain themselves.

The first contextual issue that requires clear thinking is the idea of sustainability itself.

What Is Sustainability? Politics, Ethics, and Semantics

Despite its widespread popularity, "sustainability" is far from having a clear and agreed definition. Although the core vision seems simple—a lasting and nondestructive way to live on this Earth—the questions are many. It is important for those of us concerned with landscape construction to think clearly about the local good or damage that we do and about opportunities and limits that link our site-by-site actions to a global picture.

Probably the simplest widely used general definition of sustainability is *meeting the needs of today's population without diminishing the ability of future populations to meet their needs.*[5] The concept of a sustainable *landscape* also has a significant history. (In this book "landscape" is inclusive of wild outdoor spaces and constructed ones, functional or frivolous, at scales ranging from tiny yards to biologically consistent regions—J. B. Jackson notwithstanding.)[6] The Council of Educators in Landscape Architecture (CELA) published a definition in 1988, most of which remains valid today: sustainable landscapes "contribute to human well-being and at the same time are in harmony with the natural environment. They do not deplete or damage other ecosystems. While human activity will have altered native patterns, a sustainable landscape will work with native conditions in its structure and functions. Valuable resources—water, nutrients, soil, et cetera—and energy will be conserved, diversity of species will be maintained or increased."[7]

One increasingly important concept in defining sustainability (and in measuring and verifying the performance of "green" projects) is that of "ecosystem services." This concept recognizes that almost all human work, invention, and economics depend entirely on materials and processes that are not human in origin, that is to say, on what used to be called "the bounty of Nature."[8] These more-than-human processes include fundamental life support like the creation of living soil; "provisioning," such as food, fuel, water, and materials; "regulating services," such as cleaning the air, balancing the pH of water bodies, etc.; and "cultural services," such as artistic, spiritual, recreational, and therapeutic imagery and concepts originating in nature. A more or less complete list of ecosystem services is part of Principle 11. One definition for sustainability would be "maintaining and not degrading the existing ecosystem services of a site or region." The Sustainable Sites Initiative, also detailed in Principle 11, bases much of its point-rating system on the ecosystem services concept.

Sustainability (and its near-synonyms) could also be defined in terms of priorities. Conventional modern societies have, until recently, tended to prioritize economic growth *über alles*. Sustainability sets the long-term health of humans, other species, and the planet as equal to or higher than economics per se. The field of "ecological economics" studies how this should be implemented. For practical purposes, one of the differences in sustainable priorities versus conventional ones is called the Precautionary Principle.[9] This states that, if the results of a product or technology are unknown or disputed, it should not be used, responding to risk with what lawyers call "an abundance of caution." By contrast, conventional policy makers and businesses treat risk as something to manage: if one person in a million gets sick from exposure to a new chemical that has economic benefits, some of the profits are theoretically set aside to deal with that person's illness, rather than scrapping the product. This resembles the military concept of "acceptable losses." Since

environmental risks are so often irreversible threats to whole regions or the entire planet, the Precautionary Principle argues that there is *no* acceptable or manageable level of risk. Corporate-oriented opinion considers this not to be sufficiently "business-friendly," and accuses those who prioritize sustainability of "killing jobs," etc. Both approaches have merit at the appropriate scale, but for businesses (or consumers) to put products, prices, and profits ahead of livability and health is irresponsible.

In this book, "contributing to sustainability" means primarily that a method or material appears to minimize waste, pollution, and degradation of the environment. For true sustainability, it is not enough, however, just to acquire and build with the greatest efficiency. "Do I need it?" choices about the scale and appropriateness of proposed landscape changes must also play a role. At times, humans must make sacrifices in favor of maintaining habitat and biodiversity. In these choices, landscape professionals can (sometimes) guide their clients and their communities.

To some degree, "sustainability" has become a buzzword, and fuzzy. The term is bandied about in support of widely different causes[10] and to sell products (including landscape products) only vaguely related to ecology. Some writers have proposed different terms for the concept. "Alternative" is one of these; popular in the 1960s, it implies second-rate status. "Appropriate technology" is also widely used. "Sustainability" seems preferable because it emphasizes *long-term* appropriateness.

In the 1990s the late John Lyle suggested that sustainability was not enough and that optimal design should be "regenerative"—capable of renewing the energy and materials of degraded ecosystems. Lately, this type of design has been termed "net-positive" (producing more resources—usually energy—than the project uses), in contrast to "net-zero" (using no more resources than the project produces). Sustainability in general, and LEED in specific, have been criticized for endless checklists of what *not* to do. William McDonough's concept of cradle-to-cradle material cycles, as well as the Living Building Challenge, attempt to make construction *contribute* to the planet rather than take away. Serious attempts to accomplish this rely on measuring pre-construction "ecosys-

Figure 0.2   John Lyle's Center for Regenerative Studies sets a high standard for sustainable place making. Many of the materials are recycled; the beautiful landscape functionally supports and renews the center. (*Project:* J. Lyle. *Photo:* Tom Lamb.)

tem services," then ensuring that those are still being produced, and more, after construction is complete. Tristan Roberts, *EBN*'s chief strategy officer, says being green is not doing the least harm, but is "honoring our bond with the earth at every step of the building process."[11]

By contrast, at least one group, the Bay Area Stormwater Management Agencies Association (BASMAA), talks about "less-toxic gardens" and "less-toxic methods" of maintaining them.[12] BASMAA, not without cause, implies that human activity will *always* have some negative impact on nature, particularly when concentrated in large urban areas (which is the current demographic trend).

The roots of sustainable design are in "ecological design," a term that raises still other misgivings.

"Ecology," especially as a popular movement influencing attitudes toward the land, ranges from highly emotive New Age assertions to rigidly rational species-counting, and proponents can seem bent on saving the world whether the world likes it or not. Some such accusations are so overstated that it is easy to dismiss them, but enough thoughtful concerns have been raised that they must be considered.[13]

"Environmentally responsible" is another frequently used term. Although it is a mouthful, it may yet be the best term: one can take responsibility for attempting something even when the outcome is uncertain, and one can take responsibility for mistakes. "Sustainable," "regenerative," "ecological," and "appropriate" all tend to assume that we can predict the outcome.

Two new terms have emerged to prominence since the second edition: "resilient design" and "passive survivability." "Resilience" means to take a lickin' and keep on tickin,' to use a folk phrase; sites, facilities, and communities need not only to use resources efficiently and be durable, but also to be able to *adapt* to adverse future conditions. This doesn't mean that attempts to slow or avoid climate change are abandoned, but resilient communities also prepare for what can't be avoided. Planning ahead for these possibilities greatly expands the challenge of good design. Resilience relies, among other strategies, on diversity of systems that back each other up; no one technology is "the solution." Passive survivability is, in a nutshell, buildings that can survive disasters and provide basic shelter despite prolonged supply-chain outages—in situations similar to the recent storms Harvey and Irma.[14] Both resilient and passive-survivable structures rely explicitly on "ecosystem services" to give them adaptabil-

ity, and many of those services are landscape-related.[15]

Although this book primarily uses the term "sustainability," the points raised by these alternative terms bear keeping in mind.

The limits of what landscape-makers can hope to contribute must also be acknowledged. The "present/future needs" definition of sustainability can be criticized for oversimplifying several key questions: Which population's needs are to be met? How large a human population can be sustained? Where to draw the line between needs and desires? It would be naive to ignore the criticisms that have been leveled at the very idea of sustainability. Questions about sustainability, no matter what we call it, have pragmatic and political effects on the construction of landscapes, as they do on almost every human endeavor in the twenty-first century.

The following questions illustrate some of the doubts about sustainability, in terms specific to built landscapes. Operating locally and in isolation, landscape design and construction are unlikely to resolve these questions. With coordinated effort, however, the landscape professions can and must be part of the resolution.

- If nonpolluting, low-maintenance constructed landscapes covered the globe, at the expense of wild species and places, would that be a sustainable world?
- Is there any way to avoid impoverishing the natural world without drastic regulatory limits on human population, land use, and resource consumption?
- For a majority of the world's population, "landscape" means crops, firewood, and survival. In such economies, public parks and private gardens are fantasies far beyond reach, glimpsed on TV or through closed gates. Does this mean that all landscape construction should be sacrificed to achieve subsistence-level sustainability?
- Is stewardship of the Earth as a whole system possible without dramatic changes in jurisdictional divisions of land?

For some, the answer to these questions is that sustainability is an admirable idea but can never be achieved. True, sustainability may be impossible, or the idea may merely disguise the seriousness of environmental degradation. Yet with due respect, defeatism is neither warranted nor helpful.[16] The critics rightly remind us that there are limits to what sustainability can or even should be; that within those limits, small efforts can yield important results; and that local results in turn can contribute to cumulative global change.

A dramatic decrease in materialism seems necessary for the Earth to sustain us in the long term. Will landscape construction be among the sacrificial luxuries? Drought has brought this question into stark reality in many communities, where water conservation has first been implemented by banning landscape plantings. But the functional and psychological value of built landscape makes it more than a luxury. The tradition of gardening for pleasure has deep roots and has survived many a drought. Realistically, though, if we do not reduce the environmental costs of construc-

tion, the alternative may be no construction at all. The landscape professions have a special stake, and a special responsibility, in seeking a healthy environment.

It would be foolish to mislead anyone into thinking that changes in landscape construction can *singlehandedly* reverse environmental degradation. The only possibility of a sustainable future lies in initiatives from all sides, in contributions, large and small, from great numbers of individuals and groups. The landscape professions historically have made stewardship of the environment a goal, imperfectly achieved but deeply desired. To abandon this goal because our scope of influence is limited would be irresponsible; to be smug in our greenness, equally so.

Sustainability and the Myth of Resource Efficiency

It is commonly assumed that sustainability equates to efficient use of resources, and that efficiency will be sufficient to produce a sustainable society. There is well-documented reason to be skeptical of this assumption.

In 1866, English economist William Stanley Jevons stated one of the most important economic findings that you've never heard of:

> It is wholly a confusion of ideas to suppose that the economical use of fuel is equivalent to a diminished consumption. The very contrary is the truth.[17]

Jevons observed that the increased efficiency of James Watt's steam engine over its predecessors resulted in greatly *increased* demand for coal. Ecological economics has since documented this phenomenon with other resources. Increasing efficiency means the amount of resource needed to accomplish X goes down, decreasing the cost of use and increasing consumption. For example, when auto fuel efficiency went up starting in the 1980s, the cost of driving x miles decreased, and people felt free to travel more. Again and again, the Jevons Paradox, as it is called, has combined with population growth to completely or largely *negate* improvements in technological efficiency. This applies to growing US electrical consumption despite energy-efficient technology (Principle 7) and lighting (Principle 8); to the increase in spending that accompanies increased recycling (Principle 6); to overuse of relatively cheap asphalt and cement paving (Principle 5); and most likely to the total acreage of nonagricultural irrigation, which has grown dramatically with "efficient" cheap water utilities and efficient irrigation technology (Principle 4).[18] In each of these cases, better efficiency led to *more* of the resource being used in total.[19]

Frustrated with this paradox (often without having a name for it), some writers and policy makers have declared resource efficiency impossible and, therefore, sustainability a waste of effort. This, too, is "wholly a confusion of ideas."

Efficient use of resources is necessary, *but not sufficient*, to create a system that meets present needs without precluding future ones. Resource efficiency is in fact critical, but without conservation and deliberately restrained total consumption, it backfires.

Restrained consumption, of course, is anathema to proponents of a consumer-driven, unregulated free-market capitalism, and the concomitant belief that perpetual economic growth is not only good, but mandatory. Many people associate all forms of economic restraint with authoritarian central planning. It may be that this clash explains some of the hatred and fury that is regularly directed at "enviros," who see themselves as reasonable people trying to keep human economics and the planet from imploding.

The proper response to the Jevons Paradox, in my opinion, is to *combine* efficiency with frugality. This would be a return to the values of most of our ancestors, no matter what culture we come from. As recently as the 1940s, Americans—our parents and grandparents—still lived by the saying "Use it up, wear it out, make it do or do without." Objects and tools were repaired and repurposed; buildings were made to last. Without romanticizing this attitude, it is a sound basis for a modern lifestyle—and, in fact, it seems to be reemerging among youth and young adults in the twenty-first-century "maker" movement.

From a different culture comes the idea of *oryoki*, literally "just enough," which guided medieval Japanese society. Japan, as an island, makes a good metaphor for the finite Earth. In the Edo period, from the 1600s until a time contemporary with Jevons (1868), Japan faced many of the resource issues that are arising globally today: materials, water, energy, food, and population. From these challenges, the Japanese forged a society that was "conservation-minded, waste-free, well-housed and well-fed, and economically robust," to quote Azby Brown's excellent environmental history, *Just Enough: Lessons in Living Green from Traditional Japan* (Tuttle, 2012). A major aspect of *oryoki* was what today would be called design, in which the elegant simplicity of Zen combined with an intelligent functionalism far more generous than the international Modernism it inspired. Savings from functional simplicity were harnessed to the goal of sharing "just enough" with everyone.

Making "just enough" the norm would best be accomplished as a social change in attitude, reserving our highest esteem for possessions and lifestyles that combine high productivity with simple means and graceful form. Using information technology well, for instance with apps that help foresee the consequences of unnecessary consumption and help people choose to use less, it would be theoretically possible to make "just enough" a matter of personal commitment, rather than the result of top-down planning. The aversion to central policy making, however, is part of the problem; in practice such a shift will have to come both from the people and from policies set by freely chosen representatives.

What is clear from the Jevons Paradox is that sustainability is *not* merely efficiency. Efficiency must serve a public intention to "live simply, so that others may simply live," to reduce our use so that the more-than-human world can flourish and the human sphere can know justice.

Some Things Sustainability Is Not

One sign that sustainability has become mainstream is that the concept is deliberately abused, usually to sell something as green that isn't. This is commonly known as "greenwashing." TerraChoice Environmental Marketing published "The Seven Sins of Greenwashing" in 2009. These include Hidden Trade-offs (one environmentally positive trait is touted, downplaying negative ones); No Proof (asserting greenness without evidence); Vagueness (using "natural"—a vague term—to suggest "organic," a term involving legal standards); False Labels (fake certification implied by graphic design or bogus trade names); Irrelevance (marketing tequila or wine as gluten-free, when wheat has never been an ingredient in either); Lesser of Evils (our toxic chemical is less toxic than their toxic chemical); and Fibbing (a polite way to say the advertiser is lying).[20] According to TerraChoice, 98 percent of products surveyed in its UK study were guilty of at least one of the above Sins. Landscape-specific greenwash is discussed further on p. 38.

When not being greenwashed, sustainable or ecological landscape practice comes in for frequent tar-and-feathering from *within* the landscape professions. Despite the long tradition, at least since Frederick Law Olmsted, of designing for ecosystem services (albeit without the name), some design theorists have damned recent, systematic application of the "green lungs" concept as an anti-design, anti-human "instrumentalization" of landscape. This is like saying that any building in which the plumbing, electricity, and Wi-Fi are functional *cannot be* good design. There have also been attempts to attack "the dominant moralistic posture behind the ecological and the sustainable," to quote a recent example.[21] *Any* remaking of landscapes applies values, a major and explicit premise of this book. Conventional landscapes reflect their own moralizing, which, at its extreme, gives cultural fashion greater ethical weight than any other consideration. There is no question that *all* contemporary First World approaches to landscape-making are embedded in consumer culture, and share that flawed ethic. But the issue isn't whether morality *is involved*: the hard question is *which set of ethical values* is better. Sustainable landscapes include beautiful, meaningful, healthy designs; in my view, this is an appropriate ethical balance. "Sustainable" has a moral or ethical basis, but so does the conventional land-conquering ethic that too many professionals, clients, and educators take as given.

Sustainability: Convention, Tradition, and Innovation

In discussing design and construction in this book, sustainable practices are distinguished from two other approaches: "conventional" and "traditional." It is worth defining these explicitly, because they contrast with sustainability in different ways. It is also impor-

tant to think clearly about sustainability's relationship to innovation and "progress."

Conventional practices are modern approaches, standard in much of the construction industry. Some of these practices are quite acceptable in terms of environmental impact, or can be with minor modification. Many will be part of a sustainable future. Conventional construction, however, often relies on massive energy inputs, extensive transportation, toxic materials, and removal of many if not all existing site features. There may be rare occasions when high energy use and toxic materials serve some sustainable purpose. However, changing times and conditions (for example, seesawing fuel prices) make it inevitable that conventional practices will change, even if environmental issues are ignored. The uncritical assumption that conventional practices are universally acceptable is the main thing that makes them destructive.

Traditional practices, in this book, are those surviving from pre-modern times, and in some cases learned from preindustrial cultures. Most rely on nonmechanized tools. Not *all* traditional land-use practices are sustainable. When applied in different climates or to different population densities than those of their origins, they can even be environmentally destructive. Many traditional practices, however, are extremely well adapted to their home regions. The modern focus on convenience and mechanization has displaced far too many traditions, some irreparably lost. Of those that remain, many traditional practices are worth reconsideration in the search for sustainability.

The choice of cover image for this edition reflects the conviction that many lasting landscape masterpieces are traditional in the sense used in this book. Constructed without industrial tools and materials, they have endured far longer than modern landscapes are expected to. Attentive maintenance has allowed them to evolve while staying true to their origins. They are sustained, too, in the borrowings of later designers, a fact devalued by our obsession with novelty. The previous editions' covers featured modern landscapes, among which there are also great examples. For this edition, it feels like time to acknowledge the sustainability of traditions.

A number of the techniques and materials in this book can truly be referred to as "innovative"—manufactured soil and solar irrigation controllers are examples. Many "conventional" practices, however, are or recently were innovations. As many authors have pointed out, modern American culture loves newness and invention—often uncritically. Sustainability asks for deeper thought about values and choices. Neither innovation nor convention or tradition is of unquestioned value for its own sake. To achieve sustainability, if it can ever be attained, we will have to draw on the whole range of possible practices, judging whether each one contributes to a world fit for our great-great-grandchildren.

This book evaluates specific practices and materials, old and new, as fairly as possible.[22] Conventional practices are not always the Bad Guys, and both traditional and supposedly sustainable innovations have their share of failures. Critiques are intended to *reaffirm* something that is close to the heart of almost everyone who makes the landscape his or her profession: *a desire to create beautiful and healthy places.* That desire can go tragically awry when old habits outweigh the new and important knowledge available today about the larger environment. This book presents some of that knowledge and criticizes some of those habits in the confident hope of change.

A few criticisms are offered without proposed solutions. This is not to pretend to be "greener" or more knowledgeable than everyone else—in fact, just the opposite. Somebody out there knows something useful about these unanswered problems. The only way solutions will be found is by many people thinking and experimenting, often about issues someone else saw but couldn't fix. Those who have solutions or suggestions have unprecedented ways to communicate them globally.

Green Building: Definitions and Initiatives

Moving from sustainability in general to "green construction" in specific requires careful thought. Many "simple things to do to save the planet" require only substituting "bad" products for "good" ones. Construction, however, literally changes the face of the Earth. There are many situations where building *anything* is a poor choice. Yet shelter is a genuine necessity for humans, and a healthy landscape is equally essential to human existence. It is not surprising that the growing number of associations that promote "green building" have struggled to define just what that means.

For purposes of this book, green building (including green construction of landscapes) is deliberate change to a site by grading, planting, or creation of structures that at a minimum maintains and ideally increases the level of ecosystem services existing on that site prior to the project. This definition is quite close to the concept of "green infrastructure," which advocates coordinated design for enhanced ecosystem services, but usually seems focused on water issues. Green infrastructure is an encouraging sign of maturation in green building because it coordinates, synthesizes, and integrates techniques like those in this book. It is further discussed in the following section.

When the first edition of this book appeared, many people thought of the green building movement as a fringe activity. Even then, this was hardly true, and today it is far less so. From a vanguard of activists, mainstream initiatives have grown widespread and are well established. Local adoption of green building codes began slowly in the 1990s, in places like Austin TX, Boulder CO, and Portland OR, working alongside or ahead of government environmental regulatory agencies (a stance that may be necessary once again if the federal EPA and other agencies and acts are gutted). By 2002, the influential *Environmental Building News* listed thirty-two state and local jurisdictions that had publicly available, detailed standards for green building. Today, it would be a major project to determine a complete listing of all the cities, counties, and states that have adopted green building codes, or of the green building and renewable energy groups that promote sustainability in communities large and small. Probably the most important current initiative at the national level is Architecture 2030, which aims to use green building methods to reduce fossil-fuel use and reverse global warming. (See "Landscapes Against Climate Change," p. 20.)

One significant change since the 2007 edition is that realtors, appraisers, investors, and lenders have increasingly seen the importance of sustainable development. Professional groups in those industries are offering training and certification for their members in valuing sustainable properties correctly.[23] Studies—some conducted by surprising sources—have shown repeatedly that green or energy-efficient commercial buildings command higher rents than equivalent conventional buildings;[24] that productivity is higher in spaces designed along green principles;[25] and that investment in energy-efficient renovated buildings gives returns high enough to beat the stock market average.[26]

Organizations like LEED that *rate* and *certify* green buildings and other development are discussed in Principle 11.

Green Infrastructure: Signs of a Maturing Discipline

The way in which most successful movements for professional or social change evolve is a bit like the process of learning the piano: first come hunt-and-peck notes; then a lot of (boring) practice of scales; and eventually, actual music-making. Similarly, green pioneers tinkered with hundreds of strategies, designs, and techniques for single-purpose sustainability. Gradually, after a lot of (boring) effort struggling to convince regulators, clients, and colleagues, it became possible to refocus energy on more complex and systematic projects. With what is called green infrastructure, I believe we are seeing the beginnings of the "music" phase of sustainable built environments.

Green infrastructure (which I hope never starts going by GI for short) is a subtle change, though very evident when we look back to see what has changed over the past ten years. It doesn't involve a lot of new green techniques. The EPA's very useful website on the topic (long may it survive) lists the major components that it considers part of green infrastructure. Green infrastructure pulls together rainwater harvesting and rain gardens, bioswales, permeable pavement, green streets, greenroofs and greenwalls, and site protection and restoration, all covered in this book. That's not a boast, any more than saying "I've played that scale" diminishes the value of a concert.

What makes green infrastructure important and encouraging is that the pieces are starting to come together. This is evident in how professionals present the benefits of their work in terms of the life-cycle impacts of the project as a whole, not the costs of single items. It is evident in what Howard Neukrug, former Philadelphia water commissioner,[27] calls "collective impact": instead of one agency managing stormwater, one providing tap water, and neither talking to the parks department, the focus on *shared infrastructure* creates networks that address multiple functions at once.

Making the Case(s) for Green

As green building has matured from an occasional oddity to a mainstream expectation, clients have rightly demanded *evidence* that green is worth the green. The cost of green building is still a matter of debate. Those who have tracked such costs most carefully tend to estimate that green "first costs" are 1 or 2 percent higher than conventional work, less if the contractors are experienced, but there remains a perception that green building costs up to 6 percent extra.[28] This discrepancy may reflect lack of regional experience, or contractors specifying high-end techniques or materials rather than keeping it simple. A 2014 report from the UK rating system BREEAM found that its lowest level of certification could be achieved at *no extra cost* as long as all green strategies were incorporated early in design; even the highest rating, for some types of buildings at least, added only 1.7 percent, which was paid back in two to five years;[29] a similar US study found 1.5 percent higher costs, repaid within four years.[30]

In addition to quick break-even, green properties that are rented generate 8 percent more revenue than conventional equivalents.[31] This and other factors are attracting investors[32] and, apparently, favorably influencing the insurance industry's opinion of green construction. Even Fannie Mae, which has a history of enforcing lowest common denominator standards that work against green buildings, began offering lower interest to multifamily buildings with green certification. These life-cycle monetary factors make green building financially quite viable. Although most financial studies focus on buildings, my informal tally of green strategies for buildings suggests that about a third are actually landscape techniques, particularly vegetation for heating or cooling load avoidance; stormwater management and water harvesting; and connections to nature. It is difficult to quantify the landscape's contributions to increased building value, but it is clearly positive.

In addition to pecuniary reasons, there are strong arguments that green projects result in improved occupant health and worker productivity.[33] This is a very large subject in itself, and isolating the impact of landscapes is difficult. As discussed in the section on sustainability and style (below), *visual* contact with naturalistic scenes has documented health effects. In addition, a number of recent studies have shown direct health benefits tied specifically to tree cover and landscape quality. By mapping air pollution in unusually fine-grained detail, Portland State University researchers led by Meenakshi Rao and Linda George were able to show significant correlation between tree cover and reduced childhood respiratory disease.[34] A study of 65,000 newborns in Vancouver WA found that birth weight was significantly higher if the mother's home had good vegetation cover; low birth rate is an indicator for adult health problems. This and other studies are especially interesting since they are adjusted to exclude factors that often go with landscaped neighborhoods, such as walkability, reduced noise, air quality, and family income.[35] The benefits of green sites go beyond the simple, expected explanations and are increasingly topics of serious study, with implications for health as well as environmental justice (see below).

Use "Landscape Perspective"

The European Union officially has recognized that readily identifiable *landscape* boundaries make very effective units for tailoring both social and environmental policy to local conditions.[36] This is one example of something the world needs more of: landscape perspective. Without it, issues of spatial integrity, ecological function, and community complexity are much harder to see and address.

Landscape perspective saved the National Park Service millions when the visitor center at Zion National Park was rebuilt. Because the design team agreed that the stunning canyon landscape needed to be the project focus, many visitor-center functions were moved into the open air, reducing the size, first costs, and operating costs of the structure.

Landscape perspective also changes the way environmental protection plays out. Pennsylvania State University landscape architecture professor Neil Korostoff notes that the response to the Marcellus shale-oil boom has focused on underground concerns, like aquifers, yet impacts on the surface landscape are arguably greater: massive clearance and regrading, vast toxic wastewater ponds, village-destroying heavy truck traffic. Even though these issues are critical, landscape experts like Korostoff are seldom brought to the table with activists and engineers, but when included they have been influential.

Landscape perspective is behind the ideas of local sourcing and slow food, walkable cities, and the recently documented realization that where a building is *sited* affects energy usage far more than efficient design of the building itself.

Landscape perspective combines functional considerations with spatial understanding, in ways that sometimes confound scientists, many of whom are notoriously nonspatial.[37] I once told a committee of green rating system experts that in landscape terms, 50 percent of half the site doesn't necessarily add up to 25 percent. The silence was astounding. From a landscape perspective, this conundrum makes sense: if a code or rating system allows no more than 50 percent of the site to be made impervious by construction, it matters *which 50 percent*. Paving the half that is dense clay will have a completely different outcome than paving the half that is sandy loam. This is a trivial example of a nontrivial weakness in applying quantitative measures to land-use planning without clear consideration of the spatial, open-system aspects of landscapes.

Not every green building program should be assumed to have any landscape perspective. Despite two decades of development, the major focus of many such programs is still approving *architectural* products, systems, and structures. Increased coordination between building goals and specific landscape techniques, such as shading or water management, has increased since the early days of LEED. But the full power of the spatial, open-system, relational thinking that I'm calling a landscape perspective is still far from standard.

In early versions of LEED, a project that achieved perfect site credits had 75 percent of the credits for basic certification.[38] While this appeared to be strong representation for landscape matters, there were concerns that the site credits were easily achieved substitutes for harder credits. In addition, any credit-by-credit system is better suited to addressing components of buildings than to assessing the whole-system web that produces healthy landscapes, as Philadelphia landscape architect Carol Franklin pointed out. These types of concerns led to the Sustainable Sites Initiative, a rating system specific to landscape projects (see Principle 11). Now coordinated with LEED, it overcomes some but not all of the landscape-specific problems of point-based certification systems.

As in society at large, low prioritization of landscape issues continues to keep many green rating programs from addressing significant ecological issues, particularly the effects of locating projects on inappropriate sites. Minimum energy performance, indoor air quality, recycling, and even prohibition of smoking have been mandatory for some certification schemes, yet a building could be sited on fire-prone, earthquake-prone land and still be certified. With their roots in completely voluntary systems intended to market greenness, certification has seldom addressed the issue of siting with much vigor. Few commercial developers would voluntarily give up developing a site they already own.[39] The system most likely to address siting adequately is, in my opinion, the Living Building Challenge, which, despite a growing number of successfully certified projects, many have regarded as unrealistically strict.

Including site and ecosystem protection in green building is essential, but even today input from landscape professionals is too often overlooked or added as an afterthought. A perfectly resource-green house that replaces a healthy ecosystem is a poor substitute. Badly sited, such a building destroys the site and, with it, environmental services.

Siting for access to regional infrastructure also plays a large and often unconsidered role. For example, although the very green headquarters of Patagonia makes excellent use of a degraded site and is highly resource efficient, it is located outside the Reno NV public transportation network and leaves employees little option but to drive long distances to work. Balancing these factors is difficult—and green building definitions that continue to marginalize site issues can disguise that difficulty rather than help solve it.

Including site protection in green building often highlights the fact that structures and construction are in some senses *inherently* damaging to the larger environment. The two factors that virtually *all* construction projects share are land clearance and creation of impervious surfaces—both detrimental to ecosystem function unless carefully mitigated. In an ideal world, green building should limit development to appropriate sites. Clearly, this conflicts head-on with land-use and landownership conventions. Green siting makes green building paradoxical, and to some, unpalatable—so site issues are left out.

Without site protection as a goal, green building can become a little like fat-free cookies—an excuse to consume more because it's better than other brands. Many efficiency gains, in fact, have been outweighed by a distressing trend toward larger and larger "McMansion" homes.[40] Although the design and construction industries are understandably reluctant to be put on a diet, one important part of green building is *building less*. Keeping the industry *and* the environment healthy is a great challenge.

In the growing number of green building books for architecture and engineering, landscape is usually accorded only an introductory mention. Too frequently, architectural writers assume that landscape is a minor subset of their profession, and that environmental evaluation of architectural materials can simply be transferred to landscape work. In researching this book, this repeatedly proved to be far from true. Information for architects is increasingly focused on "building systems" and on component performance for *operating* the structure. This focus has clear value, but it requires translation to have meaning in the landscape, where construction is done with simpler materials and operating energy is usually low. The very favorable reception that this book's earlier editions received from landscape professionals indicates that the architectural perspective on green building is not easily applicable outdoors. The most sustainable thing a landscape professional can do may simply be to bring a "landscape perspective" to the table.

The Landscape Professions: NOT Construction
"versus" Design

Another contextual issue affecting sustainable work is the white collar versus blue collar split. Replacing that dichotomy with broader teamwork is a hallmark of many of the projects mentioned in this book.

Most landscape "construction" books have, in the past, been written for designers by designers. In these books (and the courses where they serve as texts), physical labor, machinery, and tools might as well not exist. The focus of these books, despite their titles, is primarily on detail and structure in *design*, not on how to *build* the design at the site. There is a legitimate need for detailed design information, and the fact that "construction" books are widely read by designers shows how much the contractor and designer rely on one another in their duties. Ignoring the contractor's actual work is a shortcoming in these books, perhaps reflective of a shortcoming in professional attitudes.

At the other end of the spectrum, there are many fine books on larger-scale design and planning issues. Ian McHarg's epochal book, *Design with Nature*, turns *fifty* in 2019.[41] Since that time many books have dealt with ecological assessment, planning, and design. But even if these planning and design principles are sensitively followed, inappropriate *construction* methods and materials can still lead to unnecessary environmental destruction. Where those books start from the broad scale (design or planning), this book has its foundation at the site-specific scale of actually constructing landscapes. Although it is not so construction-focused that it includes "typical" details, doomed to be pasted into contract documentation for generations after they are obsolete, the hope has always been that both designers and contractors could learn something from this book and be persuaded to collaborate more effectively.

Prior to this book's first release, information on better landscape *construction* alternatives was very scattered and poorly documented. Much of this information was available only in homeowner format, focused on maintenance issues such as reduction of pesticide use or the value of composting. This excluded many issues of importance to professionals in landscape construction and design. The situation has improved a great deal, but homeowner/professional, designer/contractor, and other dichotomies remain barriers to deeper sustainability.

Some information in this book is of interest primarily to one-half of the landscape profession, either to contractors or to designers. Design and construction cannot truly be separated, though, and most issues affect both groups. Changes in construction materials and methods affect what designers can specify. New ideas in design affect what contractors can and are expected to build. This book has two goals: to call attention to the environmental effects and potentials of physical landscape construction, and to state the case, repeatedly, for better *integration* of design and construction as an essential step toward sustainable land use.

"Landscape professionals" and the "landscape professions" mean landscape architects, landscape contractors, and many others who support their work: horticulturists, arborists, nurseries, materials suppliers, grounds maintenance workers. Permaculturists, Xeriscape experts, consulting ecologists, and others are part of the mix.[42] Some engineers, architects, and general contractors also deserve at least honorary membership. This book is intended to go beyond current professional definitions. Thinking of ourselves as members of a larger community of *professionals whose livelihood is the landscape* has great power and value.

Breaking down barriers to cooperation is especially important for those whose goal is sustainability. The old barriers serve no good purpose in the attempt to care holistically for the built environment. Collaborative project approaches adopted by sustainability-driven firms are an entirely positive trend.

Get an Attitude

Besides appropriate techniques and materials, site protection relies on positive attitudes toward the landscape. Many "conventional" professionals share these attitudes, which are not the exclusive wisdom of environmental designers or specialists. It is too easy to assume that "They" (builders, engineers, contractors, conventional designers . . .) are insensitive to landscape issues. Landscape as afterthought is in fact a serious problem, but throughout the design and construction industries are people who know and love the outdoors and chose their profession accordingly: civil engineers who restore wetlands, or highway contractors who can quote dozens of literary naturalists.

Fundamental to protecting and making healthy sites is the recognition that each site is alive, unique, and connected to a web of off-site influences. By contrast, the common attitude that sites are just "unimproved land," blank-slate building locations, virtually guarantees site damage. Conventional concerns like practicality and keeping down costs must be balanced with respect for site health. A balanced attitude, whether among team members or in an individual conscience, is a major part of any attempt to build sustainably.

Designers and construction workers alike get great satisfaction from their power to change and rearrange the site. This power, and skill in exercising it, is well deserving of pride but can also become a "power trip." Designers can fall into the trap of arrogantly remaking the site on a whim. Cynicism and even despair are also occupational hazards, born of seeing too many good places deformed by carelessness, too many good designs denied by regulation or cost. Similarly, some construction workers begin to view site and materials as adversaries to be overcome, and use anger to crank up the energy needed to do the job. This combative attitude is expressed when existing trees are hacked unnecessarily, or equipment is driven carelessly, or construction scrap is thrown around the site. There are strong reasons, both conventional and sustainable, to avoid any of these attitudes, which poison both professional and personal relations with the land.

Successful design firms create a "corporate culture" in which creativity steers clear of arrogance. The best contractors discourage the site-as-adversary attitude; they make pride a constructive rather than destructive force. In design and construction firms, and between them, teamwork lightens the sometimes thankless task of pushing sustainability through a legal and social obstacle course. Professionals of all types work to make their *practices* sustainable. To paraphrase the basic definition, a sustainable business attitude aims for "meeting the goals of this office without diminishing the ability of other professionals to meet their goals."

The technical solutions found in this book can support, but cannot replace, an attitude that balances ecological health with human desires. This attitude,

and the creative application of sustainable knowledge, thrives best in an atmosphere of collaboration.

One of the great potential strengths of the landscape professions is that, unlike either industrialists or environmentalists, we often resist the knee-jerk tendency to take absolute positions of opposition. There is a risk of being (or being perceived as) apologists for development, but thoughtfully and honestly practiced, the ability to convince industry pragmatically of their environmental responsibilities, and communities of their accountability as consumers, is a genuine collaborative contribution.

Build a Site-focused Team

Many of the world's greatest and best-loved landscapes were built and nurtured by many hands over decades or even centuries. Part of their appeal lies in the traces of so much attention from so many people. It is certainly possible for one person to build an entire landscape beautifully, if the site is small enough and the time for building quite long. For larger landscapes, for those that are ecologically complex, or for those that must be built in a hurry, teamwork is inevitable—and can work for sustainability or against it.

One team approach that has gained widespread attention since about 2004 is termed "integrated (or integrative) design." Although there are many variations, ID calls for conducting stakeholder charettes throughout design, construction, and early occupancy; having all the experts on-board early in face-to-face meetings if possible, including contractors, code officials, and specialist consultants along with the core design team; modeling and testing assumptions, usually through several iterations; hiring a trained project manager to keep the process moving; and using communication tools that promote collaboration and keep everyone in the loop. The idea that only huge projects can use this is a myth, according to a detailed report by *EBN*;[43] for landscape firms, ID might primarily involve having the contractor on-board during design. The federal General Services Administration found that integrative design consistently produced higher performance outcomes than conventional approaches.[44] A parallel approach has the client, design team, and contractor enter a formal partnering agreement; insurance cov-

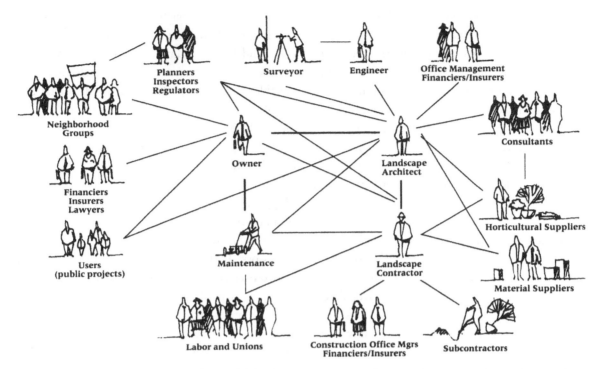

Figure 0.3   Constructing healthy and sustainable landscapes requires coordination of many specialists into a complex team. (*Illust.:* Craig Farnsworth.)

ers all the partners, promoting problem-solving rather than finger-pointing. A related contractual innovation is tying a portion of the design fee to achievement of measurable performance outcomes (see Principle 11).

The minimum team for a high-quality, sustainably built landscape consists of four roles: the client, the designer, the builder, and the maintenance person. Sometimes several roles are played by one person: the client may act as designer or do maintenance; a design-build firm may do post-occupancy maintenance. Conventional wisdom favors narrow specialization, but overlapping arrangements have great value in creating healthy places.

Nearly as often, each role may involve several people. The client may be one or more organizations. Some sites are owned by one entity but *used* by other people; users of a public landscape may have more say than the agency that "owns" it. Building codes and regulations are often an invisible "team member" (usually uncooperative) for both the designer and the contractor. Consultants and subcontractors play many roles. Lending and insuring agencies are still notorious for refusing to fund "alternative" work—but can

increasingly be instrumental in getting such methods approved.

What brings all this complexity together is a shared vision, a set of clearly stated goals that the whole team understands and supports. The vision may come from a single strong personality or from long debate leading to consensus. Unless the vision is *clear, doable, and communicated to every person involved* in the construction process, it has little hope of being realized. If the vision is some form of sustainability, clear communication is even more critical, given how wooly a word "sustainable" can be.

Even in the 1990s, the architectural firm HOK had recommended a *new design process* for sustainable results. Of six phases, the first two—where the opportunities for change and cost savings are greatest—are team formation and education/goal setting.[45]

Conventional practice tends to work against team formation and education by insisting that each expert has a narrowly defined niche. Yet nearly all designers, if asked for their most-satisfying projects, would name jobs where the contractor was a trusted collaborator. By contrast, the most frustrating projects are those that run under low-bid rules and treat collaboration as conflict of interest.

HOK minced no words: "Engineers need to be involved in the design process from the very beginning—so too must the construction professionals, including the major subcontractors, those ultimately responsible for operations, the various consultants, and in some cases key suppliers."[46] Although written with structural design in mind, this statement applies equally, if not more so, to designing landscapes that attempt ecological functions.

Many large design firms have revised their work processes in pursuit of sustainability.[47] Even governmental agencies have recognized the value of teaming with contractors and suppliers. Instead of a strict low-bid process, many agencies require prequalification for all bidders. Contractors and suppliers must demonstrate a track record, including quality work and ability to control costs, before they qualify to bid. Environmental knowledge and care may also be criteria. A graduated series of steps, from prequalification for small projects to inclusion on the large project list, opens this process to new firms and keeps it fair to all. At the same time, the client agency can have confidence that the low bidder for a project knows what is expected and has the skills to do the work. In this sense, the contractors become part of the team even within the limits of public-sector work.

The whole team needs to educate itself about environmental issues that will affect the project. On an effective team, among themselves the members already know most of the issues or how to find information quickly. Equally important, they have a well-defined way of sharing their knowledge. Once basic issues are defined and understood, project goals are set. These should be specific, and it should be possible to evaluate whether they were met. For example, a goal of "saving water" is too vague. "Reduce irrigation use of tap water to 40 percent of the average for nearby landscapes" is a specific goal. Not all testable goals include numbers, but quantifiable goals are most easily tested.

For public lands, and for many large private projects, neighborhood input is today a legal requirement. This is changing the way that land-use decisions are made, and some conventional developers, designers, and contractors resent the change. Most landscapes, however, affect the neighbors, and public opposition that is ignored often translates to neglect, misuse, and even vandalism. Building a landscape only to have it destroyed by its users or neighbors is clearly not sustainable. Landscape professionals need to look again at public input and see it as an opportunity. "Community-based planning" and "participatory design" are two approaches that are gaining more practitioners. The results can be quite remarkable. New York City Housing Authority landscape architect Leonard Hopper points to dramatic successes in making livable communities out of crime-ridden ones through redesign *by and for* the residents. It takes commitment and hard work: Philadelphia landscape firm Synterra attended over 200 community meetings in one year for a single large public-works project.

Collaborative effort may seem like a social issue, unrelated either to construction or to sustainability. In the conventional, compartmentalized mode, this is true. But that view contributes to direct and indirect waste of resources, the very opposite of sustainability. Poor coordination results in wasted site visits, consuming fuel. Incorrect drawings and specs waste paper (if they are caught and corrected) and waste materials if they go unrecognized and get built. Failing to plan for standard available sizes of materials, or for reuse of on-site materials, also leads to waste. Worst of all, a built landscape that fails to meet its goals is soon an unhealthy landscape and may take neighboring landscapes with it in decline.

Environmental Justice and the Cultural Context for Sustainability

Sustainable design is a cultural activity and occurs in cultural contexts, an aspect of which is "environmental justice." Whether it appears by name in project discussions or not, EJ can have a pronounced impact on project success.

Emerging as a movement in the 1980s, the concept of environmental justice is simple and disturbing: ethnic minorities and low-income people are significantly more likely to live or work in places affected by environmental hazards. Polluting facilities are more likely to be located in or near such communities. Members of these communities are less likely to be informed or consulted during planning decisions, and violations of existing environmental regulations are less likely to be enforced on behalf of such communities.[48]

Environmental justice is a specialized subject, and this book is not the place to examine its root causes. Evidence suggests that race, rather than economic class, better predicts whether an individual or community will face unusual environmental risks. As such, the term "environmental racism" is frequently used, with environmental justice as the hoped-for solution.

Setting aside the ethical aspects of this issue as too large to address adequately here, this issue is important for purely pragmatic reasons to landscape professionals working toward sustainability.

- Affected communities often are potent allies in pushing sustainable design past convention-bound authorities.[49] Never assume that such alliances can be easily forged, nor that community goals will align readily with design-school priorities. Extensive community involvement is required, often across cultural divides that few landscape architects can navigate without help.
- Conversely, affected communities can be formidable opponents, often rejecting projects intended to be sustainable. Environmental justice activists typically view the "classic" environmental movement as concerned only with preserving nature for the elite. What a landscape professional might consider a model sustainability project, the community may perceive as irrelevant to more pressing problems such as pollution-induced illnesses. This is especially true of projects, however well-intentioned, presented to the public as complete plans without serious local input. Complicating matters, "green" groups, including green building organizations, remain largely white.[50]
- The federal government created an EPA Office of Environmental Justice in 1992, and two years later it required *all* federal agencies to address the issue. A number of states have their own EJ agency, and these agencies may be left with sole responsibility if the federal EPA is shut down. Federal EJ efforts are governed by Title VI of the Civil Rights Act of 1964 and use federal definitions of minority and low-income status. This can cut both ways, easing

environmental quality into some projects and, in others, snarling all hope of improvements in us-versus-them politics. The difference is very often the design team's initial attitude toward cooperation with the community.

Landscape professionals can find good guidance about this thorny subject in the work of California landscape architect Randolph Hester. Hester, often working with Joe Edmiston, the visionary founder of the Santa Monica Mountains Conservancy in Los Angeles, has incorporated cross-cultural, community-based methods in all his work. While conventional wisdom has held that low-income nonwhites have no interest in nature parks and only want active sport facilities, Hester has acted on research showing the opposite to be true: poor neighborhoods vote in favor of bonds to fund nature conservation at strikingly higher percentages than do adjacent wealthy neighborhoods.[51] Hester's book *Design for Ecological Democracy* takes the interesting position that "democracy bestows freedom; ecology creates responsible freedom [through] interconnectedness with all species. [Ecology] forges the basis for civil society to address a shared public good."[52]

One promising development is Public Lab, a grassroots organization that points communities to extremely low-cost methods of mapping and monitoring conditions in their communities—literally using balloons, string, and cheap cameras, as well as homemade replacements for expensive environmental sensors. The technical aspects are noted in the section on drone surveying (Principle 1); a few landscape architects have already adopted some of these methods. By using Internet connections and open-source methods, Public Lab (which started life as the Public Laboratory for Open Technology and Science) is essentially crowd-sourcing environmental monitoring. With the ability to document conditions that governmental agencies ignore, communities are able to take more environmental justice and community-based design issues into their own hands.[53]

In addition to avoiding unfair exposure to hazards, environmental justice aims for equitable distribution of resources. Natural resources are distributed, by nature, very unequally in the world's geographic regions, something that has strongly affected cultural and technological development and, thus, differences in environmental destruction and pollution. It is well worth any landscape professional's time to read Jared Diamond's Pulitzer Prize–winning book on this subject, *Guns, Germs, and Steel*,[54] not only for background on environmental justice among cultures but also as a forceful reminder of how interdependence with ecology and place has shaped human history.

Expect Demographics, Economics, and Politics to Change Sustainability Itself

It seems obvious that economic channels create changing currents in which sustainable designers must swim. In fact, almost every junior designer hears "idealistic notions" like sustainability crushed by some crusty senior partner because they are not in line with The Economy.

Nonetheless, economic, political, and demographic trends *are* changing what sustainable practice means today. Anyone involved in construction has noted drastic increases in building material prices. Several factors are involved. China, whose rate of new building starts has often been nearly ten times that of the United States, is in effect outbidding American purchasers, with Brazil and India adding sharply to demand. Transportation costs (especially for heavy items such as building materials) rose steeply when oil prices peaked, and dropped when crude fell; this volatility makes estimating difficult, an argument for local sourcing.[55] The severe storms that appear to be part of global warming have created shortages of *re*construction materials, most evident in the United States after Hurricane Katrina, when blue tarps could not be had for any money in many major cities otherwise unaffected by the hurricane.[56]

None of these factors seem likely to go away, and the smart money says they will get worse. For sustainable design, this is bad news and good news. Some building materials have doubled in price in a matter of months, affecting both conventional and sustainable projects. Sustainable methods, however, which explicitly aim to save materials and use local and recycled products, actually gain attractiveness in such an economic climate.

The political climate between 2000 and 2008 has repeatedly been described as the worst ever for the environment (since no one was predicting 2017). Yet the federal anti-environmental posture[57] had and has unintended consequences. Groups like the Environmental Council of the States and the United States Conference of Mayors became increasingly proactive on matters from the Kyoto accord to pollution standards, partly in protest against federal gutlessness. Green building actually flourished during the same period. Despite appearances that 2017 will take "worst environment ever" to even lower depths, state and local pushback may yet be a bright spot. California, for example, is committing independently, as one of the world's largest economies in its own right, to meeting the Paris climate accord.

In about 2007, the National Association of Home Builders and construction researchers at McGraw-Hill predicted that 10 percent of US homes would be green by 2010; only 2 percent of new construction was then green.[58] As of 2014, another McGraw-Hill "SmartMarket Report" predicted that green homes would constitute 40 percent of the single-family market, with 84 percent of all homes having some sustainability-related features.[59] Green homes—a significant part of whose value comes from sustainable landscapes—are in demand from half of all buyers, and sell for higher prices than conventional homes.[60] Large "spec" builders remain, as a group, the slowest to adopt green techniques: their focus is on lowering up-front costs, which they do by sacrificing the operational savings obtained by investing in green construction. The increase in initial costs due to building green is generally reported as from less than 1 percent to about 7 percent. Benefits (considering only actual financial savings) over twenty years amount to ten times the initial investment.[61]

The marketability of sustainable design is linked to how people value the environment, and that, too, is changing as the United States undergoes *demographic* shifts. Hispanics, expected to make up nearly a quarter of the US population by 2050,[62] have become increasingly active in environmental issues, more likely to support pollution abatement and urban parks than roadless areas or endangered species.[63] Aging boomers are an increasing demographic; some will quit using outdoor facilities, while demand for handicapped access will continue to grow. What a new generation of adults will do outdoors (if anything, given the fascination of electronics) remains to be seen. As one National Park Service official put it, "Are we ready for Extreme Sports in the Parks? Because they're coming."[64]

No one can truly predict such trends, even in stable times. It is clear, however, that America's dedication to the great outdoors is changing. With it, but not necessarily in any clear parallel, attitudes toward sustainable development will change.

How people define what they value in the environment is the context within which sustainable design flourishes or dwindles. Under Obama, opportunities for green building were growing fast; whether that will continue is unknown. But the market has not been driven simply by idealism—trends such as high materials costs and the threat of climate change have made sustainable (and resilient, and regenerative, and passive-survivable) design marketable. Sustainability has not only become mainstream, but in a sense has gone beyond being optional. Landscape professionals who invest in sustainable practice must continue to assess their surroundings and adapt accordingly.

Be Prepared to Stand Your Ground

Although in general, this book steers clear of politics as much as possible, several very current political battles are bound to affect landscape practice, especially for firms focused on sustainability. For most of the past four decades, significant amounts of landscape work have come from governmental agencies charged with protecting or restoring public lands and, increasingly, agencies that have been proactive leaders in green sites and facilities. The general public acceptance of "ecology"—faddish though it has often been—also has played a role in giving landscape architects, planners, contractors, and restoration specialists work. Whatever your personal politics, it is quite clear that these values are under attack. In particular, condemning any and all regulatory law as "burdensome" and dismissing most governmental functions as part of a "nanny state" has moved from fringe dogma to federal policy; the attempt to privatize public lands continues;

and in parallel with this, anti-environmentalism has become fashionable. These trends are very likely to affect the ability of landscape professionals to practice.

If you represent your clients at zoning hearings, you may be confronted with citizens who believe zoning *itself* is illegitimate. If you get work from local, state, or federal agencies, the mandatory public hearings for your projects may be dominated by charges that all governmental spending is elitist.

Your beliefs are your own, obviously, but be prepared to be extra clear about them, and to find them challenged in ways that our profession has not routinely had to face before.

I doubt there is an American who doesn't feel that our regulations and taxes are unnecessarily complicated. Most of us also feel that certain laws make little sense, or are outdated. But ask yourself whether you believe *all* regulations should be abolished. It seems to me that there are many things, for instance building a coherent highway system, that cannot be accomplished by individuals alone, and can be accomplished most cost-effectively by working through the auspices of government. Using that highway system demands at least a few regulations, starting with agreement about which side to drive on. The decision to drive left or drive right is absolutely *arbitrary* (a term often used to dismiss the value of regulations), yet everyone's agreement to it is literally life-or-death. Wherever there is a "commons," a resource that is needed by everyone, regulations appear to me essential to prevent monopolization and misuse of that resource. My opinion isn't the point: I urge you to give thought to these questions, whatever answer you personally come to, before they are flung in your face at a public meeting.

Astonishingly (to me, at least), protection of the environmental commons has become a hot-button issue, equal in volatility to gender, reproduction, and ethnicity in the amount of intense hatred it generates. Environmentalists can certainly be strident in defense of species and places, of clean air and water, and (like most of us when we feel threatened) are prone to demonizing any opposition. Among the right wing, who feel that unrestrained economic autonomy is under threat, anti-environmentalism has reached fever pitch and is used to justify truly hate-filled attacks on scientists, elected officials, and citizens alike.

One reason for mentioning anti-environmentalism in a pragmatic book like this is that even when it is not explicit policy, it has real-world consequences that touch our profession directly. For example, several states have considered or adopted laws *prohibiting* the use of the LEED rating system for public works, at the behest of timber interests and chemical manufacturers, who see requirements for sustainably managed forests or toxin-free products as threats that would hold them accountable.[65] Many appointed officials have used anti-environmental rationales for subverting the law, as when Interior Secretary Gale Norton reported that US wetlands were *increasing* in area by counting ornamental pools, golf course water hazards, and mine reclamation ponds as wetlands.[66] Both of these examples had direct impact on people with green business strategies, whether as consultants, materials suppliers, or designers. Anti-environmentalism often goes hand in hand with negative attitudes toward environmental justice, the social aspect of land degradation, discussed above.

A second and more hopeful reason is that landscape architects are sometimes exactly the right people to bridge the divide between environmentalists and businesspeople. We understand and work daily with both the living environment and the techniques of building and development, and can sometimes be unusually effective in translating the concerns of one side into language that the other is able to hear. I can testify, from personal experience, that this works and produces results far superior to the usual confrontational process. I can also say that it is an uncomfortable position at times, with both sides accusing you of treachery. A landscape perspective, especially one that explicitly includes both the wild and the human-built environment, is broad enough to embrace apparent contradictions, with win-win results.

Whether in a positive mediating sense or simply in professional self-defense, it is more critical now than ever to take the time to think through your personal position on ecological concerns; on regulation and government; on the degree of risk that is acceptable (if any) where environmental hazards are involved; and on the claim that jobs and profits are always the most important social priorities. Without knowing clearly where you stand, you cannot have the necessary balance and flexibility to practice in today's environment.

Landscapes Against Climate Change

Any serious discussion of sustainability must include global warming, more accurately called global climate change. Denying that this threat is either man-made or urgent became official US policy in 2017; this simply adds to the necessity of the discussion. Without addressing climate change, many "sustainable" activities are almost irrelevant. Yet efforts like energy conservation or site restoration *are* important, because, at some critical mass, they *add up* to affect global climate.

Understandably, many people feel helpless in the face of what could be a worldwide catastrophe, yet the situation is not one of unmitigated gloom and doom. In fact, recent initiatives have thrust architects into the spotlight as a professional group with real potential to reverse climate change using realistic and proven methods. Similarly, recent research that connects land-use practices to weather extremes indicates that landscape professionals have a role to play as well.

Architecture 2030 and the Global Climate Initiative

Architects, according to Ed Mazria, "hold the key to the global thermostat." Mazria, a Santa Fe NM architect known for pioneering work on solar buildings, is the founder of Architecture 2030. This initiative could literally make architects the heroes that save the planet from climate catastrophe.

Perhaps that sounds like overstatement, but it is not. Mazria bases his proposal on a sophisticated re-analysis of US energy-use statistics. His work shows that when materials, construction, operation, and decommissioning are taken into account, the building industry uses *nearly half of all energy* consumed each year.[67] Urban areas, where an increasing percentage of humans live, use about 75 percent of all energy.[68] Energy use equates roughly to greenhouse gases and climate change. Thus, changes in energy use by buildings stand to have a major impact on the problem.[69]

How major? The most catastrophic effects of climate change can be averted, according to Mazria, by cutting fossil-fuel use for buildings. Goals set in 2005

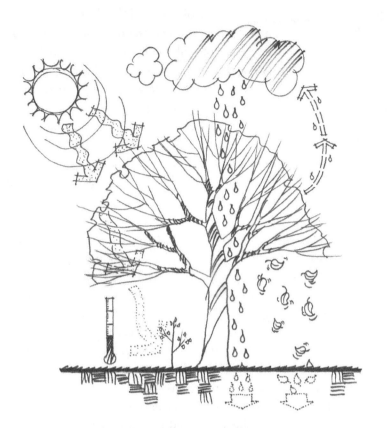

Figure 0.4 Vegetation cover, especially mature canopy, protects soil, improves infiltration, and moderates climate. (*Illust.:* Craig Farnsworth.)

Figure 0.5 Vegetation clearance depletes and bakes soil, increases runoff, and warms climate. (*Illust.:* Craig Farnsworth.)

are tracking reasonably well today. An initial 50 percent cut, plus an additional 10 percent every five years, will bring US buildings to carbon neutrality by 2030. These goals, moreover, are being accomplished using well-known and tested methods familiar to green builders.[70] What is necessary is to make these universal, and to do it consistently *and soon*.

Introduced in 2006, Architecture 2030's "2030 Challenge" was officially adopted by the American Institute of Architects (AIA), the US Green Building Council (USGBC, originators of the LEED program), the American Society of Heating, Refrigerating and Air-Conditioning Engineers (ASHRAE), and some twenty other building-related industry associations, plus the US Council of Mayors. That adoption may prove to be a watershed event, even though, by 2016, commitments by design firms to meet energy-conservation targets were common, but not yet universal.[71]

Landscapes, as this book emphasizes, use relatively little energy and fuel compared to buildings. Does that mean that landscape professionals can sit complacently on the sidelines while architects ride out in shining armor? Definitely not.

Land and Climate

The first edition of this book noted a single piece of research about climatology and landscapes—an early indicator of what has become a much broader issue. In 1998, researchers Jonathan Foley and Roger Pielke demonstrated that land development had altered Florida's climate enough to affect its agricultural industry significantly. Clearing land, draining swamps, rerouting rivers, and urbanization had resulted in measurably hotter and drier summers, and in winters that damaged citrus crops farther south than anyone had ever seen before.[72]

Since that time, there has been growing consensus that clearing land—for agriculture or for development—plays a role in climate change that must be considered alongside the better-publicized CO_2 emissions caused by fuel combustion. Pielke and others have stated that land clearance results in *as much greenhouse gas as is produced by fuel burning*. Other sources, especially official bodies, tend to put the number lower, with land clearance and related changes causing about 20 to 25 percent of the total.[73] Scientific consensus is emerging, however, that the removal of vegetation and alteration of soil conditions is implicated in *between one-quarter and one-half* of these threatening atmospheric changes. A 2011 report by scientists from the European Environment Agency raised the concern that European Union methods for estimating carbon reduction left out soil and vegetation sequestration, thus underestimating greenhouse gas emissions when land is cleared or converted from native vegetation to farmland.[74] A great deal of conventional landscape construction contributes directly to these problems, bulldozing whatever vegetation existed on-site and replacing it with limited species or monocultures. By contrast, most sustainable landscape techniques potentially affect climate for the better. Protecting healthy sites, restoring denuded ones, planting appropriate vegetation, managing stormwater for infiltration, and reducing impervious paving—in addition to localized benefits, all these techniques cumulatively have significant global implications.

Landscape professionals, even those who focus on sustainability, still tend to concentrate on local benefits of healthy sites. The evidence has become overwhelming, however, that the landscape professions must also pay attention to the *global* effects of converting land from vegetated to paved, or from dense native plant communities to sparsely ornamental horticulture. This is imperative because sustainable practices work to slow climate change, while many conventional methods hasten it.

To make a difference, individual sustainable practices need to be understood in a larger context. Thus, although this book generally focuses on practical, close-to-home matters, this section gives a brief overview of documented links between land use and climate change. Some designers and contractors will be tempted to skip this section. Doing so is asking for *business* failure, because our business is inextricable from all the things affected by climate. Seriously—if you read nothing else, read this.

Get the Facts

Doubt about climate change—that it isn't real or that humans bear little responsibility for it—has been manufactured, to be blunt, by ExxonMobil and its allies. Please download the Union of Concerned Scientists' January 2007 report documenting ExxonMobil's campaign of disinformation, which has paid tens of millions of dollars ($2 million in 2015 alone) to create deliberately false uncertainty and controversy over climate change.[75] The money funded bogus institutes where marginally qualified scientists distorted their "research" to cast doubt on climate change. The motivation for playing the American public for fools is clear—to keep making fossil-fuel money as long as possible before the switch to renewable energy sources becomes unavoidable. The contention that climate change is an invention of the Chinese or of shady environmental cabals trying to take over the Earth would be laughable if it didn't excuse this abuse of science. Imagine a judge hearing two sides present evidence in court: one side has a huge motive, almost unlimited means, and underhanded opportunity; the other has no serious financial motive, and only rational persuasion as means and opportunity.

Please consult one of the following. Not only will they give you straight, clear facts, they will inspire you that it is possible to take positive action.

- *The Weather Makers: How Man Is Changing the Climate and What It Means for Life on Earth* (Atlantic Monthly Press, 2005) is an excellent, readable book by Tim Flannery, a respected Australian scientist, author, and commentator for the BBC, ABC, and NPR.
- *An Inconvenient Truth*: the famous documentary provides a clear summary of climate issues; it is easy to follow, thought provoking, moving, and positive. (The DVD is widely available, and *An Inconvenient Sequel: Truth to Power* was released in several formats in 2017.)
- The concise graphic website www.architecture2030.org has united architects and other design professionals toward realistic climate-focused goals.
- *EBN* has devoted several issues to understanding climate change from the perspective of designers and builders. See, for example, October 2013; April and May 2014; and April 2016. All are available online at www.buildinggreen.com, which can be searched for further details.
- *Merchants of Doubt*, a book by Naomi Oreskes and

Erik Conway, details the ExxonMobil fake-science scandal and related impostures. See www.merchantsofdoubt.org/ (book) and www.imdb.com/title/tt3675568/ (documentary video).

These sources offer clear and factual background on the issue. For further detail, see the resource list for Principle 7 (energy).

Landscape Change and Climate Change

Carbon, the primary component of greenhouse gases (today often abbreviated GHGs), is also critical to all life. All plants and animals are carbon-based lifeforms; carbon is found in soil, wood, dead organic matter, and, of course, the atmosphere. Plants absorb carbon from air and bond it with hydrogen to store energy (photosynthesis), which ultimately is the world's only source of either food or fuel.[76] Oxygen breaks these bonds and releases energy (combustion, digestion, and respiration), which emits CO_2 and other GHGs like methane into the atmosphere. This release occurs at very different rates for different materials: foods hold carbon and energy for a few weeks if fresh, a few years if preserved; wood and other ordinary fuels sequester carbon and hold energy for years to decades, as do dead trees in forests. The problem with fossil fuels is that they release in an instant energy and carbon that were concentrated over unimaginably long periods. Releasing such concentrated energy makes them powerful in the extreme, while releasing eons worth of carbon in a few years is rapidly raising the percentage of GHGs in the atmosphere.

Carbon dioxide acts like glass in a passive solar design: light passes inward through the atmosphere, but CO_2 prevents heat-producing ultraviolet rays from escaping. The more CO_2 in the atmosphere, the more Earth's average temperature rises. Certain other GHGs are actually more potent than CO_2, but CO_2 appears to trigger the others.

Burning fossil fuels—which consist of carbon stored by ancient plants—creates heat directly through combustion and releases large amounts of CO_2 into the atmosphere, raising the average global temperature. In addition, as a separate cause for concern, carbon absorbed from the atmosphere has raised the acidity of the oceans by 25 percent since the Industrial Revolution. This increased acidity makes it difficult for marine animals to form skeletons, shells, and reefs; of particular concern, phytoplankton, the base of almost all marine food chains, are threatened. There is no question that this carbon is anthropogenic: it contains specific isotopes traceable only to the burning of fossil fuels.[77]

Because of the greenhouse effect and ocean acidification, CO_2 was declared a threat to humans by the EPA in 2009. Why did it take that long? Because a favorite argument of climate-change deniers has been a variation on the "you can die from too much water" deception: since CO_2 is essential to life, they have argued, it can't be called toxic and, thus, can't be regulated by pollution laws. It is likely that this battle will be refought.

The basic chemistry is excruciatingly clear. Where does landscape change fit in?[78]

Of the many planetary reservoirs of CO_2, plants and soils are the most *active* in exchanging CO_2 with the atmosphere, meaning that carbon is held for relatively short periods (compared, say, to coal, which literally holds "the energy of ancient suns").[79] Plants take CO_2 out of the atmosphere and hold it in sugars and woody tissues. Soil is also a major reservoir of stored carbon.

When plant cover is removed, or its density is reduced, several things occur, all trending toward warming. (See Figures 0.4 and 0.5.)

- No longer shaded by vegetation, soil bakes in direct sun, holding enough extra heat to raise local temperatures.
- Heated soils kill carbon-storing microorganisms and speed decomposition of organic matter, releasing CO_2.
- With less vegetation to protect it from rain, runoff, and wind, exposed soil erodes; this further releases organic matter and emits CO_2.
- Heating and erosion of soil kills more plants, leading to more heating and erosion in a vicious cycle.
- If removed plants are burned (or eaten), CO_2 stored in them is released.

Loss of soil and vegetative cover is well-known to historians under a different name: deforestation. Many of the world's deserts are the direct result of human deforestation practices.[80] Large-scale land clearance, for whatever purpose, almost always tends to increase hot-season temperatures, drought, and wildfire.

What is less commonly understood is that landscapes with sparse vegetation and dead or dying soils are also typically colder and windier in winter, less capable of infiltrating precipitation, and more prone to intense runoff and flooding.

In short, removal of any significant percentage of vegetative cover[81] from a large area, *or from many small areas cumulatively*, contributes to the extremes of heat and cold, drought, and flooding that are ever more clearly part of global climate change. Extreme weather, with records being shattered again and again, along with flooding, windstorms, and failure of infrastructure not designed for these extremes, is daily fare in the news.

Siting of buildings is a land-use/landscape issue that contributes indirectly to climate change by affecting how far materials and people are transported to build, use, and decommission the building. It has been shown that the sum of these transportation energy uses is often *double* the operating and embodied energy of the building (see Principle 7), so this is not a trivial consideration.[82] Landscape professionals, especially urban planners, can have important influence on this aspect of energy use.

Is Construction to Blame?

Construction almost always involves some land clearance. This is nearly unavoidable. In some regions, cleared areas regrow rapidly if left alone. Most projects, however, create impervious surfaces, from which vegetation and living soil are permanently excluded.

Even when a cleared landscape is replanted, this usually reduces the density and biodiversity of vegetative cover. As the Intergovernmental Panel on Climate Change states, "Conversion of natural ecosystems to croplands and pastures has resulted in . . . agro-ecosystems [that] continue to take up carbon, but at levels generally inferior to the previously forested ecosystems."[83] Ornamental landscapes are clearly agro-ecosystems in this sense and do not replace the CO_2 uptake of established regional vegetation. Most plantings also provide less shade, soil stabilization, and runoff prevention than mature forest cover.

Agriculture has been the main reason for land clearance historically, and it remains so in developing countries today. In the tropics, 500,000 trees are cut *every hour*, primarily for forestry and new agriculture.[84] In industrialized countries like the United States and Europe, however, clearance for buildings, infrastructure, and landscapes may be outpacing new agricultural clearance. The cumulative effect of clearing 1.39 *million* sites (a low estimate of annual new US housing starts)[85] is directly linked to global problems.[86] This puts landscape professionals and land-use planners in a position of serious influence and responsibility.

Estimating the extent of US land clearance is not easy. Something like 500,000 to 1.5 million acres are probably cleared per year; 3 million acres are "lost to agriculture" annually.[87] The *lowest* of these estimates equals an area half the size of Rhode Island. A great deal of this cleared land remains as "landscape" of some sort; many architectural or engineering structures, including roads, are surrounded by landscapes covering three to five times the area of the facility itself. Thus, what landscape professionals do about clearance, revegetation, soil protection, paving, and water management cumulatively influences huge areas. Areas, in fact, that are more than large enough to affect climate.

Over the past decade, two trends have linked landscape practice to climate change. One is the inclusion of GHG-emission potential as criteria in land-use planning and the issuance of permits. Since 2008, California has required regional planners to take GHG-reduction targets into account as part of transit-priority urban design; the state also successfully sued several developers and large businesses for failing to reduce GHG emissions in new facilities. In 2006, in response to severe air quality problems, the San Joaquin Valley Air Pollution Control District instituted provisions that require builders, developers, and even lawn-care operators to reduce their air-pollution outputs or pay to finance remediation projects.[88]

A second trend is design that expects to deal with climate changes, not prevent them. It appears that even if humans stop all CO_2-producing activities right now, some climate changes will still occur. As a result, designers and planners are looking hard at "resilient" design and construction—facilities that can adapt to predicted changes on an ongoing basis. Although some early thinking about resilience merely translated to overbuilt HVAC, it has quickly been realized that severe changes or disasters could overwhelm not just conventional mechanical systems, but some "sustainable" systems as well. Solar gain and air convection inside buildings will be affected by increased ambient temperatures, for example, potentially making passive solar and natural ventilation less effective than it is today. As a result, current thinking prioritizes strategies to *avoid the need* for heating or cooling, for example, over improved HVAC. Both resilient and passive-survivable *buildings* rely on environmental services and draw on landscape features, such as seasonal shading from plants, or cool paving alternatives.[89] Landscape professionals will likely see demands for these features and will need to be prepared to integrate them into overall adaptation strategies against future climate challenges.

Climate change is negatively affecting the economy, leaving less funding and resources for climate mitigation.[90] The longer we wait, the more this Catch-22 will hinder our efforts. Landscape strategies, being locally adapted and generally inexpensive, may be among the ways that we might break this vicious circle.

In order to help think about the almost unthinkable, climate modeling tools, long the purview of academia, are being redeveloped for use by designers. One such tool offers a pop-up calculator for "projected climate scenarios" inside ArcGIS.[91] Such apps are certain to increase in number and usability almost weekly.

The Landscape Architecture Foundation's 2016 "New Landscape Declaration"[92] points out the fundamental and global importance of landscapes, and of our actions in modifying them: "Across borders and beyond walls, from city centers to the last wilderness, humanity's common ground is the landscape itself. Food, water, oxygen—everything that sustains us comes from and returns to the landscape. What we do to our landscapes we ultimately do to ourselves."

What the Landscape Professions Can Do

This is good news and bad news. The bad news is that landscape business-as-usual contributes significantly to what many believe is humanity's single greatest challenge. The good news is that the strategies advocated in this book (and today being put into practice and researched by many professionals) offer practical contributions toward reversing climate change *if we act now*.

Although withdrawal from the Paris accord is discouraging, it is worth noting what the US Green Building Council said in response:[93]

> Today our efforts continue unabated and with commitment and hope that's stronger than ever.
>
> Yes, *hope*. We are hopeful for the future because we know that our movement is a community of 13 million strong, and it's growing. . . .
>
> U.S. companies, including many USGBC members, are already working to address business risks from climate change and to adapt their businesses to domestic and global opportunities created around climate-mitigation needs. Businesses and local governments are wisely seeking and investing in low-carbon fuels and technologies to stay on the cutting edge of the global economy. . . . More and more companies and government entities are tracking their carbon emissions, committing to reduction targets and taking action.
>
> Right now, "business as usual" is no longer an option.

Among the things landscape professionals can do:

- Collaborate with architects to achieve Architecture 2030's fossil-fuel-reduction goals for buildings; many landscape measures contribute directly.
- Avoid unnecessary vegetation clearing (using methods discussed in Principle 1) whether native or healthy non-native vegetation is at stake.
- Lobby against "pre-clearing" of real estate prior to sale. (See p. 50.)
- Do everything possible to increase humus in soils (up to a regionally appropriate maximum).
- Aim for canopy cover and density similar to regional plant communities, both in "restoration" projects and in planting design. (See Principles 2 and 3.)
- Find better methods of wildfire protection; especially, resist land clearance wrongly promoted as fire prevention. (See p. 127.)

- Use greenwalls and greenroofs to reinstate partial vegetative cover on structures. (See pp. 140 and 148.)
- Manage stormwater with vegetation, infiltrating it to benefit soils and plants. (See Principle 4.)
- Minimize paving to avoid soil and vegetation loss through erosion. (See Principle 5.)
- Cut down fossil-fuel use for transportation of materials, workers, and construction machinery. (See Principle 7.)
- Understand that bio-based fuels reduce (but do not eliminate) CO_2 from combustion, but they also reduce biodiversity where they are grown, and may also result in land being taken out of food production in favor of higher profits from growing fuels.
- Learn about "carbon sequestration," by which CO_2 is locked up in trees, wood, soil, and other materials.
- Don't buy the desperate or silly "solutions" proposed by industrial eccentrics. These have included giant mirrors in space, aerial spreading of tinfoil confetti, and even deliberately increasing opaque air pollutants, all to cut sunlight. One scientist has built a mini drone to replace bees as pollinators—but the average orchard tree has tens of thousands of flowers, multiplied by thousands of trees in the orchard. The unintended consequences of such actions would almost certainly worsen climate problems.

Note that working against climate change doesn't prohibit the use of any particular style or type of landscape except those that are exceptionally resource intensive; even those may be appropriate for sites of high cultural importance. In my opinion, we are looking at a redefinition of the landscape professions: by any means necessary, and in any form that works, we must restore soil and vegetation wherever development has reduced it.

One hundred trees can remove five tons of CO_2 and half a ton of other pollutants from the air each year. The same hundred trees will also capture 250,000 gallons (or 6¼ acre-feet) of stormwater per year in temperate climates. Those one hundred trees, carefully located for shade, would cut air-conditioning usage in half for thirty-three houses (three trees per house).

These effects have direct impact on climate locally and globally.[94] The vicious circle, again, is that as a region becomes more arid, it becomes harder and more resource intensive to keep plantings alive to maturity.

Carbon sequestration may well become the main economic reason for protecting and planting trees, surpassing even timber production, and may eventually provide unheard-of funding for planted landscapes. Sequestration also gives wood construction a new justification: keeping carbon out of circulation until the wood rots or burns. How much can be sequestered this way is hotly debated; clearly, plantings are only one part of a serious climate strategy.[95] A 2013 study found that sustainably managed forests store carbon, while cutting old-growth forests and replanting causes a net release of carbon.[96]

A US Forest Service research center specializing in urban trees is testing which species sequester CO_2 most effectively. Regional variation and age of trees are variables, but the following trees were found highly effective in a 2002 study: horse chestnut, black walnut, sweet gum, bald cypress, Douglas fir, and London plane; scarlet, red, and Virginia live oaks; and ponderosa, red, Hispaniola, and white pines.[97]

There has been controversy over whether mature trees sequester more or less carbon than young ones. Rapid growth of young plants was thought to trap carbon more quickly, though mature trees would hold many years of cumulative carbon. The idea that younger trees trapped more carbon was actually sometimes used as a justification for clear-cutting and replanting. However, recent research has shown that older trees actually take up *more* carbon in the same time, a strong reason for protecting mature landscapes and old-growth forests.[98]

Carbon sequestration is also the basis for "carbon-trading" schemes, such as the Chicago Climate Exchange. In theory, polluters in rich countries fund sustainable developments in poor countries through these trades. There is considerable controversy over this concept, with charges of conflict of interest, falsified reports, and lack of oversight.[99] Other "mitigation banking" schemes—for example, wetlands banking—have had poor results. Pollution and cleanup affect specific places—can they be made portable? Under carbon-trading procedures, a Texas coal-fired plant whose pollutant output was obscuring the Grand Canyon could buy carbon credits from a forest in India. Although this would positively affect global carbon levels, it would simply excuse rather than help the pollution problem at the Grand Canyon.

Until recently, only large brokerages, corporations, and governments could trade carbon futures. Individuals and small firms, however, now use a growing number of trading services. These allow a person or firm to buy enough carbon credits to offset their car or truck's annual output (about 5.5 metric tons) for around $50, or a house's worth (23 metric tons) for $99.[100] Many committed environmentalists do so. However, this looks suspiciously like paying for convenient absolution. Surely fixing the car or house, or one's own behavior, to generate less actual pollutants is more important than shuffling paper credits for them.

A more promising use of the carbon-as-commodity idea is a carbon tax, to make users more selective about consuming carbon fuels, and to generate revenues to deal with atmospheric carbon. Many permutations have been suggested, and thus far voted down due to fossil-industry opposition. One of the most plausible proposals for a carbon tax comes from the Citizens' Climate Lobby.

What the Landscape Professions Stand to Lose

Although every human being has a stake in reducing the greenhouse effect, landscape professionals stand to lose more and sooner because our livelihood *is* the environment. Warmer and drier local climates and shifted seasons are likely to snarl landscape work long before the world reaches true catastrophe. Drought has already ruined many landscape businesses, with planting or irrigation banned in many areas, while flooding and sea-level rise are all too literally destroying landscapes from Louisiana to California. Increased CO_2 is causing weeds to produce ten times more pollen, to the despair of both allergy sufferers and horticulturists.[101]

Even without obvious "natural disasters," climate change directly threatens landscape practice in unanticipated ways. Researchers with the National Oceanic and Atmospheric Administration found that hotter, and in some places more humid, weather has already reduced global labor capacity during hot seasons by

10 percent since midcentury. NOAA predicts heat-based reductions in the ability to do outdoor work of up to 60 percent if climate scenarios play out.[102] Heatstroke is a risk; metal tools can be too hot to handle, while power tools risk overheating; concrete and other materials behave differently above the 100-degree mark (see Principle 6). And heat isn't the only danger: particulate pollutants appear to increase the severity of precipitation and drought;[103] warming is predicted to create new ozone holes, making UV radiation increasingly hazardous;[104] and even solutions like working at night carry increased accident risk.

In another vicious circle, changed climate is affecting the very plants that are essential for reforestation and carbon sequestration. Over the past few decades climate change has more than doubled tree death rates in western US forests,[105] while in New England, it is implicated in lackluster fall color.[106] Storms, their intensity increased by climate change, destroy forests; Hurricanes Katrina and Rita killed or damaged an estimated 320 million trees, the largest-ever US forestry disaster, though the 2017 season may well prove worse.[107] The warming associated with climate change is causing plants to shift their distribution ranges; a study in western Europe showed that 70 percent of species studied had moved upward, toward cooler locations, by ninety-five feet per decade between 1905 and 2005.[108] The USDA's hardiness zone map was updated in 2012 (after what appears to be six years of Bush administration stalling);[109] over most of the United States, the new boundaries are on average *half a zone warmer* than the previous version (published in 1990), and two zones had to be added at the hot end of the scale. Despite this, the USDA officiously cautions that this is not clear evidence of climate change.[110]

As a profession, and as humans, we stand to lose our most beloved gardens if the climate changes sufficiently that existing species can no longer thrive in those locations. One of the saddest reports about climate change was a headline in the *Telegraph* (London): "Kyoto Protocol Fails to Save the Japanese City's Famous Zen Gardens." Your favorite historic garden may not be in the city where that accord was signed—but it too is vulnerable.[111]

The question of how built landscapes damage or benefit the environment has become considerably more central to sustainability than anyone realized a decade ago. The stakes have dramatically increased in the debate over whether native plants or nature-like landscape forms matter, and why human landscape-making so often oversimplifies those forms. "Greenwash," once merely misleading, is now nearly criminal.

The climate crisis powerfully increases the value of any activity that protects or restores vegetation and soils. Almost all the techniques of sustainable landscape-making do so, directly or indirectly. They are detailed in the following chapters. The responsibility to use them has never been more important.

Sustainability, Substance, and Style

Success is always interwoven with challenges, and never more so than in the movement for sustainability. The more the public and the profession accept green building and sustainable landscapes, and the more such places are built, the more critical it becomes to distinguish between landscapes that contribute functionally to the health of the environment and ones that do not.

Such distinctions require critical thinking, documentation of landscape performance, and the ability to see past superficial claims. None of those skills are simple, in part because of the many uncertainties about sustainability itself. It is challenging to understand how landscapes created to fit accepted, even beloved, social conventions can damage the environment. Since we raised this issue in our first edition, it has grown from a mainly site-specific question to one that influences global as well as local action. Especially as linked to global warming (see above), the pressure is on for claims of sustainability to have real substance.

Conversely, the danger of greenwash and misappropriation of sustainability as a marketing tool has clearly increased, paralleling the success and growth of genuinely sustainable practice. This amplifies the importance of ongoing discussions about what works (see Principle 11), what is a good-faith experiment, and what is self-deluding or outright deceptive.

To have those discussions requires having as much clarity as possible about the differences between built and natural *form*, and relating both to ecological function. It requires that designers train themselves to look beyond appearances, while still creating stylish and beautiful places that sustain people psychologically.

But How Can Landscapes Damage the Environment?

For those of us who love landscapes, it is troubling and confusing to think that our creations damage the environment. How can a green, growing place hurt the Earth? The question can be answered both in a technical way and in terms of attitudes and cultural trends.

Technical Issues: Resources and Biodiversity

This book also discusses materials and processes of landscape construction, mostly chosen because they protect or improve environmental health, but it also analyzes some that contribute to ecological problems. Some are very specific, such as resource depletion when redwood or tropical hardwoods are used in quantity for consumer landscapes. Toxic materials are used in gardens both intentionally (pesticides, for example) and unintentionally (fertilizer used in excess, or materials like PVC, valued while in use but with serious disposal problems). Land itself is "consumed" and "wasted" by some types of conventional construction. These are the *technical* answers to the question of ecological damage from landscapes; they are detailed throughout the book.

Landscapes and gardens, as constructed today, also have an effect on biodiversity, which can be quite negative. It may seem that some gardens, especially those of enthusiastic horticulturists, are highly diverse, and in a sense this is true. Most built landscapes, however, are planted with only a dozen or so species; in many schools of landscape design, this is actually taught as a way to avoid a "busy" or "cluttered" design. Furthermore, the main commercially available plant species have become increasingly standardized by mass marketing, so diversity is reduced *among regions* as well as at the site-specific scale. Dead plants, which in self-sustaining communities form important habitat, are usually removed from gardens, further diminishing diversity.

Real biodiversity is not merely about the *numbers* of species, however. It is about richness of interconnections *among* species. These interconnections take ages

Figure 0.6   Is this a warning sign? (*Photo:* Kim Sorvig.)

of coevolution to develop and cannot be re-created instantly in a garden. Plants brought together from different regions in a garden add visual diversity and may give great pleasure but remain akin to a diverse collection of animals in a zoo, separate and unable to interact. They do not support the great web of pollinators, predators, browsers, and symbionts that revolves around plants in their native habitats. When even a wide-ranging *collection* replaces a biodiverse *community*, there is real ecological loss. Local richness and regional identity are diminished. There is increasing evidence that these localized losses add up to something global, especially where the loss involves vegetative cover on a cumulatively enormous scale. (See p. 119.)

Natural "Look" and Ecological Function: A Paradox?

At the heart of landscape design are some expectations that are remarkably resistant to change: our expectations about the *appearance* of landscapes. Conventionally, aesthetic choices about the *style* of landscape are seen as unrelated to resource costs or environmental impact. But some styles require much higher investments in control than others. As sustainability focuses concern on the environmental costs of constructing landscapes, controversy over the appropriate *appearance* of sustainable landscapes has flared. Should a sustainable landscape look untouched by human hands—a difficult task for the contractor? Should it, at the other extreme, look like an "ecology machine," the way some sustainable houses sprout high-tech engineered appendages?

A number of studies have shown that humans seem to prefer a fairly specific type of landscape form: large, well-spaced trees over grass or low ground cover, without much shrub layer or understory—the type of wooded environment commonly called "parklike."[112] Many landscape design traditions, notably the Olmstedian one, reproduce this type of vegetation, for which there are several natural prototypes. One natural parklike landscape is the African savannah, and perhaps the most influential theory uses that fact to explain why human landscape preferences seem almost fixated on parklands. "Biophilia," biologist E. O. Wilson's concept of an innate attraction to and interest in other living things,[113] says that humans evolved in the savannah and have been trying to re-find or re-create it ever since. (The fact that significant percentages of humanity love and choose to live in forests, deserts, and mountains or on seacoasts suggests that the truth isn't quite so simple, but the effect is certainly powerful.)

E. O. Wilson's biophilia is a theory, briefly mentioned in a short book. It gives no guidance about how to design a landscape, and certainly no details about the forms such a landscape should include. Various practitioners are trying to expand Wilson's theoretical concept toward design guidelines. One formulation lists Fourteen Patterns of Biophilia;[114] these are very general, ranging from "connection with natural systems" to "biomorphic forms and patterns," but serve as inspiration for design. Alex Wilson (of *EBN*, no relation to E. O.) has summarized ways of incorporating biophilia and biomimicry into architectural, interior, and landscape design.[115]

Figure 0.7   Conventional and cheap attitudes toward landscaping abound—and often consume or destroy natural ecosystems. (*Photo:* Kim Sorvig.)

Biomimicry is another approach to designing from natural precedents. The nonprofit Biomimicry Institute defines its field as "seeking sustainable solutions to human challenges by emulating nature's time-tested patterns and strategies." The focus is on natural, usually fractal forms that fulfill specific functions in the natural world; the results tend to be more closely allied with product engineering than with landscape design, but these concepts should be inspiring to landscape professionals, including planners.

The intensely personal feelings involved in this evolving field are strong evidence for the depth of human attachment to specific landscapes. Almost everyone who cares about landscapes, whether as professional, client, or amateur, has preconceptions about what sustainable landscapes ought to look like. These biases—and unresolved differences among them—strongly affect the work of the landscape professional: how we work, and whether we get work. This controversy is worth exploring briefly here.

The Hand of the Designer

A common definition of "natural" is "untouched by human hands." Where landscapes serve natural or ecological purposes, should the hand of a designer (or builder) be evident? Stormwater ponds, for instance, are sometimes designed to look like natural ponds, with undulating edges planted with native wetland species. One example is the stormwater wetland at Fort Devens Federal Medical Center in central Massachusetts. The work of Carol R. Johnson Associates of Boston, this carefully engineered series of ponds looks as if it has always been there.

Landscape theorists like Rob Thayer, author of *Gray World, Green Heart*, have questioned whether concealing the designer makes sense. For example, applying a wild riverbank plant association verbatim to an urban drainage swale ignores its human origins, according to Thayer. Making such a constructed ecosystem look "natural" does not necessarily improve its sustainability. In fact, Thayer suggests that "sustainability requires neither the disguise nor the elimination of human influence."

On the contrary, says Thayer, sustainable landscapes represent a higher level of complexity than "cosmetic" landscapes, and they incorporate ecological relationships that may be hard to observe. Therefore, they demand "conspicuous expression and visible interpretation, and that is where the creative and artistic skills of the landscape architect are most critically needed."[116] Thayer refers to cosmetic attempts to make engineering look less engineered as greenwash. Like many others, he sees the desire to hide the mechanical systems that support modern life as unreasoning, a NIMBY ("Not in My Backyard") attitude that wants the benefits of development but none of the costs.

One thoughtful theory about whether human design and management should be visible in the landscape is Joan Nassauer's "cues to care."[117] She argues that completely unmanaged ecosystems appear messy

—to modern human eyes at least—and uncared for. Rather than tidy up whole parklands, Nassauer suggests designing and maintaining border transition areas that show that people care for the place. In some cases, making the human hand visible, even as simply as establishing a mowed threshold between developed areas and protected ones, enhances visitors' respect for the wilder landscape.

Other landscape thinkers agree that the mechanics or infrastructure of built landscapes should not be hidden—in fact, should be revealed. William MacElroy and Daniel Winterbottom, professors of landscape architecture, have coined the term "infra-garden" to describe a landscape that supports ecological and social values while incorporating landscape art.[118] As an example they cite Waterworks Gardens in Renton WA, by environmental artist Lorna Jordan.[119] Here, fanciful grottoes and basalt slabs adorn a stormwater wetland that treats runoff from several parking lots. But Richard Hansen, a Colorado-based sculptor and landscape architect, sees Waterworks Gardens as "a shotgun wedding of environmental engineering overlaid by grottoes and other large decorative elements." Hansen argues for "a better interweave—a sculptural presence integrated with an ecological process."

Another rather trendy style is the recycled industrial landscape. One of the first and best-known examples of this is Rich Haag's Gas Works Park, in Seattle. The concept is now widespread. The well-known High Line in New York City converted elevated rail lines to a linear park, as did The 606 in Chicago, while in Germany, the Landschaftspark Duisburg-Nord is a popular public space woven into industrial ruins.[120] In Albuquerque, the old railyard has become a weekend market, while in nearby Santa Fe, Ken Smith Associates won a competition to repurpose a similar facility as a park. The Santa Fe design included a proposal to water the park with collected rainwater, stored in and delivered from a mobile fleet of tanker cars; western water law killed the water harvesting, and the risk and difficulty of moving rail cars around a public garden led to abandonment of that intriguing idea. Both of these changes diminished the functional sustainability of the park. Complicating matters further, reviewers insisted that the design was an iconoclastic break

Figure 0.8   The Menomenee Valley Redevelopment produced park and property development from a brownfield, recycling 50,000 cubic yards of crushed concrete from reconstruction of I-94, and reused on-site features. (*Project:* Wenk Assoc. *Photo:* Nancy Aten.)

with the "Santa Fe style"—which applies to adobe-style *buildings*; there is no consistent Santa Fe *landscape* style. Partial recycling, iconoclasm, and sustainability make a strange mix, though I personally like most such adaptive reuse landscapes.

Another landscape that gives ecological function a sculptural form is the stormwater garden at the Water Pollution Control Laboratory in Portland OR, designed by landscape architect Robert Murase, working as part of a team of hydrologists and engineers. Runoff from a fifty-acre neighborhood uphill of the site flows to a retention/settling pond, eventually soaking into the soil or emptying into the Willamette River.

This utilitarian aim is expressed as sculptural form. The one-acre pond's upper and lower cells form converging circles. A stone-lined, curving concrete flume—an abstraction of a glacial moraine or the curve of a river—juts into the upper cell. When stormwater pours into the flume, the stones dissipate the energy in the water and allow solids to settle out; the water then seeps through weep holes in the side of the flume. Stones from the flume "spill out" and form a semicircular basalt wall that defines the second, lower pond. Although the landscape fulfills important ecological functions, Murase's design conceals neither the designer's hand nor his intent to create sculptural form on the land.

"Eco-revelatory Design"

If hiding the designer's influence is one side of a coin, making ecological processes visible is the other. Many

Figure 0.9 This Portland OR stormwater garden uses artistic form to reveal paths of runoff through the urban environment. (*Project:* Robert Murase. *Photo:* Scott Murase.)

Figure 0.10 Renton WA "infra-garden" makes stormwater visible, overlaid with garden art. Surroundings worked against naturalistic design. (*Project:* Lorna Jordan. *Photo:* Daniel Winterbottom.)

highly engineered landscapes (as well as quite a number of naturalistic gardens) *hide* the ecological processes that go on around us. Stormwater (which, after all, is just rainwater running downhill) is one of those ecological processes. Before Murase's stormwater garden was built, neighborhood stormwater ran into a sewer and emptied directly into the river—out of sight, out of mind. The stormwater flume and pond, in essence, takes stormwater out of the murky underground realm of drains and pipes and "daylights" it, revealing it in the landscape.

"Eco-revelatory design" is a label that has been applied to such landscapes by the University of Illinois Department of Landscape Architecture.[121] The department conceived a traveling exhibit of projects, design approaches, and elements that "reveal and interpret ecological phenomena, processes and relationships." Human influence is also revealed and interpreted as one part (not necessarily harmonious) of the ecosystem, in contrast with the desire to hide all trace of human work. The concept has been contentious; conventional naturalistic designers dislike the look, while some landscape architects view "eco-revelatory" as another word for making business as usual pretty.

Although he did not use the term, the spirit of eco-revelatory design was simply and eloquently expressed by John Lyle. In 1994 a visitor to Lyle's newly completed Center for Regenerative Studies noticed a compost pile in plain view and asked why he had

not bothered to screen it. "We don't want to screen things," said Lyle. "We want to *see* things. A lot of ecological problems come from hiding the way things really work."

That spirit is behind the Portland stormwater garden. By making stormwater visible, it teaches visitors about water's place in urban ecosystems. Threaded through this book are many other built landscapes that are equally honest about what they are and what they do.

The Portland and Renton examples each contrast with naturalistic landscapes, raising some important questions. The Portland garden's form and appearance are directly linked to the physical dynamics that govern water; it reveals these dynamics in a clearly constructed context, not a simulated stream. The Renton landscape allows environmental engineering to be seen (although it relies not on gravity but on a hidden 2,000-gallon-per-minute pump), decorating it with gardenesque structures and forms. In neither design will vegetation be allowed to overgrow the site, nor will water be allowed to carve its own channels. In fact, as with most built landscapes, considerable effort and expense will be spent in *preventing* these ecological processes from changing the form of either landscape. The Renton infra-garden puts an artistic veneer over both the stormwater "problem" and its engineering "solution." The Portland garden relates engineering control to natural process, although at a level considerably simplified from actual ecosystem processes.

If "ecology" is taken in the scientific sense of large-scale, complex processes, these projects, like Lyle's compost heap, are less about revealing ecology than about refusing to hide human influence. By strict definition, "eco-revelatory" would apply best to nature trails, where an educational path points out elements of an existing ecosystem and, among other things, human effects on it. Does this mean that sustainable design should always look like a nature trail? Since its earliest days, ecological design has been accused—unfairly, I believe—of being all ecology and no design. What is critical is to be clear about what is actually being revealed, and why.

The hand of the designer can be as heavy on the land as a highway interchange or strip mine. It can also be a delicate interfingering of influence, as in a Japanese garden, where the artist's touch is visible but only to thoughtful observation. (The difference, frequently, is in the contractor's level of skill, so often overlooked.) To argue that human influence should *never* be hidden, without also asking whether that influence is destructive or sustainable, is to trivialize the complexity of relations between humans and the rest of the world.

Form Follows Function in Nature, Too

Naturalism is a popular style for landscapes, and verges on being the only "look" for sustainable landscapes. There is at least one reason to argue against this. The "natural" appearance of an Olmsted park or a Japanese garden is maintained by considerable inputs of energy and materials. Especially where this maintenance is mechanized, those resource inputs are sustainability concerns. If revealing human influence reduces these inputs, it contributes to a sustainable landscape. However, there is strong evidence that some human landscapes do exactly the opposite: their form actually increases the costs of maintaining them and, in some cases, even prevents them from serving ecological functions.

The pipes and pumps of a stormwater system are a useful example. At some level, they substitute for the streams and wetlands of a watershed, fulfilling some functions (water transport) and failing others (aquatic habitat diversity, soil infiltration). The simplified forms of environmental engineering structures reveal, more than anything else, that ecological systems are far more multidimensional and complex than human engineering. Detailed study over the past two or three decades is showing more and more clearly that *the complex forms of natural systems are essential to their functioning*.

The attempt to straighten rivers and give them regular cross-sections is perhaps the most disastrous example of this form-and-function relationship. The natural river has a very irregular form: it meanders, spills across floodplains, and leaks into wetlands, giving it an ever-changing and incredibly complex shoreline. These irregularities allow the river to accommodate variations in water level and speed. Pushing the river into tidy geometry destroys functional capacity and results in disasters like the Mississippi floods of 1927 and 1993 and, more recently, the unnatural disaster of Hurricane Katrina. (A $50 billion plan to "let the river loose" in Louisiana recognizes that the "controlled" Mississippi is washing away twenty-four square miles of that state annually.[122] Breaching levees, the plan resulted in new land being deposited.[123]) The imperviousness of paving is well known as a contributor to flooding, but the vast regular plane *shapes* that paving takes are also a factor in concentrating runoff. Reducing irregularities of shape also decreases the variety of habitats available and cuts down on diversity of life, whether in a river or a lawn. Putting a stream into a pipe has an even more drastic simplifying effect, at the expense of multidimensional function.

Natural and nature-like form is an important subtheme in this book. The stiff geometry that humans favor for graded slopes actually *increases* soil erosion and slope failure. Natural wetlands have quite specific forms and locations; created wetlands do not function properly unless these forms are approximated. The branching form of wild plants optimizes their ability to compete for sunlight and soil resources, plus their ability to clean pollutants from air and water. Where "the hand of the designer" goes too far in altering these forms, ecological function is affected, most often negatively.

Since the 1970s, the forms that make ecosystem function possible have been recognized as a specific mathematical type, called "fractals."[124] The branching patterns of trees are one example of fractal shapes.

Figure 0.11 Good landscape design should tell users where they are—and do it beautifully. Recycled slate, birches, sedums, and tamarack (larch) evoke the region surrounding Warroad (MN) Port of Entry, at the Canadian border. (*Project:* Coen+Partners. *Photo:* Frank Ooms.)

Figure 0.12 Landscapes that are strongly suggestive of local ecosystems and terrain can be naturalistic without looking like English parkland. (*Warroad Project:* Coen+Partners. *Photo:* Frank Ooms.)

The name comes from the fact that these forms usually consist of endlessly repeated *fractions* of the whole, which create the overall form by growth over time. In the case of a tree, this basic element would be a single branch *and* its branching angle, proportionally repeated at many scales. River systems, landform surfaces, clouds, and whole plant communities follow fractal geometries *because their function demands it*. Human blood vessels and bronchial tubes have fractal patterns, too, which maximize delivery of blood or air; disruption of these patterns is diagnostic of serious illnesses, such as cancer.[125] Similarly, straightening a river or turning an undulating hillside into a constant 3 percent slope undermines ecological *function* because it changes environmental *form*.

The forms of natural systems also have documented effects on human beings.[126] Studies in hospitals have shown that a view of trees or other natural features improves patient recovery time and overall health when released; views of structures and machinery have no such effect. Views of natural surroundings lower blood pressure, decrease the patient's need for painkillers, and lessen the mental confusion that often goes with injury or serious illness. These benefits come from merely *seeing* the scenery, not going out into it. In fact, a photo or realistic painting of a landscape provides similar benefits, so the effect is clearly a visual one.[127] This strongly suggests that Olmsted was right: naturalistic scenes (and conserved native vegetation) have social benefits and are worth including in cities and preserving in undeveloped areas. If hard-nosed hospital administrators are increasingly paying to design buildings that give each patient a landscape view, shouldn't landscape professionals heed this research as well?

Thus the forms that "naturalism" tries to preserve or simulate are intimately linked to the ecological functioning of landscapes, as well as to human health and social benefits. Because the discovery of fractal mathematics is so recent, design theorists may be forgiven for continuing to treat natural form as random or irrelevant. In labeling as romanticism and nostalgia any attempt to mimic natural form, however, they reveal their ignorance of current science. For those concerned with sustainability, the relationship between natural form and ecological function needs to be re-

visited. Although real understanding of this relationship is still developing, it is quite clear that it is far more than a backward-looking aesthetic.

The Appearance of Sustainability

So what *does* the sustainable landscape look like?

The most honest answer is that no one really knows. Here are a few suggestions:

- The sustainable landscape does not *exclude* human presence or even human engineering. It does not, however, blindly *glorify* human intervention, nor *equate* gentle human influence with massive human domination.

- The sustainable landscape does not waste energy or resources on trying to *disguise* human influence. Rather, it *eliminates* (functionally, not just visually) those influences that are in fact destructive or disruptive. Other influences it reveals and even celebrates. In revelation and celebration, it becomes an artistic expression.

- The sustainable landscape follows natural and regional form whenever this can improve the ecological functioning of a built or restored landscape. It builds nature-mimicking forms primarily because these harbor rich diversity of life and ecological function, and secondarily because many people prefer the visual effect.

- The sustainable landscape integrates and balances human geometries with natural ones. It is not enough to allow natural form to take the leftover spaces; spatial and visual *integration* between nature's fractal forms and humanity's Euclidean ones is essential. The means to this integration are those of the arts as well as of the sciences, and can draw on vernacular traditions. Traditional Japanese landscape-makers were particularly adept at this integration of forms; of necessity, much preindustrial construction integrated with natural form because dominating it required extremes of labor.

- The sustainable landscape is visually complex, reflecting functional complexity. It is unlikely to be dominated by the visually simple and near-sterile extremes of urban or engineered space. It cannot result from theories that elevate large-scale mini-

Figure 0.13 This water/ice wall (Teardrop Park, Battery Park City) is an urban amenity constructed from quarried stone, naturalistic without being literally imitative. Besides water play, its surface offers habitat that no monolithic concrete wall could. (*Project and Photo:* Michael van Valkenburgh Assocs.)

malism or brutalism. It is likely to incorporate elements of urban space as people transform cities and industries to a more sustainable model.

- The appearance of a naturalistic landscape often contributes to ecological function but does not guarantee it. For this reason, neither naturalistic nor sustainable constructed landscapes should ever be viewed as substitutes for wild places,[128] which will remain critically important no matter how "ecological" built landscapes become—or appear.

What does this mean for the practicing landscape professional? First and foremost, that the sustainable landscape will have room for creativity and diversity, perhaps even more so than the conventional and often conformist styles that dominate our work today. It means, as great landscape design always has, an integration of the whole person—the supposedly opposite technical and artistic sides—in the work process. It means there will be less of a premium on clever ability to cover up compost bins or valve boxes, and more demand for people who can visualize and build integrally with the site. It means that fewer forms in the landscape will be oversimplified mechanical surfaces, and more will be interfingered in three dimensions, difficult to build well except by hand. It means that the appearance of the landscape will be influenced very directly by careful thought about resources and methods used to build it. It should mean a wave of creativity rising to meet one of humanity's most important challenges.

Applied Greenwash in Landscape Design

Growing public concern about planetary life-support systems has prompted some designers, developers, and public agencies to do something about it—while others think it enough to *appear* to be doing something. The latter is "applied greenwash," which should not be confused with landscapes, natural or constructed, that perform genuine ecological functions. Greenwash is for designers who want on the "eco" bandwagon without the headstrong unpredictability of the horse that pulls that wagon—ecosystem dynamics.

Much of the attention to greenwashing has focused on products that make claims deemed mislead-

ing under the Federal Trade Commission's "Green Guides."[129] However, examples of landscape greenwash abound. They include "boutique wetlands," carefully positioned, *très chic* installations that look like functioning wetlands but depend entirely on artificial support systems.

Tanner Springs Park, a new park in downtown Portland OR, is an example. Built in memory of a stream now entombed in an underground culvert, the park collects the stormwater to maintain what looks like a small wetland. Storing what it collects in an underground cistern, it requires little or no city water. That's good. Recirculating stormwater through cleansing sand and wetland plants, it demonstrates how water is filtered in nature. That's good, too. But the park is not connected to any watershed, nor does it empty (except when extreme storms cause the cistern to overflow) into the Willamette River.[130] The park is only *stylistically* a wetland. That's deceptive.

Memories of vanished pastoral scenes underlie many greenwash landscapes. Extensive technology mimics the look without the function. In St. Louis, historic Forest Park boasts a man-made river. One of the most technically ambitious hydraulic engineering projects in any park in the world creates something called, with no apparent irony, "River Returns," which looks as though it has always been there. The 2.5-mile constructed waterway roughly follows the historical course of the River des Peres, which since the 1930s has been buried in a huge concrete culvert. A team of engineers, hydrologists, and landscape architects constructed a convincing replica of the now-invisible des Peres, planting the banks with native wildflowers to complete the illusion.

Does it really make sense in the twenty-first century to create an imitation of a vanished river? This is something quite different from "daylighting" and restoring streams in cities. Forest Park's river is not a restored stream; it's a facsimile—and a profligate one at that. It takes *1.5 million gallons* of city tap water daily to keep the illusion convincing. Given the resource costs of building a 2.5-mile water feature today, why not give it a contemporary design that celebrates its ingenious technology?

Greenwashing may make some citizens feel that they are doing something to help restore local envi-

Figure 0.14 Tanner Springs Park in Portland OR, a "boutique wetland." Though totally artificial, it is designed to simulate a functioning wetland. (*Project:* Atelier Dreseitl. *Photo:* George Hazelrigg.)

ronmental systems. But boutique systems don't really restore much—they just look as if they do. They spread *ecological disinformation*: by lulling the public into thinking something substantive has been done, they dissipate the energy needed to undertake real ecological restoration.

Successful ecological design focuses on deciding what functions a given built landscape should perform and designing for those, not on setting out to achieve a certain look. Although the fractal forms of nature clearly have functional powers, natural functions can often fit into geometric shapes. The *illusion* of natural, long-established landscape can be costly and unnecessary.

A more subtle form of greenwash occurs when isolated buildings or sites are described as "green." Although energy efficient and built with minimum site disruption, these projects are undermined by their very isolation. Distance from mass transit or any other low-impact form of transportation ensures high resource costs, no matter how efficient their internal workings. When the building materials for a 15,000-square-foot mansion are trucked miles up logging roads, and the owner arrives by helicopter, the result is far from green. Custom suburban homes suffer, to a lesser extent, the same distance-based problem.[131]

A related issue is the attempt to portray modular and prefabricated buildings as green. To be sure, there are real efficiencies when buildings are produced in a factory-like setting. Efficient construction tools can be used, scrap can easily be recycled, and work-

ers may not need to drive to work. However, trucking the structure cross-country to the site, and placing it once there, requires heavy energy inputs. The need for a straight line of unimpeded movement for something as large as a house usually means significant extra land clearance. (Structures built as small assemblies, moved onto the site for final setup, are quite different.) Standardizing structures necessarily reduces the ability to make sensitive adjustments to fit building to site. Although probably not utter greenwash, the greenness of such systems appears overrated.

Another problematic claim is exemplified by *Big and Green: Toward Sustainable Architecture in the 21st Century*, a 2003 exhibition in Washington DC.[132] While many of the fifty or more skyscraper projects featured in the exhibit had innovative features for ventilation, cooling, water management, and so on, calling their *overall* performance green seems highly debatable. Plants under glass were supposed to serve ecological functions such as water purification. It was evident from the drawings that the soil volumes allowed by the architects were woefully inadequate even to support the trees shown, let alone to produce a functioning ecosystem.

Besides unworkable details, there were two issues of scale. First, natural systems, such as wetlands, take a specific amount of space to process a given volume of water; compressing such systems into small spaces, as high-rise real estate demands, is dubious. Second, most of today's large buildings, whether skyscrapers or big-box retail warehouses, function as unitary objects that are entirely the wrong scale to work with nature. Shadowing and wind-tunnel effects of tall buildings almost always decrease ecological functionality of large areas nearby, as do the monolithically impervious footprints of horizontal big-box structures. None of these giant buildings could survive without importing resources—food, water, energy—from a large supporting landscape.

It is unquestionable that natural systems are scale dependent, nor can green solutions simply be scaled up until they are Big. Concentrating population in urban areas without productive landscapes already disrupts environmental resilience. The demand for "big, tall, and all under one roof" is a symptom of that overconcentration. The intellectual temptation to think giant buildings can be "greened" needs a reality check.

"Greenwash" is not a term to be used lightly. For one thing, it implies a deliberate attempt to mislead. Far more of the kind of problems discussed in this section result from incompletely thinking through basic assumptions, the kinds that should be questioned before design begins. Is this project really needed? Is this really an appropriate place for such land use? Is this making the deepest possible cut in resource consumption or merely whittling off enough to give bragging rights?

No project is perfectly sustainable, and no one should cast stones without thinking carefully. A final example serves to underline this point.

A number of recent articles have tried to make sustainability sexier: green *and* gorgeous, as one was titled.[133] Some manufacturers fear that calling their product green will associate it with aging hippies, ugly homemade shanties, and tofu-only diets—a kind of reverse greenwashing. But the attempt to "help environmentalism go upscale" is paradoxical. At one level, if sustainability doesn't shed its back-to-basics image and get some glamour, how will it ever catch on in consumer society? Excessive consumerism and its massive distribution systems, however, are themselves clearly unsustainable. The all-luxury-all-the-time expectations of upscale markets amplify that problem. Green and glamorous is a difficult balance. Far better to change social ideas of glamour.

Until life-cycle performance analysis of sustainable projects becomes common, "greenwash" may remain one of those things that "I can't define, but I know it when I see it." Meanwhile, it is important not to rack up a few "better-than-usual" features and contentedly proclaim the whole project Sustainable with a capital S.

Rethinking Special Landscape Types for Sustainability

Almost any landscape's environmental performance can be improved, but several specific landscape types have recently attracted extra efforts. These land uses may have special "fit" with sustainable techniques, may cause extra problems if designed conventionally, or may typically be owned by environmentally attuned people.

University Campuses

College faculties have long been "talking the talk" of environmental responsibility. Academia's physical landscapes, by and large, have not kept pace. The traditional campus—trees amid vast manicured lawns and annual beds—is resource consumptive and habitat poor. The "weedy, wooly look" of a naturalized campus is at odds with the traditional groves of academe and requires reeducation to be accepted.[134]

Some campuses have created prototypes worth following. The John T. Lyle Center for Regenerative Studies at California State Polytechnic University, Pomona (Figure 0.2), is a model sustainable campus. University administration initially misjudged its value, but today it is well appreciated. The School of Architecture and Landscape Architecture at Penn State University installed an extensive system of parking-lot bioswales, native plantings, and a green classroom and studio building. Sustainability commitments are also reflected in the landscapes of the university's Center for Watershed Stewardship, a collaboration of foresters and landscape architects, and the Phipps Conservatory's research facility, the Center for Sustainable Landscapes.

At Shenyang Architectural University in northern China, seven acres of working rice paddies challenge the artificial separation between designed landscapes and food production, between campus and countryside. This working landscape (by Turenscape, Beijing)

includes strikingly patterned pedestrian paths and a student park among the paddies. Students participate in local herbicide- and pesticide-free farming methods, producing rice and vegetables consumed in the college cafeteria. Frogs and loach, a fish that eats mosquito larvae, inhabit the fields during the wet cycle.[135]

Historically, food-producing campuses (especially at agricultural colleges) were common, but Shenyang is unusual among modern universities. Growing food on campus, with few chemicals, reduces its embodied energy and follows an international trend toward locally grown food. Campuses like Shenyang's could become links in what European designers call CPULs: Continuous Productive Urban Landscapes.[136]

Campus landscapes form venues for environmental learning. Some landscape architecture and architecture departments involve their students in tangible "greening" projects. The Temple University Ambler campus and the University of Oregon contain fine examples of design-build projects accomplished by the students.

Landscape architect Meg Calkins suggests several green campus guidelines:

- Redefine public ideals of campus beauty.
- Limit lawn to culturally significant areas; promote native plantings.
- Use the campus to teach environmental literacy.
- Coordinate with facilities operations and maintenance.
- Cultivate support at the highest levels of administration.[137]

Figure 0.16 Shenyang students experience direct connection with their landscape and their food source. (*Project and Photo:* Turenscape.)

The movement toward green campuses goes well beyond the landscape, of course. As Peggy Barlett, coeditor of *Sustainability on Campus*, points out, "Campuses across the United States alone represent an enormous investment in buildings and land, and therefore how [universities] maintain and build physical plant, engage in buying practices, dispose of waste, and consume energy is critically important to the environmental health of the broader society."[138]

"Green Burial" to Preserve and Restore Land

Conventional cemeteries are extensive landscapes and, by and large, are among the most sterile landscapes imaginable: flat planes of grass with graves in industrial rows, often 1,000 per acre. Adorning the graves with plastic flowers is eerily appropriate, for these are truly deathly places. What a difference from the great nineteenth-century landscape cemeteries like Mount Auburn in Boston, with its rolling topography and lush forest canopies!

Making cemeteries sustainable requires changing cultural attitudes, a potentially uncomfortable discussion. Conventional burial bears a disquieting resemblance to toxic waste disposal.[139] The body is pumped full of toxic embalming fluids to guard against natural processes of decay, then hermetically sealed in a coffin to prevent contact with soil, water, or microorganisms: it is to be utterly removed from the cycle of life. Cremation might seem more "ecological," but it requires large inputs of fossil fuels and releases air pollutants.

Frightening as bodily decay is to many people, we are part of that cycle. Some individuals and cultures have celebrated this: the painter Edvard Munch wrote, "From my rotting body, flowers shall grow and I am in them and that is eternity."[140] Green cemeteries return to simple, unembalmed burial in wood caskets or even shrouds.

Greener treatment of the body and of the landscape are parallel issues. Green cemeteries address both issues by burial in landscapes that are then reforested. The Natural Death Centre, a British nonprofit, began with a single cemetery in 1993. Today there are ninety. In the United States, there was only one such cemetery in 2006; as of 2017 there are over 300. The Green Burial Council certifies these operations, and provides lists and maps to locate them, at https://greenburialcouncil.org/find-a-provider/.

At Ramsey Creek Preserve, the first US green cemetery, near Westminster SC in the Appalachian foothills, graves are scattered throughout an existing forest,

Figure 0.17   At Ramsey Creek Preserve in the Appalachian Mountains, the deceased decompose naturally in the soil of a trust-protected woodland. (*Project:* Memorial Ecosystems. *Photo:* Sam Wang.)

which, aside from walking paths, is under conservation easement. Gravestones are simple rocks from the immediate watershed. All plantings must be native to the region. As the cemetery's website explains: "The use of the woodland as an environmentally conscious graveyard will help preserve the ecosystem intact—[preservationists can] tap into the $20 billion per year funeral industry to provide funds [for] endowments that save and restore beautiful land that might otherwise be lost to development."[141]

Joe Sehee, founder of the Green Burial Council, points out how graveyards and nature sanctuaries overlap: their intent to preserve land in perpetuity. Many states require that cemeteries be managed under long-term trusts. Land trusts have closely parallel organization and almost always need sources of funding. People routinely pay large amounts of money for tiny plots in sterile conventional cemeteries. The same money can fund protection for landscapes disturbed only by the occasional, carefully managed burial and a few visitors.[142]

Sehee notes that although he expected people to be squeamish about discussing this concept, his experience has actually been just the opposite. "People find it liberating," he says. "They are looking for meaningful alternatives to the conventional funeral industry." Green cemeteries offer such an alternative.

Ski Areas

Downhill skiing requires clear slopes, often carved out of some of the nation's wilder landscapes. Their impact on wildlife, erosion, and visual quality can be significant. In addition, a large ski area like Aspen uses 45 million gallons of water each season for snowmaking and other purposes.[143]

Global warming seriously threatens the ski industry; US areas have declined in number, from 727 in 1984 to 478 in 2017, often due to waning snowpack. The National Ski Areas Association (NSAA) introduced an environmental charter in 2000, which was updated in 2005. Aspen Skiing Company produced one of the first LEED-certified buildings; in 2006, 22 ski areas were 100 percent wind or solar powered. As of NSAA's 2016 annual *Sustainable Slopes* report,[144] over 200 ski resorts had endorsed the charter; together these areas receive 75 percent of all ski visits. The eighteen-page charter has guidelines for structures, but it also has more than the usual focus on outdoor practices; as such it is relevant to landscape professionals in general.

The voluntary NSAA charter lists techniques to decrease the environmental impact of skiing. Water used in snowmaking can be recaptured, not only for ski area reuse but also for summer uses, such as maintaining streamflow; grading soil moguls requires less snow cover (and less water use); ski-trail signage and print on snack-bar cups can educate the public. Forest clearing remains an issue unless everyone turns to cross-country skiing, but short of such drastic measures, ski companies are reducing their environmental footprint.

One aspect of NSAA's approach is worth copying: its online database of case studies, keyed to each technique in the charter, promotes sustainable design to members and to broader audiences.

Eco-resorts, Parks

In many national parks, such as Zion and Yosemite, pressures from increasing numbers of visitors have forced reassessment of transportation and facilities. A natural-gas shuttle system, for example, has replaced almost all private-car access to Zion, dramatically improving visitor experience and reducing impacts on the park.[145] Public-sector landscapes, often overlooked in glamour-focused professional publicity, are often sustainability models.

These changes are not without critics. At Yosemite, a $440 million project balances resource protection with public access but has been assailed as for-profit development excluding all but the rich.[146] Less camping and more hotel rooms will be provided—but where 80 percent of 1970s visitors stayed overnight, today 80 percent are day-trippers. The plan includes a shuttle, removal of a dam to let the Merced River flow through the park, and installation of raised boardwalks to protect the floodplain while accommodating visitors.

Even with sustainable facilities, tourism's sheer numbers have real impacts on some of the world's best-loved landscapes. This issue sparked a national debate in 2000, when the Sierra Club sued to require the Hawaii Tourism Authority to perform an environmental impact assessment before spending public funds to attract more tourists.[147] Despite lengthy appeals, the question raised by this case remains: do heavily visited landscapes have a carrying capacity, and if so, what roles do design, planning, and policy play in making them sustainable?

Amenity Migration

Many exceptional wild landscapes were once strictly visit-and-leave destinations. Today, however, people increasingly live in or adjacent to these landscapes, empowered by communication and transportation technology. These people are "amenity migrants."

Laurence Moss, who coined the term "amenity migration," describes it this way: as the biosphere becomes degraded by unsustainable development, "a very influential but growing minority of humankind is seeking what remains, especially the best of it. Owning high-amenity landscapes or proximate property now constitutes a global driving force."[148]

Amenity migration is two-edged. Those communities that have protected their amenity landscapes, and that mandate sustainable development, are seeing economic booms. But in many desirable places, existing communities are overwhelmed by new people and money. Similar conflicts occur in the so-called Urban Wildland Interface, where wildfires and residences collide (see p. 127).

Many amenity communities are leading markets for sustainable design. Yet privatization and intense development (green or otherwise) in fragile ecosystems give this trend a dark side. For both reasons, resort communities are a landscape type that bears watching.

Industrial Ruins

As noted in the "Sustainability, Substance, and Style" section, above, restoration of derelict industrial facilities has become a stylish mode of creating new landscapes and parks. The work is challenging, given the pollution and other hazards inherent in many postindustrial brownfields (see Principle 2), but the results have been well received. Although ruins are often very exciting and attractive spaces, this approach often seems to harbor confusion about sustainability. The fact that abandoned structures are left standing means that this is a type of recycling. Yet using the word "recycled" to describe reuse at this scale (which this book does, too) can be misleading; economically at least, such reuses are closer to "downcycling." Using a factory skeleton in place of a gazebo is vast overkill in terms of material usage. Careful analysis is needed to compare the salvage value of the materials with the recycled facility's value to the community. For communities left behind by overseas outsourcing or other forces, a huge converted park may not be at the top of the wish list, and for tourists, once the novelty wears off, interest may well wane. Nonetheless, reuse of ruins is a form of site restoration, which appears to be an important and growing source of employment for landscape professionals. It is more important than ever, though, to ask what the restored land will be used for, and who will benefit.

One of the bitter ironies of the sustainability movement is that when society had apparently unlimited energy to build, we didn't have the wits to design for disassembly or reuse, and we were in the grip of the Modernist design fad, which produced more demolition-worthy monster structures than any other era. Now that we have the idea of reuse, we are constrained by the costs, financial and environmental, of demolition and rebuilding.

Walkable Communities

The goals of sustainable design include human health, not just landscape preservation. Increasingly, sprawl landscapes are blamed for the US obesity epidemic. Of average Americans' daily trips, fewer than 6 percent are made on foot, according to the Federal Highway Administration. Reshaping the urban landscape toward walkability has become a focus for several research groups.[149]

Any planning initiative against sprawl will have major impacts on design work. Public spaces that encourage regular walking, but avoid overpaving, will require sustainable design and construction expertise. Walkable cities rely on relatively small residential buildings, often multifamily, which may decrease opportunities for residential landscape services. Nonetheless, I believe that sustainability-minded landscape professionals should welcome this trend without qualms.

In 2017, it is becoming clear that a new generation of potential homeowners is gravitating toward walkable cities, many of which are renewed urban centers.[150] This demographic actively seeks diversity, both economic and cultural, and prefers the mixed-use development and relatively small accommodations that make services accessible by walking or biking. They prefer to rent, or to own condos rather than stand-alone houses. This in turn lessens the demand for private cars, and eases the burden on public transit as well. To me, this trend is one of the most hopeful for sustainability, along with the financial viability of on-site solar and wind energy. In both cases, demand for change is not idealistic, or even focused on The Environment, but has percolated down into public demand for a preferred lifestyle. This may, I hope, give it momentum that the "old" sustainability movement has never fully gained.

Sustainable redesign of campuses, cemeteries, resorts, parks, and even The Suburbs is encouraging: the concept is maturing. Sustainable practices can be applied to a very wide range of landscape types, some of which offer more immediate incentive than others for this effort. The results can make a substantive change and be very stylish—or they can be all style and no substance. The ability to judge the difference, and to recognize the trade-offs, is what makes the practical techniques of sustainability mean something in practice.

Subtopics and Search Terms for Basic Principles: "Sustainability" in Context

Note: Subtopics are also useful search terms; add "innovation" or "controversy" to search terms as appropriate.

General sustainability
Search terms: sustainability OR environment OR ecology

Ecology
Search terms: ecology || forest ecology || aquatic ecology || desert ecology || soil ecology || activism AND ecology OR environment || environment publishers || deep ecology

Climate change
Search terms: "LUCC" || climate change || global warming || land use + climate

Green building
Search terms: green building || green construction || sustainable building || LEED

Construction
Search terms: landscape construction || outdoor construction || construction || landscaping

Technology
Search terms: landscape technology | | technology

Style and sustainability
Search terms: sustainable living | | sustainable home | | eco living | | eco friendly | | biophilic design | | biomimicry | | naturalistic design

Planning, design, and management
Search terms: land + (use OR planning OR management OR design) | | land-use planning | | landscape + (design OR management OR planning) | | urban design

Teamwork
Search terms: sustainable collaboration | | environmental collaboration | | interagency OR teamwork

Community-based planning
Search terms: community-based planning | | sustainability + teamwork

Resource List:

Links to information sources related to this chapter are posted at http://islandpress.org/sustainable-landscape-construction

Principle I:
Keep Healthy Sites Healthy

The first rule of the tinkerer is to keep all the pieces.
—*Aldo Leopold, quoted by E. O. Wilson in* Biophilia

Every site resembles a living organism, and like organisms, sites vary in health. This chapter discusses what "site health" means, and methods for preserving it during construction. Like human health, site health is not easy to define in a simple formula. Prevention is usually more successful—and less expensive—than cure.

Protection of sites—particularly those with mature vegetation and healthy soils—is of increasingly critical importance because deforestation links to global climate change (see p. 20). Site protection can make both local and cumulative differences.

Landscape construction that accidentally or deliberately damages a *healthy* site is doubly wasteful. While restoration methods can repair many site injuries, there is a point of no return, beyond which restoration is neither cost-effective nor ecologically sufficient. Mature trees needlessly destroyed in construction are not effectively "restored" by planting saplings, for example. Thus, the first principle of sustainable landscape construction is self-evident yet easily overlooked: *avoid harm to healthy sites.*

Protecting a healthy site requires care *throughout* the design and construction process, from initial reconnaissance through final cleanup. Sustainable *design* anticipates and integrates appropriate construction methods, influencing choices about siting, structures, and materials. The quality and coordination of such choices can make the difference between irreparable damage and minimal impact.

What Is a Healthy Site?

"Health" is one of those conditions everyone knows when they see it, but which remains impossible to de-

Discussed in This Chapter

Identifying healthy and unhealthy sites.
How site knowledge forms the basis for sustainable work.
Dealing with pre-construction impacts through teamwork.
General protection strategies applicable to any important site feature.
Protection of specific features like soil, vegetation, or water bodies.
Choice of construction equipment and construction planning.

fine completely. Despite this difficulty, it is important for both ecological and economic reasons to develop at least an operational definition of what "site health" means.

It is fairly easy to say when a site is *unhealthy*: stripped of topsoil by natural erosion or human carelessness, polluted by chemicals, supporting only a small percentage of the richness of plant and animal life found in the region, or overrun with invasive species, sick sites are often obvious eyesores.

Some site "illnesses" are brief ones, with quick recovery. A site drowned in sediment by a flood, or burned by a forest fire, may look unhealthy but usually retains vitality and soon begins regrowth. In fact, many plant communities and soil types depend on such events for long-term health. A site that is healthy and has plentiful resources (water, soil fertility, sunlight) can recover from minor construction damage, too.

More serious ill health results when toxic chemicals are involved, or when soil is removed, massively eroded, compacted, or paved. Some plant and animal species invade the site in much the way that parasites, microbes, or even cancers invade the human body.[1]

The cumulative effect of small, normal stresses also affects site health. Individual factors like wind, temporary drought, or increased ultraviolet radiation can add up over time to weaken plant life that holds a site together. Human use of a site produces new stresses. A site that had limited resources to start with may be unable to adapt to added stress.

Like healthy humans, healthy sites are productive, have vitality enough to keep growing despite some stress, and generally have a satisfying "look" and "feel." The appearance of a site can tell much about its health. Some healthy sites, however, go through messy-looking phases, and some landscapes conventionally viewed as stylish conceal serious ill health. Conventional landscape aesthetics are not a reliable guide to site health. (See Figures I.1 and I.2.)

Healthy ecosystems provide what have been called "environmental services," such as keeping air and water clean, improving local climate, and creating food—services on which human life depends.[2] (These services are discussed in more detail in Principle II.) Healthy sites also provide many amenities. Compared to landscapes cleared and flattened for convenience in construction, healthy sites have significantly higher property values (by at least 5–20 percent).[3]

Healthy sites are recognizable by several characteristics:

- They support *diversity* of plant and animal life *adapted to the region* and *linked to one another* in a web of interdependence.
- They are *seldom dominated exclusively by one species*, and especially not by species imported there by humans. (Criteria for agricultural sites are different, but crop monocultures are also unhealthy, sacrificing health for high productivity.)
- Their communities or ecosystems (soil, plants, and animals) are essentially *self-maintaining*, not dependent on outside resources supplied by people.
- Their living species are *actively reproducing* at rates typical of each species.

- The geological portion of the site is *not changing too rapidly* to support the living community, nor poisoned or infertile.
- The site has sufficient vitality and resilience to *overcome* a variety of stresses.
- The community changes with age through a process called *succession*.

Succession is a regionally characteristic series of changes. Healthy meadow or bog may be superseded by healthy forest. Unlike invasion by imported species, succession is healthy. It is like the changes in a healthy human from infancy through adolescence, maturity, decline, and death—and in the case of plant communities, succession includes rebirth. Accelerating or holding back succession without weakening the site's health is one of the most sophisticated methods of site management. Excessively slow or fast succession, like unusual aging in people, can indicate ill health.

It is seldom up to a single construction or design professional to decide precisely how healthy a site is. However, if developers, designers, and contractors learn to *recognize* relatively healthy sites, such sites will be valued and protected more often. Some clients still insist that unhealthy is good: less brush to clear. But recognition and protection of site health is increasingly required of landscape professionals.

One extremely valuable way of assessing the health of land at a site scale is the Floristic Quality Assessment (FQA). The method was developed at the Morton Arboretum (Lisle IL); published in 1994,[4] it offers a consistent means of evaluating any site. Plant species are known as "opportunistic" (a.k.a. wide) if they adapt easily to different site conditions, including disturbance by human activities; plants that are adapted to and require more specific conditions are termed "conservative." FQA uses a regional list of all plants known to occur there; each species is assigned a "coefficient of conservatism" (CC), a value between 0 (extremely adaptable, likely invasive) to 10 (dependent on and indicative of specific undisturbed local soil and ecosystem conditions). For a specific site, an inventory of species found on that site is taken, and the CC values for all species are averaged. The higher the average, the more healthy the site and the more valuable to protect.

The value of FQA is that it integrates complex information about soil health, species interactions and coevolution, and disturbance into a single metric that can be applied to field data. The method is used in all fifty states (each using a regional database of plant species) and by many federal agencies. It has proven ecologically accurate as well as legally defensible, so it is used in mitigation and restoration planning, including monitoring of mandatory restoration projects. It also correlates to the level of ecosystem services, with low FQA scores predicting decreased levels of air and water quality and other critical "services." An online calculator, with several dozen regional databases, is available free to anyone wishing to test the floristic quality of any site.[5] By sharing FQA reports, a kind of crowdsourcing is rapidly improving site and regional understanding of ecosystem health.[6]

There are a number of other commonly used "biodiversity index" methods, easily found online. They vary in whether they simply count the number of species, or weight more complex concerns (e.g., whether in a mix of many species, a few species dominate while most have only a few individual representatives). It is the weighting of "conservatism" that distinguishes FQA for site evaluation and facilitates crowdsourced floristic data collection.

Take a Role in "Pre-construction"

Prior to what is conventionally considered the beginning of either design or construction work, a great deal can happen to the site. The pre-construction actors are likely to be realtors, surveyors, developers, utility companies, and governmental agencies. Increasingly, projects stand or fall on the input of neighborhood groups as well.

Landscape professionals can influence most of these groups toward sustainable practice—but only if they form strong channels of communication and give input at the right time. Failing this, these same groups will act on the site, often by default, before landscape professionals are involved. Some standard practices—including hiring a landscape consultant only at the last moment to "shrub up" an already completed design—attempt to disguise unsightly or unhealthy results. Although not easy, winning influence

Figure I.1 Assessing site health visually can be misleading. This site fits the conventional image of landscape health, but it may use or pollute resources unsustainably. (*Photo:* Kim Sorvig.)

Figure I.2 Messiness is commonly equated with ill health, but this site is growing back from flooding—an important part of a healthy life cycle in any floodplain. (*Photo:* Kim Sorvig.)

over land-use planning is critically important to sustainability. The teamwork required among landscape architect, contractor, architect (or other consultants), and client or user is a good place to start forging community connections.

Prevent "Pre-clearance"

One very specific pre-construction practice is increasingly unacceptable in light of the clear links between vegetation loss and global warming (see p. 20). This is the practice of "pre-clearance"—bulldozing a site flat and removing all vegetation and much of the topsoil *before* putting up a For Sale sign. Although realtors clearly believe flattened sites are attractive to commercial buyers, pre-clearance is truly destructive. Convenient, perhaps, for a big box or parking lot, but what if a corporation wanted to create a model green headquarters? Much of the incentive, and many "environmental services," are now destroyed. Pre-clearance is likely an end run around development permit processes—if the site is cleared before the regulatory process begins, there is nothing left to regulate.

Sometimes pre-cleared sites lie naked and vacant for years, waiting for sale, planning, design, and construction. During that time, for absolutely no reason, all the air and water benefits of healthy plants and soils are lost.

Site clearance not only should be kept to a minimum but also should not be done any longer *in advance* than truly necessary. Responsible, sustainability-oriented developers will not pre-clear. Unfortunately, some conventional realtors and developers have to be threatened with legal penalties before they consider anything beyond their own interests. No site should *ever* be cleared until a *specific* master plan or design has been approved.

Do Your Homework First: Knowledge as Sustainability

Those who think that site analysis before design or construction is expensive need to consider the costs of ignorance, which are always far greater.

There are two kinds of "homework" involved in protecting a healthy site. The information gained from each applies to every subsequent step of sustainable

Figure I.3   "Pre-clearance" destroys potential and actual site benefits, for reasons that aren't even commercially valid. (*Photo:* Kim Sorvig.)

landscape work, from design through maintenance. The first involves attitude; the second, facts.

It is impossible to protect what you don't respect. Even with a strong love of nature, working on a site involves carefully setting priorities, and in many cases, reeducating clients and coworkers. Attitudes about preserving natural conditions have a strong influence on design and construction priorities. Is the desire for home soccer practice worth flattening the backyard? Is impressing the neighbors justification for using extra resources or replacing native plants with lawn? Choices like these are never easy and involve basic attitudes about human relationships to landscapes. This book's introduction includes thoughts about cultivating sustainable attitudes, as does the conclusion.

Concepts and models are used to understand and organize complicated subject matter. Mental models are not neutral but reflect attitudes and judgment. The model that a landscape is a decorative architectural space is quite different, both in attitude and outcome, from models based on social science, which in turn differ from those based on the biological sciences. Landscape ecology is one important concept whose influence continues to grow. Around 1994–95, at least five federal agencies developed land-management principles based on landscape ecological concepts.[7] These policies treated landscapes and ecosystems as nested systems at several scales, with fuzzy boundaries, interacting with other units to form the whole. A related conceptual system that is useful for understanding landscapes in a dynamic way is called complexity science, which studies and digitally models systems made up of many independent "agents."[8]

Even with respectful attitudes and sound models, protecting what you do not thoroughly understand is difficult. Information gathering is critical to sustainable work, from the earliest preliminary feasibility studies, through design and construction, and into maintenance. As noted in Principle II, data gathered before development form an indispensable baseline for monitoring and assessing site performance, which is essential to evaluating whether designs are actually sustainable. Data gathering, both informal *site reconnaissance* and technological *surveying* and *monitoring*, benefits from a team effort, clear communication, and information sharing.

Reconnaissance should identify and evaluate site features *before* design begins. (In fact, this knowledge should inform selection of properties to develop, but rarely does; most site selection appears to be based on transport, location, and economics.) Although online resources are changing this, much reconnaissance is visual, observing and noting conditions without technical equipment. Published sources, such as soil and topography maps or land-use records, are also important in effective reconnaissance. Ideally, archival research is done before an on-site visit, so that maps and other records can be carried while observing. For genuinely site-specific design, there is no substitute for the multisensory experience of reconnaissance on the site. Contractors usually carry out their own reconnaissance, separate from such work by the design team, just before bidding a contract. Ideally, their insights should be part of the design process, though this is rare.

Surveying with technical instruments is too often used only to establish ownership boundaries, general contours, and a few construction control points. Global Positioning Systems (GPS), Geographic Information Systems (GIS), and, most recently, drone surveying equipment (see below) leave little excuse for not locating all major site features prior to starting design. Too many conventional designers assume they should remake the site without reference to anything existing; this assumption is often at the root of inadequate surveying.

Whether done with survey instruments or camera and sketchbook, detailed site-specific mapping is a critical part of building sustainably. Homework left too late may be of poor quality or may be overridden by assumptions made before good information is gathered. Much conventional construction is undertaken from site plans that are nearly blank. (I once saw a plan on which the surveyor, clearly no botanist, had marked every tree either "Maple" or "Pine.") Given clearer site data, designers can work with existing topography or trees, while contractors can prioritize site-protection zones and avoid hazards to construction. With 3D scanning, on-site resources like boulders can even be modeled accurately enough to incorporate them into very specific construction details.

Site-specific data have long been considered prohibitively expensive to gather using conventional survey methods. In 2000 GPS and GIS were new technologies. Today they have become standard tools. They have generated more, better, and cheaper site-specific information. Despite a few attempts to monopolize this information for profit, the overall result is better public access to site data.

Increasingly, online information sources are helpful site reconnaissance tools. (They should seldom become substitutes, however, for field observation.) Extremely valuable site information formerly available only in print—the US Soil Survey, climate data, geological diagrams, native and invasive plant lists—is available via the Internet. A wide variety of maps and air photos are also online, some updated almost in real time.

With current software, it is simple, fast, and cheap to pull relatively recent air photos of most places on Earth, convert a photo to a scaled site plan, overlay soil type boundaries and other biological factors, and take the result to the site on a tablet computer or a printed sheet. The same preliminary plan can quickly be turned into a 3D site model that is good enough to permit early planning of site access, parking and staging, and other potentially damaging activities, long before "construction documents" begin. This is particularly valuable to the collaborative process of integrative design, which especially benefits sustainability-oriented teams.

Doing this kind of homework has been costly and time-consuming in the past, perhaps excusing the tendency to treat existing site conditions and materials as irrelevant items to be removed or remade by design. In the same way that the Internet puts an unimaginable library at your fingertips, online geographic data, carefully used and ground-truthed, is dramatically increasing how well professionals know their sites.

Locate Features During Site Reconnaissance

The best and most vulnerable features of any site should be inventoried early. Many will be items of clear ecological value; others will be historic or cultural; some may be of personal importance to the owner, client, or user group. All are likely to need protection during construction. A basic checklist includes:

- all trees, and any unusual or specimen plants
- meadows, groves, thickets, and other identifiable vegetation communities
- wildlife dens, breeding areas, and pathways, including seasonal ones
- streams, wetlands, ponds, and lakes
- rock outcrops
- any potential source of on-site reusable materials
- soils: erodible, fragile, and especially fertile areas
- cultural features (archaeological, historic)
- items or locations of personal or sentimental importance to owners or users
- connections, links, and pathways among these features.

Responsible design firms will make such an inventory the first step in their work. Analysis of the site may reveal other reasons for protecting certain features: for example, a common and none-too-beautiful tree may need to be protected because it acts as a windbreak or moderates solar gain.

Pay Special Attention to Streams, Lakes, and Wetlands

The care of water bodies is a very specialized topic (Principle 4). Because of the difficulty, expense, and legal complications involved in restoring them, it is critical to *identify and protect* streams, lakes, and other wetlands at the earliest possible stage. In fact, the presence of wetlands should be researched before *buying* a property for any sort of development. Horror stories about wetlands regulation usually reveal an owner who didn't know, or didn't want to know, about site conditions. Despite regulation, many commercial land

buyers still limit their site research to the proverbial "location, location, location." That is a mistake no designer or contractor can afford.

Once wetlands are identified, they need protection during construction. The techniques discussed in this chapter, particularly fencing to limit access, are used to safeguard wetlands as well as other site features. Because of the biological complexity and legal status of wetlands, however, their protection often requires going well beyond generic site-protection techniques. For this reason, protection of wetlands is discussed in its own chapter (Principle 4), along with other issues involving water.

At the site research stage, remember that wetlands:

- must be delineated according to legal definitions, not just a layperson's observations
- are highly susceptible to sediment, which erodes off adjacent land surfaces (see "Preserve Healthy Topsoil," p. 70)
- vary seasonally much more than most other landscape features, to the point of disappearing in dry periods
- have life cycles and may be "healthy" or "unhealthy"; either protection as-is or restoration may be appropriate
- are linked to and influenced by off-site and possibly underground water sources, which need to be included in protection planning
- often require the addition of a specialist to the team
- can cause special difficulties for construction workers and machinery.

Even where no wetland exists on the site, protect the existing *drainage* patterns carefully. A featured grove or meadow, thoroughly fenced for protection, can die from flooding or drying if grading outside the fence redirects the flow of water. For sustainability, the movement of water on a site should be changed only with great care.

Tap Local Knowledge of Sites and Seasons

Contractors with years of experience in a specific region know that weather and seasonal changes can make or break a project. The same conditions dramatically affect the need for site protection. Erosion on recently graded soil may be minimal in most weather, until a summer rain squall or seasonal high winds sweep the soil away overnight. Frozen or muddy soils cause practical and engineering problems; equipment may damage wet soil that would be unharmed if worked when dry. Plants may be especially susceptible to breakage or root compaction during seasons of rapid growth, or may tolerate damage better when dormant. Seasonal vulnerability of endangered wildlife has delayed many public projects.

For sustainable construction, consider whether a change in construction *schedule* can minimize disruption. For example, in Bouctouche NB, work on a large boardwalk for Le Pays de la Sagouine was done in winter, with heavy machinery positioned on ice.[9] Working in the summer would have been more complicated *and* more disruptive to the river-dune-island site.

No book or website could possibly include appropriate advice for protecting all sites, in all seasons, for all aspects of construction. A growing literature on site conservation (or "geoconservation") is available, mostly from the United Kingdom. Local contractors often have a remarkable store of seasonal, site-specific knowledge, used to plan ahead for practical matters, scheduling around periods when the site will be inaccessible. If sustainable construction and protection of site features are recognized as goals, this local knowledge is invaluable in achieving results. Large national firms can do sustainable work if they subcontract local experts and heed their influence. The tendency of large firms to standardize all procedures must not overrule adaptation to local conditions. Applied globally and in all seasons, rigid standardization is incompatible with sustainable landscape work.

Avoid Survey Damage

Although detailed site-specific mapping is often key to reduced construction impact, the *process* of site surveying can be the start of site degradation. Fortunately, new technology combined with new attitudes makes survey damage avoidable.

Manage Line-of-sight Surveys

Conventional surveying relies on a clear line of sight between a known point or "datum" and any point whose position is to be determined. Optical surveying instruments, including lasers, must be able to "see" in a straight, uninterrupted line from the instrument to the point being recorded. Sonar and ultrasonic instruments, which bounce sound off a target and back to the instrument, also require a clear shot at the unknown point. To ensure clear line-of-sight connections, surveyors clear brush and small trees with machetes or similar tools, a process known as "brashing."

Depending on region, climate, and vegetation, brashing can cause anything from minor injury to long-term harm. It is least critical in regions where vegetation grows back quickly, such as deciduous forest. Even in these areas, brashing, like careless pruning, can spread plant disease and may affect both species diversity and age distribution of vegetation. In bioregions with fragile vegetation, brashing may be less necessary, but regrowth takes decades. Vegetation removal in linear patterns opens paths for soil erosion. Conventional surveys concentrate on lines, such as property boundaries, which arbitrarily cut across slopes or watersheds, thus increasing disruption.

Modern surveyors plan their fieldwork carefully in advance to minimize wasted time and backtracking. The same planning skills can minimize site damage from brashing, as well as from unnecessary vehicle access, even where line-of-sight tools are unavoidable.

Because much conventional development starts with total regrading of the site, existing site features, other than landmark-quality specimens, may seem unimportant to site crews. In the worst cases, surveyors, like other construction workers, thoughtlessly destroy any inconvenient item found on the site. Drone surveying does not require human access to the site, a fact that can avoid damage. If minimal site damage is an explicitly stated goal of the project, the survey team becomes an important ally in meeting that goal.

Use Alternative Survey Technology

Several methods of surveying that do not rely on line of sight are appropriate for landscape construction surveying. These include both high-tech and low-tech options.

GLOBAL POSITIONING
Global Positioning Systems have been in the surveyor's toolkit for over two decades; widespread use of

GPS was still news in 2007, but by 2017 it had become commonplace. GPS chips are tiny, and anyone who has a cell phone has likely used the technology. The concept of triangulating on several geosynchronous satellites, whose location relative to Earth is constant, is widely understood by nonspecialists. Russia, the European Union, and several other countries have launched their own GPS systems (sometimes referred to as GNSS, Global Navigation Satellite System); some receivers can triangulate on multiple systems, increasing the number of available satellites and the accuracy of results.

Conceptually, GPS technology has not changed much since this book's first edition, but GPS has become easier, cheaper, more accurate, and more widespread.[10] GPS survey results are digital and can be fed directly into computerized drafting, mapping, and analysis programs. GPS data are "georeferenced," meaning that every site survey is easily related to latitude and longitude and, thus, to all other sites. A site survey can be precisely placed within regional data (for example, the US Soil Survey), as well as being "in registration" with surveys done at different times. Georeferencing means that CAD drawings, uploaded into a GPS field unit, guide construction staking, while GPS-gathered field information makes accurate "as-built" drawings and maps.

One major development has been the combination of GPS and GIS with other technology. The GPS in your phone shows your location on a map that could not have been created without GPS data-gathering and GIS mapping. Similarly, studies of complex environmental data can be done by linking unrelated mapped data. A study on the effects of light pollution used satellite imagery to determine actual light levels in specific communities, then correlated those levels to cancer rates in those communities. Without combining the accuracy of GPS and the storage and mapping capacities of GIS, such correlations would be nearly impossible. A second example of synergy is mounting sensors and GPS on a small radio-controlled plane, resulting in a drone that can survey land many times faster than any other method (see the following section).

In terms of site protection, a major advantage of GPS is that Earth-surface line of sight is not required.

In most cases, brashing can be entirely eliminated and access to the site is simpler and safer. Anywhere the surveyor (or drone) can carry it, a GPS unit can record horizontal and vertical location. (Dense tree canopy, very narrow canyons, or tall buildings may block communication skyward to the satellites.[11] Such obstructions can be worked around or surveyed with line-of-sight instruments.)

Simple recreational or street navigation GPS is accurate to within ten feet (three meters), costs in the hundreds of dollars (or is free on your phone), and is adequate for many general site-inventory purposes. (For all types, accuracy refers to *horizontal* measurement; vertical elevation, if measured, typically is about half as accurate.) Mapping units are accurate to one yard or meter horizontally; these cost a few thousand dollars and link easily and directly into GIS maps.

Survey-quality GPS is accurate to less than half an inch (one centimeter) horizontally, plus or minus. This degree of accuracy requires two units in a "differential" system (often called DGPS): one mobile, plus a stationary "base station" at a known point. By comparing satellite readings from the mobile unit to those taken at the known point, small deviations can be corrected. A differential system is "real time" (or RTK, for real time kinematic) when corrected data are beamed directly to the mobile unit in the field, rather than doing batch corrections back at the office after completing fieldwork. Such systems cost tens of thousands of dollars. It is increasingly common that differential GPS uses a regional "reference station," often provided by local government, which corrects mobile GPS readings for anyone within about a twenty-mile radius. Subscription charges and password access are required, but the end user needs only one GPS, significantly reducing costs. A similar concept, covering all US states, is WAAS (Wide Area Augmentation System). Set up by the Federal Aviation Administration, it uses independent satellites to correct GPS accuracy. It is free and works even with many inexpensive GPS models; the unit usually must be specifically set to use WAAS.

For landscape professionals, there are several ways to take advantage of GPS technology. Most surveyors offer GPS, and contracts can specify it. A second option is renting (budget about $2,000 per week); setup, calibration, and data-file conversion may be included. Once set up, fieldwork can be done by people not trained in surveying—for example, a botanist could produce very accurate tree inventories, a designer could walk and map desirable paths, or a contractor could locate construction hazards. A third option is to purchase GPS equipment and be trained in its use. This remains a big investment, and teaming with a skilled surveyor is often more productive.

A few project examples hint at the range of landscape uses. Design Workshop (Denver and Aspen CO and Tempe AZ) has used GPS on several projects where accuracy, environmental sensitivity, and speed of site analysis were important. At McDowell Mountain Ranch in Scottsdale AZ, new community trails had to be integrated with regional trails, and strict environmental laws were involved. Starting with rough sketches on a topographical map, landscape architect Stuart Watada leased a handheld GPS unit to refine trail locations and collect data on trailside vegetation and features. Design Workshop uses an inexpensive GPS unit to field verify potential home sites at large developments, and for early site planning in countries like Bolivia, where no published survey information is available.

For the Alaska Botanical Garden in Anchorage, Jeff Dillon of Land Design North had GPS data collected by University of Alaska students. Existing vegetation and features were incorporated directly and accurately into design work. Dillon has also used GPS to lay out miles of ski trails in Anchorage parks.

Ohio State University's Center for Mapping developed a "GPS van," the forerunner of Google's mapping cars. Combining GPS and stereo-photo methods, the van could locate any item it could "see" to an accuracy of approximately fourteen centimeters (five inches). OSU's research, among others, has made semi-automated GPS-controlled site grading and agricultural seeding and fertilizing widespread.

GPS has been welcomed in conservation work. Rob Corey, a landscape architect with the Natural Resources Conservation Service, produces "virtual landscape animations," which allow users to visualize land-use changes and then compute environmental-impact statistics from the images. GPS is important in collecting the data on which Corey's innovative system

Figure I.4   GPS units, often backpack sized, make surveying quicker, easier, and potentially less destructive to site vegetation, and are an essential part of UAS surveying, below. (*Photo*: Magellan Corp.)

is based. In The Nature Conservancy's Parks in Peril program in Latin America, landscape architect Brian Houseal and colleagues use GPS to establish accurate legal boundaries for nature preserves and to locate endangered plant communities. The information greatly increases the Conservancy's ability to win protection for remote, ecologically critical sites.

UNMANNED AIRCRAFT SYSTEMS FOR SURVEYING
A very recent, and potentially revolutionary, addition to the surveying and remote-sensing toolkit is

Figure I.5a, b Unmanned aircraft systems (UAS, or drones) are removing the last excuse for inadequate site data. Fixed-wing (*right*) and rotor types (*below*) make surveying fast and cheap enough for ongoing performance monitoring, and produce 3D models of whole landscapes or specific features. (*Photos:* Lumpi, Pixabay.)

unmanned aircraft systems (UAS) carrying cameras and sensors. These are simpler versions of controversial military drones. Surveying UAS include both fixed-wing and multi-rotor or "hexicopter" craft. Fixed-wing models are lightweight, on the order of one and a half pounds, with a photogrammetric camera, on-board GPS, electronics, and communications hardware. Larger fixed-wing and 'copter models, often weighing twenty pounds, are needed to carry LiDAR (Light Detection and Ranging), which measures location by bouncing laser pulses off objects in the same way radar uses radio waves.[12]

Unlike hobbyists' radio-controlled aircraft, UAS are controlled by GPS software on precisely predefined flight paths; only in an emergency does the operator take over with a joystick. For surveying, they fly much lower than conventional manned planes; thus, assuming use of the same camera, the lower-altitude flight produces more detail. Accuracy varies: "mapping grade" UAS can usually achieve about three-inch

resolution; "survey grade" models produce one centimeter per pixel horizontally and about five centimeters vertically. Much of this accuracy depends on on-board RTK GPS, which constantly monitors the aircraft's actual position in three-dimensional space, correcting for wind and other distortions. Correlating the flight log to the imagery and a GPS base on the ground allows images to be stitched together and processed.

In addition to conventional (but very high-resolution) air photos, UAS can produce multispectral maps, such as infrared or UV. Both photographic and LiDAR models can also produce dense "point clouds" bounced from surfaces of infrastructure, buildings, or landforms (but not, apparently, water). Once collected, point clouds can be processed semi-automatically into topographic contour maps and 3D models in CAD and other formats. These remarkably detailed scale models show actual conditions. They are used by engineers to inspect industrial and transportation

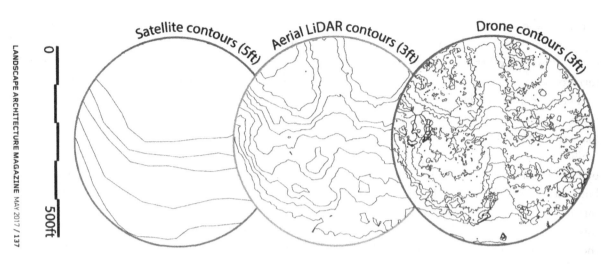

Figure 1.6 This image represents the dramatic increase in resolution between satellite, conventional aerial, and drone imagery. (*Image:* Prof. Karl Kullman, UC Berkeley.)

infrastructure, by archaeologists and preservationists to document prehistoric sites or ornate historic structures, and by developers to get accurate site maps early in the planning process.

UAS surveying is comparable in accuracy to ground surveys with the best GPS equipment, but can be done far more quickly and cheaply. Several current sources claim half the time and one-fifth the cost of conventional surveying. These advantages are heavily, even overly, emphasized by current vendors, but cost and speed should make *better site data* the norm, rather than merely shaving pennies off the cost of the same old inadequate information. UAS have other benefits related to sustainability. They do not require any kind of site clearance (although 3D points under tree canopy are difficult to obtain) nor placement of GCPs (ground control points), and they can access rough terrain and polluted or unstable sites where survey teams could not safely enter. They can be quickly deployed after disasters. Because they are GPS-based, it is easy to coordinate hybrid methods, such as incorporating tree inventories done on the ground with an overall site map using UAS. The fact that they are fast and cheap makes ongoing repeated surveys affordable, which has promise for monitoring baseline and performance of sustainably designed sites (see Principle 11).

The amount of raw data UAS collect is overwhelming: one report estimated a *million* surveyed points *in fifteen minutes*. Such accuracy enhances both site pro-

tection and context-sensitive construction. UAS have been used for population counts of wildlife, and, with extra software, they may be able to track and monitor some species.[13] The Denver firm THK Associates has its own fairly low-resolution UAS, producing 3D site models with the help of a cloud-based processing service.[14] Low-res 3D models, perhaps produced in-house, bring existing conditions like slope into design discussions from the earliest phases; more precise mapping is done as needed by a surveying service. In many cases, the *lowest*-quality UAS map is dramatically more accurate than the plat maps and boundary surveys on which past projects were so often based.

UAS can, in theory, go almost anywhere, including inside buildings and under tree canopy, provided there is room to fly and signal from the controller. They have been used to show potential tenants of skyscrapers what their view will be—before the building even exists. This might have creative parallels in landscape design.

THK's in-house UAS cost about $1,500 including license; processing is outsourced at under $20 per site. This is well within reach for landscape architects, contractors, and maintenance firms, and could improve results while cutting costs. Survey-grade equipment is another matter, ranging upward from $50,000,[15] with a steep learning curve, and produces such large data files that many office computers cannot handle them. A growing number of surveyors (as well as other operators who do only reconnaissance, not legal surveys) offer complete packages including conversion to CAD or other formats. Some offer one-day turnaround.

There are a few problems with these robotic surveying machines. The fixed-wing models are often made of Styrofoam, which raises concerns about durability and long-term disposal. All types are powered by batteries, limiting average flight times to under an hour. Some animals are spooked by drones, and in one project near Quito, Ecuador, a surveyor's drone was downed by a hawk after flying close to a nest; the wings and propellers were ripped off and never found, though the body was salvaged. As noted, LiDAR can't survey water surfaces or below vegetation canopy, and optical point clouds are blank in areas covered by shadow. Complex shapes like bare winter trees can theoretically be modeled precisely, but actual success varies.

The Federal Aviation Administration realized the need for UAS safety regulations only recently. In the United States, private drones are limited to an altitude of 500 feet; in other countries they can fly near 1,000 feet. High altitude allows faster area coverage but decreases accuracy. Lighter-weight models are exempt in Canada and elsewhere from some regulations, since crashing a two-pound foam plane is far less dangerous than a 'copter weighing ten times that. Licensing is required, operations must be within sight of the pilot, and generous no-fly zones surround airports and some other facilities. None of these seem to be seriously slowing the adoption of this powerful form of land data acquisition.

Some of the capabilities of drones can be had for next to no money from Public Lab.[16] This grassroots organization sells balloon and kite mapping kits as well as inexpensive sensors to monitor water and air quality, vegetation, pollution, and other data on landscape health. These "poor person's drones and dataloggers" provide detailed basic information that often would be sufficient even for professional landscape work, and certainly for activism and educational use.

Low-tech, Non-line-of-sight Tools

While GPS looks to satellite technology to free itself from line-of-sight limitations, a much-simpler method relies on the oldest of all leveling tools: water. The tube level or hose level is available in several forms. Like a surveyor's transit, it determines vertical level only; separate distance measurements make a complete survey. Where sight-line clearing must be minimized, and for some types of construction layout, it is an inexpensive and valuable tool.

In a U-shaped tube partially filled with water, the water surfaces in each arm of the U always lie at the same level. In a hose level, the U is replaced with twenty or more feet of clear flexible tubing. The water line at one end of the tubing is held at a known elevation, and the water at the other end of the tube adjusts to exactly the same level.

Hose levels can be used around blind corners, without clear sight lines, and at considerable distances across rough ground. They speed construction layout because no calculation is required: the two water lines are simply at the same level. Laser equipment provides similar functions, but it is more costly and requires line-of-sight clearance.

Some manufacturers have added electronic sensors to the traditional tube level; an audible signal sounds when the ends of the tube are aligned. This allows one person to use a hose level more efficiently. Even these enhanced versions cost only about $50. If a site is free of visual obstructions, line-of-sight tools are more convenient for most surveying. But where clearing would be costly and intrusive, tube levels offer cost-effective site protection.

Another remarkably simple site-surveying tool is the "A-frame level," in use since ancient Egypt. Three light boards nailed together form a rough capital "A"; a mark is made at the center of the cross arm. A weighted string, like a plumb line, is hung from the top of the A. When the string intersects the cross arm exactly at the center mark, the two "feet" of the A are level. Walked across the land like old-fashioned drafting dividers, the A-frame quickly establishes a series of level points. For terracing and other erosion-control work, the A-frame can level earthworks or find contours quickly, without any math calculations, and without line-of-sight clearance.

Sometimes what needs to be measured is not the size or layout of the landscape, but the rate at which some aspect of it is changing. Some remarkably sim-

Figure I.7 The Egyptian A-frame is a simple, site-friendly way of establishing level and the fastest way to lay out points along a contour line. (*Photo:* Kim Sorvig.)

ple tools can serve this purpose. For example, rebar "benchmarks" (usually with bright plastic caps for visibility and safety) can be used to mark the edge of vegetative cover or the level of soil. Set deep enough that they can't move, such markers can reveal loss or movement of soil or plants between site visits. These simple measurements can be critically important for planning and performance monitoring of sustainable projects. Even with UAS monitoring, creative use of on-the-ground marking can be valuable.

Use Flexible, Accurate Visualization Tools

Having good survey data doesn't help much if the data can't become visible in the design process. Although design graphics are well outside the scope of this book, it is worth noting that some methods are better suited than others to visualizing irregular existing site

features like rock outcroppings or specimen trees, or displaying complex interactions such as a stream channel's wanderings over time. The choice of the right tool can directly affect the ability to transform sustainable intentions into on-the-ground success. Although skill with graphics is often dismissed by ecologically oriented designers as just a way of making pretty images, it can be an important link between the reality of the site and the proposed construction—a tool for site protection.

Hand-drawn measured perspective sketching techniques are very valuable for fieldwork and charettes at the client site, and in the right hands they are as fast as software; in some situations, faster.[17]

Software like SketchUp increasingly makes it easy to overlay digital field photos, hand sketches, and 2D or 3D wireframe images, as well as offering "model libraries" that include thousands of objects that can populate a project visualization. SketchUp, and most modeling software, can import or export from Google Earth and other software.

Software for organizing and visualizing Earth data is improving rapidly. Google Earth, released in 2005 and rating a speculative mention in the second edition, has transformed these possibilities. Originally developed by the US Central Intelligence Agency, it provides a level of instant geographic information that was inconceivable ten years ago, and goes well beyond the conventional map. It permits fly-throughs of existing topography, single-click latitude and longitude data, plotting of surveyed points and other data, exporting of contour lines and topographic models, and links to photos and documents posted by anyone. It is beginning to be used as a central repository for links to other site-specific information, which could include site photos, as-built drawings, regional soil or climate data, or local history. The software has been used to expose "mountaintop removal" coal mining in Appalachia[18] and to map forest fires as they happen. There still appears to be no systematic effort to store "site-indexed" ecological and social background information in such software. Doing so could be a quantum leap toward making sustainable design the norm rather than the exception.[19]

This is not a book on computer technology, and there are far too many new and excellent tools to cover in detail. Thus, one of the more comprehensive tools will serve as an example of visualization software that works at a landscape scale. CommunityViz, now in version 5.1.2, is a software add-in for ArcGIS that produces 2D and 3D visualizations of "what-if" land-use scenarios. The transition from planning graphics (three colors of dots representing three house designs on a 2D subdivision map) to conceptual drawings (a bird's-eye view of the whole subdivision) is fast enough to test multiple scenarios during a public meeting. 3D models (in this case, the three prototype houses, but also of trees and almost any object occurring often in a plan) are added from built-in libraries, or created in software like SketchUp. CommunityViz also includes a Suitability Wizard that visually ranks parcels, for example, on how well they meet a set of factors. A demo video[20] shows this being used to select an ideal neighborhood for a family with school kids, near parks and libraries, but the wizard could presumably use any mappable characteristic as a factor. Using geology, soil, hydrology, and other environmental factors, the result would be a McHargian analysis, produced in minutes instead of hours and readily updated for what-if analysis. CommunityViz doesn't appear to do very well with site grading and its 3D impacts, nor can it (or any other software I've seen) transform an air photo into a 3D visualization with topography, buildings, and vegetation automatically extending into vertical space. Like most of the rapid-modeling software available today, the library of trees seems to me to encourage an entirely horticultural approach to planting design; a user would have to work much harder to visualize a restored native plant community than to image a backyard with "plopped" trees and bushes. This isn't specific to CommunityViz, which remains a remarkable tool. Similar software is available, but there tends to be a split between the GIS/analytical capabilities and the 3D visualization. As recently as May 2015, a thread on the AutoCAD Forum decried the lack of software combining all the functions needed by landscape professionals, who often have to cobble together civil engineering, architectural, and general drafting to accomplish their project work.[21]

Esri, the maker of ArcGIS, has recently launched a Green Infrastructure Initiative, another major aid for visualizing land-related issues. It provides a trove of mapped data, assembled over many years of Esri's experience, along with accessible tools for mapping and analysis—available free to everyone. Its strengths are primarily in looking at issues one or two scales larger than ordinary landscape sites: habitat loss, water management, land-use impacts, and so on. In an interview with *LAM*, Esri's founder, Jack Dangermond, says he hopes the tool and its users will be "a counterforce, particularly at this time, that speaks with the voice of science."[22] Professionals, especially those who integrate sustainability concerns into their work, will benefit from the huge data-set represented by the maps. For many of us, software with a shorter learning curve than high-end GIS will offer geographic analysis to those who aren't computer specialists.

"Agent-based modeling" (ABM) uses simple rules of interaction programmed into large numbers of individual "agents," and produces remarkable simulations of complex systems. For example, many of the armies in Peter Jackson's *Lord of the Rings* were composed of agent soldiers individually following very simple rules (if X move in, if Y strike, if Z fall back, etc.)—on the basis of which some Orcs deserted! This unexpected behavior is an example of an "emergent property" resulting unpredictably from the simple repeated interactions of large numbers of agents. ABM is perhaps the most promising trend in realistically envisioning actual ecological and social processes (which tend to be emergent, as opposed to a top-down design approach). Easy-to-learn but robust software for ABM is NetLogo, downloadable for free; for understanding any process where many small forces over time produce large results, NetLogo is a powerful tool that few landscape professionals yet use.

Visualization is an essential part of design, but it is also critical in public presentations; relatively few laypeople can easily read technical drawings. A recent addition to public-focused visualization is a line of on-site virtual-reality (VR) viewers from the company Owlized. The hardware (and the name) is a take on the classic midcentury "tourist viewer" (the kind mounted at scenic viewpoints across the United States).[23] But as the user of the OWL VR turns its binocular head, virtual reality imagery adjusts to give a 360-degree immersive experience of what the site might be, or what it once was. The VR imagery can show a proposed streetscape overlaid on an actual treeless block; simulate flood conditions seen from the viewer's location; or show historical images of how the site looked in the 1800s. The VR imagery can be created in SketchUp or other common modeling software and uploaded. The viewer can also be programmed to collect survey responses, either by on-screen input or via audio. The viewer can be AC or battery powered, and a solar canopy is available, which doubles as a shade over viewers. A version of the viewer that uses a cell phone to display the simulation is also available. Owlized's equipment capitalizes on something that landscape architects know instinctively—that being in the actual place brings visualizations new power.

Simtable, another new entrant, takes a different approach. Sand tables (sandboxes on legs, the sand sculpted to model topography) have long been used in firefighter training. The portable Simtable keeps the flexibility (and public accessibility) of sand modeling but can project detailed imagery onto the sand and, more remarkably, read the sand topography back into digital mapping. Using a camera carefully in register with a projector, this system allows the physical model to *interact* in real time with digital simulations. A typical sequence might be to project a color-coded elevation map onto flat sand, then pile up the sand until it matches the digital map. (By reading the sand surface repeatedly, the software indicates where sand is too high or low.) With experience, the three-by-five-foot surface can be accurately sculpted or resculpted in a matter of seconds. A USGS map—or any other spatial data from the Web—automatically orients and scales to the sand model, and the user can run simulations such as runoff, road traffic in an emergency, or wildfire behavior based on real conditions like humidity, wind, and slope.

The camera recognizes the light of a laser pointer so that projected menus can be selected; for dramatic effect, when starting a wildfire simulation, inventor Steve Guerin uses a lighter instead. Using the device "in reverse," a client could scoop away sand to represent a graded development site, or pile sand across a valley as a dam, and immediately see the "what-if" effect this would have on runoff. The projector-camera combination can do many similar interactive modeling tasks on a flat surface; a firm might start with those

capabilities, expanding to the sand modeling if client or public input is a frequent need. Another cool trick: Guerin and his team have worked out how to get accurate 3D point-cloud models on-site and nearly in real time, using nothing but two cell phones and the Simtable software. See the company's website for photos, which don't reproduce in black and white, and for videos that, though focused on wildfire, give a clear picture of how Simtable works.

Visualization helps us dream and, at the same time, avoid nightmare miscalculations. Simtable, Owlized, and CommunityViz illustrate how rapidly this essential tool set is evolving. It is important to recognize that new tools are often relegated to conventional purposes by default, but that such innovations can open up new possibilities, like sustainable design, if we recognize those capabilities.

Minimize Utility Damage

Many modern landscapes are crisscrossed with buried and overhead utilities. Although some of these systems are invisible, constructing and maintaining them seriously alters the landscapes through which they pass.

Irrigation, site lighting, and storm-drainage lines are part of landscape construction, their functions landscape specific. Other utility systems, like sewage, power, phone, and cable TV, serve the buildings on the property; some alternative methods of heating, cooling, or energy storage involve underground pipes or tanks. The site may also be affected by systems that serve larger communities (main power, sewer, or phone lines) or commercial interests (oil and gas pipelines), along with easements for such systems.

Landscape construction has direct influence over landscape-specific utilities. Landscape architects and contractors have also had significant effects on public-utility impact (below). The difference between planning carefully for utilities and dismissing them as necessary evils can be like night and day and is an important aspect of site protection.

Make Maximum Use of Narrow Easements and Trenches

Access is required to construct, maintain, replace, and repair utilities. Significant decreases in site impact can be achieved by reconsidering how utility access is provided. Public utility easements are usually far wider than actual pipeline or cable. Rural utility easements cut across country, requiring their own access roads. In urban areas, utility companies frequently dig up buried lines and keep street trees clear of overhead wires. Ways to decrease the impact of access in each case are discussed below.

According to the Edison Electric Institute, no one keeps national records of the total length or land area occupied by utility easements.[24] Pacific Gas and Electric (PG&E), as a single example, has 14,000 miles of electrical transmission lines. A fifty-foot-wide easement uses about six acres per mile. At this common width, PG&E's transmission lines alone could require as much as 80,000 acres. Multiply this across the continent and it is clear that utility easements have a major impact on landscape health nationally. Utilities are recognizing the potential for lessening these impacts and for creating habitat corridors in easements. The Edison Institute, for example, publishes EPA-approved guidelines for maintaining easements.

Because easements of any width are linear, they can disrupt wildlife movements and invite invasive plants. In addition, these lines follow not the topography but the shortest route between source and user; as a result, cleared easements often run up and down very steep slopes, hastening erosion. Conventional transmission and pipeline systems necessitate easements, which is a strong reason to advocate on-site wind and solar power. Because so few decision makers apply any landscape perspective, false comparisons between distributed and grid utility strategies are common.

Reduce Clearing for Access Roads

Access roads are required when utility lines do not follow existing transportation. Main branches of utility systems are often routed to avoid populated areas by going through rural areas or urban parks, where they require dedicated access roads, on top of pipelines or below overhead wires.

Easement clearing can often be narrowed.[25] Minimize width to a single lane for maintenance or construction vehicles, with wide turnarounds at strategic points. Using the smallest and lightest possible machinery can further decrease the access space required. Decisions about machinery use are made at many levels, from corporate purchasing offices to the job supervisor renting extra equipment for an emergency. Landscape professionals have a variety of opportunities to influence these decisions.

Special construction techniques, such as trenchers that lay pipe or cable behind them as they go, can cut easement width dramatically. At Loantaka Brook Reservation in Morris County NJ, landscape architects Andropogon Associates challenged both conventional routing design and conventional construction methods for a gas pipeline through mature beech-oak forest. Space-saving methods of pipe installation, devised with the contractor, reduced a proposed fifty-foot right-of-way to thirty-four. Using a tracked loader specially adapted for the project, the contractors were able to replace slabs of vegetation-rich soil along the pipeline trench, guaranteeing revegetation.

In Loudon County VA, a developer installed a sewer line across park authority property. Two landscape architecture firms, HOH Associates and Rhodeside & Harwell, persuaded the county sanitation authority to reduce construction width from their standard seventy-five feet to thirty-five. With an arborist and engineer, they worked out three main guidelines for the project:

- Keep construction and final easements to thirty-five feet.
- Eliminate straight utility swaths longer than 1,000 linear feet. Follow topography and natural features. (This principle is particularly important in steep or forested areas.)
- Keep openings into or out of woodlands—the points of greatest visual impact—as narrow as possible. In this project, the opening into the woods was pinched to ten feet.

These principles proved so successful that they became standard in Loudon County.

Utility easements should, wherever possible, be thought of and constructed as multifunctional space. Combining an easement with a public road, trail, or

Figure I.8 This easement, in Loudon County VA, is less than half as wide as the utility's standard. Note the site protection fence. (*Project:* Park Authority, HOH Associates, and Rhodeside and Harwell. *Photo:* Doug Hays.)

bike path is a common example, used in the Morris County project above. Combining utility easements with trails is an increasingly common way for park systems to pay for needed services. The Washington & Old Dominion Trail in northern Virginia combines four major functions and "recycles" an older right-of-way. What began as a disused rail corridor first became a power-line easement. A paved trail was added, managed by the regional park authority. Later, sewer line and fiber-optic cable were installed under the trail; leasing fees ($250,000 annually) pay for trail maintenance.[26] The result is a much-needed recreation corridor. Sharing functions achieves more with less site disruption.

Utility corridors can share with wildlife, too. Their linear and interconnecting patterns can form wildlife corridors and habitat—*if* they are not ruthlessly cleared of all vegetation. Despite costs and impacts, mowing (or spraying) the entire right-of-way is still common practice. Even where a certain width of easement is legally required, clearing can be selective. Where easements are extra wide to allow for future expansion, clear only the area in actual use. Leave the access road grassed to reduce runoff and erosion. Except for the road itself, shrubs or small trees can be allowed to remain. As long as the road is kept drivable, clearing the location of a specific repair when it occurs is often cost-effective, compared with ongoing clearance of the whole easement.

Keep Urban Utilities Accessible

In addition to sharing space with wildlife or bicyclists, carefully designed utilities can also share space with each other. Landscape contractors frequently lay irrigation and low-voltage supply lines in the same trench. The same concept applied to municipal utilities can save energy, simplify maintenance, and reduce space for easements. Excavation costs money and energy, during both initial construction and subsequent maintenance. Shared-trench construction reduces excavation and should be part of sustainable construction.

Not all utilities are suited for shared trenches. In particular, natural gas cannot run in the same trench as any electrical utility, including phone, cable TV, and low-voltage wires. The bending radius required for large pipes may prevent routing them with other utilities; consider designing the more flexible system to follow the less flexible. Similarly, gravity-flow systems have strict limits on slopes and lengths of run; other systems might follow their layout.

Shared trenching is most likely to work for "main" supply lines, because the starting and ending points of different utilities seldom coincide. For example, streetlights and fire hydrants are spaced differently along a street but are supplied by main lines running parallel to the street, which might be shared. With careful planning, some utility fixtures can be located together (streetlights sharing poles with electric lines, for example), reducing both materials used and space required. Such arrangements require clear cooperative agreements between utility companies for maintenance, future expansion, and similar issues.

Easy access to buried utilities can save materials and energy otherwise wasted. Locating utilities under roads saves easement space, but digging though asphalt or concrete pavement to repair lines is costly and disruptive. Patched pavement is frequently inferior to original construction, and excavated material contributes to solid-waste problems.

A European solution relies on interlocking pavers (like bricks with jigsaw-puzzle edges). Europeans call these concrete block pavers, or CPBs; in the United States they are usually called CMUs (concrete masonry units). Laid without mortar, they provide a strong paved surface that can be removed and replaced for access to buried utilities. Although initial cost is higher than for sheet paving, lifetime savings on labor alone may justify installation of unit pavers. From a sustainability perspective, almost no material waste is involved because interlocking pavers can be pulled up and replaced repeatedly (or reused elsewhere). To excavate through solid paving requires heavy machinery, but to remove and replace unit pavers, smaller machinery or even manual labor is used. This not only saves energy but also decreases access widths. Lest anyone worry about strength, interlocking pavers support huge commercial aircraft at Hong Kong's international airport, Chek Lap Kok.

Interlocking pavers offer other practical and aesthetic advantages over standard sheet asphalt or concrete. Different colors can designate pedestrian crossings or make elaborate mosaics: for example, a miniature baseball diamond in multicolored block greets baseball fans at Anaheim CA's Angel Stadium.[27] Streets surfaced with interlocking pavers give a traditional cobblestone look to New Urbanist streetscapes; an example is Riverside Village in Atlanta, by progressive land management firm Post Properties.

Compared to mechanized street-paving methods, interlocking blocks may seem labor-intensive. European companies like Optimas, however, have developed small forklift-like tractors to pick up and place pavers about eighty at a time, plus tools for preparing the sand bed and edging. The same machine can pull up groups of pavers three feet square during maintenance, setting them aside for quick replacement. If ease of maintenance is included, interlocking blocks may actually use less labor than sheet paving over their life cycle.

Edging required to keep interlocking pavers from moving sideways is often made of polyvinyl chloride (PVC). This is a material that should be phased out of landscape use wherever possible (see p. 295). For edging, many alternatives exist.

Plant the Right Street Trees and Prune Them Right

Where overhead utility lines follow streets, they frequently conflict with trees, which get pruned away from the lines. Most affected are street trees, planted

Figure I.9 Interlocking pavers set on sand are easily removed and replaced for utility access, saving energy, cost, and waste. Some pavers also permit water infiltration. (*Photo:* Courtesy of Interlocking Concrete Pavement Inst. / David R. Smith.)

along roadsides at public expense and increasingly important to urban environmental quality. Utility crews have been notorious for butchering trees near their lines, a practice that fortunately is changing.

Prevention is the preferred solution. For new construction, utility lines and trees should be placed to avoid conflict. New plantings that cannot be relocated should use ornamental species that will not grow tall enough to touch the lines.

Where existing or poorly selected trees do conflict with utilities, thinning the tree *selectively* is in everyone's best interest. The temptation to lop the entire treetop like a hedge results in increased costs as well as environmental damage. Although lopping is initially quick and cheap, and requires little skilled labor, the tree will sucker vigorously at every cut, producing a dense thicket of branches. These fast-growing shoots soon threaten the utility lines again and must be trimmed every year or two. (Huge tractor-mounted circular saws, buzz-cutting everything in their path, do a particularly destructive "drive-by" lopping.)

Selective thinning, by contrast, carefully removes those branches that extend toward the wires. Far fewer cuts are made; aggressive sprouting does not occur. For many species, thinning once every five years is sufficient to protect the utility. In the long run this makes thinning as cost-effective as lopping. Savings in transportation energy are high, because distance is a major factor in utility corridor tree work. Thinning is far less

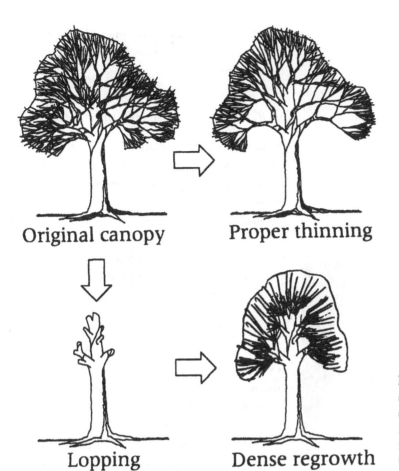

Original canopy   Proper thinning

Lopping   Dense regrowth

Figure I.10 Dense tree canopies should be selectively thinned (top) to solve utility, shade, or view problems. Lopping or "pollarding" (bottom) disfigures the tree, and regrowth is denser than before. (*Illust.:* Craig Farnsworth.)

stressful on the tree, and much less likely to spread disease. Selective thinning done well is hard to see. Thus, without extra cost, thinning prolongs the life and appearance of valued trees, maintains their ability to filter air and provide shade, and reduces energy expended on line maintenance.

Increased awareness of costs and environmental issues has led many utility companies to contract tree maintenance with knowledgeable arborists. Public disgust with the ugliness and ill health of butchered trees, as well as outrage at destruction of tax-financed street trees, has helped change older practices, a trend that landscape contractors and landscape architects should encourage.

Look Ahead to Make New Utility Technologies
Less Intrusive

Cellular and wireless telecommunications utilities are a concern for sustainability-focused landscape professionals. More than 245,000 transmission towers are already in place, each covering about a twenty-mile radius; expect more as cellular companies battle for profitable markets.[28] Industry-sponsored federal law forbids communities from regulating tower placement or requiring shared towers. A few communities have succeeded in forcing cell companies to use existing steeples or towers or new decorative clock towers[29] to accommodate transmitters. Even this much compromise is the exception. With growing demand, towers and access roads are proliferating.

Cellular facilities rely on height to function and cannot be buried, making landscape integration awkward. Disguising the towers as trees[30] is not the solution, but cell equipment is ever more intrusive. One cellular tower may serve an area equivalent to hundreds of telephone poles and, in this sense, saves resources. Towers are not *replacing* poles, however, but are built *in addition*. The ideal system would eliminate most poles and miles of wiring, using unobtrusive towers. Realistically, common easements and shared towers for telecom should be a policy goal.

Figure 1.11 Cell-phone towers, even when disguised as trees, mar the landscape visually and harm wildlife; access roads cause environmental disruption. (*Photo:* Kim Sorvig.)

One manufacturer, Phazar Wireless Antennas, makes boxlike cell antennas intended to be building mounted. The company will print a photo-based "Chameleon Covering" that matches the mounting surface—for example, a brick pattern—making the antenna all but invisible.

Technical alternatives to towers continue to evolve. "Cable microcell integrators," or CMIs, are box antennas so small that they hang from existing utility poles, providing phone and data service over cable-TV wires, which already has nearly 97 percent coverage in the United States. About four CMIs can replace a tower system, often at 30 to 50 percent cost savings. Visual impact is much less than with towers, and CMIs can provide service in tower technology "holes." DAS (distributed antenna systems) and HetNets (heterogeneous networks) are two common terms for such

infrastructure. Educating designers and engineers that there are practical alternatives to new towers is one of the main challenges.[31]

Specify and Lobby for "Alternative" Utility Systems

Because utilities are shared services, their location, use, and maintenance are strongly influenced by legal agreements. Such agreements can be used to encourage environmental care.

Many subdivisions have covenants requiring buried utilities. Such covenants could include requirements for shared trenches, limited easement widths, and selective clearance and pruning. Community associations can use maintenance contracts to minimize utility damage.

Many public utility regulations date from a period in which the only concerns were mechanical efficiency, cost savings, and safety. Recent cellular regulations continue this tendency to favor utilities over the public or environment. As older infrastructure decays, technical, cost, and safety concerns are pushing utility issues to the fore. Large-scale infrastructure is ripe for financial abuse, as in the Enron scandal, while arguments like "energy independence" are used to exclude public voices from utility decisions. In addition, some alternatives, like on-site solar electricity, have become viable enough that public utilities are attacking them. Strategies to discourage on-site solar have included charging solar customers for linking to the grid instead of paying them for energy they produce, and lobbying for extreme reporting requirements for alternative energy suppliers, disguised as "consumer protection."

Current laws favor centralized utilities, which require extensive infrastructure networks for distribution (electricity or natural gas) or collection (sewage, crude oil). These networks cost materials, energy, and maintenance. Constructing them laces whole regions with environmental disruption, temporary or permanent. Operational losses (leakage from pipes, voltage drop from cables) and accidents increase with distances and age. On-site alternatives avoid these problems.

Many "alternative" systems are local: for example, photovoltaic panels generate power at the point of use; constructed wetlands treat waste on-site. These "near-the-need" systems can eliminate distribution and collection infrastructure entirely, at least in theory. On-site power generation eliminates the 60 percent voltage drop losses common to grid electricity.[32] Similarly, on-site sewage treatment eliminates the use of huge amounts of water merely to transport waste. Some "alternative" systems have flexible infrastructure: for example, pressure-based sewage systems can follow topography in small trenches, unlike gravity systems.

In natural and historic parks, where overhead pylons and wires are forbidden, and buried cable is impossible for reasons of geology, safety, or cost, dispersed power generation, especially solar, gains an extra advantage. On-site systems, carefully integrated, are often the lowest-impact way to provide power to remote sites (see p. 317 and Figure 7.9).

Two promising alternatives to utility power exist but have been slow to market: fuel cells, which produce electricity by reacting hydrogen and oxygen; and micro-turbines, which are generators fueled by natural gas (see p. 320). Widespread adoption of these on-site energy sources would transform landscape design and construction. Eliminating power lines may be a real possibility. Even a director of the Edison Electric Institute, a utility company group, has said that the era of big central power generation plants "is certainly over."[33] Hiding a generator in every backyard will sorely test conventional landscape aesthetics, challenging sustainable designers to integrate decentralized "utility" structures into residential and public landscapes.

The policy bias *against* alternative, localized systems has decreased slowly, and an increasing number of professionals now design and build such systems. Even solar and wind power advocates, however, often overlook the problems of the grid. Several projects and landscape products that rely on "alternative" localized utilities are described in the sections on constructed wetlands (p. 228) and solar electricity (p. 309).

Physically Protect Sites During Construction

Construction, even appropriate and sustainable construction, is a forceful process. The forces used in construction, whether small and cumulative or large and intense, can easily damage a site. Unintentionally backing a few yards too far with heavy equipment can irreparably damage fragile site features; so can a work crew's thoughtlessly placed hand-warming fire. Prevention means physically keeping construction activity out of protected areas, no matter what the project size.

Careful decisions about what to protect must be made throughout the design and construction process. As a goal, aim to keep clearing, grading, and other site disruption minimized: one model development guideline recommends that clearing extend no farther than ten feet from the building footprint, and that construction access coincide with permanent roadways.[34] This may need adjustment in some regions. These protection goals, often backed up by covenants, actually raise property values; developers who think of site protection as a hindrance to business, or merely as lip service, are behind the times. (See the discussion of the Dewees Island covenants, p. 82.)

Carbon sequestration (p. 27) may make protecting existing trees directly profitable. Nor would it be any surprise if, in some jurisdictions at least, tree protection became mandatory, as it has been for decades in Europe.

Clearly Designate Protected Areas

Based on site inventory, all areas to remain undisturbed should be clearly marked on the plan *and* on-site. This may require additional fieldwork, especially if the initial inventory was generalized or approximate; UAS surveying (see above) can increase accuracy while reducing costs.

It is important to mark protected areas on *all* construction plans before contract bidding begins. Site-protection requirements affect contractor procedures and costs. Requirements added after bids are accepted cause disagreements and are often disregarded. *All plan sheets* should include protected areas, so that subcontractors (who may see only the irrigation plan, for example) are clearly informed. Copies for the supervisor, the crew, and the office should *all* include these markings, as should any change orders. With CAD software, producing such documents is simple.

Areas to be protected are best staked out during a site walk with designer, contractor, and client all

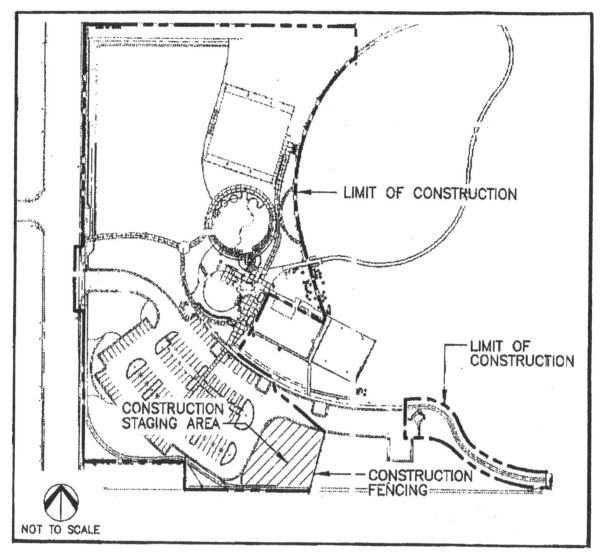

Figure 1.12   Fencing, protected zones, and staging areas should always be clearly marked on all plans. (*Plan:* Design Workshop.)

present. This allows decisions to be made in the field to protect *that* tree and *this* piece of meadow. On-site communication is much clearer and simpler than trying to work strictly on paper. As soon as the protected areas are located in the field, they must be fenced.

There is no substitute for temporary fencing to protect landscape features. Even conscientious crews can be tired and inattentive. Snow fence or bright plastic mesh fencing will not physically stop a vehicle or even a determined pedestrian. But it provides a tangible, visible boundary, reminding construction workers to keep clear. More than one specimen tree has been saved by the sound of snow fence snapping as heavy equipment backed into it. Tree root systems, though

invisible, need to be part of protection planning (see Figure 3.22); contrary to popular belief, roots don't extend straight down! To prevent overreaching by backhoes and loaders, place fencing six or more feet beyond the edge of the protected area.

Fencing must be erected before *any* other work begins, including site clearing. On densely overgrown sites, placing fence before clearing may be very inconvenient, but the risk of not doing so is great. At the least, fluorescent marker paint or flagging should be used around (not on) protected features to guide preliminary clearing, followed immediately by fencing.

Protection fencing should remain until all work and cleanup is complete—at an absolute minimum,

Figure I.13 Fencing to protect site features is critical and should remain throughout construction. Much plastic fencing used today is at least partially recycled. (*Photo:* Kim Sorvig.)

until all heavy machines (including delivery vehicles) have left the site.

With few exceptions, all fenced areas should be *completely* off-limits. This includes foot traffic as well as machines. A dozen trips with a loaded wheelbarrow can compact some soil types enough to kill plant roots. Where there is foot access, crew members often dump buckets or mix and spill gas or chemicals. Plan site protection fencing and designate work staging areas so that there is no reason for any access to fenced locations during the entire construction period.

Modify Grading to Protect Site Features

Grading plans usually assume plane slopes at consistent grades. Especially on large projects and along roadsides, these regular computations can be "flexed" around important existing features. For example, even under AASHTO road design standards (which so many engineers treat as engraved in stone), regular side slopes can be "warped" to protect trees, rock outcroppings, or cultural features. What appears on the plan as a regular 3 percent slope might actually vary from 2.*x* percent to 3.*x* percent as it bends around site features. Working with contractors and engineers to make these adjustments costs almost nothing but can have a significant effect on site protection.

Limit On-site Stockpiling, Parking, Etc.

Even outside fenced protection zones, the whole site needs protection from some common construction activities. This protection is best accomplished by designating areas for certain uses, enforced by careful supervision. Specific areas should be established for activities such as:

- chemical mixing and disposal (even "harmless" chemicals can damage soils when concentrated)
- disposal of waste concrete and asphalt; many jurisdictions require dumpster-like "concrete washout containers" for excess wet concrete, while demolition rubble is recyclable
- on-site parking (construction equipment, large or small, *and* private transportation); repeated parking compacts soils; oil and gas leaks contaminate soils
- fires (if permitted at all) must be contained and well away from vegetation
- cutting and drilling metal, plastic, concrete, some stone, and treated wood, which can contaminate soils, affecting pH and plant growth
- stockpiling of supplies (heavy weight can compact soil; chemicals can leak or leach).

The need to stockpile materials on-site can sometimes be reduced by "just-in-time (JIT) delivery."

Suppliers deliver materials just when they are needed for use. Common in factories, JIT delivery is not always feasible for construction materials. Where it is possible, however, reduced stockpiling can limit site damage and avoid loss, theft, or damage of stored materials.

Choose Staging Areas Carefully

Locations designated for construction activities are often called "staging areas" and may be as large or larger than the area of actual construction. Staging areas limit damage to other parts of the site by serving as sacrifice zones where soil compaction, spills, and other damage are concentrated. A thoughtfully planned staging area avoids treating the entire site as disposable (a worst-case situation that is unfortunately still common).

Where a busy road or path exists on the site, maintenance of uninterrupted vehicle or foot traffic is often a high priority, especially for businesses. Space for detours expands the staging area, in effect. Careful planning limits temporary roads and paths, decreasing ecological and monetary costs.

The ideal staging area, from a sustainability perspective, is a future driveway, patio, plaza, or tennis court, already designed to be permanently "hard" landscape; building foundations can sometimes be used temporarily. Existing paving makes good staging areas because dust and mud can be a serious problem, both on-site and for neighbors. Be certain that construction equipment is not too heavy for the pavement. In urban areas, permits allow public streets as staging areas; traffic backups caused by this practice can seriously increase air pollution, not to mention commuter stress.

Before an unpaved staging area is used, topsoil should be removed and stockpiled (p. 107). Unless the staging area is to become hardscape, it must be restored and revegetated once the project is complete, using stockpiled topsoil and appropriate restoration techniques (Principle 2). Soil compaction is almost inevitable in staging areas, which should be well away from important trees. Tilling to loosen compacted soil is usually necessary as part of restoration.

On large sites, it may be necessary to plan construction access roads. Where possible, use existing roads, or follow future permanent roadbeds. Temporary construction roads are extensions of the staging area. Their overall area should be minimized as far as possible. This must be balanced against total distance covered by machinery, an energy-efficiency concern. Within reason, the *number* of trips across the site should also be minimized. Crossing streams or wetlands should be avoided; special restoration will be required if crossings are unavoidable (Principle 4). Temporary roads generally require topsoil removal and restoration, as do staging areas.

Access needs are strongly influenced by the size of machinery used. Consider extra-small machinery (p. 323), and plan for the effects of working space (see Figure 10.2).

Preserve Healthy Topsoil

Topsoil, the top few inches in which 70–100 percent of all root activity occurs,[35] is a living part of every site, composed of billions of life-giving organisms interacting with organic materials and mineral components. Protecting soil during construction is one of the most fundamental sustainability practices—and one of the most easily overlooked. When not protected adequately, soils are easily damaged and must be restored (Principle 2). This costs both money and scarce resources and should be avoided wherever possible.

"In 1978, 80 million tons of soil was eroded from construction sites and 169 million tons from roads and roadsides . . . nearly 90% of this takes place on land under development."[36] The rate of erosion from construction sites is two thousand times (or more) greater than normal rates on healthy vegetated sites (see Figure 6.22), equivalent to the worst erosion from mine sites. Although there has been some improvement in development practices since the time of these statistics, soil erosion caused by conventional carelessness is still a serious problem. Agriculture, mining and drilling, utilities, pipelines, and forestry also cause major soil erosion—but as with all sustainability issues, each industry must do its part, not point fingers at others.

Saying that soil is alive is no poetic exaggeration. It is difficult to imagine the microscopic life teeming in healthy soil, but estimated numbers can help

Figure I.14   Staging areas (this one is for a fairly small road project) can permanently damage an expanse larger than the site of actual work. (*Photo:* Kim Sorvig.)

form a picture.[37] In just one pound of soil, there are more than 460 *billion* organisms; in a cubic yard of soil, something like 740 trillion; and in an acre covered with one foot of soil, the truly mind-numbing figure of 1,000,000,000,000,000,000 living things. This counts earthworms, but nothing larger. It has been said that if the nonliving part of the Earth's soil mantle were somehow vaporized, leaving living organisms undisturbed, the shape of the land would not change noticeably. Thus, treating soil "like dirt" is truly life-threatening behavior.

Avoid Soil Compaction

Healthy soil is permeable, with spaces between solid particles where water, air, and soil organisms can move. Soil compaction occurs when weight on the soil surface collapses these spaces, creating a hard solid mass. Compaction can result from a single intense force or small repeated forces such as persistent foot traffic. Water, air, and roots may be completely unable to penetrate compacted soil, reducing or destroying its capacity to sustain life. The susceptibility of soils to compaction varies greatly by soil type and is an important reason for knowing the soils of each site before beginning work.

The sections on staging areas (p. 70) and on the choice of construction machinery (p. 320) discuss specific ways to decrease the danger of soil compaction. Compacted soil may already exist on the site due to previous land-use patterns. Compacted areas will

need to be tilled and will often require added amendments to restore fertility and porosity.

Protect Healthy Native Soils from Unnecessary "Improvement"

Soil is conventionally viewed simply as *more* or *less* fertile, with the goal always to "amend" or "improve" it toward more fertility. For sustainability, think of different *types* of soil fertility, not just different *levels*: that is, some soils have the appropriate type of fertility for rich grassland, while other soils have the right fertility for desert plants. This is not strictly a scientific concept, but does point out that fertility is directly linked to characteristics of ecosystems. Complex interactions between available minerals and a host of organisms (from microbes to grazing herds, from fungi to trees) are specific to each region, site, and soil type. Fertility is also influenced by how *long* this soil-creating interaction has been happening, and in what climate. Looked at in this way, raising the chemical fertility level of the desert soil may be an "improvement" if the goal is to grow grass, but is *detrimental* to the type of fertility that sustains native vegetation and animals.

Increased fertility can be inimical to native plants in almost any biome. At Freedom Parkway in Atlanta, an overzealous contractor fertilized soil intended for common broomsedge (*Andropogon virginicus*) and other natives that thrive on depleted soils. Added fertilizer hastened growth of invasive weeds.[38]

Soil fertility is changed out of a desire to alter the plant community, usually toward agricultural crops or horticultural ornamentals. This is an important sustainability topic for two reasons. The process may be too energy and material intensive to be sustainable. Second, changing the ecosystem may have unsustainable results. Some soil amendments, especially heavily processed ones, concentrate in runoff and cause serious water pollution. Especially when existing soil is an undamaged local type, "improving" the soil may have negative effects. Appropriate uses of amendments in site *restoration* are discussed on pp. 110–119.

Air pollution deposits significant extra nutrients (especially nitrogen and sulfur) in many "untouched" soils. The conventional impulse to add still more fertilizer is doubly wasteful in such cases. Even compost, which is almost universally a good idea for soil management, needs to be used with care on healthy native soils. It should not be imported from dramatically different sites. For instance, composted grassland vegetation will not support the best microorganisms for forest soils. Compost made from vegetation *similar* to what is being reestablished may *aid* the process with appropriate seeds and microbes. The balance of woody, dry, and green matter, as well as its age, should be matched to organic accumulations found on healthy sites. Leafy compost decomposes more rapidly than woodland compost. Replacing a layer of twigs and rotting logs with fully rotted and sieved commercial compost may satisfy a desire to tidy the site but actually changes the nutrient status for the worse.

Exotic plantings (for whose benefit the soil is usually improved) can bring a great deal of pleasure and beauty in a landscape. If they begin to outnumber native plants, loss of habitat, climate deterioration, and other serious problems can result.

For these reasons, healthy soils need protection. Limit the "improvement" of soil to carefully chosen areas. Specimen plantings that require high soil fertility can be grouped together in locations to provide most impact and pleasure. The remainder of the site can then retain unamended soils, an unirrigated water regime, and native plants. This design approach (cf. Xeriscape, p. 216) is likely to reduce resource and energy use, pollution associated with manufacturing and transporting soil amendments, and ecosystem disruption caused by overuse of non-native plant species.

Amending only selected areas of soil is not a new technique. Planting beds and vegetable gardens are often selectively amended. Some extra planning and care is required. Selective soil amendment using small, light equipment may in fact help protect sites from compaction. Closely targeted soil fertilization using GPS (above) and computer-driven tractors is used in agriculture; the concept, if not the machinery, could be adapted for some landscape purposes. Drip irrigation can also deliver exact amounts of liquid fertilizer to precise locations.

Many situations cause loss of soil fertility and create conditions where soil improvement *is* appropriate. Amending and improving soils that have been damaged or have lost fertility is an important goal of site restoration. Restoring damaged soil can re-create habitat, stop erosion, and even break down some kinds of pollutants. Unlike the questionable "improvement" of healthy native soils, restoring damaged soils to match regional norms is almost always a sustainable practice. See the following chapter for discussion of site restoration.

Save Every Possible Existing Tree— Even Just One

Existing trees are among the most valuable features a site can have, from both ecological and real-estate perspectives. While individual trees do not affect warming or greenhouse gases as much as forests do, they still provide localized temperature modulation, water, air, and soil protection, and CO_2 sequestration. Economically speaking, carbon sequestration may soon make every tree bankable. Their value is already well-known to experienced realtors, who always note "mature trees" as selling points (sometimes with comically differing definitions of "mature"). A well-maintained landscape is reported[39] to increase property value by up to 75 percent; merely mentioning "landscape" in real-estate ads sells properties 20 percent faster.[40] Yet damage to trees during construction is common, and often fatal; one study estimates such losses for a single medium-sized US city at $800,000 annually.[41] This problem is entirely preventable, though often overlooked. For sustainable landscape construction, prevention is a must.[42]

Get Professional Evaluation of Existing Trees' Health

Tree species vary widely in lifespan. Individual trees also vary in health, affected by soil nutrition, disease, and physical injury. Ideally, clearing for construction would remove only those trees that are already in poor health or near the end of their life (leaving some dead trunks for wildlife habitat). Although this ideal is seldom fully achieved in practice, careful planning can greatly reduce the number of healthy trees destroyed. Success requires evaluating the site's vegetation in detail.

If possible, existing trees should be mapped and their health evaluated before either design or construction begins, as part of the surveying and site inventory process. GPS and UAS surveying leave no excuse for substandard inventories. Both design (siting of new features) and construction methods (access and staging) affect the need for clearance. Designing a new structure to fit beautifully among ancient trees is of little use if construction requires removing those trees for access. Site-protecting construction methods should drive the design on sites with high-quality vegetation.

A professional arborist or tree surgeon is the best person to evaluate health and expected life of trees. Thorough evaluation requires knowing species characteristics and hidden signs of weak health. Determining the health of specimen trees may require climbing them with tree surgeon's equipment. Rough visual surveys of site vegetation are useful first steps, but specialized knowledge and equipment are required to make a reliable evaluation.

The cost of an arborist's evaluation, which conventional developers often avoid, is small compared to the value of trees saved (see Table 3.1). Consulting cost can be lowered by limiting the number of trees evaluated. To do this in a way that contributes to sustainability, set a "construction envelope" (see p. 82). Outside the envelope, all trees and other site features are to remain undisturbed unless clearly dangerous; thus it is only necessary to evaluate in detail the trees inside the envelope. Laid out during site inventory, or at the early stages of conceptual design, envelopes reduce both costs and environmental damage and raise property values.

Although trees are the most prominent vegetation on most sites, and may have historical significance, the health of other vegetation may be equally important in some regions. Large cacti and shrubs, meadows, hedgerows, windbreaks, and groves strongly affect both site character and ecological function. The health, lifespan, and growing requirements of such features may also require professional evaluation. A botanist, forester, or range management expert may be the appropriate consultant.

One caution: arborists usually sell pesticide-spraying services. Some are like doctors who are too quick to recommend expensive, heavy-duty medicine. Cultivate working relationships with arborists who respect preventive approaches to tree health, and who practice Integrated Pest Management (see p. 381).

Evaluating trees and other plants is usually easier and more accurate when done during the growing season. Judging a plant's condition when it is leafless and dormant is not impossible but requires extra skill. A dormant evaluation is better than none, but where possible, plan for this task to occur at the proper local season.

Remove Trees Early, If at All

Where it cannot be avoided, tree removal should usually be one of the first construction tasks, along with fencing of protected areas. Although competent tree surgeons can drop a tree piece by piece in a very restricted space, this is costly and there is always the risk of damage by falling timber. After construction, felling may destroy new work. Large branches or trunks can leave deep gashes in soil where they fall, and stump removal leaves a crater, so it is better to complete these tasks before site grading.

Removing felled logs raises several sustainability questions. In "sustainable forestry," logs are winched out of the forest to avoid tractor access. This limits soil compaction and clearing and is often practical for landscape construction.

Remember the Health Benefits of Death

An important option is not to remove dead trees, logs, or stumps at all. (Those that are in danger of falling must of course be trimmed or felled, but may be left lying.) Standing snags, in particular, are home to many species of wildlife—about two-thirds of all forest species use snags for some purpose. In an undisturbed natural system, decomposing wood fertilizes soil and nurtures young trees.

These benefits are lost when dead trees are removed. Stump and root removal, in particular, has conventionally been done with heavy equipment, extremely strong chemicals, even dynamite. Cost and environmental damage from these methods makes leaving dead timber in place even more attractive. Clearly, not all landscape design styles or construction methods can integrate relic timber. Richard Haag's mysterious, stump-strewn moss garden at the Bloedel Reserve near Seattle proves that a sustainable approach can produce great beauty from what is conventionally considered an obstacle.

Several land management agencies and environmental groups offer guidance on deadwood habitat. The Washington Department of Fish and Wildlife goes so far as to advocate *creating* snags and occasionally erecting a dead tree from one location on a gravel foundation in another.[43] This extreme measure is a response to the lack of large dead trees due to fire suppression (see p. 127).

Fence All Protected Trees Thoroughly

Around trees it is especially critical to exclude all traffic and to prohibit stockpiling, parking, and toxic materials. One common mistake is to pile excavated soil under a tree "temporarily." This can kill many species.

There is no foolproof way of knowing where an existing tree's roots lie. The horizontal zone of root spread is not "a neat and tidy radially circular or concentric pattern, but one that is strictly determined by the path of favorable subsurface conditions."[44] Rule-of-thumb practices should always be considered the *minimum* area to fence and protect. One such guesstimation is the "dripline," an imaginary line formed by projecting the edge of the tree's canopy onto the ground (see Figure 3.22). The actual root zone is irregular, and often two or more times the diameter of the dripline. Likelihood of major root damage decreases with distance from the trunk. Especially for very old, very large, or shallow-rooted trees, the protected area should be increased by at least 50 percent beyond the dripline.

Species like aspen, sassafras, and sumac spread in roughly circular groves by underground runners. The runners extend far beyond the dripline of any individual trunk, joining what appear to be many trees into one plant (a "clone"). Damage to roots near one trunk can spread to other trunks. If possible, groves of any species should be fenced as a group, enclosing an area *twice the diameter of the grove* if there is any reasonable way to do so. This is especially important, however, with clonal species.

Trees that "weep" or trail branches near the ground may require an extra buffer space beyond the branches. Similarly, tall machinery used near trees is responsible for many unnecessarily broken branches.

Build with Great Care Under Trees

People love the sheltered space under a tree or within a grove, which by definition is within the dripline. This presents a special challenge. Seating, gazebos, and other construction close to trees are often important garden features. Such construction should avoid changes in drainage or permeability and be lightweight, set without foundations or on the least intrusive foundation possible, such as pilings. Work should be done by hand, because even the smallest lawn tractor can compact soil around roots or injure the tree's bark.

Pliny Fisk, of the Center for Maximum Potential Building Systems in Austin TX, has developed a highly unconventional foundation system to place even large buildings very close to trees. Auger-like soil anchors form the foundation, screwed into the soil with little disruption. If additions or remodeling increase the building's weight, anchor foundations can be screwed in deeper to provide extra holding power. Once it is no longer needed, the whole foundation can be unscrewed, leaving none of the long-term disruption of abandoned masonry foundations. (Some solar streetlight systems include auger foundations for flexible placement.) A commercial system based on a different anchoring concept, called Pin Foundations, is gaining popularity, especially for wetlands use (see p. 194; also Figure 6.18). For any landscape structure requiring a foundation, removable systems should be seriously considered.

Working closely around existing plants requires craftsmanship and care. The attitude of some conventional construction crews is a real hazard to existing plants. Part of widespread cultural carelessness toward nature, this attitude treats existing plants as inanimate obstructions rather than living specimens. It is not uncommon to see construction workers hack or tear off branches they feel are in their way, leaving jagged stubs that invite disease. Such branches should be either tied back or properly pruned. Experienced contractors take the extra care required to build around existing trees, reaping improved profits and reputation, as well as a healthier environment.

Avoid Grade Changes near Trees

Ideally, no cutting, filling, or tilling of soil should occur within the protected area around existing trees. On some projects, however, financial and other pressures may mean a choice between grading around a tree or removing it entirely. Keep such changes to a minimum, and consult an arborist. As a rule of thumb, no more than six inches of soil can be added or removed within the dripline. (Even this is too much if it applies to the *entire* dripline area.) Trees "breathe" in large part through their roots, which take up oxygen as well as water and nutrients. Building up soil can smother the roots, while removal of soil exposes them. If a lowered soil level causes water to collect around the trunk, many species will eventually drown.

Sometimes it is impossible to avoid grade changes around existing trees without abandoning construction altogether. In such cases, special soil-retaining structures called tree-wells and tree-walls can be built to give the tree a chance at survival. These structures enclose the dripline (or more), keeping the soil and the tree at their original level while the new grade steps up or down at the edges. On a slope, a well or wall may be semicircular, either protruding from the new slope or cut into it. Many decorative variations are possible. Drainage into and out of these structures must be carefully designed and constructed.

If buried pipes and wires cannot be kept out of the root zone, a counterintuitive rule applies. Place the line across the tree's *diameter*, tunneling carefully under one edge of the main trunk. Because roots generally spread radially, this tactic avoids cutting across them; trenches farther from the trunk usually damage more roots.

Don't Half-save a Tree

Unless most of the above guidelines are followed, leaving a tree on a drastically changed site and expecting it to survive is mere pretense. Some species are more adaptable than others, but most require rigorous protection; err on the side of extra protection. Many ignorant or disreputable developers have "left" (rather than protected) a large tree on-site, only to have it die within a year or two. By that time, the developer has made the sale and can deny all responsibility, and in any case it is too late: the magnificent old tree can only be replaced, if at all, with a nursery sapling. Nothing about such a practice is sustainable.

Use Appropriate Construction Machinery

Mechanical construction equipment is a part of most landscape projects. Available equipment varies widely in size, weight, energy consumption, and clean or pollution-prone operation. Each of these factors affects the site directly and influences the need for staging and access areas. Careful choices of equipment are essential in sustainable construction, especially for site protection.

Don't Assume a Need for Heavy Equipment

Most experienced contractors have encountered at least one project where machinery other than hand power tools was impossible to use: a back garden for a row house, with access strictly through the house, or a terraced landscape too steep to drive onto without extreme risk. A can-do attitude finds ingenious ways to complete such work without heavy machines. The same approach can serve a sustainable agenda.

Many of the world's most admired construction projects have relied on limited machinery. Thorncrown Chapel, in Eureka Springs AR, was deliberately designed by architect Fay Jones to be constructed with materials no larger than two men could carry.[45] This deliberate decision kept the chapel and surrounding forest in intimate contact, a prime quality of this beloved building. Fallingwater and many other Frank Lloyd Wright buildings were constructed without heavy machinery.[46] Many preindustrial landscapes and buildings, entirely constructed with hand labor and nonmechanized tools, are revered design ideals. Their enduring quality, health, and popularity can be attrib-

Figure 1.15   Sitting under trees seems to be an innate human desire. Furniture or construction under trees must use minimal foundations (if any); erosion from constant use is a concern, but paving is risky unless very porous. (*Photo:* Kim Sorvig.)

uted at least partly to the appropriate technology used in their construction.

Conventional construction workers often default to powerful, heavy equipment, a "we can, so we do" assumption. When planning a fleet of landscape construction machinery, it seems easier to purchase the biggest, most powerful tools, on the assumption that they can do any job, large or small. Sustainability requires matching the size and power of the machine to the job and the site. Mechanical "overkill" has many costs that are not accurately reflected by the monetary price of purchasing or operating a machine.

The larger and heavier the machine, the greater its turning radius and, as a result, the more cleared area it requires for working and staging. Heavier machinery also means greater soil compaction: the weight of the machine is concentrated through the relatively small area of wheel or track in contact with the ground. An

Figure I.16 Thorncrown Chapel is a national treasure, in part because nonmechanized construction preserved its relationship to the woods. (*Project:* E. Fay Jones. *Photo:* Stephen Schreiber.)

average-sized car or small truck occupies about 16,500 square inches, but only 140 square inches of tire meet the ground, multiplying pressure per square inch by over 100 times. Balloon tires and tracks are designed to decrease per-square-inch ground pressure, lessening soil compaction, erosion, and vegetation loss.

Even on paved roads, AASHTO estimates that a tenfold increase in vehicle weight results in *five thousand* times the damage to the road.[47] A dump truck with dual rear axles, at about 30,000 pounds, wears down the road 5,000 times more than a private car at 3,000 pounds.

In Table I.1, note that some vehicles, especially tracked ones, have lower ground pressure than a person exerts when walking. (Wheels or tracks churn the soil, however, so walking can still be less damaging.) In general, damage to soil is reduced by any decrease in mechanical power and ground pressure. Often, re-

Table 1.1

Ground pressure of vehicles and pedestrians

Vehicle Type	Ground Pressure (psi)
Mars Sojourner	0.14
Tracked, small all-terrain vehicle	1.0
Cuthbertson tracked Land Rover	1.9
Person standing, flat shoes[a]	2.5–3.3
12.5-ton Rolligon timber hauler (loaded)	3.2
Person walking or running	3–12
Low Ground Pressure Vehicle (legal definition, Canada)	5 or less
Person standing, in "sensible" heels	9–12
Bulldozer or military tank	10–80
Work trucks	18–36
Spike heels (standing weight on toes and heels)	26–33
Spike heel (120 lbs. on one ¼ heel)	1,920

[a]Low value: 40 sq. in. soles (both shoes), weight 100 lb. High: 75 sq. in., weight 250 lb. The obesity epidemic is raising these averages. Pressures increase when pushing off to stand, walk, or run.

ductions can be made without compromising work. In other cases, benefits of doing the work must be balanced against damage done by heavier machinery.

Use the Lightest Machinery Available

To match the tool to the job, consider both traditional construction tools and newly refined modern machinery. Many of the former accomplish construction tasks without internal-combustion engines. The latter are miniaturized, efficiency-improved, motorized tools. Both approaches have benefits.

In many cities of the eastern United States, there are sidewalks made of huge slabs of granite, up to twelve feet square. These were hoisted into place, and set with remarkable accuracy, using a tripod of poles and a block and tackle. In the great gardens of Japan and China, massive stonework was constructed with similar tools. This system is cheap, simple, portable, and energy efficient. To get equal precision in placing boulders and similar objects from a crane, loader, or backhoe requires unusual skill on the operator's part.

The traditional pole sling, carried on two people's shoulders with the weight centered between them, is a remarkably efficient lifting and carrying tool. Widely used in Asia, and in Europe and America until the 1800s, two- and four-person slings are an energy-efficient way of moving objects weighing several hundred pounds. They are especially useful for irregularly shaped items, where the main difficulty is not the weight, but getting a handhold. On awkward slopes, a sling or similar device may offer access where wheeled carriers cannot go. A recent innovation on the basic sling, the Potlifter, uses self-adjusting straps buckled to handles for easy attachment, allowing two people to lift almost anything bulky, up to 200 pounds: ball-and-burlap (B&B) trees, large pots, boulders, garbage bins, or bagged materials.

"Ball carts" for B&B trees are available in various sizes. Low slung like a furniture-mover's dolly, ball carts are also good for moving boulders and other heavy, irregular objects. Victorian horticulturists moved trees with root balls nearly six feet across in special tree-moving frames. Drawn by horses or large crews of workers, these frames were practical only on fairly flat land. (A modern relative is the Tree Toad, a hand-operated, cart-mounted tree spade.) In Venice's canal-and-bridge environment, modified carts even negotiate stairways with ease.

Roller panels can also move large, heavy, irregular objects. A frame several feet long and a foot or more wide holds rollers every few inches—updating the technique that built the Egyptian pyramids. Winches and "come-alongs" can also drag heavy landscape construction materials into place, on the ground, on skids, or on a ball cart or roller. Powered and hand-cranked winches are available for moving objects up to several tons. The Appropriate Technology movement has invented several innovative ways for a winch to replace a tractor in pulling a plow or tiller across a field. As long as fossil fuels remain artificially cheap, these tools will not replace trucks or tractors, but they are far more energy efficient and avoid most soil compaction.

Not all modern equipment is "heavy." Since the 1980s, construction machinery has become available in smaller and more efficient sizes. Today very small power equipment is widely available to buy or rent. Tractors, backhoes, trenchers, and other common landscape machines are often half the size and weight of their 1970s counterparts. Powered wheelbarrows, walk-behind forklifts, and small "site dumpers" are

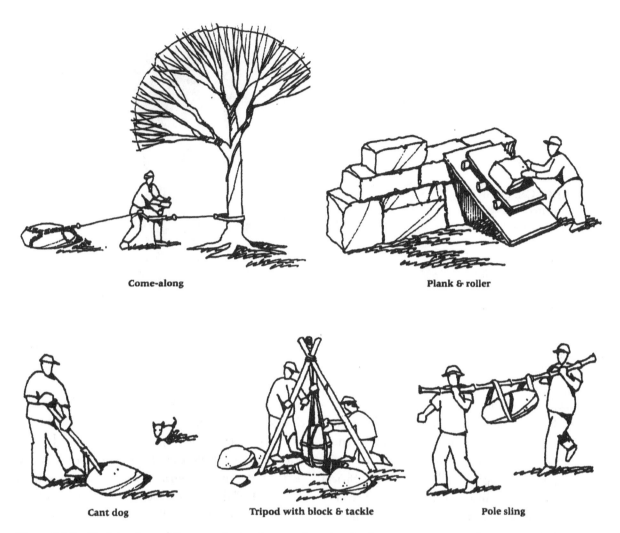

Come-along **Plank & roller**

Cant dog **Tripod with block & tackle** **Pole sling**

Figure I.17 Traditional ways of moving heavy objects still work in landscape construction (often more flexibly than modern machines) and can reduce environmental costs. (*Illust.*: Craig Farnsworth, based partly on R. Daskam [in Dubé and Campbell, *Natural Stonescapes*; Storey Communications, 1999].)

available. These are maneuverable and light; their decreased weight increases efficiency. Several of these mini heavy machines are illustrated in Figures 7.10 through 7.14, in the section on fuel consumption.

At Mill Brook in southern Maine, the team (a landscape architect, forester, and wetland scientists) needed least-destructive methods of reclaiming a sensitive eighteen-acre site. Noting that "standard methods of large-scale soil installation using bulldozers, excavators, etc. often trample or bury vegetation in the process," the team found a mulch spreader designed for steep slopes and reforestation areas. This "air spreader" caused minimal disturbance and applied soil evenly, following existing contours.[48] For a stream res-

toration project on Staten Island NY, small "power wagons" by Honda transported boulders down an erodible embankment. On sensitive sites, small equipment may be *more* effective than heavy machinery.

The ability to move under power is *not* essential to all backhoes, augers, cranes, small mowers, or cement mixers. Running a relatively small tool by connecting it to an engine large enough to move a tractor is not fuel efficient and may result in increased pollution and necessitate wider access clearance. As fuel costs rise, self-propulsion will very likely be reserved for tools that truly require it.

Hand-*carried* motorized equipment should also be considered in sustainable construction. A two-person

Figure 1.18   Col. Greenwood's Treelifter (1844) allowed one worker to transplant a thirty-foot-tall tree. The "ship's wheel" cranked the axle, pulling up the lifting chains. In transit, the axle rotated independently of the chains. (*Illust.*: From "The Tree-Lifter," London, 1844; thanks to Tim Brotzman, Brotzman's Nursery, Madison OH.)

motorized auger for digging postholes is a good example. The handheld auger may be slightly slower than a tractor-mounted one, but it can dramatically reduce soil compaction and the need for clearing. A muscle-powered posthole digger is still more energy efficient but in some soils is unacceptably hard to use. The small engines used on hand-carried machines must be compared to larger engines case by case, because both fuel efficiency and pollution rates vary.

A recent addition to the hand-carried landscape toolkit is the chainsaw trencher. Although a kit to convert a standard chainsaw was offered in the 1980s, both chain design and RPM were suboptimal for cutting dirt. Weighing about thirty pounds, current models cut trenches wide enough for irrigation and electrical lines, can turn tight corners, and can run in tight spaces where large trenchers can't. Videos show them cutting faster than a conventional trencher, probably because of the narrow cut. Two parallel cuts define wider trenches, easily cleared by hand. A wheel attachment, much like a dolly, facilitates long, smooth cuts. Several models are available; at $3,000 and up, they are expensive but potentially useful tools.

Similarly, not all heavy equipment is equally unsustainable in all uses. Given a suitable staging area, a crane may be used to "fly" heavy materials into a site, replacing trucks, barrows, or other wheeled machines, which would otherwise cross the site repeatedly. Concrete-pumping systems are often used in this way. Such equipment can lift materials *over* protected parts of the site. Whether this should be considered "sustainable" depends on the energy efficiency of the individual machine, as well as the importance of preserving existing site features.

Related Design and Planning Issues

The pursuit of sustainability requires teamwork, and the issues involved often cross conventional boundaries between design, construction, and maintenance. Many approaches discussed in this chapter refer to design choices that link to construction methods. The following are some areas of site protection where, in practice, the designer, planner, and/or owner have more influence than the construction professional.

Advocate Sustainable Site Selection

Landowners (and designers if they are involved in identifying suitable sites for proposed projects) can protect healthy sites by simply choosing other places to build. In particular, prime agricultural soils are of

Figure I.19 This may be taking the "lightest tool possible" theory a little too far. (*Photo:* Courtesy of Hammacher Schlemmer.)

exceptional importance to any sustainable society. The financial drive to subdivide such land is powerful but shortsighted, because it diminishes society's food reserves. Many communities limit building on such lands to ensure continued crop production, conserve habitat, and protect migratory corridors. Timberlands are also at risk, with less public input: the nation's largest private landowner, Plum Creek Timber, decided in 2008 to turn real-estate developer. In a hush-hush deal with the Bush-era Forest Service, Plum Creek got permission not only to develop mountain lands it owned but also to convert logging roads across public lands to paved access. Though environmentalists have opposed timber interests in many places, converting forestland to subdivisions may be worse. "A clear-cut will grow back," said Ray Rasker, executive director of Headwaters Economics, which has stud-

ied the changing land use of the West for years. "But a subdivision—that's going to be that way forever."[49]

Consultants may influence individual decisions to subdivide and develop; landscape professionals should support planning initiatives that encourage development on more appropriate land types. Among these, two stand out. One is the "hurt site" or "brownfield" (see Principle 2), where land damaged by previous use can be repurposed. This approach decreases demand for "greenfield" development on healthy sites. A second, sometimes overlapping idea is "infill development," which encourages development of the many leftover spaces found in most urban areas. Skill, commitment, political backing, and innovation by designers and contractors support these land-saving strategies.

Since McHarg's *Design with Nature* became influential in the 1970s, broad-scale planning has been used to protect many land types from inappropriate development. These include steep hillsides, fire-prone forests, and coastal beaches, to name only a few. Without appropriate site selection at both regional and individual scales, the construction techniques described in this book cannot be truly sustainable and can in fact cause great damage. (Site *selection* is a weak point of green building certification systems—see Principle 11.) Site selection, and even unpopular limitations on the right to use certain categories of land, is an essential part of progress toward sustainability.

Collaborate with Community Stewardship Organizations

A relatively new type of nonprofit called a Community Stewardship Organization (CSO) can keep development from being the one-sided, divisive activity it so often is. CSOs are formally chartered partnerships among community groups, conservationists, governmental agencies, and potential developers. By anticipating how an area *could* develop, and balancing multiple interests about what *should* happen, CSOs tend to avoid adversarial situations. Involved citizens give the local environment—built and natural—better care. Local CSOs network with experienced peers, seminars, tools, and concepts to help them succeed.

Lay Out Building Envelopes

Even if site selection is a "done deal" before the designer is hired, site *planning* can still limit disturbance. One of the most useful concepts is the "building envelope." Based on careful site inventory, this is an area of the site within which all construction will be contained. This envelope is best located on already-disturbed areas, away from fragile areas, with views to the site's best features. Locating at the best features often results in views of the least desirable ones. The envelope is sized to include new construction as well as a carefully limited work zone. Everything outside the envelope is treated as a protected area during construction (see pp. 52, 66). Around the building, the envelope is either restored to native vegetation or planted with horticultural gardens, depending on owner preferences.

Building envelopes have become a familiar part of many landscape architects' repertoire. Protective covenants require each landowner to respect such envelopes in subdivisions like Desert Highlands (Scottsdale AZ, by Gage Davis Associates) and the similarly named High Desert (Albuquerque NM, by Design Workshop). Non-native plants and constructed landscape features must be within the envelope; outside it, only native plantings are permitted. This approach balances the resident's desire for personalized outdoor space with the goal of preserving the native landscape as a community feature. The transition from garden to native landscape fits water-saving Xeriscape principles (p. 216) and enhances visual integration.

Promote Reasonable Grading and Clearing Regulations

Grading and clearing is regulated by law in many communities. This can be two-edged, however. One study found that only 40 percent of communities *enforced* their regulations with inspections; less than 20 percent set specific, measurable targets for how much of the site could be cleared.[50] The climate-change effects of removing healthy soil and vegetation make both voluntary and regulatory limits on clearance and grading imperative.

Grading limits can be too specific, resulting in site damage. Many communities set a *steepest* allowable slope. Because a gentle slope takes more horizontal distance than a steep one, such regulations may force removal of trees or features that could be saved if steeper grades were allowed (within limits of soil stability, of course).

In general, regulations of this sort should be *performance based*: they should set a clear goal, such as preserving a specific percentage of the vegetated area on a site, but avoid narrowly regulating the *methods* used to meet the goal.

Use Covenants for Site Protection

Covenants are contracts between private parties and can be more specific or flexible than governmental zoning laws. Covenants and conservation easements can be used to protect traditional land uses, specific views or landmarks, habitat for particular species, or

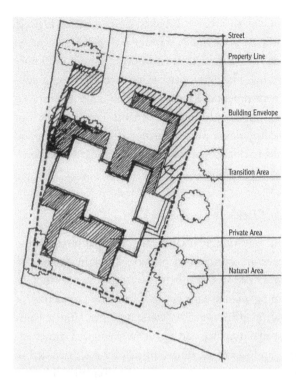

Street

Property Line

Building Envelope

Transition Area

Private Area

Natural Area

Figure 1.20 Development "envelopes" can help integrate new construction with protected landscapes. (*Project:* Design Workshop. *Graphic:* High Desert Investment Corporation.)

Figure 1.21 High Desert, Albuquerque, used building envelopes, roads on existing grade, and other design strategies to preserve vegetation, encourage walking, and save 80 percent of the development's city irrigation allocation. The resulting amenities have increased return on investment. (*Project:* Design Workshop. *Photo:* D. A. Horchner.)

the character of a neighborhood or region. They can also prohibit certain types of development or construction. "Reversion clauses," which give the land back to the community or the donor if misused, can add teeth to covenants. (Misused, conventional covenants often enforce bluegrass lawns and penalize native plantings.)

Dewees Island, a residential development off the South Carolina coast, has been called by *EBN* "a model of what development can and should be."[51] The covenants used at Dewees Island will seem aggressive, even extreme, to those who think of themselves as "bottom-line" advocates—yet the project's return on investment has been *double* the investors' expectations. Clearly, something is being done right when good for the environment proves this good for business.

The Dewees covenants:

- limit total disturbance per site to 7,500 square feet, including house footprint, all paving, and utility easements; houses may not total more than 5,000 square feet, nor stand over forty feet tall
- require restoration of any temporary disturbance
- prohibit removal of any tree over twenty-four inches in diameter and require permit review for removal of *any* vegetation
- require native plants from a 136-species list
- limit driveways to twelve feet width and require all roads, driveways, and paths to be surfaced with sand, crushed shell, or wood chips
- allow only collected rainwater for irrigation
- permit only organic fertilizers and pest control, except for development-wide mosquito control using Integrated Pest Management (purple martins and bats first, pesticides only if unavoidable)
- prohibit solid lumber larger than two by twelve inches, metal or plastic siding, asphalt or fiberglass shingles, several types of insulation materials, and high-VOC paints and varnishes
- require a construction waste management plan, including sorted recycling of building materials
- prohibit garbage disposals and trash compactors as obstacles to recycling
- provide constructed wetlands for each house.

These covenants pull together many recommendations made in this book. Together with conservation easements, they have protected 65 percent of Dewees Island's 1,200 acres. A transfer fee of 1.5 percent on all lot sales supports environmental and community programs. The developer has invested in ongoing public environmental education in low-income communities nearby. Although covenants usually start out in wealthy developments, many of them can, do, and should trickle down into zoning standards that benefit whole regions.

Think of Landscapes in Zones

In any well-designed landscape, compatible uses and features are grouped in patterns for efficient use of space. Xeriscape explicitly extends this principle, grouping plants with similar water requirements for irrigation efficiency. Designing zones of similar landscape maintenance can result in savings of time, energy, and materials. These principles are discussed in chapters on water and maintenance, but they have relevance to site protection too. Combining similar uses into carefully designed zones can accomplish more in less area—leaving more of the site undisturbed.

Specify Site Protection in Contracts

Cooperation between owner, designer, and contractor is the best way to achieve effective site protection. By selecting contractors who are responsive and cooperative, and cultivating strong working relationships, designers and landowners can do much to ensure a healthy site.

Especially in public-sector projects, contractor selection is strictly by lowest bidder, although there has been some improvement in contractual procedures. Because the cheapest construction methods frequently rely on wholesale site clearance, low-bid selection often guarantees site damage. Especially in such situations, clear, strong specifications are essential to site protection. As sustainability grows in importance, better site protection is becoming part of *standard* specifications, local and national building codes, and covenants attached to land deeds.

Among the most important items to specify are:

- explicit methods of determining what areas are to be protected

- physical fencing of protected areas, in place before construction begins and removed at the latest possible date
- and strict limits on the activities noted above (pp. 71–80).

Because damage to existing landscape features, especially living plants, is usually irreversible, specifications *must* include financial motivation for protecting them. A positive incentive approach offers a bonus if all features are undamaged at final inspection. A liquidated damages clause sets financial penalties for damage. The two ideas can be used together. Without such financial motivation, site protection specifications lack teeth and will be ignored by those contractors who are ignorant or unconcerned about sustainability. It is often cheaper for a contractor to buy nursery stock and "replace" a mature tree than to pay a crew extra to work carefully around it. Contractual language and financial penalties can only go so far in overcoming this problem. Selecting and working closely with a contractor whose work is conscientious is far preferable. Fortunately, more and more contractors are becoming convinced of the value of sustainable practices and have the skills to protect construction sites from unnecessary damage.

Coordination and Follow-up

Protecting a healthy site requires coordination. Like a bad haircut, damage to a healthy site can't just be glued back. It must grow back, perhaps with the help of expensive restoration techniques, always with a requirement for time. Planning, surveying, design, physical protection, machinery use, cleanup, maintenance, and monitoring all play a role in keeping healthy sites healthy.

Because design, construction, and maintenance are conventionally organized as separate professions, monitoring and follow-up are often neglected. On-going attention is required to sustain those increasingly rare sites that have retained their health in today's stressed environment.

Contractual partnerships among client, designer, and builder improve site protection by encouraging collaborative work, simplifying team insurance, and avoiding blame games if problems do occur.

Subtopics and Search Terms for Principle 1: Keep Healthy Sites Healthy

Note: Subtopics are also useful search terms; add "innovation" or "controversy" to search terms as appropriate.

Surveying and mapping
Search terms: surveying OR mapping || land surveying || land mapping || GIS || GPS || drone surveying || UAS surveying

Site inventory and visualization
Search terms: site inventory || site inventory method || site assessment || site assessment tools || site protection || site visualization || 3D mapping

Site protection: vegetation
Search terms: protection + (vegetation OR trees)

Vegetation: consultants
Search terms: biologist || range (scientist OR manager) || plant ecologist

Vegetation: native plants
Search terms: native plants || native vegetation || native landscaping

Utility impact
Search terms: utility + (impact OR environment OR easement)

Energy generation
Search terms: (energy OR power) + (generation OR production OR technology) || renewable energy || photovoltaic || fuel cell || hydro power || fossil fuels || fracking || waste water injection

Resource List:

Links to information sources related to this chapter are posted at http://islandpress.org/sustainable-landscape-construction

Principle 2: Heal Injured Soils and Sites

And they shall build the old wastes and repair the waste cities, the desolation of many generations.
—*Isaiah 61:4*

In a consumer society, landscape development too often becomes a form of consumption. As development sprawls outward along an ever-expanding urban fringe, forests are leveled and farms destroyed to make way for cul-de-sacs, backyards, malls, business parks, and the accompanying transportation.

Instead of *consuming* virgin landscape to make places to live and work, think in terms of *recycling* existing sites. Degraded sites in cities and older suburbs can be rendered fit for new uses. At the same time, managed growth must preserve farms, forests, and natural areas surrounding cities.

There are various tested models of growth management; greenbelts and "urban growth boundaries" are probably best known. Such initiatives lie in the realm of politics and land-use planning, not landscape construction. But landscape construction that recycles existing sites has its own role to play in reinhabiting waste places.

Techniques of soil and site restoration may occasionally apply to healthy landscapes, but primarily offer help for abused landscapes—what most of us would consider wastelands. Fortunately, landscapes, like people, have a remarkable ability to heal, and numerous precedents exist for turning even wastelands into gardens.

Restoring sites that have lost vegetation and soil takes on new purpose and urgency with recent research that links such losses to global climate change (p. 22). Local land restoration techniques and global climate-related issues overlap. Restoration that decreases wildfire danger, for example, decreases soil erosion, flash flooding, and drought as well.

Discussed in This Chapter

Types of sites requiring restoration.
Evaluating whether restoration is appropriate.
Social and organizational aspects of site restoration.
Structural restoration techniques.
Restoring soil to health.
Using plants in site restoration.
Restoration as the proper approach to wildfire dangers.
Getting professional help for heavy-duty site toxicity.

Turn Wastelands to Gardens

Urban and suburban landscapes may be degraded in various ways, from minor damage to Superfund sites. Three levels of damage are considered here, recognizing some overlap. In order of severity, these are:

- derelict sites—damage to health and structure, but not particularly toxic
- brownfields, including contained landfills
- toxic waste sites.

Outside urban areas, sites are frequently damaged by vegetation removal or topsoil loss, by vegetation changes due to suppression of processes like fire, and by introduction of invasive species. Restoration of such "nontoxic" damage is discussed in the latter half of this chapter.

Arid regions present special problems for any kind of restoration, and for biotechnical erosion control (Btec), greenwalls, and greenroofs (see Principle 3). One promising resource is David Bainbridge's *Guide for Desert and Dryland Restoration*, released in 2007 by Island Press. It covers techniques, tools, planning, and community issues, focusing on rather large-scale and mostly rural restoration—all invaluable in adapting the strategies presented below to the land of little rain.

Mend Derelict Sites

Every community has derelict sites, stripped of topsoil, littered with debris, and capable of supporting only noxious weeds. Buildings or paving cover some of these sites—"improvements" from a real-estate point of view—making them impervious. As such, derelict sites cause harm without necessarily harboring toxic waste: they prevent recharging of aquifers, seal off the soil, and support neither oxygen-replenishing plants nor wildlife. For derelict sites, soil revitalization may be enough restoration, permitting normal gardening techniques to work once more. Removal or reuse of structures is also realistic.

Reuse Brownfields

Brownfields are polluted lands—"the neglected sites of the postindustrial landscape," in the words of Harvard landscape architecture professor Niall Kirkwood, an expert on such sites. Brownfields go beyond derelict, usually suffering from polluted soil or groundwater or both.[1] Landfills can be considered deliberate brownfields. Some sources also refer to "greyfields," abandoned sites that are 50 percent or more paved or impervious, which though not technically "polluted" are heavily damaged.

Landscape construction can play an active role in reclaiming these sites, usually in conjunction with engineering solutions. In addition to significant structural repair, use of plants that actively remove toxins ("phytoremediation") and "manufactured" soils are important techniques.

Kirkwood believes cleaning up brownfields could return landscape architecture to "the nineteenth-century vision that the landscape is the body and the lungs of the city. A lot of Olmsted's work," says Kirkwood, "was really environmental engineering. His Emerald Necklace [in Boston] is essentially a drainage project. Our roots [are] in issues of health, infrastructure, and open space—the Olmstedian concept of regenerating the city."

Kirkwood's forecast has been borne out by the number of ASLA Professional Awards going to brownfield projects in the past fifteen years. In 2004, Seonyudo Park in Seoul, a renovated island water treatment plant, won a Design Award of Merit for SeoAhn Total Landscape. In 2006, Michael Van Valkenburgh Associates received an award for Alumnae Valley, the former site of the physical plant at Wellesley College, a campus laid out by Olmsted. Shanghai's Houtan Park by Turenscape, a former industrial site, was a 2010 winner. Klopfer Martin Design Group of Cambridge MA was recognized in 2011 for The Steel Yard in Providence RI, which turned an industrial brownfield into a business incubator and "learning landscape." And in 2016, the "living filter" called Ningbo Eco-Corridor in China was a Professional Award recipient, taking historical canals abused by industry and turning them into a linear park. Clearly, brownfields have become a source of work for landscape architects and contractors, at a level worthy of real pride.[2]

Recognition of brownfields' potential value was initially slow to dawn but today is growing rapidly. Early attempts at redevelopment were daunting: owners were liable for any site contamination, even if caused by previous users. Today, however, federal regulations have been streamlined, states like Massachusetts initiated their own brownfields-cleanup programs, and banks now lend money for sites previously deemed untouchable. In 1998 the *New York Times* estimated that there were 6,500 brownfields in and around New York City alone; in 2007 it reported that restoring such sites was a chief priority of the city's economic development officials.[3] Nationally some 450,000 brownfields await return to productive use; between 2002 and 2013, the EPA granted $190 million outright, plus tax incentives, to over a thousand cleanup projects.[4]

Reuters reports that as part of slashing the EPA, funding will be cut by 42 percent for brownfield resto-

Figure 2.1 Brownfields take up large areas in most modern cities. Neither society nor the environment can afford this waste, and restoring the potentially toxic sites is a priority and a challenge. (*Photo:* Eric Carman.)

Figure 2.2 Restoration of mines, heavy industry, and Superfund sites requires specialized engineering, but should not exclude landscape concerns such as habitat and visual fit with surroundings. (*Photo:* New Mexico Department of Mining and Minerals.)

ration, in addition to a 30 percent cut for lead cleanup.[5] Ironically, Trump properties in New York include a number of that city's most toxic brownfields, including a golf course on a city landfill, acquired rent free.[6] Beyond irony, cutting these kinds of programs will directly remove jobs and spending from the economy, a considerable portion of it coming straight from the pockets of landscape professionals. Ignoring the potential of brownfields may also push recently promised infrastructure projects onto greenfield land, doing double damage.

Get Specialist Help for Toxic Sites, Tanks, and Hazmats

On sites such as those covered by the EPA's Superfund, landscape construction is not the primary solution. Only after highly technical environmental engineering might surface landscape construction be appropriate. Remediation and restoration of sites at this level is outside this book's scope. For this category of injured sites, seek consultant help. Resources for Principle 6 also offer information on identifying toxic materials.

Removal of hazardous buried structures like fuel-storage tanks and remediation of heavily contaminated soils is a very specialized branch of construction. This work requires both special permits and special skills. It is critical to long-term sustainability that these tasks be thoughtfully planned and skillfully carried out. What effect the current administration's frontal attack on the EPA will have on this economic sector is unknown.

Any site remediation involving toxic materials is likely to require input from environmental engineers. The degree of engineering involvement *should* correspond to the severity of contamination. Current regulations, however, are written and administered largely by engineers, and sometimes exclude biological solutions. It is critically important to balance both types of approaches in ways that meet safety requirements, minimize financial costs, and truly restore the site (rather than making it inert, safe but dead).

Landscape professionals can work to educate engineering colleagues and the public about biological site remediation. This must be done thoughtfully and diplomatically. No purpose is served by insisting on "natural solutions" that fail and tarnish the credibility of more careful site-specific approaches. Although bias against biological solutions is frustrating at times, landscape professionals *must* know when engineering help is truly the most appropriate solution.

Balance the Environmental Costs and Benefits of Restoration

Restoring landscapes costs money, energy, labor, and time. Hindsight is clear: avoiding contamination in the first place is much cheaper. But faced with undeniably injured landscapes, choices must be made. There are both economic and ecological limits to what can be restored. For some sites, only full restoration to preindustrial conditions is worth doing; for others, any remediation is better than nothing. Not all technologies are appropriate for all restoration sites, nor for the communities in which they exist. As with most sustainable practices, site specificity is the key concept.

When Restoration Is Called For

Site restoration is usually appropriate if:

- Disturbance resulted from human land use (construction, grazing, mining, logging, fire suppression, legal or illegal dumping, abandoned structures, off-road vehicles, regional economic decline, etc.).
- Use of the *restored* site can prevent developing or disturbing a *healthy* site.
- "Recruitment" (vegetation regrowth from relic seeds in existing soil or from adjacent sites) can be a major strategy.
- Restoration costs are likely to yield long-term savings by stopping erosion, rebuilding productive soils, buffering or treating noise or air or water pollution, or protecting threatened species. The crucial need to reduce global climate change is changing the equation significantly in favor of revegetation.
- Restoration is legally required, a condition for permitting land use, with costs borne by the parties who profit (e.g., mine restoration).
- The site has strong cultural significance, as in national and historic parks, or was significant before becoming degraded.
- Degraded forests, wetlands, estuaries, or aquifer recharge zones are involved.

When Restoration May Be Feasible

Site restoration *may* be worth considering if:

- Disturbance resulted from disaster "provoked" by humans (landslides due to soil abuses, floods due to failed "flood control," etc.).
- Restoration will yield economic or aesthetic results

valued by people (but of no particular ecological value).
- Restoration can create jobs, educate workers, or support local industry (a native-plant nursery, for example).
- Restoration involves community participation, increasing community cohesion and identity.
- Restoration educates community members about sustainability through planning, fieldwork, or activities at the completed site.

When Restoration Is Inappropriate

Site restoration is usually *not* practical or appropriate if:

- Disturbance resulted from natural processes not accelerated by humans.
- The site is so small that outside influences will overwhelm restoration.
- The true cause of disturbance is off-site, with no likelihood of cooperation from the source site's owner.
- The so-called restoration is cosmetic (disguising persistent problems, not self-maintaining).
- Restoration requires major use of materials whose removal damages other sites (e.g., wild-dug plants or imported topsoil).
- Restoration cannot be expected to sustain itself without long-term intensive maintenance, irrigation, or similar intervention. (Maintenance during establishment and minor periodic maintenance should be expected.)
- Restoration defers the real problem onto another site or into the future (in which case, it is probably cosmetic).
- Restoration may attract poaching, destructive or motorized site access, illegal use, or other problems, unless these can be monitored and prevented.
- Cost of restoration is excessively high, even when figured as life-cycle costs and taking environmental services, intangibles, and job creation into account.
- Cost of restoration would be borne by taxpayers, but the benefits would be private ("externalization of cost" by the polluter, or below-cost deals to sell the restored land).

Involve the Community in Site Restoration

Abandonment of defunct industries and deteriorated neighborhoods often makes site reuse a desperate need. Demolishing 800 vacant row houses at once, as happened in Baltimore in the 1990s, is unusual only in scale. There, reduced demand meant only a quarter of the housing would be replaced, leaving 600 lots to transform into green space.

Technical solutions to such challenges are invented, communicated, and used in social *context*. Infill development and neighborhood revitalization are common steps toward local sustainability, and with federal abandonment of such efforts, a growing percentage of the landscape professional's clients are likely to be community groups, rather than top-down agency or commercial entities. Community-based recycling of derelict spaces isn't landscape business as usual. The contractor or designer who wants to be part of this process will need to learn and adapt.

Know the Site's History

Restoring something implies going back to an original condition. For something as complex as a landscape, knowing what condition was "original" is not always simple. Sites are living, changing entities; both natural succession and human land use change every site over time.

It is important to distinguish between *historic* restoration, which attempts to re-create the site at a particular point in time, and *environmental* restoration, which attempts to restore site health. Both forms of restoration have their purpose, and overlap significantly. "Health," however, is a much more dynamic goal than period restoration. Consider the human equivalent: the health of a sixty-year-old can be restored; the sixty-year-old cannot be restored to being sixteen. (Landscapes can be set back in time, but re-creation is never exact.)[7]

A person who recovers from ill health continues, once healthy, to age and change. So does an environmentally restored landscape. Suppose a forested site were developed, abused, and left derelict. Restoring it to health would primarily mean restoring its ability to support life. The restored parcel might look like a meadow and still be "restored" in health. It might also, given many years, use its restored health to grow back to forest. People could, of course, also choose to restore its health by planting forest trees. That would restore it both environmentally and historically, at an increased cost in resources.

Thus restoration requires both knowledge (What was the site before? How did it develop?) and decision (Is health the goal, or history? Are conditions in 1800 the target, or 1492?). In both knowledge and decision making, local community input is indispensable.

No matter what kind of restoration is planned, decision-making knowledge almost always includes history, of natural processes as well as of human land use. Resources from the fields of historic preservation and historical ecology are frequently helpful. Environmental and historic restoration may be separate goals; but the environmental past of a site is seldom separate from human influences. This is especially true of the derelict lands most in need of restoration, because that need is due to human abuse or neglect.

Think Big, and Across Boundaries

An example of a site abused by history is the Colorado River wetlands at Yuma AZ.[8] The river, once flowing at 300,000 cubic feet per second (cfs), has been reduced to 4,000 cfs, the remainder diverted for agriculture. That same agriculture, and city settlers, demanded that wetlands be pumped to keep fields dry and septic tanks working. Former wetlands succumbed to nearly impenetrable plant invasion and became home to smugglers and meth labs, a dumping ground in more ways than one.

Starting in 2002, a collaboration to restore hundreds of acres of wetlands and river began to grow between the City of Yuma, the Quechan Indian tribe across the river (and the AZ-CA border), and the Yuma Crossing National Heritage Area, including the old territorial prison museum. Four private landowners, over a dozen federal and state agencies, and affected citizens like farmers all were involved.

Fred Phillips, a young landscape architect drawn to both river restoration and tribal history, led his small staff and what became an army of volunteers. Wearing clothes reinforced with duct tape and dust masks that turned black in a single day, they hacked back the reeds and other invasives, sometimes literally tunneling through them to map site conditions and understand restoration possibilities. In a few places, simply restoring water to historically wet places made bulrushes resprout from long-suppressed rootstocks. In others, overgrown vegetation was bulldozed.

Water to restore the wetlands was a problem, with the river so low and flooding tightly controlled. Phillips found a creative (and ironic) solution: using the groundwater pumped out of nearby fields.

Among other reasons to take note of this project is that scientific monitoring and documentation were built into the land restoration budget by Phillips. Summarized in one of the Landscape Architecture Foundation's Landscape Performance case studies, the data provide insight into ecological performance as well as social benefits. At last report, 373 acres had been restored; 300,000 plantings had achieved a 90 percent survival rate, even in arid, saline conditions; sightings of two endangered species had doubled, as had total numbers of species. The project has educated about 200 volunteers per year and created 150 full- and part-time jobs involving professional restoration skills that are in demand up and down the Colorado, employing Quechan tribal members, among others. Some 100 to 250 people visit the restored site daily, year-round; it has a TripAdvisor listing with 4.5 stars, and a virtual tour via ArcGIS.

The project challenges what "restoration" means. The conventional idea is an accurate re-creation of past conditions. On the scale of this project, that would be impossible. Restoring broad ecosystem patterns and healthy vegetation, however, has clearly proven possible. While it could be wonderful to bring back precolonial conditions, the Yuma East Wetlands Restoration Project looks likely to be a model for sustainable restoration, not only of land but also of human communities. It is a model that may provide direction, and work, for many landscape professionals.

Start an Urban Barn-raising

Transforming, regenerating, and restoring neglected lands is crucial to restoring the *human* communi-

ties that have been abandoned on these unpromising sites. One individual who pursued land-and-community restoration was the late Karl Linn. Landscape architect, psychologist, and social activist, Linn was concerned about the decline of inner cities where shrinking populations or economies result in derelict land.[9] Conventional municipal-park landscaping generally fails or cannot be funded in such areas. Instead, drawing on experience of grassroots groups like New York City's Green Guerillas, Linn worked with inner-city residents to construct "neighborhood commons."

Linn proposed that derelict tracts be turned into urban farms or wildflower meadows, at least until further development. His methods rely primarily on natural plant succession, with help from humans, to improve soil and transform neighborhood appearance. Linn envisioned Newark NJ (then stigmatized as America's most squalid city) becoming "the Garden City of the Garden State," bringing together vast acreages of urban land with an ecological vision.[10] After relocating to Berkeley CA, Linn worked with community groups to create city gardens and farms in the Bay Area.

Community-based methods are critically important to urban restoration in particular. They parallel environmental protection efforts in less-developed countries, where participation of local and indigenous people has proved vital to success.[11] Clearly, they also link with the community-garden concept, a well-established movement in many parts of the world.

Follow the Lead of Community-garden Groups

One group Linn worked with is the San Francisco League of Urban Gardeners (SLUG), in 1994 one of the country's most active community-gardening groups. SLUG's work crews have constructed over forty neighborhood gardens, plus San Francisco's only working farm, the four-acre St. Mary's Urban Youth Farm in low-income Hunter's Point. St. Mary's has utterly transformed a blighted inner-city site. Twenty-three years later it continues, as Alemany Farm, to "teach a man to fish"—or, at least, to grow.

The site (adjacent to a housing project) had been used by contractors for dumping; it had been littered with spoil dirt and waste concrete, soon followed by

Figure 2.3 St. Mary's Farm (now Alemany Farm) relinks urban residents with the land and their own skills. Most cities could benefit from similar community landscapes; where soil is not toxic, they produce food as well as social activity. (*Project:* SLUG. *Photo:* Karl Linn.)

old refrigerators, wrecked cars, and household garbage. SLUG workers filled several sixteen-foot-long Dumpsters with debris. The site featured thirty raised garden beds, nearly one hundred fruit trees, and herb gardens. These provided produce for residents' use, for distribution to food kitchens in other low-income communities, and for a cottage industry of salad vinegars made by local residents. A composting operation produced and sold garden mulch from yard waste collected throughout San Francisco. Under management of Friends of Alemany Farm, this urban garden has evolved and survived.[12]

The community-garden movement is quiet but widespread, a potent grassroots force for site restoration. With many urban residents isolated from any notion of how food is produced, and others living in "food deserts" where healthy food is scarce, it is also a social force alongside farm-to-table and slow food movements. Its thesis (quite foreign to supermarket culture) is that food should be grown close to where people live. Thousands of community gardens thrive across the United States, most of them in major cities. In Philadelphia alone, 1,500 such gardens involve over 600 families in producing $1.5 million worth of food.[13]

European cities devote significant land to "allotment" gardens. A 1980 survey of urban soils in England and Wales found only two main types: sterile soils

disturbed by construction, engineering, and dumping; and the fertile soils of community gardens. The survey described allotment-garden soils as "man-made humus soils . . . , dark well-structured topsoil from particularly deep cultivation (double digging) coupled with heavy organic manuring."[14] This is dramatic evidence that gardeners can reinstate site health in urban areas.

Despite their immense value, urban community gardens are seldom safe from development pressure. In 1999, for example, New York mayor Rudolph Giuliani coerced community-garden and environmental groups into paying $4.2 million to ransom eleven acres of gardens they had revived from trash-strewn abandoned lots. Giuliani equated the gardeners' efforts with communism and did his best to create conflict with people on the eight-year waiting list for public housing. Like the environment-versus-jobs ploy, setting community landscapes against community housing is the worst sort of dishonesty and shortsightedness.[15]

Invest in a Garden Festival

The garden festival, more capital intensive and ambitious than a community garden, is nevertheless a valid restoration approach, widely used in Europe. Abused sites (both derelict and brownfield) are redeveloped as large, themed public gardens. Festival gardens oper-

Figure 2.4   Chicago's Gary Comer Youth Center turned 8,000 square feet of bare roof into a "community-garden green-roof" that produces 1,000 pounds of vegetables and fruits yearly, feeding 175 kids at the center itself and sold to a local farmers market and restaurants. (*Project:* Hoerr Schauldt LAs. *Photo:* Scott Shigley.)

ate like fairs for some months, then are "recycled" as parks or housing space. Essentially, such festivals create landscapes as a catalyst for reinvestment. Garden festivals were effective in rehabilitating bombed-out German cities after World War II, then were applied to other European sites, including Britain's urban and industrial brownfields.[16] Despite high costs, they show how much can be accomplished quickly when society decides to reinvest in damaged sites.

Nearly all British garden festivals were constructed on industrially degraded sites. Liverpool Garden Festival (in the 1980s) was built on spoil tips from coal mining and inner-city garbage dumps. The "Nature in the City" portion of that festival, showcasing Britain's native plants, was built on an eighteen-acre mountain of garbage more than a hundred feet high.[17] "The people of Liverpool through the event were made aware," wrote one festival designer, "that you could transform a totally useless, severely polluted area of

land into a major visitor attraction of international standing."[18]

Ebbw Vale in South Wales was also developed on a brownfield site. The 57-hectare (141-acre) site of this festival had been an air-polluting steel mill, with adjacent mines. The Welsh Development Agency reclaimed the site at a cost of 20 million pounds. The festival garden included a 5-million-gallon lake, a 120-foot waterfall, 33,000 trees and shrubs, and 550,000 bedding plants. *Landscape Design* magazine's description read: "Where there used to be satanic mills and furnaces there is now a fantastic array of lakes, gardens, floral displays, marquees, exhibitions, and fun rides." After the six-month festival, the landscape was developed as a business park.[19]

Garden festivals are costly and may fail to meet ecological goals. As fast-track projects they require installation of semi-mature trees and other plantings, trucked in from distant nurseries. Like other social

Figure 2.5   Peralta Community Art Gardens in Berkeley CA is a decorative meeting place made by neighbors from leftover land and materials. (*Project:* Community and Karl Linn. *Photo:* Karl Linn.)

issues affecting landscape reconstruction, decisions about speed of restoration are seldom simple. Instant landscape, however, manifests a commodity-driven society. Emphasizing speed strongly affects choice of techniques and may rule out gradual, community-based reclamation. Instant plantings also can *miseducate* festival visitors, obscuring understanding of plant succession. A community that accepts the concept that built landscapes grow and evolve has an expanded range of cost-effective and ecologically sound restoration methods available.

Educating the public about landscape ecological processes is integral to the Earth Center in South Yorkshire, England. Although the center is as big as many festival gardens, its stated mission is "to promote understanding of sustainable development and to help people become involved in the process of achieving it in their own lives." The Earth Center is built on a pair of abandoned collieries (coal mines) on the River Don, near Doncaster. It is the biggest landscape project in the United Kingdom based on sustainable principles—"to demonstrate," in the words of Andrew Grant, the landscape architect, "how regenerating land can provide rich opportunities for play, production of food, wildlife, and general public enjoyment."[20]

In designing the Earth Center, all decisions had to be justifiable in terms of sustainability. Materials specification required local materials, suppliers, and labor. This minimized environmental costs of transportation and bolstered the local economy. Many materials came from the site itself: for pedestrian paving, burnt coal shale—a pinkish by-product of historical coal-washing activities—produced an attractive surfacing at very little cost.[21]

Planting at the Earth Center was the antithesis of "instant landscape." Instead, "the Earth Center landscape is designed to make people look at, think about, and react to the issues that affect our future landscapes," says Grant. "It is to be a visual and ecological response to the process of regeneration on this site, and is deliberately planned to evolve and redefine its character well into the next century."[22] Plant succession and change is on display, contrasting not only with instant landscape, but also with attempts to "freeze" landscapes unchangingly through intensive maintenance.

Despite different methods, the Earth Center and garden festivals are public celebrations of the ability to regenerate blighted landscapes.

Make a Virtue of the Necessity for Landfills

Landfills, unlike other brownfields, are created deliberately to contain society's enormous quantities of waste. Once filled, they become environmental problems (and eyesores) if simply closed. If restored, landfills offer remarkable open-space opportunities—

what might be called "postconsumer landscapes." The oldest urban precedent for this may be Rome's eighth hill, Monte Testaccio, which probably received its first broken amphora in about AD 50 and closed in about 300. Materials from this dump were recycled into, among other projects, St. Peter's Basilica, and the hill itself has been repurposed repeatedly ever since.[23] Recycling such sites today requires interagency cooperation, but still offers unusual opportunities to create new and diverse spaces. Restoration may be cheaper than acquiring urban land for parks and recreation and can relieve development pressures elsewhere.

Recycling landfills is no substitute for waste-stream reduction. Entombing garbage within a clay liner, cut off from water and air, preventing natural processes of decay, is fundamentally questionable. Actively mining these sites has been suggested, but except in developing countries where the poorest of the poor provide labor, this concept is not yet widely feasible.[24] As solid-waste authorities find more effective resource-recovery and recycling methods—or, for that matter, as consumers buy fewer throwaway products—landfills and landfill restoration may fade into history. Until then, reuse is better than abandonment.

The scale of possible landfill reclamation is vast, with a conservatively estimated 10,000 "retired" landfill sites in the United States alone.[25] The Trust for Public Land has estimated that, as of 2006, about 4,500 US landfills had been converted to parks.[26] One of the oldest is Virginia Beach VA's aptly named Mount Trashmore. Cambridge MA added 20 percent to its total open space with one landfill restoration, fifty-five-acre Danehy Park. Featuring turf and naturalized plantings, this popular park also incorporated recycled "glasphalt" (see p. 275) in an ADA-accessible path.

A landfill project in Yarmouth MA, on Cape Cod, shows how many functions—ecological, social, and economic—a well-reclaimed site can serve. The designers of Danehy Park, Camp Dresser & McKee (CDM), have developed landfills as office parks, sports fields, and parking facilities, says Vice President John Kissida. The fifty-seven-acre landfill at Yarmouth, however, stands out for its integration of functions.

Federal and state regulators forced closure of Yarmouth's forty-year-old dump; among other problems, it was located in one of Cape Cod's scarce aquifer recharge zones. A community-based, participatory process created a golf course, park, bike path, and recycling facility for residential, construction, and demolition waste. Revenues from recycling and the golf course offset the cost. Effluent reuse provides nearly half the water (and fertilizer nutrients) for the golf course.[27]

Landfills have become golf courses in climates as diverse as Charlotte NC, Phoenix AZ, and St. Petersburg FL. (Some, like the New York City example noted above, have raised questions about environmental justice and who benefits.) Harborside International Golf Center, on Chicago's South Side, is one of the largest (425 acres) landfill-to-golf projects to date and quite spectacular, comprising two eighteen-hole courses, a

Figure 2.6   At Quarry Hills outside Boston, a 130-acre closed landfill (in background) became twenty-seven holes of golf. (*Project:* Quarry Hills Associates. *Photo:* Art Cicone.)

Figure 2.7 Chicago's Harborside International Golf Center makes beautiful reuse of a landfill. Industrial buildings in the background show the context of this massive site restoration. (*Project:* Nugent Associates. *Photo:* Sally Hughes.)

forty-five-acre practice facility, and a golf academy. Above the flat Illinois landscape, the site is a plateau built up of fly ash from a closed garbage incinerator. A recycled product provided fertility: processed sewage sludge from Chicago Metropolitan Water Reclamation District. Sinuous greens meander through tawny grassed mounds and steep hillocks where fescue and rye, unmown, wave in the unfailing breeze. Harborside has won several awards, including the 1996 Superior Achievement award from the American Academy of Environmental Engineering.

One of the world's largest dump sites, at 2,400 acres, is Staten Island's Fresh Kills Landfill (the name, ironically, means "fresh brook"). The site is poised to be "refreshed" as New York City's most expansive "lifescape," to use James Corner's trendy term. A draft master plan by Field Operations landscape architects (New York and Philadelphia) may be downloaded from the Freshkills Park website, www.nyc.gov/freshkillspark. The first recreation facility of a thirty-year plan, Owl Hollow soccer fields, was completed in 2007. The New York City Department of Parks and

Figure 2.8 Fresh Kills Landfill on Staten Island, one of the world's largest garbage dumps, is being reclaimed as a twenty-first-century park. (*Project:* Field Operations. *Photo:* City of New York.)

Recreation oversees construction, with an initial allocation of $100 million in capital funds.

Freshkills will undoubtedly be the country's largest, most elaborate landfill park, containing a memorial from World Trade Center rubble. Some unusual activities will be accommodated, like mountain biking and kayaking. Beyond notoriety or sheer size, Freshkills is important for scientific monitoring that provides hard data on the safety and cost-effectiveness of structural restoration methods for landfills.

Understand Structural Issues of Landfills

Landfills are structurally unique in the built environment. By law, landfills closed since the 1990s are sealed to isolate the polluting materials abandoned in them; they are huge buried containers that cannot be moved and must not be punctured. The technology of capping and sealing landfills is well developed. Planting over such structures, however, requires unusual techniques. Some, like manufactured soil (p. 116), are widely applicable; others are specific to contained landfills.

Fear that tree roots might pierce the strictly regulated clay or plastic "cap," allowing dangerous gases to escape or rainwater to enter, has led some states to ban trees and plant landfills with unvarying swaths of turf. Research (some at Fresh Kills) suggests that banning trees is unwarranted. None of a dozen scientific studies shows conclusively that tree roots will damage a properly built clay cap, yet a 2016 case study by five Rutgers landscape architecture and environmental science professors states that "the majority of design options for landfill reuse typically do not include natural vegetation patterns, biodiversity of plant species, or woody species."[28] Unfortunately, this situation has changed only a little in the past decade.

Root penetration of a properly constructed cap is highly unlikely because:

- cap density physically prevents root penetration
- anaerobic conditions in and below the cap kill roots
- tree roots are concentrated in soil surface layers above the cap[29]
- geosynthetic fabrics are often used, further decreasing the chance of root penetration.

A compelling reason to *permit* trees is to reduce landscape maintenance. Local trees will colonize unless actively prevented by mowing and herbicides, with energy and pollution costs. Trees also reduce erosion, a serious issue on landfills, where slopes may be 3:1 and 250 feet high. With shrubs and trees, landfills gain potential as wildlife habitat or corridors and provide increased environmental services, such as slowing runoff, as well as visual variety.

A related issue complicates tree planting over capped landfills: the depth of soil above the cap is *not* set by law and is usually shallow (on the order of two feet). A number of studies, reviewed by the 2016 Rutgers researchers, have shown trees over landfills to be extra susceptible to windthrow, and to have high mortality due to limited soil depth and nutrient availability. This sets up a conflict between the value of woody plantings and the extra resources needed to provide adequate soil.

In the late 1980s the New York City sanitation department devoted six already-capped acres at Fresh Kills to testing. One goal was to determine whether the landfill could support anything approaching Staten Island's indigenous vegetation, which of course includes many species of trees.

The restoration team reshaped uniform steep slopes, interrupted every fifty feet by wide, flat benches, creating dune-like slopes that mimicked the island's coastal landscape. (Compare with landform grading, p. 101.) They rescued plants from sites slated for development elsewhere on Staten Island: 3,000 shrubs, 523 native trees, and native perennial grasses and wildflowers.

Landscape architect Bill Young, one of the team members, advocated irrigating with leachate (water that drains from landfills, often picking up contaminants). This was controversial, but Fresh Kills leachate was tested and found to be within EPA toxicity limits. Because it could not be allowed to flow off the landfill, it was recirculated on-site. Young notes that irrigating with leachate would be much more feasible if toxic items like batteries and household cleansers were eliminated from waste. Increasingly, landfills do require that such materials be sorted out (for reasons other than watering trees).

A team of restoration ecologists was hired to monitor the Fresh Kills plantings. Test plots showed moderate tree growth and excellent shrub growth. Woody plants in "habitat islands" provided much-needed perching sites for birds, which reciprocated by dispersing seeds, spreading volunteer trees to other areas. Surprisingly effective, seed dispersal from the habitat islands boosted woody species from eighteen to fifty.

Perhaps the most important finding from the Fresh Kills study, however, was that tree roots did *not* affect the clay cap.[30] Excavating selected trees, the Rutgers team found wide, shallow root systems. Planting directly in a sand-compost mix, with neither imported topsoil nor excavated "tree pits," may have encouraged horizontal rooting.

Even with these encouraging early findings, revegetating an area as large as Fresh Kills is a major challenge. Soils are thin and of poor quality, moisture levels are generally low but also highly variable, invasive species dominate, and there is little species diversity. Woody plantings, even from habitat islands, are unlikely to thrive everywhere, and other techniques will be tested. One is an adaptation of agricultural strip cropping. Fast-growing plants will be grown in contour furrows, then plowed into the soil to create "green manure," adding organic matter. This potentially cost-effective technique for improving poor soils on an industrial scale will be part of ongoing research at Fresh Kills.[31]

The Rutgers case study team took a different approach, more suited to ordinary-sized landfills. Their sites were two former New Jersey landfills, in Voorhees Township (46 acres) and Somerville (116 acres). In each case, covering the entire landfill with soil deep enough for trees was rejected as too costly. Both designs used contained areas of raised soil to introduce trees, adapting this concept to two very different sites. At Voorhees, a large, nearly rectangular site that had been closed before the 1990s regulations took effect, about one-third of the area was covered with solar panels to generate both power and revenue for the city. A raised promenade lined with trees and supported by gabions (which require no excavated foundations and are flexible if the buried materials settle) was irrigated with runoff from the solar panels. This stormwater had been causing erosion that threatened the integrity of the landfill. At Somerville, raised soil was configured as terraces flanking an existing stream and wet-

land. The terraces were designed to match predictable water levels during 2-, 10-, 25-, 50-, and 100-year storms and to provide rooting depth for plantings patterned after the site's remnant riparian forests. In both cases, reclamation provided public amenities, as well as increasing potential biodiversity and urban habitat and contributing to management of stormwater.

The study's authors made an interesting observation about the attitude shift required for this kind of restoration: environmental science, they noted, has "over the past two decades, shifted attention from analyzing negative human impacts on natural systems toward investigations of the interaction between humans and their environment."[32] Instead of thinking only of human economics, or only of saving ecosystems, the interactive viewpoint uses ecosystem services as both linkage and measurement spanning the two systems. It is within this context that "waste" lands can be reincarnated as beneficial places.

Suggested Practices for Landfill Sites

Build a multidisciplinary team early. For restoration of huge sites as amenity facilities, overlapping systems must be well integrated for environmental and human benefits.

Consider educational and interpretive design to shed light on the site's history. The way consumer society generates and hides waste is an important factor in long-term sustainability. Landscapes on landfills should not simply make those processes invisible.[33]

Grade the site using landform or stepped slope methods (below).

Plant in uniform soil cover, possibly in raised terraces, but not in pits. Pits can constrict roots and might force them into the cap.

If additional soil is needed, consider manufactured soil (below).

Plant trees and shrubs for erosion control and habitat. Trees pose little risk to the cap and offer many benefits. Use turfgrass for active-recreation areas. Native grasses and wildflowers are also satisfactory.

Try bare-root stock or an on-site nursery. Allow seedlings to acclimatize to landfill microclimate and soils. Commercially grown trees, aside from being expensive, may not survive transplanting to landfill conditions.[34] Low-cost bare-root stock is sometimes available from governmental sources, usually mixed native and non-native species, which should be carefully evaluated.

Plant habitat islands (above), from which no-cost seedlings spread.

Recognize Agricultural and Rural Restoration

Urban and industrial restoration projects are often dramatic, gaining media coverage because they restore lost services to downtrodden neighborhoods. Where they involve reuse of industrial ruins, they also are popular with the design avant-garde. In terms of sheer acreage, however, there is probably more restoration activity *outside* the city. Mine reclamation deals with sites similar to urban industrial land, but often at a huge scale. Reforestation of recent or historical timber clear-cuts can involve small armies of workers, as can rangeland restoration after overgrazing.[35] Agricultural fields may seem benign, but many have suffered fertility and topsoil loss or worse abuse. They, too, are candidates for restoration, especially where they were created by draining wetlands (see Principle 4). Consulting firms such as Prairie Land Management have found that restoring native vegetation to marginal farm soils reliably increases efficiency and profitability.[36]

These site-restoration projects have much in common with their urban cousins, but differ in scale and location. When hundreds or even thousands of acres are being restored, cost and practicality require simple methods. Some, like broadcast seeding, or prescribed burns in place of weeding or thinning, produce a naturalistic result. Other mass techniques result in functional landscapes: forests are restored for the next timber crop with one shovel-cut per seedling, hundreds per day. Highly designed landscape restoration might not fit rural settings.

Landscape architects and contractors may not often do this kind of large-scale, non-urban restoration, but should be aware of it. The County Extension is often a good place to find regional expertise in large-scale restoration.

Use Techniques Appropriate to Both Community and Site

As the previous sections illustrate, there is a very wide range of approaches to site restoration. Tiny lots may be repaired by the loving hands of a few volunteers. Where abandonment of a major industry has left huge gaps in the community, significant funding and professional work are required. Thus, the techniques described here must be adapted to the *community* as well as to the site.

Abandoned land often goes hand in hand with meager resources: such a community needs simple, inexpensive methods, cooperation, and patience. Compost and planting to restore soil health may initially be the only options. A surprising amount can be done with well-planned volunteer labor, however, and some intensive approaches can be scaled down. Inventive ways of funding such projects have been found by programs like the Massachusetts Heritage State Parks program and Philadelphia's linkage of public-art money to vacant site restoration.

Larger-scale restoration often involves agencies of the larger community—municipal, state, or federal. Creativity and inventiveness apply, but methods and funding are inevitably different. It is more difficult as an official agency or a nonresident investor to win the local support that makes did-it-ourselves projects so powerful. Nonetheless, truly public projects can take on problems too big for individual neighborhoods, and many succeed extremely well. It is critical to avoid moving in and taking over. Incorporate community-based planning and participatory design and expect to adjust to local standards. Community participation linked to serious reinvestment can be truly uplifting.

Restore Landscapes Structurally

Although healthy soil and vegetation are the most evident goals of site restoration, it is often necessary to deal first with *structural* damage to the site. This includes site topography and drainage damaged by inappropriate grading or erosion, and impervious structures that interfere with environmental functions. The unique structural issues of capped landfills, above, have parallels on other sites. Many emerging restoration methods address damage caused when structural forms fail to integrate with ecological dynamics.

Restore Environmentally Appropriate Grading

Grading changes the surface shape of the Earth. Conventional thinking assumes that such changes are purely a matter of human convenience and aesthetics. But recent evidence, both scholarly and practical, shows that Earth-surface forms are a critical *functional* part of the environment.[37] Partly because modern society tends to see all natural patterns as "random," the irregularities of landform surfaces are conventionally viewed as unimportant, even as nuisances. Nothing could be further from the truth.

Most conventional grading is based on straight lines and planes, in plan, section, or both. Such grading produces level or near-level surfaces for human use and unvarying slopes on "in-between" areas (such as road cuts or embankments).

Until recently the acceptability of such large planar slopes was seldom questioned. Their grim shapes often raise public outcry because they are ugly, but engineers overrule these concerns with arguments about safety, slope failure, erosion, and cost. All of these, conventional thinking insists, require the mathematically regular patterns of conventional grading. The evidence suggests otherwise. Two alternatives are discussed in this section.

Grade to Follow Regional Landforms

Horst Schor, whose Anaheim CA consulting firm specializes in what he calls "landform grading," began questioning convention while a senior vice president of Anaheim Hills development company. "We, like every other developer," he says, "were taking natural (hilly) terrain and transforming it into rigid, mathematical shapes for building. It was a practice based on the idea: We've always done it that way." Public resistance to stark, ugly results was a heated issue in Anaheim. Schor himself didn't like the look of the engineered slopes.

His solution was to study and photograph natural hill forms across the world, and then retrain his

Figure 2.9 Conventional grading insists on uniform, planar slopes. Until recently, objections to this approach have been aesthetic, but recent research shows environmental disadvantages, too. (*Photo:* H. J. Schor.)

team of designers, engineers, surveyors, and contractors to construct landforms based on geomorphic, fractal patterns. The bulldozer operator turned out to be key to success. Schor writes, "We finally had to go into the field and call a bulldozer operator off his machine, show him the drawings and photos and explain the ideas. 'Sure, I can do that. Why didn't you say that in the first place?'" was the response.[38]

The resulting slopes were carefully engineered but looked natural. Still, engineers and planning agencies were doubtful, if not hostile, at first. Engineers in particular predicted that naturalistic slopes would cause *increased* erosion. Schor proved them wrong by landform grading an experimental hill slope seventy feet high, deliberately leaving out all the drains and pipes usually required by code. After three years of unusually heavy rains and no maintenance, the landformed slopes were free from erosion. Similar-sized conventional slopes were gullied and severely damaged by the same rains.[39] In California, where developed land is regularly washed away in landslides, Schor's grading practices had immediate practical appeal, and won professional and public acceptance.

Schor has carefully documented comparative costs of conventional and landform grading.[40] The first time a contractor is asked to do landform grading, costs of learning (and of resistance to learning) can push costs up by 15 percent. Once the learning curve is overcome, however, surveying costs on average only

Figure 2.10 Landform grading creates forms that resist erosion by being in equilibrium, and that increase habitat diversity and aesthetic appeal. Lifetime costs of creating and maintaining these forms are less than for conventional grading. (*Project and Photo:* H. J. Schor.)

1 to 5 percent more than with conventional methods, and design costs 1 to 3 percent more. Construction costs (once the contractor is experienced) are typically only 1 percent higher than for conventional grading. (GPS and/or drone surveying may help; see p. 55.)

Offsetting these costs are strong benefits. Construction costs were *reduced* by 20 percent on one project because landform grading required much less total earthmoving. Contractors often like doing landform grading because it does not require extremely tight geometric control. Residential density on landform graded sites equals that on conventionally graded ones; commercial sites, which demand huge level pads, may be 1 percent fewer. Costly delays due to public opposition can be avoided. Buyers perceive landform grading as attractive, which can result in quicker return on investment, higher property values, or both.

Landform grading has been shown to decrease erosion, and it fits well with scientific theory about geomorphologic evolution of natural slopes.[41] It clearly helps blend restored land with undisturbed areas. Compared to flattened slopes, landform graded slopes revegetate more quickly and cost-effectively and offer a diversity of concave and convex, shaded and sunny, exposed and sheltered plant habitats.

Because of its combination of ecological and social benefits, landform grading deserves to be a major part of sustainable construction, and indeed, as of 2017, an online search reveals a significant number of jurisdictions that have made landform grading either optional or mandatory. It is applicable both to site restoration and to work at the edges of protected healthy sites. "A willingness and an open mind to depart from old concepts are essential," says Schor.[42]

Like porous paving (p. 251) and BTEC (p. 134), landform grading remains underused despite nearly thirty years of well-documented results. Rethinking, retraining, and overcoming entrenched resistance are one-time hurdles in each firm, agency, or community. (Schor uses clay models of typical landforms, along with slides of natural hillsides, to help both design and field workers get a feel for the desired results. The Simtable, p. 61, may have similar uses.) A more general change is also required: slightly increased up-front costs must be viewed as investments with rich, long-term payoffs, rather than as immediate gouges in the monetary bottom line.

Grade Long Slopes in Steps

"Stepped slopes" are another effective approach that avoids some problems of conventional grading. Used on highway slopes in hilly topography from California to Appalachia, they are applicable to other grading situations. Essentially, stepped slopes are small horizontal benches, constructed during grading—modern versions of the terraced agricultural hillsides used for centuries by traditional societies.

Water collects on each bench, then drops to the step below, dissipating its energy. Because it flows slowly and puddles on each step, it has time to infiltrate, aiding plant establishment. Over time the steps do erode, but this only deposits loose soil on the benches below as rooting medium for seeds. Once plants have stabilized the slope, the steps are difficult to detect.[43]

Steps are typically cut at about two-foot vertical intervals; their width is proportional to the slope. They can be created during ordinary excavation by a bulldozer traveling in alternate directions so that material does not pile up at one end of the slope.[44] Step "tops" must be truly level or slope back into the hillside. Otherwise, erosion can actually be speeded.

Stepped slopes have costs comparable to conventional grading. On some projects costs are reduced because slopes are not fine graded after excavation. Change orders have added stepped slopes to contracts at no increase in price, according to one Federal Highway Administration engineer.[45]

Although designed to erode, stepped slopes must be able to stand long enough for stabilizing vegetation to become established. Caltrans erosion-control specialist John Haynes, with extensive experience with stepped slopes, has found that compost and mulch protect the soil while providing nutrients (see p. 112). The steepness of many California highway cuts has not prevented use of composts; Caltrans has applied wood-chip mulch on slopes up to 1.25:1.

Grade Subsoil, Not Topsoil

Whatever form grading takes, always grade *subsoil* to change site topography. Differences between subsoil and topsoil are discussed on p. 108; topsoil should usually be stockpiled and reapplied to graded or otherwise altered areas. The top surface of regraded subsoil must be several inches lower than the designed finish grade. This difference, usually about six inches, allows for topsoil to be re-spread; note that topsoil may expand or compact during stockpiling and replacement. The completed site has a blanket of topsoil over structural subsoil. Avoid mixing subsoil into topsoil during spreading. In many areas, exposed grading must be protected with spray-on tackifiers to prevent dust storms.

A common problem of subsoils, including many urban soils, is compaction. Probably the best single volume on problems of urban soil remains Phillip Craul's *Urban Soil in Landscape Design*, which describes ways of ameliorating compaction. These include deep water jetting and air injection to fracture compressed soil; fractures are then backfilled with some dry material such as vermiculite.[46] Applying humic acid will also loosen some soils.

Deep plowing or subsoiling, an agricultural technique for breaking clay "pans," is applicable to urban soils. Deep plowing shatters compacted soil, creating large pore spaces that aid water drainage, aeration, and root penetration. Two caveats: subsoiling must be repeated every two to three years, and it cannot be used around trees and shrubs because of damage to the root systems.[47] On construction sites, a backhoe is often used for the same purpose as construction nears completion but before re-spreading topsoil and doing final grading.[48]

Balance Cut and Fill

Transporting soil is costly, in both money and energy (see Table 7.9). "Balancing" cut and fill, so that no soil needs to be trucked in or carted away, is standard practice for large engineering projects. This concept can contribute to sustainability and should be considered for all sites. Many construction projects, however, create large new impermeable surfaces (buildings, pavement), resulting in more topsoil than should be re-spread on remaining areas. Rather than placing topsoil to a depth that does not benefit plants on-site, it *may* be appropriate to truck the excess to another site where soil remediation is required. This should be a last resort, given energy costs and differences in soil chemistry or fertility. It is far preferable, wherever possible, to limit impermeable surfaces and to avoid contamination and other conditions that require remediation of soils.

In roadway construction, strictly balanced cut and fill can lead to raising or lowering the roadbed far beyond what is needed for safety. Although energy and cost savings result from not hauling the soil, excessively raised or lowered roads tend to disrupt natural drainage patterns, compromise traffic safety, and require increased maintenance. Sustainable construction should *first* minimize the *total* amount of grading, and then come as close as possible to balancing cut and fill.

Note: Re-grading and Wetlands

Poor grading often creates areas of standing water. If these ponding areas have persisted for a number of years, they may be legally classed as wetlands. Even if no regulatory situation exists, ponded water may be a desirable site feature or can become one with design help. Normally, however, badly engineered grading should be corrected as part of restoration.

Grading to eliminate *naturally* swampy or marshy ground is never sustainable, and is usually illegal under Section 404 of the Clean Water Act (a.k.a. Wetlands Protection Act)—a good example of how concerns for sustainability are changing landscape construction.

Remove Damaging Structures

Land restoration frequently involves *removing* existing structures. Most structures have environmental costs: they are designed to keep out water and wildlife, to block or absorb sunshine. These costs are offset by human benefits when a structure is in use. The same structure, abandoned or poorly used, has most of the costs without the benefits. Derelict houses in declining cities are one example of failed structures that hinder sustainable site use. On a much larger scale, the Army Corps of Engineers has demolished its own dams on some rivers where they disrupt river wildlife, especially the economically valuable salmon.

Some "greyfield" structures can be renovated for productive reuse as buildings. However, market forces and American attitudes often preclude this. (Adaptive reuse is a centuries-old accepted practice in Europe and Asia.) Structures may also be so deteriorated that reuse is truly impossible. Any of these situations create a candidate for structure removal.

Greenroofs and greenwalls can turn impervious structures, including relics no longer in use, into plantable surfaces (Principle 3). They provide air and water quality benefits and replace hot, sterile surfaces with habitat area.

Remove Excess Paving

Paved surfaces, in the United States at least, almost seem to grow by themselves. A net *decrease* in paved area anywhere remains inconceivable to conventional thinkers. However, when a closed factory is renovated as shops, or a single firm takes over what was once several offices, parking needs may decrease. Many writers on sustainability envision major reductions in single-occupant vehicles.[49] Such changes call for restoration of paved areas.

Even where demand for parking has not decreased, pavement removal may be justified. Many lots in current use are never more than one-quarter filled, due to excessive planning formulas for parking requirements (see p. 238). Where land is affected by increased runoff and erosion, or by extremes of flooding and drought, successful restoration may depend on removing excess hard surfaces upstream. For parking still in use, porous pavement may replace all or part of the impervious surface and biofiltration can infiltrate runoff on-site (see pp. 247).

On the Upper Charles River just outside Boston, impervious surfaces have been removed on a grand scale. Here, in the early 1990s, the Metropolitan District Commission (MDC) decided to reclaim several miles of abandoned, overgrown public riverbank as a greenway. For years, however, riverside businesses had encroached on the banks with impromptu parking lots. The MDC forced encroachers to pay for pavement removal, soil rehabilitation, and planting by landscape architects Carol R. Johnson Associates.[50] Removal of these paved areas restored the riverbanks to health and to their rightful use—a green riparian park for Boston's citizens.

Reducing runoff at the *top* of a watershed is usually more effective than trying to combat erosion with expensive engineering *downstream*. Ownership boundaries often hamper this approach, however. Watershed-wide cooperative control of stormwater, including removal or replacement of impervious paving on upstream sites, is an important trend.

Standard paving specifications require removal of all organic soils and placement of gravel "base course." These materials are highly compacted and chemically infertile. For revegetation, base course must be removed

Figure 2.11   Hunt's Point Landing removed a Bronx street and restored access to the confluence of the East and Bronx Rivers. Its treatment of the renewed shoreline received funding from NOAA (the National Oceanic and Atmospheric Administration). (*Project and Photo:* Matthews Nielsen LAs.)

Figure 2.12   The Upper Charles River was the site of miles of illegal paving. Note the ironic No Dumping sign. (*Photo:* Carol R. Johnson Associates.)

Figure 2.13   The same site, with paving, trash, and signage replaced by restored vegetation and public access. (*Project:* Carol R. Johnson Associates. *Photo:* Dan Driscoll.)

along with asphalt or concrete surfacing and the soil tested and revived before planting can be successful.

When paving is removed, conventional practice (or simply habit) is to dump the removed materials. Sustainability requires better practices. Both asphalt and concrete can be recycled using high- or low-tech methods (Principle 6); rubble, a.k.a. "urbanite," is potentially reusable. Base-course aggregate is so cheap at present that it is seldom reused. Demolished roads and buildings may become on-site material sources, as was done for the Chesapeake Bay Foundation's headquarters (Annapolis MD).[51]

Replace Overengineered Drainage Structures

Conventional drainage practice focuses on quickly getting water away from desirable structures (especially buildings and roads), often at the expense of adjacent land and aquifers. Water considered "excess" is piped or shunted into ditches for delivery to a surface water body. This deprives land of infiltrated rainfall and increases erosion, sedimentation, and flooding. The true source of these problems may be the "drainage" structures themselves; restoration downstream may not be possible without removing them.

Many "hard" erosion and flood-control structures deflect and concentrate the force of water onto other surfaces. Just beyond the hardened edges, soft soils erode more quickly than normal and undermine the structure, causing its collapse. In extreme climates, many municipally funded concrete drainage structures break down from undercutting and weathering *many years before* the bond issue debt is paid off.[52]

Where poorly planned grading *dams* natural drainage, stagnant water may produce anaerobic soil conditions and drowned plants. Examples are often seen along interstate highways. Where roads are raised on fill, cutting off drainage in surrounding low places, eerie dead forests stand like ghosts of misdeeds past.

Drainage methods should infiltrate more and harden less. These include Btec and appropriate planting (Principle 3), porous paving materials and infiltration structures (Principle 4), and landform grading (above). Each may require removal of damaging structures first.

Restore Damaged Soils On-site

Once structural problems have been corrected, or if they are not an issue, restoring soil health is an important next step in most site restoration. Compaction may need to be reversed, or soil that has been hauled away or allowed to erode may need to be replaced—erosion rates on construction sites are disastrously high if not controlled (see Figure 6.22).

Urban soils are called "made land" for good reason. They are "produced by mixing, filling, or contamination of land surfaces"[53] and support little vegetation without help.

Methods of re-creating healthy soil range from simply adding organic material to complete replacement with "manufactured soil." Unless the site has been stripped of all soil, sustainability is best served by methods that rebuild soil on-site. Only rarely should soil materials be imported in quantity, and never at the expense of another site.

Avoid "Topsoiling"

One of the most common—and most questionable—practices in contemporary landscape construction is "topsoiling." Some sites may truly lack topsoil, due to prior abuse. But more commonly, soil is imported on the assumption that on-site soils lack fertility—or that stripping topsoil and hauling it away is easier than stockpiling it.

In most urban areas, companies specialize in collecting topsoil from land under development and reselling it as "new" topsoil for *other* developments—a game of musical soils. The excuse is often that source sites are being disturbed anyway, so making off with their topsoil is no crime and saves it from destruction. The energy and pollution costs of transporting bulk soils, however, make good on-site soil management during construction the preferred alternative.

Importing soil also carries an *unseen* environmental cost—it often comes from developments that destroy productive farmland. Planning policies that allow this are unconscionable. "I feel strongly that landscape architects should never use the word 'topsoil' in spec-

Figure 2.14 Rigid structures protect only the soil they can shield from water. Along the hard edges, erosive undercutting is actually increased. (*Photo:* Kim Sorvig.)

ifications," says Vancouver BC landscape architect Cornelia Oberlander.

From a strictly practical standpoint, topsoil mixes have a significant disadvantage compared to sand plus compost (a.k.a. manufactured soil). Topsoil is usually of unknown origin and may contain near-inert subsoil, residues including pesticides, or depleted agricultural soil. In fact, the most likely time to sell soil is when its productivity declines.

Fortunately, alternatives to importing topsoil do exist. Where saving existing topsoil and reapplying it is impossible, try the soil restoration methods below before trucking in topsoil.

Stockpile Existing Topsoil

Depth of topsoil varies widely depending on soil type, from an inch or less in the desert Southwest to several feet in fertile farmland. Beneath it, subsoil contains far fewer organic materials and soil organisms. Subsoil can be thought of as primarily structural, while topsoil is alive.

The best way to preserve topsoil is to leave it strictly alone. Construction usually disturbs some areas, however, no matter how carefully minimized by planning and design. Prior to construction, topsoil should be scooped off all parts of the site that will be built on, as well as access paths and staging areas. As a practical rule of thumb, the top six inches are removed, but in unusually thin or deep soils this may vary.

Stockpile topsoil on-site in piles covered with breathable material. This slows drying, keeps down dust, excludes windblown weed seeds, and avoids mud, sedimentation, and erosion. On large projects, stockpiles are sometimes planted with a quick-growing crop of erosion-preventing groundcover.

Inevitably, many organisms in stockpiled soil die from lack of oxygen, drying, or other factors. Stockpiling longer than a month is particularly likely to kill the microorganisms on which soil health depends. Cases where construction cannot be phased to avoid long stockpiling are one of the few times when selling topsoil may be justified. Despite these concerns, and calls for reevaluation of how to protect topsoil that must be moved during construction,[54] stockpiling is clearly better than simply destroying topsoil. In order to keep soil organisms alive, observe the following suggestions.[55] The local Natural Resources Conservation Service or County Extension office may also provide advice on keeping stockpiled soil healthy.

- Make several small piles, not one large one.
- Depth of piled soil should be no more than six feet for sandy and four feet for clay soils.
- Keep piles moderately damp.
- Protect piles from wind and water erosion with tarps or temporary planting.
- Handle soil as little as possible, and stockpile as short a time as possible.

On large projects, the guidelines present a challenge of logistics and space. Nonetheless, studies by Caltrans have shown in no uncertain terms that topsoil reapplication works. On test slopes, where topsoil was reapplied after highway construction, plant growth after three years was 250 percent better than without reapplied topsoil—even with identical applications of nutrients, seeds, and erosion-control materials.[56] Under the even more demanding conditions of mine reclamation, "high sodium content, nutrient deficiencies, toxicities, and soil-water relationships were mostly alleviated by replacing topsoil."[57] There are limits, however: the same study found that two inches of replaced topsoil produced up to 70 percent as much grass regrowth as thirty inches.

One possibility to preserve topsoil and the "seed bank" found in healthy soil is to treat it like sod. Andropogon Associates pioneered a modified front-end loader to scoop up huge sheets of intact soil and plants, on the Algonquin pipeline in Morristown NJ.[58] A similar machine is now commercially available. Small plugs of seed-bearing soil are commonly used to plant wetlands (see p. 195).

Grow Soil, Not Plants

Although it sounds quixotic, growing soil instead of plants is a watchword in organic agriculture, Integrated Pest Management, and natural turf care. The same should apply to landscape efforts.

With some four billion microorganisms in a teaspoonful of healthy soil, 60 percent or more of the

Figure 2.15 In this test pit, living organic topsoil contrasts clearly with light-colored subsoil. A precious resource, topsoil is created from subsoil only by major resource inputs, either from humans or from time. (*Photo:* Natural Resources Conservation Service.)

metabolic activity in soil is microbial. Recycling organic materials, microbes allow soils to support plants—the mineral soil is just a structural matrix. The living parts of soil are responsible for binding mineral particles together, absorbing water, holding and releasing plant nutrients, and sequestering CO_2. The complex soil ecosystem suppresses excessive (disease) concentrations of any microbe species, maintaining itself dynamically like more visible ecosystems.

When soil organisms are few, or their populations are unbalanced and low in diversity, these beneficial processes are diminished. With less organic binder, soils erode more easily and hold less water and nutrients. In high concentrations, not balanced by other organisms, some microbes begin to act as pathogens,

with plant diseases as visible results. Soggy anaerobic soils also favor pathogens.

Construction, along with many other human activities, frequently diminishes soil health. Common landscape activities that can damage soil include topsoil removal; compaction by equipment or day-to-day use; mowing, pruning, and harvesting unless organic matter is returned to the soil; and "plant care" chemicals, not only pesticides but also high-nitrogen quick-release fertilizers.

"Growing soil" means keeping the web of microorganisms healthy or restoring its health. Almost as a side effect, landscape plants, lawns, and crop plants thrive with reduced amounts of irrigation and fertilizer, and few or no pesticides.

Growing soil involves several simple techniques in coordination. These include correcting compaction and sometimes improving mineral soil structure; stopping the broadcast use of pesticides and high-intensity fertilizers; and restoring microbial life and organic content, primarily by adding composts and compost teas (see below).

Soil development in nature takes decades to centuries. Human efforts to grow soil need not take so long, but even so, it takes time. Compost tea sometimes produces results as quickly as chemical methods, and more lasting. In other cases, soil restoration may take two or three years in transition, during which the landscape may look scruffy. Convincing clients (and neighbors) that instant green is a deceptive short-term idea can be the most difficult part of the soils-first approach.

The negative effects on a regional scale of unhealthy soils, and positive effects of soil restoration, are profound enough that King County WA developed a program for the Seattle region called Soils For Salmon. This in turn has become a model for other regions to manage stormwater, pollutants, vegetation cover, and wildlife by focusing on soil health.

Franklin Roosevelt once said that "a nation that destroys its soil destroys itself." In the United States, where agricultural soil has lost more than 40 percent of its soil nutrients since 1860, this is not idle rhetoric.[59] The good news is that the region that invests in maintaining its soils reaps comprehensive environmental dividends, at less cost (in money, resources, and energy) than conventional methods of landscape "care."

Analyze Soil Both Chemically and Biologically

Until relatively recently, soil analysis meant sampling physical sand-clay-loam structure and major chemical nutrients only. While this is useful information, it leaves out what is arguably the most important component of soil and the biggest factor in its health: the microbiological community of species that process and even create soil as part of their life cycle.

Truly modern soil analysis laboratories test soil microbiology and can recommend ways to bring soil flora and fauna into balance. Restoring microbiological balance to soils usually involves composts, which full-service labs also test. Two such testing services are Soil Foodweb, based in Oregon and with several labs worldwide, and BBC Laboratories, in Tempe AZ. Such labs are increasingly common; check for a local one.

Sending soils for microbiological testing has sampling requirements that may be unfamiliar: be sure to check with the lab in advance. Procedures are likely to include submitting accurate information on where and from what depth the sample was taken; express delivery on ice to ensure live microbes when tested; and deciding among several available types of testing. Tests to determine how to manage a specific soil for a specific "crop" (such as a turfgrass species) are simpler than those that give a more comprehensive picture of soil health in relation to its region. The latter are generally more useful to landscape projects, where single-crop plantings are less relevant. Simple tests can cost $25 per sample or less, with more complex ones ranging toward $75 each. For very large areas, AgRobotics's tractor-drawn AutoProbe takes up to 2,500 soil samples per hour on a GPS-controlled grid and at the same soil depth each time.[60]

Consultation is usually available to help interpret test results. Dr. Elaine Ingham, founder of Soil Foodweb, teaches courses about testing soil and composts; her published work is extremely useful. For long-term maintenance, especially of heavily trafficked landscapes, routine testing shows what groundskeeping activities to prioritize; Battery Park's playing fields

(p. 386) use this approach. Testing's relatively small investment yields big returns and should be part of most landscape projects, especially those that aim to restore damaged sites.

"Amend" Soil—But with Restraint

Particularly on abused urban sites, any topsoil worthy of the name may have been stripped away long ago or covered by rubble and fill. Even in the worst cases, however, existing soil properly amended may be better than commercially available "landscape" soil, according to Simon Leake, an Australian soils scientist.[61]

Unpromising soils may actually be surprisingly viable. For example, "urban renewal" leaves large tracts of land strewn with demolition rubble. Research in Great Britain suggests that brick rubble can be amended as planting medium, particularly if it has lain on-site for years. Soil-forming processes work on raw bricks and mortar to form a kind of stony soil.[62] Soil texture, drainage, and aeration are excellent. Nitrogen is typically deficient, although it may be rebuilt by nitrogen-fixing plants (or acid rain). Brick clay provides sufficient phosphorus, potassium, and magnesium; mortar offers calcium. The ancient Roman landfill, Monte Testaccio (above), is largely made up of clay potsherds; not only is it well vegetated, but its high porosity keeps things cool—including wine cellars.[63]

Other types of rubble, especially broken concrete, have fewer nutrients but so much calcium that the soil becomes alkaline. Concrete rubble is harder and denser than mortar or brick, and breaks down more slowly. Plastics, metals, woods (treated and untreated), paints, sealants, and petroleum fuels can be present in demolition debris in widely varied proportions. The unpredictable, spotty patterns in which debris may be scattered on a site make testing more complicated *and* more necessary.

Gardens on rubble are not easily created, nor always feasible. The above research suggests, however, that removing *existing* debris may not be the best or only way to rehabilitate derelict land. (This applies only to existing debris: responsible contractors must reduce waste and avoid leaving trash.) Rubble-strewn lots, a seemingly hopeless urban situation, show how biological processes and human practices together can resurrect damaged sites.

Materials and Energy for Soil Amendment

A wide range of materials are marketed for improving soils. Many are appropriate for use where existing soil is badly damaged. As noted on p. 71, however, it is possible to amend soil too much. As landscape architect Leslie Sauer puts it in *The Once and Future Forest*, "Researchers have shown repeatedly that fertilizer benefits weeds." *Decreasing* fertility and changing pH often favors native species.[64] Avoiding overfertilization is especially important on relatively undisturbed and healthy native soils. In general, the goal of restoration should be a soil with chemistry and fertility *comparable to healthy regional soils*. Regional variety allows for most reasonable landscape purposes.

Robert Nold, an expert on wildflowers of the *Penstemon* genus, puts soil amendment in regional perspective. "Dryland gardening, if it is to be successful," he writes, "must not attempt to compensate for 'inferior' conditions [by using] notions of 'soil improvement' left over from agriculture. Soils do not need to be improved—the plant choices do."[65]

Experts are not fully in agreement on the appropriateness of soil amendments, and indeed these practices are site or region specific. Some general guidelines can be stated, however:[66]

- Compost (rotted vegetative material) is the most universally valuable of all soil additives, a paradoxical substance that helps sandy soils hold water and clay soils release it. (See next section.) Compost tea, an increasingly important way of applying compost, has its own section, below.
- Sand is often specified to improve drainage. Impractical amounts, however, must be added to most clays. At least one-third of the final result must be sand; for an existing volume of clay, half that volume must be added. Smaller amounts of sand can bind soil tighter (as in adobe bricks). Add compost instead.
- Clay well mixed into sandy soil can readily improve its *structure*. Remember the farmer's adage: "Sand on clay, money thrown away; clay on sand, money in

hand." Compost, however, is a better choice for *both*.
- Gypsum is useful on unusually calcium-deficient soils, or those affected by salt. Most western US soils are already too alkaline to benefit from gypsum. It can improve structure in compacted soils, and has the advantage of being soluble, so it can be surface applied without digging. "Organic" gypsum, though it sounds ludicrous, is a naturally occurring mined material, as opposed to gypsum as a by-product of water treatment, electrical power station "flue gas," manufacture of certain acids, or recycling of wallboard.[67]
- Wood ash is useful on acid soils in the eastern and southern United States, but can increase existing pH and salt problems in western soils.
- "Biochar" is charcoal produced from wood and other greenwaste under controlled oxygen-poor conditions (a.k.a. pyrolysis). It was discovered in the Amazon, where it was used by pre-Colombian civilizations; soils with biochar are called *terra preta* (black earth). Waste wood, sugarcane bagasse, and even poultry manure can be converted to biochar by burning in special ovens or pits. Bartlett Tree Experts has done trials of biochar in street-tree conditions and found that it improves fertility (without being a fertilizer), increases soil-moisture retention and decreases leaching, and promotes beneficial microbes.[68] Bartlett produces biochar for tree maintenance. According to Bob Pine, director of environmental planning and engineering at Pine & Swallow Environmental in Boston, biochar must be carefully produced because under some conditions pyrolysis results in hazardous by-products (polyaromatic hydrocarbons) that are undesirable in a soil additive. Assuming high-quality biochar, Pine says, poor soils (low in organic matter) will benefit, while richer soils show less improvement, or none. Biochar persists in soil, sequestering carbon, but the "residence" (how long it persists) varies from years to centuries, depending on the type of waste used to produce it and the soil type into which it is worked.[69] Some breathless claims have been made that biochar will save the Earth from CO_2 while feeding a rapidly doubling population; this should not deter serious study and experimentation.

- Peat moss is widely specified as a soil amendment. It can structurally improve drainage and water holding, but contributes little to living soil. Coir, from coconut palms, similarly provides drainage but few nutrients. Peat is harvested from wetlands in vast quantities and shipped long distances; many experts consider its use entirely unsustainable. Coir is sustainably produced, though shipping distances are long. Use compost instead, from local leaf litter.

- In many areas, soils today contain *extra* nutrients from acid rain and air pollution. Adding fertilizer may be unnecessary or harmful. A major nutrient from pollution is nitrogen; elevated levels encourage weeds.

- Some soils, especially if irrigated where evaporation is high, have high salt content. Avoid adding to this with salty fertilizers (fresh cattle and poultry manure, as well as ammonium nitrate and other high-nitrogen mixes).

- Microbes that decompose organic material require nitrogen. Amendments that are high carbon and low nitrogen (a "C/N ratio" higher than 20:1) cause microbes to *take* nitrogen from the soil to fuel their work. This can make nitrogen unavailable to plants until decomposition is finished. Amendments with high C/N ratios include horse manure, dairy (but not beef) cattle manure, straw, wood chips and sawdust, and some composts if not well matured. Such amendments may be *good* for high-nitrogen soils, or for woodland soils where leaf and twig litter naturally composts slowly. Elsewhere they should be used with caution.

- Many plants live cooperatively or symbiotically with soil organisms. Roots of such plants work in cooperation with mycorrhizae (fungi that process nutrients and exchange them with the plant). If the correct symbiotic organism is not present in soil, these plants cannot survive. Mycorrhizal "inoculants" are commercially available for some species. They should be used with local expertise, however, because the wrong mycorrhizae can displace beneficial ones native to the soil. Deliberate fluctuations in soil moisture can stress plants just enough to encourage symbiosis. Despite practical and successful applications in Permaculture and forestry, landscape architects in 2017 still overlook this important aspect of soil fertility.[70]

- Apart from composts, super-absorbent polymer granules can increase available moisture. One pound of such granules absorbs nearly fifty gallons of water; an almost bizarre amount of water disappears into dry polymer when mixed. Polymers in planting mixes reduce irrigation needs. Bare-root or live-stake BTEC materials (Principle 3) can be dipped before planting directly into a slurry of the water-absorbent material. Salt holding by polymers has been a concern, but they have been widely accepted both in horticulture and in dryland reforestation.

Embodied energy and potential toxicity of soil amendments vary widely. Some amendments are simple materials like sand, clay, compost, or manure. Such materials are toxic only if contaminated, but energy to "mine" the materials and transport them can be significant. As noted above, topsoil should rarely be imported or exported. Toxicity by overuse of fresh manure is a possibility. Unless carefully researched, "organic" may be a misleading or meaningless label on soil products. Processed soil amendments range from simple ground limestone to completely artificial chemical fertilizers or water-holding polymers. A responsible approach to sustainable construction does not simply reject these materials because they are processed. Rather, each material must be analyzed for embodied energy, toxicity, and related concerns, and used accordingly. The number of available products continues to increase.

Even if soil-amending materials are energy efficient and nontoxic, widespread change in site soils may have undesirable ecosystem effects. Anyone who has overwatered or overfertilized a houseplant will understand this problem. In some regions of "poor" soils, increased soil fertility actually *decreases* the health and hardiness of native plant species. At the same time, it makes the soil more hospitable to weeds that are not picky. The result is unsatisfactory both horticulturally and ecologically, and increases maintenance.

To repeat an important point: soil restoration should usually aim to bring damaged soil back to conditions *similar to healthy regional soils*. In landscape use, this implies design emphasizing native plants, since these actively affect soil composition. Dramatically increased soil fertility should be reserved for the lim-

Table 2.1
Cost-benefit comparison of soil amendments for trees.

Treatment	Materials (g/tree/yr.)	Equipment (g/tree/yr.)	Labor (g/tree/yr.)	Total (g/tree/yr.)	Growth (g/tree/yr.)	Efficiency ($/g)
Null	0.0	0.5	7.5	8.0	22.8	0.35
Compost tea	7.5	28.5	30.0	66.0	24.1	2.74
Biological products	3.5	3.5	11.3	18.3	23.9	0.77
NPK fertilizer	6.5	3.5	11.3	21.3	38.7	0.55
Wood chips	3.0	1.0	15.0	19.0	61.3	0.30
Compost	3.0	1.0	15.0	19.0	62.8	0.30
Biochar	10.0	1.0	15.0	26.0	70.1	0.37
Biosolids	0.0	1.0	15.0	16.0	73.0	0.22

Source: Bryant Scharenbroch, PhD, University of Wisconsin and Morton Arboretum, presentation at the 2015 ASLA Annual Meeting, Chicago.

ited number of exotics planted as special accents in such designs.

Use Greenwaste and Other Composts

Compost for private yards or community-garden plots is everyday practice, but what about large-scale landscape construction? Some of the very largest-scale landscape projects—highway rights-of-way—routinely employ composted materials. A 1997 study by the University of Florida found that thirty-four of the fifty state departments of transportation used compost on roadsides routinely or experimentally; the practice has only increased since.[71]

For large-scale projects, compost is usually applied hydraulically in a slurry, often mixed with uncomposted greenwaste. Compostable materials are countless: grass clippings and leaves from suburban backyards; chicken and livestock manure; brewer's waste; biosolids (composted sludge) from municipal sewage; trees chipped after felling; farm by-products like walnut shells and peach pits; and chopped wood waste from demolished buildings.

The range of applications is equally wide: as a soil amendment, as mulch or topdressing, for erosion control, and as a planting-soil ingredient. Frequently noted benefits from compost include:

- better plant growth, with less fertilizer, due to balanced organic matter, slow-release nutrients, and microbial populations

- effective erosion control, slope stabilization, water-holding, and drainage
- fewer weeds, fewer herbicides (where used as mulch).

With compost, says Caltrans's Haynes, "you're effecting real soil improvement, since we often install landscape plantings in subsoil." The term "improvement," often used too casually about soil additives, definitely applies to compost.

Compost has been a standard specification for Minnesota DOT (MNDOT) for over two decades, completely replacing topsoil or peat moss. MNDOT uses 20,000 cubic yards of compost annually on roadsides, largely in planting trees and shrubs. DOTs in California, Florida, Illinois, Maine, North Carolina, Washington, and Massachusetts also report substantial—and successful—compost applications. Caltrans's erosion-control toolkit emphasizes compost; among other benefits, it meets California policy by diverting recyclable materials from landfills.

These agencies have tested the performance of compost against results obtained from peat, humus, bark, topsoil, or fertilizer. Compost compares favorably in almost every trial. Caltrans finds compost to be as effective for slope protection as erosion-control blankets. Maine's DOT finds that turf grown on a fifty-fifty mix of compost and subsoil, with compost mulch, resists erosion better than grass grown on loam topsoil.[72] In short, compost has immense value on almost every landscape project.

Availability and Quality of Compost

In most urban areas there is a glut of yard waste. (If processed into boards, the volume of wood-like wastes is enough to replace all wood harvested for timber; see Figure 6.20.) In the past, this valuable organic matter was trucked to landfills, a practice increasingly banned by municipalities. Leaves and grass have made up as much as 18 percent of landfill volume, with another 7 percent composed of soil, rocks, and woody landscape waste. Thus *one-quarter* of landfill volume could be eliminated by making good use of organic materials. With landfills bulging at the seams, the value of greenwaste has been recognized. California legislation in the 1990s required communities to reduce landfill greenwaste by 50 percent by 2000, a goal easily met by separating yard waste.

As of 2013, 3,560 community compost programs existed in the United States.[73] Along with yard waste, Christmas trees, agricultural by-products, scrap wood, animal manure, biosolids (see below), and food wastes from food services and restaurants are frequently composted. (In Vancouver BC, one composting firm makes high-quality compost entirely from restaurant wastes. Landscape architect Cornelia Oberlander's use of this product is discussed below.) Occasionally, mixing two kinds of waste can neutralize problems with both, similar to phytoremediation (below); for example, brewery waste consisting of spent yeast has been used to pull heavy metals out of computer-chip wastewater.[74]

Despite generally large volumes of raw greenwaste, large-scale landscape use of compost can run into availability and quality issues. Several state DOTs have found it difficult to obtain compost in quantities required for highway projects. This can affect application rates and product quality. Hauling charges can be substantial for these bulky materials—particularly in large and sparsely populated states.[75] In such cases, environmental costs of energy use and air pollution must be carefully weighed against benefits of compost. Considering long-term health of plantings, reduced erosion, reduced chemical use, and decreased landfill disposal, however, transporting compost may still be environmentally viable, despite financial cost.

Specifications that spell out characteristics of qual-ity compost are important in ensuring consistent product. Fortunately, model specifications do exist. One is the *Suggested Compost Parameters and Compost Use Guidelines* developed by the US Composting Council.

Contaminants in and maturity of compost are the most common quality issues. Weed seed, heavy metals, salts, and other contaminants should be limited by specification. Some substances, such as small pieces of plastic or glass, pose no horticultural problem (see "Manufactured Soil," below). Of course, foreign objects that may cause injury to construction workers, to users of the site, or to wildlife must be eliminated. Special concerns when using compost on relatively healthy and undisturbed soils are noted on p. 71.

Compost that is not fully mature—that is, still decomposing—can steal nitrogen from the soil, depriving plants. The Washington DOT requires producers to provide maturity-testing kits with compost deliveries.[76] Soil-testing labs that include microbiology analysis can also test compost and advise on modifying it to accomplish specific landscape goals. The US Composting Council, a trade organization, certifies compost after standard testing through its Seal of Testing Assurance (STA) program.[77] This voluntary program was formed with the explicit goal of avoiding state regulation; potential users of certified compost should read the testing standard to ensure that it meets their specific soil management goals.

There is no technical problem in turning raw materials into compost. At present, more raw material is available than is collected or processed. In many areas, increased demand would help municipal governments fund increased compost production. Ideally, wastes generated at a site should be composted and used on that site, saving transport costs, but this is not always feasible. Landscape professionals should make a commitment to putting this valuable product to use.

Use Compost Teas

Compost teas are one of the most interesting innovations of organic maintenance. Unsurprisingly, skepticism about them is not unusual. Made from ordinary soil-like compost by "brewing" in water, teas enhance the microbial composition of the mix. As liquids, they are convenient to apply and quick to be taken up by plants. Compost teas are sometimes referred to as "effective microorganisms" and are available as "mother culture" that is mixed with molasses and water, fermented a few days, and applied to soil or foliage.[78] To be effective, they must be live and in the proper mix and concentration.

For compost tea, water is mixed with compost plus agents like soy, flour, kelp, fish emulsion, or molasses, which stimulate reproduction of specific types of soil microorganisms. The mixture is usually agitated with air to keep oxygen at optimum levels. Tea recipes are frequently based on biological soil tests (above). The finished tea is diluted in a water-to-tea ratio between 3:1 and 5:1. For turf, 50 to 100 gallons per acre are applied once a month. Foliar sprays are applied directly onto plant leaves (whose surface microbial populations are important to plant health). Foliar applications average one gallon per large shrub and four gallons per tree, adjusted per species. Horticulturalists have even developed a technique to inject teas into the sand joints of pavers around street trees.[79]

Compost tea must be brewed to match specific requirements and applied within a day after production. Commercial compost tea should be produced near the site, and generally remains the province of specialists. There are about twenty small US companies that brew teas to order. An Internet search may help locate brewers in your region. Bottling compost tea may be a possibility, although effects on the living organisms are unpredictable. An alternative is brew-it-yourself; equipment to do so is available from several companies. A growing number of landscape and turf maintenance companies produce and apply their own compost teas.

Although compost teas are very popular, almost to the point of being faddish, they work best in a coordinated program of "growing soil." Such programs were discussed earlier in this chapter; their successful application to landscape maintenance is discussed in Principle 10.

Use Yard Waste On-site

Although municipal composting and use of compost in construction are desirable, most American yards would be healthier if yard waste were composted and reapplied *on-site* (see p. 383). As with most environmental technologies, on-site reuse also saves transportation and associated costs. If garden maintenance (and agriculture) becomes more sustainable, it is possible that current sources of greenwaste may decrease. In the meantime, however, municipal compost should be a mainstay in reclaiming damaged soils.

Plant "Green Manure" Crops

"Green manure" plants are aids for soil enrichment that farmers have known about for millennia. Grown on-site for one or more seasons, they are then tilled into the soil to compost. Most green manure plants are leguminous (pea family). Their roots fix nitrogen, available to later plantings as the green manure breaks down. For regionally appropriate green-manure practices, contact a local agricultural school or County Extension. Be sure to pick species not likely to become invasive—a few leguminous crops, such as alfalfa, spread aggressively in some climates.

Watch for Lead in Soils

Community gardens on derelict urban land must beware of lead. Although no longer used in consumer paints or gasoline, lead is not biodegradable and persists in soil. Sites near older buildings painted with lead, heavily traveled roadways, or service stations may be contaminated. Former industrial locations should always be researched carefully for persistent soil pollutants.

Community-garden sites where food crops will be grown should *always* undergo a soil test. For lead at levels less than 500 parts per million (ppm), the Ohio State University Extension recommends incorporating one-third organic material (compost or manure) by volume: twelve to sixteen cubic feet for a 100-square-foot plot. If lead levels are higher, build raised beds that separate planting medium from contaminated soil.[80] Raised beds are a convenient, traditional gardening method, favored for maintenance and handicapped accessibility, and common in European intensive vegetable cultivation. Whenever chemical residues are found, reconsider whether to use the garden for food plants. Decorative gardens are also an appropriate use of community allotments.

Use Biosolids Appropriately

The urban environment produces many by-products in need of recycling. Few are more appropriate for use in restoring landscapes than biosolids—yet none is so underutilized. Many fears and misconceptions surround biosolids, processed from municipal sewage. Although some concern is legitimate where food production is involved, for most other types of landscapes, biosolids are too valuable to waste.

Many traditional societies around the world prize composted human waste as fertilizer. Small-scale, on-site treatment, using composting toilets, constructed wetlands, and other "alternative" systems, is common—but not common enough—even in industrialized countries. Such systems are close to the source and relatively easy to keep free of chemical contaminants. In modern societies, however, sewage is too easily piped away underground, out of sight and out of almost everyone's mind.

At the other end of the sewage pipe, treatment plants used to simply dump the treated sewage. Beginning in the 1920s, the practice was recognized as neither cost-effective nor environmentally intelligent. In 1926, Milwaukee began marketing the granddaddy of US biosolids products, and still the best known, Milorganite.

In 1988, federal law banned dumping municipal sludge in the oceans, narrowing disposal options for wastewater-treatment facilities. Landfilling and incineration are expensive and environmentally questionable. The 1988 ban created a full-fledged biosolids industry, products with names like Biogrow, GroCo, Nutramulch, and Technagro.

Increased biosolids availability has decreased costs—from $120 to $42 per ton in Florida between 1990 and 1994, for example.[81] Since supply is never-ending, some wastewater-plant operators even supply biosolids at no cost, especially for public-sector projects.

Not everyone concerned with the environment supports biosolids use. Despite extensive standards set by the US EPA, some biosolids contain heavy metals and contaminants dumped ignorantly or maliciously into sewer systems. These are of particular concern on food-producing fields. Many experts consider the EPA standards very low risk even for crops, but not ev-

eryone accepts these definitions. A 1998 proposal to allow foods fertilized with biosolids to be labeled "organic" raised serious public objection, and to this day, some activists view all biosolids as a corporate conspiracy. Ordinary manufactured fertilizers, for which there are *no* standards, arguably pose far greater threats than biosolids; some even include toxic wastes merely relabeled as fertilizer.[82] (See "Toxics as 'Fertilizer,'" p. 301.) When produced and used in accordance with EPA standards, biosolids seem highly appropriate for *landscape* use, with the possible exception of aquifer recharge zones or little-disturbed, near-natural sites. On brownfields, where the site itself is toxic, biosolids can be an important tool.

Biosolids are soil conditioners, essentially similar to compost, increasing water and nutrient retention in soil. Like compost, they improve soil tilth and boost fertility, with significant nitrogen, phosphorus, potassium, and beneficial trace metals. Used as mulch, often mixed with wood chips or yard waste, they control erosion—a multipurpose, low-cost soil amendment.

How safe are biosolids? The EPA recognizes two main classes, A and B.[83] Both undergo a process known as digestion, which reduces pathogen levels by approximately 99 percent and heavy metals to required levels. This produces class-B biosolids; application requires a state permit and site monitoring for up to a year.

Class-A biosolids are further composted, heat dried, or irradiated, sterilizing and deodorizing the product. Sea World of Ohio uses class-A Technagro on flower beds next to public walkways, stockpiling it for two weeks to dissipate any lingering odors.

The chemical composition of sludge varies greatly from one treatment plant to another. Because lime is sometimes used to stabilize it, pH may reach eleven, far too alkaline for most soils. Soluble salts and nitrates are not uncommon. According to one noted soil scientist, any contaminants can build up with repeated application, although they dissipate if application stops for several years;[84] a study on golf courses showed that metals did increase in grass tissues, but still below EPA-permitted levels.[85] Site remediation using plants (phytoremediation, p. 124) or microbes (bioremediation, p. 126) removes very similar contaminants and might provide extra treatment for biosolids, before or after they are applied to landscapes.

Biosolids are not totally risk free; that claim cannot be made for commercial fertilizers either. Properly applied, they solve two major environmental problems—sewage disposal and soil fertility—with minimal health or environmental risk. One caveat: quality compliance varies from one *producer* to another, or at different times. Bob Rubin, professor of agricultural engineering at North Carolina State University, has conducted extensive research in landscape applications of biosolids. He recommends buyers and specifiers ask their state regulatory agency these questions: What facilities in the state are producing class-A pathogen-free biosolids? Has the agency analyzed nutrients, salts, metals, and other elements in those products? Which producers consistently comply with state and EPA guidelines? Such information, available in every state, identifies producers of quality products. This information may or may not survive the gutting of the EPA.

Satisfactory biosolids products may not be available in quantity in every locality. If no local options exist, the cost of transport may be more than that of the biosolids (see energy costs, Principle 7). Life-cycle costs may make even imported biosolids viable, and availability continues to spread.

The range of projects in which biosolids have played a role is broad. Applying biosolids on the White House lawn sounds like a contractor's nightmare or partisan political joke. Nevertheless, the White House has used biosolids. In the late 1980s, 825 tons of ComPro—biosolids from Washington DC sewage composted with lime and wood chips—were applied to the south lawn for compaction. The head White House groundskeeper reported no problems. A few blocks away, 6,000 tons of biosolids were applied to the National Mall's Constitution Gardens. The Washington Monument, Mount Vernon, and Dumbarton Oaks are other sites in the nation's capital maintained with biosolids. Washington-area landscape architect James Urban specified ComPro for the National Geographic Society headquarters. (Despite what humorists might predict, Washington's sewage is relatively benign; it has few of the heavy metals that plague waste in historically industrial cities like Boston.)

Seattle Parks and Recreation landscape architect Barbara Swift specified biosolids for Discovery Park, a 500-acre expanse degraded by years of logging and farming. On a fourteen-acre demonstration area, two inches of class-B biosolids from King County's wastewater-treatment plant were spread and tilled to a fifteen-inch depth. Project manager Kevin Stoops notes that odors dissipated quickly when exposed to air and sunlight. Shifting winds led to neighbors' complaints late in the process; after that, the city switched to a class-A mixture. The site now exhibits luxuriant growth, says Stoops. Parks and Recreation obtained the biosolids free, realizing enormous cost savings over other fertilizers.[86]

In general, Washington State has led other states in biosolids application since the mid-1970s, when Seattle's world-famous Gas Works Park was treated with class-B biosolids. Mountains to the Sound, a greenway initiative along Interstate 90, used biosolids to revegetate highly visible logged slopes and logging roads along a scenic mountain corridor, while in Everett, biosolids were tested for wetlands restoration.

Elsewhere, use of biosolids sometimes encounters public resistance.[87] Kentucky DOT has been apprehensive about biosolids' potential for fouling water supply, and Minnesota DOT uses biosolids only in pilot projects. Wyoming DOT tried to use biosolids but encountered backlash that forced it to stop—even though the product in question easily met EPA standards. States like Massachusetts, however, are moving confidently ahead with biosolids, while in Nebraska, farmers use it as fast as it is made.[88]

A darker form of resistance to biosolids comes from entrenched conventional interests. Producers of wood mulch and fertilizers see any form of compost as cutting into their markets; at least one attempt to legislate roadside use of biosolids was "shot down by chemical industry lobbyists."[89] Special-interest resistance really argues in *favor* of biosolids. Public and professional education is key to its appropriate use.

Manufactured Soil

Many derelict sites have fill and rubble where topsoil should be, while landfills and highway cuts may be soilless, their huge size prohibiting imported topsoil. To cover Fresh Kills Landfill with as little as twelve inches of soil would require 104,551,200 cubic feet, or nearly 5 million tons. The question at such scales is where to get that much soil. ("Excuse me, can you spare five million tons?")

That question can be answered by another: Why not recycle discarded materials to reconstruct a dump? Manufactured soil does exactly that—and not only on landfills. Although it seems an oxymoron, manufactured soil is technically quite feasible and often the ecologically responsible option. The constituents of soil—its mineral, organic, and chemical components—can be assembled mostly if not entirely from recycled materials. (The concept of making soil is familiar from household "potting soils" combining perlite and vermiculite with peat or compost.) Once the mix is applied, microorganisms and plants complete the "manufacturing."

Phil Craul, the author of *Urban Soils*, has taught at Harvard's Graduate School of Design and is a leading interpreter of soils science to landscape professionals. Craul has consulted on many projects using manufactured soils and written guidelines for specifying them. Here is Craul's definition of manufactured or, as he calls it, "sustainable soil": "Sustainable soil is comprised entirely of recyclable products, alone or in a mixture with derelict soil material, the latter useless without supplementation. It contains few, if any, nonrenewable resources."[90]

Soil components are usually available on or adjacent to even the most abused sites. Examples include the following:

- sand from river dredging
- recycled ground glass
- washings from aggregate plants
- certain smokestack fly ashes
- derelict soils such as mine tailings (selectively)
- fine-ground till from glacial deposits
- various composted or recycled organic materials.[91]

The soils Craul envisions would *not* include sand specifically mined for the purpose, only the types of materials listed above. In most cities, says Craul,

"you've got all the components you need for making soil—and it's all recycled."

A futuristic article about agricultural soils for space colonies led Craul to use ground glass. Lunar dust, noted the article, resembles ground glass, a possible silica matrix for man-made soils. "If they think they can use that stuff on the moon," mused Craul, "why can't we use ground glass as a matrix here on Earth?" He soon learned that others were thinking along similar lines, using ground glass as a sand substitute in drainage, from a landfill near Syracuse NY to septic drain fields in Washington State. Manufactured soils could make inner-city restoration feasible where little if any topsoil remains. "So there's a movement afoot," says Craul. Design of manufactured soils, however, is still new, and few professionals are experienced.

Craul's biggest project to date was Spectacle Island, gateway to Boston Harbor Islands National Park, opened in 2006 with public access by ferry. The 105-acre island served as a landfill, capped with clay, for 2 million cubic yards of contaminated spoil from Boston's Central Artery tunnel. Craul and Boston landscape architects Brown & Rowe calculated that 582,000 cubic yards of topsoil would be needed to cover the island. "To find that much soil," says Craul, "we would have had to strip all the remaining farms in Suffolk County," which neighbors Boston.

Instead, topsoil was manufactured. The first ingredient was stone grit, derived from the glacial till of which the island is composed. Other materials were barged over from the mainland: coarse sand from New Hampshire, and compost. Obtaining the inert till and sand proved relatively straightforward. The compost was another matter: 21,000 cubic yards was needed. The Rochester NH firm of AllGro was contracted to supply a mixture of 70 percent brewery waste and 30 percent biosolids.

The brewery waste ran out during the project's first phase, replaced by biosolids. Because of the volume needed, AllGro had to contract for much of it from other processors in the region. Shipments arrived full of large sticks and wood chips—low-cost bulking agents that settle inconsistently as the wood decomposes. Quality fluctuations are symptomatic of compost industry growing pains. Far from arguing against

Figure 2.16 Spectacle Island in Boston Harbor is a recreational landscape salvaged from a toxic dump. (*Project:* P. Craul with Brown and Rowe. *Photo:* Massachusetts Turnpike Authority.)

compost or manufactured soils, they indicate need for better specifications and monitoring of delivered products.

With manufactured soil in place, the island was bare and without seed sources. Brown & Rowe protected the 3:1 slopes against erosion with multilayered plantings in bands along contours. Deciduous trees and shrubs were underplanted with grasses and legumes to stabilize slopes and increase water retention while the woody plants matured. Heights and densities alternated to counter winds buffeting the site. The plant list was somewhat experimental; the designers chose self-seeding, naturalizing plants, knowing some would thrive and others not. "Basically we designed for low or no maintenance," Rowe recalls. During establishment, sprinkler irrigation pipes and two water cannons were employed. Water was barged to a large tank on the north drumlin. By the summer of 2002, irrigation was no longer needed. The wisdom of installing a wide range of species has been confirmed: the plants are beginning to form a forest and give shape to the island.[92]

Other projects for which Craul has designed soils include cover on underground parking beneath Boston Commons; South Cove at Battery Park City, Manhattan; and J. Paul Getty Center, Los Angeles. The Fresh Kills revegetation (above) used manufactured soils, with ratios of between 3 and 4 parts sand to 1 part compost, depths varying from 1 to 2.5 feet. Discarded, chipped Christmas trees also provided organic mulch.

Suggested Practices for Soil Restoration

- Cardinal principle: *Wherever possible, avoid removing or bringing in topsoil.*
- Use soil analysis services to understand site soil and to plan any amendments. Analyze not only chemical components, but also microbes and soil organisms. Consult a soil scientist.
- Amend to match healthy regional soil types, not agricultural ideals. Use regional plant species rather than widespread soil amendment and irrigation.
- Wherever possible, stockpile topsoil from construction areas on-site and re-spread as soon as possible.
- Where there is only fill dirt on-site, amend that to create viable soil rather than bringing in topsoil. Add compost or plant restorative plants.
- Specify *recycled local* soil amendments and erosion-control materials if possible.
- Get over your inhibitions about biosolids and help clients get over theirs. Promote this material (within limits noted above) to turn waste into a resource.
- Become knowledgeable about biosolids production and standards. Locate reliable local producers through appropriate state agencies. Use class A to avoid odor, class B for less public sites.
- For soilless sites, or if on-site soil must be removed due to contamination, consider manufactured soil.
- Once restored, ensure good soil maintenance (Principle 10). Inappropriate irrigation and fertilization can *damage* soil fertility.

Restore Regionally Appropriate Vegetation

Restoring site soils is essential to reestablishing healthy vegetation. The process, however, is two-way. Vegetation interacts with mineral earth, microbes, and climate to produce regional soil types. Regional plants and regional soils mutually depend on each other.

Landscape architects often use native plants both for restoration work and in garden design, placing new demands on landscape contractors. Although a few contractors and nurseries specialize in native plants, others still need to develop knowledge and skill to work successfully with these species. Standard construction often fails to create site conditions that favor native plants (sometimes quite different from conditions favored by human users).

Site restoration is not just about replanting appropriate species, but also about control and removal of inappropriate plants. Some derelict sites are literally green, due to an unhealthy mix of weedy plants. Restoring such sites requires attention to changed soil, grading, and drainage patterns that invited weedy species. Thoroughly eradicating aggressive introduced plants also requires methods not common in conventional work. A useful and widely accepted way of evaluating vegetation before, during, and after restoration is Floristic Quality Assessment (see p. 48).

There are many books on site restoration using native species. Because restoration is specific both to region and to the type of site damage, no single book or resource can detail all practices. The following is an overview of main issues affecting landscape professionals.

Remove Invasive Plants and Restore Native Succession

In purely economic terms, invasive plants, imported by people and allowed to overrun fields and forests, do an estimated $140 billion worth of damage annually in the United States.[93] This problem continues to grow, but is also increasingly recognized. The federal government's National Invasive Plant Management Strategy, drafted in 1996, estimated that 4,600 acres of public lands *per day* are lost to noxious weeds in the western half of the United States alone, reducing both economic yield and ecological viability of these lands. (Oddly, these very real losses evoke far less outcry than the belief that lands are "lost" if designated as national monuments.) Removal of these invasives, and restoration of diverse native plant communities, is expected to be the largest public-works project *ever* undertaken. It is a task that could largely have been prevented, in hindsight, if horticultural and agricultural plant introductions had been more carefully screened for invasive characteristics.[94]

Of the several thousand non-native species that have naturalized (adapted to survive without human help) in North America, only about 10 percent (still, 400 species) are truly invasive. "Invasive" has varied definitions (and some critics vehemently reject the concept as a whole), but it essentially means a plant that not only survives where introduced by humans, but takes over and damages significant parts of the local ecosystem.[95]

Two examples show that the concept of invasives is complex, but that the damage done by such plants is real. Tamarisk, or Salt Cedar (*Tamarix* sp.), like about 60 to 85 percent of invasive species in the United States, was deliberately imported as an ornamental plant.[96] Two circumstances made it invasive. First, two separate tamarisk species from Asia and the eastern Mediterranean "met" for the first time in cultivation and hybridized, becoming tougher and spreading more vigorously.[97] Second, major water projects dammed western US rivers and sharply decreased reproduction of native cottonwoods. The hybrid tamarisk then invaded these river areas—up to 90 percent of such habitat in many western states.[98] It can live in salty soil (often produced by irrigation) and "sweats" salt onto its leaves, which it drops. Its leaf litter makes topsoil too salty for other plants.

Ironically, after getting its foothold thanks to water-supply dams, Salt Cedar has proved to take up huge amounts of water. One estimate is that, throughout the West, the invader sucks up 800 billion gallons a year *more* than the native plants it replaced. Eradication of this one species from the arid West is estimated to cost $500 million.[99]

A second example is Spotted Knapweed (*Centaurea maculosa*). Seed was accidentally imported in alfalfa in the late 1800s. It has now spread to almost every American state and Canadian province. In Montana alone, it covers 4.5 million acres and costs ranchers an estimated $40 million annually.[100] Even among invasives, it is unusual in forming monocultures, completely enveloping huge swaths of landscape. Most animals except sheep find it inedible; its dominance of some valleys has actually changed elk migration patterns.

Spotted Knapweed releases a soil toxin. In its native Europe, other plant and insect species have evolved ways of coexisting, but North American plants have not had the centuries necessary to adapt. Worse, even if knapweed is physically eradicated, soil toxicity remains.

These examples show that each invasive species is a unique problem. Not only do invasives change vegetation communities, but they have varied detrimental effects on hydrology, soil erosion and sedimentation, nutrient cycling, and wildfire susceptibility.[101] Remedies require both ecological and historical knowledge, and clear evaluation of environmental and economic damage. Climate change may favor some invasive species and curb others. Species like tamarisk and knapweed are truly destructive to existing ecosystems, not just a threat to some romantic concept of nature. As noted above, "invasiveness" or any substitute term applies to no more than 10 percent of non-native species: those capable of abruptly and drastically reducing communities that have coevolved high levels of diversity and interdependence.

Today, however, responses to invasive species are undergoing forced changes, for two reasons. The changes in plant hardiness zones, as well as extreme weather, that appear to be inherent in climate change are forcing many of us to the position that any plant is better than none. No matter that coevolved plant communities provide ecosystem services with highly effective synergies; as regional conditions destabilize, we may have no choice but to accept the unintended monocultures that invasive species tend to produce. Second, the cost and complexity of removing the most aggressive imported species are vast today, and likely to become even less feasible if the economy is undermined either by climate disruption or by attempts to defund climate-related programs. Conversely, carbon sequestration may generate an entirely new source of funding for vegetation restoration.

Since the 1996 strategy was released, federal, state, and local agencies have been attempting to control invasive species. The US Forest Service, the National Park Service, and the Natural Resources Conservation Service have their own programs. ASLA has a National Policy Statement on Non-native Invasive Species on its website.

Removing invasive plants has not been without controversies. Although control of human-introduced invasive *animals* is widespread and based on exactly the same principles, part of the public has a much harder time accepting that plants can be considered undesirable. Except for obvious threats like Kudzu and Porcelain Berry, "aggressiveness" or "destructiveness" are not nearly as obvious in plants as in animals. Diseases that invasive plants might spread are never as frightening as animal diseases threatening livestock or human health, though they should be, given their ability to wipe out monoculture crops. Plants, to many people, are just green backdrop; any species will do.

A prime example of this dilemma was a raging controversy over proposed restoration of oak savannah and tallgrass prairie near Chicago around 1996.[102] The restoration would have removed some areas of naturalized—that is, human-introduced—forest, dominated by sugar maple and the impenetrable invasive shrub European Buckthorn. Thanks in good part to sensationalist press coverage by writers whose biological knowledge was pitiful,[103] the public attacked the restoration process and eventually stopped it.

This is clearly not an issue this book can resolve. However, design and construction professionals involved with landscape sustainability in any form, but especially with site restoration, need to be aware of the potential for such controversies. Approach restoration via community-based planning, educating the public about benefits of restoration and problems of invasive plants, and listening carefully to what they value about both native and non-native landscapes. The pressing need to increase vegetative cover as a brake on climate change (see p. 20) is influencing restoration processes and politics. Ability to sequester carbon gives an objective measure for restoration cost-benefit decisions. Careful analysis might favor leaving non-native woods alone; planting native vegetation; or planting whatever species are available—probably decided case by case.

Figure 2.17   The curving floodplain (center right) of this New Mexico river has lost all native vegetation to two invasives, Russian Olive and Salt Cedar. (*Photo:* Kim Sorvig.)

Age, species type, growth rate, and (probably) degree to which a planting fits the web of ecosystem interconnections are all likely to affect carbon uptake. Restoration of self-sustaining forests should get a major boost from this concern, but the crystal ball is down today.

The remainder of this section discusses practical issues involved in controlling invasive plants and restoring native vegetation. Landscape designers and nursery operators will probably see more bans on some invasive ornamental plants.[104] Design and construction professionals concerned with sustainability can expect to see removal of invasives and reintroduction of native species as a new source of work, requiring new knowledge and practices.

Removing invasive plants is hard work. One mower manufacturer advertises a list of "the Toughest Weeds in America." Of these, fully 50 percent were introduced from Asia or Europe, deliberately transported outside their original range.[105]

Invasive plants can either cause or result from site damage, and they figure prominently as targets of restoration projects. (For discussion of what constitutes a "native," and how they are used in new planting, see "What Is a Native?," p. 172.) Invasion by weedy plants often indicates other disturbance, such as overgrazing, soil erosion, declining water table, or pollution. Correcting these problems is essential to restoring healthy plant communities. Some invasives, however, actively displace all other species and must be physically removed before the soil or desirable plants have any chance of recovery.

Conventional plant removal, called "grubbing," tends to be hit or miss, the largest plants ripped out with heavy equipment or sawed down. Eliminating invasive plants is not so simple: these species are among the world's most vigorous. Many can re-sprout from a small piece of root left behind in the soil, or multiply explosively from a few seeds. Ridding an area of invasives may require careful hand labor, such as forking the soil, to remove roots or tubers. Some invasives can be eliminated by changing soil conditions to favor native plants, requiring unusually careful analysis of soil nutrients and knowledge of plant metabolism. Controlled burning or flooding may be part of a strategy for "plant regime change," but carry their own risks and limitations.

In the case of truly damaging invasives, selective use of herbicides may be essential. (Some federal attempts to eradicate invasives have "crop-dusted" with herbicides, both ineffective and dangerous.) Workers on selective-removal projects will need to be familiar with advanced techniques of herbicide application, such as ultra-low-volume targeted application. Considerable plant identification skill will be necessary. Full eradication of invasive species often requires repeat visits in different growing seasons. Most of these practices are unfamiliar to conventional landscape crews.

Replanting diverse and appropriate native plant cover also requires new skills and knowledge. While horticultural plants are commonly selected because they transplant or propagate easily, native plants demand a much broader range of nursery skills. For example, many natives can grow only in cooperation with specific soil organisms. Regional native plant societies often have excellent information on propagating and planting native species.

In contrast to horticultural care for *individual* plants, native plant restoration usually involves management of *communities*, and of *succession*. A plant community is a group of species that grow closely and codependently together, usually supporting an identifiable animal community. Every plant community undergoes succession, a series of changes in the composition of the community over time. Succession is considered to "start" from bare ground, whether exposed by natural events like fires or landslides, or cleared by humans. Small nonwoody plants usually pioneer bare ground, especially on poor soils. Over time, these are crowded out by shrubs, small trees, and, eventually (if soil fertility, water, and sun permit), by forest. Ecologists originally considered the forest or other "climax community" as the end of succession, but more recent work shows that succession is cyclically set back a stage, or even restarted, on a given site. This idea is extremely useful in site management.

The stages of succession (for example, the change from meadow to shrubland) are fairly distinct for most regional vegetation. Each stage requires certain conditions before it can develop and can be set back by other conditions. As an example, for woodlands to take over from shrubs, a high level of organic matter is often required, left in the soil by earlier meadow and shrubland plants. Many tree species germinate only in shade, which must be provided by their shrubby forerunners in succession. Thus, shade and organic soil might be human *management strategies* for hastening succession toward its forested phase. Similarly, changing soil pH, or burning a meadow annually, can "set back" succession, so that woody plants cannot occupy meadow territory. In fact, these ways of managing succession were widely used by pre-agricultural cultures, for example, burning the Great Plains to favor grass for the buffalo.

Some stages of succession are more desirable, socially, than others: many people favor meadows and woods over the big-shrub stage called "oldfield." It is crucial to note that, although native shrubs may be "invaders" in a native meadow, this is an entirely different process than invasion of an ecosystem by imported species. As just outlined, native invaders are frequently set back by natural disasters, or by aging of the community; in the process, other native species have their day again. When imported invasives that have few natural enemies take over, all other plants may be permanently suppressed, to the point of extinction. For example, the floodplain in Figure 2.17 will never see native cottonwoods again unless massive human effort eradicates the imported Tamarisk and Russian Olive that have overrun it.

Professional restoration skills, including work with native plants, are likely to be in demand as sustainability grows in importance. For most designers and con-

tractors, collaboration with a native-plant nursery is the most practical route to this knowledge.

Follow Field-based Planting Patterns

Restoration planting is best based on *patterns* of plant growth that occur naturally in the region. Natural plant patterns are often seen as random, disorderly, and too irregular to reproduce (compare issues in landform grading, p. 101). In addition, many designers, influenced by avant-garde artistic theories, have developed deep-seated prejudice against any "mimicry of nature." As discussed in "Sustainability, Substance, and Style," pp. 28, nature mimicry *as cosmetics* over socially objectionable structures is a questionable practice. Practical experience, however, indicates that *pattern* is as important to long-term health of plant communities as species composition, soil condition, or microclimate.[106] In site restoration, by definition, getting the pattern right is fundamental.

Leslie Sauer, in her book on forest restoration, *The Once and Future Forest*, urges, "Plant in patterns that you have observed on the site or in analogous habitats."[107] Sauer and her colleague at Andropogon, Carol Franklin, have for years taught a simple method: field-sketched mini maps showing growth patterns of regional trees and shrubs. Selecting a little-disturbed grove of trees, pace off distances and draw, on graph paper, a roughly scaled plan of the major plants. The plan is like a designer's planting plan, but derived from naturally occurring patterns. It should show approximate trunk size of each tree and a dotted line representing the canopy—which will seldom, if ever, be perfectly round, because trees growing in groups compete for space and sunlight. A file of such sketches is a model on which to base landscape plantings. Computer modeling of succession, using agent-based or fractal methods, could also simulate regional patterns (p. 60). Used this way, naturalistic patterns are not greenwash but are critical to survival and ecological function of plantings.

Construction professionals and nursery employees are frequently responsible for laying out planting plans on site. Conventional attitudes treat accurate planting layout as optional, "close enough for convenience." For sustainable construction, careful adherence to well-patterned plans is a must. Although it is easier to locate and measure points along straight lines, planting crews need to relearn skills of laying out irregular, but not random, patterns. Baseline-and-offset measurement is one such skill. Some GPS units can be programmed to signal when the user reaches a known location, making pattern layout accurate and simple.

If You Mess It Up, Put It Back

About thirty miles east of Phoenix, US Highway 60 was a winding mountain road that killed people. About 2009, AZDOT decided it had to be upgraded to a four-lane divided highway where it crossed Gonzales Pass.[108] Two-thirds of the project ran through Tonto National Forest, meaning US Forest Service viewshed protection goals were important. The resulting project is an example of Context-Sensitive Design (see p. 240), but also involves a rather common reason for site restoration: what construction messes up has to be put back.

The project has a lot to teach about how to do naturalistic restoration design well, and even more about why that effort is worthwhile.

Landscape architects were involved, unusually, from the conceptual design stage, by a very collaborative and forward-thinking team of highway engineers. The landscape architects promoted the concept of landform grading (see p. 101), modeling these designs in 3D to get public input but also to communicate with the engineers and equipment operators. They also GPS inventoried over 7,000 of the site's large cacti, including the iconic saguaros, noting each plant's health and suitability for transplanting along with an exact location. These plants were individually labeled and moved to a holding nursery. So were nearly 30,000 smaller plants, whose existing density was tallied. Detailed conceptual planting patterns were drawn up, and once the road was completed, over 35,000 transplants went back onto the freshly graded slopes.

AZDOT has developed an unusually progressive attitude toward and process for roadside planting, in part because Arizona's native species are so emblem-

atic. Also driven by decreased funding, they have moved away from horticultural roadsides to the type of accurately naturalistic restoration used on US 60. If the cost is challenged by legislators or the public, AZDOT staff have figures to defend their approach. An already-established local plant is the most resource-efficient planting of all, and holds soil, as does landform grading. By contrast, almost every storm erodes conventional slopes, costing AZDOT $10,000 per event, minimum, in cleanup; one complete slope failure cost $125,000. Native plants, too, outcompete tumbleweeds, which are a maintenance issue as well as an accident hazard. All in all, naturalistic design in these situations is no decorative frill; it provides ecosystem services that benefit AZDOT and the public in financial terms, as well as maintaining the scenic beauty that is financially and culturally important to this desert state.

Match Plants to Restoration Purposes

In restoration work, plants serve both general purposes of stabilizing and enriching soil, and more specific purposes like reattracting wildlife or processing toxic soil materials.

PLANTS FOR WILDLIFE RESTORATION

Reintroducing wildlife is a frequent motive for land restoration. Plants and wildlife in any region are a co-evolved community, depending on one another for survival. Some plants (or their fruits), however, may attract wildlife *undesirable* to people, either pests, like rats, or desirable animals (such as bears) too wild to coexist well at close quarters with humans.

For wildlife restoration, plant species and patterns must match animal preferences. A simple and well-documented example: the three North American bluebird species are attracted to sassafras, cherry, dogwood, and juniper trees. Bluebirds are reluctant to nest unless surrounded by a clearing nearly one hundred feet across, which forms a barrier to their most aggressive competitor, the house wren.[109] Thus, a large, dense *grove* of their favorite species would fail to attract nesting bluebirds, while a *single tree* planted in a meadow might succeed.

Restoration projects intended to attract wildlife must be designed with detailed knowledge of the whole community and consideration for human impact. Constructing such landscapes offers unique challenges. Designer, contractor, scientific specialists, and client must work closely to achieve success.

Phytoremediation for Brownfields Cleanup

Correctly chosen, plants can be active workers in remediating many kinds of pollution. This approach is called phytoremediation. It has great but largely untapped potential for hundreds of thousands of brownfields that litter the North American landscape.

In innovative phytoremediation efforts, the United States lags far behind Europe. Early work was actually catalyzed by environmental artists like New York sculptor Mel Chin. In 1989 Chin teamed with US Department of Agriculture agronomist Rufus Chaney, who was experimenting with pollutant-absorbing plants. Because little was then known about increasing plants' uptake of toxins, Chaney suggested that Chin's artwork be configured as a scientific testing ground.

Chin's site was Pig's Eye landfill (St. Paul MN), contaminated with heavy metals. Here Chin and his team created Revival Field, a 3,600-square-foot garden. The design was a circle within a square.[110] Walkways formed an X, outlining ninety-six test plots with various plant species. Three years of digging up plants each spring to analyze their metal content showed Chaney that Alpine Pennycress was best at extracting zinc and cadmium. In 1993 Chin and Chaney collaborated again in Palmerton PA, and Chin started a third such garden in Baltimore in 1998.[111] Other artists, such as Stacy Levy, have created beautiful and educational artworks that also rehabilitate toxic sites.

Where artists or landscape professionals aren't involved, cleanup is typically viewed as an engineering problem, ignoring biological or horticultural possibilities. Some approaches that have been tried on brownfields are not just prosaic, but brutal—sealing the entire site with paving, encasing the soil in concrete, or vitrifying it (turning it to glass with high-voltage electrical probes). Trucking the soil off to be cleansed by chemical and mechanical processes and returned, even if ef-fective, drastically raises remediation costs, economic and environmental. These brute-force "solutions" often cost society all future productivity of the land.

For some situations, harsh engineering methods are unavoidable. Everywhere else, phytoremediation offers significant benefits to the environment, to the public, and to the landscape industry, which is well qualified to learn such work.

The basic concept of phytoremediation is familiar in constructed wetlands for water treatment (see p. 228). In wetlands, aquatic plants take up pollutants and cleanse water, often outperforming conventional treatment. Pollutants typically remain in the plants, periodically harvested as toxins build up in their tissues. In many cases, the toxic materials have industrial value and can be reclaimed. Constructed wetlands could, in fact, be called aquatic phytoremediation, because the same processes are at work.

Today phytoremediation is being developed for a range of substances considerably more toxic than the stormwater or sewage typically treated in wetlands. Briefly, phytoremediation is:

- useful against a wide variety of pollutants: crude oil, solvents, pesticides, landfill leachates, and such metals as chromium, mercury, and lead
- generally best for relatively low concentrations in upper soil layers
- solar powered, unlike energy-intensive mechanical methods
- far cheaper to install, maintain, and operate than other decontamination methods, although slower ($80 per square yard; $1,000 to $6,000 per acre; 4 to 32 percent of other methods[112])
- aesthetically pleasing.

New species are constantly emerging for phytoremediation. Tumbleweed and Jimsonweed take up radioactive waste; Watercress has been genetically engineered to detect land mines. Salt-tolerant species might remediate soils made saline by desert irrigation.[113] "Phytomining" even uses plants to extract gold and nickel from marginal ores.

As of 2017, it appears that research on phytoremediation has focused on identifying new species to deal with more pollutants. The use of "trans-species," or genetically modified, plants has been a subject of testing as well as of public controversy; it may be more appropriate to modify plants for remediation than for crops. The Timbre Project (Tailored Improvement of Brownfield Regeneration in Europe, under EU auspices)[114] has done considerable work on phytoremediation, but concludes that the techniques are too slow for many uses, ineffectively used due to uninformed expectations, and best suited to very large-scale remediation projects, such as mining districts or former military sites. This pessimistic view is not shared by everyone, however, and phytoremediation continues to be part of the site restorer's toolkit.

"Public acceptance of a phytoremediation project on a site can be very high, in part because of the park-like aesthetics, shade, dust control, and bird and wild-life habitat," notes Steve Rock, an engineer with the EPA's National Risk Management Laboratory. "There is a widespread intuitive agreement that a site covered in vegetation is less hazardous than a bare abandoned lot. When the plants are growing the site is apparently being cleaned."[115] Of course, healthy growth is not a perfect indicator of improved health and must be backed by instrumented monitoring.

Phytoremediation operates through three principal mechanisms: by extracting, containing, or degrading contaminants.[116]

Extraction takes up and accumulates contaminants in shoots and leaves. (Phytoremediation experts like to compare plants to solar-powered pumps bringing contaminants out of the soil.) Harvested, the plant removes the contaminants from the site. Plant tissue may be dried, burned, or composted under controlled conditions, sometimes reclaiming the extracted chemical. *Phytovolatilization* extracts pollutants from soil or water, converting them into gaseous form that breaks down safely in air.

Containment uses plants to immobilize contaminants permanently. Certain trees, for example, can sequester large concentrations of metals in their roots. Although harvesting and carting away whole trees is impractical, the contaminants at least no longer circulate within the environment. *Hydraulic containment* uses deep-rooted (phreatophytic) species to keep contaminated groundwater from spreading, while *phytostabilization* keeps soil contaminants from moving through the soil.

Figure 2.18a, b Phytoremediation of a petroleum-contaminated site in Wisconsin. Photo (a) shows willows at planting; (b), after one year. (*Project:* Geraghty and Miller. *Photo:* Eric Carman.)

Degradation breaks down or digests contaminants —principally hydrocarbons and other organic compounds—so that they are no longer toxic. Degradation often occurs in the root zone through microbial or fungal interactions, chemical effects of roots, or enzymes they exude. Degradation also occurs inside the plant itself. Degradation may also convert a chemical from a water- or fat-soluble form (easily taken up by animals and people) to insoluble forms that pose little danger.

Phytoremediation is no cure-all, nor effective on all sites. Besides limits noted above, most phytoremediation plants also seem to require a soil-chelating chemical (one that binds metals to itself, allowing plant uptake). Recent research, however, isolated a gene that allows *Arabidopsis thaliana* (a relative of Alpine Pennycress) to produce its own chelating chemical—and could be bred into other plants.[117]

A relatively new science, phytoremediation still invokes suspicion from some regulators. Certainly, valid questions have yet to be answered. What happens in the food chain if wildlife consume leaves or shoots of phytoremediation plants? How is air quality affected if plants pull pollutants out of soil and release them via evapotranspiration? More research is needed to answer such questions.

Alan Christensen, a landscape architect from American Fork UT who has studied brownfield remediation, raises another question: "What if you could plant trees to get rid of the contamination, and at the same time use the trees as landscape buffers or to create shade for parking lots and buildings?" Despite one National Park Service pilot project reportedly begun in Charleston SC, this idea has yet to be implemented, and results would be very long term.

The number of plants that can remediate a specific contaminant is limited; there may not be *any* frost-hardy shade tree with yellow summer flowers that can degrade cadmium. Capacities and hazards differ for every contaminant or plant species. Examine the possibilities for permanent phytoremediation doubling as parks.

Bioremediation

A related strategy is bioremediation: use of soil bacteria and microorganisms to cleanse pollution from soil or water. Like phytoremediation, it is a low-tech, environmentally sound approach that harnesses a benign force of nature—microorganism enzymes—to biodegrade pollution.

Bioremediation is already a mainstream approach to toxic site cleanup. It is widely used on petroleum spills and has proved successful against toluene solvent, naphthalene moth repellent, and pentachlorophenol fungicide and wood preservative. Especially if a chemical resembles natural substances, there is a good chance that a microbe can be found to metabolize it. Governmental agencies and for-profit consultants are expanding bioremediation capacities.

Petroleum leakage from old, corroded underground storage tanks is a widespread environmental problem. Minnesota's DOT uses bioremediation for routine remediation of gasoline, diesel, and used motor oil, according to senior environmental engineer Brian Kamnikar. Indigenous soil bacteria treat petroleum as a free lunch, a source of energy. MNDOT accelerates natural biodegradation by mounding up contaminated soil ("biomounds") and adding nutrients (typically sheep manure). MNDOT adds moistened wood chips to reduce the soil's density, provide moisture, and keep oxygen flowing, thus promoting aerobic bacterial activity. MNDOT has successfully reused decontaminated soil, after testing, as topsoil on highway-construction projects—completing a cycle that turns a problem back into a resource.[118]

At the federal level the EPA is actively promoting bioremediation and has published field-testing results. The National Ground Water Association offers courses in what it refers to as "natural attenuation" of soil and groundwater pollution. Bioremediation consultants can be found via the Internet; the Web has played a significant role in the growth of this specialty.

Bioremediation is not a panacea for all hazardous wastes. For example, in mixed wastes, heavy metals may kill bacteria that could metabolize the organic pollutants. Bioremediation is particularly valuable for dispersed, dilute soil contamination. In soils that air cannot readily penetrate, anaerobic conditions can hinder the process; relatively simple aeration methods, such as using blowers or compressors to pump oxygen into the ground, may enhance bioremediation.[119]

Perhaps the greatest appeal of bioremediation is its low cost. According to one summary on the Internet, "The cost of restoring the burgeoning global inventory of contaminated ecosystems is virtually incalculable. . . . Bioremediation . . . is a safe, effective, and economic alternative to traditional methods of remediation."[120] Like many sustainable strategies, bioremediation is based on services that the environment has been providing to humans throughout history. A 1999 study found that bacteria living in lake- and stream-bottom mud can remove 35–85 percent of two carcinogenic water pollutants.[121] As emphasized in the section on soil preservation (p. 70), microorganisms exist by the billions in soil and are among the best-known defenses against pollution. Bioremediation is simply advancing human ability to make specific use of what the Earth has been doing for eons.

Restore Forests and Coexist with Wildfire

Until very recently, wildfire was not a landscape professional's concern. Several factors have combined to make it one today. Homes in wild places like forests and mountains are increasingly popular and feasible. Population growth is pushing development into new lands, some covered with "fire-adapted" vegetation that *requires* periodic burning to reproduce or compete with other species. Flight from cities perceived as dangerous and suburbs perceived as boring has motivated a new back-to-nature exodus. Instant communication, telecommuting, and four-wheel drive allow living comfortably in the wilds. Around and even within many cities and towns, residential development is colliding with relatively undeveloped forests, creating what is called the Urban Wildland Interface (UWI) Zone or, more bluntly, the Wildfire Danger Zone.[122]

The second factor in making wildfire a landscape issue is what ecologist George Wuerthner calls "a century of failed forest policy."[123] This policy, with Smokey the Bear as its mascot, suppressed all fires to protect timber interests, scenic parks, small towns, and a few homesteads. Suppression, however, produced overly dense stands of small trees that, when they do burn, do so explosively. Years of drought have dangerously amplified this situation.

Thus, exurban development has collided not just with forest, but with unhealthy, tinderbox forest (Figure 2.19). It is for this reason that wildfire is a landscape-scale restoration issue.

In 2000 a spectacular wildfire started when a National Park Service preventive burn got out of control. Public outrage focused on the federal government, which predictably threw money and regulations at the problem.[124] These regulations make wildfire an issue for landscape professionals, especially when trying to work sustainably.

Regulations imposed in UWI areas typically focus first and foremost on vegetation clearance, which fire activists call "fuel reduction." These regulations typically require removing 60 to 80 percent of vegetation for at least 30 feet around every structure, and in some cases over *600* feet. The only plants allowed are those considered fire resistant, almost always nonnative, irrigation-dependent species. Similar clearing is required for 10 feet on either side of driveways, which must often be widened to urban standards: 20 feet wide and all weather, which for practical purposes means paved. These regulations are often retroactive, requiring removal of existing landscape plantings. In some jurisdictions, authorities have the power to carry out clearance and add the bill to property taxes; a citizen can theoretically lose ownership of property for not clearing it.

The federal government offers millions of dollars for state and local fire departments that institute such policies, and a massively funded publicity campaign called "Firewise." As *Audubon* magazine put it, "The press and politicians called fire season 2000 'a natural disaster.' The fires were natural, but the 'disaster' was how much the United States spent to fight them."[125] San Diego landscape architect Jon Powell declares that in many places "the fire marshal has become the only land-use authority."

Clearly, such regulations severely limit or prohibit many standard landscape practices. Of much greater concern is the sustainability effect of so much clearance and prohibition of native vegetation. Typical clearance requirements, applied to a 2,500-square-foot residence and quarter-mile-long rural driveway, removes most vegetation from over 1.25 acres.[126] In an average-sized county, total annual fire clearance could be over 45 *square miles*, or nearly 3 percent of total land area.[127] This amount of clearing would generate enough greenwaste to cover an acre five feet deep (20,000 tons or more), much of it hauled to landfills.

The unintended consequences of Firewise clearance requirements are major:

- increased runoff and topsoil loss, and with it, loss of organic soil and soil water retention capacity
- exposure of soil to direct sun, with heating and drying (and further soil loss)
- changes in microclimate that trend toward warming and drought—and thus toward *more frequent and more intense wildfires.*

In fact, "fuel reduction" is cumulatively the same as deforestation, and has the same effects on regional and global climate (see p. 20 and Figures 0.4 and 0.5). Clearance aimed at fire prevention contributes to drought, making wildfires worse.

Figure 2.19   In fire-adapted ecosystems, structures must adapt. Plastic fencing melted and the house (right rear) narrowly escaped (San Diego area). (*Photo:* Kim Sorvig.)

What should landscape professionals do? Primarily, work to create regionally specific and well-reasoned fire policies.

• Emphasize that fire policy must be *coordinated* with other environmental management: stormwater and erosion, water quality, soil health, water conservation, restoration of wooded areas and grasslands, and reduction of greenwaste in landfills.

• Object strongly to fire codes imported word for word from other regions. The attempt to apply pine-forest fire codes to chaparral was one reason that 2002 fires in southern California did extreme damage despite code-compliant clearance.[128]

• Explain that clearance is ineffective against wind-blown flames and flying embers. US Forest Service fire researcher Jack Cohen states that "the evidence suggests that wildland fuel reduction for

Figure 2.20 The "Firewise" focus on clearing fire-adapted forests merely gives a false sense of security. This sign barely avoided being burned down in the 2002 San Diego–area conflagrations. (*Photo:* Kim Sorvig.)

reducing home losses may be inefficient and ineffective."[129]

- Recognize that vehicles and power tools frequently spark wildfires; consider shared transport in UWI areas. Ensure all developments have two access/escape routes. Use single-lane-with-pullout designs on private driveways to provide safe access while minimizing runoff. Push fire departments to use the smallest reasonable vehicles.

- Where vegetation clearance is essential, be sure cleared plant material is returned to the soil by burning, chipping, or composting. Alternatively, use goats or other browsers that eat young woody material, recycling plants as manure.

- Be very cautious of proposals to use thinnings commercially, because this permanently removes large amounts of organic material. Commercial use of small-diameter thinnings can benefit local economies, but only if managed for long-term sustainability.

- Similarly, "salvage logging" (removing standing dead trees after a fire) has long been justified as reducing future fire danger. A June 2007 study shows clearly that this is not the case: areas salvage-cut and replanted burn up to 61 percent more intensely in subsequent fires than areas left to natural regrowth.[130]

- Where possible, design firebreaks for whole communities or clusters of houses, based on healthy grove-and-meadow patterns. Wetlands, sports fields, and other features can do double duty as community firebreaks.

- Work toward restoration of the health of whole forests, including periodic fires.[131] "Mimic nature's fire," in both vegetation patterns and planned fire schedules.[132] When fires occur at regular intervals, they tend to be less intense, to burn in patchwork patterns that increase species and habitat diversity, and to leave older trees as seed sources. Less intense fires are also far easier to control.

- Work to focus protection policy on fire-resistant *buildings*, especially metal or tile roofs, which are known to be far more effective than clearance. A nonflammable roof increases a structure's odds of surviving wildfire from 19 percent (no preventive measures) to 70 percent. Vegetative clearance can at best add another 20 percent and often fails to add any safety. Fire-resistant glass and paints are increasingly available. Not only materials but design details offer important protection against fire.

Along with fire-resistant construction, a nontoxic spray-on gel called Barricade has been available since about 2000 that will prevent structures and even trees from igniting. A liquid concentrate is applied about one-quarter inch thick with a garden-hose sprayer, without need for special protective clothing. Demonstration videos show it stopping half a plywood shed, and one of two adjacent evergreen trees, from burning. After the fire, the gel rinses off. The company states that it will not damage sound paint, and can actually clean old paint. The required 30 gallons per minute (gpm) is more than some wells can supply; some users have installed secondary systems for firefight-ing. The concentrate has a guaranteed three-year shelf life, and will last longer if vigorously shaken every six months.[133]

Wuerthner points out that fires are like floods: many small ones occur each year with little damage, but the "100-year fire" is also inevitable in fire-adapted ecosystems. In a given year, one or two "megafires" account for 90 percent or more of acreage and structures burned, says Wuerthner.[134] Policy and design for development in fire-adapted landscapes need to acknowledge this distinction. Controlling the many small fires is feasible. Stopping megafires is possible only, if at all, with what a contributor to Wuerthner's book calls the "Fire-Military-Industrial Complex."

Because clearance is costly, environmentally destructive, and often entirely ineffective against wildfire, landscape professionals should resist fire ordinances that rely primarily or exclusively on vegetation removal. Ultimately, clearance is politically expedient, giving the appearance of preventive action, but creates a false sense of security. (See Figure 2.20.) Fire-resistant construction plus forest restoration is by far the more sustainable goal, and one that landscape professionals should advocate.

Subtopics and Search Terms for Principle 2: Heal Injured Sites

Note: Subtopics are also useful search terms; add "innovation" or "controversy" to search terms as appropriate.

Site restoration
Search terms: ecological restoration | | site contamination OR cleanup | | historic preservation | | landscape ecology | | historical ecology

Brownfields
Search terms: brownfields | | site contamination OR cleanup | | greyfields | | Superfund | | pollutants

Grading
Search terms: land grading | | grading drainage | | grading landscape

Compost and mulch
Search terms: compost | | mulch | | vermicompost | | organic garden | | compost tea

Biosolids
Search terms: biosolids | | composted OR treated "sewage sludge"

Soils
Search terms: soil | | soil profile | | soil science | | soil testing

Soil amendments and manufactured soil
Search terms: soil amendments || soil enhancer || manufactured soil || soil microbes

Phytoremediation
Search terms: bioremediation || phytoremediation || soil mycorrhizae

Bioremediation
Search terms: bioremediation || phytoremediation

Wildfire
Search terms: UWI || WUI || Urban Wildland Interface || Wildfire || Firewise

Resource List:

Links to information sources related to this chapter are posted at http://islandpress.org/sustainable-landscape-construction

Principle 3: Favor Living, Flexible Materials

He that plants trees loves others beside himself.
—*Thomas Fuller, 1732*

Plants are the only truly productive organisms on Earth. Their ability to photosynthesize—the original solar-powered production—is the ultimate source of all food and fuel on which humans, and all other animals, rely.[1] As the Bible puts it, "All flesh is grass."[2] It often seems, however, that we as modern humans are busily forgetting our debt to the plant kingdom—biting the frond that feeds us.

This book does not deal with agriculture or forestry or "economic botany" as such, but it is critical to remember that landscape-making depends on plants for far more than decorative specimens. The ecosystem services that plants provide are, without exaggeration, the inescapable foundation of human civilization. The list of these services (see Principle 11) is often quoted, but humans remain careless toward individual trees and whole forests. This raises the question of whether the significance of those services has really sunk in to human consciousness.

Without vegetative food and fuel, there would be no society within which landscape-makers could practice design, and no materials with which to work. Plants play a major part in creating soil, as well as stabilizing it against erosion by water or wind; together, plants and soil sequester significant amounts of carbon. Coevolved communities of plants support biodiversity of animals both terrestrial and aquatic. Vegetation cools the land surface by shade and evapotranspiration. Plants are remarkably effective at purifying air, water, and soil, even neutralizing many recent, toxic human inventions.

To oversimplify only a little, the "ecological crisis" has largely resulted from ignoring the limits on the

Discussed in This Chapter
Controlling slope erosion with the strength of living plants.
Using "greenwalls" to retain slopes and clothe buildings in growth.
Revitalizing wasted acreage on the skyline with planted "greenroofs."
Designing and building appropriate structures for sustainable planting.
Selection, substitution, and handling to ensure plant survival.
Native plants for sustainability.

productivity of the world's vegetation. Sustainability (by its many names) can legitimately be considered a quest to restore that productivity, often using plants in the process.

The ability of the world's plants to sustain life has been impacted directly by human activities that decrease the number and diversity of plants (clearing, grazing, and monoculture cropping). Their life-sustaining capacities have also been strained, indirectly, by our releasing substances toxic to plants, and concentrating benign substances until they become harmful. With nearly 40 percent of the land surface of the Earth converted to croplands, pasture, and logging, the cumulative impact of vegetation reduction is massive.[3]

Thus, in addition to practical and local purposes like reducing erosion and cooling buildings, the planting strategies that follow share with the previous chapters a larger goal: simply revegetating as much of the planet as possible with these astonishing life-forms on which all earthly life depends.

Highlight the Benefits of Vegetation

Landscape professionals can get so caught up in designing, constructing, or maintaining outdoor spaces for human activities that trees and other vegetation almost become secondary. Drought, massive forest die-offs, and the need to sequester carbon are primary arguments for keeping the value of vegetation front and center.

The financial value of a tree can be estimated in various ways. Table 3.1 (p. 158) shows one approach. The US Forest Service Climate Change Resource Center offers a large number of tools to calculate energy savings and carbon reductions from trees, which can then be translated into monetary values.[4] A 2012 study published by the American Chemical Society found that pollutant reduction by vegetation was eight times greater than previously estimated (40 percent reduction of NO_x and 60 percent for particulate matter; earlier studies estimated less than 5 percent reductions of these pollutants).[5] Harder to measure are psychosocial benefits. Using electroencephalographs, one team tested subjects' brain responses when walking among trees versus walking in both sterile and stimulating but un-treed locations. The walk among trees produced significantly more positive states of mind.[6] Residents in treed neighborhoods produce babies with higher birth weights, have lower asthma rates, and experience less crime; explaining these correlations is still difficult.[7]

Strangely, despite all these benefits, some urbanites actively hate trees. The MillionTreesNYC program has had dozens of its plantings pulled up or cut down. Interviewees (apart from those who just hate any governmental activity) rejected trees for reasons from emotional (it would remind them of a deceased spouse) to selfishly pragmatic (they don't want to maintain it) to ill-informed (they see it as a waste of tax money that should go to graffiti removal, etc.) Sadly, all these rationales leave health and ecosystem service benefits out altogether.[8]

Vegetation, of course, has another benefit: providing food. Informal back-lot gardens, Permaculture, and a concept called CPULs (Continuous Productive Urban Landscapes) integrate croplands into places that would conventionally be either "landscaped" or ignored. These are powerful tools for diminishing hunger, undoing "food deserts," and empowering people. While some techniques used in food-producing landscapes are discussed in this book, agricultural strategies aren't covered in detail, not because they lack value but because they are a huge topic in their own right, and well covered elsewhere.

Hold Slopes in Place with BTEC— Biotechnical Erosion Control

A quiet revolt against conventional approaches to erosion control came of age at the turn of the twentieth century, known as biotechnical erosion control (BTEC) or soil bioengineering.[9] During the following two decades, the revolt has continued to spread.

BTEC combines living and inert structures into something stronger and more flexible than either. These *living structures* reinforce vulnerable interfaces between soil and water, especially on steep slopes, stream banks, and shorelines. Despite well-established use in Europe, and publication of guidelines[10] by both the USDA and the Army Corps of Engineers in the 1990s, BTEC was slow to take off in the United States. In researching the first edition, it was difficult to find a dozen practicing experts. There are now established and new firms, books and best-practice guidelines for landscapes as diverse as Nepal and the Caribbean, even specialized software. Perhaps most encouraging, state and local agencies have Web pages dedicated to biotechnical approaches. At least part of the official world is recognizing these methods, in addition to or instead of conventional rigid engineering.

The *techniques* of BTEC are mature and well tested, and the basics are unlikely to undergo major change. Basic knowledge of these methods belongs in the repertoire of every landscape professional, although a specialist consultant should almost always lead any BTEC project.

Rigid structures of concrete and steel, the conventional erosion technology of choice, are *so* twentieth century—and barely a century old. By contrast, BTEC is a modern adaptation of age-old "green" technology. For centuries before the industrial revolution, in cultures as ancient as the Inca, constructed banks were held in place by grading and terracing, by pervious walls of local stone, and by dense-rooted plantings.[11] These tested systems were rejected by conventional engineering, insistent that rigid structures were always cheaper, more durable, safer, and mathematically more predictable.

Detailed observation has shown, however, that these conventional claims obscure problems *caused* by rigid erosion- and flood-control structures. Hard, engineered structures certainly have their place, but as a one-size-fits-all standard they trigger the problems they were designed to solve. Concrete ditches and pipes transform precious rainwater into a problem to be whisked away. Wherever it is shunted, stormwater becomes a concentrated and destructive force and fails to nourish the ground or replenish the water table. Hard structures, especially flood-control ditches, preempt wildlife habitat. Engineered for "safety," they traverse many cities—lifeless, armor-plated canyons, usually posted with Danger signs.

BTEC and its near relatives can also be applied to building walls and roofs, and are closely related to sustainable use of water (Principle 4). Increased acceptance of these techniques reflects a new—or renewed—respect for an essential landscape component: living vegetation.

BTEC includes a wide array of applications, almost all using certain plants' remarkable ability to sprout from freshly cut twigs stuck in soil. The most vigorous are willows, poplars, and dogwood; poplar fenceposts reliably sprout leaves. These are the live materials of BTEC. When cut, they have neither roots nor leaves, making them almost as convenient to work with as wood stakes—yet they are alive, and within days or weeks are beginning to weave new roots deeply into the soil.

In the simplest form of BTEC, live woody cuttings and branches provide both structure and growth. Mulch and natural or synthetic fabrics—geotextiles—also play a major role, preventing surface erosion un-

til cuttings leaf out. Once the cuttings take root—usually within one growing season—they provide long-term slope stability and are self-repairing and self-maintaining.

BTEC does not rule out hard structures, however. Inert structures of concrete, wood, metal, or plastic—through which plants grow and water drains gradually but freely—are also important. Greenwalls (next section) are related live-plus-hard techniques, along with a whole menu of vegetated structural approaches.

Biotechnical methods recall one of this book's themes—that many supposedly "outdated" traditional techniques warrant reexamination. Twig-and-wattling erosion control has been in use for millennia in widely different cultures. In the 1930s, Works Progress Administration (WPA) and Civilian Conservation Corps (CCC) workers repaired gullies and restored stream banks with native stone and cuttings from local plants.[12] Modern BTEC was pursued most energetically in German-speaking countries, first spreading to North America in the 1970s. Some specialized supplies for BTEC are still imported.

BTEC provides:

- a flexible, self-sustaining, self-repairing structure
- cheaper installation and maintenance than hard structures, in most cases
- greater strength than standard surface plantings, due to deep burial of cuttings, and interwoven stems, roots, and geotextiles
- a practical alternative where heavy equipment cannot be used
- wildlife habitat, air and water filtering, and other functions of plants.

Bind the Soil with Living Plants

Some common soil bioengineering techniques are:

Live stakes (sturdy cuttings an inch or more in diameter) can be driven directly into slopes with a mallet, typically two to three feet apart. Live stakes provide initial structural slope protection (similar to rebar in concrete); rooting, these systems further stabilize the soil; sprouting leaves intercept stormwater before it hits (and erodes) the ground.

Wattles and brushmattresses ("woven" pads of live branches) are staked to slopes for coverage.

Fascines (tied, linear bundles of branches or whips) are buried lengthwise in trenches along contours to reduce surface erosion and stabilize slopes. (Some companies refer to these as wattles, too, but fascine is the preferred term.)

Brushlayering places branches on excavated terraces perpendicular to contours. The terraces are backfilled with soil, covering the branches except for the tips. When the branches take root, the tips leaf out.

Live crib walls, boxlike structures of interlocking live logs, backfilled with alternating layers of soil and branch cuttings, can stabilize the toe of a slope. Roots of cuttings extend into the slope, providing structural support.

Although not strictly soil bioengineering, Land Life Company's Cocoon is a promising aid to establishing saplings in arid or harsh conditions. Made of paper pulp, the Cocoon resembles a deep baking ring-form with a cover. The seedling is placed in the central hole, inside a protective sleeve. The surrounding container is filled with six gallons of water, then covered and buried, with mycorrhizal fungi added to the soil. Moisture seeps through the biodegrading container slowly, irrigating the plant for its first year, while training roots to go deep. The Cocoon degrades into organic soil, leaving a rain-catching depression around the plant. The concept is based on clay jar plantings traditional in India. The company has installations in more than twenty countries, including monitored tests at New Mexico State University. No follow-up is required, and the company claims survival rates of 80 percent and more. Cocoons are lightweight and stackable; for small projects, they are shipped from the Netherlands, but for large reforestation works, local manufacturing is contracted.[13]

Control Surface Erosion with Mats and Mulches

New BTEC slopes need some form of cover until plants take root, either erosion-control nets, blankets, and mats, or organic mulches. Both work primarily by blunting the force of raindrops, which dig into bare soil surfaces. Both have proven effective, but mulching, in most cases, is by far cheaper. Mulch can slow runoff moving across the surface, but the structure and weight of a mat may be more effective under such conditions.

Biodegradable products are usually preferred. Typically they comprise fibers such as jute, straw, wood, excelsior, or coconut fiber (coir). Pins and stakes secure blankets to the slope; biodegradable examples are North American Green's Bio-STAKE and Eco-STAKE, made of lumber scraps. Like mulches, biodegradable mats add organic nutrients to the soil.

For extremely steep or erodible slopes, some practitioners prefer products bound together with long-lasting synthetic fibers (see project examples, below). Avoid plastic or similar meshes likely to trap birds or mammals. Biodegradable mesh could trap animals, but is easier to gnaw or break and eventually disappears.

"Landscape architects, like engineers, are too ready to use manufactured products," says John Haynes of Caltrans, a longtime BTEC practitioner. "All these products have their niche and can be very effective in the proper application; but some of them are pretty darn expensive. We need to be looking at locally available, inexpensive materials for use in erosion control." For large-scale highway-construction projects, even inexpensive blankets cost ten times as much per acre as tackified straw mulch from local sources.

Except for unusual soils or extreme conditions, consider composts, biosolids, and proprietary "soil tackifiers" applied directly to soil or mixed with straw or other fibers. Loose wood chips will protect a surface against rainfall as long as running water is not channeled under them. For erosion control, all types are usually applied as slurry, using hydro-seeding machinery.

Tackifiers made of guar gum are environmentally preferable to asphalt-based ones; asphalt's fumes are moderately toxic, and asphalt can contaminate soil. Polymer tackifiers have various formulas; each should be evaluated for biodegradability.

The many uses of compost are discussed in more detail in Principle 2. Further information on these practices is available from Caltrans.

Evaluate and Monitor Each Site Carefully

When is BTEC appropriate for a project? Landscape architect Andrea Lucas of Berkeley CA, who has

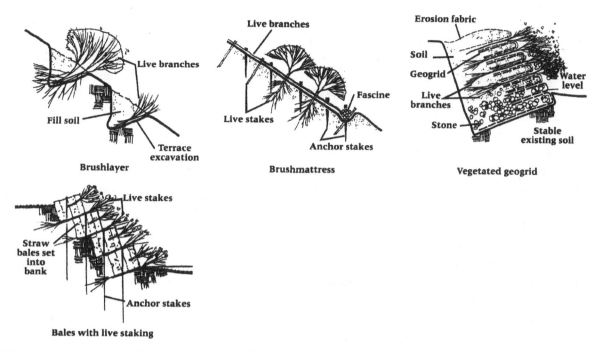

Figure 3.1   Btec holds soil with structural assemblages that later root. Correctly installed, these resilient solutions often outperform rigid structures at less cost. (*Illust.:* Craig Farnsworth, based on R. Sotir and Stan Jones.)

Figure 3.2   Lakeshore stabilization at Whiskeytown CA. Soil wraps are being constructed on top of brushlayers. (*Project:* Salix Applied Earthcare. *Photo:* John McCullah.)

Figure 3.3   Three weeks later, willow twigs are sprouting between wrapped soil layers. The willows will be at water level once the lake is refilled. (*Project:* Salix Applied Earthcare. *Photo:* John McCullah.)

wide Btec experience, recommends it for any steep slope subject to excessive runoff. "If you see a long, cut slope with rills occurring," says Lucas, "this is the perfect place to reduce runoff velocities by adding contour wattles and contour straw rolls." Hillsides already planted with standard techniques but continuing to erode are also prime candidates, as are banks of streams and lakes (p. 197). Extremely steep slopes or abrupt grade changes may require a "greenwall," the

bioengineered version of a retaining wall (see below). On extremely unstable or undercut banks, prone to collapse in what geologists call "slumping" or "mass wasting," Btec is probably not appropriate.

Lucas recalls Btec initially being presented as a foolproof miracle cure. Despite continued enthusiasm, Lucas warns against taking that view. As part of her research for a graduate degree, she visited bioengineered stream banks across California. All had eroded at least 20 percent after Btec was installed. This does not mean that Btec is invalid, says Lucas, but that it requires monitoring and maintenance for the first few years—patching unexpected gullies in particular. Follow-up makes the difference between success and failure—and increases expertise for future projects.

Btec cannot always stand alone against major off-site influences, such as expanded upstream pavement and increased runoff. Btec provides structural solutions as *part* of watershed-wide water and erosion management. Btec adds living and structural strength to eroding slopes. In addition, it slows and absorbs runoff, unlike conventionally armored slopes. Surface roughness, irregularity, and permeability relate directly to landform grading (p. 101), Permaculture (p. 205), and near-the-source solutions (p. 410). Used together, these concepts reinforce each other.

Btec is usually cheaper than hard alternatives, but more expensive than hydro-seeding. Compared to simple planting, it involves more grading, filling, or extra-deep plantings; some methods are hand-labor intensive. Where labor is scarce or high priced, Btec becomes less cost competitive. Btec is also knowledge intensive for design services and on-site supervision. Nevertheless, says Lucas, Btec "is always cheaper than building a concrete wall," and will generally outlast the wall.

To evaluate specific Btec products or approaches, observe a completed one- or two-year-old installation. Erosion-control publications, manufacturers, consultants, and agencies may provide a list of projects and contacts in your area; the federal government has sponsored hundreds of demonstration projects. Web searches make them easier to find. Examples below and in Principle 4 give some idea of the diversity of existing installations.

Many state highway departments use Btec on at least some types of work. John Haynes has used Btec techniques on many Caltrans projects and has compared various approaches on test plots. On a 1.5:1 slope with highly erodible soils near Redding CA, Haynes employed brushlayering (defined above). On bulldozed terraces, willow stems were laid twenty per yard; backfilling was also done by bulldozer.

Four weeks into this 1993 project, a major storm dumped fifteen inches of rain on the test site. Some slopes treated with erosion-control fabrics failed, but the willow cuttings held. Those slopes suffered some gullying—a problem that could have been avoided, Haynes feels, if he had specified about three times as many cuttings as were actually used. The results of Haynes's test plots are summarized in *Proceedings of the 1994 IECA Conference*, available from the International Erosion Control Association.

Brushlayering also stabilized a large mudslide on slopes from 2.5:1 to 1.5:1 near Pacifica CA, above a residential area. Andrea Lucas collaborated with Btec pioneer and author Andrew Leiser. In addition to brushlayering, Lucas planted rooted seedlings of native pine and cypress, and seeded the slope with an erosion-control mix of grasses, perennials, and annuals. Although installed during California's rainy season, the work immediately reduced sediment transport dramatically, Lucas reports, and continues to perform well.

In gullies, watercourses, and drainage channels securing fill is particularly difficult; soil tends to liquefy during storms and flow downhill. At Sanders Ranch in Moraga CA, one drainage ditch, though lined with pieces of concrete, was eroding ever deeper with each storm. Lucas began stabilizing it with "burritos" (fill soil wrapped in geotextile). At the edges of these devices, the crew buried locally gathered live willow cuttings with only the tips exposed. These quickly rooted, tying fill, geotextile, and existing subsoil together as a strong flexible channel.

Side banks were seeded with fast-growing annual grass and perennial native bunchgrass, covered with

Figure 3.4 Brushlayer installation can be done by hand or aided by equipment. (*Project and Photo:* Biohabitats Inc.)

Figure 3.5   Fabric anchored with logs, live stakes, and fast-sprouting grass, in place only a few weeks when this storm struck, survived with no losses. (*Project and Photo:* Andrea Lucas.)

geotextile blankets. Stout willow "live stakes" two to three feet deep, plus cables, held the geotextiles to the ground to withstand storm flows. Storms soon after installation are a risk that must be anticipated by design. A storm struck the Moraga project one month after installation during an El Niño winter—and the system held.

Robbin Sotir, of Marietta GA, is an active consultant, even working as a mediator where brute-concrete projects raised public outcry. She has built over 200 biotechnical projects, even in desert areas, across the United States and abroad, including a 2015 project installed, under supervision, by ninth-grade students at Walton High School, Marietta GA. Her Crestwood project in Houston TX (see Figure 3.6) is an excellent example of how BTEC combines techniques to fit a site, or even specialized conditions within a site.

At Crestwood condominiums, twenty-foot banks were eroding into Buffalo Bayou (a shipping channel leading to Houston's port). Virtually all the techniques diagrammed in Figure 3.1 were used to stabilize this bank. At the toe of the slope, rubble wrapped in erosion-control fabric provided a strong footing above and below mean water level. Above that, the main slope was held with vegetated geogrid—soil wrapped in fabric or stronger plastic grid sheets or both, with layers of branches between soil layers. Fascines and bare-root plantings were used at transitions: between rubble and geogrid, and along the top of the slope.

Carefully monitored since construction, the slope shows no sign of moving. Bayou sediment is now trapped by vegetation and deposited, gradually building even more strength.

It is too early to know how these installations fared during Hurricane Harvey—and important to remember that no human technique, including "sustainable" ones, can withstand truly extreme storms.

Even Walden Pond, ur-environmentalist Henry David Thoreau's home near Concord MA, has benefited from BTEC. Annually 80,000 visitors come to swim or sightsee. By the late 1990s the pond was suffering from severe bank erosion. Using live staking, coir mats, and cellular containment systems (see p. 146), Walker Kluesing Design Group of Cambridge MA reconstructed 3,800 feet of pond edge, bank, and path. The project won a 1998 Boston Society of Landscape Architects award.

There is a growing body of information in English on soil bioengineering techniques, including computer programs for planning. Sotir tirelessly continues to educate the public about alternatives to standard engineering. Among her hundred or more publications are some of the most comprehensive books on BTEC, as well as a half-dozen extensive articles posted on her website. Sotir has seen many enthusiastic do-it-yourself BTEC projects fail because seasonal or regional conditions were overlooked, plants were misidentified, or cuttings were harvested at the wrong time. Sotir

Figure 3.6a–c BTEC techniques form a flexible toolkit, often used in combination, as in stabilizing this bank at Crestwood (Houston TX). Note the large stump, left as added protection, visible in the before, during, and after photos. (*Project and Photo:* Robbin B. Sotir.)

emphasizes that even though BTEC is straightforward in concept, success depends on adjusting to complex site-specific conditions, and requires well-honed ecological expertise. Lucas seconds this: "As a designer or practitioner you need to respond to each site in-

dividually," she says. "Along with the specific plants you choose, soils, compaction, slope angle, amount of sunlight, runoff forces that the site must weather—all affect the design."

SUGGESTED BTEC PRACTICES
- Employ an experienced practitioner.
- Tailor techniques to geology, topography, plant species, and site conditions.
- Consider greenwalls (below) on steep slopes.
- Get regional guidelines for rocky, gravelly slopes, or in arid regions; dryland BTEC is feasible with a limited palette.
- Where possible, obtain cuttings of native species locally. Do not harvest on ecologically sensitive sites.
- Protect the project, especially exposed soil and existing vegetation.
- Be sure structures can withstand storm flows before plants root, or divert runoff until vegetation is established.
- Maintain BTEC like any other planted work, for at least a one-year establishment period.[14]

Make Vertical Structures "Habitat-able" with Greenwalls

What can hold up a truck, protect a prince, foil graffiti—and clean the air too? It's not the Incredible Hulk; it's the "greenwall."

These strong structures with a green face resemble BTEC on near-vertical slopes.[15] Viewed from another angle, they apply the greenroof concept (below) to the rest of the building. Greenwalls are an important use of flexible, living materials for functional purposes.

Understand Advantages of Greenwalls

Jon Coe is a persuasive advocate of greenwalls. Both in his Philadelphia firm, CLR Design, and in his more recent practice in Australia, he uses them in zoo exhibit design. But Coe sees much wider possibilities for the greenwall. "Contemporary technology," he says, "spends inordinate effort to stifle biological succession on built surfaces. What if we set out to design structures that *welcomed* plant growth?"

Where conventional landscape and engineering design use retaining walls of concrete, metal, or wood, greenwalls offer compelling alternatives. Vegetated surfaces suit many aesthetic preferences; they deaden and diffuse noise, make graffiti impossible, cut heat and glare, slow rainwater, trap air pollutants, and process CO_2. One 2012 study shows that greenwalls offer significant habitat for birds;[16] other wildlife probably benefit as well. Most landscape greenwalls are built from small, light masonry, mesh, or fabric, installed without heavy equipment, then filled with soil. Reduced materials, no formwork, and (for some types) no footings save money and resources. Most systems deal flexibly with unstable soils, settling, deflection—even earthquakes. Careful attention to irrigation and microclimate is richly repaid. Various designs are discussed below, from residential to heavy-duty.

Architectural Greenwalls

With commercial greenwall systems proliferating since the mid-2000s, greenwall products appear to be differentiating into architectural and landscape systems. There is some overlap, but the purposes and methods are fairly distinct.

Architectural systems are applied to the walls of buildings, either interior or exterior. They usually rely on a mesh-like scaffolding support system, on which various proprietary troughs, wires, trellis-like or solid panels, or pockets of geotextile hold plants. Soil for rooting may be at the base of the wall, or in containers supported on the scaffolding, ranging from nursery pots to fabric wrapping. Given the limited volume of soil, irrigation is critical to building-attached systems, as is managing any overflow. Drip irrigation onto individual plants, or uptake from the supporting troughs, appear to be the most common approaches. Systems that use potted greenery allow replacement of plants that die, or even seasonal shifts in the composition.

An alternative approach to greenwalls over structures is the use of stainless steel cable to support climbing plants. The British company Jakob offers a thoroughly worked-out system of cables and hardware, as well as a remarkably detailed downloadable booklet covering types of cable structure that work best for different types of climbing species.[17] Twin-

ing vines such as wisteria can grow up vertical cables; scramblers, which have thorns, are best supported by horizontal wires; and true climbers like clematis and grape need a lattice of vertical and horizontal cables joined by clamps at each crossing. Jakob's booklet also offers information on weights of various plants, wind and precipitation loads, and other engineering considerations. The Australian tensile architecture company Ronstan Rigging offers similar cable-trellis systems, used, for example, on Brisbane's dramatic kilometer-long South Bank Grand Arbour by the Melbourne-based firm Denton Corker Marshall. Both Jakob and Ronstan have offices in the United States; Seco South, a Largo FL supplier of cable railing systems, also offers a cable trellis.

One concern with mesh or cable as plant supports is that the metal could heat sufficiently to burn leaves and stems that contact it. However, the University of Arizona Architecture Building (see Principle 4) used vertical stainless cable to support a living shade screen. The cables, because of their small cross-section, did not heat enough to be a problem; larger pipe cross-supports did heat up, but hardware kept the cables (and vines) distant from the pipe system. The Edith Green–Wendell Wyatt Federal Building in Portland OR (also Principle 4) used a similar greenwall as part of a major remodel over one of the dullest 1970s facades ever.

Architectural greenwalls provide a certain amount of insulation for the building on which they are constructed, though the actual benefit is still under debate. These greenwall systems have been used dramatically by artists like Patrick Blanc. Since plants are placed into the grid individually, striking compositions of contrasting foliage can be created, including naturalistic patterns of diversity, arcs of color contrast, regular Euclidean patterns, and even single-species uniformity. In fact, one installation on a thirty-foot wall outside London's National Gallery arranged some 8,000 plants to "reproduce" Van Gogh's *Wheatfield with Cypresses* in monochromatic green.[18]

Indoors, architectural greenwalls can bring the landscape in; outdoors, they can merge the building, from certain angles, into surrounding vegetation. Nonetheless, they are adjuncts to the building and, in most cases, are a type of facade. Many are expensive; a Italian study indicated a range of $3–$10 per square foot for simpler systems, with proprietary panels priced at $40–$120/sq. ft.[19]

Landscape Greenwalls

Outdoor greenwall systems serve as freestanding fences or barriers, or as retaining walls. This makes them quite different from the architectural systems discussed above. (Constructing a potentially freestanding greenwall of this type against a building is possible, though probably not cost-effective.) A wide range of structural concepts have been developed for landscape greenwalls. Not all are commercially available in the United States; some can be built with on-site materials. Some of the main strategies (illustrated in Figure 3.7 and detailed below) are:

block—engineered with gaps where plants root *through* the wall.
crib wall—concrete or wood elements stacked "log cabin" style.

frame—stacked interlocking O- or diamond-shaped masonry (mostly in Europe and Japan).
trough—stackable soil-filled tubs (retaining or free-standing).
gabion—stone-filled wire baskets, strong but permeable; sometimes planted.
mesh—like mini gabions, holding a thin layer of soil to a surface.
cell—flexible, strong honeycombs filled with soil, also used horizontally.
sandbag—geotextiles wrapped around soil; formally called "vegetated geogrid."

Two definitions: *Geotextiles* are woven or felt-like synthetic filter fabrics. *Geogrids* are stronger sheets that look like plastic construction fencing. Geogrid is also (confusingly) a trademark for a type of cellular honeycomb. Several good publications give further detail on methods and definitions.

Landscape greenwalls derive their strength primarily from their inert elements; planting protects the surface and adds some strength. This contrasts with soil

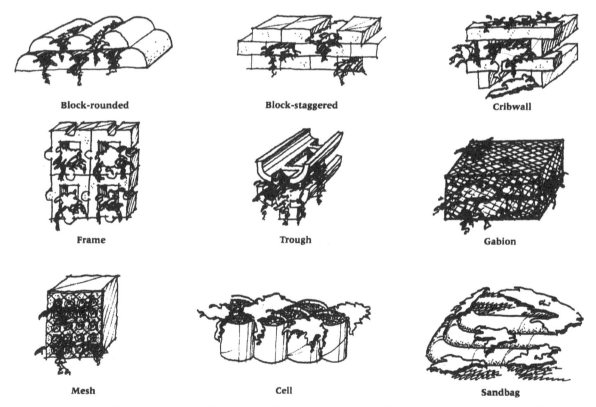

Block-rounded   **Block-staggered**   **Cribwall**

Frame   **Trough**   **Gabion**

Mesh   **Cell**   **Sandbag**

Figure 3.7   Greenwalls combine BTEC with a variety of hard structures; several basic concepts are diagrammed here. (*Illust.:* Craig Farnsworth.)

bioengineering, with which greenwalls are often combined as part of systematic whole-site design. With many materials to choose from, it is essential to get technical assistance from manufacturers and specialists. Costs are often 25–50 percent less than for cast-in-place concrete, but analyze case by case.

Greenwalls are as effective for slope retention as conventional structures. Most are porous, and do not require the weep-holes used for solid retaining walls. Add their soil, stormwater, and vegetation benefits, and greenwalls clearly perform *better* in landscape construction than impervious, monolithic retaining walls.

Newly planted greenwalls require maintenance; weeds may move in before plantings establish, or if plantings fail. At least a year's monitoring and maintenance should be planned for any new greenwall. Mulching and other preventive measures should be carefully considered. Once weeds are present, hand removal or selective herbicide use may be unavoidable. With proper design and vigorously established plantings, however, a mature greenwall requires less maintenance than hard surfaces—especially if graffiti is an issue.

Many landscape greenwall structural systems could be adapted for use indoors for air quality and soothing ambience, or in zoo or botanical displays. In general, though, the advantages of these systems for outdoor use are disadvantageous indoors: they are bulky and freestanding.

Build Plantable Masonry Structures

The simplest plantable retaining structure is a drystone wall. Constructed against the toe of a slope by stacking local stones, these one-rock-wide walls require considerable skill to lay.[20] If rocks are readily available nearby, such walls are particularly attractive.

Drystone must usually not exceed six feet in height. For taller structures, gabions (rocks encased in heavy galvanized wire mesh) are an alternative. Usually, the empty basket is set up and filled on-site; moving prefilled gabions requires heavy equipment. Gabions may be stacked in a battered arrangement, tilted into the slope. They can look mechanical and raw, but soil can be added to establish vegetation over them.[21]

Crib walls are somewhat more sophisticated—open faced, interlocking wood or concrete beams embedded in the slope. Normally battered to improve stability, crib walls may be vertical with appropriate foundations. Plants grow through openings between beams. Preserved wood is often used (see p. 298 for concerns). As mentioned earlier, "live" crib walls may be assembled in the field from living logs, then filled with soil and fast-rooting cuttings.[22] These persist because they are living, rather than preserved.

Where crib walls must be extremely high or nearly vertical, concrete may be a better choice. Concrete "logs," notched for stacking, resemble parking wheel stops in size and shape. Short walls of this kind can be built with hand labor.

Figure 3.8 Gabions cause fewer problems than impervious walls because they allow water to seep through. Over time or by design, gabions can support vegetation. (*Photo:* Kim Sorvig.)

GREEN TROUGHS

Imagine earth-filled bathtubs in a tapering stack up to sixty feet tall. Each trough has holes in the bottom, forming a continuous soil core throughout the wall and allowing moisture to reach each level. The proprietary Evergreen system offers a narrow footprint, and can be freestanding, planted on both faces for noise reduction or security (an example surrounds Jordan's royal palace). To retain soil or rock faces, trough units stack against the surface. Philadelphia's Synterra used a 600-foot Evergreen wall along the Blue Route expressway. Affected neighbors favored its appearance, and after testing, the Pennsylvania DOT used similar walls elsewhere, according to Synterra principal Bill Wilson. The National Park Service used Evergreen for huge earthworks at Cumberland Gap Tunnel. Trough units are sixteen feet long, weighing up to three and one-half tons without soil. Unlike other greenwall systems, they can only be installed with heavy equipment.

A similar trough wall, but made of mixed recycled plastic, has been used in Europe as a sound-wall. It would certainly be lighter for installation than concrete troughs, being made of a varying mix, 60–95 percent polyethylene and/or polypropylene, "supplemented" by recycled PVC, polystyrene, and polyethylene terephthalate (PET). A 300-meter-long, 3-meter-tall stacking trough wall (roughly 1,000 by 10 feet) uses one year's worth of plastic waste from 10,000 people. Much of the green building community retains doubt about any use of PVC, but this way of recycling it appears to be a responsible approach.[23]

GREENING THE BLCOK WALL

Any wall can be *draped* with trailing or climbing plants, rooted above or below it. True greenwalls have plants growing *through the surface*, which requires soil spaces. Two basic masonry designs achieve this: leaving out blocks in each course, or rounding the corners of each block.

The so-called "S-block" system, a European product distributed by US licensees, leaves out occasional blocks. The blocks' S or Z shape and weight lock courses together, so missing blocks don't compromise strength. S-blocks require poured footings, and must

Figure 3.9   The Evergreen "trough" greenwall serves both as retaining wall and as noise wall on Philadelphia's Blue Route (I-476). (*Project and Photo:* Synterra Ltd.)

slope at least ten degrees. In earthquake-prone California, these walls withstand Richter-7 tremors, settling tighter afterward.

Verdura blocks, patented by Soil Retention Structures (Oceanside CA), are small, twenty-three-pound trough-like blocks with elliptical front faces; planting spaces occur at the rounded corners, into soil behind. A fish-scale texture provides interest until covered by growth. A similar system, known as Hercules (St. Louis MO), uses a face shaped like an M, planted at both sides and in the middle.

Standard block systems, like Keystone, Anchor, and Rockwood, are plantable if terraced. Attempts to put planting "pockets" on the face of such blocks (without root access through the wall) have fared poorly, resulting in root-bound plants and awkward irrigation.

Unanchored, some block systems can be fifty feet tall. Anchoring is done by geogrid sheets, pinned to the blocks and buried behind the wall. This is a variation on the "sandbag" system, described in more detail below. Geogrid anchors, with or without block facings, are standard fare in heavy-duty civil engineering, giving them a clear track record for stability.

Use Flexible Soil Support Systems

A variety of flexible materials can be used to make soil and plants stand upright.

WIRE MESH (SEE ALSO "ARCHITECTURAL
GREENWALLS," ABOVE)
An ultrathin greenwall made of three-dimensional
wire or polypropylene mesh is one of the offerings
of the German site engineering firm System Krismer.
The mesh is pinned to rock, concrete, or soil, and
filled with soil-gravel mix using hydro-seeding equipment. The metal mesh does not appear to affect plant
growth, at least in temperate climates. Krismer has also
used this product sculpturally, producing what looks
like topiary; at Längenfeld thermal springs in Austria,
a wooly green mammoth commemorates Hannibal's
crossing the Alps on elephants.[24]

GreenScreen offers a modular system of galvanized
welded-wire panels surrounding two or three inches
of "captive growing space." GreenScreens are double-
sided trellises; plants root below, in the ground or a
planter. It is what the name says: a screen system that
can completely or partly cover structural walls, or be
used as a freestanding (but not load-bearing) space-
divider. It is also available as cylindrical columns or
traditional fan trellises. One variant, combining a lightweight wheeled planter with a GreenScreen, is dubbed
the "Rolling Bush."[25] Panels may be "prevegetated" for
instant effect, and maintained by switching out panels
showing deteriorated growth. Eco-Mesh is a similar
system by McNichols, manufacturer of "hole products" (grates, meshes, etc.); two rectangles of mesh are
framed by metal channel, and can be used freestanding as well as attached to structures. Both of these systems are thin variations on the gabion, a structural wall
made of mesh filled with stone (see below).

GreenScreen's website lists recommended plants,
mostly nonwoody vines, plus succulents (like those
for greenroofs). The plant list suits moderate climates,
and would need modification for other regions. Like
any freestanding landscape wall, these screens face climate extremes: depending on compass orientation,
one side may be in full sun while the other is completely self-shaded, with severe temperature, moisture,
and wind exposure differences.

The great majority of projects illustrated on
GreenScreen's website are in the company's home state
of California and in Florida, probably the most favorable climates for such a system. Photos of other instal-

lations in Arizona, New York, Texas, and Maryland
show rather sparse growth, possibly because installations were new.

Firms like EDAW and SWA have used custom-
fabricated GreenScreens to create vegetation-covered
gazebos and shade structures. GreenScreens have also
been integrated with signage and lighting. By covering or replacing hard surfaces with plants, this system
combines visual novelty with environmental benefits:
purification of air, microhabitat creation, and decreased heat retention. GreenScreen does not appear
to be appropriate, as greenwalls are, for soil erosion or
stormwater management.

GreenScreen was innovatively used at the National
Wildlife Federation's headquarters in Reston VA, designed by HOK. GreenScreen panels cover the south-
facing windows, mounted about four feet out from
the facade. By using deciduous vines in these trellises,
the building is screened from solar gain in summer
and open to solar heat in winter. This takes the mesh
greenwall beyond mostly cosmetic planted surfaces
(as at Universal Studios in California, or the recently
opened Quai Branly Museum in Paris) and into the
arena of significant energy savings through design.

SANDBAG VARIATIONS
At zoos in Seattle and Rochester, Jon Coe developed
a simple, cost-effective greenwall. Reinforcing fabric
is laid down wider than the wall's footprint. A one-
foot layer of soil, as wide as the final wall, is placed on
the fabric; the extra width is then folded over the soil.
More layers of fabric folded around soil are added,
stepped to final height. Soil weight holds fabric, and
fabric holds soil. If the height-to-width ratio exceeds
about 2:3, fabric is pinned to the ground or structure; footings are sometimes needed. Geogrid may be
wrapped around fabric-lined "bags" for extra strength.
The wall face is seeded or turfed; woody seedlings or
cuttings are planted through the fabric. At Seattle's
Woodland Park Zoo, grass covered the wall immediately, with Arctic Willow taking over by the third year.

Coe layers geogrid and porous mat together, or uses
Enkamat Type S, which fuses grid and mat into a single sheet. He avoids "the ziggurat look" of a stepped
face for two reasons. In zoos, kids who climb the steps

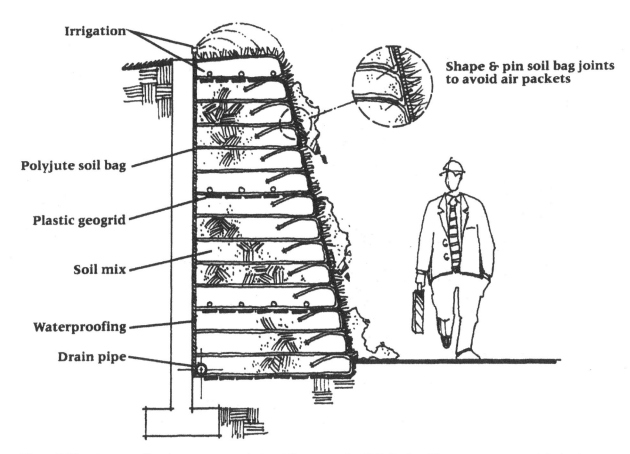

Figure 3.10   A greenwall against a structure, designed for zoo use by CLR Design. The same concept used for bank stabilization is called vegetated geogrid (Figure 3.1). (*Illust.:* Craig Farnsworth, based on Jon Coe.)

risk falling off—and being eaten. Second, sharply stepped angles can produce root-killing pockets. So Coe's workers soak the finished wall, then beat the face flat with shovels.

Landscape architect Kevin Kleinhelter used a similar system for Post Properties (Atlanta GA), whose management emphatically values landscape as a prime client attraction. Using Tensar's Sierra system (geogrid stabilization with plantable-mat surfaces), Kleinhelter avoided massive concrete retaining walls that didn't fit Post's landscape-focused marketing philosophy.

For exhibits, sandbag greenwalls can simulate natural slopes or historical sod construction (CLR used them to re-create Kodiak Island pit houses). In other settings, greenwalls could be ornamental, patterned with colored sedums or blooming displays. One limitation: fabric-reinforced systems rely on fill weight and wide footprint. For this reason, they are best used on fill slopes or to cover built walls. If used on cut slopes,

significant extra excavation is required, affecting existing vegetation and offsetting greenwall benefits.

CELLULAR CONTAINMENT

These polyethylene-sheet honeycombs fold flat for shipping, expanding when pulled like crepe-paper holiday decorations. Once staked at the edges, the expanded cell sheet is strong enough to walk on while being filled with soil. Each cell is about eight inches square, available in two-inch to six-inch depths.

A single layer of cells can blanket an existing slope for stabilization; filled with gravel, it substitutes for paving; with perforated sidewalls, it stabilizes stream crossings. To make a greenwall, cell sheets are laid horizontally on top of one another, stepping upward as steeply as 4V:1H. Edge cells, exposed by the stepping structure, are filled with planting soil; the remaining cells, with gravel. The polyethylene edge of each layer remains exposed, but is quickly covered by plants.

Figure 3.11   Cellular containment materials are flexible honeycombs filled with soil or gravel. A single layer can form a drivable surface; stacked as shown, cells form a greenwall. (*Photo:* Webtec.)

At Crystal Cove State Historic Park, near Newport Beach CA in a historically certified landscape, undercutting by a creek and the ocean threatened the Pacific Coast Highway. Landscape architect Steve Musillami replaced the highway's original vegetated fill slope with Geoweb, a Presto cellular product. Filling cells with local "duff" soil produced a healthy mix of native plants from seed. By steepening the slope, Musillami widened the creek bed to accommodate the real source of the problem: increased runoff from upstream development. The landscape architect's solution went far beyond the riprap suggested by highway engineers—and did it in record time. The cell material, Musillami says, easily installs to curves, without massive formwork or heavy equipment. Presto cites a similar creek-bed project that flooded ten feet deep without damage.

Some greenwalls benefit from underdrains; Musillami used one to return water to the stream. At Minnesota's Grass Lake, state highway engineers underdrained a cellular greenwall to keep potentially polluted road runoff out of the lake. The engineers noted that the geocell (Terracell by Webtec) avoided disruptive excavation, resisted road salts better than concrete, and softened vehicle impact in accidents.

Design for Greenwall Maintenance

Many design choices go into a successful greenwall:

Figure 3.12a, b   Greenwalls can reduce the "footprint" or horizontal extent of a high bank by steepening it. This approach protects Crystal Cove State Park (CA) from increased upstream runoff—shown during (a) and after construction (b). (*Project:* California State Parks, Steve Musillami. *Photo:* Alan Tang.)

- Microclimate on any vertical surface depends on compass orientation and is usually severe—hot/sunny, cold/shady, or alternating daily.
- Soil mix and plant selection are critical.
- Irrigation can be sprayed onto the wall, channeled down from the top, or (using drippers) run on or behind the face. For trellis-like systems, irrigate the soil, not the climbing vegetation.

- Be sure to plan for maintenance during plant establishment.
- Especially if the greenwall covers a building, plan scrupulously for maintenance of the underlying structure.

Turn Barren Roof Spaces into "Greenroofs"

Of all strategies cited in this book, none has seen more dramatic growth since the first edition than greenroofs (a.k.a. ecoroofs). In the late 1990s, greenroofs were rapidly emerging in northern Europe, especially Germany. At that time, however, there were virtually no examples on any major US building.

Today there are scores of fine examples, and not just on "alternative" buildings: the greenroofs on Chicago's City Hall and Ford's truck factory at Rouge River MI show how far this technology has come. According to Green Roofs for Healthy Cities (GRHC), the US greenroof industry's main association, 2.5 million square feet of greenroof were constructed in the United States in 2005 alone. Greenroofs even put in an appearance at the 2002 Philadelphia Flower Show, winning a Best of Show prize for Temple University's landscape architecture and horticulture department. The 2008 recession slowed all types of construction, but by 2015, the industry was reporting 18.5 percent growth and 1.6 million new square feet of greenroof.

Nonetheless, by European standards the North American greenroof movement is just starting. "We're still in the very early stages," confirms Steve Peck of GRHC. Two and a half million square feet sounds impressive, but by comparison, Peck notes, "Germany averages eleven to twelve million square feet of greenroof construction per year," with a population roughly one-third of the United States.[26] Germany's density, size, and relatively uniform climate may have helped, but progressive cultural attitudes have Europe outstripping the United States in many types of sustainable construction.

Promote Greenroofs' Environmental and Economic Benefits

Every contemporary city has, in the words of Toronto environmental designer and author Michael Hough,

"hundreds of acres of rooftops that for the most part lie desolate and forgotten." Hough's description conjures a city in decline, yet is true even of economically vibrant cities: at ground level, they are lively, but up on the roof, lifeless. [27]

Conventional roofs are severe microclimates, impervious to water, exposed to high winds. Every square foot of sterile roof corresponds to a square foot of life missing from the ground surface, linked to various urban environmental problems, and even to global warming (see p. 20). Greenroofs have great potential for reversing these problems, as Hough and Vancouver landscape architect Cornelia Oberlander has long advocated.

Requirements of greenroofs are relatively modest, yet environmental benefits are considerable:

- Improving buildings' thermal insulation.
- Reducing the urban "heat-island" effect, by absorbing less heat.
- "Pre-conditioning" air, cutting the amount of air-conditioning required.
- Reducing glare and reflected light pollution.
- Producing oxygen, absorbing carbon dioxide, and filtering air pollution.
- Storing carbon.
- Providing wildlife habitat, especially for birds.
- Absorbing up to 75 percent of rain falling on them, thus slowing runoff.[28]

About eighty cities in Germany promote greenroofs by regulation or incentive, according to Peck. "Their primary motivations are stormwater management, urban heat-island reduction, and provision of green space," he says. In Germany, builders must provide new green space equal to the amount dislocated through construction. Greenroofs are usually a good way to comply.[29]

Greenroofs also make economic sense: they protect conventional roofs from ultraviolet (UV) radiation and temperature extremes—the two main sources of roof-membrane degradation. Roofing materials like Bituthane are vulnerable to UV breakdown; a greenroof completely shields such waterproofing materials from light, often doubling (or more) their service life. On a conventional asphalt roof, temperatures may fluctuate 170°F over the course of a year. Green-roofs dramatically decrease this. The Chicago Depart-ment of Environment found that on a 100-degree day, the surface temperature of a blacktop roof reached 165°F, while a greenroof was only 85°.[30] When coor-dinated with air intake design, greenroofs "pre-condi-tion" air enough to reduce the size of air-conditioning units required, as well as their operating costs. Green-roof insulation can cut summer cooling costs by half, and winter heating by 25 percent.[31] Both savings—energy and membrane life cycle—have environmental and economic benefits.[32]

The costs of greenroofs (and greenwalls) is often overstated, says Rick Scaffidi of Environmental Qual-ity Resources, a stormwater engineering firm active in the Washington DC to Baltimore area. In the United States, greenroofs are often estimated at between $15 and $20 per square foot.[33] Scaffidi says that adding the hidden costs of conventional roofs, and subtract-ing the hidden benefits of greenroofs, makes green-roofs quite competitive. Greenroofs reduce runoff, saving costs associated with enlarging stormwater sys-tems and resetting an estimated 20 percent of existing drain inlets, thus requiring repaving, and disrupting traffic. Preventing disruption of traffic in urban ar-eas can add up to 40 percent to total project cost.[34] On the other side of the ledger, solar panels com-bine effectively with greenroofs, the former perform-ing better because the latter cool the roof.[35] Irrigating the greenroof with "orphaned" water like air condi-tioner condensate gains benefits while avoiding costly disposal of valuable resources. So-called blue and green roofs increase water-holding capacity, usually by leaving some modular growing trays empty to catch precipitation.[36]

Quantifying the economic value of greenroofs is not simple, but several studies have used advanced sta-tistical methods to estimate it. San Francisco, which in 2016 became the first US city to require green-roofs and/or solar panels on all new buildings, com-missioned Arup, the global engineering consultants, to evaluate costs and benefits. The study compared a standard white membrane roof to a greenroof over a twenty-five-year life cycle. Even with simple meth-odology, it was clear that the greenroof's energy and stormwater benefits balanced its extra up-front costs.

However, more sophisticated analysis considered ten-ant productivity, effects on surrounding property val-ues, increased rental value and occupancy, as well as environmental services and taxes resulting from prop-erty value. This method found that, under San Fran-cisco conditions, greenroofs added $60.90 per square foot value for the owner or renter, plus $28.10 per square foot in social benefits including tax revenues. A study of 15,000 condo purchases in Portland OR determined that buyers were willing to pay a "green-roof premium" of 4.2 percent before the 2008 crisis, and even more (6.3 percent) afterward. With condos averaging about $300,000 during the period of study, the greenroof increased the condo value by roughly $19,000.[37]

The oddest rationale for greenroofs appeared in 2006 in the *Los Angeles Times*: "Thanks in part to the surging popularity of Google Earth—a bracingly new, if detached, way to interact with the built environ-ment—rooftops are shedding their reputation as for-gotten windswept corners of the urban landscape and moving toward the center of architectural practice."[38] In this case, aesthetic visibility is driving sustainability, which is certainly the exception rather than the rule!

Understand Greenroof Definitions, Approaches, and Materials

As greenroofs become more widespread, it is important to be clear about what distinguishes them from con-ventional "roof gardens." Despite some general simi-larities—soil and plantings on top of a building—the two are quite different in intent and execution.

Conventional roof gardens are usually called "in-tensive greenroofs" by people in the industry; I pre-fer "roof garden" for clarity. They are typically used like street-level gardens. Shrubs and trees are often in-cluded. These require deep soils (a foot or more, add-ing 80–150 pounds per square foot) and irrigation, resulting in two structural options: reinforce the whole roof, or grow plants in containers. The former is costly and in some cases structurally impractical; the latter limits planted surface area and, with it, limits envi-ronmental benefits. Conventional roof gardens may be "better than nothing" environmentally, but energy and materials costs must be carefully considered. Homeowners shouldn't abandon rooftop container gardening, but landscape professionals should think honestly and rigorously before justifying conventional intensive roof gardens as sustainable. While rooftop Edens are delightful to the favored few who have access (including birds), they are too costly and resource intensive to help the urban environment as a whole.

"Extensive greenroofs," by contrast, are not intended for regular access, and generally do not feature woody plants. This keeps them lightweight, covering the entire roof with a continuous layer of specialized growing medium, as thin as 50 millimeters (about 2 inches, adding 15–50 pounds per square foot), supporting low-maintenance vegetation. In concept they are lightweight, modern sod roofs, updating centuries-old tradition.

This different intent is reflected in different structure. First, extensive greenroofs require relatively modest additional load-bearing capacity and may be retrofitted to many existing roofs. Second, they do not require flat roofs, but may be installed on slopes up to thirty degrees. On steeper roofs, greenwall techniques could be adapted. Third, they may require little or no irrigation (except during establishment and in some harsher climates). Fertilizer, if any, should be formulated for healthy minimal growth.

Greenroofs are built of materials found in conventional roof gardens, but in dramatically different configurations. Below the soil, they consist of waterproof membrane, insulation layer, and drainage layer. Insulation may be above or underneath the waterproof membrane; insulation above waterproofing is far easier to salvage if the roof is replaced. On roofs pitched five degrees or more a drainage layer is not needed.

Greenroofs *hold stormwater on the roof* rather than sending it down gutters into storm drains. Thus, every greenroof requires reliable waterproofing, properly coordinated with architectural and structural design. Different methods of waterproofing affect not only reliability, but also how easy it is to detect and repair any leaks that may develop. Sheet waterproofing laid on the roof deck may allow leaks to migrate long distances. Fully adhered waterproofing solves this problem, but can cause difficulties at expansion joints and structural edges. Some greenroofs incorporate sophisticated leak detectors, especially in Europe. Electrically conductive primer, sensors, and other methods are improving leak detection.

Roots penetrating waterproofing would cause leakage. A PVC sheet is often added below the substrate to prevent this; given PVC's environmental difficulties (see p. 295), high-density polyethylene (HDPE) sheeting is preferable. Some systems incorporate copper-based root-killing barriers. This has been ques-

Figure 3.13 Ecoroofs are an update on traditional sod roofs— an example of revisiting past technologies to meet sustainability goals. (*Photo:* Kim Sorvig.)

Figure 3.14   A greenroof ready to plant, showing porous-aggregate lightweight planting mix. (*Project:* Emory Knoll Nursery. *Photo:* Ed Snodgrass.)

tioned both because of copper's toxicity, and because the chemical effect is likely to wear out long before the rest of the greenroof.[39]

Greenroof soil conditions differ markedly from conventional roof gardens, which rely on deep, high-quality soil. Greenroofs generally make do with poor and relatively thin growing medium (a.k.a. "substrate"), adequate for sedums, grasses, wildflowers, and other tough small species. Depending on the slope of the structural roof, the soil may have to be held in place against slippage. This is done in various ways: baffles, modular trays, and geotextile cells (see greenwalls, above) are some of the options.

Growing media specifically manufactured for greenroofs are at last available in North America. No one substrate is suitable for all sites, however. Some designers develop their own regionally adapted mixes. Expanded shale, a widely available lightweight material of which the brand Permatill is an example, is often combined with sand and humus (recommended by author Ted Osmundson, who uses 9:9:2 proportions). For sedums in some climates, pure sand may be sufficient. Cornelia Oberlander has successfully used one-third sand, one-third pumice, and one-third Humus Builder, a food waste compost that adds an extra dimension—recycling—to greenroof benefits. Crushed brick waste and concrete are among substrate materials (mixed with organics) that have been used in Eu-

rope. By crushing rubble and other on-site materials for substrate, the double environmental cost of hauling rubble away and fresh materials back is avoided.

Some mixes incorporate hydrogels for water retention. There is some question of how long these products will last in a roof environment, where replacement is physically difficult and costly. Another question concerning greenroof mixes is how best to protect lightweight soils from wind erosion, especially during establishment.[40] Erosion-control blankets have been used for this purpose; tackifiers might also be appropriate. Wind uplift (i.e., blowing the roof off) can be a problem on some building types in some regions; GRHC has standards for this type of construction, and for fire prevention on greenroofs, available on its website.

What plants do well in thin, nutrient-poor greenroof substrates? Begin by looking at plants that spontaneously colonize local hard surfaces, including roofs never intended to support plant life. Many gravel roofs are colonized over time with mosses and stonecrop.[41] Develop a list of regional drought-resistant plants. At least one US nursery now specializes in such plants: Greenroof Plants, in Street MD.[42] Its founder, Ed Snodgrass, coauthored a greenroof planting manual. For arid regions, there is still a great need for research and testing of soil and plant combinations suitable for greenroofs, greenwalls, BTEC, and constructed wetlands. Properly planted, greenroofs need little or no irrigation, except during extended dry spells.

Like their cousins, the greenwalls, greenroofs can be invaded by weeds if poor establishment or maintenance leaves bare soil exposed. Many invaders are weeds that cause problems wherever they grow. Most greenroofs, however, approximate a meadow, successionally replaced in most regions by shrub or tree communities. Shallow, nutrient-poor soil mixes prevent shrubs and trees from thriving for long—but not from sprouting in the first place. Although a few woody ground covers fit right in, removing woody seedlings is a necessary greenroof maintenance task.

The 2016 GRHC Awards of Excellence give a little idea of how creative greenroof design has become and how widely they are used. The winners included a research park in Calgary; an infill office building in Mountain View CA; in Manhattan, retrofits on a condo

Figure 3.15   Edgeland House, built on a brownfield in Austin TX, contrasts sloping greenroof with dramatic hard-edged structure, and feels integral to its site, a well-restored brownfield. (*Landscape restoration and greenroof:* John Hart-Asher, Lady Bird Johnson Wildflower Center. *Architect:* Bercy Chen Studio. *Photo:* Paul Bardagjy.)

building and on the 6.75-acre Javits Center, where the light weight of the greenroof made it cheaper than a conventional roof that would have required structural reinforcement. The Javits roof retains more than 70 percent of precipitation falling on it, keeping a significant amount out of New York's storm drains. At Trent University, in Peterborough, Ontario, a large greenroof was designed for food production and botanical research. Toronto's Bridgepoint Active Healthcare, another winner, used its greenroof as part of a strategy to give green views from every room; post-occupancy evaluation provided yet another validation of the theory that naturalistic scenes improve patient recovery.

Edgeland House, built on a brownfield in Austin TX, is the only detached residential building among the winners. Its striking greenroof is like a pyramid split down the middle, with the two halves enclosing a courtyard. The designers, Bercy Chen Studio and John Hart-Asher of Lady Bird Johnson Wildflower Center's Ecosystem Design Group, didn't want the usual "nod

to nature," and so they "blurred the lines so the house and landscape were truly one."[43] The contrast between glass walls, hardscape, and greenroof are proof that brownfields and greenroofs can be the basis for very stylish and beautiful work.

Some of the earliest projects in the United States are still going strong. The greenroof atop Chicago's City Hall is still among the most widely publicized US greenroofs. This pioneering example cools the building considerably, but its design was too expensive to be widely replicable.[44] Its prairie wildflowers reportedly contribute to about 200 pounds of honey per year, produced by several hives of bees.

One of the Windy City's most impressive greenroofs—and a more affordable model—is the Chicago Academy of Sciences' Peggy Notebaert Museum. This 17,000-square-foot retrofit illustrates various concepts: "extensive" design (shallower soils, groundcover-type plants) and "intensive" (deeper soils, taller prairie grasses and wildflowers).[45]

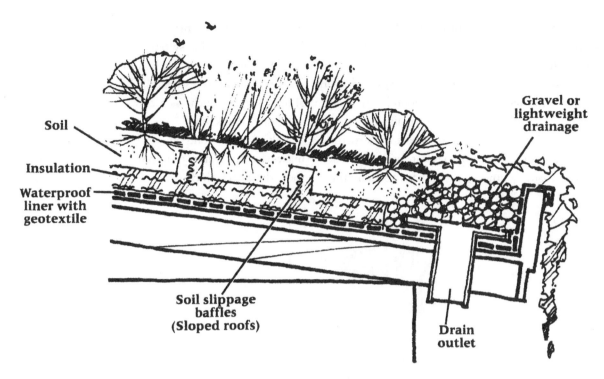

Figure 3.16   Unlike conventional roof gardens, greenroofs are light enough to retrofit on existing structures. (*Illust.:* Craig Farnsworth, based on Re-Natur.)

Figure 3.17   Lightweight, "extensive" greenroof covers Peggy Notebaert Nature Museum in Chicago. (*Project:* Conservation Design Forum. *Photo:* Andrea Cooper, Conservation Design Forum.)

The roof section most visible to the public, a 2,400-square-foot intensive demonstration completed in 2001, is the only irrigated area. In 2003, when more funds became available, the museum added two extensive greenroofs to cover its large south and north wings. These were designed to weigh no more than twenty-two and a half pounds per square foot

when saturated, well within the building's structural capacity. On the existing roof, waterproof membrane was installed, followed by root barrier and moisture-retaining fabric—all manufactured by Sarnafil, one of several North American greenroof suppliers. An inch of gravel followed by two and a half inches of lightweight soil mix were blown onto the roof from trucks below. The roof was hydro-seeded with wild-flowers, native grasses, and sedums, and hand planted with sedum cuttings. Hose bibs were installed to permit watering in case of drought—Chicago has long, hot summers.[46]

Now fourteen years old, the Ford Motor Company's Rouge River truck plant (Dearborn MI) remains North America's largest greenroof, at 10.4 acres.[47] Its installation was motivated by the stormwater discharge needs of the huge factory. The greenroof is one component of architect William McDonough + Partners' natural stormwater management system, which includes a network of underground storage basins, porous pavement installations, wetlands, retention ponds, and swales.

Ford undertook a lengthy series of greenroof trials

with the Michigan State University (MSU) horticulture department. They finally chose the XeroFlor system, in which mats of sedum are grown in a very thin substrate—just 2 centimeters (¾ inch)—and then installed. This system weighs 9.7 pounds per square foot fully saturated; the substrate remains intact, and can be rolled up if necessary to inspect the structural roof underneath. Fewer species can withstand such thin soil, basically limiting the choice to sedum; thin-

medium greenroofs may require ongoing irrigation. In MSU's trials, this system retained 66 percent of rainfall; commercial gravel holds only 25 percent.[48] A Ford representative estimates, "We ended up paying about twice as much [as a conventional roof], but it will last twice as long."

Baltimore's Montgomery Park Business Center makes a central feature of its retrofitted 30,000-square-foot, three-inch-thick greenroof. Installed in August

Figure 3.18　Montgomery Park Business Center (Baltimore) boasts a thriving lightweight greenroof. (*Project:* Katrin Scholz-Barth. *Photo:* Kai-Henrik Barth.)

2002, it was designed by Katrin Scholz-Barth, a Washington DC greenroof expert. The project was driven by strict regulations on nonpoint-source stormwater pollution affecting Chesapeake Bay. The developer's proposal qualified for a $92,000 EPA grant[49]—an example of incentives for greenroofs (which may, of course, be going away in 2017). Once fully vegetated, the roof is expected to reduce runoff by 50 to 75 percent. Any remaining roof and parking-lot runoff is collected in a 30,000-gallon underground cistern and reused for flushing toilets.

This roof consists of a single-ply PVC waterproof liner, covered with 2.5-inch insulation board, and two geotextile layers that keep soil from migrating downward and washing out. Sloping 7 percent, the roof provides gravity flow without a drainage layer. The planting medium (15 to 25 pounds per square foot, saturated) consists of 75 to 85 percent expanded slate, plus composted mushroom substrate from a nearby farm. The expanded slate, which puffs up like popcorn when heated in a rotary kiln, was mined in North Carolina.[50]

Monitor Greenroof Benefits

An astonishing eight-acre rooftop landscape in Salt Lake City shows that evaluating greenroofs is complex. Conifer-forested terraces climb the north and east walls onto the rooftop of the Conference Center of the Church of Jesus Christ of Latter-Day Saints (LDS, or Mormon). Sweeping off to a meadow framed by mountain views on the west, the roof drapes hanging gardens along south-facing ledges. Designed by Philadelphia-based Olin Partnership, it is a stunning example of planting on a structure.[51]

The LDS design was driven by a religious vision and regional aesthetics, not primarily by sustainability. By sheer size, it must have stormwater, air-purification, habitat, and insulation value, though no monitoring is done to substantiate this. But in Salt Lake's climate, it requires irrigation, seriously offsetting environmental gains. The LDS garden's drama also came at high initial cost: the auditorium roof, already a huge clear span, required extra steel to support full-size trees, shrubs, and pedestrian access.

Greenroof pioneer Charlie Miller of Philadelphia noted the difficulties with comparative studies of greenroof performance. "The same greenroof," says Miller, "will provide different benefits depending on the climate in which it is installed, the elevation of the structure, whether or not it is irrigated or fertilized, and so on." Professor Milind Khire, formerly with the greenroof research center at Michigan State (which consulted on the Ford plant), points out that even though better data are accumulating about performance of greenroofs on individual buildings, the cumulative effects on a city are harder to study; Khire worked on a program to model these citywide effects.[52]

Europe's head start on greenroofs makes projects

Figure 3.19 The LDS Convention Center in Salt Lake City supports lush "intensive" roof gardens, even forest. (*Project:* Olin Partnership. *Photo:* Craig Widmier.)

there worth watching; some are well monitored, tracking almost thirty years of performance.[53] Amsterdam airport's extensive green terminal roof, and Ecover's greenroof on its green products factory, are well-documented examples; Ecover's used treated effluent for occasional irrigation.[54] Ecover's home page contains project information, including lessons learned from a few repairable problems. In Britain, researchers are testing greenroofs designed to purify wastewater like constructed wetlands.[55] Starting with the 2008 Olympics, China has embraced greenroofs in a huge way; given the severe environmental problems of Chinese cities, these installations may prove to be exceptional test cases.

Among the earliest North American greenroofs are two that still exemplify the wide range of situations in which they can be used. Library Square, a Moshe Safde high-rise occupying an entire city block in Vancouver BC, has a greenroof by Cornelia Oberlander that covers more than 70 percent of the roof. Almost diametrically opposed in scale and construction, Tom Liptan's modest homemade retrofit greenroof in Portland OR has been an influential example, helping to convince others of the concept's feasibility. This ten-by eighteen-foot greenroof was actually monitored for performance—as all greenroofs should be. Liptan reported that a 0.4-inch rainstorm produced only three gallons of runoff (7.5 percent of the forty gallons that fell on the roof). Overall, the roof retains 15 to 90 percent of precipitation. Intense storms saturate it; after a 2-inch storm, runoff flows slowly for two days. Plants thrive without irrigation. This sort of specific, observation-based information is needed for greenroofs in each bioregion. Where no full-scale greenroofs exist locally, Liptan's approach offers a quick, cost-effective, low-risk feasibility assessment. (Data loggers, p. 397, facilitate monitoring.)

Greenroof pioneer Charlie Miller, interviewed on PBS's *The Green Machine*, urged that "greening our cities should not be an act of atonement for the environment that we've destroyed; rather, this should be a fundamentally positive adventure creating a better world for ourselves with nature as our partner." And in fact, the idea of structures with a living skin has inspired some wonderfully playful designs. These include "Bus Roots" (greenroofs on NYC buses) and

Figure 3.20 The ecoroof atop Ecover's headquarters helps meet the company's goal of a green factory producing green products. (*Project:* Ecover. *Photo:* Peter Malaise.)

Figure 3.21 Even small-scale ecoroofs decrease runoff, support habitat, and clean the air. Tom Liptan replaced his conventional garage roof with this one. (*Project and Photo:* Tom Liptan.)

a comparable program by a different artist in Stuttgart, Germany; the interior greening of an entire Chicago Transit Authority commuter rail car, complete with grass-covered seats and ferns and philodendrons draping the ceiling. A whale-shaped, green-skinned, solar-powered river cruise-ship has been proposed; from it, tourists might go ashore to see Renzo Piano's "Volcano Buono," a truncated cone structure with an Italian market in its "crater," its side covered, rather bizarrely, in lawn.

All these were featured in GRHC's 2011 "Top 10 Hot Trends," a virtual conference that can be accessed on YouTube.[56] Although it also includes many "green skyscrapers," an idea that seems credulous at best, this video shows how much "positive adventure" greenwalls and greenroofs can inspire.

Suggested Greenroof Practices

- Think of *every* roof, especially if large, as a greenroof candidate.
- Understand waterproofing, insulation, and structural requirements.
- Specify lightweight growing medium from locally available ingredients. (See "Manufactured Soil," p. 116.) Where feasible, use recycled ingredients. Do not make the mix too fertile. Use the shallowest soil layer that will support herbaceous plants.
- Select drought-tolerant, shallow-rooted regional plants.
- If possible, rely on rainfall alone. If necessary, irrigate with graywater, treated effluent, or water harvesting (Principle 4).

Many US cities offer greenroof incentives. Designers and developers can help draft and lobby for ordinances that fit their region. Density bonuses allow developments with greenroofs to build more square footage than otherwise permitted. In some jurisdictions, greenroofs are allowable toward requirements for open space, landscaping, permeable surface, energy efficiency, or stormwater management. Minneapolis, for example, will reduce utility fees for buildings with features that improve stormwater quality or reduce quantity—and greenroofs do both. Tax credits, low-interest loans, and outright grants are also possible. Fast-track or "streamlined" permitting, which risks slipshod plan review, is nonetheless a common incentive.[57] Of course, as of mid-2017, it seems likely that any federal money for something as useful as living architecture will dry up for at least four long years; on the other hand, this may prompt local authorities to get even more creative about advancing this concept. To explore policy tools and precedents, start with the Green Roofs for Healthy Cities website.

Construct for and with Plants

Much of the "hard" construction of any landscape is created to support or control plants. Landscape plants represent a significant financial investment, whether purchased, transplanted, or protected on-site. Healthy plants, and the construction that keeps them that way, are essential to functional, ecological, and aesthetic success of built landscapes.

The US urban forest is in severe decline and needs restoration. John Cutler, landscape architect with Houston's SWA group, points out that amid alarm over tropical deforestation, "the media is basically ignoring the equally disturbing disappearance of our urban forests."[58] In the decade bracketing Y2K, the largest US cities lost a total of 3.5 *billion* trees, according to the advocacy and research group American Forests. Cutler notes many new neighborhoods have *no* trees because "developers don't want to spend the extra money." American Forests offers a useful tool, GIS-based CityGreen software, that tracks existing or proposed urban forests and quantifies their environmental and economic benefits. A more recent study at SUNY-Syracuse shows that *rural* tree losses are catching up with declines in urban forests.[59]

As vegetation's many crucial roles in sustainability are recognized, plant-friendly construction methods are more important than ever. Despite the fact that these methods are long established, *careless* planting still wastes millions in money, materials, and energy. Many plants of all sizes are unavoidably removed during construction—damaging any more by carelessness or poor planning is utterly wasteful. The city of Milwaukee WI, for example, estimates its *annual* street-tree losses from poor construction practices exceeds $800,000.[60] Milwaukee publishes a thorough manual to help avoid this destruction.

The purchase cost of a landscape plant is far outweighed by value it adds to the environment. The Michigan School of Forestry has estimated the value of a single mature tree at $163,500—based solely on quantifiable services it provides.[61] Other values, such as wild bird habitat, or aesthetic and historic worth, are hard to put in dollars, but cannot be disregarded. Computer software, and a manual for legally defensible tree appraisal, can help; the Council of Tree and Landscape Appraisers (CTLA) offers such aids. Contact the International Society of Arboriculture for regional experts.

Table 3.1 compares initial costs of landscape plantings against some estimates of their true worth. These

Table 3.1

Comparison of costs and values of landscape plantings.

Service, Value, or Cost	Amount	Notes
Purchase or replace nursery stock up to 6″ caliper size	$25–$750	Varies regionally; based on informal survey of nurseries
Cost to install and establish one tree	$75–$3,000	Through second year; based on CTLA[a] rule of thumb, two to three times initial cost of tree
Annual maintenance investment, one tree	$0–$75	Informal estimate of likely costs
Oversize replacement (> 6″)	9″ = $955–$5,725 36″ = $15,270–$91,620	CTLA: $15–$90 per sq. in. of trunk cross-section area
Oxygen production, one mature tree	$32,000	Michigan School of Forestry[b]
Air pollution control, one mature tree	$62,000	Michigan School of Forestry
Water cycling and purification, one mature tree	$37,500	Michigan School of Forestry
Erosion control, one mature tree	$32,000	Michigan School of Forestry
Energy saving (heating and cooling adjacent structure),one mature tree	$26,000	50 years times annual $520 (40 percent of EPA heating/cooling national average; equivalent to 10.7 million Btu savings per home)
Insurance limit for one tree under ordinary property-owner policy	$500	Informal survey of several policies
Litigation value of one tree destroyed	$15,000	1981 Arlington VA US tax court case on record
Annual losses of trees caused by construction in Milwaukee WI	$800,000	R. J. Hauer, R. W. Miller, and D. M. Ouimet, "Street Tree Decline and Construction Damage," *Journal of Arboriculture* 20, no. 2 (1994): 94–97
Annual energy savings of entire US urban forest	$4,000,000,000	Rowan Rowntree, US Forest Service— no other information; cited at http:// www.treelink.org

[a]Council of Tree and Landscape Appraisers.

[b]For other studies, search for "compensatory" or "ecogical" + "value of urban trees."

figures vary by region as well as species and age; historic and cultural values are also reflected.

Cornell ecologist David Pimentel estimates the economic value of environmental services provided by nature to humans at $320 billion for the United States and $2.9 trillion globally—*not* including the value of agricultural crops.[62] A US Forest Service scientist estimates urban forests save the United States about $4 billion annually by moderating climate.[63] Three trees, properly located around a home, can cut air-conditioning energy use by half; planting about 7 million trees (a medium-sized urban forest) could eliminate demand for 100 megawatts of power-plant capacity. Trees slow runoff enough that San Antonio TX plans to increase urban tree cover by 8 percent as an alternative to a $200 million stormwater facility;[64] Philadelphia's water supply agency is behind an ambitious effort to regreen 10,000 acres that are currently impervious.

Clearly, plants contribute greatly to sustainable environments, and sustainable construction must be done *with plants in mind*. Botanical expertise—general plant biology and ecology, protection on-site, and cultivation requirements—is essential on landscape teams. A surprising number of landscape architects have only cursory plant knowledge; fortunately, many plant specialists can provide this expertise.

It is in the interest of the *contractor*—who must guarantee plant survival—to select, transport, handle, and maintain plantings properly. Careless hardscape construction practices, such as compacting soil or burying debris in planting pits, can also kill plantings. Sustainable structures often require innovative construction skills, as well as knowledgeable design that avoids specifying the impossible.

Inappropriate species substitutions for specified plants can undo the intended function of plantings, or the substitutes may not thrive. Substituting cheaper, easier-to-find non-natives for specified native species is especially inappropriate. (Even experienced designers and contractors need help from nursery professionals when substitution is necessary.)

Construction professionals should not assume that the designer never makes mistakes about planting design. Planting structures require buildable, maintainable, well-dimensioned designs; some contractors have considerable experience with such structures. From the pre-bid meeting through the last change order, the contractor may spot problems that the designer may not have noted, or that are site specific. Challenging the design may be tricky, but a team approach focuses on protecting plantings, not egos.

The following sections give some plant-focused guidelines about structures and handling. Always modify general rules in light of regional experience. Unusual climate conditions, soils, and plant species may require additional or different care.

Follow Up-to-date Planting Structure Guidelines

Alan Blanc, a British lecturer and author on landscape construction, had a sense of humor about his topic. His term for undersized street-tree pits was "dog-graves." (Really tiny ones were "Chihuahua-graves.") The image is morbid, but appropriate. Without adequate soil *volume* for roots and nutrients, and adequate *surface* for water and air to pass through, even the toughest plant is doomed to die, leaving its pit empty and grave-like, with a stump for a headstone.[65]

Their roots severely cramped, some street trees wither, while others rebel, heaving and cracking the oppressive pavement. Controlling errant roots with barriers may save sidewalks, but further stresses trees. That stress is extreme: Jim Patterson, retired National Park Service soils scientist, once saw three successive street-tree plantings die, finally replaced with artifi-

cial trees—which soon rotted away in "the most hostile environment we know," an ordinary streetscape. Older conventional tree-planting specifications focus on squeezing plants into minimum space. Because clients demand maximized buildable and rentable area, the landscape industries continue to build lethal, undersized planting structures. Sustainable practice does not waste trees where they cannot survive, but makes survivable space for plants a priority. This is ever more critical in light of the need for healthy trees to sequester carbon, clean the air, and cool streets and parking.

Several special structures in which to plant urban trees have been developed. These are the focus of the following section.

Street-tree Structures

Inadequate planting structures are a leading cause of urban street-tree deaths: the average lifespan of urban trees has been estimated as low as two years, and few experts give them longer than ten years to live.[66] These are trees that could live fifty years or more in suburban settings or in the wild. Clearly, this epidemic is an economic and environmental disaster. As one expert puts it, "Elaborate and expensive designs are produced and installed only to have the plant materials succumb to some malady even before the grower's guarantee expires."[67]

What is "adequate" soil space for a tree? A widely accepted *minimum* is 300 cubic feet, that is, a pit 10′ × 10′ × 3′ deep. This is much more than many street trees ever get, yet it is truly adequate only for trees whose *mature* trunk diameter (DBH) is less than 6 inches. For a 24″ DBH tree, about 1,500 cubic feet of soil is recommended—a pit about 22′ × 22′ × 3′ deep. (Increased *depth* is of little value to most trees, because root growth stays mainly in the top foot of soil.)

The relationship between tree canopy and soil volume can be expressed by a rule of thumb: the volume of root space (cubic feet) is roughly 1.5 times the area under the canopy (square feet). (See Figure 3.22.) This relationship is "the most critical factor in determining long-term tree health," according to James Urban, an Annapolis MD landscape architect and national street-tree expert. Some plants probably

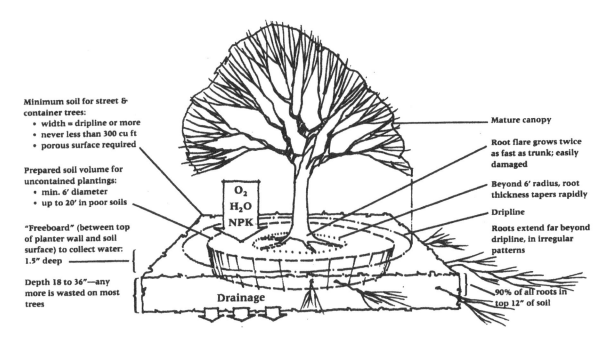

**Minimum soil for street &
container trees:**
- **width = dripline or more**
- **never less than 300 cu ft**
- **porous surface required**

**Prepared soil volume for
uncontained plantings:**
- **min. 6' diameter**
- **up to 20' in poor soils**

**"Freeboard" (between top
of planter wall and soil
surface) to collect water:
1.5" deep**

**Depth 18 to 36"—any
more is wasted on most
trees**

**O₂
H₂O
NPK**

Drainage

Mature canopy

**Root flare grows twice
as fast as trunk; easily
damaged**

**Beyond 6' radius, root
thickness tapers rapidly**

Dripline

**Roots extend far beyond
dripline, in irregular
patterns**

**90% of all roots in
top 12" of soil**

Figure 3.22   Root volume requirements for trees. Recent research indicates the minimum soil volume, especially for contained plantings, is greater than conventional standards provide. (*Illust.:* Craig Farnsworth, based on James Urban et al.)

use more than this volume in the wild; many can survive on less. As a general principle, the more root volume is reduced from this ideal, the more stress the plant must cope with, and the more maintenance it requires. Avoidable stress and maintenance are costly and unsustainable.

Aboveground, plants may be domed, columnar, or pyramidal; root spread varies widely, depth less so. A narrow columnar tree does not necessarily have a deep, narrow root system. Thus the "dripline" concept, while handy, seldom accurately represents actual roots. Because roots taper and fork as they grow away from the trunk, the dripline usually covers a majority of the largest roots.

Available root volume may be even less than it appears at the surface. Utility lines frequently run through tree pits; steam lines are lethal, but all utility lines steal root volume. Flared footings, bedrock, and other invisible barriers may rob even more. Many trees survive only by sending roots immense distances, following any line of soil weakness and permeability. This stresses the tree and can result in heaved sidewalks, broken planters, and clogged sewers. (Contrary to popular belief and marketing, few trees actively attack foundations except when severely root-bound.)

The conventional bias is toward protecting structures, unnecessarily destroying many trees as a result. Relatively few tree species are capable of attacking masonry. Most "problem" species are "gross feeders" whose roots follow the soil surface, thus requiring extra-broad planting areas. In new construction, such trees should not be planted near structures.

There are proprietary physical or chemical barriers to stop the spread of roots. Unless the plant can spread in other directions (which may cause problems elsewhere), the barrier is merely another reduction of root space, producing increased stresses. Barriers are usually short-term solutions at best and, especially for sustainable construction, a last resort. Avoid placing structures and vigorous-rooted trees too close together. Make sure that water, irrigation, stormwater, and sewer pipes do not leak in root zones, attracting roots toward the leak and eventually into the pipe. ("Frost free" faucets, which intentionally release water below the standpipe to avoid freezing, need special consideration near trees, especially if the local frost line is shallow.)

Reduced root volume can have several effects. The most striking example is bonsai, in which root pruning dwarfs the aboveground plant. Bonsai can be kept alive and healthy for hundreds of years, but only with devoted maintenance. (Bonsai are regularly turned out of their pots for root care; don't try this with the average street tree!) The stress of inadequate planting space makes trees short-lived, highly vulnerable to pests, diseases, and storm injury.

Despite new research-based standards, widely published in the *Graphic Standards* and other references, many horticulturists, landscape architects, and contractors are *still* using outdated planting details, especially for containers or limited spaces. Current standards recommend significant increases in volume per tree, and introduce two alternatives to street-tree "pits." These

are "continuous trenches" and "root path trenches," illustrated below. (Figures 3.23-3.25)

Soil under pavement is deliberately compacted to support sidewalks. In the United States, an engineering compaction standard is used, significantly denser than proven European specifications (see below). This creates a wall around conventional pits, often as hard as concrete. The *continuous trench* stretches from tree to tree, under reinforced paving that bridges the planting area, greatly increasing soil volume available to each tree. It requires slightly different sidewalk construction details, which any experienced contractor can readily learn; however, if such pavement is later cut, it

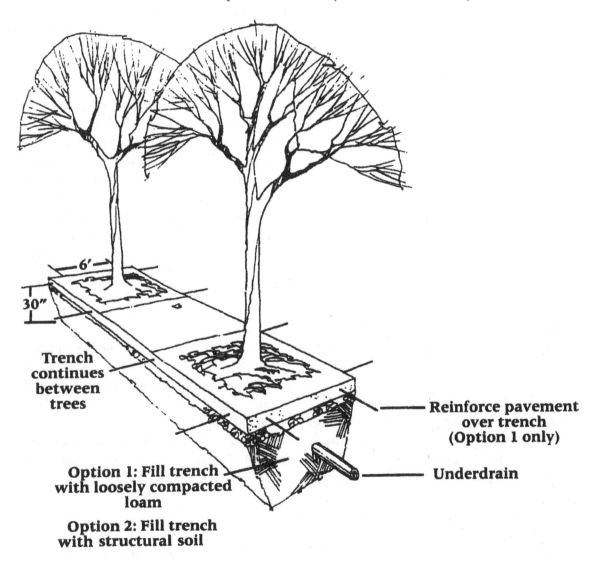

Figure 3.23   Continuous trench plantings gain enough root space to survive in urban settings. The trench may be filled with loam (reinforced paving is required) or with "structural soil." See Figure 3.24. (*Illust.:* Craig Farnsworth, based on James Urban et al.)

Figure 3.24 Continuous trench plantings can unify a streetscape. Paver joints are open to admit air and water. (*Project and Photo:* Henry Arnold.)

may not retain strength to support itself. Variations on the design are used for plazas, sidewalk plantings, and other urban situations. Modular suspended pavement takes the bridging concept a step further: see below.

The *root path trench* leads roots out of the pit in small radial trenches, about four inches wide by twelve inches deep. Each trench contains a drainage product, a plastic "waffle" core wrapped in geotextile, which brings both water and air through the length of the trench. Surrounded by good planting soil, this air and water source provides conditions roots need to grow; thus roots follow the trench. Beyond the narrow trenches, soil does not need to be replaced wholesale, but must be good enough for roots to spread eventually.

One planting structure for street trees that did not make this book's second edition is the "modular suspended pavement" system; the first commercial US installations occurred the same year as the book

came out. The concept of pavement "suspended" over planting soil is part of continuous trench design, but reinforcing pavement to be self-supporting is costly and limits the width of soil that can be spanned. Modular systems use "cells" resembling oversized milk crates that support paving from below, and are filled with lightly compacted soil through which roots readily grow. As with continuous trench systems, all or most of the area under the sidewalk or other paving is excavated; depth varies by species, commonly three and a half feet. The cells are stacked to fill the trench, leaving openings for installing root balls. The open "crate" structure allows utilities to be routed through the stacked cells if necessary. (Figures 3.26, 3.27).

Two systems typify the modular suspended concept: Silva Cell 2, manufactured by DeepRoot,[68] and Strata (which has both a cell and a "vault" product) from CityGreen, which has US and foreign distributors. Sizes and assembly methods vary; all are usually stacked several layers deep.[69] Both brands are plastic (although Silva started as plastic-embedded steel), using recycled material and glass reinforcement in some cases, and are engineered and rated to support traffic up to large semi-trailers. Strata products are designed to nest for transport, cutting bulk and thus shipping energy costs. Plastic cells can be cut in the field to fit odd-shaped spaces, providing structural integrity is not compromised. Both systems can (and should) do double duty by harvesting and storing stormwater. Both are relatively costly, but not if a life-cycle approach is used.

An important advantage to suspended-pavement systems is that no special soil mix is required, which means that the mix can be tailored to the site and the tree species used, and soil excavated on-site can often be part of the mix. This contrasts with "structural soils," discussed in the next section. Comparisons of these differing approaches to urban planting follow the description of structural soil.

Pros and Cons of "Structural Soil"

In addition to redesigning structures in which urban trees must survive, there have been attempts to redesign soil itself. Various forms of "structural soil" attempt to protect root zones from compaction, while

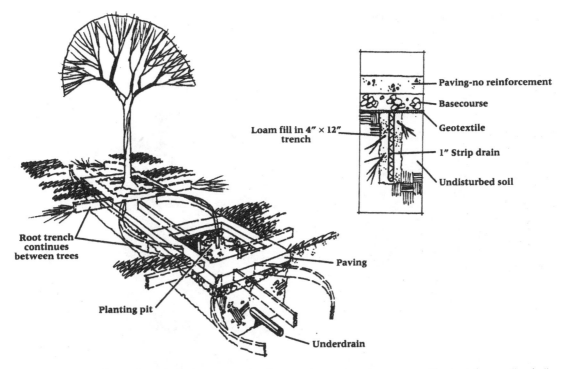

Loam fill in 4″ × 12″ trench

Root trench continues between trees

Planting pit

Paving

Underdrain

Paving-no reinforcement

Basecourse

Geotextile

1″ Strip drain

Undisturbed soil

Figure 3.25 Root path trenches require less excavation than continuous trenches, yet provide air and water "paths," which lead root growth. Pavement reinforcing is also eliminated. (*Illust.:* Craig Farnsworth, based on James Urban et al.)

Figure 3.26 "Cells" to support suspended pavement are a relatively recent addition to the toolkit for protecting street trees. Strata Cells, shown here, are designed to stack for efficient shipping (right rear). (*Project and Photo:* Citygreen.)

Figure 3.27 "Pits" are created by leaving out cells; the whole trench is backfilled after placing trees, and pavers rest atop the cells. Rectangular Strata Vault system is shown; Silva Cells are similarly shaped. Roots (and utilities) pass easily through such support structures. (*Project and Photo:* Citygreen.)

supporting sidewalk traffic. The term "structural soil" covers several materials:[70]

- natural "compaction resistant" sandy loams
- sand-based "Amsterdam tree soil"
- lightweight porous-aggregate mixes
- crushed-stone-and-soil mixes.

The first edition of this book gave crushed-stone-based structural soil a cautious thumbs up. Since that time, however, serious controversy has emerged over this material. Cornell University's Urban Horticulture Institute (UHI) catalyzed the debate by *patenting* its crushed-stone structural soil recipe, called "CU-Soil."[71] Even structural soil advocates have deep doubts about patenting a mix that cannot work without adjustment for local conditions. Among others, street-tree guru Jim Urban and soil scientist Phillip Craul have expressed reservations about the patented mix.

Phil Craul ran a thirty-year test of a sand-based mix at the Syracuse (NY) College of Forestry. Trees planted in it withstood 115-mph winds that toppled trees in ordinary soils; brick paving over the mix neither heaved nor sank, even under snow-removal equipment. "The main reason I'm critical" of UHI's exclusivity, says Craul, "is that there's a long-tested, cost-effective alternative that works." Sand mixes, he says, are horticulturally better, structurally almost equal, and far less costly than CU-Soil.

Henry Arnold independently developed what he calls "air entrained soil." The aggregate he uses is internally porous; minerals like expanded shale or slate, heated until they swell like popcorn, are similarly used for greenroof soils. Arnold uses 50 to 65 percent porous aggregate, 5 to 10 percent organic matter, plus loam topsoil; the mix is adjusted for each site. Many of Arnold's installations have been in place for over thirty years (thirteen years before UHI published its recipe); he reports vigorous trees under heavy foot traffic. He points out that structural soil mixes require aeration and underdrainage and that pavement over structural soils should be pervious. Any landscape professional who understands soil basics can specify his nonpatented system.[72]

In concept, structural soil using crushed stone is simple, even elegant. An open matrix of stone provides support; soil for root growth fills voids in the matrix. To ensure stability of both support and void space, the stone must be angular, locking together under pressure.

For maximum voids, the stone is sieved to close size tolerances with only traces of smaller or larger particles. This is called "open grading," "gap grading," or "no-fines sorting," also important in porous concrete and porous asphalt paving (p. 251).[73] Proportions must be carefully controlled, and the soil portion must be sticky enough not to sift out of the matrix during placement.

UHI's specification for structural soil starts with 100 lb. crushed stone, sized ¾ to 1½ inch. To this are added 20 lb. clay loam and 0.03 lb. (½ oz.) of an artificial copolymer (hydrogel) tackifier. Moisture content should be about 10 percent. The mix is placed in 6-inch layers and compacted to 95 percent, sufficient to support heavy-duty paving. The mix, according to an article[74] by UHI director Nina Bassuk, costs $40–$75 per cubic yard, or $1.50–$2.75 per cubic foot.

UHI's early experiences convinced Bassuk that ordinary landscape contractors couldn't guarantee quality, so UHI patented its mix, requiring licensed installers; as of 2017 there are seventy-six of them. Although Bassuk credits 1,700 projects across the United States, Canada, and Puerto Rico to license-enforced quality control, the CU-Soil *patent* has probably caused as many problems as it has solved.[75]

"Everybody wants to use the stuff, but how can you patent a base-course material?" asks David Dockter, managing arborist for the city of Palo Alto CA, a strong advocate of structural soils. Indeed, those happiest with UHI's system seem to be people who, like Dockter, have adapted the formula to their region, with or without help from UHI. Where suppliers or city ordinances have enforced the patent word for word, dissatisfaction is common.

Michael Mills, consulting arborist with Vancouver's DMG Landscape Architects, has probably installed more structural soil than any individual in North America. Like Dockter, he credits UHI, but has significantly modified the mix for British Columbia's wet climate. Water-holding hydrogels were useless in Vancouver; Mills eventually substituted a binder called Soil Stabilizer. He's not sure how necessary it is, but because "the first question from engineers is al-

ways, how do you keep it from separating," it remains in his mix.

In UHI's original mix, the soil-to-stone ratio is 1:4. Mills uses a gravel-yard machine called a "cone separator," which removes flat stones that sieves can't catch, and achieves a 1:3 mix with more space for soil, aeration, and drainage. This innovation has widespread potential.

In Palo Alto, Dockter found that CU-Soil needed 50 percent more clay, low in silt to prevent clogging. It took Dockter's Cornell-licensed supplier several tries to find the right material, and supplies are limited. Regional availability, says Dockter, "is a tough one."

Regional problems can be aggravated by "boilerplate" specifications written into local codes. Bernie Jacobs (of Jacobs Ryan, Chicago) underscores how inflexibility can backfire. After what Jacobs calls "a real hard sell," Chicago-area planners wrote CU-Soil into municipal ordinances, enforcing them retroactively

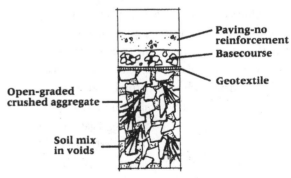

Figure 3.28a, b Structural soil resists compaction by incorporating crushed stone (top); soil fills voids, providing space for roots, air, and water. Diagram (bottom) shows components; paving over structural soil may be either porous or not. (*Photo:* J. Grabosky.)

on already-designed projects. Crushed limestone was used, based on UHI's experience in New York, but Illinois limestone is much softer, affecting soil pH. Lime-intolerant trees had already been purchased for Jacobs' project, but the contractor claimed (incorrectly, according to UHI) that changing stone would infringe the patent. Here the patent was misused to *prevent* adaptation.

UCLA Berkeley landscape architecture professor Patricia Lindsey, who studied at Cornell, also advocates designing structural soil mixes regionally. "There is no one perfect compaction-resistant, aggregate-based tree soil mix," she writes in an article outlining the mix-design process. The list of "Street Trees Appropriate for Use in Structural Soil" published by UHI's Bassuk is quite limited, and heavy on imported horticultural species.[76]

CU-Soil excels in one regard: it can be compacted above 95 percent "Proctor density," the standard test level required for base course under highway and industrial paving. The fact that the other mixes score only 85 to 90 percent compaction is less a technical concern than a matter of professional politics. US sidewalks, viewed as minor adjuncts to roads, are built to codes set by engineers, copied from highway specs. In Europe, where streetscapes are better valued, sand mixes compacted at 85–90 percent are almost universal under walkways. Acceptance of these proven standards would permit a much wider range of solutions. According to Bruce Ferguson, 85 percent compaction is becoming near standard for use under *porous* pavement, where excessive compaction defeats permeability.[77] Unfortunately, many US planners and engineers still insist, "We want thirty-year sidewalks, and don't care if we have to replace the trees," as Jacobs reports.

Engineer-friendly compaction may distinguish CU-Soil from other structural soil types, yet its "horticultural viability remains untested," says Mills. Amsterdam soil and porous-aggregate mixes have forty-year track records. The oldest CU-Soil installations are about thirty years of age; UHI published initial results in 1995. Since that time, says Jim Urban, "it has been embraced as almost a fad, a panacea for trees in urban areas. We just don't have good science on what happens to tree roots going through this mix long-term."

To study root growth, UHI and Palo Alto researchers dug up trees grown one or two years in structural soil. Roots showed vigorous long, thin growth, kinked from squeezing around matrix stones. Dockter found eighteen inches of new root growth after one year. Roots also tended downward, away from pavement, which should prevent heaving. According to proponents, plantings in CU-Soil always outperform those in conventional pits, but their methodology, especially of early testing, has been questioned.[78]

Arnold's air-entrained installations have been revisited periodically and appear to be robust.[79] They indicate that structural soil based on porous aggregate and carefully designed for drainage and aeration can seriously improve urban tree survival. They suggest that gels and other additives may be unnecessary, at least in some regions.

The key question, though, is long-term documentation. Craul has seen several recent cases of trees dying, apparently of root strangulation, in mixes based on the CU-Soil spec.[80] Although small roots and young trees thrive in short-term tests, Craul fears that mature roots may become too big to fit through voids— a problem that will only appear over time.

Bassuk counters that failures are only due to improper mixes or procedures. "People typically think the mix is too stony, and add extra soil," she says, which interferes with stone-to-stone locking. The mix then settles, producing compacted stony soil. Skimping on depth is another risk. UHI recommends 24 to 36 inches depth; one failed test, says Bassuk, used only 4 inches.

Structural soils have real promise and need real testing. But in an applied profession like landscape architecture, how should such things be tested, and how much testing is enough? Horticultural testing in particular can't be hurried: as one urban forester puts it, "It still takes a hundred years to grow a hundred-year-old tree."

Until many different species have been tested to maturity, structural soil users are beta testing an experimental method, says Urban. Especially for landscape sustainability, testing and verification are critical. Inflated claims can doom an otherwise worthwhile product in the fickle court of public opinion. Jacobs suggests the structural soil debate is a wake-up call for landscape architects. In an increasingly quick-fix world, "we need a Green Industry Review Process," he says. A decade later, at least on the topic of street-tree planting methods, research may have progressed enough to be the basis of sound decisions.

The Great Soil Debate

At the ASLA's 2010 annual meeting, Jim Urban, Nina Bassuk, and Bob Pine of Pine & Swallow Environmental held a panel[81] in which each championed a street-tree system. Pine advocated for Sand-Based Structural Soil, or SBSS, similar to Amsterdam soil; Bassuk presented CU-Soil; and Urban advocated cellular suspended pavement.

Pine's presentation illustrated a wide trench filled with thirty inches of uniform sand compacted to about 85 percent. Pavement over the sand is supported by a six-inch layer of gravel, in which perforated pipes run. These pipes provide aeration, and irrigation lines run inside them that can be removed or replaced easily. Pine emphasized several advantages: sand is a widely available, familiar, and relatively inexpensive local material; its fast drainage removes the risk of anaerobic conditions; and the system is not proprietary. It conforms easily to odd shapes, and can be installed around existing utilities (with care during compaction).

Bassuk emphasized the need for 95 percent Proctor compaction as a given, stating that in her experience, this cannot be achieved with sand mixes without limiting root spread. (As noted above, the lower compaction values used for SBSS and similar systems are accepted and proven in Europe.) She noted that CU-Soil is also well drained, holding about 8 percent water, and that trees must be selected that prefer fast-draining soils. CU-Soil should be two to three feet deep. It is the only system that specifies a minimum-sized unpaved opening around each tree; this should be fifty square feet, about seven by seven feet, which is larger than most conventional tree-grates.

Urban summed up his argument by saying that "approaches that try to make the planting soil meet both the compaction requirements of the pavement and the growth requirements of the trees result in a compromise to tree growth potential." Modular suspended pavement systems, he emphasized, use only a small percentage of the excavated volume for structural support, so that the soil volume (and nutrients and moisture) available to trees is large. Not required to serve as structure, the soil can be compacted to a degree that fosters root growth. This loose compaction means that almost any soil can be used. Reuse of on-site excavated soil is a major advantage; even subsoils and heavy clays can be used with compost added. Reuse can save a major amount of transportation energy, both for disposing of excavated material and for hauling in replacement material. In addition, the soil mix can be tailored to the plantings, rather than the other way around, greatly expanding the list of species that can thrive. (The extremely well-drained character of structural soils works against the long-standing tradition of using floodplain species, which are adapted to dense soils, extreme moisture fluctuations, and physical abrasion, as street trees.) For these and other reasons, Urban concludes that on-site mineral soils must be reused as much as possible, minimizing imports such as sand.[82]

The panel's moderator stated that there was "no settled science" on urban tree plantings, and that the panel was intended to give landscape professionals decision-making tools. However, an ongoing study by Dr. Thomas Smiley had already been under way for six years at Bartlett Tree Research Labs, and it comes close to settling at least some of the science. In 2004, Dr. Smiley had planted identical (cloned) trees in beds of identical volume, side by side so that local soil, sunshine, and weather would be identical. The only difference was the planting system: two control plantings used loamy soil, one compacted, the other not; three structural soil beds—sand-based, expanded stone-based, and gravel-based; and two suspended-pavement cell products, Silva and Strata (see above). As the photo shows, the trees in beds with either brand of suspended pavement were visibly larger and continued to outpace the others, starting early in the study.

Smiley uses a measure that should help landscape professionals evaluate these situations fairly and pragmatically. In the study, he refers to the "net available soil," meaning the percentage of total planting-pit volume that is soil-filled (subtracting volume occupied by structural materials, whether stone, cells, or other materials that contribute neither water nor nutrients).

Figure 3.29 Identical saplings were planted in suspended pavement (Silva and Strata products, front row) and various sand- and rock-based supportive soils. The trees in cellular suspended pavement are noticeably larger, as visible in this photo after several years' growth. (*Project and Photo:* Dr. Tom Smiley, Bartlett Tree Experts.)

He also refers to this as the "soil efficiency" of each design. (Undisturbed loam soil is used as a baseline, representing 100 percent "soil efficiency.") Suspended pavement systems use engineered, strong, low-volume materials for support, so their soil efficiency is over 90 percent. Sand-based structural soil is about 50 percent efficient, while gravel-based systems are 20 percent efficient.

Soil efficiency is important in understanding some hidden considerations about design and cost of urban planting systems. Figure 3.30 shows the various tested systems; a bar shows their efficiency. Under each graphic tree, a schematic rectangle represents the volume required to provide as much "available soil" as the control loam. At 50 percent efficiency, for example, sand-based systems require twice the pit size and twice the volume of material as the loam.

First, soil efficiency affects design. Street trees, by definition, are located where space is limited, in both volume and surface area. The less soil efficient a planting method is, the more space is required to give the tree an equal chance of survival. The sand system requires twice the volume as loam, while the gravel system requires five times that amount. Assuming both are 3 feet deep, this translates to a surface area of 665 square feet per tree in sand (about 26 feet square), and 1,665 square feet for gravel mixes (a square about 41 feet on each side). Even when placed under the sidewalk (as with continuous trench designs), these per-tree areas can rarely be accommodated in any urban setting. This means that a recommendation of 600–1,500 cubic feet (common to both sand- and gravel-based structural soil specs) is likely an underestimate, even though it is dramatically more than convention-

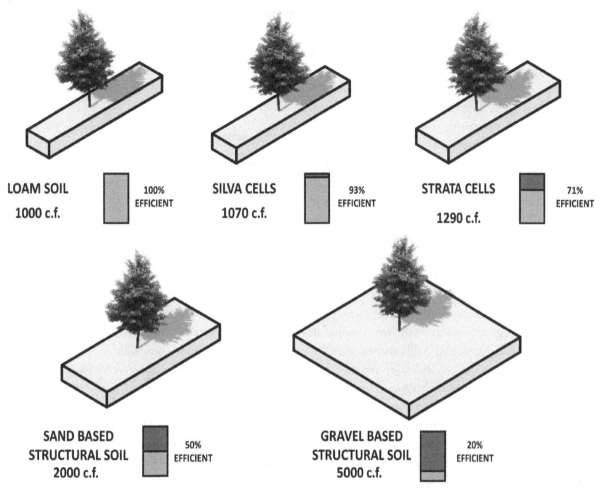

LOAM SOIL
1000 c.f.   100% EFFICIENT

SILVA CELLS
1070 c.f.   93% EFFICIENT

STRATA CELLS
1290 c.f.   71% EFFICIENT

SAND BASED STRUCTURAL SOIL
2000 c.f.   50% EFFICIENT

GRAVEL BASED STRUCTURAL SOIL
5000 c.f.   20% EFFICIENT

Figure 3.30 Net available soil, also called "soil efficiency," for various street-tree planting systems. Further testing showed both types of cellular support to have 90+ percent soil efficiency. (*Study:* Dr. Thomas Smiley and Bartlett Tree Research Labs. *Diagram:* James Urban.)

ally planted trees ever receive. This could explain reports of trees thriving in structural soil for a decade or so, and then declining—a large volume for a small tree becomes a small, soil-inefficient volume for a mature one.

Second, soil efficiency affects attempts to compare prices. Suspended pavement systems are not cheap. DeepRoot estimates, based on actual bids for installations under US conditions using two layers of cells, that the system costs $14–$18 per cubic foot, installed. (To facilitate comparison to other systems, this price includes only the cells, excavation, and soil, not base course, pavement material, or trees.) CU-Soil, according to Bassuk, averages between $40 and $75 per cubic *yard*—roughly $1.50 to $2.75 per cubic foot; SBSS is reported as being significantly cheaper,

although I found no precise figures. Thus it might seem, on the surface, that structural soils cost about one-tenth the price of cell suspension.

Jim Urban, however, cautions that the true price should be based on net available soil. On this basis, the quoted CU-Soil prices translate to $7.50 to $13.75 per cubic foot because only 20 percent is net available soil. This brings at least the upper end of the structural soil price range equivalent to the lower end of cell-suspension systems.[83]

My interpretation of these results is this: trees are simply too important and valuable, increasingly so in these days of carbon concerns, to cut corners. Planting trees at public or private expense, only to have them fail to thrive or die prematurely, is a waste of resources. Sand-based plantings have been *documented* for fifty years (probably longer in Europe), CU-Soil for twenty, Strata (via a sister company in the United Kingdom) for sixteen years, and Silva for thirteen. None of these is a full lifespan for most trees; each improves on the average lifespan of conventionally planted street trees. The Bartlett study clearly shows that growth is consistently better in cell systems; strong growth normally translates to better health and greater longevity. A life-cycle costing approach must consider long-term health (where poor performance would lead to replacement) as well as first costs. Add to that the difficulty, at 20 percent or even 50 percent soil efficiency, of providing enough volume anywhere in most cities, and the prudent investor might well lean toward suspended pavement. As with so many sustainable systems, the up-front cost is higher, but the long-term benefits appear to be significantly greater.

Urban plantings are critical to the environment in which an increasing percentage of humanity lives. Pit and soil innovations may considerably improve tree survival. The main reasons such systems are needed, however, are social: the value of urban land is so inflated that landowners refuse to allow adequate space for plantings, and standards set by engineers sacrifice trees to exaggerated cost and safety demands. Changing social expectations to recognize trees as essential to healthy urban places would be truly sustainable; special engineering for squeezed trees is a distinctly second choice.

Recommended Street-tree Practices

- Advocate adequate planting volume and surface area for urban trees, factoring in "soil efficiency."
- Always analyze and design soil mixes for aeration and drainage, using on-site soils where possible.
- Advocate compaction policy appropriate to traffic type, not "boilerplated" from vehicular paving standards.
- Base system cost comparisons on "soil efficiency," factoring in life-cycle costs (early replacement, utility access) and carefully evaluating cost-performance trade-offs.
- Use continuous trenches with modular suspended pavement as the gold standard, and structural soil if first cost is an overriding factor.

- Test and specify structural soil mixes locally; specify "or-equal" to permit proprietary and nonproprietary mixes.
- Cultivate experienced, but not necessarily licensed, contractors.

Planters, Raised Beds, and Containers

Growing any plant in a container or planter is similar to the tough situation of street-tree planting, and far more stressful than planting the same species in the ground. Limited soil volume means containers dry out, heat up, or freeze quickly, and can easily become waterlogged or nutrient deficient. Containers are most often set on hard surfaces, amplifying temperature and exposure. These stresses make large container plants particularly hard to sustain, especially if containers are undersized. Carefully selected shrubs and herbaceous plants are usually more successful.

Container plants require water and air. If the container has sufficient "freeboard" (see Figure 3.22), it may collect enough rainfall to sustain the plantings, assuming precipitation is adequate. Otherwise, irrigation is required. Container plantings without adequate irrigation are generally an unsustainable waste. Drainage for excess water must also be built in.

Similarly, plants that require maintenance they will never get cannot be part of a sustainable landscape. Containers usually require *increased* maintenance, but are frequently located in inaccessible places, making maintenance nearly impossible. Contractors' practical experience can often help landscape designers avoid such costly mistakes.

Updated Standards for Uncontained Plantings, Too

Trees and shrubs have been planted in lawns and other unconstrained areas using the same standard details since roughly 1900. These standards have changed[84]— but are still frequently reproduced from old books, cut and pasted onto blueprints, and taught in university courses.

In particular, the recommended size of planting holes has grown. An older standard of "twice the width of the root ball" is now considered a *minimum*. Depth should be six inches deeper than the root ball;

for trees at least a six-foot width is now preferred. In poor, clayey, or compacted soils, pit width goes up dramatically, to fifteen or twenty feet.

The bottom and sides of the pit must be roughened. Clay soils particularly will glaze when dug, creating "virtual container" conditions. In slow-draining soils, space for good soil *below* the root-ball level helps prevent waterlogging. Soil for filling the pit should be amended with compost or other organic matter up to about 5 percent by weight. Making the soil too rich can discourage roots from leaving the pit—and voilà, virtual container again. Mycorrhizae (fungi symbiotic with plant roots) are important in many planting mixes, purchased commercially or incorporated from native leaf litter and soil. Grade the surface to form a water-collection saucer, but not so deep that water stands.

Many experts now feel that staking and wrapping the trunk of trees is to be avoided. In addition, the tree should be oriented in the same direction it was growing in the nursery. This is not just a reference to the old horticultural jokes about "green side up." Rather, it means marking the north side of each tree in the nursery, and turning that side northward when planting it on-site.

Select Sustainable Species (and Substitutes)

Landscape architects select plants for aesthetic and practical reasons: color and flowering season, or capacity as a windbreak or shade tree. When sustainability is a goal, these reasons must be balanced carefully with environmental costs of planting and maintenance. Resource costs can vary greatly between different species. When *substituting* because the specified plant is unavailable, basic understanding of ecological issues is essential.

Every species of plant evolved in, and is adapted to, a fairly specific region with its own range of soils and climate. Individual species are also "coevolved" to depend on other species of plants, animals, insects, fungi, and microbes in their community. Some species are very narrowly limited to exact growing conditions, while others, informally known to plant ecologists as "wides," are adaptable within a broad range of conditions. Selection of cultivars for specific traits affects the coevolved capacities of the species, but the intent of selection and hybridization is usually to override the complex mix of evolved traits in favor of supercharging a single characteristic. This tends to make the tree less adaptable, even if stronger in a narrow sense.

When people plant landscapes, they must help plants survive in one of two basic ways. The conventional approach is to *provide the conditions* that each plant requires—watering, shading, warming, even cooling the garden environment to match conditions where the plant evolved. The second approach is to *select plants that are adapted to conditions* similar to the new landscape. These plants tend to survive in the new location with little maintenance. Thus the second approach is *generally* more compatible with sustainability.

One way of ensuring well-adapted landscape plants is to select species that grow nearby without human assistance—the *native* plants of a region. There is some controversy over how to define "native" (see p. 172), and their maintenance performance is not conclusively documented. Nonetheless, a growing number of professionals have found that landscapes based *primarily* on native species save water and other resources. This is not an argument for using natives *exclusively*. Exotic or non-native species, adapted to similar conditions, are used in many regional gardens as specimen or accent plants.

Few, if any, plants, including natives, are "no maintenance" in a built landscape. Even the most hardy natives are stressed by being transplanted. Isolated from the diversity of their coevolved ecosystem, and placed in close contact with human activity and human chemicals, even native plants require care. This is especially important during an establishment period of one or two years after planting.[85] After that time, natives require less maintenance than most exotics—but not "zero maintenance." The only zero-maintenance landscape is solid concrete, and even that will begin to break down after about thirty years.

Because they are adapted to a range of conditions, "wide" species are among the easiest to match to new sites. Most common horticultural species are "wides," because they survive in many settings. Some of these species, however, adapt *so* easily to new conditions that they become invasive, disrupting native ecosystems and causing extinction of unique regional species. Loss of regional species and ecosystems, like high maintenance of poorly adapted imports, is a serious sustainability issue. It is also a tragedy for design, since the results tend toward homogeneity around the globe.

Native plants, ironically, are not as easily available in nurseries as globe-trotting imports. As a result, it may take *more* work to locate a native species, and to find an appropriate substitution when the specified native can't be found. Some natives require specialized planting techniques. Contractors and designers committed to sustainable landscape construction *must* be prepared to go the extra mile and, in particular, to communicate extremely clearly about substitutions.

In general, if a specified plant is native, the substitution should also be. If a suitably similar native can't be found, then the substitution should be well adapted to survive without extremes of artificial maintenance. Non-native species that are invasive under local conditions should *never* be specified for outdoor use. (Nursery catalogs often refer to "naturalizing species"; their ability to naturalize is an environmental problem if they spread rapidly and aggressively.)

Trying to match these sustainability concerns to desired form, color, flowering season, and so on, is not easy. In some regions, such as the desert Southwest, no substitutable species may exist. For example, except for river and mountain areas, the Southwest lacks "canopy" trees. In such cases, design should usually change to achieve sustainability, not the other way around. Those who have mastered the art of native-plant gardening produce stunningly beautiful landscapes that eloquently tell the story of their region. This regional awareness in turn contributes to sustainable attitudes about specific places.

What Is a Native?

At first glance, it seems simple to define which plants are native to a region, and which are not: a native grows someplace naturally and always has—right? But this apparently simple issue provokes one of horticulture's hottest controversies.[86] This book is not the place to throw more fuel on that fire, but native plants are an important part of sustainable landscape construction. Without respecting native species, it is difficult to protect or create self-sustaining, diverse plant communities.

Several criteria can be used to distinguish native plants, but no single one will define them:

- The species *reproduces* in the region without human intervention.
- The species *survives* in the region without human care (irrigation, fertilization, removal of competitors, or other maintenance).
- The plant shows distinctive *local variations* that it lacks when growing in other regions.
- The species *coevolved* with and depends for survival on regional plant and animal species.
- The plant (or its ancestors) was not transported to the region by humans, purposefully or accidentally.

The basic concept of a native plant is not overly complicated. It has practical value in maintaining healthy ecosystems, not to mention a sense of regional place. Scholarly and geographic *certainty* about what is native is hard to achieve, however, and controversy has been surprisingly bitter. Landscape professionals can benefit from considering some of the difficulties in pinning down the concept.

- Plants do extend their ranges without human help, dispersed by wind, tides, or animals. However, like species extinction or soil erosion, dispersion is a naturally occurring process that has been dramatically and selectively speeded by human actions.
- Prehistoric and precolonial people frequently managed the plant communities around them, for example using fire to keep grasslands from being overtaken by shrubs and trees. The "managed" species, however, both those favored and those hindered by management, usually remained parts of the native plant community; only their balance was changed.
- Prehistoric and precolonial people also introduced seed from distant regions, usually for food. Relatively few imported crop plants colonized aggressively or survived without cultivation, unlike the many weedy invaders imported by colonial settlers.
- Defining the "region" can be difficult. For example, Red Fir (*Abies magnifica*) is found in the Sierra

Figure 3.31 Converting Sausalito CA's historic Fort Baker to a National Park Service conference center involved restoring native coastal vegetation with seed sourced on-site. The landscape architect's influence was unusually broad, prohibiting cars, reducing total building footprint by 30 percent, reusing non-historic building foundations for new construction, and combining sustainability with historic preservation and adaptive reuse. (*Project:* Office of Cheryl Barton. *Photo:* Marion Brenner.)

Nevada at elevations of 6,000–9,000 feet. Saying that the species is native to the Sierra, which few would dispute, is still risky: there are many areas in the Sierra above or below the species' altitude range where it would never grow well. Stating that a species is native to a *political* region (for example, a state) is even more misleading. Red Fir is considered an *Oregon* native, because it grows in the southern edge of the Cascade Mountains there, yet its current range includes less than 5 percent of Oregon's land area.[87]

- The "range" of a plant is a snapshot in time. During the most recent Ice Age, Red Fir grew at much lower elevations and farther south than it does today, and may have been totally absent from areas where it now thrives. Climate change due to greenhouse emissions is redrawing range maps of many species, an effect likely to be increasingly dramatic.

None of these points, in my opinion, seriously discredits the idea that coevolved, self-sustaining plant communities are critical to sustainability. Natives should be planted and protected *at every opportunity*. The alternative is an anything-goes horticulture favored by critics of the native-plant movement. Historically, that type of horticulture is responsible for many of the four hundred species of invasive plants now threatening vast areas of US ecosystems (see p. 119). A working definition of "native," even if not perfectly precise, is appropriate—and necessary—for sustainable landscape construction.

For landscape purposes, the most appropriate snapshot or baseline for native plants is fairly clear: just before modern colonization and industrialization began their trend toward unsustainable environments. In the United States, the list would include plants growing here between the end of the Ice Age and the arrival of European settlers. This is clearly not a "pure" historical or botanical yardstick. Rather, it is a value-driven choice reflecting the goal of reestablishing *self-maintaining* plant communities that conserve environmental resources and regional diversity, and offer a maximum of ecosystem services.

From a practical landscape perspective, there is no need for a vendetta against non-native plants. Only those non-natives that are invasive should be eradicated or prohibited or both. The remainder should be used sparingly, with consideration for their higher resource demands (including, often, transcontinental shipping) and lower value to coevolved regional species.

Use of primarily native species is often hindered by official and commercial attitudes. Many municipalities maintain officially approved plant lists. Some lists are based on native and regionally appropriate species. More often, unfortunately, the lists were drafted long ago, aimed at avoiding "messy" seeds, keeping branches away from utilities, protecting sidewalks from "terra-ist" roots, or preventing allergies. Commercial horticulturists, often advisors on these lists, saw (and some still see) no profit in native plants. The lists are now changing in many areas to promote drought-tolerant species.

One other commercial hindrance to native species is nursery stock grading. Standards rate uniformity of growth and form above most other considerations. Because many native plants never produce lollipop forms even under ideal conditions, they may be ruled out by default when Grade One Fancy stock is specified. There are times when uniformity is desirable—but be careful not to let it exclude valuable species unintentionally.

Designers interested in applying the idea of native species can get a clear, graphic, and scientifically based resource in Robert G. Bailey's trilogy of Ecoregions books. These explain the concept thoroughly, map out major species and ecosystems that make up bioregions, and relate region to design. Travis Beck's *Principles of Ecological Landscape Design* is an excellent recent work that brings real scientific knowledge to planting design and vegetation management.

Handle with Care

Besides requiring appropriate structures and conditions to support them, landscape plants need careful handling during the "unnatural" moving and planting process. Observing a few guidelines can cut losses—financial losses for the contractor, and waste that affects sustainability on a larger scale.

These guidelines are relatively common knowledge—conventional nurseries and contractors follow them for business reasons. When sustainability is a goal, these points increase in importance. Energy and materials costs involved in preparing, transporting, and planting nursery stock may be estimated roughly using data in Principle 7.

Choice of Nursery Stock

Landscape plants are supplied by nurseries in temporary containers, ball-and-burlap (B&B), or bare-root. They may also be transplanted directly from one site to another. The choice among these options significantly affects energy and labor costs, and plant survival rates, all of which are environmental issues worth considering.

Bare-root stock must be protected from drying; even a few minutes of exposure to air and sunshine can kill roots. Moist sawdust or wet paper, often under plastic sheet, holds in moisture.

Handle bare-root plants while dormant; this restricts the planting period. Refrigerated storage keeps plants dormant longer, but has serious energy costs.

Bare-root plants are least expensive, in resources and dollars. Survival rates are reasonable, especially when plants are fairly small.

Containers and burlapped root balls protect plants during transplanting, with generally higher survival rates. This is offset by resource costs of containers, and extra transportation weight. Be sure the ball or container size complies with or exceeds minimum industry standards.

Most containers are plastic; some are metal or wood. Resource issues are discussed in Principle 6.

Large mature plants, in great demand for landscape use, are always B&B or container; they cannot survive as bare-root. Large specimens represent long growing time and, like old-growth forests, are becoming rare and expensive. The ecological appropriateness, and even legality, of removing large trees from their original location deserve more consideration than they get. In Arizona, saguaros and other large cacti are routinely stolen from public land and sold.

On-site transplanting may save plants located in construction zones. Hand-dug transplants are usually bare-root. Root balls of transplants can be burlapped; this requires skill and must be done in season.

"Tree spades," large truck-mounted machines that lift trees, soil and all, provide the only option to save most mature trees. They represent significant energy costs and may risk compacting soil very near new planting pits. A hand-operated tree spade for small trees, the Tree Toad, is discussed in Principle 1.

All plantings, regardless of method, require significant time to recover from "transplant shock." Smaller stock recovers more quickly and usually "catches up" in size with larger plantings that take extra seasons to resume full growth.

Moving and Storage

Highway speeds generate wind, which along with sunshine and high temperature can wither plants rapidly, especially if recently dug or repotted.

In winter, wind-chill affects plants in transport, creating freeze-dry or frost conditions even when temperatures are not below freezing.

Plants in transport should *always* be completely covered with opaque tarps; in summer, spray the load before tarping. Do not use clear plastic; it has a greenhouse effect, and polyethylene blackens leaves.

Spray chemical anti-transpirants on leaves to slow water loss into the air, in both summer and winter.

Enclosed delivery vans, covered trucks, and semi-trailers protect plants, and can double as on-site storage. Enclosed vehicles *must* be ventilated to prevent overheating, and heated to avoid freezing, especially while parked.

Ideally, deliver and plant all in one day. Realistically, weather, available labor, and incomplete hard construction require just-in-time delivery or careful on-site storage, partially shaded and protected from wind.

For longer storage, or in hot, dry, or very cold weather, consult a nursery professional. "Heel in" roots or root balls with loose soil or moist sawdust, water regularly, and mist leaves.

Planting Practices

Comply, *at a minimum*, with up-to-date industry standards.

For bare-root plants, spread roots in the planting pit. Place the plant on a cone of soil.

Dipping bare roots in super-absorbent polymer

slurry increases water availability during the critical period after planting.[88]

Rough handling of container and B&B plants cracks soil away from roots. Never lift B&Bs by stem or trunk; use the wire cage, or nursery hooks.

Most contractors remove containers at planting, but it is not uncommon to see dying plants buried in their containers.

Slide plastic and metal containers off the root ball, sterilize, and reuse. If containers must be cut off, try to recycle them.

Remove wire from B&Bs to protect soil wildlife and future gardeners.

Cut back burlap around trunks. Leaving burlap at the trunk may stabilize the newly planted tree for the first year, after which it should be removed.

Disassemble and reuse wood from large-stock boxes (but not in new boxes, because of potential for spreading diseases).

Loosen or cut strangling container-bound roots before planting.

Set plants at the same depth indicated by the "nursery line," a color change on the trunk. Collect water toward or drain water away from the plant by regrading surroundings or adding soil amendments, *not* by "planting high" or extra deep.

Completely fill soil around roots. Air pockets commonly kill new plantings. To avoid them, water-in the plant immediately and thoroughly.

Use root stimulants and vitamins, especially vitamin B, to help the plant recover from stresses of being moved; apply immediately at planting.

Fertilize the plant only after it establishes new roots, based on local experience with soils, climate, and species. Conventional contractors usually fertilize at planting, to save a trip.

Mulch planting surfaces about three inches deep to hold moisture, but keep mulch several inches from the trunk itself.

Sod, bulbs, seeds, and potted herbaceous stock must be selected, handled, and maintained with equal care as larger plants.

Wildflowers

Meadow-like wildflower plantings have become popular for naturalistic, low-maintenance gardening. Not all commercial wildflower mixes are composed of natives; work with local suppliers, and carefully evaluate species.

Homeowners and professionals often assume "wild" flowers require no maintenance. As with other native plantings, this is not true.

For most sites, do *not* deeply till soils prepared for wildflowers. Loosen the top inch of soil. Deeper tilling releases dormant weed seeds.

Don't bury seed too deeply. Follow supplier recommendations. Many wildflower seeds should simply be broadcast, then rolled or tramped in.

Protect seed from birds during germination with mesh or mulch.

Keep seed evenly moist during germination, even for dryland species.

One wildflower supplier points out that the main cause of failure is *impatience*, followed by incorrect site evaluation, improper soil preparation, and inadequate early maintenance.[89] This reminder applies equally to all plantings, not just wildflowers.

Maintain New Plantings

Even with careful planting, many landscape plants die within their first year or two. Some losses are unavoidable, but many are due to inadequate maintenance. Watering, pruning, protection from extreme weather, and pest and disease monitoring are especially important during this "establishment period." Yet this is the time when these tasks are *least* likely to be done, at least in landscapes built under contract.

Unlike homeowner plantings, residential or commercial contract planting is often completed long before the buildings are occupied. Between planting and occupancy, *no one* may remember to do maintenance. For new plantings, this can literally be a matter of life or death. Watering, particularly critical just after planting, may be forgotten; plumbing may not be hooked up, or irrigation may not be programmed. Post-move confusion may keep clients from noticing the landscape for weeks after occupancy. The result: dead or stressed plants, remedial maintenance costs, and loss of "environmental services" that plantings were supposed to provide. Such waste is unacceptable in landscapes designed for sustainability.

To avoid this undesirable situation, contractor, designer, and client must plan in advance for maintenance responsibility. Some landscape design firms provide a written landscape maintenance schedule as part of their services; a few do scheduled maintenance as part of the contract.

Every client's needs and abilities are different—when they will move in, whether they will do maintenance themselves or hire groundskeepers—but the common factor is a transition period when responsibility passes from contractor to client. Because the landscape construction contractor is already familiar with the plantings, and is in many cases responsible for guaranteeing them, that contractor is best positioned to ensure plant survival during the establishment period. In my experience, planting contracts should include complete maintenance services *for the first two growing seasons after planting*. By that time, the guarantee on plants has been fulfilled, the client is in occupancy, and the contractor can hand over an established maintenance program or bid to continue services, which some species need more than others.

To cover two growing seasons, maintenance contracts for spring plantings must run eighteen months; for fall plantings, twenty-four. Including such long-term maintenance requirements in construction contracts is *not* common practice. It certainly increases initial client cost and requires landscape construction contractors to do (or subcontract) horticultural maintenance. Lack of maintenance, however, is the most common cause of unsatisfactory landscape performance. Such failures are costly in dollars and environmental wastefulness. Good maintenance *during* the establishment period almost always decreases maintenance needs *after* that period by establishing strong plants from the start—a form of preventive medicine. Planning and paying for competent maintenance up front is a cost-effective investment in sustainability (Principle 10).

Organic Maintenance

"Organic" or "natural" gardening has become well-known and popular, for both food crops and decorative gardening. Many excellent reference works are available. Many are home oriented, and not all organic practices can easily be used with large-scale landscapes or paid labor. Decreasing toxic chemical use in *all* landscapes, however, clearly benefits sustainability.

Energy costs of synthesizing, transporting, and applying chemicals are also of concern.

The conventional separation between construction and maintenance sometimes blurs this issue. Likewise, many professionals who maintain commercial and institutional landscapes continue to opt for machinery and chemicals. Design, construction, and maintenance of built landscapes at all scales benefits from keeping organic gardening principles in mind.

Some information on landscape-scale organic maintenance is included in Principle 10. Related information on composts and compost teas, important in organic maintenance as well as construction and restoration, is found in Principle 2.

Evaluate Turf: The Green, the Bad, and the Ugly

In general, almost any vegetation contributes to sustainability. Turf, the three-quarter-inch fuzz that covers more than 30 million acres of the United States, may be the exception, a sustainability paradox. As author Ted Steinberg puts it in his excellent book *American Green*, "Grass by itself can indeed prevent soil erosion and stormwater run-off, but the quest for perfect turf is another story altogether."[90]

Books like Virginia Scott Jenkins's *The Lawn: A History of an American Obsession* offer in-depth coverage of this contentious topic, America's number-one cultural landscape. Increasing use of and controversy over *artificial* or *synthetic* turf, however, requires a hard look.

Severe and prolonged drought has been widespread in many parts of the country during the first decades of the twenty-first century.[91] Drought-stricken municipalities, before any other response, usually place limits on landscape irrigation and outright bans on new landscape planting, especially turfgrass. While this may be unfair to the landscape industry and potentially counterproductive (lost vegetation eventually makes drought more severe), these water constraints have had unavoidable impacts. Among these have been increased use of native plants and Xeriscape, but also replacement of living turf with plastic.

For homeowners, water restrictions plus no-maintenance fantasies make artificial turf very attractive. For similar reasons, many communities have installed artificial sports fields, dog runs, and road medians;

maintenance costs go down to one-tenth or -twentieth of live grass, water use theoretically drops to zero, and playing surfaces become all weather and all season, an alluring economic justification.

It requires a deeper look to evaluate whether artificial or living turf is "greener." An excellent source of information, and one on which the following discussion draws extensively, is Jessica Boehland's article in April 2004's *EBN*.[92]

Living turf is huge business. Upward of $40 billion is spent annually on US lawn care, with three-quarters of a million going to seed for new installations. Planted turf cumulatively covers an area larger than Pennsylvania. Six million *tons* of fertilizer plus 70 million pounds of pesticides are applied to lawns each year. Homeowners, many of whom would not eat a vegetable grown with poisons, typically apply lawn pesticides at *ten times* the rates used by farmers on crops. Overuse is leading to resistant pests and increased dosages. Runoff from yards is the single largest source of water pollutants in many urban areas. Lawn irrigation consumes an estimated 60 percent of urban water in the western United States and 30 percent in eastern US cities. Overwatering escalates grass growth, thus increasing mowing and greenwaste, and contributing to fungus growth, which in turn increases pesticide use. Mowing lawns uses hundreds of millions of gallons of gas yearly and puts out 5 percent of US total air pollutants. Gas mower noise reaches 90 decibels, beyond levels known to cause hearing damage. Finally, 31 million tons of yard waste is generated annually, accounting for 17 percent of municipal solid waste in the average US city.

Artificial turf—in theory—eliminates many of these problems. Ideally, it requires no water, fertilizer, or pesticides. In practice, artificial playing fields are often hosed down twice a day because they heat up. Water is also used to *wash* artificial turf: windblown dirt lodges in it, dogs do the usual on it, and blood and vomit are common from sports mishaps. Unlike living grass and soil, fake turf does nothing to biodegrade such contaminants and health hazards. Persistent weeds will also grow *through* artificial turf, requiring pesticide treatment. Still, none of these equals what living grass requires. The Institute of Real Estate Management estimates that living turf costs $3,500 to $10,000 per acre per year to maintain.

Artificial turf, when it first appeared under the name Chemgrass in 1964, was stiff plastic mounted to asphalt or even concrete. Sports injuries on early fake grass were high. "Second-generation" artificial turf uses smaller, softer plastic blades, "infilled" between stems with sand and recycled rubber chips. This is far softer than early versions, and due to absolute regularity, artificial turf surfaces are now considered safer for players than divot-pocked, worn living turf.

Although artificial turf avoids many problems of living lawns, it has few of living turf's environmental benefits—such as they are. Living turf, even monocultures of locally ill-adapted species, is *living*. It produces oxygen and cleans air, like any living plant. It can trap half a ton of airborne dust per year and, like bioswales (p. 249), filters pollutants from stormwater. It also dramatically decreases soil erosion because its roots stabilize soil. Turf is up to 15°F cooler than bare soil on a hot day, 30°F cooler than asphalt. It reduces ambient noise by 8 to 10 decibels.

Artificial turf, by contrast, is inert, in many ways a form of paving; its suppliers are often outgrowths of the flooring or carpeting industry. It does not produce oxygen, or trap CO_2; in fact, being made from petroleum-derived plastic, it is on the wrong side of the carbon balance-sheet. Drainage problems have been common (even though in some installations it is a cure for the muddy field), and if it filters stormwater at all, the process is passive, without biological breakdown.

Artificial turf has been suspected of outgassing from plastic blades and crumb-rubber infill. Despite several studies, people still state as fact that plastic grass gives off volatile organic compounds (VOCs); most studies have found such chemicals, but at non-hazardous levels. (In indoor facilities, concentrations of VOCs could still be a problem.) Some have questioned whether, since the crumb rubber may go home in a child's hair or clothing, the studies have underestimated the time and intimacy of exposure. There are also questions of whether the source or processing method for either rubber or plastic makes a difference. Many concerns relate to proprietary additives in colorants for the plastic leaves, and other chemicals used in rubber tires, safe enough while the tire is intact but possibly released by grinding for turf-filler. Another concern, skin infections, is often cited; the same studies indicate that while abrasions are more common on plastic, fake grass harbors fewer bacteria than the real thing, reducing opportunities for infection.[93]

Permeability (to water and air) of many artificial turf products is limited. Most manufacturers' information and marketing gloss over this extremely important point. Even for permeable products (especially those with granular infill), ground beneath fake turf is at least compacted, often paved, to guarantee that it doesn't move. A new form of artificial turf, patented in 2004, features "horizontal drainage": an impermeable bottom membrane, a permeable layer that shunts water to the edges, and artificial turf on top. The South Nevada Water Authority accepts artificial turf as the water-saving equivalent of mulch, but only if it is permeable.

Thus, although it protects surfaces from precipitation, artificial turf does not actually stabilize soil. Like paving, artificial turf is probably vulnerable to being undermined by flowing water. Like pavement, it sterilizes soil if it excludes light, water, and air. Even types that permit some water infiltration may be air-impervious enough to create anaerobic soil conditions that potentially harbor nasty microbes. Impervious artificial turf concentrates runoff (and pollutants) rather than infiltrating it.

Artificial turf is promoted for airport runway edges, where *elimination* of wildlife is desirable for safety. The website of Act Global, producers of AvTurf, states bluntly that artificial turf "does not support food, water or shelter—which wildlife depend on and build their habitats about."[94] For runways, this is logical, but is the antithesis of sustainable landscapes.

Artificial turf is 5°F–15°F hotter than grass in hot weather. (The higher figure is equivalent to bare soil.) Artificial turf appears green from ordinary viewing angles, but from above is nearly black because of ground rubber "infill," which greatly increases heat holding.

Artificial turf, like any plastic, is susceptible to breakdown by ultraviolet radiation. This effect is most pronounced in the arid, sun-drenched regions where drought makes artificial turf seem most attractive— at least to those who are too homesick for temperate lawns to appreciate desert flora. Sunlight in the American Southwest is intense enough to make plastic trash bins crumble in a couple of seasons. Thus, while many brands of artificial turf have an eight-year warranty, they may not last that long in the places where drought

inspires their use. Living lawns, properly maintained in suitable climates, can last many decades.

Living lawns *can* be created and maintained more organically. In 2003, for example, New York City's Battery Park City Authority completed playing fields grown without conventional pesticides or fertilizers. Instead, organic soil nutrition products like compost tea (p. 113) maintain healthy soil and, thus, healthy turf. Soil nutrients and microorganisms have to be regularly monitored. IPM (Integrated Pest Management) keeps pesticides as a narrowly targeted last resort. Using native or regionally adapted species, and allowing lawns to go dormant with normal seasonal changes, such lawns meet most purposes of turf, while avoiding the worst problems of excessive water and chemical usage.

The most recent entry in the turf wars is hybrid or reinforced turf, which uses artificial "leaf" fibers to stabilize living grass. It has been used in Europe and Asia since the early 2000s; a few distributors (of Italian, Dutch, and Korean products) are trying to introduce it in the United States. Hybrid turf has tufts of plastic "leaves" spaced an inch or so apart, partly buried in soil, with seed sown among these reinforcing fibers. The concept is essentially a novel form of soil bioengineering, with inert and living components working together. It has similarities to fiber reinforcement of building materials such as adobe, fiber-reinforced cement, and fiberglass-reinforced plastics.

Two of the three systems that appear to be available in the United States have a backing and come in rolls. XtraGrass uses a partly biodegradable cloth, while EZ Hybrid Turf is fastened to something like coarse fishnet. In both cases, the openness of the backing encourages the live grass to root through the fabric. A second approach, Desso Sports's GrassMaster, plugs eight-inch-long fiber bundles into soil, leaving an inch above the surface. Plugging requires a large, computer-controlled tracked machine that resembles a multi-needle sewing machine on steroids; in operation, it appears to be a large tent grazing slowly down the field, like something out of *Harry Potter*. Completing most standard sports fields takes ten days or more, with the machine making multiple passes. Plugging (even as a conventional maintenance task without synthetic grass) improves drainage and rooting depth of the live grass. The fabric-backed methods can be installed with ordinary groundskeeping equipment and local labor, but the plugging approach can be installed into existing grass or bare soil. Desso's website shows the cost of hybrid turf as higher than artificial turf (six stars compared to five); the more numerical Field-Turf website lists natural turf installation at $4 per square foot and its artificial turf at $4.75, down from $5.50 in 2004 but still almost 25 percent more in first cost. All artificial and hybrid turf suppliers justify the extra cost in terms of extra playable hours compared to living turf. Some of this is legitimate—using a living field for two games in a day risks damage and time needed to repair the field that can interfere with the second event—but some estimates of the extra possibilities seem inflated. It may be possible, as some sources report, to use artificial or hybrid turf nine hours per day, ten and a half months per year, but seasonal weather, darkness, and limited local team numbers can make such projections moot. Hybrid turf, alive but reinforced with artificial fibers, using minimal artificial fertilizers and pesticides, seems to be a promising alternative that still allows more intense use, including some revenue-generating events like outdoor concerts. Resource costs remain, however: installing the GrassMaster system at London's Wembley Stadium used an estimated 75,000 *kilometers* (47,000 miles) of synthetic (petroleum-based) fibers.

Ultimately, the question of which turf is greener may have to be answered, "None of the above." It may be that the *idea* of turf—the perfect surface, nature subservient to human geometry—is the problem, not whether that surface is grass, plastic, or mixed.

Although turf is living, it is misleading to call it "natural." "In most places, flawless carpets of green simply cannot be grown in an environmentally benign manner," says one scientist quoted in *EBN*.[95] Natural meadows are seldom grass monocultures, nor an even, ground-hugging height. A natural meadow, furthermore, almost always is an early stage of succession, quickly invaded by woody plants. Preventing this—also known as maintaining the lawn—requires heavy inputs of labor, energy, and materials. Almost none of the fifty or so grass species used for US turf are native to North America.

Artificial turf, however, only avoids problems of living turf—it does not really offer benefits unless one assumes that turf-like expanses are inevitable. This assumption is perhaps the final criterion for judging both artificial and living turf. As Jessica Boehland succinctly notes in *EBN*, "By maintaining flawless living greenscapes, we teach that the control of nature is possible. Worse, we teach that it is to be expected."

Landscape architects such as Capability Brown and F. L. Olmsted bear considerable responsibility for popularizing turf lawns as essential parts of the English and American scene, as do gardening organizations and magazines. The fact that a layer of shaggy impervious plastic can substitute for turf may be the best indication that the idea itself needs to change, and that landscape professionals who care about sustainability must advocate that change.

Count on Plants to Sustain

All animals, including humans, burn energy, or, in terms of physics, degrade it toward entropy. Plants capture solar energy, making life possible. Globally, one plant species in eight is on the verge of extinction, while in the United States nearly one-third of known species are threatened—now with the added threat of removing endangered species protections altogether.[96] The destruction of rainforests and oceanic algae are well-known strains on global sustainability. What is less widely considered is that every tree damaged in "developing" land contributes to the same problems—and every tree planted offsets them, however slightly.

Planted trees serve many functions that decrease other resource use. They can perform a number of functions better than any technological equivalent yet invented. Because of their essential role in making life possible, as well as the social and financial costs of raising them, cultivated plants are too valuable to abuse. Sustainability requires that the very best of human horticultural and ecological knowledge become a universal standard for landscape work.

Subtopics and Search Terms for Principle 3: Favor Living, Flexible Materials

Note: Subtopics are also useful search terms; add "innovation" or "controversy" to search terms as appropriate.

Bioengineering
Search terms: soil bioengineering || biotechnical erosion control || wetlands creation || ecological restoration || stream-bank stabilization

Erosion control

Greenwalls and greenroofs
Search terms: greenwalls || ecoroofs || greenroofs || roof gardens

Plants: valuation
Search terms: tree appraisal || urban forest assessment

Plantings
Search terms: planting design || horticultural design || garden design

Plantings: native plants
Search terms: (native OR regional) + planting OR plants || plantings "native plants" || native plants design

Plantings: structures
Search terms: planting structures || plantings "trellis" || planters || street tree || "protect planting"

Horticultural products
Search terms: (horticulture OR garden OR yard OR landscape) + supplies

Resource List:

Links to information sources related to this chapter are posted at http://islandpress.org/sustainable-landscape-construction

Principle 4:
Respect the Waters of Life

A mighty mercy on which life depends, for all its glittering shifts water is constant.
—*Donald Culross Peattie, 1950*

Water covers nearly 70 percent of the globe, and makes up almost 99 percent of the human body. Essential to life, it is also a powerful force of change and destruction. Despite its global presence, far less than 1 percent is *fresh* water suitable for sustaining land animals and plants.[1] In Ambrose Bierce's wonderful phrase, "Water occupies 2/3 of a world made for Man—who has no gills."[2]

Besides regional and seasonal water *scarcity*, water *quality* is threatened by pollution. Even in such apparently waterlogged and water-surrounded places as Florida, scarcity of fresh, clean water is a serious issue.[3] Paul Simon (the US senator, not the musician) has predicted that wars over oil will soon take second place to wars over water.[4] Drought and increased flooding spread simultaneously over whole continents, their occurrence linked to both air pollution[5] and global climate change (see p. 20). Even places that receive increased precipitation actually see a decrease in available water, due to high runoff, violent storms, higher evaporation rates, or changes in seasonal arrival of moisture.[6]

If any single issue seems likely to push landscape sustainability into the foreground of public awareness and to change professional practice, that issue is water. Since the first edition of this book, the seriousness of water problems (which have been there all along) has become far more evident. Consumers, businesses, and governmental agencies have taken active interest in what were once fringe concepts—rainwater harvesting, BTEC, or constructed wetlands. In addition to better acceptance of existing solutions, water conservation has driven technological innovation in the irrigation

---

Discussed in This Chapter

Understanding natural water patterns.

Protecting surface water features, such as wetlands, lakes, and streams.

Restoring water bodies that have been damaged.

Special techniques for balancing human water needs with regional conditions.

Harvesting and storing water.

Getting more out of each drop with graywater.

Efficient irrigation, and new savings through "smart controllers."

Water purification by vegetative and mechanical means.

---

industry. Even the civil engineering and regulatory community is slowly changing, although it remains far too dominated by the pave-and-pipe paradigm.

Cultural and legal attitudes toward water are huge hidden influences on how it is used and distributed. The difference in water law between the eastern United States (share and share alike, to oversimplify) and the western states (first claimant takes all, use it or lose it) are responsible, perhaps more than weather or streamflow, for many of the West's notorious water problems. By contrast, religious teachings obligate traditional Muslims to share water, and denounce those who would deny it even to a stranger—attitudes adapted to arid lands.[7]

Construction affects water and water quality in many ways. Direct water use during construction ("embodied water") is discussed in Principle 6. By changing natural patterns of water movement, structures and paving can change water from a life-giving force to a destructive one. During construction work, sediments and pollutants enter water on or near the site. Collecting and distributing water for human use also affects the site's hydrology—and that of its neighbors. Carefully planned landscapes can compensate for some of these changes. As traditional societies as different as Mayans and Balinese have shown, well-integrated construction can make some ecosystems more productive without detriment to others. Unfortunately, this is the exception rather than the rule where modern construction is concerned.

Water is well-known as a poetic metaphor for patient, slippery, flowing power, gentle yet unstoppable. Yet the conventions of engineering frequently take a confrontational stance toward water—as if it could be pinned down by brute force. Conventional texts on landscape construction continue to indoctrinate students with ideas like "water causes scouring action when left uncontrolled."[8] Destructive water flows, ironically, result more often than not from human attempts at control. Unlike hard construction materials, water *never* responds well to heavy-handed methods. It must be worked *with*, like plants, people, or any living thing.

This chapter looks at ways of protecting the most critical resource of all.

Work with the Site's Water Regime

Water is more a system than a substance. Using water sustainably, and protecting natural water bodies, begins with understanding this system. Although it is possible to think of a pond as an object, its boundaries are muddy, and its connections to other objects are many. The pond (perhaps the simplest form of surface water) cannot be properly protected just by fencing it, as a tree or historic sculpture might be. Protecting water features means understanding their links to larger patterns.

For this reason, water protection merits a separate place in this book, rather than treating it as part of

site protection. The techniques discussed in Principle 2 are *part* of protecting water on-site. What differs is how these techniques are applied to the web of water, a web that weaves together rivers and wetlands, evaporation and rainfall. In this web, surface waters are linked to one another, to underground aquifers and springs, to water vapor and precipitation, and ultimately to the oceans. Protecting any part of this system is valuable in itself, and also contributes to conserving the health of the whole. For maximum benefit, protection of water bodies needs coordination throughout each watershed or river basin.

Respect Natural Drainage Patterns

Because river geometry is complex, many people still think of stream channels as random in shape and location. Nothing could be further from the truth. Each channel where water runs, and each pocket where it collects, matches the quantity and speed of water that normally flows through it. A similar relationship between shape and capacity is simpler to see in roadway design: a four-lane avenue with distinct turn lanes can handle more and faster traffic than a two-lane street where turning cars wait in traffic. Likewise, the shape of any landscape feature touched by water is dynamically related to the way water flows there. So is its location. For construction, the important point is this: change the shape and you change water's performance, how much soaks in to benefit soil and plants, and how much runs off or collects. Too much or too little of either can dramatically change the site, sometimes overnight, sometimes over many invisible years.

Three major factors interact to determine how water performs on a site. These are:

- the *quantity* of water itself
- the *material(s)* over which it runs, including vegetation
- the *shape*, particularly the steepness, of the surface on which flow occurs.

A small quantity of water running on porous soil at a gentle slope will mostly be absorbed. On the same material and slope, a large quantity (from a huge storm, or hard surfaces upstream) will erode the soil quickly; erosion is also speeded if the slope is steeper or the surface softer. Surfaces stabilized by vegetation erode more slowly, as do hard surfaces. Hard materials are vulnerable, however, where they meet softer soils.

Construction can change any of these three factors. Impervious constructed surfaces shed water, concentrating water quantity. Soil materials are compacted, loosened, and amended. Grades are changed, and plant cover removed or altered. Once the dynamic balance between these factors is changed in any part of the system, all links in the water web must readjust toward new balance. This readjustment happens gradually all the time in natural watersheds and is a key concept in construction involving water.

Planning for water on a site demands understanding local patterns that have evolved over centuries. This is site specific and region specific, but there are several key questions to ask. If you cannot answer these yourself, or don't understand what they imply, get specialist help. Water is too important to ignore.

- From where does water come to the site, and where does it go from the site? Even standing water has a source and a destination, if only rain and evaporation.
- Does on-site runoff move in sheets, or in channels?
- Are surfaces hard or porous, and where does water spill from one kind of surface to another?
- Where does standing water accumulate, and why? How are standing and moving water linked?
- Regionally, what are the shapes of river systems? Do they branch like trees at acute angles, or make sudden right-angle changes in direction? Large-scale patterns often indicate that geology is shaping the drainage, making it hard to construct new channels "against the grain."

If there is any kind of stream, creek, or river on the site, or affecting it, the following questions also need answers:

- Does the channel meander (bend from side to side)? This indicates a stream that is slowing and dissipating excess energy. Its force may be due to steep slopes or to increased volume from upstream. Straightening the meanders is ill-advised; forceful

flow will cause erosion and flooding until meanders are reestablished. Working upstream from meanders involves different conditions and methods than working downstream.
- Is the stream cutting away its banks, or depositing soil? Cutting indicates high volume and speed. Expanding into a larger channel, water slows and drops sediment. Planting or stabilizing areas of cut requires a different approach than for areas of deposition.

Besides answering such questions in the present, it is important to respond to changes over time. Upstream, development may increase runoff, or agriculture and industry may divert water. An example of a response to upstream development is Crystal Cove State Historic Park (pp. 146–47). Monitoring development proposals may forestall some problems. (Downstream changes usually have less impact, although wells or dams affect whole regions.)

Accept Regional Limitations of Water Supply

Conventional water management imports and exports water hundreds of miles by pipe or ditch for municipal, industrial, and agricultural use. Water conflicts are continually escalating: farmers versus cities versus river restorationists, for example. Areas lacking political defenders lose their water. Water is diverted from regions, particularly undeveloped mountain areas, said to have "excess" water, to supply demand in locations that have used up their local supply. Water is impounded in reservoirs before it can "wastefully" run away downstream. Clearly, this affects the ecosystem from which water is taken, or to which it no longer flows. The smaller the quantity of water, the shorter the distance diverted from natural flows, and the sooner the borrowed water reinfiltrates, the less likely to do harm.

Regional water management has stark impacts on landscape-related businesses and land users. Particularly in the western United States, municipal water conservation ordinances, in response to drought, typically target horticulture first. The 2002 drought, for example, cost landscape industries in Colorado 2,000 jobs and $60 million in revenue.[9] In response, many

Figure 4.1   This Guadalajara convent garden makes elegant, sparing use of water for tranquility. Roof drains replenish the pool. (*Project:* Arq. Alfonso Peniche-Banisteros. *Photo:* Kim Sorvig.)

landscape-related firms *increased* revenue by providing drought-tolerant plants, Xeriscape designs, and water-saving maintenance.

Thus, although water management and policy may seem a planning issue, it impacts and is influenced by site-specific construction. Demand for water is affected by where and how people build. Conventional water features, like fountains, can be great sources of pleasure, but ostentatious designs waste water—often imported, purified water. Modern recirculating tech-nology combined with traditional designs gets stunning effects from tiny amounts of water.

Demand for water is also affected by plantings. Minimizing water import and export is a strong argument for gardening with native plants (pp. 172). In some regions, the native-plant list may not include plants for every use. For example, in the high desert, there are simply no native "shade trees" except along watercourses; upland trees are small and shrubby. Cottonwoods planted on dry mesas around Albuquerque

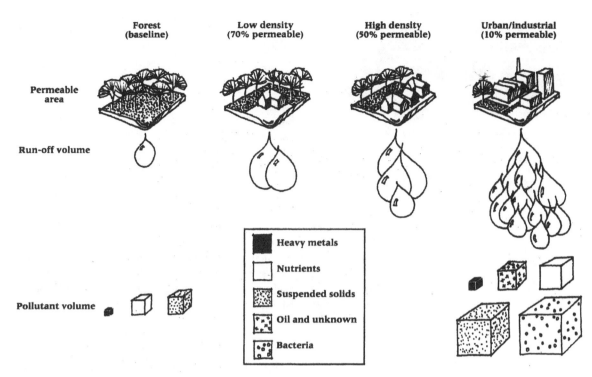

Figure 4.2 As impervious development reduces infiltration, the volume of runoff increases dramatically, as does pollution. Even nutrients, harmless in forest runoff, become serious problems at higher concentrations. (*Illust.:* Craig Farnsworth, based on data from Groesbeck and Streifel.)

require imported water, even though the plant is technically "native." The region's Indians created shade structures of brushwood. Many beautiful Southwest landscapes have adapted this idea instead of shade trees, truly respecting the regional water regime.

Deal with Stormwater near Where It Falls

When rain cannot infiltrate the ground where it falls, it becomes runoff. Runoff supplies water in most natural streams, lakes, and wetlands, but *excessive* runoff causes problems for humans (and disruption in aquatic ecosystems) through flooding and erosion. With increased runoff comes a dramatic increase in water pollution. Loss of infiltration due to development is one of the single most serious barriers to sustainability.

Fortunately, since the first edition of this book, stormwater issues have gone public. Revisions to the Clean Water Act require stormwater management on virtually every construction project (although oil and gas producers have lobbied themselves too many exemptions). Stormwater "management" poses intriguing opportunities to transform runoff into design features. Stuart Echols and Eliza Pennypacker, of Penn State University's landscape architecture department, call this strategy "artful rainwater design"—combining the utility of stormwater management with the amenity of rich place making.[10]

Many techniques are available for controlling runoff, but their success depends on one simple principle: *control runoff near its source.*

The farther runoff travels, the faster it moves as increasing volumes move together in a steady flow. Speed and volume give water erosive and sediment-carrying force. Thus, controlling water quality and runoff damage "is most easily and economically achieved if stormwater management *starts at the point that water contacts the earth.*"[11]

Many specific techniques in this and other chapters follow this close-to-the-source strategy. These include bioswales (p. 249) and water harvesting (below). For dispersing water or collecting it, a single centralized system almost always adds pipes, pumps, and other hardware, which dispersed, close-to-source systems do not require. Other infrastructure (sewage treatment,

Figure 4.3   Contour-line infiltration trenches, plus check dams in the gully at bottom, stop erosion and raise soil moisture in this Permaculture project in arid New Mexico. (*Project:* Arina Pittman. *Photo:* Kim Sorvig.)

Figure 4.4   More effective than a single massive dam, a series of small check dams stop and infiltrate water throughout a stream or gully. Only the highest floods overflow spillways. (*Photo:* New Mexico Department of Mining and Minerals.)

below, or power generation, p. 66) is also most resource efficient if *decentralized*—that is, close to the resource or to the point of use, or both.

In water management, there are two reasons why this principle is not followed. A landowner may have no influence on upstream neighbors and must deal with runoff they have neglected. For this, there is no simple cure. Second, conventional practice favors massive solutions instead of multiple ones; conventional wisdom believes larger structures offer economy of scale. Particularly for runoff control, this is a false economy, considering only capital costs, ignoring performance, maintenance, and durability. Several small infiltration devices in the upper part of a watershed are more effective than a single large one in a lower lo-

cation. At the lower spot, fast-moving water will not infiltrate as effectively, and the sediment it carries will clog the drainage structure much more quickly.

Where runoff is controlled early, slower speeds and lower volumes also allow BTEC to be used effectively (Principle 3). Despite BTEC's modern track record and ancient pedigree, engineers sometimes dismiss it because performance calculations are more complex than estimates for hard structures. New methods of computer simulation and modeling (see p. 59) offer potential for persuasive calculation of such "soft" approaches. Designers, contractors, and even some engineers are increasingly recognizing that "small and close to the source" is the key to sustainable water management.

One study suggests that, at least in the eastern United States, every gallon of water properly managed on-site saves at least two dollars in engineering costs downstream.[12] This "avoided cost analysis" has persuaded many municipalities to offer incentives for close-to-the-source water management like infiltration and, especially in the West, for "smart irrigation" retrofits (see below).

These three general strategies—know the patterns, accept regional supply, and deal with water near its source—underlie all the specific techniques discussed below.

Figure 4.5 Straw bales pinned to the ground provide temporary control of erosion and sedimentation. (*Photo: New Mexico Department of Mining and Minerals.*)

Understand, Protect, and Restore Natural Wetlands

Wetlands may well be the most unique and challenging kind of site for landscape work. Part land, part water, wetlands are often in the news, often misunderstood. Conventional landscape work, not long ago, needed no knowledge of what wetlands were, how to recognize them, or how they function. Today, even though the majority of wetland work is still done by specialists, almost everyone in the construction-related industries knows: watch out for wetlands. Landscape professionals need to go further, because wetlands health is closely linked to sustainability of human land use.

Scientific and practical aspects of working with wetlands have changed only gradually since the first edition of this book. What has changed more rapidly is acceptance of their importance—despite an adversarial stance from property-rights and industry groups, and those who confuse conservatism with op-

position to anything enacted by any government. Although the damage likely to be done by an EPA full of climate deniers cannot yet be predicted, construction professionals, with some irresponsible exceptions, have learned to respect wetlands and make them a positive part of the human landscape.

Despite controversy over their legal definition, it is not difficult to understand what a wetland is. According to international wetlands consultant Donald Hammer, wetlands are places that are *wet enough long enough* each year to produce *oxygen-poor soils* favoring *specially adapted plant species*.[13] Contrary to popular misconceptions, wetlands are not constantly wet. They are transitional zones, or "ecotones," between land and water, both spatially (edges where land meets water) and over time (land and water in the same place at different seasons). Understanding this shifting, transitional character is essential to working with wetlands. Misunderstanding this, or trying to force wetlands to fit stable-state expectations, has distorted and amplified controversy over wetlands regulation.

Wetlands are a critical link in the water web, crucial to food webs and habitat diversity. US wetlands are home to 190 amphibian species, 270 birds, and 5,000 plants, many of which can survive *only* in wetlands. Of all US endangered species, 26 percent of the plants and 45 percent of the animals are wetlands species.[14]

Recognize "Services" Provided by Wetlands

The many ways wetlands serve humanity warrant their protection:

- Filtration: wetlands purify water, trap sediment, and biodegrade many pollutants.
- Aquifer recharge: wetlands are often porous gateways to groundwater.
- Floodwater overflow basins: wetlands slow stormwater.
- Economic productivity: some of the richest and most diverse ecosystems, wetlands influence fisheries and other industries. Estuaries (wetlands where fresh and salt water meet) are particularly productive; sea-level rise will hit estuaries early and hard.
- Recreation and aesthetics: enlightened developers

increase property values by including protected wetlands as amenities.

Wetlands have provided free "services" to humans since prehistory and are cost-effective today, even when constructed. For example, Ed Garbisch of Environmental Concern, one of the first wetlands specialists, could provide coastal erosion control with a strip of salt marsh created for 17 percent of the cost of stone revetments.[15] For sewage effluent treatment, wetlands are built for one-tenth of conventional facilities' cost, and are simpler and cheaper to operate.[16]

A wonderful example of what can be accomplished in protecting and conserving wetlands is the Crosby Arboretum, a Mississippi State University facility in Picayune MS. Architect Fay Jones, curator Ed Blake, and landscape architects Andropogon Associates (Philadelphia) made the wetlands accessible to visitors through carefully planned construction. The result carries a message of hope for sustainable construction on unusual sites—and is a supremely beautiful place as well.

Know the Issues Before Working in or near Wetlands

"Homework first" is especially critical in wetlands. Wetlands are a resource from which sustainable development, design, and construction benefit. Careful planning is required to do so without diminishing or endangering the resource for the future.

To work successfully in or around wetlands, both ecological and legal understanding is essential. Major issues are summarized here.

Understanding and Recognizing Wetlands

Scientists recognize over one hundred types of wetlands: marshes, swamps, bogs, mangroves, and seasonally flooded bottomland forests.[17] While design and construction professionals can recognize wetlands generally, classifying wetlands and understanding their particulars usually requires specialist advice. An ideal team would include a wetland ecologist/botanist, hydrologist, soils specialist, and landscape architect with strong engineering skills.[18] Some projects need wild-life specialists, geologists, and experts in environmental education, recreation, and cultural archaeology. Much of this expertise has been available through governmental and educational institutions and will perhaps remain so. The National Hydrography Dataset, a GIS-based map of the nation's watersheds, water resources, and pollution sites, became available in 2000; a national Wetlands Mapper was released by the US Fish and Wildlife Service in 2014. Though not as fully detailed as would be ideal, such online information leaves little excuse for approaching wetlands without thorough understanding.

To restore or create a wetland, observe natural wetlands in the region. This is no place for aesthetic theories that condemn the mimicking of nature. Wetlands consultant Hammer emphasizes that "the created wetland must closely imitate natural systems adapted to that region if it is to succeed without excessive operating and maintenance costs."[19] Diversity of species and habitat, and varied, fractal physical forms, are *functional* essentials.

Several general points are critical to wetlands protection and restoration:

Wetland plants *tolerate* flooding that would kill dryland plants, but more and deeper is not always better. Like all plants, wetland species require air and sunlight; most have at least their leaves above water. Species that grow underwater require *clear* water to get sunlight. Many wetland plants need *alternating* flooding and drier conditions. Too deep or too long inundation can stress or kill wetland species.

In natural wetlands, alternating flood and dry states control nutrient availability, set up conditions for germination, influence wildlife behavior, and keep weedy invaders out—especially important in newly planted wetlands. Built or restored wetlands require precise water-level control and seasonal draining of the basin. Use a "stop-log" or "flash-board," an adjustable spillway formed by boards or logs set into a vertical channel in a dam. Valves only control flow volume, but stop-log spillways set water *level* directly and simply. A T-shaped slot in a riser culvert drains a small volume through the stem of the T, setting normal water level, and a larger volume through the cross-stroke of the T, for quicker flood release. (See Figures 4.7 and 5.9.)

Any natural wetland is a temporary landscape feature. Ecological succession changes wetlands to drier communities as sediment fills the basin and creates soil. Built wetlands are only prevented from disappearing over time by management practices.

Essential information for any wetlands work includes source(s) of water supply, "hydroperiod" (seasonal water-level changes), soil type(s), plant species, adjacent land uses, and project objectives.

Wetlands, like most natural systems, usually serve multiple functions. To truly "replace" or "mitigate" destruction of existing wetlands, the replacement must match *all* the functions of the original.[20] Increasingly, there is evidence that replacing a natural wetland with a reconstruction on a different site is not functionally adequate to restore lost ecosystem services.[21] For constructed wetlands, a single function may be primary, but secondary functions offer large returns for small investments. For example, constructed wastewater-treatment wetlands in places as diverse as Arcata CA and Minot ND include wildlife habitat and environmental education. Such "secondary" functions increase public acceptance and value of wetlands.

Legal and Political Issues

Most US states have lost between half and 90 percent of precolonial wetlands area.[22] Wetlands were first protected under US law in the 1970s, although hunting groups, concerned about waterfowl, had been restoring wetlands earlier. State and federal laws responded to wetlands' value and rapid loss. Before wetlands regulation began, 700 square miles (nearly 450,000 acres or 180,000 hectares) of wetland were destroyed *per year*. After regulation, that rate dropped to 300,000 acres annually, and today it is about 100,000 acres. This alone ought to demolish any argument for deregulation, but shortsighted self-interest seems to be reemerging as a desired quality among policy makers.

Important though such reductions are, wetlands continue to be lost, and construction professionals should be aware of two concerns. First, present losses are slowing, but past losses are far from being restored. Second, successes in slowing wetlands loss have been mostly agricultural; losses due to development and

construction have declined very little, and now make up 80 percent of the total.[23]

Protection of wetlands remains a priority for sustainability, on a par with protecting rainforests. The construction industry and landscape professionals especially need to do everything possible to reduce impacts on wetlands.

Filling and draining wetlands, once common practice, is largely prohibited. Erosion and sedimentation requirements enacted in 2003 include *permanent* soil stabilization (almost always by revegetation) of any project *disturbing more than one acre*.[24] Many conventional developers see such laws as restricting their freedom to build on what were once cheap lands, and some contractors complain that wetlands interfere with their ability just to do their job. While frustration is understandable, wetlands are too important to sustainability to allow negative attitudes to destroy them. Fortunately, demographic shifts that favor truly urban development are decreasing the incentive to build on cheap exurban land, and are doing so through largely apolitical market trends.

Some conflicting laws and definitions exist; some legislation aims to make wetlands regulation more consistent nationally, more responsive to regional differences, and more straightforward.[25] Legal definitions have moved close to Hammer's (above), while developers and the public are learning to understand and recognize these transitional areas *before* damage and regulatory penalties happen. Although there have been horror stories about making mountains out of mud-puddles, wetlands protection deserves everyone's support.

Wetlands "Creation" and Brokering

Legislation protecting wetlands often permits their destruction if they are replaced on another site. This process is called "mitigation." Brokering (also called "mitigation banking") goes one step further and allows developers to trade rights to destroy and mitigate wetlands across projects.

Some mitigation wetlands have succeeded in replacing wildlife and plant habitat, water filtering, and recreational and amenity value. Others, as reported in several studies, replace less area than was destroyed and create a completely different type of wetland (23 percent were essentially "tanks," steep-sided ponds built for ranch livestock). Only half are ever monitored for function. Permits, justified by these inadequate "replacements," allowed destruction of endangered species habitat "in most states evaluated."[26] There is strong doubt whether even the best created wetland is interchangeable with a natural one.[27]

A major concern is whether re-created wetlands can function as aquifer recharge zones. Aquifers—porous underground reservoirs between impervious soil or rock layers—recharge where surface water gets into the porous layer. Such zones are usually low areas where water collects—that is, wetlands. Unless a wetland is re-created in very similar conditions, it will be unconnected to groundwater and offer no recharge.

Wetlands are also related in complex but logical ways to surface drainage patterns. Wetlands linked to flowing water serve as flood dispersal basins. Susan Galatowitsch, formerly of Iowa State's Landscape Architecture Department, points out that (in prairie regions) a wetland area must equal at least 0.5 percent of its watershed to be effective for flood control.[28] Location relative to streamflow is also critical.

Especially for recharge and flood control, mitigation wetlands of different size, location, or type may fail to replace functions. Such mitigation is primarily decorative and can disguise environmental damage.

Proponents of brokering argue that it allows regional planning, restores the most valuable wetlands in larger units rather than piecemeal by each developer, and provides profit motives for protecting wetlands.[29]

By the EPA's own analysis, however, wetlands brokering seldom re-creates functions or values of the destroyed wetland.[30] Rather, "replacement" is located on land the developer can acquire cheaply enough to make the trade worthwhile. In highway construction, ordinary route-planning difficulties make wetlands removal very attractive. Highway engineering does not preclude ecologically appropriate wetlands mitigation, but in practice acts against it.

Proposals for mitigation banking are often linked to stricter function-for-function replacement. Even advocates of wetlands creation and brokering, however, acknowledge that "our ability to replace functional values, with a few exceptions, is limited because

of our poor understanding of these functions . . . [and even] existing information has often not been used."[31] Most forms of environmental "banking" and "brokering" raise similar questions: are they convenient ways to allow continued destructive behavior by paying a remote price?

Neither mitigation nor banking of wetlands is indisputably sustainable. *Restoring* wetlands on sites where they previously existed has much higher chances of success. Simply in terms of energy and materials, *conserving* an existing wetland is more efficient than either creating or restoring it. Protection of these important ecosystems is *always* the preferred alternative.

Protect Wetlands During Construction

Many general site protection techniques (Principle 1) are used in protecting wetlands. The main difference is that wetlands will almost certainly connect off-site in one or more directions. This requires extra care and ingenuity when restricting access. Nonetheless, preventing construction traffic from entering or crossing wetlands is very important.

If there is no alternative to crossing a stream or wetland, temporary access must be provided, removable without damage on completion. Some work can be carried out from boats and other specialized equipment. (Launch or landing sites still need protection or restoration or both.) If land vehicles must cross a wetland, protect bottom soils from being churned by wheels, tracks—or feet. Use temporary bridges, planks, mats, or removable structures filled with gravel. Dumping gravel directly into wetlands forms a passage, but is hard to remove.

Banks of any water body are especially susceptible to damage and require protection well beyond actual crossings. Temporary shoring may be an option. Banks attract people and animals, sometimes causing inadvertent damage. Expect to rebuild and replant the banks at the end of the project.

Construction runoff must be prevented from entering wetlands, or at least filtered through straw bales, sediment fencing, or other standard erosion and sedimentation (E&S) controls. Natural rates of erosion can increase by a factor of 2,000 during construction, unless controlled (Figure 6.22), often washing into water bodies. Polluted runoff threatens streams and wetlands. However, Dawn Biggs, a Virginia landscape architect with strong experience in wetland and stream management, notes that wetlands are resilient concerning water purification (see bioremediation, pp. 124–26). Potentially more serious than chemical pollutants are dense sediments that choke wetlands, and mechanical soil disturbance that admits invasive species.

Certain stages of work (site clearing or paving, especially) can lead to temporary danger of flooding. E&S controls, designed for severe storms, *must* be in place before such work. Even wetlands designed to hold floodwater cannot be suddenly inundated during their establishment period. It may be critical to deal with problems of the whole watershed before attempting to protect or restore a wetland.

Use Wetlands-specific Protection Strategies

Wetland conditions may need special protection techniques.

- Soil compaction risk is generally greater on saturated soils than on dry ones.
- Wet zones should have generous buffers, above and beyond what would be fenced for dry site features.
- Plan for seasonal variations in precipitation, water table, and flooding. These, as well as tidal motion, can dramatically change wetlands during construction.

Use Low-impact Construction if Building in Wetlands

Nature centers, water recreation facilities, and other special projects may require construction *in* a wetland. This involves specialized techniques and materials.

Work in standing water stirs up bottom sediments. Sedimentation curtains, hung from floats, keep muddied water within the construction zone, and out of other waters. These function like filter fencing on land, but form a boundary between two areas of water.

Structures built in or at the edge of wetlands are best supported by minimal-footprint foundations. Pilings are commonly used, as is a patented system called "Pin Foundations" (below, and see Figure 6.18). These minimize disruption, permit water motion around the structure, and work with unstable wetland soils.

Pilings are available in many forms and materials. Tubular forms driven into the soil and filled with concrete are common; a conical plastic mold called Bigfoot creates quick and economical footings for tubular concrete pilings, with minimal excavation. Wood pilings are also widely used. Rot resistance is important, but beware of toxic preservatives, which can leach into the water (see p. 298). Some woods, like elm, are rot-resistant if they *remain* underwater; in ancient ports, centuries-old pilings of such woods have been found in perfect condition. These timbers rot only if alternatively wet and dry (as in fencing or decking). Not all species of naturally rot-resistant wood will function as well when submerged.

Recycled "plastic lumber" is also used for waterside construction; structural limitations apply to some types, but have been resolved in others (see "Plastic Lumber," p. 279). It is waterproof and rotproof and cannot leach, making it a good choice for wetlands construction.

Boardwalks have traditionally provided dry-footed access into wetlands. Treated lumber may contaminate water and kill wildlife.[32] Well-designed boardwalks leave spaces between boards, permitting precipitation and light to the area underneath; aquatic life can be excluded by lack of light.

At Juanita Bay Park in Washington, landscape architects Jongejan Gerrard McNeal used two different methods of supporting boardwalks.[33] One, requiring considerable skill, was to lay logs across the wetlands as grade beams. The contractor had to match variable-thickness logs to the ground surface, without digging, to keep upper surfaces level. The second system, for wetter ground, was to drive two-inch steel pipe as pilings. This avoided heavy equipment: one worker with an air hammer and scaffolding installed the pipes. Cross-tie pipes were added for stability, plus four-by-twelve beams. Both support systems were decked with ACZA-treated lumber, clearing the ground by eighteen inches so that visitors would think twice about stepping off.

An innovative foundation system for sensitive sites is the "pinned foundation," from a company in Gig

Figure 4.6   Boardwalks can make an art form of the necessity for minimum disturbance in wetlands. This is at Spring Peeper marsh in the Minnesota Arboretum. (*Project and Photo:* Fred Rozumalski.)

Harbor WA. Grade beams or short aboveground wooden posts are fitted with metal brackets. Through slots in these brackets, the "pins" (four- to eight-foot-long sections of galvanized pipe) are driven by hand or jackhammer into the ground at diagonal angles. The structure's weight locks the pins into the slots. They can be pulled up, adjusted, or removed with minimal site disturbance. Pinned foundations can be placed even closer to existing trees than conventional pilings. Another adjustable, removable system is auger foundations, developed by Pliny Fisk (p. 74).

Pin Foundations has recently developed two variations on this system. One, the Diamond Pier, is essentially a precast concrete footer with holes for pins and a bolt on top for attaching one four-by-four post. The second, called Low Impact Foundation Technology, or LIFT, attaches the metal pin-sockets to formwork for on-grade cast-in-place concrete foundation walls. The sockets are thus cast into the walls, and after removing the forms, pins are driven through them to anchor the foundation, with conventional construction on top. Pin spacing is engineered for each structure. The on-grade system uses 20 to 30 percent less concrete than conventional foundation walls, according to the manufacturer. Pinned systems greatly reduce site disturbance, compaction, and grading for drainage, and have applications beyond wetland areas.

Floating walkways, where feasible, are assembled in segments, off-site; one section is placed from the bank, providing a platform for placing the next, and so on. If sized for a crew to move by hand, very little site disruption occurs. Such a system was used by Bruce Dees & Associates, at the Hood Canal (Washington) Wetlands Project. Styrofoam-stuffed used tires may serve as floats if sealed to prevent waterlogging or degrading into the wetland.

Restore Damaged Wetlands

Wetlands damaged or drained by prior land use can be restored; these techniques may also apply to postconstruction repairs or to creating new wetlands. Reconstruction takes advantage of existing links to aquifers, streams, and ponds, and taps remnant soils as a "seed bank" of dormant wetland species. A restored wetland is much more likely to function as a recharge zone or flood basin than one created at a site of convenience.

First, reestablish water flows and levels. If the original level is known, this may be simple, but more often a specialist must determine what level to restore. In wetlands drained for agriculture, removing or altering drainage structures may be enough, with plants and animals soon reestablishing themselves.

On other sites, a dam or dike may be needed, usually constructed of earth, often with a clay core, and welded wire mesh buried in the center to exclude burrowing animals. A "stop-log" (p. 190 and Figure 5.9) in the dike sets normal water level. The flood spillway is a separate "emergency exit"; in wetlands under twenty acres, design for the ten-year storm. A grassed spillway, reinforced with geotextile, is preferable to concrete in cost, functionality, and appearance.

Once the surface level and rate of water flow are known, grading may be needed. The basin should not be steep sided, even if deep water exists in the center. A broad, shallow basin offers the widest area and diversity of plantable shore.

Grading must be unusually accurate, because wetland plants require precise water depths. Because the water surface is always horizontal, it is the basin bottom that determines water depth. Zones of different depth support diversity of species. Stepped horizontal terraces work better than sloped grading. A very small slope (as little as 0.05 percent) can cause a major difference in depth over one hundred yards, so that the same plants cannot survive throughout the zone.[34]

During grading, wetlands soil should be stockpiled *underwater* to preserve seeds, tubers, and anaerobic chemical conditions. Some artificially created wetlands require a liner of bentonite clay or waterproof sheeting. The liner is covered with 16 to 24 inches of soil for planting. Either an artificial liner or a natural impervious surface can be punctured by careless construction work, causing the wetland to fail.

Another reason for care during grading is that soil disturbance invites invasion by aggressive aquatic plants like Giant Reed or Loosestrife. Once established, they can be difficult or impossible to weed out, actively displacing native species. Invasive species (sometimes deliberately planted) are responsible for decline of many existing wetlands; creating a haven for them defeats the purpose of restoration. In general, select wetland species native to the region and suited to the specific type of wetland.[35]

Wetland planting techniques are specialized. Only a few species float freely; most must be rooted in the bottom even if their leaves or flowers are above the surface. When replanting existing wetlands, plants or seeds are often weighted and dropped from a boat, a technique that has mixed success. Where possible, flooding the wetland and then draining it produces ideal muddy planting conditions. Tubers, seedlings, and "live stake" cuttings may be planted by hand or with specialized machinery. Furrows, cut across the di-

Figure 4.7 The T-shaped opening in this wetland structure sets the water level. Small rises in level flow out through the "trunk" of the T; if major flooding raises the level higher, the top of the T permits faster drainage. (*Project and Photo:* Rick Scaffidi, EQR.)

rection of water flow, can speed planting. In soft soils or where wildlife are feeding, plantings may need to be anchored and protected with erosion-control matting or biodegradable mesh.

When previously existing wetlands are restored, planting may be unnecessary. Seed of wetland plants can survive for a decade or more in drained or filled soils, germinating once wetland conditions are restored. Soil "cores" collected from nearby wetlands are sometimes used to seed restored or new wetlands. In collecting cores, extreme care must be used to avoid damaging the donor site. Small cores (a few inches across) should be dug in a scattered pattern, leaving undisturbed soil to support regrowth.

Managing water level is critical to plant establishment. After planting, the water level needs to keep pace with plant growth. Hammer describes water management schedules for various newly established wetland types, in some cases filling and draining the wetland weekly. After establishment (two to five years) management needs decrease, but annual or seasonal manipulation of water levels is still common.[36]

The final aspect of restoring wetlands is monitoring and adjustment. Flows and levels, plant and animal establishment, and water quality should be recorded. Final field adjustments of inlet and outlet grades may be needed. Responsibility for these adjustments must be carefully spelled out in specifications. Wetlands construction exemplifies the teamwork, coordination,

Figure 4.8a–c This constructed wetland was (a) carefully excavated to specific depths required by wetland plants, then (b) lined. Planted with marsh-tolerant sedges (c), the completed wetland treats graywater organically for reuse, reducing this Michigan convent's water use by half. (See p. 239 for project description.) (*Project and Photo:* Veridian Landscape Studio.)

Table 4.1
Plants to avoid (or use very cautiously) in wetlands.

Botanical Name	Common Name(s)
Eichornia crassipes	Water Hyacinth
Lysimachia sp.	Purple Loosestrife
Melaleuca quinquenervia	Melaleuca, Bottlebrush
Phalaris arundinacea	Reed Canary Grass
Phragmites australis	Giant Reed
Salix sp.	Willows (some shrub and tree forms)
Tamarix sp.	Tamarisk, Salt Cedar
Typha latifolia and T. angustifolia	Cattail

and inclusion of long-term maintenance essential to sustainable landscape work.

Las Vegas NV doesn't seem like a wetland sort of place to most visitors (although many do take a soaking). But the Las Vegas Wash, which empties into Lake Mead, had 2,000 acres or more of wetlands as recently as the 1970s. Used for sewage effluent discharge, as much as 1,600 tons per day, the Wash lost all but 10 percent of those wetlands.

Las Vegas drinks from Lake Mead, and in 1998 the EPA found bacterial pollution and traces of rocket fuel in the lake, which galvanized the county government into action. Early in 1999, they unveiled a plan to build fifteen erosion-control dams, with wetlands behind each one, and trails expected to attract a million visitors a year. The restored Wash today offers clean drinking water to Vegas residents (those who don't follow W. C. Fields about drinking water). Called Clark County Wetlands Park, these reconstructed wetlands have interpretive exhibits, a small visitor center, and a theater. Interior Secretary Bruce Babbitt called the plan "a model for the West," and the park has been welcomed by local residents. Harvard landscape scholar Robert France recognized it as one of the most innovative wetlands projects in the world in 2001.

Spring Peeper marsh, at the Minnesota Arboretum near Minneapolis, won an ASLA award for original educational design. Simple color-coded stakes show how water depth coincides with vegetation types (see p. 195). Wetlands need interpretation because they are so rare and misunderstood; the good news is that they

Figure 4.9   At Spring Peeper marsh, lines of color-coded stakes show water-depth contours and coincide with vegetation changes. Wetlands are prime sites for education and interpretation. (*Project and Photo:* Fred Rozumalski.)

attract and educate people so successfully. (See more examples under "Let Constructed Wetlands Treat Water," p. 228.)

Restore Rivers and Streams to Full Health

Eroding stream banks are an environmental problem close to many people's backyards, degraded by two main forces: first, channelization, culverting, and burial to make watercourses fit human development patterns; and second, massively increased stormwater runoff from impervious urbanization. In many communities degraded streams have catalyzed local restoration projects.

Restoration is much more complex than simply stabilizing eroding banks. Holistic restoration takes into account the entire watershed and how water entering the stream has been affected by development. According to Tom Schueler, executive director of the Center for Watershed Protection, simply repairing the bank—even by environmentally progressive methods—is little more than a short-term fix. "A lot of people have been doing that kind of work because, quite frankly, it makes for great before-and-after pictures," says Schueler. "I don't mean to imply that it's just cosmetic, but that alone is not stream restoration. It's stream-bank stabilization."

Stream restoration entails a considerable learning curve, but many aids exist: a growing how-to literature, courses and workshops, and environmental action groups. Much of the real work involves regional design and policy measures that reduce impervious surfaces, especially near the top of the watershed (see Principle 5).

Keith Bowers's design-build firm, Biohabitats (Towson MD), has increasingly worked in stream restoration. "Stream restoration doesn't start in the stream channel," Bowers says. "It starts in the watershed. If you just patch a stream, that improvement may be blown away in the next big storm. You have to recapture some of that off-site flow and try to release it slowly." Thus, restoring upstream wetlands may be essential; the Center for Watershed Protection calls upstream ponds and wetlands "a watershed manager's most reliable tool . . . to successfully improve a stream's overall operating health."[37] Best results are achieved by looking at the whole watershed and all the communities—human and ecological—in it.[38] Invasive aquatic plants, dispersed by water, are also a threat in some areas.

The overall goal, says Bowers, is to "get the water into the ground as fast as possible in as many places as possible," through infiltration. This is easiest in new design, but applies to retrofits, too. Control stormwater runoff from existing paving *before* it enters the stream, and do so prior to restoring stream banks. Otherwise, problems will return periodically.

One leading stormwater expert, University of Georgia landscape architecture professor Bruce Ferguson, emphasizes that flood-control basins must be selectively sited, or they can do active damage. A watershed-wide plan is the only way to determine proper locations. Basins sited at random or uniform locations

fail on two counts: overflow from these ponds may join downstream to create a delayed flood; and infiltration at wrong locations may never reach groundwater, nor seep back into streambeds to replenish "base flows."

Local policies often mandate a detention basin on every site. This, however, produces excessively numerous and wrongly located basins, according to several studies cited by Ferguson. Such basins actually *increase* flooding downstream and seldom reduce storm flows to predevelopment levels.[39]

To avoid these problems, runoff must be infiltrated into (not just detained in) drier soils in the upper watershed. Basins should be designed as diverse wetlands (above) rather than simple holding tanks, with water-level control devices and grading for varied depth. Engineers and regulators increasingly see the benefits of such design; watershed-wide management, however, transcends property boundaries and still causes consternation.

With stormwater infiltrating and base flows normalized, restoration of the stream itself can finally be addressed. To bring back some semblance of the structure, function, and dynamics of the predevelopment stream often requires regrading the banks, and even the streambed.

Two patterns of stream dysfunction are common. In *incised channels*, erosion cuts (incises) into the bed; in *aggrading channels*, the stream fills with silt, becoming broad and shallow without pools or riffles. Incised channels generally reflect increased flow volume from upstream; they may also be caused by increased speed, if the streambed is lowered downstream (into a culvert, for example). Aggrading streams reflect decreased speed, blockage downstream, or increased amounts of sediment from upstream erosion.

In general, an incised channel needs to have the volume and speed of flow decreased, and banks strengthened. An aggrading channel needs deposits cleaned out, and more steady flow. The source of the sediment (often an incised channel upstream) may require repairs, too.

There are several approaches to bank erosion. Conventionally, riprap or "river rock" is dumped down the banks. At best, this offers local, short-term relief, often accelerating trouble elsewhere. Riprap is easily swept away or buried by floods and provides no resting and feeding places for fish (as shade and roots of vegetative stabilization do). It is unsightly, neither tidy nor naturalistic; the stone is seldom local, and its out-of-place color exposes it as imported, often over long distances. (Strategically placed boulders can help restore a stream's natural structure of pools and riffles.)

Most restorationists recommend plant cover, not riprap, to stabilize stream-bank soils—BTEC in a specialized, partly submerged use. As in other forms of BTEC (Principle 3), hard but permeable structures (crib walls, gabions, etc.) are used in extreme situations. (An unusual approach, described on p. 276, combines rubber tires with tree saplings to rescue collapsing banks.)

Branches, roots, and even entire tree trunks are widely used stabilizers. The Missouri Department of Conservation has perfected whole-tree revetments, cabled along stream banks. The trees are salvaged from development or road building, or after storms.

Live trees also protect stream health. Streams and rivers in many parts of the world are buffered by forests, or were before development. Streams with wooded banks have channels that are cooler, shallower, and up to four times as wide as streams running through pastures or meadows. Replacing tree cover restores channel form, increasing habitat as well as resilience to pollutants, according to the National Academy of Science's Stroud Water Research Center (Pennsylvania).[40]

Most BTEC materials and methods (p. 134) are useful for stream restoration; the number of suppliers and qualified consultants has grown significantly. Biodegradable fabric blankets hold stream banks and streambeds until plant growth is established. At the toe of the bank, where water and soil meet, rolls or "biologs" made of coconut fiber have proved effective. For extensive bank restorations, ready-made products can be expensive. The University of Oregon, stabilizing a stream bank on campus, put design students to work assembling and installing cost-effective soil-filled "burritos." This may be an option for cash-strapped community groups.

One BTEC technique that California stream restorationist Ann Riley and many others recommend is live willow or cottonwood stakes. Riley calls these "the underused workhorses of restoration," reinforcing soil like rebar in concrete, and far better than riprap (which she considers a last resort).[41] For tall banks, live stakes can be driven through straw-bale walls to root—another technique used at the University of Oregon.

BTEC consultant Robbin Sotir often uses plants alone (mostly willow cuttings) to stabilize stream banks while providing excellent wildlife and aquatic habitat. Such techniques are attractive for a number of reasons. Materials are often available at little or no cost from the site, or from other client- or contractor-owned property.

"Conventional stream and river practices," says Ann Riley, create "community blight where natural resources once existed."[42] This observation was reflected in the history of a meandering woodland stream in Silver Spring MD, Wheaton Branch. Its highly urbanized watershed gradually became 55 percent impervious, creating cascades of new runoff. Years of such torrents reduced it to a broad, shallow channel with eroding banks and scant vegetation, its cobbled bed buried beneath inches of silt. Aquatic life was reduced to two pollution-tolerant species.

Today Wheaton Branch again meanders between densely vegetated banks; whole trees buried, roots outward, stabilize the bank. The water runs clear, scouring the cobbles clean. Plentiful small fish and crayfish dart in pools and riffles created during restoration.

The interagency project[43] was the first phase of restoring Sligo Creek, of which Wheaton Branch is a tributary. Rather than simply "patching" eroded stream banks, the team addressed Sligo Creek's entire 13.3-square-mile watershed. Interconnected ponds detain runoff, allowing pollutants and sediments to settle out, then gradually release water into the stream. Wheaton Branch's streambed was reconfigured with stone "wing deflectors" and log weirs; banks were rebuilt and reinforced; and the riparian zone was revegetated with shrubs and trees. Finally, fish were reintroduced by a "bucket brigade" of neighborhood volunteers. Monitoring indicates that aquatic life—perhaps the best indicator of water quality—is flourishing.

At Wheaton Branch, upstream runoff was accepted as a given—a common, realistic approach, but not inevitable. Repairing uplands infiltration to restore a stream is an opposite approach and, at least in theory,

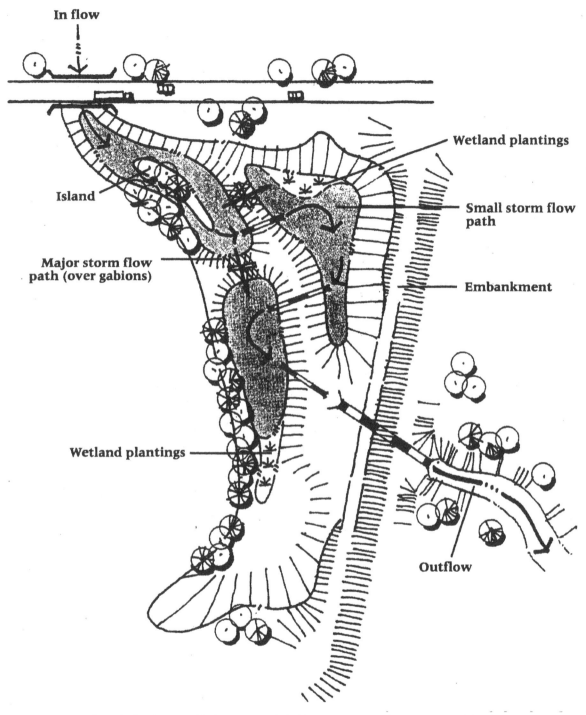

Figure 4.10 Ponds at the headwaters of Wheaton Branch hold stormwater, infiltrating part and slowly releasing it into the stream. (*Illust.*: Craig Farnsworth, based on Center for Watershed Protection and Loiederman Association.)

is more cost-effective and lasting.[44] A truly holistic approach requires both mending upland problems and rebuilding stream structures.

One guru of stream restoration is hydrologist Dave Rosgen, of Colorado-based Wildland Hydrol-

ogy. Rosgen is the author of a profusely illustrated book classifying the many different types of streams according to morphology. At the risk of oversimplifying, Rosgen's scientifically based approach restores a stream's ecological functions by re-creating its natu-

Figure 4.11   University of Oregon landscape students fabricated "soil burritos" of fabric, soil, and chicken-wire for a campus restoration, demonstrating a simple, inexpensive method. (*Project and Photo:* Professor Stan Jones.)

Figure 4.12   Students installing "burritos" and brush-layer to stabilize the stream bank. (*Project and Photo:* Professor Stan Jones.)

ral dimension, pattern, and profile.[45] This may involve excavating an entirely new channel for a disturbed stream, requiring more room than is available in many dense urban situations. Combined with upstream run-off reduction, the end result should approximate a predevelopment stream.

A Staten Island restoration project demonstrates just how challenging it can be to renovate urban streams to anything resembling original ecological structure and function. Sweet Brook, one of Staten Island's major streams, alternates between aboveground fragments of natural channel and underground storm sewers, a common urban condition. One aboveground segment flows through a quarter-mile wooded valley alongside Sweetbrook Road, but its source is a culvert. Only manhole covers mark its upstream corridor, and

Figure 4.13   Stone deflector in restored Wheaton Branch unobtrusively guards the stream bank from floods. (*Project:* Washington Council of Governments. *Photo:* Walt Callahan.)

it empties into another culvert. The valley—a designated open space that also included private homes—is "a little remnant, an island in an otherwise man-made environment," says Dana Gumb of the New York City Department of Environmental Protection (DEP).

Receiving far more water from the culvert than its narrow channel could possibly handle, the stream regularly flooded the valley, tearing out a pedestrian bridge and turning Sweetbrook Road into a linear lake. In 1995 the DEP moved to restore the valley segment as part of its Staten Island Bluebelt program, a watershed-scale effort to infiltrate stormwater. Bluebelt planners argued successfully that restoring natural systems was cheaper than installing storm sewers, thus guaranteeing good funding.

Sweet Brook's tight, urbanized situation precluded most current stream-restoration principles—treat the whole watershed, control runoff at the headwaters, excavate a new "natural" channel. Even though the stream was part of a 12,000-acre watershed, there was not even room to construct a retention basin directly upstream to slow stormwater.

A technical compromise was developed. Normal "base flows" would run in the restored aboveground channel, while a device called a flow splitter diverted storm flows into large new pipes below Sweetbrook Road. To restore the visible channel, dumped rubble was removed, flood-damaged retaining walls were rebuilt, native stone reshaped the streambed, and na-

Figure 4.14 Tons of accumulated sediment were removed from Sweet Brook and used to fertilize the restored banks. (*Project:* New York City Department of Environmental Protection. *Photo:* Dean Cavallaro.)

tive plants—including ferns long absent from the island—were reintroduced.

The six-acre, quarter-mile corridor restoration cost $1.1 million. "Whether such projects are worth the investment is widely debated," says Richard Claytor, principal engineer with the Center for Watershed Protection. Pointing out that stream restorations in fragmented watersheds are not uncommon, he cites Strawberry Creek on the campus of the University of California, Berkeley. It, too, says Claytor, is in pipes above and below the restored, "daylighted" segment.

Claytor considers such projects "less valuable than a continuous stream. Aquatic exchange of plant and

Figure 4.15 Sweet Brook after restoration, just downstream from the previous photo. (*Project:* New York City Department of Environmental Protection. *Photo:* Dean Cavallaro.)

Figure 4.16   Erosion undercut pavement at Maguire Avenue and prevented plants from re-establishing. (*Project:* New York City Department of Environmental Protection. *Photo:* Dean Cavallaro.)

Figure 4.17   Maguire Avenue after installation of gabions, boulders to deflect culvert outflow, and plantings. (*Project:* New York City Department of Environmental Protection. *Photo:* Dean Cavallaro.)

animal species is severely limited, so it has limited value from a biological standpoint. But it has great value as an educational resource. It sharpens nearby residents' ability to appreciate the watershed."

At Maguire Avenue, another Staten Island Blue-belt project, a 250-foot stretch of stream had become a drainage ditch. Armoring the adjacent road simply created extra erosive power, and the channel undercut and collapsed the pavement. Creative Habitats (White Plains NY) used gabions to stabilize the steep banks. Gabions, BTEC's method of last resort according to Riley, are still "softer" than solid concrete. Boulders and fibrous "biologs" slowed the flow of water. Within a year, the banks were revegetated and protected from further collapse.

A small but growing number of landscape architecture firms undertake such restoration, but most still require consultant help. There are many more stream, shoreline, and wetland restoration specialists since the first edition of this book; check the International Erosion Control Association. Many consultants are also suppliers of specialized products like mats or wattles. This is not necessarily a conflict of interest, because localized knowledge is often essential in producing appropriate supplies.

Go for a Riverwalk

There are twenty-eight "Riverwalk" parks in eighteen US states:[46] landscape promenades along a restored

Figure 4.18   Riverwalks range from modest urban bank restoration to major engineering projects. Many revitalize their watercourses while providing a high return on social and financial investment. (*Project:* Sasaki. *Photo:* © Christian Phillips Photography, courtesy of Sasaki.)

river, in most cases. American towns have historically turned their backs on the rivers that run through them, converting a landscape feature into an alley or ditch, and often setting up conditions for extreme runoff and flooding. By restoring such rivers and developing their banks as public spaces, riverwalks have reversed the fortunes of both river and town.

Estes Park CO had been the tourist gateway to Rocky Mountain National Park for more than a century when in 1982 it suffered a flood that tore out its streets and filled businesses counter-high with sediment.[47] (Entrepreneurs advertised Free Mud.) Someone recognized this as an opportunity, and took a first step: hiring EDAW's Herb Schaal to create a master plan. This called for hydrological restoration as well as landscape improvements—but how was a small, recently devastated town to afford it? The next decision was to create the Estes Park Urban Renewal Authority (EPURA), and designate the main street business district (paralleling the river) as a Tax Increment District (TID). This method of funding could help many communities improve both ecological and social amenities.

TIDs are simple in concept. Total sales tax revenue, at the beginning of the project, is set as a benchmark. If revenue increases (because more sales are occurring, not because the tax rate changes), the difference goes to an agency (EPURA, in this case) charged with reinvesting that money in improvements in the zone. (The concept also works with property tax: if revenue increases because property values go up, the difference is earmarked for the district.)

The design and implementation of the Estes Park project (by Denver's Design Studios West) are beautiful; it won two ASLA awards in 2007, for Design Excellence *and* Land Stewardship.[48] But the point of including it here is that it directly demonstrates the financial value of landscape restoration, both of streetscape and of rivercourse. EPURA invested $20 million over its twenty-five-year state authorization period, and generated $50 million—without raising the tax rate at all. The entire investment was landscape focused, to which the return can legitimately be ascribed. Establishing the value of landscape improvements has seldom been as clear-cut. The funding mechanism, as well as the concept of ecological restoration partnering with urban restoration, are valuable strategies that sustainability-oriented communities, planners, and designers can use to great effect.

Collect and Conserve Water

Reducing human use and waste of water protects natural water systems. Conflicts between diverting water for human use and leaving it in-stream to support aquatic life are increasingly common, especially in the western United States. Much is at stake if rivers or aquifers dry up from overuse, as some, like the Lower Rio Grande, already have. Biodiversity, habitat, and human survival depend on water, but diversion from distant sources is a risky way to meet these needs. Conserving water, through a wide range of techniques, is necessary in its own right, essential to protection of wetlands and streams, and important in keeping water supplies clean.

Harvest Water from Roofs and Landscapes

Water harvesting means close-to-source collection and storage of rainwater from roofs, paved surfaces, and landscapes. Roof collection was common in older US homes, often filling basement cisterns and moderating indoor temperatures in the process. In 1997 the American Rainwater Catchment Systems Association estimated there were about 250,000 roof systems in the United States;[49] they are common in Australia and the Caribbean.

Harvesting from ground surfaces has an even longer history. Ancient Israelites, Chinese, Pueblo Indians, and Australians (both aboriginal and recent settlers) have used landscape water harvesting to survive. Variations on terracing, usually small scale, and low stone walls or check dams infiltrate water at strategic points in a watershed. This traps fertile sediment and moisture in some of Earth's most arid environments. Shallow ditches roughly following contours (often called "key lines") are also used to gather sheeting water into linked hillside ponds.

The results of arid-land water harvesting can be startling: stopping gully erosion, raising the water table, and greening the desert without artificial irrigation. In recent years, such techniques have been revived and somewhat systematized by Australian author Bill Mollison, under the name Permaculture. Many techniques from this agriculturally focused system of sustainable construction are adaptable to nonagricultural landscapes.[50]

Evaporation and precipitation "distill" rainwater, so it is free of many surface-water pollutants. It is "soft" water, holding few minerals and no municipal chlorine or fluorine. Unless contaminated by materials on the collecting surface, its purity makes it desirable for drinking; many plant species prefer rainwater irrigation. (For purifying harvested water, see p. 227.)

In roof systems, stainless steel, along with tile, terra-cotta, and slate, are frequently used. Metals may leach from galvanized roofing; some color coatings, solder, and fasteners may contain lead. Especially if collecting for drinking water, be sure the chosen roof material does not pose such risks. In water collected for irrigating ornamentals, this may or may not be a problem. Where rain is frequent and plentiful, as in the Caribbean, limestone roofs sweeten the water. In any less-wet climate, the porous stone surfaces would collect impurities and grow algae, bacteria, or mold. Wood shingles share these problems of porosity, and if treated with preservative should not be used on collector roofs. Asphalt (with gravel, or as shingles) may contaminate water, and the rough surfaces hold dust; spray-foam and membrane roofing must be evaluated per material.

Costs of harvesting equipment vary widely. The Sustainable Cities Institute estimated (as of 2013)[51] that rooftop systems for non-potable water ranged from $10,000 to $30,000 (not including the roof itself). This figure includes a tank, at $0.50 to $4.00 per gallon; gutters, professionally installed at $3.50 to $12.00 per foot; and filtration before water enters the tank ($50 to $800). A pump, if gravity cannot be used, adds $300 to $1,000. Filtration and disinfection to potable standards potentially adds another $1,000.

Figure 4.19   Water harvested from roof and landscape is stored for dry-season use at Mariposa Port of Entry, Nogales AZ. A I-million-gallon tank holds the rainwater. Solar hot water and electricity, as well as recycled materials and native plantings, are other features of this building, one of many commissioned by the General Services Administration. (*Project:* Chris Winters & Assoc. and Jones Studio. *Photo:* Bill Timmerman.)

For much less expense, any paved surface can be a water-harvesting collector, though not for drinking water. Asphalt can produce contaminants; most other paving materials are relatively inert. Paved surfaces collect residues from air pollution, spills, automotive sources, dumpsters, and industrial processes. Paved non-vehicular or lightly trafficked surfaces are generally suitable for water harvesting. Runoff from potentially polluted surfaces (driveways, Dumpster pads, etc.) should be routed through a vegetated biofilter (Principle 5, p. 249) before flowing to final use. Lawns, unless maintained with excessive pesticides, also serve as collecting surfaces, although like any porous surface they yield less runoff.

Perhaps the simplest form of water harvesting for landscape use is simply grading the site to drain toward planted beds or ponds. Permaculturist Ben Haggard of Tesuque NM used this approach for the landscape of New Mexico's first Energy Star–compliant house.

In a region where annual precipitation averages about twelve inches, Haggard's design supports mature shade and fruit trees without supplemental water.

The volume of water collected by any surface—paved, roofed, or planted—can be calculated using standard engineering formulas; treat the resulting volume as a *resource* rather than a nuisance. The same formulas make it possible to size collection basins. Without careful planning the collected water may drown some plants while others parch. Planting beds,

Figure 4.20   (opposite) "For the GSA, water is a prevalent issue," says Christian Gabriel, the agency's national design director for landscape architecture. The Edith Green–Wendell Wyatt Federal Building in Portland OR could hardly be more different from the Mariposa Port of Entry, but water harvesting is central to both. The twenty-story EGWW building also has a green facade of vines on vertical supports. (*Project:* GSA with Sera Architects. *Photo:* © Nick Lehoux.)

which are low points in such a design, must be sized to prevent water standing in them. If ponds are to collect water, size them to accept the ten- or twenty-five-year storm and provide spillways to avoid washout. Plantings in such areas must, ironically, be adapted to drought as well as flood, since those conditions will alternate in any temporary pond. Using occasionally flooded areas for photovoltaics may be better use of space than plantings.

Most water-harvesting research focuses on drinking water. For landscape irrigation, which can consume two to three times as much as indoor uses combined, potable purity is not needed; heavy metals and lead should still be avoided. Collecting enough for all irrigation is desirable, but difficult unless use is reduced. Even as a backup irrigation source, water harvesting makes good sense, reducing use of pumped groundwater or treated municipal supply. Even in Arizona, demonstration homes have shown that harvested water supplemented by graywater can meet irrigation needs.[52] Water harvesting is also extensively used at Lady Bird Johnson Wildflower Center in Austin TX.

Water harvesting turns impervious surfaces into assets; irrigation becomes a form of close-to-source infiltration. The combination may, as in the following example, moderate both peak flows and seasonal water availability. Water availability in the local ecosystem as a whole increases with infiltration.[53]

Water harvesting demonstrates the saying that if the people lead, the leaders will follow. In Arizona, a study found that 13 percent of the population was harvesting water—which was illegal under "western water law," in which seniority rules, and harvesting by others is considered "an injury to senior rights holders." This misguided system is gradually changing; between 2007 and 2017 a great number of states approved, or at least considered, new water-harvesting laws, usually in favor of the practice. Arizona legalized the practice, and Colorado, after a 2007 study showed that only 3 percent of precipitation actually entered streams, passed a 2016 law allowing limited harvesting.[54] A plan to harvest water for Santa Fe's Railyard Park[55] demonstrates the absurdity frequently resulting from western water law: water harvested from rooftops (the park includes historic buildings) was legal,

but water that fell on the ground could not be harvested, because it belonged to the state!

Intense water harvesting could *delay* in-stream flow, especially if sent into sewers after use rather than infiltrated; however, delaying flow is actually *desirable* in many urbanized areas, and harvested water used for irrigation generally reenters streamflow gradually. Local small-scale water harvesting for on-site infiltration benefits sustainable communities, and is increasingly used around the world.

Parque da Cidade in Oporto, Portugal, offers an intriguing example of contemporary water harvesting to maintain water levels in a man-made lake through Portugal's six-month dry season. Project engineers initially specified plastic lake liner on the premise that the sandy soil would not hold water. Instead, landscape architect Sidónio Pardal and a hydrologist sited fifty infiltration basins throughout the park. Some are grassy swales, others edged with city-salvaged granite. The basins interrupt overland flow during Portugal's rainy season, collecting rainwater that slowly infiltrates. This groundwater reaches the lake during the dry season, taking months to seep from the infiltration basins. Almost no drains or pipes were used, because speeding up flow was undesirable. The approach is worth trying in similarly wet/dry climates, like California.

Even major downtown areas have places to capture and conserve rainwater. Combining designs with ecological principles can create extraordinary urban places that celebrate rain's beauty and life-giving effects. In a number of recent design competitions, using only harvested water has been a major selling point.[56]

Thirty projects that address rainwater environmentally and artfully were studied by Stuart Echols and Eliza Pennypacker (Penn State University landscape architecture department). One of these projects is called "10th@Hoyt," an urban apartment courtyard in Portland OR's Pearl District designed by landscape architect Steve Koch. Copper downspouts convey runoff from the building roof to tall, thin concrete structures resembling skinny ziggurats, stepping down and cantilevering over raised concrete basins filled with round river rocks. In two of these stepped aqueducts, Cor-Ten steel sheets perforated by colored glass dots

Nichols
Arboretum

Figure 4.21a–c The Nichols Arboretum (Ann Arbor MI) creates beauty from stormwater management structures. The sequence shows construction and planting of stepped pools to control runoff. (*Project:* The Nichols Arboretum. *Photo:* Robert E. Grese.)

Figure 4.22 Rainwater from a roof drain is caught in a gravel basin and routed to furrows in the garden at the Denver offices of designer Bill Wenk. (*Project and Photo:* Bill Wenk.)

spread the water cascading onto the river rock, hard counterpoints to lush planting. The spreaders are lit from below, making the glass dots glow at night. In this inward-oriented, private oasis, thanks to the "chutes and ladders" conveyance system, visitors can watch rainwater flow.

At 10th@Hoyt, captured rainwater is stored in a buried 4,000-gallon cistern for up to thirty hours, then slowly released to the city stormwater system. Some recirculates to steel fountains in the courtyard. It might have been more educational to spill water into planting beds, visibly sustaining vegetation. Nevertheless, this project incorporates many principles of artful rainwater design:

- Make rain visible as it flows through the system.
- Incorporate a cistern or other receptacle to handle overflow.
- Use rainwater for irrigation or other needs.
- Design the flow system artfully for sound, reflection, and aeration.[57]

Infiltrate Water Simply On-site

Until the mid-1990s, a focus on *getting rid of* water virtually displaced the many varieties of water infiltration devices. European texts on landscape construction were well ahead of most US counterparts (Ferguson's work was ahead of its time). For example, a standard

Figure 4.23 Collected on the Portland Water Pollution Control Lab's roof, water spouts from scuppers in rhythmic jets. (*Project:* Robert Murase. *Photo:* Tom Liptan.)

British text from the *1970s* contains no fewer than four detail drawings for infiltration devices, plus calculations showing how large a land area each can drain in normal soils.[58]

On-site infiltration may be overlooked because it is so simple. It relies on two basic principles: slowing or holding water flow, and increasing soil permeability. Both are easier to achieve close to the source of water, because large volumes and fast flow are harder to hold and require extreme porosity to infiltrate quickly.

Bioswales (p. 249) use vegetation and gentle gradients to slow and infiltrate water. Wetlands (whether natural, restored, or constructed) slow and hold water due to topography and vegetation, and frequently are

Figure 4.24 The 10th@Hoyt courtyard (Portland OR) makes rainwater visible and artful en route from roof to cistern. (*Project:* Steve Koch. *Photo:* Stuart Echols.)

major infiltration sites. Porous paving over a reservoir provides on-site infiltration (p. 251). Water harvesting, sometimes put into storage, often has infiltration as its ultimate goal. Check dams, terracing, key-line trenches, and many other techniques of BTEC and Permaculture hold water in small, even tiny, reservoirs, from which it soaks into the soil. Conventional retention basins do the same thing, though generally on an overcentralized scale.

Two structures especially designed for infiltration are the French drain and the "soakaway." Conventional construction recognizes these only as minor weapons in the arsenal of water control. For sustainability, they should be everyday tools for making peace with water and winning its benefits.

The French drain is simply a pit or trench filled with rubble or gravel. The rubble should be graded, large at the bottom to small near the top. Over the smallest gravel, several inches of soil match the original surface. Modern French drains are lined with filter fabric, which permits water to move through the rubble, while keeping out sediment that would eventually fill the voids.

Prior to invention of filter fabric, French drains had to be dug up and cleaned of silt, or replaced, every few years. Conventional concrete catch basins can also be overwhelmed by silt, but are somewhat easier to clean.

Silting, however, really indicates that the structure is serving a quickly eroding area; more structures, closer to the source, may solve this. A single drain for a large area may seem economical, but only in terms of initial costs. Shorter flow lines, and vegetated surfaces for the flow, significantly cut maintenance costs due to siltation.

Soakaways are quite similar to French drains, but usually receive water from a small drainpipe or downspout rather than overland flow. Some soakaways are rubble filled, while others are called "dry wells." Infiltration occurs through unmortared stone walls and an earth floor. Without rubble, soakaways hold a larger volume of water. Unlike French drains, they are usually covered with a grate or manhole. If incoming water is very silty, a conventional silt trap can be added. Like wells, dry wells may pose accident dangers. Where this is a concern, the filled soakaway or French drain with filter fabric may be a better choice.

In soils with ordinary drainage and rainfall typical of Britain, a 60-cubic-foot-capacity soakaway can infiltrate runoff for about 2,200 square feet (1.6 cubic meters for 200 square meters). Larger soakaways collect from areas almost 100 feet square.[59] This gives an idea of the small scale appropriate to these methods. For larger areas, terraces or check dams may be simpler and cheaper.

A number of commercially available drainage systems use filter fabric around a core with large voids (usually waffle-like plastic). In effect, they provide a French drain in the shape of a pipe or sheet (laid vertically or horizontally), very useful for collecting and filtering sediment-laden water. Old-fashioned perforated pipe serves some of the same purposes, but may clog with sediment. Filter drains are important in some updated tree-planting standards (Principle 3) and valuable in water harvesting. For harvesting, similar "wrapped waffle" materials are available in modules, for example AquaStor, for constructing updated versions of the French drain.

Store Water for Later Use

One common complaint about water harvesting results from underestimating required storage volume. Precipitation usually comes in one season and must be held for use in another. Thus, the total *season's* accumulation determines the size of storage tank needed.

Most people are surprised by how much water can be harvested from a single storm, and tend to skimp on storage.

Harvested water can be stored in tanks above- or belowground, or in ponds. Ponds lose too much to evaporation to make efficient irrigation holding tanks and are unsuitable for drinking water. These limitations may be offset, however, if ponds also serve for raising fish, for solar collectors or heat pumps, for slowing flood flows, or as decorative features.

Tanks are available ready-made in metal, fiberglass, plastic, or precast concrete. They can also be built on-site from stone or ferrocement (thin cement over steel reinforcing mesh). Wood tanks should be of sustainably harvested lumber. If located aboveground, tanks should be opaque; sunlight promotes algae growth. Buried tanks must be heavy-duty, but have the advantage of protection from freezing. Not all tank materials are suitable for drinking water. Energy and toxicity in manufacture should be considered as well (see Principles 6 and 7).

Figure 4.25   Despite the severity of desert runoff, Cavalliere Park captures 100 percent of Scottsdale AZ's 100-year storm (49.5 acre-feet, 16 million gallons, or 61 million liters, enough for 400 people for a year). It also cools the microclimate, provides wildlife habitat, reduces resource use, and generates 25,000 kWh annually. (*Project:* JJR/Floor. *Photo:* Bill Timmerman.)

Concrete tanks and box culverts installed under paved areas are increasingly common as developers try to maximize space, conserve water, and manage runoff. To some extent, these substitute for "reservoir porous paving" (p. 251), but lack the biological benefits. In a few places (for example, Houston TX), dense clay soils virtually prevent infiltration, and tanks may be important in managing storm flows (though not the size of Hurricane Harvey's). With safeguards against collected pollutants, water from tank storage may be reusable as non-potable irrigation.

Water storage designs can be highly creative. One recent storage system is the Rainwater Pillow, a heavy reinforced polymer bag holding from 1,000 to 200,000 gallons. It is particularly useful when installed in crawl spaces or under decks in otherwise wasted space. The smaller pillows need only three feet of clearance. Above about 50,000 gallons, the pillow edges must be supported by berms or other structures. In a similar spirit, Rainwater Hog tanks fit between framing members in ordinary walls or floors. Another system, WaterFence, fits modular tanks into a six-foot-tall fence with various facades; it holds about forty-five gallons per linear foot, and was invented by a fourteen-year-old as a science fair project. Another inventive example is the Danish firm Nordarch's design using the basins of a skateboard park as emergency floodwater ponds.

Use Pumps if Needed

Where possible, gravity-flow water systems are most energy efficient. Harvested rainwater, however, is normally stored lower than the collecting surface; if this is a roof, gravity flow into the same building's plumbing is unlikely. Water is too heavy to locate tanks on upper floors of buildings without structural reinforcement. Carefully located tanks might provide gravity-fed flood irrigation at ground level, but water pressure for modern irrigation is hard to achieve using gravity alone.

For these reasons, water harvesting often requires pumps. Water pumping is one of solar electricity's most efficient uses (see p. 311), common in agriculture and at remote campgrounds. For water supply, it is cheaper to store water than electricity—that is, pump to a high tank during sunny periods, supply-

ing users by gravity, rather than pump on demand using storage batteries. Decorative fountain pumps can be solar powered; sunshine intensity could regulate pumped volume, creating a climate-responsive fountain. For constant pump operation, a small solar-charged battery is practical.

There are many types of pump design. Look for low energy usage, good service life, and low maintenance. Many suppliers offer pumps designed for solar power, or even paired with photovoltaic panels as kits. DC-powered pumps can be operated directly from solar panels without an inverter, keeping systems simple.

Find Hidden Waters

The Sonoran Landscape Laboratory at the University of Arizona, Tucson, was built outside the architecture school with a budget of zero in a former parking lot.[60] Plantings that represent five vegetation zones of the Sonoran Desert get their water, as the garden got much of its material, by "living off the waste of the building," as the designer, Christine Ten Eyck, puts it.

The main source of water for this landscape is air-conditioning condensate, about 95,000 gallons of it per year, or 34 percent of the irrigation supply. Filter back-flushing provides another 14 percent, and is rich in minerals the plants need. Ten Eyck found that condensate and similar lost water sources are common in the Middle East, a response to desert necessity, high-tech construction, and Islamic water teachings that have long emphasized stewardship. Water harvested from the building's roof provides another 30 percent of the irrigation budget; all these sources are pooled in a tank built into the building itself. Compared to equivalent-sized landscapes in Tucson, the Landscape Lab uses 83 percent less tap water for irrigation. Like the Yuma East wetlands (Principle 2), on an entirely different scale, it uses an unnatural water situation to accomplish biological sustainability. Ten Eyck says that "buildings are the new aquifers." As at Yuma, there's a risk these unconventional sources might dry up as sustainable water use matures; meanwhile, there is functional and educational benefit in experimenting.

Urbanite (a.k.a. debris from demolition) was placed by hand to create a pool and a series of stream-like channels and micro-basins. It looked all wrong, until

Figure 4.26   This University of Arizona native-plant garden is watered with reclaimed air-conditioning condensate, a technique widely used in desert countries with a strong heritage of Muslim water ethics. (*Project and Photo:* Ten Eyck Landscape Architects.)

smaller gravel was broadcast across it, then allowed to wash into place with storms. The result is what might be called "process-based urban naturalism" that even purists among the faculty and students came to love. University of Arizona landscape alumni contributed materials and time, completing the project after the university cut its budget to zero.

This landscape, like several other new third-edition entries, exemplifies an integration of individual sustainable strategies into something vital. It tells the Sonoran story, in a botanic garden way; saves water overall, and demonstrates very creative reuse of resources. And it was instrumented for research from the first; a monitored arid-zone greenroof, the ability to meter water use precisely, and unusually specific and numerous irrigation zones all allow experimentation to produce documentable results.

Besides being a beautiful and comfortable outdoor space, this is truly a laboratory for teaching and researching Tucson's unusual landscape.

Irrigate Intelligently and Sparingly

The irrigation industry underwent major changes between the first and second editions of this book. Fortunately, these changes have substantially improved irrigation's alignment with water conservation, to such an extent that systems over a few years old may be obsolete, and in some states, water-saving replacements may be eligible for rebates.[61]

In writing about irrigation in the first edition, it was difficult not to treat it as fundamentally unsustainable, deeply associated with bluegrass obsession.[62] Apart from drip irrigation, most of the industry seemed unrepentantly devoted to unlimited water.

Today, by contrast, the irrigation industry is outpacing the landscape professions in walking conservation's talk. Perhaps the handwriting on the wall has been more blunt about water issues than other aspects of landscaping. Faced with a choice between changing direction or shriveling away, irrigation industry associations, manufacturers, and contractors have made water conservation a priority.

As a result, many idealistic and even radical ideas suggested in 2000 are now incorporated in new technologies and advocated as best practices. Artificially redistributing the Earth's waters to fit market demands will always raise sustainability issues, but landscape irrigation today involves a serious conservation ethic.

Change Attitudes, Incentives, and Technologies

The quantity of fresh water on Earth is a fixed amount,[63] of which some is unavailable due to pollution and drought. Much available water is essential to nonhuman life-forms and in that sense "spoken for." Yet human demand is growing. In many countries, population growth is outstripping water supply; US "lifestyle improvements" have increased water usage *four times* as fast as population growth, doubling every twenty years since 1900;[64] as of 2008, total US use was 400 billion gallons *per day*.[65] Water supply takes energy, and energy production takes water (see Principle 7).

The concept of a "water footprint" reveals hidden water usage in products as diverse as T-shirts and electronics; the movement of such products amounts to the export of "virtual water."[66] One 2007 study found that while construction *processes* use little water, "embodied water" in construction *materials* can be many times the volume enclosed by the building, and many years' worth of operational water use.[67] In addition to actual scarcity, water infrastructure is becoming inadequate to meet demand in many regions, and water demand is "hardening": the easy reductions have been made, and further conservation will be more difficult.[68]

For anyone interested in a holistic view of one city's water infrastructure over time, enter "aquae urbis romae" in your browser for an interactive map of Rome's natural and built water systems, including its famous fountains, over hundreds of years.

As water has become an international resource concern, this has affected irrigation. Usage restrictions have become common, many targeting landscape irrigation first. Between 1984 and 2008, costs of water in the United States rose 310 percent, while the Consumer Price Index rose only 207 percent for the same period.[69] This has forced real efficiencies and generated heated debate about irrigation's role.

Landscapes use a major portion of US water, but far from the largest. Landscape irrigation consumes 30 to 50 percent of municipal water in many areas, and in dry regions or hot months can account for 75 percent.[70] Cities use about 12 to 21 percent of the US total; at 30 to 75 percent of this, landscape use is 4 to 16 percent of the national total. Industry uses 10 percent, equivalent to landscape usage; the remaining *69 percent* goes to agriculture and hydropower.

Two issues differentiate landscape irrigation from industrial and agricultural use, however. First, unlike either agriculture or industry, much landscape irrigation unnecessarily uses *treated* municipal water. Second, agriculture and some industries use water for tangibly productive purposes. By contrast, landscapes are considered ornamental, their benefits far harder to quantify than crops or manufacturing. Thus, when drought or supply problems arise, landscape irrigation is curtailed before agriculture or manufacturing. Restricting the relatively small landscape industry, rather than take on larger ones with more clout, is also politically expedient. It is increasingly clear, however, that this approach is shortsighted.

As a result, "the first reaction to drought and water shortages tends to be . . . shutting off the taps" for landscape use.[71] This is arguably unfair to landowners and to the landscape professions. More important, it risks destroying environmental services provided by planted landscapes, such as heat-island abatement and runoff control. Studies from Australia and New

Jersey also suggest that when on-again-off-again water restrictions are lifted, water consumption *increases* 4 to 10 percent over pre-restriction levels.[72]

Instead of waiting for droughts and shutting off irrigation, proactive jurisdictions mandate certain types of irrigation equipment, such as drip systems and efficient controllers. California offers rebates of several hundred dollars for such installations, and requires all irrigation systems installed after 2010 to have "smart" controllers and meet other efficiency criteria (see below).[73] From 2008 until about 2015, Denver Water offered large irrigators as much as $7,000 for each acre-foot they could save.[74] The EPA announced, in October 2006, a program called WaterSense to certify water-conservation products, services, and specialists.

Irrigation means addition of *any* water *above and beyond normal precipitation.* Although some irrigation techniques save more water than others, *all* irrigation requires extra water. The *baseline* for evaluating *ecological* costs and benefits of irrigation should always be the unirrigated landscape and its natural water regime. This baseline, of course, is variable, and the variation is becoming more extreme due to climate change.

This does not mean that irrigation should be excluded from sustainable design. Rather, irrigation should be used where it can produce outstanding results in resource-efficient ways. Truly saving water requires considering all options, from irrigating with surplus water to eliminating irrigation for most or all of a site. Comparing relative efficiency of different irrigation systems is not, by itself, sufficient to make a landscape sustainable. In this, both irrigation and landscape professionals have a significant blind spot: we habitually assume that irrigation is a given, and that efficiency is enough. This bias, unfortunately, has proved stubborn to change.

Water efficiency is not just a matter of technology, though. "The most important feature of a water-conserving landscape is the preservation of as many existing [native] trees and shrubs as possible."[75] Thus the issues and techniques raised in Principle 1 are critical to water conservation. This constant interlinkage of good practices cannot be overemphasized. The first step toward truly sustainable irrigation is to plan, preserve, and design landscapes that *minimize the need* for water.

Design Xeriscapes for Real Water Savings

Xeriscape designs landscapes to use water efficiently. This system, trademarked by the Denver Water Department and the National Xeriscape Council, promotes seven basic principles, corresponding to many themes of this book.[76] They are:

- planning and design
- soil analysis and improvement
- practical areas of turf
- appropriate plants
- efficient irrigation
- mulching
- proper maintenance.

These principles (which, taken individually, are not new to gardeners) are all essential to the system. Xeriscape's central concept, however, is that plants with like water requirements are grouped together; this corresponds to well-designed irrigation, both conventional and leading-edge (see IrriGreen, p. 221, for example). Xeriscape reserves water-intensive plants for locations of maximum effect. Exotic, water-hungry specimen trees might be used at focal points. A small, drought-tolerant lawn might be a special feature. Moving away from the house, however, planting zones contain more drought-tolerant plants. On larger properties, only a reasonably sized garden contains irrigated plants; outside that zone, the native landscape predominates. In the native zone, any plantings are species that survive without watering once established. (Climate and carbon considerations require adjusting this idea to value well-established non-natives too, while generally not planting new ones.)

Clearly, Xeriscape offers far greater water savings than irrigating the entire lot, no matter how efficiently. With efficient irrigation technology where any is used, Xeriscape gardens live up to their name: "xeric" means dry, despite the misconception that it is "zero-scape."

Like native-plant use in general, Xeriscape requires changes in attitude, encouraging people to see well-adapted plants as beautiful. Too many (laypeople and professionals) still assume that only certain horticultural varieties have merit, and that all others are scruffy weeds. Xeriscape encourages attention to the qualities that make a place unique. This attitude is critically important to sustainability.

A simple approach to water efficiency, emphasized by Xeriscape and many other systems, is organic mulch. (Inorganic mulches, like gravel, can protect soil moisture, but lack other benefits.) In addition to increasing soil fertility, applying two to four inches of mulch as part of regular maintenance dramatically decreases evaporative water loss (see Principle 10).

Healthy soil produces healthier plants while demanding or wasting far less water. Before increasing site irrigation, test and maximize existing soil's ability to store water and release it to plants. Recall that excessive soil "improvements" are counterproductive in some regions (p. 71).

Install Water-efficient Irrigation Technology

The main forms of irrigation are flood, spray, and drip. Flooding a field or bed requires the least equipment, but is labor intensive. Spray can use simple hoses and fittings, which are easily moved and aimed, although dragging hoses is many a gardener's complaint. As a result, buried pipe with fixed spray heads and automated controllers is popular. Drip irrigation delivers water to precise points on or under the ground. Like buried spray systems, it requires considerable pipe runs, but can easily be automated.

Comparisons of water efficiency between these three systems are straightforward. (Ease of maintenance and other issues may be more awkward.) Flood and spray systems lose significant amounts of water to evaporation, and spray systems waste water by overspraying unless very carefully installed and maintained. Micro-spray systems have been developed that suffer less loss, but still more than drippers. Compared to older aboveground systems, drip saved up to 90 percent of water used; despite important recent improvements in spray technology, drip continues to outperform spray by 30 to 65 percent.[77] Instead of going to waste, nearly 95 percent of water supplied by drip is delivered where plants need it.[78]

Water-efficient design is not more costly than conventional landscapes. In fact, at least one study concluded that for two equivalent landscapes, one water conserving and the other conventional, the low-water design's overall operational and maintenance costs were less than *half*, including labor, fuel, pesticides, fertilizer, water, and energy. Because operation and maintenance represented 80 percent of each landscape's total cost (design and construction representing only 20 percent), this difference is significant.[79] One reason for these savings is that over- or underwatering affects soil and plant health, contributing in turn to costly erosion and soil subsidence and requiring more pesticides, water, fertilizer, and staff attention.

Drip irrigation systems are, for many people, the main mode of environmentally responsible irrigation. In general, this remains true even with recent innovation. Aboveground irrigation, however, has been enough improved, and controllers have taken such a predominant position in efficient irrigation, that they warrant expanded coverage.

Irrigation work involves specialized skill, and many landscape companies subcontract it. (Those who do both often say, resignedly, that landscape is a sideline to their irrigation business.) This section focuses on sustainability of irrigation systems. For basic design principles, and equipment details, consult irrigation-specific reference books, software, and manufacturer catalogs.

Use Controllers and Sensors for Efficiency

Controllers, when this book first appeared, were time clocks, some fancier than others, occasionally equipped with a sensor to override the clock in rainy or windy conditions. These controllers were important attempts at water conservation, but have truly been supplanted by "smart controllers," which have themselves rapidly evolved through several generations.

Even when irrigation hardware is highly efficient, immense waste occurs if the system runs during rainstorms, on saturated ground, or during midday heat. Few people can remember to turn irrigation on and off at precisely the right times. The best times for residential irrigation are often when people are asleep or not home. Time-clock controllers were the first attempt to solve this problem.

Weather, however, doesn't happen on a clock schedule. From one day to the next, a site's soil moisture, relative humidity, temperature, light levels, and wind can vary dramatically. All affect how much moisture is in the soil, and how much a given plant actually needs.

Irrigating at the same time every few days actually has had the unintended and unexpected consequence of making water waste *worse*. A number of studies have shown that set-and-forget time-clock controllers apply up to *twice as much water as is actually needed* by landscape plants. (An attentive person hand watering does far better, wasting only about 10 percent.[80] One clock-based trick can be valuable: if soil absorption is slow, repeated short waterings of each zone give time for infiltration and decrease runoff. Water needs are complex; convenient, predictable settings give very poor conservation results). Timer-controlled systems are dinosaurs, despite early attempts to add sensors and seasonal adjustment factors. In many places they are banned for new installations, and rightly so.

Smart controllers achieve far great water efficiency by basing irrigation times and amounts on actual environmental conditions. They do this in three basic ways. Because most manufacturers now offer at least one of these options, and many offer all, in different combinations, trade-name examples have mostly been dropped from this section.

The simplest and most accurate indicator of site-specific growing conditions is soil moisture. When sensors register soil moisture below a set threshold (due to depletion by plants, or hot, dry conditions), the controller opens valves until the threshold is reached. If the soil is moist from rain or earlier irrigation, the sensor-linked controller stays off. Similarly, as plants slow their moisture uptake in late fall, or begin uptake in early spring, sensors gradually reduce or increase irrigation. Some soil-moisture systems have a single sensor, giving an overall picture of site conditions; others have a sensor for each valve or zone.

"ET controllers" use evapotranspiration (ET) data to determine when and how much to water. (In 2000, these data were available in California for computing irrigation *design*. Data are now available throughout the United States and used directly by the controller.) Older ET controllers relied on built-in databases of past seasonal ET levels and guesstimated current conditions. Newer models download current ET values from regional weather stations and other Web-based sources daily, or even hourly. Some compare current data to a database before "deciding" whether to water. Since weather stations may be dozens of miles from the irrigation site, ET controllers use interpolation to estimate localized weather, but in arid regions, where irrigation and conservation are most critical, even a quarter-mile difference can mean totally different weather.

Integrated multisensor systems put a mini weather station at the irrigation site, calculating ET values from site-specific information. Some models use relative humidity (RH) and temperature to predict rainfall (RH rises dramatically before storms and remains high afterward). In theory, local data provide most accurate control.

The ongoing revolution in communications not only provides data to on-site irrigation controllers, but also exchanges field data with remote devices by two-way communication in real time. (This concept was pioneered, primarily for remote system management, in the 1990s by LEIT solar irrigation controllers, noted below.) Irrigation controllers, and even individual heads, are becoming part of the much-ballyhooed "Internet of things." Older, dedicated radio or landline linkage is being replaced with cloud-based systems; many manufacturers have recognized that requiring a monthly fee for such connectivity hampers sales, though others still charge. Complete control of single or multiple systems from a cell phone or computer is nearly standard. For irrigation companies or large institutions, this can significantly cut fuel usage by reducing site visits.

Many recent controllers offer leak detection and auto-shutoff, pressure regulation (high pressure causes mist and overspray), and electrical troubleshooting. Useful for single-site systems, these are essential for centralized control of multiple sites. Leaks that would otherwise consume huge amounts of water are recognized almost instantly; the zone is turned off, and a message sent to the maintenance person's phone. According to the Boulder (CO) Energy Conservation Center (BECC), 5 percent of average residential use is wasted via leaks.[81] With US residential use around 250 gallons per day,[82] leaks waste some *4,500 gallons annually per household.*

Smart controllers significantly improve water conservation. By replacing a clock-only controller (with-

Table 4.2
Leaks consume surprisingly large amounts of water.

	Leak Size (line pressure 60 psi)	Water Waste (gallons/month)	Equivalent Water Use if Not Wasted
Drops per minute	60	192	
	90	310	1 average household for 1 day
	120	429	
Length of smooth stream	3 in.	1,095	1 super-efficient household for 1 month
	6 in.	2,190	
	9 in.	3,290	
Opening diameter	1/32 in.	6,300	1 average household for almost 1 month
	1/16 in.	25,000	
	1/8 in.	100,000	1 average household for more than 1 year
	3/16 in.	225,000	1 church, hotel, or retail store for 1 year
	1/4 in.	400,000	1 acre turf irrigated for 6 months, or a 100-student elementary school for 1 year

Sources: Drip rates: California Urban Water Conservation Council, "Practical Plumbing Handbook," 2001, www.cuwcc.org. Equivalent uses: City of Santa Fe (NM) Planning Department, 2001 pamphlet.

out changing the rest of the system), 50 percent of water waste and 70 percent of irrigation runoff can be eliminated.[83] An increasing number of jurisdictions either require or offer rebates for smart controllers.

No controller can completely overcome poor design, inadequate plumbing, or negligent maintenance (some can detect such problems). Smart controllers come very close to applying exactly what plants need. This is an impressive achievement—and also means that further improvements in efficiency are not likely to be easy.

Related to controller improvement, companies like SprinklerMaps are making it easier to gather as-built irrigation information in the field. This smartphone app for groundskeepers can map irrigation heads onto satellite maps; calculate areas and rates of water and fertilizer application; and flag items needing repair. A different approach is the Mesa and Mesa 2 "hardened" tablets from Juniper Systems, which offers standard tablet software in a dust- and waterproof case with an all-day battery life.[84] It must be only a matter of time until design and construction documents are uploaded into phones and tablets, annotated with as-built information, and used to control irrigation and other systems as well as to record changes, repairs, and operational issues. Thus far, I have not found a system

that truly integrates all these aspects of professional landscape work.

Make Drip Irrigation First Choice

Drip technology was already highly efficient as of the first edition of this book. Although it has continued to evolve, the changes are aimed at overcoming drip's reputation (largely undeserved) for being "complicated." The broad principles relating drip to sustainable practice have changed relatively little.[85] These are:

In-line emitters (built into the supply tube every few inches) are most reliable. Most manufacturers offer standard spacings (twelve or eighteen inches); some offer custom-spaced tube. It has become common to color-code both in-line tubes and individual emitters according to flow rate.

Other drip types are useful for some conditions, including emitters that "punch in" to the supply tube wall or connect via small "spaghetti tube." Some can be disassembled for cleaning. Porous or "leaky" pipe, in which water oozes through the whole tube wall, is used in some drip systems.

Pressure-compensating emitters adjust for supply pressure, topography, and pressure drop over distance, increasing efficiency. Recently, check valves have been added to some in-line drippers, which will shut down the zone if pressure falls below a minimum.

Self-cleaning emitters are preferred. The most common design uses turbulent flow to clean the dripper. An "air gap" in some designs creates a barrier to root intrusion. Some drippers are impregnated with root-inhibiting chemicals to prevent clogging; longevity of these chemicals varies. Drippers exposed to strong sunshine may become caked with evaporated mineral salts.

Filters are essential, upstream from all valves, even with self-cleaning drippers. So-called Y-filters are preferred over straight in-line designs, providing a larger filter surface and simplifying draining and cleaning. Many filters are self-flushing.

In addition to pressure-regulating drippers, each valve should have a master pressure regulator.

Backflow preventers are required on all irrigation, especially important where harvested water or graywater (below) supplement tap water.

Drip irrigation relies strongly on zones of similar water need—the Xeriscape concept. Although much has been made of drip systems delivering water to individual plants as needed, in landscapes (as opposed to containers) the system actually waters a zone. Putting each *plant* on an individualized watering schedule would require separate valves and pipes per plant.

Individualized water delivery has misled many designers into placing a single dripper per plant, which irrigation author Robert Kourik refers to as "water bondage." Kourik recommends that emitters be on a zone-wide grid, uniformly watering that area.[86] Grid spacing needs to match plant types, rates of percolation, and spread in local soils. Another approach where grids are awkward (e.g., rock gardens) is "hubs" that supply several easily adjustable spaghetti-tube drippers. Each hub is fed by a riser from a buried supply line; the hubs are not movable, but the drippers are.

One situation where drip may not be optimal is on soils that are extremely quick-draining. Drip (as the name implies) puts out water as a series of drops, all at exactly the same location. For the system to work, the soil must hold water and cause it to spread horizontally; the size of the grid needs to equal the diameter of this spreading. In very sandy soils, water in effect migrates straight down and becomes unavailable to plants (not an issue in agriculture, with its

one-plant-one-dripper regimen). Failure of water to spread can, in turn, mislead sensors: a sensor precisely at the drip would register very wet, but located anywhere else, would register dry no matter how much water was applied. The only potential solution I have heard for this problem is to run the irrigation in extremely short repeated cycles, on the theory that small amounts of water will bond to the soil before the next drops are applied. Since there likely are limits even to this fix, carefully designed and controlled spray irrigation may be more effective in such situations.

Drip systems can be buried successfully, and improvement of subsurface performance has been a theme over the past decade. Rain Bird, for example, has added a copper film to each emitter, which deters root penetration without being toxic. Extra care is required in burying drip; the emitter tubes, which must be near the surface to deliver water, tend to heave up out of the ground, possibly due to frost action. (Supply tubes without emitters can always be buried, and pipes or wires that cross walkways should be buried for safety.) Attaching emitter tubes to buried mesh has been suggested, but seems likely to harm soil wildlife. A better approach is to stake the system before burying it, using landscape staples (those with a kink in each leg hold better than plain ones). Rain Bird offers tube joint fittings with attached stakes, and a "staple gun" for landscape use won a 2016 innovation award from *Landscape and Irrigation* magazine.

Even with self-cleaning emitters, some models clog easily if buried. Under lawns, drippers may need to run briefly every few hours to keep grass roots from growing into emitters.[87] A buried drip system, however, is completely belowground and unlikely to be damaged by surface traffic or vandalism. One improvement that would be extremely valuable in drip tubing and fittings would be built-in or clip-on metal markers to allow buried lines to be traced magnetically. (Wire and valve locators are available, and can sometimes be rented; but no instrument can directly locate plastic pipes.)

If left on the surface, drippers should be covered by mulching for efficiency and to protect the emitters from salt buildup caused by exposure to strong direct sunlight. Unburied drip systems can be an unsightly sprawl of piping, but as long as the owner is committed to regular mulching, drip systems stay invisible. By leaving them on the surface, pipes remain accessible, reparable, and adjustable. Adjustment is important as plants mature or site usage changes. No other fully automatic irrigation system can easily be moved.

Drip's inherent efficiency can be defeated by poor design or maintenance, or by an ineffective controller. Coupled with smart controllers, however, drip remains the system of choice for water-conserving irrigation.

Consider Spray and Rotor Systems

Conventional aboveground irrigation includes a variety of aboveground (or pop-up) heads, which cover circles or partial circles. Impact heads, originally developed for agriculture, cover large areas with a characteristic *pft-pft* sound;[88] spray heads put out a sheet of water; rotors shoot one or more rotating streams. Relatively recent additions to the arsenal are "rotary nozzles" (small rotors that mount on spray-head risers) and "bubblers" that flood the ground, generally used for trees and shrubs.

All aboveground hardware suffers evaporative losses that drip avoids. Overlapping arcs of coverage pose challenges in design, aiming, and maintenance, producing variable coverage and tending to put water where it is not wanted—on fences, sidewalks, windows, or plants that don't need it.

Aboveground hardware has gradually improved in several ways. Low-volume and ultra-low-volume systems are available; they lose less water, and more heads can be put on a single line or zone. Spray patterns (including rectangular coverage) have been made more accurate.

Pressure regulation is important for spray heads. If line pressure is higher than the head is designed for, it will produce rapidly evaporating mist and overspray.

Spray heads can clog, but are fairly easy to clean. They have moving parts, however, while drippers do not. Risers and pop-up heads are easily jammed, broken, damaged, or vandalized. Flexible mountings between supply line and riser have improved spray-head survival. Regular readjustment to keep spray heads vertical and high enough to clear surrounding vegetation is essential to maintain performance and avoid ponding or runoff.

Aboveground systems often drain from the lowest head in each zone after shutoff. Many manufacturers have added check valves to prevent this. The valves will also prevent geysers from broken, vandalized, or stolen heads. More recent systems have leak detection and the ability to notify the user.

Some landscape professionals believe that combining micro-spray with drip produces a humid soil surface, microbe populations on periodically wetted leaves, and water to break down mulch. I have been unable to confirm this theory, but would welcome further information.

Introduced in 2014, the IrriGreen Genius system uses one computerized rotor centered in each zone, relying on inkjet technology for precision water placement. Each rotor has about a dozen jets "stacked" vertically on one side; at any given rotation angle, the jets throw water to evenly spaced points on the line from the rotor to the zone edge. The length of this "line" of jets can be programmed to reach exactly to the zone edge, no matter how irregular; a phone app allows the installer to define the zones.[89] Once the zone shape is programmed, the system computes the volume of water to be applied, and constantly adjusts the distance of all the streams of water, as well as the speed of rotation, to give equal coverage. The maximum distance to the zone edge is 30 feet (assuming normal water pressure, which the system calibrates to ensure consistent coverage). This results in a maximum zone of about 2,000 square feet.

The inventor, Gary Klinefelter, an inkjet-printer engineer, "set out to save water, but ended up saving labor." Because each zone has a single valve, a single supply line is trenched reasonably close to laid-out head locations; there are no lateral lines, just short connections from supply line to head. According to IrriGreen, this cuts labor to one-third; the savings pay for the difference in equipment cost, resulting in cost comparable to a conventional system of similar size. Heads are located in the middle of lawns rather than at paving edges, where they are more vulnerable. In addition, where a conventional system might have 50 heads for 8 zones, IrriGreen's one-zone-one-sprinkler design uses only 8, with similar reductions in fittings. IrriGreen has calculated that 85 percent less plastic is required for its system than for comparable cover-

Figure 4.27a, b Centrally located in each irrigation zone, the IrriGreen "Genius" sprinkler is set to variable-length sprays to fit irregular outlines (top) and varied volumes per jet to achieve even coverage (bottom). (*Product and Photos:* IrriGreen.)

age by either spray or drip tubing. As for water, tests at the Center for Irrigation Technology at California State University, Fresno, showed a minimum savings of 40 percent, compared to mechanical aboveground sprinkler systems. This brings the calibrated jet system close to the water savings associated with drip irrigation (although no comparative study with drip has been conducted).

The calibrated jet system is intended for use on lawns; it *can* spray around trees in a lawn, but such obstacles impede even coverage. For watering shrubs, trees, or flower beds, the controller can also run zones with conventional irrigation equipment, both drip and spray. Extra adjustments are needed to water evenly on slopes. Because IrriGreen zones are fairly small, and only one zone runs at a time, the system is primarily used for residential and small commercial projects, though the company is working on larger-capacity heads and added controller features.

IrriGreen is intended as an evolving platform. At present, the suppliers recommend connecting a soil sensor to the controller; they consider ET data (which can be "cobbled" in) less accurate, but will eventually add this as a supported function. Calibration is done by a flow meter, which monitors usage but is not yet programmed to detect leaks. Settings are done by logging in, via cell phone, to IrriGreen's site; a more direct remote control is another future feature. IrriGreen is also working with OmniEarth toward a mapping application that can analyze map data to plan zone irrigation and compare costs.

IrriGreen has been called the future of irrigation, and it is certainly a game-changer for turf areas. It appears the company recognizes the need to keep innovating, especially to add control apps that users, especially in large installations, have come to rely on.

There have been a number of "contour sprinklers" for hose-end use that can be set for odd-shaped areas, but the only apparent competitor for IrriGreen is the German manufacturer Gardena. It produces the Vielflächen-Versenkregner (multi-area pop-up) Aqua-Contour. With a spray pattern resembling the old-fashioned oscillating lawn sprinkler, the AquaContour is set similarly to the IrriGreen method. Permanently installed or portable hose-end units are available; the portable type uses ground pins to mark its position

when set, and can recall several area shapes, thus covering many zones by moving one pre-programmed unit. It is primarily suited to residential use, for the same reasons affecting IrriGreen.

Remember Other Irrigation Options

Some irrigation suppliers now offer "root-watering" fixtures,[90] primarily for trees and large shrubs. These are tubes, three or four inches in diameter, run from the soil surface to root depth, usually a foot or two. Plain pipes have been used in this way for years, filled periodically from a hose. The updated version is filled by the automatic irrigation system. For some species, and with a separate valve controlling only them, root waterers may have value and conserve water.

A low-tech option is the Treegator drip irrigation bag, a heavy fourteen- or twenty-gallon plastic sack that drip irrigates one tree for up to ten hours. Careful placement of the bag is important: with all but small trees, it is a mistake to place it next to the trunk. Compared to hose watering, Treegators reduce evaporative loss and runoff. The manufacturer estimates that this system cuts weekly watering visits from four to one, and laborer time per tree from fifteen minutes to two. By this estimate, labor cost is only 3 percent of that for hose watering, and some fuel costs may be saved. Average wholesale price is $17.50 per bag. The manufacturer suggests that landscape contractors save enough on labor that they can use the bags to establish plantings, then give them to the client.

Hose watering is an often-overlooked option. Professionals profit on irrigation systems, but should not forget that for some situations (occasional watering of tough species, or early establishment where a permanent system is not desirable), hose watering is a reasonable, water-conserving alternative.

Use Non-potable Water for Irrigation

Non-potable water can and should be used for irrigation. Very few plants benefit from treated water; chlorine and fluorine harm some species. Infrastructure and treatment costs are significant. Many manufacturers offer non-potable pipes and fittings (usually color-coded purple). These are identical to conventional components except where valves and filters must be redesigned to avoid clogging or attack by impurities in non-potable water.

Brackish water from deep subsurface wells, plus "produced water" (waste from oil drilling), are coming under scrutiny as possible irrigation sources. The legal rights to deep water deposits are contested. Both types of water require desalinization, and are so saline that biopurification is not an option. Reliable forms of water "softening" involve filters, which need cleaning, and salts, which must be renewed and disposed of. Some companies market magnetic water softening; this is controversial and with mixed scientific results at best.

Aim for Energy-efficient Irrigation Systems

Controllers, sensors, and valves all require electricity. A few models run on 9V batteries. Solar-powered systems are available from a number of manufacturers. These take advantage of photovoltaics' greatest benefit: flexible location. Solar-powered controllers have proved popular with street and highway agencies for irrigating road medians and other non-electrified areas. One large California developer, McMillin Properties, installs Photocomm solar controllers temporarily at new sites during the vulnerable period before utility power is turned on. Solar-powered controllers can be located close to valves, decreasing wire runs and reducing both voltage drop and materials costs.

Solar irrigation controllers are available both for retrofitting and new construction. Most non-solar systems use solenoids that are held open by constant electrical current and close when current stops. Supplying constant current has until recently only been possible with utility power; solar panels could not generate enough electricity. So-called latching solenoids are much more energy efficient: they open on a brief energy pulse and close with a second pulse. Whether a latching solenoid can be retrofitted to a standard valve depends on the model of each. Units with inverters can supply 12V or 24V AC, which powers most standard irrigation, simplifying retrofits and replacement parts.

Costs of these solar systems are significant, sometimes two or three times the cost of conventional con-

Figure 4.28   An early solar irrigation controller with an inverter to provide 110V AC power to standard valves. (*Photo:* Photocomm/Golden Genesis Co.)

trollers. They are most cost-effective for new, rather than retrofitted, work. Depending on the site, savings may well pay for these costs. Savings are primarily from installation, operating, and maintenance costs, not from the electrical bill, but may still represent energy savings.

At one time, Solatrol (one of several early solar-irrigation companies that have passed into the great beyond) advertised its solar-powered irrigation controller with a photomontage of irrigation on the moon. Theoretically, this clever image is possible now

Figure 4.29   Small, solar powered, and radio controlled, LEIT irrigation controllers were among the first to save electricity as well as fuel used in site visits. (*Photo:* Altec Co. [now DIG Corp.].)

that lunar water has been discovered. It also is a reminder, however, that solar-powered irrigation makes it easier to bring irrigation to truly remote sites, where irrigation may be quite inappropriate. Used with good judgment, however, solar irrigation can significantly increase irrigation efficiency.

Reduce Materials Use in Irrigation Systems

Pipes, valves, and components of irrigation systems "embody" energy in their manufacture. This concept is discussed in Principle 7 and relates to other environmental impacts, such as toxic materials, introduced in Principle 6. Relative costs of energy and materials in irrigation is important to long-term sustainability.

Irrigation is a significant user of PVC and other plastics. PVC is a cheap but controversial material (see p. 295). Organochloride materials, of which PVC is one, are highly toxic during manufacture and disposal, and many experts have called for phasing them out. Solvents for PVC and other plastics pose health risks for installers. Thus, irrigation designers and contractors have a stake in how these materials are used.

Materials impact can be reduced by cutting the amount of material used, and by using materials with low embodied energy and toxicity. Non-PVC pipe is available, but costs more. Reusing or recycling materials also reduces overall environmental costs, although serious take-back programs have been slow to develop. Agricultural associations, which generate pipe and other plastic waste in bulk, have been the primary organizers of take-back arrangements; check if such a group exists locally, and might welcome landscape plastics as well.

The irrigation system that uses the least *materials* is simple flooding. In old-fashioned agriculture, this was done with nothing more than soil channels cut with a hoe. Labor intensiveness, evaporative losses, and imprecise application offset savings in materials.

Although it is popular to bury them, spray irrigation systems and, to a lesser extent, drip systems can be based on a single supply hose moved around the landscape. Crawler sprinklers were once the only "automated" systems, still common for home use. Large parks sometimes use movable metal irrigation pipes. These use less piping than buried systems, but involve high labor costs. Homeowners do not like to move hoses constantly; moving large-scale pipes requires tractors. The Treegator system, discussed above, uses material-efficient movable bags.

Buried controller-driven systems eliminate operational labor and save water. They crisscross the site with pipes, however, which must connect every head to a valve. Wires must link the controller to each valve; if the valve box is distant, this uses significant materials. Material costs for subsurface drip are reportedly 10–15 percent greater than for buried sprinklers; here, costs probably reflect resource consumption. Installation, however, was reported by the same author to be 10 percent *less* for buried drip than for buried sprinkler with its more-complex assemblies of risers, pop-ups, and so on.[91] As noted above, the one-head-per-zone design of IrriGreen and AquaContour systems radically reduces the amount of pipe and wire used; IrriGreen claims an 80 percent reduction in plastic usage, and correspondingly less trenching and other machine work.

Embodied energy of plastic pipe is about 20,000 Btu per foot, and some plastics have toxic ingredients. Copper wire ranges from 500 to 1,700 Btu per foot, depending on gauge.[92] These factors, along with monetary cost, make efficient irrigation layout important. Connecting a set of points with the fewest and shortest connectors is a classic mathematical riddle called the "random walk." New research has recently proposed computerized solutions to this puzzle.[93] These algorithms might be combined with pipe-sizing and pressure-drop software to optimize irrigation layout.

Follow the Irrigation Association's BMPs

The Irrigation Association (IA) offers training as well as informative literature (much of it online). Among IA publications are extensive best management practices and practice guidelines for irrigation.[94]

The IA has been a positive force in moving the industry toward water conservation and sustainability. Although the guidelines cover other topics, the following IA recommendations relate to sustainable practice.

- Start with site analysis.
- Encourage non-potable water use.

- Make avoiding runoff a priority.
- Specify equipment by make and model to ensure compatibility.
- Design sprinklers/emitters in any zone to have the same water delivery rate.
- Ensure that line pressure matches heads and emitters.
- Field test actual system performance after installation, and periodically.
- Maintain and adjust system parts regularly.
- Provide each client with information (as-built plan and parts inventory) and instructions, not just hardware.

One important concept embodied in IA guidelines is the "Drought Response Plan." Designers should plan each system so that in a drought, it can be set to distribute minimal water to high-priority plants while sacrificing low-priority ones (such as lawns, which can be replaced far faster than mature trees). Also called "Water Budget Deficit Design," this proactively minimizes the impact of almost-inevitable water shortages and restrictions.

Drought response planning goes beyond irrigation. Reducing fertilizer slows growth, reducing water needs, as does increasing mower height. Mulch and soil-health practices reduce irrigation, as can Integrated Pest Management (see p. 381). During drought, careful monitoring for stress-induced plant health problems is extra critical.

Don't Expect Miracles

The Irrigation Association's emphasis on drought planning underscores one reality: irrigation efficiency can make big differences, but is not a cure-all.

For now, smart controllers, efficient hardware, careful design, and conscientious maintenance can, as some irrigation advertising suggests, "conserve water without sacrificing landscape design." The efficiency of these systems, however, appears to be approaching a maximum. Once efficient systems become standard, irrigation technology may not be able to offset rising water demand and population growth any further. Therefore, landscape professionals have a strong stake in regional, national, and global water conserva-

tion initiatives. A good source of information is the Water Footprint Network.[95] Without these larger solutions, even maximally efficient landscape irrigation could once again become the first use of water to be prohibited.

Reuse Graywater

Graywater means all "used" household water except from toilets. If biodegradable soaps are used, laundry wastewater may be included. (Some definitions exclude kitchen water, for fear of food particles.) Graywater systems use separate plumbing from "blackwater" sewage pipes, allowing reuse. Graywater typically amounts to 60 percent or more of household wastewater; using it "twice" offers significant savings.[96] Although some systems use graywater to flush toilets, the most common use is landscape irrigation. Graywater is the most common source for non-potable irrigation.

Concerns have been raised about health and safety of graywater, which is banned under some building codes. Australian researchers concluded, however, that there was little evidence for disease spread from graywater in ornamental landscapes.[97] Few disease organisms will survive once applied to soil. In 1992 California established a US precedent by allowing untreated graywater for landscape irrigation. Since then, many jurisdictions have followed suit. Especially for owner-occupied single residences, and where volume is small, restrictions on graywater are being lifted. Homeowners can often install their own systems (as simple as fitting a hose to the washing-machine drain). In 2012, the first national graywater standard was published.

An opposite approach is also emerging: in-house high-tech water treatment. For graywater, such systems are mechanized, often self-cleaning, the size of a water heater; systems that treat sewage are also available, often as add-ons that aerate septic tanks.[98] The complexity, expense, and (in some) addition of chlorination work against the simplicity that attracts most graywater users. Others prefer the plug-and-play aspects of higher tech.

Graywater should be applied directly to soil or mulched surfaces for quick absorption; some overcautious standards require that it never "daylights," for fear that ponding, spraying, or residue on plants could expose people to pathogens. With proper filtration, surface driplines covered with mulch are the best no-daylight graywater design. Alternatively, graywater drip can be buried in the top three to six inches of soil. Deeper burial puts the water below plant roots, and below the soil organisms most effective at breaking down impurities. (For these reasons, many experts believe that the California code requirement for nine-inch burial is a mistake.[99] A 2016 study concluded that long-term graywater application improved soil fertility, but raised pH.[100]) As a precaution, graywater should not be used for vegetable gardens. If used with drip systems, graywater needs filtration to remove materials that clog emitters.

Homeowners must be informed and willing to maintain graywater systems. Filters and tanks need periodic cleaning; gloves, eye protection, and a simple mask should be worn (decomposing materials could in theory cause health risks). The household must adapt to alternative cleaning solutions; paints, solvents, and other toxic materials must be strictly kept out of graywater. Powdered detergents high in sodium, bleach, boron, or softeners can build up in soil and must be avoided. Acid-loving plants dislike graywater, often alkaline from soaps, according to Sacramento CA's *Water Conservation News*. Thus, graywater may be of limited value if site soils are already alkaline.

An even greater water savings is possible by eliminating water-flushed toilets entirely. By substituting a composting toilet, *all* wastewater is graywater. Especially in arid climates, this may be a more sustainable solution than using water to flush, then building a constructed wetland to purify the water. These options must, as always, be evaluated using site- and user-specific criteria.

Purify Water at Every Opportunity

Conventional thinking has centralized water-purification processes in large facilities relying heavily on chemical processes. Conventional treatment tends toward a one-size-fits-all approach: contaminated water in, drinking water out. The dark side of conventional centralized treatment is that it makes water quality "someone else's problem," almost encouraging local abuses of rivers and lakes on the assumption that water dirtied *here* can be fixed *over there.*

Several alternatives exist. Although large-scale treatment for drinking water is likely to continue (and even increase, with desalinization plants), near-source approaches should be part of the toolkit. A number of these are within the landscape realm.

Bioswales and small-scale stormwater filtration for use with paving are discussed on p. 249. The following sections note several other water-cleansing methods for harvested rainwater, swimming pools, and piped stormwater retrofits, as well as constructed wetlands for stormwater and industrial wastewater.

Purify Collected Water for Drinking and Swimming

Collected water may need to be purified, although for landscape use this may be unnecessary and even wasteful. Water is purified by physical filtration, ultraviolet (UV) light, or chemicals. For sustainability, chemicals should be a last resort; for irrigation, many water-purifying chemicals are harmful to soils and plants, and could contribute to the worrying rise in resistant disease organisms.[101]

Physical filtration ranges from simple screen or sand filters to high-tech ceramic filters. Ceramic filters are commonly sold for camping and can remove bacteria and viruses sized less than one micron. Similar systems can be installed at the faucet. For drinking and cooking water, filter-as-used may make more sense than treatment in storage. Filters require periodic cleaning or replacement or both.

For drinking-water systems, "roof washers" or "first-flush" diverters reroute the first few gallons of stormwater, which carry dust and contaminants, before allowing water into storage. There are many designs; some can be adapted to pavement-based water collection.

Solar power is a trusted technology for purifying water supplies in the Third World, and at some US campgrounds. Photovoltaic power can run standard ultraviolet purification systems; these require significant energy—80 kWh per year or more.[102] Filter the water first, to remove particles that hide microorganisms from UV light. With carefully designed storage, perhaps in dual tanks, water can be pumped and purified during the day, eliminating the need for storage batteries.

A related application is a floating swimming-pool purification system manufactured by Floatron. This unit ionizes water in which it floats, eliminating the need for chlorination. A twelve-inch unit can treat 50,000 gallons continuously. Another swimming-pool purification option is the "natural swimming pool," of which there are many thousands in Europe, both private and public. Such pools are ponds designed with open water at their centers for swimming, and constructed wetlands (see below) around their edges that continually purify the water.

Test Modern Hardware for Cleaner Piped Stormwater

Pave-and-pipe stormwater "control" contributes to pollution and is not a recommended practice. Piped systems, however, remain an article of faith among engineers, and many cities, large institutions, and even national parks have legacy systems of stormwater pipes.

Over the past decade or so, engineering ingenuity has been applied to making stormwater cleaner in the pipe. Recently a number of engineering product suppliers have taken the approach of packaging a few plants and some high-tech growing media into concrete structures, and selling it by advertising that directly attacks biological treatment designs. Such systems appear to derive little or no treatment from bacteria or plants; rather, special inert filtration is the focus, even if adorned with plants. Names like Modular Wetland continue the engineering myth that nature ought to come in interchangeable parts. Marketing for such devices attacks bioremediation and even infiltration ponds as inefficient, space-wasting, and allegedly dangerous to the public. Perhaps such attacks can be taken as an indicator of green infrastructure's success, enough to put engineers on the defensive. Particularly against the allegation that biological solutions are dangerous, designers and suppliers of living systems should mount a vigorous legal defense; the claims are unfounded.

Nonetheless, faced with existing piped systems or where no other solution is workable or permitted, some of these relatively new devices may be worth considering.

Mechanical water-cleaning systems replace or can be inserted into older catch basins or stormwater system components. In general, they are called "stormwater separation or filtration devices." Using inflow and outflow pipes at different levels, filters, baffles, and vortex flows created by the shape of the device, such in-pipe systems are widely available. According to manufacturers' claims, they remove oils, fats, suspended solids, nutrients (fertilizers, etc.), metals, and other pollutants. Effectiveness, again according to manufacturers, ranges from 80 percent upward. Even in stormwater trade journals, however, there is debate among engineers as to which devices work best, or even at all.

Chemical treatments for stormwater are also available. Like mechanical systems, these have costs and consequences not found with vegetative and soil filtration.

Related systems for improved septic-tank performance are also available, for example the Pirana and SludgeHammer systems. These may be relevant to constructed wetlands for sewage treatment (below), most of which rely on septic tanks to remove solids.

Landscape professionals concerned with sustainability should be aware of these engineered water-cleansing systems for two reasons. One is as a last resort, where lack of space or budget, regulatory insistence, or heavy-duty pollutants truly require such systems; occasionally, mechanical pretreatment might be appropriately combined with biological methods. The second reason to know these systems is to challenge their use on projects where sustainable solutions are more appropriate. A good source of information on these products, as well as for consultant help, is the trade magazine *Stormwater*.

Let Constructed Wetlands Treat Water

Constructed wetlands are beautiful water gardens with a new ecological twist: they transform sewage effluent into growing medium for plants—and the plants, in turn, filter the effluent, turning it into water fit for swimming and fishing. Natural wetlands have provided similar services to humans since prehistory, yet people still find the concept novel—half treatment

Figure 4.30   Treatment wetlands in raised beds are the focal point of gardens at the Albuquerque home of green architect Paul Lusk. (*Project:* Paul Lusk. *Photo:* Kim Sorvig.)

mechanism, half nature center. In fact, constructed wetlands form a bridge between two main issues of this chapter: sparing use of water supply, and restoration of water bodies.

As Alex Wilson, editor of *EBN*, notes, "Constructed wetlands can become valuable assets to the landscape around buildings, especially if we call them 'flower beds.' It is quite conceivable that within a few years it will be landscape professionals who deal with wastewater treatment, not sanitary engineers."[103]

Constructed wetlands are more widespread than many people realize. When the subject comes up, the famous Arcata CA wetland is typically the only one mentioned; there are, however, probably over one thousand functioning constructed wetlands in the United States, with more under construction each year.[104] The EPA actively promotes their spread as an alternative to conventional sewage and stormwater treatment.

Constructed wetlands are fairly straightforward, although various configurations exist. Modern wetlands

Figure 4.31 Mississippi State University's Crosby Arboretum epitomizes the beauty, as well as ecological and educational value, of wetlands. (*Project:* Ed Blake, Andropogon, Fay Jones. *Photo:* Ed Blake.)

for sewage/stormwater treatment originated in Germany in the 1960s, introduced to the United States in the 1980s. Constructed wetlands are shallow ponds, often divided into "cells." Wastewater flows over gravel substrate supporting vegetation. Plant roots, and the many microorganisms that live in the root zone, actively filter and absorb pollutants. Mechanical equipment (other than a pump) is not involved.

Some waste treatment terminology: *primary* treatment removes solids, *secondary* treatment removes most remaining impurities, and *tertiary* treatment "polishes" the effluent. "Tertiary treated effluent" is water clean enough to swim in, irrigate with, or discharge into lakes or streams, often exceeding standards for municipal drinking water. Wetlands can provide all three stages of treatment, but in most US facilities, mechanical pretreatment removes solids before effluent ever reaches the wetland. Most of today's constructed wetlands in the United States do tertiary "polishing" only. A fair number provide secondary treatment, and a primary-treatment wetland on the border between California and Baja California was proposed by students of visionary landscape architect John Lyle.[105] It is certainly fair to say that wetland capabilities remain underused.

There are two design options for constructed wetlands: (1) "subsurface flow," in which water flows *beneath* gravel through which emergent wetland plants grow, and (2) "surface flow," in which water is vis-

Figure 4.32 The "business end" of any treatment wetland is the root zone and the billions of microorganisms that live in its complex geometry. (*Project:* City of Albuquerque and MFG. *Photo:* Michael D. Marcus.)

ible among the plants, closely resembling a natural wetland. Subsurface-flow wetlands are often recommended for applications near housing or office buildings. Water is never at the surface, and some designers take this to mean less risk of mosquito breeding, odor, or human contact with effluent. Wetlands expert Donald Hammer, however, states that hiding the effluent under gravel is less reliable than surface-flow designs. As he puts it, "The latest designs . . . are quite simply [returning to the initial concept] that patterned constructed wetlands after natural wetlands. [These] have proven to be the least costly to build, have higher removal efficiencies for a wider variety of pollutants,

Figure 4.33 Increasing clarity is visible in water from Arcata CA's constructed wetlands, sampled at progressive stages of wastewater treatment. From left: inflow to system; outflows from oxidation pond, treatment marsh, and enhancement marsh. (*Photo:* Professor Joe Meyer, University of Wyoming.)

[and] are less costly and complex to operate."[106] Surface flow also provides greater wildlife habitat and is more feasible in poorer communities with most to gain from simple waste treatment. Both designs are legitimate alternatives and should be compared for site-specific advantages.

A typical subsurface system is one to three feet deep, with impervious (plastic or concrete) bottom and sides, filled with gravel and planted with wetland species. With the wastewater out of sight below gravel, small-scale subsurface-treatment wetlands are easily integrated into housing, park, and office landscapes. One prototypical subsurface wetland, at Indian Creek Nature Center in Cedar Rapids IA, lives up to Alex Wilson's image as a "flower bed." Designed by North American Wetland Engineering in Forest Lake MN, it treats all sewage from the visitor center. The wetland has become locally popular for its show of aquatic

plants and wildflowers. It is clearly not an objectionable feature—the deck overlooking the wetland is a favorite place to hold weddings.[107]

Despite some people's reluctance to do so, surface-flow constructed wetlands can also be installed quite close to buildings—for example, at the Crosby Arboretum. A small pond system provides *secondary and tertiary* treatment for the site's two public restrooms. It was designed by Mississippi-based scientist Bill Wolverton, a pioneer in natural sewage treatment. When the director of the arboretum, landscape architect Ed Blake, saw Wolverton's design concept— a standard engineer's rectangle—he asked, "Can we loosen this up a bit?" With Wolverton's consent Blake reconfigured the treatment pond as a naturalistic river meander. The resulting pond fits seamlessly into the arboretum landscape, an amenity in full view of all visitors—who learn from interpretive guides that it treats on-site sewage.

Constructed wetlands can fulfill many functions in addition to water purification. Two wetlands built several years apart by the town of Gilbert AZ (a suburb of Phoenix) make an excellent case study of the *process* of multifunction design. The wetlands are fine examples of their type, but more important, variations in public perceptions and team approach between the two projects are a valuable lesson.

Comparing these two projects is easier because the same firm worked on both, in different capacities— the multidisciplinary Sacramento CA firm Jones & Stokes. Landscape architects Joe Donaldson and Sheri Brown were involved in habitat restoration and interpretive exhibit design for both projects. Donaldson in particular speaks of wetland experience reinvigorating professional practice.

In the early 1990s, Gilbert's wastewater reclama-

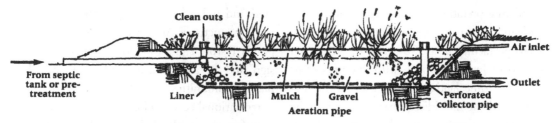

Figure 4.34 Constructed wetland (subsurface type; surface-flow type would have water at surface instead of mulch). Treatment wetlands discharge to infiltration basins, irrigation systems, leach fields, surface water, or tanks. (*Illust.:* Craig Farnsworth, based on NAWE [North American Wetland Engineering].)

Figure 4.35 Indian Creek Nature Center (Cedar Rapids IA) illustrates Alex Wilson's vision of constructed wetlands doubling as flower beds. (*Project and Photo:* NAWE.)

tion complex built the Cooper Road Recharge Ponds, a series of shallow ponds designed for the single engineering purpose of recharging groundwater. After the boxy, functional ponds were already laid out, the town saw an opportunity to create urban habitat for birds, bats, and other fauna, and was able to get funding from the state game-and-fish department. Jones & Stokes was hired to enhance the ponds' habitat value. Donaldson planted riparian and marsh plants around the banks and upland species on levees, with assistance from desert-plants purveyor Wild Seed and community volunteers. Although not able to alter the basic pond layout, Donaldson and Brown constructed nesting boxes, and added interpretive exhibits and a ramada (shade structure) for visitors. Despite their initial functionalist layout, the Cooper Road Ponds garnered a Governor's Pride award for environmental leadership, as well as the Arizona Planning Association's 1994 Best Project Award.

Perhaps more important for the continuing story, habitat and interpretation won the approval of Gilbert residents. When the opportunity arose for another recharge facility in a 130-acre park, the town again turned to Jones & Stokes, with one important difference: this time landscape and restoration specialists managed the multidisciplinary team from the start. Engineers, as well as local landscape architect Carol F. Shuler, became part of the team.

The result of public support and consistent plan-

Figure 4.36 Cooper Road Ponds treat wastewater, support waterfowl, and attract birdwatchers. The square ponds were already excavated when landscape architects were called in. (*Project:* Jones and Stokes. *Photo:* Joe Donaldson, ASLA.)

ning is clear. Named the Riparian Reserve, the park is a highly visible feature, beside the public library where two main bike paths intersect. Permanent marshes, wildlife islands, roosting structures, and varied wetland and upland planting are managed as an urban wildlife sanctuary. At nearly seventy acres, the recharge ponds restore significant lost habitat. Xeriscape design and botanic-garden exhibits of rare Sonoran plant communities make this an educational as well as recreational center. The public had been convinced: multifunction wetlands have much greater value than single-function ponds.

One issue raised by the Gilbert ponds is that of

Figure 4.37 Coordinated by landscape architects from the start, Gilbert AZ's Riparian Reserve will go beyond its Cooper Road predecessor to create a full-fledged public park. (*Project:* Jones and Stokes. *Photo:* Joe Donaldson, ASLA.)

access. Interestingly enough, there is no consistent standard for access around wastewater ponds. Some facilities allow visitor access to *secondary* treatment ponds, yet the tertiary-treated Cooper Road ponds are fenced. At the Riparian Reserve, the town weighed benefits of education and recreation against risks of liability. Because this facility infiltrates tertiary-treated water, they decided in favor of public access. Similarly careful planning could open many more wetlands to amenity use.

Consider Wetlands for Industrial Wastewater

Nature's filters can purify some of humanity's least "natural" water wastes, from mining and manufacturing. Wetlands absorb phosphates, nitrates, and other toxins through phytoremediation (p. 124). There is a growing literature on industrial treatment wetlands, and an increasing number have been built near factories and mines.

One highly visible treatment wetland is the award-winning Living Water Garden, covering six acres along the banks of the Fu-Nan River in Chengdu, western China. This elegant example of environmental education is the core of an urban park, growing out of a larger water quality improvement project. The garden draws 200 cubic meters of water from the Fu-Nan each day, removes bacterial pollutants and heavy metals, and returns the water to the river. This is not meant to have an appreciable impact on a river the size of the Fu-Nan; major improvements can be achieved only by reducing pollutant emissions. People go to Living Water Garden for relief from an intense urban setting, and the park seduces them into learning about natural water purification. The impact of Living Water Garden lies in its effects on the thinking of the people of Chengdu: increased awareness of environmental issues and pride in progress the city has made toward resuscitating the river.[108]

The principle of respecting water comes full circle, like the hydrological cycle itself. When water is wasted, shoved aside as a problem, or contaminated, humans and the environment both suffer. When humans work thoughtfully with water, even contaminated water, it repays them in health, in livable surroundings, and in recreation and learning.

Subtopics and Search Terms for Principle 4: Respect the Waters of Life

Note: Subtopics are also useful search terms; add "innovation" or "controversy" to search terms as appropriate.

Wetlands
Search terms: wetlands || freshwater wetlands || saltwater wetlands || wetland ecology

Wetlands restoration
Search terms: wetland restoration || wetland mitigation || wetland protection

Construction in wetlands
Search terms: removable foundations || pinned foundations || auger foundations || wood preservatives

Stream restoration
Search terms: stream-bank (protection OR restoration OR planting) || fish habitat

Stormwater
Search terms: stormwater || stormwater management || runoff || erosion sedimentation || hydrology || NEPA || stormwater infiltration

Water harvesting, storage, and purification
Search terms: water harvesting || water storage || water purification || rain barrel || ponds

Graywater
Search terms: greywater OR graywater (or as two words or hyphenated)

Xeriscape, Permaculture

Irrigation
Search terms: combine the following with "irrigation": drip, spray, rotor, agricultural, solar

Irrigation controllers and sensors
Search terms: smart controllers || ET controllers || "web based" + irrigation || (weather OR moisture) sensor

Constructed wetlands
Search terms: wetland construction || constructed wetlands || treatment wetlands || biological water treatment

Resource List:

Links to information sources related to this chapter are posted at http://islandpress.org/sustainable-landscape-construction

Principle 5:
Pave Less

Little by little, roads eat away at the hearts of mountains.
—*Gary Lawless, First Sight of Land, 1990*

The United States paves more area every two years than the Roman Empire did in its entire existence.[1] Since 1980, an average of 25,500 miles has been added yearly. The US Department of Transportation counts a total of 8,766,049 "lane miles" of public highway, as of 2014.[2] Assuming an average 12-foot lane width, plus 4 feet for shoulder and other auxiliary areas, one lane-mile equals 84,480 square feet, or nearly two acres. The total—17 million acres—is enough paved area to cover New Hampshire, New Jersey, Connecticut, Rhode Island, and Delaware. Add to this an estimated 4.7 million acres (1,921,582 hectares) devoted to parking in the United States.[3] The US road network is "perhaps the biggest object ever built."[4] By one estimate, the US Interstate Highway System alone excavated enough soil to cover Connecticut knee-deep, and used concrete enough for 80 Hoover Dams, steel for 170 Empire State Buildings, and drain pipe to match water and sewer for Chicago six times over.[5] It is easy to see that paving is an environmental issue of colossal proportions.[6]

As of 2017, what has changed regarding pavement is less about techniques and materials than about understanding of paving's impacts. Research showing the economic, social, and health costs of the road-and-parking system is noticeably more common and accurate than ten years ago. Demographics are changing America's love affair with The Road, in ways that may have more impact on sustainability than any other trend today. These issues are covered by added material in this chapter.

Widespread paving is a very recent phenomenon. Even a century ago, the normal condition of city

---

Discussed in This Chapter

Paving impacts and trends.

Planning and policy strategies to reduce paving requirements.

Design options to decrease paving area and its site impact.

Techniques for infiltrating more of the runoff from pavement.

Infiltration to reduce pollution potential of pavement runoff.

Porous and partially porous paving materials.

When it's most appropriate *not* to pave.

Reducing the heat-sink effect of paved areas.

---

streets was a muddy morass (recall, for example, Sherlock Holmes's deductions from clay on urban trouser cuffs); many rural roads were still "paved" with logs. All that changed in the mid-1800s, when "macadam" (compacted stone bound with asphalt) was introduced by a Scottish contemporary of the fictional detective. The past hundred years have seen paving cover unprecedented areas. By the early 1970s paving was referred to as "the nation's biggest publicly endowed business."[7]

Paving's relationship to car and truck traffic and carbon emissions is obvious; what is less well-known is that the American Suburb, totally reliant on cars, was deliberately shaped by a coalition of auto, realty, mortgage, road-building, oil, and tire interests. As J. F. P. Rose documents in his thought-provoking *The*

Well-Tempered City, "When the federal mortgage assistance program was created, the nation's housing and auto industries quickly realized that the more federal policy shifted toward suburban single-family homes and away from urban multifamily homes, the more money they would make." In lobbying to make federal mortgages unavailable for urban housing of any kind, they embroidered on the idea that urban dwellings were "communist" while the suburbs were "capitalist." Their chief hired gun, before he went on to infamy, was Joseph McCarthy.[8]

Portrayed as a matter of personal preferences and free markets, the rush to pave and extend our road system was in fact deliberate. This is important to understand, since it is now being challenged by genuine market forces, ones that will likely be giving landscape professionals much of our work in the near future. First-time home-buyers of the post-Boomer generations strongly prefer to live in walkable, mixed-use, diversely populated urban areas.[9] This demographic prefers not to own a car; ridership on public transit in the United States is growing twice as fast as either the population or the number of driving miles. If they drive, they turn to car-share and ride-share options. Encouraged by Fitbits and reports linking walking to health and sedentarism to disease, they support the rapid growth of urban residential infill. The link to sustainable design is explicit: LEED-certified neighborhoods are predicted to generate 40 percent fewer car trips than conventional ones. Since repeated studies have shown that the transportation energy used to bring people and supplies to a building most often outstrips direct uses of energy (like heating and cooling), a cultural preference of walkable living is a revolution in the making. The impact of this trend may well be more important than any formal move toward sustainability in cutting carbon emissions.

For all its popularity and functionality, paving has been implicated in a wide range of ecological problems. Most paving materials create surface stability by excluding water from the soil, causing serious difficulties. Soil absorbs rainfall and nurtures flora, fauna, and humans, but impervious surfaces increase runoff, causing erosion and flooding, depleting soil water, and contributing to siltation and water pollution; any and all of the above contribute to drought, vegetation loss,

and wildfire. Modern construction has created such vast nonporous areas that many communities are being forced to limit creation of new impervious surfaces.

Parking lots, for example, constitute an ever-increasing blight on the American landscape. As metropolitan areas sprawl away from transit-friendly cores, surface parking becomes the urban fabric's common denominator. From the air, parking is *the most visible feature* of many communities. This hardening of the American landscape shrinks the biologically productive surface of the Earth, replacing cornfields, meadows, forest, or desert. Moreover, "paving the planet" (as it has been called) consumes nonrenewable resources both in building the lots and in fuel to truck materials to the site. Asphalt, the material for most parking lots, is a complex mix of hydrocarbons; extraction, mixing, and application of these entail air and potentially water pollution. Asphalt has been shown to have adverse health effects on workers exposed to its fumes.[10] Meanwhile, traffic fumes not only are increasingly documented as direct health hazards, but also are implicated in reduced productivity even of indoor workers. Diesel exhaust appears to leave honeybees disoriented and cyclists winded.[11]

Parking lots can directly affect microclimates and overall city climates. Since the automobile conquered America, summer temperatures in urban areas have risen two to eight degrees Fahrenheit higher than in surrounding rural areas.[12] Surface parking is the prime land use in most American cities, making parking and road paving a major factor, if not *the* main factor, in this heat-island effect—not to mention spiraling land costs. A 2013 study also shows that rural areas are being heated indirectly by urban conditions.[13]

Low-speed roads—suburban residential streets, in particular—are often wider and more impervious than necessary. Thirty-six feet or more is a typical width. The total width of the average residential street has increased by 50 percent since World War II.[14] Blanket application of standards for high-speed, high-volume highways to low-speed, low-volume streets has created unwanted pavement in thousands of urban neighborhoods and rural byways. Overbuilding of roads has serious sustainability (and safety) implications and has even been challenged by several national *engineering* organizations.

The most egregious impacts of overpaving have to do with stormwater.[15] Conventional parking lots, for example, seal off enormous areas of soil, preventing rainwater from soaking in and replenishing crucial groundwater resources. Concentrating rainfall, paving and subsurface drainage systems send erosive torrents of runoff into local streams. Erosion, sedimentation, extremes of flooding and drought, and habitat loss are among the results—a central problem for sustainable landscapes, and repeated, of necessity, throughout this book.

There are many practical, well-tested alternatives to overpaving. Many have been known for almost as long as the automobile—yet are ignored in conventional design predicated on ever-increasing road speed, volume, and "convenience." Highway and parking engineers cater to such social demands, which today are changing. Interestingly, much of the most positive change is "top down": from the Federal Highway Administration to the Institute of Transportation Engineers, official research and design standards are focusing on the benefits of better integration of roads with community, ecosystem, and scenery.

"Context-sensitive" roadways and traffic calming have been officially accepted by many transportation authorities since the twenty-first century began; what was once an all-cars-all-the-time attitude has broadened. A few states have been slow to catch up; county and local public-works departments harbor more than their share of dinosaurs. Individual engineers remain resistant, fearful that they might be liable for not following set-in-stone standards, despite (literally) an act of Congress that says otherwise.[16] Today overpaving remains one area of landscape design and construction where the *main* culprit is outdated, unthinking habit—stoutly defended by industries with vested interests, and by a society still addicted to cars.

Plan and Design to Reduce Paving

Although this chapter will focus on building parking lots and streets with *fewer environmental impacts*, the crying need in North America is to *reduce the total area of paving*. This constitutes an enormous challenge to planners, designers, and policy makers for the simple reason that parking is generally regarded as a universal

good. American cities are built around auto use, with destinations so spread out that walking from home to the grocery store is no longer possible.

Where driving is the only option, congestion soon follows. In major US metro areas, a given trip takes 30–50 percent longer during peak hours; the average commuter spends fifty-four hours annually waiting in standstill traffic (that's 1¼ workweeks); and idling in traffic jams wastes 60 to 120 gallons of gas per driver per year.[17]

Many urbanists are reviving pre–World War II patterns of development—walkable communities effectively served by mass transit.[18] This goes against many national habits, but is successfully promoted by Walkable Communities, the Congress for the New Urbanism, and others, a movement sometimes called Neo-Traditionalism. Aiming for livability rather than accepting suburban sprawl or urban jam, these models treat streets as public spaces primarily for *people*, shared with cars where needed.

Urban growth boundaries (UGBs) are a related planning strategy to rein in sprawl, encourage infill, and increase urban density, thus reducing need for paving. A well-known (if sometimes controversial) US example is Portland OR. In 1976 politicians and planners took the unprecedented step of drawing such a boundary around Portland and prohibiting expansion beyond it. The UGB has not completely abolished sprawl—housing prices have risen, and Portland still has strip malls and cookie-cutter subdivisions. Such development, however, is all within three to eighteen miles of Portland's compact, walkable downtown, on which an exemplary light-rail system converges.

Walkable-density ideals have received a real boost, where paving is concerned, from skyrocketing materials costs. Between 2000 and 2005, the cost of asphalt paving rose 37 percent, according to the US Bureau of Labor Statistics.[19] This has promoted "pavement preservation" (preventive maintenance and thin, strong surfacing techniques) and recycling of roadway materials, and has made governments more cautious (slightly) in undertaking new paving. Unfortunately, it is still true, as the Foundation for Pavement Preservation notes in a 2001 report, that "there has always been more management interest (and Federal funding for that matter) in building new roads than maintaining existing ones."[20] Even if vast paving operations were sustainable, building them and then *not* maintaining them is clearly not.

A trade-off exists between compactness and green open space: Densely compact communities are walkable, with fewer miles of street per person; overall, the ratio of impervious to planted areas is high. Communities with high proportions of green open space have decreased stormwater problems but are less dense, requiring more miles of traffic infrastructure and more trips per person. One solution is "skinny streets and green neighborhoods," the title of a useful book on these planning choices. New research on the health value of trees is noted in Principle 3.

Several specific policies are valuable for avoiding unnecessary paving and decreasing negative effects of existing pavement.[21] These include:

- Density zoning: local policy based on number of units per acre (or percentage of acreage devoted to structures) works better than minimum lot sizes, allowing flexible adaptation to site topography.
- Cluster development: several buildings centered in open space, rather than each in the center of its separate lot, can greatly reduce infrastructure costs, including paving. This is a scale-dependent technique, however; Le Corbusier's horrid "tower-in-park" developments are, unfortunately, visible proof of this in almost every country with any modern economy.
- Combined land uses: zoning that allows residences, shops, and workplaces to coexist makes walking, biking, or public transit realistic; often forbidden by existing zoning laws.
- Impervious surface (IS) limits: cap the percentage of site area that can be impervious (both paved and roofed areas, existing and new). Protecting streams requires IS of 10 percent or less; above 10 percent, impacts will require mitigation, and at 30 percent IS, ecosystem degradation is almost inevitable. In urban areas already far over this threshold, incentives for reducing impervious cover can be effective (see Principle 2).
- Street-width limits: set a *maximum*, reversing laws that require minimum widths. Besides reducing total paving, narrower lanes give Context-Sensitive Design and traffic-calming benefits (below).

- Planted islands: paved traffic islands are of no use to drivers and should be replaced with permeable, planted surfaces. Select tough, usually native species with compact or dwarf growth habit to minimize maintenance.
- Isolation of pollutant-collecting pavement: separating runoff from gas stations, car washes, Dumpster pads, and other pollutant "point sources" keeps stormwater on ordinary streets much cleaner.
- Labeling of storm drain inlets: knowledge of where pavement runoff goes can decrease public dumping of pollutants onto pavement and into drains.

Truly paving less begins at the policy level. Some of the above policies aim at existing problems, but the most important are forward-looking. The central intent of policy must be to *establish growth management that encourages denser development and decreases automobile dependence.* Construction methods can help, but only a concerted effort can create compact cities. Decreased paving will be both *result* and cause of more people traveling by foot, bicycle, rail, ride-share, or bus. As noted above, in 2017, this is actually happening, and in a way that cutting federal funding can't really touch.

Put New and Renovated Development on a "Parking Diet"

Even cities that are fundamentally auto-oriented can reduce parking. In 1996 Olympia WA completed large-scale research, the Impervious Surface Reduction Study, aimed at reducing need for new parking and decreasing environmental impacts of new or existing paving. The study carefully documented effects of runoff from roads and parking on Olympia's water quality and quantity, and articulated a set of strategies with the remarkable goal of *smaller and fewer parking lots in future developments* throughout the city.

To accomplish this intent, which flies in the face of current development practices, a central strategy is to get developers to *size parking lots to reflect real needs.* Olympia's study uncovered a fact that applies across the United States: developers routinely *oversupply* parking to meet a single "peak-day" (or even "peak-hour") projection—the height of the Christmas retail rush, for example. In Olympia, parking supply was *51 percent above nonpeak needs.* Retailers fear that without this excess, customers will be turned away for lack of parking. In

Olympia, this fear proved groundless. On those peak shopping dates, the study team surveyed thirty-one parking areas, representing fifteen different commercial uses. Eighteen of the lots had less than 75 percent occupancy rates *during their peak periods*. Although not part of the Olympia study, it is clear that the trend away from car ownership will only increase the degree to which existing parking exceeds actual need.

Armed with such data, Olympia formed new policies.[22] One is *to encourage cooperative or shared parking*. This combines parking quotas for land uses with different hours of operation—a church and an office, for example, or a movie theater and a paint store. Shared parking works best for long-term tenants whose parking needs do not fluctuate much over time. It may require legal agreements between neighboring tenants; local governments should actively promote such agreements. Shared parking is already working in some cities, according to the Institute of Transportation Engineers, which endorses the practice.[23]

A related principle is to enforce the *maximum* amount of parking for any land use. Typically, local governments enforce *minimum* parking requirements. Many developers and designers, who have struggled to fit in required parking spaces at the expense of site amenities, would welcome an enforced-maximum approach. Minimum parking ratios confer license to overpave. Suburban office parking is routinely oversupplied by one-third.[24] Townhouse developers commonly provide the actual spaces required, *plus 103 percent*—fully *double* what anyone needs, even when visitor parking is considered. The Center for Watershed Protection recommends parking codes that impose a maximum number of spaces unless compelling data clearly justify more.[25] Olympia's new parking code requires developers to build according to "median" parking ratios that reflect day-to-day use.

Mass transit lowers paving demand by reducing the number of vehicles driven and parked. For developments close to a bus or rail stop, regulations should reduce the number of parking spaces. A number of farsighted communities have encouraged or required developers to reduce parking when mass transit is available. These include Chicago; Hartford CT; Montgomery County MD; Albuquerque NM; and, of course, Olympia.[26] When Portland OR added 20,000 new seats to its sports stadium, it did not add a single

parking space: a light-rail stop served the arena. Excellent mass transit is obviously essential to such a solution. Acceptance and use of transit are growing, even in the United States, and even "normal" amounts of parking may soon be going unused.

On a smaller scale, Seattle landscape architects Berger Partnership prescribed a "parking diet" for the Washington State Department of Ecology headquarters in Lacey. The agency's original proposal called for 1,150 parking spaces, nearly one per employee. This would have claimed four and one-half acres, more than twice the building's footprint. In the final design, parking used just over one acre. The number of spaces was slashed to 900, and stacked in a land-saving garage. The new design challenged employees to adjust their commutes, but also served, in the words of partner Tom Berger, as "a model for what the Department of Ecology should expect from other planners." Besides cutting runoff, the reduced parking footprint made it easier to put the main building close to bus and foot access. In the garage, the closest spaces were reserved for carpoolers; not even the director got an individual reserved space. Still, the farthest spaces in the garage were closer than most surface parking would have been, and state officials call the experiment a success.[27]

"Parking diets" offer major opportunities for site restoration. In Monroe MI, the historic convent campus of the Immaculate Heart of Mary order was being renovated. Landscape architects Rolf Sauer and Partners were actually able to change the campus's zoning by showing that carpooling and shuttles had reduced on-site parking needs. The sisters also convinced the local bus line to add a stop. These changes eliminated more than 300 parking spaces. Some roads were converted to pedestrian paths, and others were demolished, along with old parking areas, and converted to wildflower meadows and stormwater wetlands (Figure 4.8c).

Mark Childs, author of *Parking Spaces*, notes that every driver who parks is also a pedestrian. He advocates improved design of parking that accommodates pedestrian and public-space possibilities. Childs's book details many methods, plus insights into the history and social perception of parking in the United States.

Questioning assumptions about the *need* for parking is becoming more feasible, as the previous examples show, but still requires careful and persuasive planning. Fortunately, literature and assistance are increasingly available from sources like the Institute of Transportation Engineers, the Center for Watershed Protection, and the City of Olympia.

Parking reduction is largely a task for local government. Planners and designers should advocate and implement such policies wherever possible.

Take Advantage of Context-sensitive Road Design

Road standards can be even more difficult to update than parking policies. Overengineered roadways, and standards that enforce overbuilding, have many of the same environmental impacts as excessive parking. Oversized roads also have negative effects on traffic safety and diminish the quality of life for communities through which they pass. Since about 1998, however, a major change in US attitude and policy has at last developed serious momentum. This is Context-Sensitive Design (CSD; or CSS, context-sensitive solutions; or CS[3], context-sensitive and sustainable solutions). Where past policy explicitly designed for the safety and convenience of motorists and no one else, CSD gives communities and environments through which a road passes equal consideration.[28]

CSD is a very positive change, wholeheartedly adopted by many transportation departments throughout the country; some states have full-time CSD staff, often landscape architects. Unfortunately, some agencies still ignorantly or deliberately disregard CSD. Smaller jurisdictions, such as counties, are often the worst offenders. Chronically underfunded, they resent CSD and environmental protection as imposed costs, and are extra-paranoiac about imagined liability.

In Santa Fe County NM, for example, I have documented county road projects with *no* stormwater management or revegetation at all, resulting in destructive soil erosion of over a foot per year on adjacent private property, despite strict regulations requiring no net increase in runoff leaving any site.[29] Many public-works agencies get away with such negligence, for which any other agency, developer, or private landowner would be severely fined. What highway departments call "erosion control" merely armors the right-of-way, still

dumping increased runoff onto the neighbors.[30] Road "improvements" remain so popular, however, that such damage often goes unchallenged, especially at the local level. Landscape professionals can hasten change, especially if they seek allies among young progressive engineers, who are often frustrated with outdated official attitudes.

One important policy change related to CSD concerns transportation department funding. Strictly separating capital costs (design and construction) from operating budgets defeats any attempt to analyze life-cycle costs (see Principle 7). Some DOTs use this split deceptively: during design, the public is promised that issues like revegetation will be addressed by the maintenance branch (and are then dropped). Even when a DOT is being up front about such issues, many sustainable design techniques are vetoed because the design engineers cannot require the maintenance necessary to make these techniques work.

Legalize Narrower Streets and "Traffic Calming"

"Traffic calming," closely allied to CSD, improves road safety for everyone, motorists and others alike. Designed to motivate drivers to slow down and be attentive, traffic calming has been gaining acceptance in the United States; in Europe, Canada, and Australia, it has a thirty-year track record. Traffic calming originated from safety concerns, but also has significant environmental benefits, especially where it results in narrower roadways.

Conventional street and road statutes, although often imposed by local agencies, tend to be carbon copies of state and federal requirements more suitable for major highways. Ironically, at the Federal Highway Administration (FHWA), the Institute of Transportation Engineers, and many state agencies, progressive research has cast doubt on older requirements for extra-wide, straight, flat roads. Updated standards, including the FHWA's computerized Interactive Highway Safety Design Model, are available, but many local governments continue to enforce design standards decades out of date. Local agencies often adopt the American Association of State Highway and Transportation Officials (AASHTO) guidelines, which the local engineers enforce far more inflexibly than do most state DOTs. These standards are often presented to the public as cut-and-dried matters of safety: the "AASHTO Green Bible," as it is called, is (wrongly) considered by many engineers to be completely mandatory and inflexible. Although actually specifying acceptable *ranges* of design criteria, AASHTO standards are usually interpreted as requiring widening, flattening, and straightening of all roads, everywhere.[31] The assumption, however, that bigger roads are always safer (like the assumption that more parking is always better) is increasingly questioned, even by otherwise conventional agencies and professional organizations.

Where did bigger-is-safer come from? American society (with industry encouragement) has demanded that an exploding number of private vehicles should always be able to drive door-to-door at full speed. This single-minded focus on speed and capacity has disguised crucial safety issues. Current research shows that the real cause of most accidents, serious ones especially, is *speed itself*, and that wide, straight, flat roadways *encourage* drivers to speed. Conventional engineering has struggled to make *speeding* as safe as it can be, which is not actually very safe at all.

Traffic calming takes a different approach. In the words of Robert A. White, a Norwich VT landscape architect who consults on traffic calming, "measures that reduce lane width, introduce roadside 'friction' features like street trees, and prominently define pedestrian crossing points can [significantly reduce] roadway speeds—from 20% to 50% reductions depending on the technique and location. It has been shown that similar safety improvements can reduce crashes by as much as 80%, and those that do occur tend to be less severe."[32] Similar results were found in a 2011 study of data from Portland OR from 1991 through 2010, which showed that the more bicyclists were on the road, the *fewer* crashes; this suggests that the presence of bicyclists is itself "traffic calming." The study also notes similar findings from Germany and Denmark.[33] A welcome side effect: in 2013, another Portland study showed that bicyclists *outspent* car drivers by 20 percent, attributed to ease of stopping and, thus, more frequent patronage of local shops.[34]

Traffic calming relies on self-preservation instincts, rather than on fear of punishment. "Most drivers ad-

just their speed more readily in response to road and traffic conditions than to speed limit signs and the often remote possibility of enforcement penalties. . . . 85% of drivers tend to adopt a sensible speed for prevailing road conditions. . . . [Drivers] unconsciously respond naturally to the physical cues presented to them."[35] Thus, making a road narrower (or even making it *look* narrower with grassed shoulders or roadside shrubs) is something highway designers can do to get drivers to observe safe speeds. Recognizing that no amount of design can "idiot proof" a road puts responsibility back where it belongs: on the 15 percent of drivers who speed, rather than on the designer or public agency that built the road.

Robert White considers traffic calming as "a set of roadway design tools and principles where *community values* as they relate to traffic management are more fully represented and integrated into the actual roadway design." Streets and roads once again become multipurpose spaces. Narrower roads release space for bike lanes, walkways, and bridle paths; in residential neighborhoods and small business districts, streets become truly public; on scenic highways, conflicts between tourists and local drivers are reduced.[36] Traffic calming provides practical methods of achieving these "Neo-Traditional" goals. Conventional design and exclusive use by automobiles remain appropriate for freeways and major highways. For any road where access cannot be limited, however, the multiple-user approach is safer, less disruptive, and frequently cheaper. Traffic-calming projects are eligible for funding under federal "intermodal" or multiuse transportation acts.[37]

"Traffic Fatalities and Injuries: Are Reductions the Result of 'Improvements' in Highway Design Standards?" is a critically important 2001 paper by traffic researcher Dr. Robert Noland. Traffic injuries and fatalities *have* gone down during the past few decades; it is an article of engineering faith that this is due to flatter-wider-straighter improvements. By sophisticated analysis of statistics from all fifty states, Noland shows that the reductions *actually* result from better vehicle-safety design, increased seat-belt use, demographic decline in fifteen- to twenty-four-year-old drivers, and greatly improved emergency response and medical triage for injured motorists. The traffic engineers' claim that their bigger roads are safer may be an innocent mistake, but it is false.[38] In fact, to quote the paper, "as arterial and collector lane widths are increased up to 12 feet or more, traffic fatalities and injuries *increase*."[39]

For rural roads, recent FHWA research from Turner-Fairbank Highway Research Center has shown that "9-ft lane widths have lower accident rates than 10-ft lanes with narrow shoulders . . . at least partly due to reduced vehicle speeds." The report suggests that it is *safer* to retain existing nine-foot lanes unless a community can afford dramatic widening of both roadway and shoulder.[40]

Alex Wilson, in an *EBN* summary of traffic calming, notes several compelling facts. Traffic-calming techniques reduce collisions by anything from 51 to 94 percent. Slowing traffic decreases pedestrians' chances of being killed: 83 percent fatalities at 44 mph, only 37 percent at 31 mph, and less than 4 percent at 15 mph. (Similar reductions apply to motorist risks.) Calming from 56 to 48 mph decreases noise as much as 90 percent. Reductions in crime (due to presence of more pedestrians) have also been credited to traffic calming, as have increased property values: 63 percent for residences, and, for commercial properties, 80 percent increase in occupancy and an astonishing 967 percent increase in average rents.[41]

Those landscape professionals who deal with streetscapes and roadsides should remember a simple summary of the reasons for traffic calming:

Wider + flatter + straighter = faster driving
Wider + flatter + straighter = inattentive driving
Faster + inattentive = more dangerous

As one traffic official put it, "Roads aren't dangerous; drivers are." Traffic calming and Context-Sensitive Design try to influence the most effective safety device in every car: the person behind the wheel. The safety and community benefits of traffic calming are clearly of concern to landscape professionals—especially those who are tired of being steamrolled by outdated arguments in favor of overbuilt roads.

A closely related trend is banning motor vehicles from selected streets on specific days, or permanently, to encourage pedestrian and bicycle use. Begun in Bogotá, Colombia, the *ciclovía* (bike road) is widespread in Latin America and Europe; more than twenty US cities have adopted it to date.[42]

Traffic calming has been bitterly attacked by special interests like the American Road and Transportation Builders Association (ARTB). ARTB took the position, *despite a 63 percent increase in federal funding* for highway construction between 1993 and 1999, that "environmental and community extremists" were out to deprive road builders of their livelihood.[43] Although such associations represent part of the construction industry, contractors and designers concerned with sustainability need not feel too much sympathy for the poor starving highway-construction lobby. Like developers who produce 50–100 percent more parking than necessary, ARTB treats paving as an unqualified good—and for their pocketbooks, it clearly is. For society, less is more, while more can be lethal.

If it ever materializes, the much-touted self-driving car stands to change a great deal about private transportation. As currently proposed, the concept is modeled on *cars*: completely private, not shared; ample cargo space, even though unused for most trips; and running on roads rather than tied to rails. The concept of taxi-on-demand would vastly reduce the number of cars per capita if Americans would accept it; this would decrease, but not eliminate, the need for large expanses of paved parking and driving surfaces. There are still many doubts about the self-driving concept, despite a number of theoretical advantages.

Community Benefits of Narrower Streets

Narrowing of roads is the traffic-calming technique with clearest *environmental* benefits. For safety, *visual* narrowing, even an illusion created by painted lane lines, is effective for slowing traffic. To have an environmental effect, the narrowing must be physical, reducing the amount of paving material and decreasing impervious surface.

When existing narrower roads are maintained, instead of being widened and flattened, both construction and maintenance costs are avoided. Because older rural roads tended to follow topography, simply repairing them avoids the environmental destruction common to so-called road improvement. Where a road runs *across* a slope, small increases in paved width are drastically magnified by wider-cut-and-fill slopes to either side. On a 30 percent side slope, adding just one foot on either shoulder increases fill by *two-thirds*, and widens the road-construction "footprint" by ten feet. For one inch of rainfall, the two-foot added pavement width increases runoff by nearly 700 gallons per mile of road.

Conventional residential street standards frequently call for two 12-foot lanes plus 6-foot shoulders, totaling 36 feet. National engineering organizations now suggest that residential streets can be as narrow as 22 feet in neighborhoods that generate fewer than 500 daily trips (about fifty homes).[44]

Compared to the 36-foot-wide standard, a 22-foot street saves nearly *1.75 acres* (75,000 square feet) of paving *per mile*. Assuming a city block of 700 × 500 feet, or about 8 acres, the 22-foot street on all sides saves nearly an acre. That land savings can be used for open space, stormwater or wetland functions, or additional lots. At the same time, the narrowed streets reduce infrastructure costs both for paving and for utilities. Costs of maintenance are usually propor-

tional to the distance a crew must travel (sign replacement, for example), and/or the area that is maintained (pothole repair). Narrower streets reduce both. By slowing traffic, they also protect children, pets, and pedestrians, and contribute to walkability. Last but not least, narrower streets increase the effective density of homes and facilities; more density means destinations are closer together, on average, and this reduces fuel consumption.

In most states, local governments have the option to permit narrower streets, and communities such as Bucks County PA and Boulder CO have done so. One of the most important achievements of New Urbanist communities like Seaside FL and Kentlands (near Washington DC) is using narrower streets than the nationwide norm.

Unfortunately, in many localities, narrow streets are still *illegal* under local or DOT codes. Broad streets were portrayed by early civic boosters as patriotic and sanitary; today, emergency access is often the argument.

Traffic calming in fact causes little delay for police and ambulances; delays for larger fire trucks average

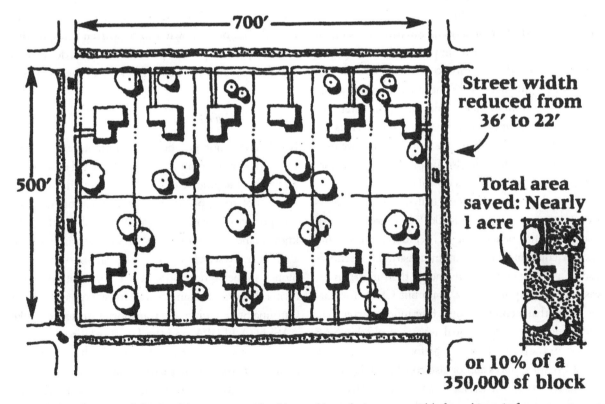

Figure 5.1   One acre of developable or protected land is saved by reducing street width from thirty-six feet to twenty-two feet around an eight-acre city block. (*Illust.:* Craig Farnsworth.)

5 to 20 seconds,[45] compared to delays of 10 to 20 *minutes* commonly caused by sprawl distances.[46] Delays vary by traffic-calming technique. Only speed bumps, raised intersections, and large roundabouts, however, cause as much delay as ordinary stop signs. Mini traffic circles, which eliminate stop signs, often *reduce* delays at intersections, actually lowering pollution from idling, stopped vehicles.[47] Traffic calming also reduces the frequency and severity of accidents; this cuts emergency vehicles' responses overall, so the effect on public safety is definitely positive. Challenges to narrowed streets on the basis of the "right to drive" or "right to park" are entirely outweighed by public benefit; even some drivers' groups say these attacks on traffic calming smack of conspiracy theory and lack credibility.[48]

Standards that ban well-designed narrow streets are outdated and should be seriously reconsidered. Appropriately narrow streets restore a sense of community to places deadened by the dominance of the car. For sustainability, the Center for Watershed Protection's model development standard recommends narrower streets as principle number one.

AASHTO published "A Guide for Transportation Landscape and Environmental Design" in 1991; starting in 2000, it underwent extensive revision by landscape architect Donal Simpson of HNTB (Charlotte NC), but this appears to have been derailed by AASHTO in 2016.[49] What this implies about AASHTO's commitment to improving the often dismal community impacts of roadways and streets is unclear. The draft document was a major improvement and would have given landscape professionals real leverage; perhaps that was its downfall.

Increasingly sophisticated analysis of transportation patterns since the mid-2000s has revealed social and economic benefits of denser development and shorter commutes. In suburban densities, households use nearly 40 percent more energy than in urban areas. A 2007 report for the nonprofit CEOs for Cities found that a commute only four miles shorter than the twenty-four-mile national average resulted in $2.6 billion in transportation savings for an urban area of 500,000; the report's author also concluded that those dollars tend to stay in the local economy. A 2013 study from Harvard University and the University of California, Berkeley, found that urban sprawl hindered not

Figure 5.2 Narrow streets enhance livability of older cities, especially in Europe. Recent US developments use narrowed streets to save land and infrastructure costs, and to protect watersheds. (*Photo:* Kim Sorvig.)

only literal but also social mobility, a concept proven in the remarkable transit-focused turnaround of the city of Medellín, Colombia. Perhaps most telling, calculations by *EBN* staff showed that for many buildings, including very "green" ones, commuting to the building used 30 percent more energy than the building itself did. Excessive paving is a major cause of the urban heat-island effect, a problem in itself, but recently has been shown also to worsen smog by disrupting wind dispersion patterns.[50] Urban design that reduces paved area has an impact on all these issues.

Consider the Critters

Roads affect not just human communities, but animal and plant communities as well. "Road ecology" is a rapidly emerging science devoted to understanding impacts of roads on ecosystems. It is a strongly cross-disciplinary outgrowth of landscape ecology; the well-known landscape ecologist Richard Forman has been a pioneer. Research centers and databases of techniques are being developed at the University of California, Davis; Montana State University; and North Carolina State University; transportation agencies like AASHTO, FHWA, and the Transportation Research Board sponsor research and maintain their own programs. Whether infrastructure reinvestment promised during the 2016 election will include or attack such innovations is anyone's guess. The findings of road ecology confirm concerns that observant drivers, environmentalists, and designers have had for years.[51] Roads interrupt the flow of ecosystem processes and fragment populations. They cause mortality, disease, and suppressed reproduction in both plants and animals within a zone fifteen to twenty times as wide as the road itself. In addition, roads are primary vectors for the spread of invasive species.[52]

Two aspects of road ecology are expanding horizons for applied landscape work. These are roadside habitat management and wildlife crossings.[53]

The Surface Transportation Policy Project (STPP), a Washington DC think tank, notes that public highway right-of-ways occupy 12 million acres of land, and that there are 90,000 miles of road on public lands. "Transportation agencies are land managers on a grand scale," according to STPP, which recommends that all roadsides should be revegetated with their original vegetation communities.[54] Hedges to block wind and snow (instead of fences) provide extra wildlife habitat; decreased and seasonally coordinated mowing schedules increase habitat value. Road structures like bridges can be modified to provide nesting sites and hunting perches for birds. To prioritize the roads most dangerous to wildlife, the Society for the Protection of Nature in Israel asked drivers to use Waze, a traffic-conditions app, to report roadkill sightings; the results not only warned other drivers, but also indicated where design solutions would be most effective.[55]

Wildlife crossings have put road ecology in the news, and landscape professionals are frequently involved, collaborating with wildlife specialists. Wildlife crossings, which are still experimental, vary according to the species expected to use them. Crossings have been developed to protect deer, elk, moose, foxes, panthers, badgers, gophers, tortoises and turtles, frogs, toads, snakes, and alligators. A number of websites share ideas and track projects. One such site, https://arc-solutions.org/new-solutions/, is especially useful because it attempts to standardize terms for the structures and includes clear sketches of each major type. These types are:

- Wildlife overcrossing: a bridge-like overpass for animals (sometimes called ecoducts or biobridges), or a traffic tunnel under natural or naturalistic crossings.

- Wildlife underpass: a road bridging the wildlife corridor, or a soil-floored culvert or tunnel for animals.
- Wildlife barriers: fences, Jersey barriers, or walls (including noise walls doing double duty) that funnel animals to crossings, and in-road barriers similar to "cattle guards" (grate-covered pits across the road where it passes through fence lines).
- Escape structures: one-way gates and ramps for animals accidentally trapped inside barrier fences.

For easily caught animals in small numbers, radio collars have been successfully used to trigger flashing lighted signs when an animal enters the roadway. Infrared beams can detect large species like moose and elk without collaring, but specific knowledge of crossing locations is essential.

In 2010, a new international group called ARC, dedicated to landscape connectivity, wildlife mobility, and human safety, sponsored the first International Design Competition for Wildlife Crossing Infrastructure. A number of landscape firms are partners with ARC, and its website is a good source for illustrations of existing projects and new concepts. Because bridges for animals are generally much wider than long (the opposite of vehicular bridges), design and materials can differ significantly. Modular planting methods, similar to greenroof methods, are becoming popular, while the need for multiple crossings (within a state or for a single highway) is pushing toward standard, perhaps precast, structural components. ARC's philosophy is that wildlife crossings should be beautiful, in order to draw attention to a landscape that vehicular speed has made invisible.

The cost of wildlife protection varies widely, offset by accident costs. The Virginia Transportation Research Council found that even structures costing hundreds of thousands of dollars saved the state money if they prevented between three and nine deer-auto collisions annually. Deer, elk, and moose collisions cause hundreds of human deaths and tens of thousands of injuries yearly; property damage, road cleanup and repair, and other costs add up to many millions of dollars. A 2003 lawsuit held Arizona liable for not providing wildlife protection on Interstate 40, awarding a driver $3.1 million. Wildlife value

Figure 5.3 This wildlife crossing reunites two halves of Phil Hardberger Park, San Antonio, for humans as well as animals. (*Project and Rendering:* Stephen Stimson Assoc., D.I.R.T. Studio, and Rialto Studio.)

Figure 5.4 A wildlife crossing finalist in the ARC competition (**above**), this proposal recognizes that excellent and aesthetic design, in addition to function, engages and educates the public and thus advances support for sustainable facilities. (*Proposal and Rendering:* OLIN, courtesy of Arc-solutions.org.)

Figure 5.5   Wildlife crossings come in all shapes, sizes, and speeds. (*Project:* Logan Simpson Design, AZDOT, and team. *Photo:* Rod Stanger, ASLA.)

to hunting and tourism provides other economic incentives, if ethical and ecological arguments are not enough.

Use Techniques That Reduce Runoff from Paving

Even where planning and design efforts reduce the total area of roads and parking, some new paving is inevitable. Its environmental impact can and should be limited by appropriate choice of materials and methods.

A good starting point for this discussion—in opposition to the prevailing tendency to pave every piece of ground in sight—is "Haag's Theory of Softness." Propounded by Seattle landscape architect Richard Haag, this simple principle states that *no ground surface should be hardened any more than absolutely necessary for its function.* Paving, for instance, should not be used where crushed stone will do, nor crushed stone where a path of bark chips is sufficient. Many conventional paved areas are much harder than function requires them to be.

Softness is not necessarily literal—porous concrete, for instance, is quite hard. The same principle can be restated for permeability: *no ground surface should be any more impervious than necessary.* Any technique or material that works *with* environmental dynamism, rather than resisting, is "softer" than conventional engineering.[56]

Just Say No to Paved Parking

This concept is self-evident, yet almost radical: *not all parking areas need to be paved.* In fact, many lightly used parking lots are much improved (from a sustainability standpoint) by simpler surfacing.

Professor Bruce Ferguson, an expert on stormwater management, says that crushed aggregate was common for surfacing until the 1930s, but now largely abandoned. Crushed oyster and clam shells are still similarly used in some regions. Both persist where overengineering is not mandatory. In the upscale suburban community of Medford Village NJ, this humble paving material formed part of a township-wide stormwater infiltration plan by environmental planner Ian McHarg. Seeing crushed stone used with consistency and sensitivity in historic Medford, Ferguson "really concluded that gravel pavements had a future."

Although it may be porous, not just any gravel will do. Technically "gravel" is rounded small stones, washed by a river; for loose surfacing, it is highly unstable. Crushed stone, which interlocks under pressure, is preferable despite the extra energy costs of producing it. (Sand and gravel mining's environmental impact is considerable.) In specifying crushed stone, Ferguson notes, coarser grades drain more readily; finer grades are more walkable and ADA-accessible. Open grading (sorting so all particles are the same size, a.k.a. "no fines") improves drainage and reduces dust; it is important in porous asphalt or porous concrete (see below).

Like most materials, crushed stone should be used selectively. Best suited for relatively low traffic, it is commonly used in parking stalls served by asphalt travel lanes, with adjacent grassed swales to handle overflow from large storms. Gravel surfaces on clay soils can become highly compacted and impervious under traffic, offering little stormwater advantage over asphalt.[57] Six inches of aggregate is a minimum depth; use a filter fabric or geotextile under the stone to keep it from mixing into soil. The surface layer will almost always become compacted as cars pack the top stones; hand raking yearly will restore porosity. Contain the loose materials on either side with substantial edging, or incorporate cellular containment (p. 146) or meshes similar to those used for grassed paving (see below).

Stone chips or screenings are widely used for pedestrian surfaces in parks. Many famous European gardens, such as the Jardin des Tuileries in Paris, are "gravel" surfaced. Henry Arnold used such surfacing, supported by air-entrained soil at MetroTech plaza in Brooklyn.

Figure 5.6   Porous parking is separated from standard driving lanes. This stormwater management tactic can also create strong aesthetics. (*Project:* Spaceplan [arch.]; Petrus [pervious paving]. *Photo:* Bruce Ferguson.)

For garden paths and very-low-use areas, organic materials such as bark chips or mulch can be used as a truly soft surface, possibly combined with cellular or mesh support. Some (but not all) are acceptable for handicapped access when properly designed. All must be maintained and replenished.

Make Gutters and Curbs Permeable

Many municipal standards require a concrete curb and gutter along both sides of any residential street. Curbs collect and concentrate pollutants deposited on paving (from spills or airborne). Conventional road drainage usually dumps these into the nearest stream.

To avoid this, in most residential neighborhoods it makes sense *not* to add curbs and gutters—a seem-

Figure 5.7 Stone screenings over air-entrained soil at MetroTech in Brooklyn create a permeable surface with the feel of traditional French public spaces. (*Project and Photo:* Henry Arnold.)

ingly simple design strategy, but one that may require a variance from the municipality. If curbs are absolutely required, add multiple openings that allow water to flow through the curb, into grass (or, if possible, into bioswales, below). Gutters of pavers laid on sand can also infiltrate a considerable amount of precipitation. Curbs are sometimes considered to act as safety barriers to keep cars from leaving the road, but they are quite ineffective in this role; the purpose is better served by street trees, other plantings, or bollards. For low-speed streets, a bioswale (below), while not a physical barrier, can act as a reminder to drivers who stray into it, which is really about all that curbs accomplish.

Infiltrate Road and Parking-lot Runoff in Bioswales

Beyond (or instead of) the curb, install grassed or vegetated areas called "bioswales"—linear, planted drainage channels. A typical bioswale moves storm-water runoff as *slowly* as possible along a gentle incline, keeping precipitation on-site as long as possible to soak into the ground—contrary to conventional engineering practice. At the lowest point of the swale there is usually a raised drain inlet taking any overflow to storm sewers. This is insurance, however, because well-designed bioswales completely infiltrate all but the most intense storms. Bioswales' plants and soil microbes cleanse runoff, a simple form of phytoremediation (p. 124).

Bioswales for road drainage are common (and in some counties, mandated) in the Pacific Northwest. In Vancouver WA, more than five acres of bioswales at Heritage (a planned-unit development) were configured as roadside park with handsome plantings, winning a Portland/Vancouver Metro Area Stormwater Design Award. Bioswales can enhance streetscapes, rather than looking like ditches.

Bioswales function particularly well in parking lots, where stationary cars often drip pollutants. Such plantings also improve the pedestrian environment. At Portland's Oregon Museum of Science and Industry (OMSI), a demonstration project features seven bioswales where the raised parking-lot medians would typically be. The OMSI bioswales improve water quality by filtering pollutants from the museum's 800 parking spaces before runoff enters the Willamette River. Quite unlike conventional catch basins and sewers, OMSI's system actually protects the river.

Designed by Murase Associates, OMSI's bioswales are graded to a very gentle incline, retaining water rather than hurrying it out of sight. River rocks and small wooden check dams at thirty-foot intervals cause water to pond, giving it time to soak into the soil. Native wetland plants—cattails, bulrushes, and iris, among others—further slow the water while biologically breaking down pollutants. Contaminants that escape this gauntlet are attacked by soil microorganisms. Thus filtered, the stormwater seeps through

Figure 5.8 Bioswale at OMSI filters, slows, and infiltrates run-off from parking. Raised grate overflows to storm sewers only in very heavy storms. (*Project:* Robert Murase. *Illust.:* Jeff Foster, Portland Bureau of Environmental Services.)

the subsoil into the water table. Raised overflow inlets were installed, but in practice rainwater rarely gets that far.

The city's Bureau of Environmental Services asked OMSI to build the bioswales, prompted by pioneering work on grassed bioswales at the University of Washington. Tom Liptan, a Bureau landscape architect, felt the idea should be tested in Portland, and OMSI management agreed. "Stormwater should be part of the landscape architect's design palette," says Liptan. "We need to be much more involved in the water that falls on a site than most of us are currently." Liptan notes that conventional details for parking lots raise landscaped area *above* curbs, mounded so that any rainfall runs off onto the pavement—exactly the opposite of bioswales, and contrary to the concept of harvesting stormwater into planted areas.

OMSI directed the project engineer to pitch the lot so that it would drain *into* the medians between parking rows, where the swales would be; most lots are pitched *away* from the median strips. Murase Associates designed the richly planted swales, using native plants in lieu of turf, as an "exhibit" to reveal water fall-

ing on the site. To widen the swales, the Murase team convinced the engineers to cut nearly 2 feet off each parking stall (only 16.5 feet). Computer stormwater modeling indicated the swales would hold runoff *longer* than the engineer had calculated, fully infiltrating 0.83 inch of rainfall in a twenty-four-hour period. This is sufficient for 75 percent of all the storms that fall on Portland, says Liptan. The computer model estimates that the swale's topsoil captures 60 percent of suspended solids in the runoff; with a few improvements Liptan expects 90 percent pollutant capture. The parking design won an honor award from an Oregon consortium of municipal governments.

Not surprisingly, visitors to OMSI often ask whether the swales are breeding grounds for mosquitoes. "They don't hold water," is Liptan's response. "The water drains into the soil quickly enough that mosquitoes are not an issue." This might not be true on all sites, Liptan cautions; much depends on the soil and its permeability.

Most encouraging for the future of such projects, the OMSI parking-lot design saved $78,000, compared to a conventional lot, catch basins, and drainage system. This cost savings has helped Bob Murase market the bioswale concept to several Portland-area clients. One is the Bureau of Environmental Services itself, which practiced what it had been preaching and installed bioswales at its Water Pollution Control Laboratory. There, bioswales capture runoff not only from the parking lot but from the laboratory's roof as well. The building has no gutters; instead, scuppers extend from the roof and send water spurting in graceful trajectories to land in a rock-lined bioswale several feet from the edge of the building. The Water Pollution Control Laboratory won several important awards, regional and national.

Bioswales are gradually appearing at other sites around North America. One is the new School of Architecture and Landscape Architecture at Penn State University.[58] Such functional systems on university campuses can also provide on-site demonstration of ecological principles for students. As noted in Principle 4, some engineered stormwater separation filters are being marketed as better than bioswales, a doubtful claim probably based on convenient and fast installation, not biological performance or cost.

Subdivide Impervious Surfaces

With or without bioswales, it is a good idea to break up paved areas so that they drain to unpaved areas rather than to other paving or to storm drains. "Directly Connected Impervious Areas" (DCIAs—paved surfaces that drain straight from one to the next) should be minimized in design.[59] Instead, for example, insert a narrow band of porous material, perhaps just gravel, dividing a driveway from the street, and routing runoff to soil at the sides of the drive. It is especially important that the "first flush" of rain off paving, which carries most surface pollutants, go to a grassed or vegetated area. If stormwater is routed first to a bioswale, and only enters a drain system if ponding is deep enough to reach an overflow outlet, most first-flush pollutants are kept out of further flows, and broken down.

Use Porous Paving Materials

Paving can be made permeable so that infiltration occurs *through the surface of the paving itself*. (Not all alternative paving materials are porous. For soil cement, glasphalt, and plasphalt—using recycled glass or plastic as aggregate—see Principle 6.) Porous paving comes in several forms.

Porous Asphalt and Concrete

Porous paving combines surface stability with permeability. Since the 1970s, landscape profession-

Figure 5.9 This bioswale, part of Glencoe School's green street in Portland OR, uses check dams, a "flash-board" level-setting device in the weir, and overflow drain to treat and infiltrate stormwater. (*Project:* Portland Bureau of Environmental Services. *Photo:* Kevin Robert Perry and Portland Bureau of Environmental Services.)

als have been pioneers in its development and use.[60] Considering how often the profession is involved in (and frustrated by) pavement design, familiarity with these materials is a must for being "part of the solution" rather than part of the problem. As of 2017, an increased number of asphalt and concrete suppliers have at least some experience with porous versions of their material; national industry organizations promote (separately) porous asphalt and concrete, and can help locate project examples to visit.

One major step toward full integration of porous materials into mainstream practices was the publication, in 2005, of Bruce Ferguson's handbook *Porous Pavements*. This book finally offers the documented detail necessary to make porous paving understandable and acceptable to clients, engineers, and regulatory agencies, including information on suppliers and existing projects.

Porous asphalt and porous concrete are similar materials that go by a variety of names: no-fines paving, pervious paving, permeable paving, and percrete (for "percolating concrete"). Stone aggregate is held together with either asphalt or Portland cement; high-tech versions have used epoxy binders. The aggregate must be angular crushed stone, usually three-eighths of an inch in size, carefully sorted to exclude all the "fines" (sand-sized particles) that normally fill voids between larger stones. Without fines, voids make the material porous. (The same concept creates root space in "structural soil," Figure 3.28.) Two-inch no-fines crushed rock, used in reservoirs under porous paving, results in about 40 percent void space.

Whether held together with asphalt or cement, porous paving is strong enough for parking, pedestrian use, and some road surfaces. The asphalt version was originally developed for airport runways, where it prevents dangerous surface ponding. Many state highway departments use it for road surfacing, and asphalt plants routinely carry it, specified as "open-graded mix," "popcorn mix," or "porous friction coat." As a surface over conventional impervious paving, it gets water off the road quickly (the focus of conventional pavement engineering), but does nothing to solve runoff, erosion, or infiltration problems. Porous paving, even if only surfacing, reduces noise as much as halving the traffic (or doubling the distance to the hearer).[61]

It can also be elegant, especially if edged with traditional materials.

In order to affect infiltration or erosion, the porous surface material must be underlaid with a bed, or "reservoir," of larger aggregate surrounded by filter fabric. The reservoir supports the porous surface and holds precipitation until it can percolate into the soil. The reservoir may be as shallow as nine inches on some well-drained soils.

Filter fabric is placed in the reservoir. Extra material, wide enough to completely wrap the crushed stone, is left at all sides, partly raised (like erosion-control fencing), to keep *all* sediment out of the reservoir during installation. Large crushed stone fills the reservoir. A "choker course" of half-inch crushed stone laid on top evens the top surface. Keep heavy equipment out of the excavation; if unavoidable, drive only on previously placed layers of stone and minimize the number of trips. Folding the temporary "fence" fabric onto the top of the reservoir, the porous pavement (either asphalt or concrete based) is then laid.

For porous asphalt, binder is about 6 percent of the aggregate's dry weight, and the porous course about three inches thick. It is slightly flexible and will withstand freezing and thawing. In hot weather, vehicle tires that repeatedly take the same path may rut the surface (as they will on any asphalt paving). Thus in warm climates, and for constant in-and-out traffic, porous concrete may be a better choice.

Porous concrete uses Portland cement binder in a ratio of four or four and one-half parts aggregate to one part cement by weight. This layer is usually five inches thick for ordinary vehicular traffic, and thicker for heavier use. Porous concrete is frequently laid directly on compacted soils in areas with very good soil drainage. It will withstand heavier and more repeated loads than porous asphalt, and it does not soften under heat. Concerns are often raised about freeze-thaw damage. Water drains so quickly through porous asphalt or concrete that ice never forms either in the paving or on the surface. A large reservoir enhances this effect. Air-entrained or otherwise strengthened concrete mixtures can also combat freeze-thaw problems, although concrete additives are frowned on by many in the green building movement. In all, Ferguson considers freeze damage and frost heaving extremely rare.

Figure 5.10   Even at as ceremonial a place as Washington DC's National Cathedral, porous pedestrian paths fit in while protecting the site. (*Project:* Andropogon Associates. *Photo:* Peter von Pawel.)

Both the mixture and timing of porous concrete must be carefully controlled. The contractor must keep to the narrow range of a 0.34 to 0.40 water/cement ratio. With too much water, the cement runs off the aggregate and seals the bottom of the layer; with too little, material bonding is weak. Porous concrete must be placed within sixty minutes of mixing, finished immediately, and covered with plastic sheeting within twenty minutes of placement, to cure for three to ten days. New concrete delivery systems may make all this easier to achieve (see Principle 6).

Reservoir porous paving reduces both runoff volume and concentration of overland flow. This decreases disruption of on-site groundwater recharge and slows downstream erosion and siltation. While water is percolating through the porous system, significant amounts of waterborne pollutants may also be filtered. On some soils, microbes will further neutralize contaminants during infiltration.

In addition to its ecological advantages, porous paving can save construction, real-estate, and maintenance costs—a clear example that working *with* natural systems yields economic benefits. These cost savings happen because porous paving serves two purposes at once—or, perhaps more precisely, in the same place.

Porous-paved surfaces absorb rainfall near where it falls, making the storm drainage system for the site significantly smaller and simpler. Considered strictly as a paving material, porous paving may cost 10 percent more than conventional asphalt. By doubling as a stormwater system and eliminating storm drains, however, it may be 12 to 38 percent cheaper overall.

A second, greater savings occurs where a porous paving reservoir substitutes for stormwater detention or retention basins. Land area otherwise required for basins is freed for other uses—to create more buildable space, which can offset several times the added paving cost; or to conserve site features that would otherwise have been destroyed. In Lower Merion PA, Cahill and Associates was able to create porous tennis courts over reservoirs, an amenity that met stormwater management regulations.

A third advantage is reduced maintenance costs, particularly where snow removal is significant. Snow that falls on porous paving melts quickly and drains into the pores. Only after heavy snowfall will any removal be required, and dangerous surface icing can be virtually eliminated.

Soil around any porous installation must percolate at a minimum rate of a half-inch per hour and should contain no more than 30 percent clay. The reservoir bottom must be at least three feet above bedrock or water table for unimpeded drainage. If clay lenses or other impermeable barriers exist on-site, the reservoir must be either well above them or deep enough to reach permeable soils. On sites sloping 3 percent or more, terrace paved areas so that the bottom of each reservoir remains relatively level; extra depth at the lower side, however, may be needed in some cases.

The size and depth of the reservoir must be designed to fit site conditions: soil permeability, slope, and the local design storm. (Cahill and Associates uses a computer program to do this.) The reservoir must be sized to accommodate the water generated by the design storm and to hold it long enough to percolate into that specific soil. Some conditions (and nervous authorities) may require underdrains or overflow pipes set to catch water if the reservoir fills. Ferguson's book shows a variety of overflow solutions.

Runoff from roofs and nonporous pavement may also be directed into the reservoir, assuming it is sized accordingly. Sediment-bearing runoff, such as flow from wooded areas, should not discharge directly onto porous paving. It may, however, be channeled or piped into the reservoir once sediment is removed by routing the runoff via bioswales, sediment traps, or filter fabric.

With all its advantages, why hasn't porous paving become a standard material? The primary reason appears to be resistance from some engineers and regulators. Porous paving goes against conventional "pave-and-pipe" notions of stormwater management. Moreover, successful design requires more sophisticated site-specific data than standardized pipe sizing; in particular, soil, bedrock, and groundwater characteristics must be tested and respected. As with any new technology, porous paving has a learning curve and requires educating both clients and colleagues.

Among concerns raised by engineers and planners, the fear of clogging is most common. Unfortunately, some "tests" of porous paving were reportedly built on unsuitable soils and at toe-of-slope locations where clogging was virtually assured. Yet initial porosity is far in excess of any storm event (1,000 inches per hour), and most researchers have found that proper design, installation, and maintenance can prevent loss of porosity over time. In one test, an inch of loose fine material was deliberately applied to a porous concrete surface. The pavement never became less porous than turf, and full porosity was easily restored by cleaning with a device called a HydroVac.[62] Porous asphalt may lose surface porosity in areas deformed by traffic; drilling compacted areas with a small bit can restore performance. A relatively minor loss of porosity occurs in all porous materials over the first four to six years and should be assumed in design calculations; even after this loss, porous surfaces still infiltrate no less than 200 inches per hour, still far more than any normal regional precipitation.[63]

Underdrains, overflow drains, and edge drains have been installed on some systems in case the reservoir should ever clog and cease to percolate. Cahill and Associates states that in more than twenty-five years of experience with porous paving, these added features have had only one real purpose: not to deal with clogged or overfilled pavement, but to deal with the "clogged" thinking of skeptical planning commissions.

Most designers familiar with the material recommend porous paving, especially asphalt, for areas of lighter traffic where repetitive movement will not be severe. Employee parking, generally once-a-day in and out, is an example. Main traffic lanes are paved with ordinary asphalt. Porous paving can also be used for many light vehicles, such as golf carts or bicycles, for pedestrians, and for some sports surfaces. Increasingly, these limits are giving way to improved design and materials, so that porous pavement can at least be considered for almost any use.

Porous paving should generally not be used where site soils or bedrock drain very directly into a vulnerable aquifer, or where particularly toxic pollutants are likely to be deposited on the paving. The gravel reservoir and ordinary soils filter ordinary pollutants well enough that this is not a widespread concern. If the subgrade is mostly fractured rock, however, or if the water table is high, consult with soil scientists and hydrological experts before using porous paving.

Pave with Grass

Grassed paving systems allow turfgrass to grow through permeable, structural cells that support the load of vehicles. A variety of commercial products are

Figure 5.11 Porous concrete, shown here, and porous asphalt support vehicles but permit water to infiltrate rapidly. (*Photo:* Florida Concrete and Products Association/Dennis Graeber.)

available, including large sheets of plastic mesh, precast open concrete blocks, and form systems for casting concrete cells in place.

The environmental benefits of grassed paving can be considerable. According to one manufacturer's study, every 1,000 square feet of grassed paving infiltrates nearly 7,000 gallons per ten inches of rainfall, which would otherwise be runoff; converts enough CO_2 to oxygen to supply twenty-two adults for a year; provides significant cooling (equated to 1.7 tons of air-conditioning annually); and, if made of plastic, recycles more than 400 pounds.[64]

Grassed paving is somewhat limited in its applications because grass will not survive constant daily traffic. (Grass for parking stays healthy if used not more than about one day a week—less in dry climates.) It is excellent for emergency fire lanes and temporary overflow parking. But as the Olympia study documented, many more parking areas receive temporary use than is generally supposed. Sports arenas, for example, are typically used on one or two days a week; grassing the entire stadium parking would greatly reduce the need for storm drains (see project examples).

An active operating plan may increase grassed paving's capacity. A large grass-paved area can be divided into two or more subareas, using fences or barriers (permanent or temporary). By alternatively using and resting the subareas, each can be given a chance to recover from wear. This works especially well for overflow parking, where, for example, the *whole* area is only needed occasionally, but filling the lot to *half* capacity is fairly common. Base plans on realistic, not speculative, numbers.

"Grassed" paving systems do not have to be filled with sod. A number of ground covers, such as thyme or chamomile, will flourish in some climates. Fine gravel, oyster shells, or other permeable materials can substitute for grass where frequent parking is expected (or in climates in which grass does not readily grow). Such materials provide strength and permeability without worry about the health of grass. At least one paving-systems manufacturer, Invisible Systems, manufactures a system, Gravelpave^2, designed to be filled with a gravel mixture. This system was employed in 1999 as part of a demonstration project for the head-

quarters of the Riverside/Corona Resource Conservation District in Riverside CA. (Gravelpave^2 is only one of the innovative materials used at the center; others include car stops made of recycled tires.)

A drawback of grassed paving is its cost, which can be higher than that of solid asphalt or concrete parking lots. In fact, the Olympia study found that concrete grass pavers average two to four times the per-square-foot cost of asphalt. A parking area with 20 percent grassed pavers would cost approximately 60 percent more to install than an equal all-asphalt area. But the Olympia study found that permeable paving systems are less costly to maintain over time than asphalt.[65] Moreover, the initial expense of grassed pavers may be deceptive because it does not take into account the *reduced* need for storm drains and sewers. Subtracting the cost of such drains, the overall cost of grassed systems (like porous concrete or asphalt) may actually be lower than that of conventional, impervious paving.

Three general types of grassed paving systems exist: *Poured-in-place* systems such as Bomanite's Grasscrete consist of steel-reinforced concrete and are typically the most expensive systems. They require skilled workers to install.

Precast concrete pavers resemble interlocking concrete pavers (p. 64) and provide rigid structural support. Typical pavers are heavy and require equipment for hauling and lifting. Precast and cast-in-place concrete systems have a lattice-like or checkered concrete grid framing areas of grass. This can be very attractive in some designs and may help make it clear that the area is for parking.

A large number of the available systems are *plastic pavers*, some manufactured from recycled plastic.[66] Although they do not have concrete's rigidity, these flexible pavers conform to irregular surfaces. They appear to support grass growth better than the thick-walled concrete cells if moisture is scarce. Plastic grid systems come closest to disappearing entirely under the grass, giving the appearance of ordinary lawn. Invisible Structures, founded by Denver landscape architect Bill Bonhoff, makes all its products of recycled plastics. Invisible Structures grass pavers have been tested up to 5,700 psi bearing strength when filled; the empty structure will support over 2,000 psi.

The introduction of "hybrid turf"—live grass reinforced with plastic fiber—may offer another porous surface that could withstand light, infrequent traffic. (See p. 279.)

In general, it is better to use a mix of sand and water-absorbent polymer as grass-paver growing medium than to use topsoil. Topsoil usually is loamy or clayey and will compact. Sandy fill is also most permeable. Porosity of the system depends strongly on the native soil underneath it. Over clay or loam soils, 50–80 percent of rainfall may run off (compared to 95 percent from hard pavement); over sandy soils, runoff from grassed paving can be as little as 15 percent.

A key requirement of grassed paving is maintenance. This includes mowing, which is important because tall grass matted down by vehicles can decrease porosity. People are less likely to park if grassed paving does not appear stable and well cared for.[67] Invisible Structures states that snow can be plowed off its systems if inch-thick skids are attached to the snow-plow blade. An irrigation system is also recommended even in areas of high rainfall to counter stresses of compaction, shallow rooting space, oil drips, and, with concrete cells, heating and water wicking by the concrete.[68] Maintenance costs appear to be comparable to or less than for conventional pavement, although such comparisons are hard to make. Durability is likely to vary with soil type and climate.

In choosing between different grassed systems, evaluate ease and weight of installation, durability, grass growth and maintenance issues (preferably by comparison of projects in your region), and finished appearance.

Grassed paving is well suited for periodic "event parking"; the City of Miami used a recycled-plastic system for new parking stalls at the Orange Bowl, with conventional asphalt driving lanes.

"Overall, it's working out really well," says Enrique Nuñez, a landscape architect with Miami's Department of Community Planning and Revitalization. Nuñez confirms that grass pavers have helped to eliminate runoff; the site has a conventional stormwater system as a backup.

Because much retail parking is used only at peak periods, grassed paving may be appropriate for areas not used day-to-day. Westfarms Mall (Farmington

CT) seized this opportunity. When the mall proposed adding 4.7 acres of parking, primarily to accommodate the Christmas rush, the local zoning board pointed to a percentage green-space requirement. A grassed paving system of recycled plastic pavers enabled Westfarms Mall to get its parking while meeting the green-space quota, and without enlarging existing storm drains. Although this particular project incorporated tree plantings, too, grassed paving is certainly a minimal form of "green space," and should not be a way to *get around* planted-area regulations. Converting excess *existing* parking to grassed paving would be more appropriate; removing the excess altogether, better yet.

Figure 5.12   Gravelpave² uses recycled plastic grids to stabilize gravel. Similar plastic or concrete grids strengthen grass paving or combat slope erosion. (*Photo:* Invisible Structures.)

Figure 5.13   Overflow parking at Westfarms Mall uses Grasspave² instead of impervious asphalt. (*Photo:* Invisible Structures.)

Olympia WA tested the effectiveness of grassed paving in a demonstration project: a public-school parking lot from which storm runoff regularly flooded adjacent athletic fields. An 8-foot-wide, 2.5-foot-deep infiltration trench was dug along the edge of the lot and backfilled with porous sandy gravel. Honeycomb-like cellular containment units, filled with a gravel and soil mix, bear parked cars while allowing rainwater percolation into the trench. For quick vegetative cover, turf was installed over this. The soil mix was designed to hold enough water for grass to survive.

Post-construction evaluation was done for forty-eight days, of which thirty-four were rainy. Ponding on the athletic field occurred on only six of these days, a marked improvement. Parks and Recreation vehicles drove over the test; tire tracks were found on several occasions but did no irreparable damage to the lawn or to infiltration.[69] People tended not to park on the area, however, apparently averse to driving on grass. Turf, a loose carpet over such a system, may have looked muddy or unstable, a problem that grass-in-cells avoids.

Unit Pavers on Permeable Subgrade

Another potentially permeable surface uses unit pavers (set as individual pieces, rather than poured as a continuous sheet). Such pavers may or may not be permeable themselves, and must be laid on permeable material: sand, crushed stone, or stone screenings. If set on concrete—as unit or interlocking pavers so commonly are—the resulting surface is no more permeable than the concrete.

Unit pavers are time-honored materials in many older cities: the brick that makes the undulating historic sidewalks in Washington DC and Philadelphia so appealing; the hexagonal pavers used in New York; or even flagstone, granite setts, or cobblestones. Interlocking concrete pavers in many styles and colors also provide some percolation. (Because permeability is not their primary environmental benefit, interlocking concrete paver systems are discussed in Principle 1, Figure 1.9.) A few manufacturers have made pavers with fly ash (see Principle 6).

Some unit pavers are cast with spacers on each edge, which automatically creates extra-wide joints, while maintaining paver-to-paver contact for stability. These

Figure 5.14 Traditional granite setts being laid on sand in Philadelphia's historic district. Joints are somewhat permeable if not mortared. (*Photo:* Kim Sorvig.)

"spaced" systems are probably the most permeable of any unit paver, unless precast grass pavers are included.

Because percolation actually takes place in joints between the pavers, joint width and fill becomes critical. A Cornell University study[70] recommends:

- small pavers, to maximize total joint area
- thicker pavers to increase rigidity
- ¼-inch-wide joints; wider reduces stability
- joints lower than the walking surface to increase infiltration
- coarse, sharp sand bound with bitumen (a sort of miniaturized porous asphalt) as permeable joint filler
- extra joint filler after initial settling, to avoid finer debris that blocks porosity
- coarse, lightly compacted base course for under-drainage.

Similarly, the National Concrete Masonry Association recommends *not* compacting sand under interlocking concrete pavers. Ferguson has found that joint fill coarser than sand is more permeable and stable.

As with porous paving, above, unit paver permeability may decline over time as joints become compacted by traffic and filled by debris. This decline levels off after about five years, leaving considerable permeability.

For landscape architect Henry Arnold, the major benefit of such systems is that easy percolation supports healthier plantings and cuts irrigation costs. As an example, Arnold used colored concrete unit pavers set on a bed of finely crushed stone in downtown At-

Figure 5.15 Henry Arnold has used open-jointed unit pavers at large plazas in Atlanta GA, Brooklyn NY, and Newport NJ, usually with extra aeration vents. (*Project and Photo:* Henry Arnold.)

Figure 5.16 Dispersed parking for Simmons headquarters reduced disruption and infiltrates runoff near its source. (*Project:* Robert Marvin Associates. *Photo:* Bruce Ferguson.)

lanta's Peachtree Plaza. This beautiful walking surface collects and infiltrates water, helping to irrigate plaza plantings.

On Sensitive Sites, Scatter the Parking

One problem with extensive parking lots is that they require leveling landforms and clearing vegetation. For forested and other sensitive sites, scatter the parking throughout the site, keeping disturbance small-scale. The Simmons Mattress Company outside of Atlanta used this strategy successfully for 200 parking spaces. Instead of the typical monolithic lot, Robert E. Marvin & Associates created "woodland parking" throughout the forest. A sinuous one-way driveway connected one- to three-space clusters. Flexible layout required much less cutting of trees and disturbance of the forest floor; the one-lane access kept total

paving equivalent to a single lot for similar numbers of spaces. Stormwater from the slender roadway and small groups of parking spaces runs directly onto the woodland floor (there are no curbs or gutters) and soaks in.

This approach requires much more detailed siting and staking than a single lot; GPS and UAS surveying can help. It requires extra care during construction, preferably with small, light machinery. Landscape contractors who forgo the convenience of grading a single large space will gain satisfaction from very attractive results and reduced environmental impact. A reputation for care brings repeat business and an edge over more conventional competitors.

One objection to the scattered approach is that, because the parking is so dispersed, an employee may have to walk farther from her or his car to the building. The only appropriate response is: Get over it! Like the "right-to-drive" arguments mentioned above, this

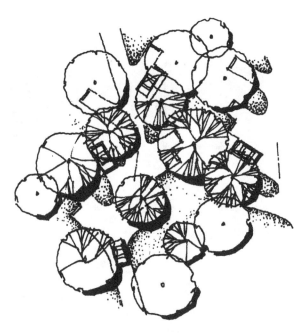

Figure 5.17 Plan of Simmons dispersed parking shows small graded areas integrated with the existing site, rather than one large flattened area. (*Illust.:* Craig Farnsworth, based on Ferguson.)

objection has little merit. Dispersed parking should be tried at many more low-density sites where trees or other site features need to be preserved.

In general, even where preservation of site features is *not* a major issue, it is advisable to break up any paved surfaces into smaller units so that each can drain to an adjacent unpaved area. By reducing runoff-flow distances for near-source infiltration, this system protects the site's water regime, a concept discussed in more detail on p. 184. Breaking up level surfaces also reduces grading significantly. On hillsides especially, parking lots, roads, and trails should be terraced. This requires subdividing the parking, and separating roads and trails into independent parallel lanes, a technique beautifully used in parkway design.

Install "Green Streets"

An important innovation in managing runoff from paving is the "green street." A green street, essentially, is one that cleanses and infiltrates its own stormwater through a coordinated combination of techniques similar to those in this chapter. A green street decreases stormwater burden on both sewer systems and streams.

In concept, green streets work like bioswales. Water runs down the street in the gutter and drops into a series of planted basins for cleansing and infiltration. Vegetated, porous areas divide impervious surfaces (see DCIAs, above); for example, they are typically inserted between sidewalk and street. Excess can flow into a conventional storm sewer during heavy storms.

Green streets can be new streets or retrofits. Typically, their many elements are shoehorned into existing urban fabric: wrapping around elementary schools, wedged into boulevards, growing at grocery-store entrances, and planted in residential parking zones. They are *constructed ecological networks* designed to treat urban stormwater. When a street is redesigned for traffic calming, bump-outs, medians, and other calming techniques are opportunities for green-street planting.

Not unexpectedly, green streets are most frequent in the rainy Pacific Northwest. Portland OR has installed several as ongoing demonstrations. All are capable of infiltrating at least two inches per hour and have measurably reduced impacts on the larger stormwater system. They are generally low maintenance, requiring occasional sediment removal and annual plant trimming. Soil quality is monitored for heavy metals (currently within safe levels). These demonstrations show that the concept works, and if applied on a citywide, master-planned scale could be significant for stormwater management.

Kevin Perry, a landscape architect formerly with Portland's Bureau of Environmental Services, suggests four key concepts for green streets:

- Manage water at the source: Infiltrate water where it hits the ground. Green streets reduce downstream flows by at least 80 percent; that much less water reaches the next pipe, basin, or treatment facility.
- Manage water at the surface: Avoid pipes, which are expensive to install, and can clog or freeze. Overland conveyance is easier to install and maintain, and allows evaporation, use by plants, and infiltration.
- Let nature do the work: When plants and soil slow runoff, filter minerals, and prevent erosion, costs for construction and operation of infrastructure such as treatment plants are reduced.
- Create community assets: Pipes and catch basins don't do anything for anybody except the dubious service of whisking away water. Green streets bring

Figure 5.18 In small-scale, low-traffic areas, unit pavers can even support wildflowers. (*Project:* R. and V. Sorvig. *Photo:* Kim Sorvig.)

beauty to urban neighborhoods, make pedestrian crossings safer, and calm street traffic.[71]

Green streets exemplify multifunctional and geometrically complex design, increasingly recognized as a core concept in sustainability. Conventional streets and drain pipes are designed with simplified geometries to optimize one exclusive function (flat surfaces for vehicle movement, simple cylinders for water removal). Like ecosystems, green streets are a step to-

ward approximating ecosystems' geometric complexity, functional openness, and diversity. (See p. 34.) Sadly, engineered products are being touted as equal to biological stormwater treatment, despite failing almost all of Perry's guidelines.

Cool Asphalt with Planting and Albedo

Conventional parking lots, as noted above, are major contributors to urban heat islands. Black asphalt is

Figure 5.19   "Green streets" (like Siskyou St., Portland OR) collect water from wider areas with parking, and infiltrate it in "bump-out" planted areas that also help traffic calming. (*Project:* Portland Bureau of Environmental Services. *Photo:* Kevin Robert Perry and Portland Bureau of Environmental Services.)

particularly heat-absorbing. Concrete and some other light-colored paving materials reflect more sunlight, absorbing less heat. Dark brick and stone, and colored concrete, may be almost as heat-absorbent as asphalt. (Meg Calkins gives surface reflectivity index [SRI] values and other heat-island data for fifteen materials; conventional asphalt ranges from zero—black—to 6; concrete and colored asphalt, from 35 to 85. LEED gives a credit for SRI over 29.)[72]

Grassed paving is significantly less absorptive of heat than any hard surface. If the climate is not too harsh to support grass, this alternative paving can cut heat retention. Initial test results indicate porous paving, with its built-in air space and moisture, also holds less heat than conventional paving.

Reducing the *amount* of paving should always be the first consideration where heat is an issue. Where a hard-surfaced lot is essential for a project, however, the EPA recommends two ways of reducing the heat increases from paving.[73] The first is to plant shade trees—a seemingly simple move. Some city tree ordinances, however, actually ban true shade trees in favor of small convenient species. Vine-covered trellises can be an alternative, but the magnificent street trees of older cities shade more area more economically.

The second EPA approach is to increase pavement's reflectiveness (or "albedo"), thus reducing heat absorption. Too much reflectance equals glare and

must also be avoided. Given the prevalence of asphalt (nearly 75 percent of all US paving), and the fact that its oily composition makes it hard to paint or stain, methods of lightening these surfaces take on particular importance for sustainability.

Fortunately, asphalt can be lightened in several ways. Specify light-colored aggregate and fines in asphalt mixes; although surfaces are initially black, wear exposes this aggregate. Many conventional "black-top" roads are in fact the color of local aggregate. Ensure that neither construction workers nor maintenance staff apply the conventional pure-black "wearing coat," often done routinely for a new and tidy look. Light-colored aggregate can be used for porous as well as nonporous asphalt.

Color-coating for asphalt developed as a decorative system, but has environmental possibilities. Slurry seals, composed of sand, cement, and acrylic-polymer binders, have been developed to adhere to the slightly oily surface of asphalt. These can be almost any color; light-colored coatings make asphalt paving less heat-absorptive.[74] These coatings are often used with metal templates that, pressed into the hot asphalt by a vibratory roller, produce surface patterns: brick, cobblestone, even custom logos or artwork. Normal cracking of the asphalt is reduced because template-compressed areas act as expansion joints, while the coating seals out water. The first installations in the United States, made in the early 1990s, have required much less routine maintenance than conventional asphalt.

The main environmental reason to consider these coatings is to reduce heat absorption. To the extent that these coatings reduce maintenance and extend the life of asphalt, they save resources. They may also solve the difficulty of trenches cut through paving for utility repairs: using templates, trenches can be recoated to match original work. Coatings do not address asphalt's imperviousness, nor health problems that exposure to hot asphalt can create, nor general issues surrounding petroleum production.

Coatings, which can be applied by ordinary laborers, add 30–50 percent to the price of plain asphalt. Similar in appearance to patterned concrete, they cost 50–80 percent of high-end stamped concrete systems like Bomanite.[75]

In addition to coatings, asphalt can be colored in the hot mix. Provided by Asphacolor (Madera CA), this relatively new process was used for Los Angeles Union Station. Heat-island reduction was not apparently a goal of this project, but probably occurred incidentally.

Bagged colorant is batch mixed with asphalt and aggregate at the plant; as with coatings, almost any color can be produced. Compared to ordinary asphalt, mixing is slightly slower, more coordination is required, and extra cleanup is necessary before mixing other colors or plain asphalt. Only the top 1 to 1.5 inches of paving are usually colored. Costs are somewhat higher than for asphalt-coating systems, but still less than for colored concrete. Because it is integral to the mix, the Asphacolor process may wear longer than coatings. It offers some interesting design possibilities in combination with contrasting colored aggregate and is the only way that *porous* asphalt could be colored.

Asphalt, as one of the cheapest ways of meeting society's massive demand for paving, is likely to remain a major component of the built environment for a long time to come. Being able to achieve color more cheaply than with colored concrete may actually expand the marketplace for asphalt. Whether these decorative systems can make asphalt paving significantly more sustainable remains to be seen; for discussion of the material itself, see Principle 6. Colorants clearly affect the heat-island problem,[76] however, and may somewhat reduce asphalt maintenance and replacement. Like any impervious paving, colored asphalt requires runoff management.

As stressed throughout this book, technical solutions to sustainability problems can only succeed if paralleled by social changes. This is particularly true anywhere cars are involved, as with paving. Creative and high-quality work by landscape designers and contractors is one of the best hopes for raising public awareness and acceptance of new paving methods. Museums, nature centers, and educational institutions, as well as national and regional parks, even some progressive corporations, have environmental goals and offer high-profile opportunities to showcase sustainable methods.

One of the few things that the new federal administration shares with its predecessor is stated commitment to infrastructure renewal. With Chinese and other foreign investors actually buying distressed high-

Figure 5.20   Decorative color coatings for asphalt can lighten the surface, decreasing heat-island effects. Integral color, mixed into hot asphalt, is also becoming available. (*Photo:* StreetPrint, Scott Hind.)

ways and bridges,[77] there could be major changes in infrastructure by 2020. Whether these changes are a feeding frenzy or a "paving diet" is something landscape professionals should try to influence.

Subtopics and Search Terms for Principle 5: Pave Less

Note: Subtopics are also useful search terms; add "innovation" or "controversy" to search terms as appropriate.

Overpaving
Search terms: paving excessive || impervious surfaces || parking quotas || "pave the planet society"

Paving
Search terms: paving || paving materials || pervious paving || permeable paving

Roadway design and traffic calming
Search terms: traffic calming || context sensitive design || roundabouts || speed bumps

Heat islands
Search terms: pavement + (albedo OR cooling)

Biofiltration
Search terms: bioswales || vegetated (swale OR filtration) || biofiltration

Road ecology
Search terms: "road ecology" || wildlife crossings || vehicle wildlife accidents

Resource List: see http://islandpress.org/sustainable-landscape-construction

Principle 6:
Consider Origin and Fate of Materials

Nature resolves everything into its component elements, but annihilates nothing.
—*Lucretius, 57 BC*

One theme of this book is that inappropriate landscape design and construction—such as overpaving or invasive plantings—damages sites. Even landscapes that seem perfectly harmonious with their sites, however, can impact environments far *beyond*. Pliny Fisk, codirector of the Center for Maximum Potential Building Systems in Austin TX, illustrates this: "One can disturb a site to the least possible degree and be causing utter havoc on Earth at the same time—because of what you're *bringing to* that site. Let's say that landscape architects are going to do a large paved area and they decide to use granite pavers quarried in Minnesota. There's a good chance that the granite is shipped to Italy, sliced up, sent back and delivered to Houston, or wherever the building site is. That's an incredible imposition on the well-being of this planet."[1]

Fisk is referring, of course, to energy costs (and concomitant air pollution) required to move that granite around the globe. *Materials* used in landscapes have many such impacts. Extraction of raw materials for landscape products has environmental and energy costs, including what are called "hidden flows" (e.g., mine spoils) that are seldom accounted for but can be triple the "direct flows" (e.g., the mine's actual product, ore).[2] Materials processing and assembly of products also generates impacts far from the site. Even debris hauled off-site has impacts—energy costs of removal and space taken up by landfills.

While designers have become increasingly aware of sustainable techniques, the majority of landscape projects still specify virgin materials. "Such landscapes, no matter how sensitive they are to the ecology of a site, are still destructive," says Kathleen Baughman, a land-

> ## Discussed in This Chapter
>
> Eight basic guidelines to simplify choice of sustainable materials.
> Using on-site and local resources.
> Recycled products for landscapes.
> Recycling construction materials.
> Recognizing and avoiding toxic materials.
> Impacts of transportation, mining, and other general processes.

scape designer in Portland OR, "for they promote the continued environmental degradation associated with resource extraction."[3]

Almost every construction material is extracted from somewhere. Some extraction processes are more destructive than others; some products are renewable or reusable. Hidden costs can be high, from nonrenewable petroleum products used in asphalt to destruction of rainforests for tropical hardwoods—or, for that matter, felling of domestic redwoods for decks and site furniture. This chapter focuses on recognizing hidden costs of landscape materials, and hazards to landowners and landscape workers.

Realistic alternatives do exist: local materials, reused or recycled materials, and materials found onsite. Acceptability of these materials was growing rapidly when the first edition of this book was released: a contest to win a custom home built of "top-of-the-line recyclables" attracted *seven times* as many entries in 1998 as in 1997.[4] These trends continue: wider acceptance of alternative materials, and more detailed materials research. In product design, recycled materials are a hot trend, and many landscape professionals now view alternative materials not as limitations, but as opportunities—not only imposing lesser burdens on the planet, but also inspiring some of today's most creative landscapes.

The Devil Is in the Details

Like the rest of this book, this section on materials is intended as a strategic guide to concepts and methods. One of the most promising advances in "green" perspective on landscape materials was the 2009 publication of Meg Calkins's *Materials for Sustainable Sites*. The fact that she could take what this book covers in a chapter, and expand it into an encyclopedic book, shows how much the profession has matured. Besides Calkins's thoroughness, her book reflects the collected expertise of the SITES (formerly Sustainable Sites Initiative, or SSI) Materials Technical Subcommittee.

I am happy to recommend Calkins's exhaustive book as the go-to for detailed information on materials. Readers need to be prepared to convert between metric and US measures (one of the book's strengths is that it draws on European and Australian experience, but units appear to be given in whatever form was used in the original research). Calkins's training is in both architecture and landscape architecture, which gives a broad perspective, but also means that some of the materials and applications discussed are not landscape specific. These minor issues are more than made up for by extensive comparison tables, full citation of sources, useful bibliography, and a detailed index. I'm very happy that Calkins champions life-cycle methods of evaluating materials, as well as embodied energy, to which she adds data about carbon footprint.

Recall Some Simple Guidelines

As a simple set of operational rules, consider this short list of principles from Maurice Nelischer, a landscape architect in Guelph, Ontario:[5]

- Whenever possible, specify locally produced products.

- Use less-processed materials (rough-sawn or air-dried lumber, for instance).
- Perform at least a rough audit of energy required to mine, produce, ship, and install materials. (See Principle 7.)
- Explore recycled materials. Specify reusable materials—for example, stone, brick, or concrete pavers rather than poured concrete.
- Avoid petroleum-based materials whenever possible. Asphalt and plastics are indispensable in a few uses, but not for every purpose.

These guidelines offer a starting point. Some additions to the list:

- Use durable materials and designs. Conversely, prioritize reuse of structures and site elements.
- Minimize use of materials that are toxic, either on-site or during manufacture or disposal.
- Offset CO_2 at every opportunity. Lock up carbon by using wood durably; Fisk speaks of "CO_2 balancing" a project's materials. Use living materials (plantings or BTEC) that take up CO_2 while serving structural purposes.

Let Reuse Be Re-inspiration

Recycling is worthwhile for simple pragmatic reasons. But like necessity, it can be a source of invention, inspiring both designers and users of landscapes.

The uniqueness of specific places has been diluted by modern communication and transportation; many people feel adrift in a featureless landscape of convenience. Reusing cast-off materials is a link to other people and times, giving a deeply desired sense of continuity. The results may be as quiet as "character" from worn, used stone, or as blatant as an old tractor planted with petunias. Large or small, tasteful or garish, reused materials have an identity that can't be bought new.

Use Local, Salvaged, or Recycled Materials

The simplest single way to cut down material impacts is to obtain them locally. Trucking one ton of material one mile typically uses between 2,000 and 6,000 Btu;

Figure 6.1 Landscapes that reuse neglected materials can be a much-needed source of pride and identity in a homogenizing world. (*Photo:* Kim Sorvig.)

Figure 6.2 "Recycling" a power turbine into a picnic umbrella (New Zealand) saves no materials, but humanizes a massive postindustrial artifact. At this scale, reuse and recycling can be both whimsical and transformative. (*Photo:* Kim Sorvig.)

air freight can easily use twenty times this energy.[6] Fuel consumption for transporting materials from afar can be greater than energy used to extract and manufacture the items. Rising fuel costs make local materials economical.

Not only is long-distance transportation an energy cost, but fuel combustion is a primary source of pollution and greenhouse gases. For every mile less between supplier and site, nonrenewable fuel resources are saved, and emissions that cause health problems and contribute to global warming are reduced.

Some materials are easier to obtain locally than others. Steel, for instance, is produced in a few centralized mills, while cement and brick are frequently manufactured locally. Buying from your local steel mill is not often an option: production efficiency requires centralization. For other materials, such as lumber, it may be possible to find a local supplier, but conventional business practices (such as supplying all US lumber from the Pacific Northwest or Georgia) keep local materials artificially expensive. Distant or foreign ownership of local material production can also distort costs. Intense demand from China for construction materials is destabilizing prices. Monetary cost is often a misleading indicator of environmental costs, and sustainability requires better true-cost estimating of materials.

Salvaged or reused materials are often local, serving twice for roughly the same energy cost. Clearly, some salvage methods use so much energy that they offer no real environmental savings, but the bulldoze-and-dump approach uses as much and wastes more. Salvage work is typically done by hand or small power tools, using less nonrenewable energy and more renewable human energy, and thus creating more jobs than conventional demolition.

Recycled materials are *remanufactured* between first and second use. Careful analysis is required to know which materials are environmentally cost-effective to recycle. Popularly equated with sustainability, some forms of recycling do not save enough energy to be environmentally sound. While aluminum can be remanufactured using a fraction of new production energy, other materials cannot. Collecting and transporting materials for recycling may evaporate net energy savings. For some materials, recycling can only produce a second-rate material; this is called "downcycling." For example, plastics pure enough for medicine containers generally are only downcycled. Recycling, like salvage and reuse, does keep materials out of landfills; sometimes this is reason enough to recycle even when energy savings are borderline.

A few consumer products have "take-back" programs (formally "extended producer responsibility," or EPR); dead cell phones and exhausted printer cartridges are examples. Only a few building materials have similar programs, voluntary or mandated. Carpet, vinyl siding and shingles, agricultural irrigation plastics, and drywall are among the few products where take-back has been tried. In general, it is collection and participation problems, rather than remanufacturing issues, that have prevented such programs from taking hold.[7]

Participation in recycling programs fluctuates dramatically. Recycling as a percentage of total waste generation has risen fivefold since 1960, to 34.3 percent; but for the same period, per capita waste generation has risen by 60 percent, compounded by population growth of 77 percent. Most studies show that the more people recycle, the more trash they also produce (see Jevons Paradox, p. 6).[8] Recovery rates vary for materials; 99 percent of lead-acid batteries are recovered, while plastic bottle recovery, generally perceived as the core of recycling, is only around 30 percent. If a community recycles a large amount, recycled materials may flood the market, making them less valuable; recycling then becomes costly, rather than profitable or break-even.

The market for recycled materials is also unstable and distorted by artificially cheap fossil fuels. Aluminum scrap, for example, dropped dramatically in 2003, but hit an eighteen-year high price in 2006, according to the Institute of Scrap Recycling Industries; since then it has seen two major peaks and two deep valleys. In the mid-1990s, recycled newsprint was worth $100 per ton; in 2003, it had fallen to one-tenth that value; by 2017, advertised prices were $80–$150. Metal recycling prices, at their highest, can induce *theft* of landscape items. Aluminum bleachers, park benches, and irrigation pipes; steel highway guardrails, light-rail tracks, and railroad spikes; copper downspouts; all have been stolen—even power lines, which have electrocuted several would-be thieves.[9] As natural resources become scarcer through unsustainable use, they change social behavior, often negatively.

These are issues far larger than the landscape industry, but affect many landscape practices. Refuse from construction and demolition ("C&D waste") is tracked separately from municipal solid waste (often abbreviated MSW). In 2013, 530 million tons of C&D waste was generated; 96 percent was from demolition, indicating that lack of reusability is a more urgent problem than wasteful construction practices. Portland cement accounted for 67 percent of C&D waste in 2013 (355 million tons); asphalt at 18 percent and wood at 8 percent follow, percentages paralleling relative ease of recycling. No other single material exceeded 2 percent of the total.[10]

Yard waste has made up about one-fifth of municipal solid waste, and more in some areas; many jurisdictions now ban it from landfills (see p. 383). In 2013, an estimated 60 percent of greenwaste was diverted to composting, counting as both recycling and reuse. For organic material, the landscape is the *medium* of recycling and of renewability.[11] Renewability depends on proper management of forests or fields so that these can continue to produce resources.

Sustainable use of materials has many complexities, and the well-known slogan "Reduce, Reuse, Recycle" needs to be understood as a list *in priority order*. Using less materials, reusing them in their present form, and finally recycling them is a sustainable path. When recycling, or even reuse, becomes an excuse to continue using more materials, or to use materials with extremely poor environmental records, it makes a mockery of hopes for sustainability. Likewise, using a locally produced but highly toxic material is of little environmental benefit.

For better or worse, environmental choice of materials is seldom cut and dried. As Sandra Mendler points out in HOK's *Sustainable Design Guide*, these choices will become easier the more professionals practice them. "It took about 100 years to arrive at a generally accepted set of 'rules' to deal with basic issues of safety in 'modern' buildings. We must now move forward by focusing on sustainable design as our 19th century predecessors emphasized life safety."[12]

Use On-site Materials

If using local materials follows "close-to-source" principles, then the closest source is the site itself. The great majority of materials for traditional construction—soil, wood, or rock—were from the site or very nearby. Limitations on locally available materials played a strong role in development of regional technologies and design styles. For example, the high deserts of the southwestern United States and Mexico have tall trees only in limited mountain areas. This led directly to adobe—earth from within the building's footprint, in many cases—as the main building regional material, with timber reserved for roof beams and lintels.

Far from being just a constraint, these local materials awakened creative design: southwestern adobe has become one of today's most popular and imitated styles. With creativity, a wide range of on-site materials may be productively reused in landscapes. In an era when the homogenizing effects of industrial, Modernist design are widely regretted, creative use of on-site materials offers not only environmental benefits, but artistic rebirth.

Boulders, Stone, Brick, and Timber

As well as earth and plants, many sites contain stone, either cut or rough, bricks, or old lumber. Mario Schjetnan, a Mexico City landscape architect, made extraordinary reuse of on-site volcanic stone at Malinalco golf club south of the capital. The stone—some of it sizeable boulders—was unearthed during excavation. Instead of reinterring it at great cost, Schjetnan constructed massive stone walls to define the entry, and a spacious entrance plaza built entirely of smaller

stones. The project won an honor award from the American Society of Landscape Architects in 1998. (Another Mexican landscape featuring on-site volcanic stone is Luis Barragán's famous Pedregal.)

The stones at Malinalco were placed by hand—a labor-intensive process not replicable in nations with high labor costs. Social issues are part of construction, and reuse evolves to fit different societies.

On-site rubble can be used in developed countries, though. In Oslo, Norway, demolition permitted creation of a garden court in a historic area. Landscape architect Rainer Stange transformed roof tiles and other rubble into retaining walls. Following the former buildings' footprints, the walls are a ghostly reflection of history, restating the recycling concept. Steps were made of reused stone curbs. Tiles and other salvaged materials fill plantable gabions, while for contrast, clean high-tech metal trellises tie the space together. Careful selection of climbing plants, one species per wall, helps orient users to this charmingly offbeat garden.

Demolition rubble, reconstituted as paving surfaces or wall blocks, has become a common reuse of C&D debris. At the Institute for Regenerative Studies, broken concrete slabs were pieced together and cemented to form a new driveway and parking area. This reduced new cement requirements significantly. Asphalt is directly recycled on-site by modern road machinery; concrete is increasingly recycled as aggregate.

There are strong arguments for removing old paving and structures and restoring soil underneath. But where the structure can be adapted, or where energy costs of removal are high, it may make more sense to leave such structures in place and *reuse* them. An example is Monnens Addis Design in Berkeley CA, where a defunct warehouse was rehabilitated as a graphic-design studio. The owners wanted a garden, but the only available spot was the former loading dock, covered with a concrete slab eight inches thick. Landscape architect Jeffrey Miller chose an unusual strategy: instead of demolishing the slab, he built the garden atop it.

Cost was an obvious factor; transporting and dumping demolition debris has become a significant expense in most cities. But beyond this pragmatic consideration Miller believes in reuse of on-site materials. "If you can leave things where they are," he says, "you're not spreading more junk around the planet."

Figure 6.3   Stone from site excavation, reused in walls and paving at Club de Golf Malinalco, makes a stunning argument for inventive use of site "waste." (*Project:* Mario Schjetnan. *Photo:* Courtesy of Grupo de Diseño Urbano.)

Miller punched through the slab to create planting pits for four weeping acacia trees, a queen palm, and two species of bamboo, using a diamond-blade saw. Cement from the holes was piled against the building to create raised, planted seating areas. Compacting the rubble mechanically by vibration, Miller filled any voids with gravel and sand, and finally added eighteen inches of soil. The striking results can be seen in Figure 6.8.

Adobe, Soil Cement, and Other Earthen Materials

Mud, that most elemental of materials, has been used in dozens of cultures, not just the familiar Santa Fe style. Ironically, architects and historians are more likely to be aware of this than most landscape professionals. Although scarcely familiar in contemporary landscapes, earth-building techniques are intimately linked to landscape history.

Historically, the earliest Persian gardens and Babylon's Hanging Gardens were probably earth walled. North Africa and the Arab world have a vibrant mud-building tradition with arches, domes, and incised decoration. The Great Wall of China is cored with rammed earth; many of Japan's most sophisticated gardens are mud walled, often whitewashed. Even in rainy European climates, each country has its earthen architecture: "cob" and "wattle-and-daub" in England, *leichtlehm* in Germany, or *pisé* in France; each emigrated to the colonies, where examples still survive.

A few landscape architects use earth structures to-day, appreciating soil's sculptural, geomorphic flexibility, plus the unparalleled intimacy it creates, site specific and understated. Albuquerque landscape architects Baker Morrow and Bill Hays have used adobe blocks for garden shelters, walls, seating, even patio pavement. In New Mexico's dry climate, adobe will last nearly twenty years without even a coping. Russell Beatty, a California landscape architect, uses rammed earth for garden walls. The firm of Cochran and Delaney used rammed earth walls based on South African tradition in their African Healing Garden in San Francisco. Although earth building is almost never taught

Figure 6.4   Salvaged during demolition, roof tiles form curbs and gutters, and fill gabion-like planted walls in this urban garden in Oslo, Norway. Crushed tile surfaces paths, and serves as concrete aggregate. Stone, too, is second hand. (*Project:* Snøhetta Landskapsarkitekter. *Photo:* Rainer Stange.)

Figure 6.5   Broken concrete, reused in slabs or crushed as aggregate, demonstrates John Lyle's concepts at the Institute for Regenerative Studies. (*Project and Photo:* John Lyle.)

Figure 6.6   This unpromising site was reborn as a garden for Monnens Addis Studio—without major demolition. (*Photo:* Jeffrey Miller.)

in landscape courses, it is energy efficient, nontoxic, and self-recycling.

Technically, only sun-dried bricks of earth are "adobe."[13] Other earth building includes "puddled" or "coursed" adobe, a poured-in-place approach. Rammed earth uses forms filled with moist (not wet) cement-stabilized earth, tamped solid in six-inch lifts; "pressed adobe" is rammed blocks; and "stabilized" adobe is the old-fashioned sun-dried brick, with a little asphalt emulsion added. *Adobe quemado* is a porous, low-fired brick, made on-site, typical of Mexico and parts of Arizona.

Soil cement is ordinary soil mixed with a few percent Portland cement. Many examples survive from New Deal public works and national parks structures, most still in good shape today. For soil paving that blends

Figure 6.7 The Monnens Addis renovation in progress. (*Project:* Miller Co. *Photo:* Jeffrey Miller.)

Figure 6.8 The finished Monnens Addis garden gives no hint of its former derelict status. (*Project:* Miller Co. *Photo:* Jeffrey Miller.)

Figure 6.9 Earthen landscape construction graces hundreds of historic sites, including Japan's most refined gardens. (*Photo:* Kim Sorvig.)

aesthetically with the site, several companies offer binders or stabilizers. These save importing bulk materials. The resulting surface is impervious, with runoff problems similar to asphalt or concrete.

Many but not all types of soil can be used for earth building. Highly organic, silty, and shrink-swell soils should be avoided. The National Bureau of Standards even has a formula: 17 percent clay, 24 percent silt, 19 percent coarse (angular) sand, and 40 percent fine sand. More than 30 percent clay causes shrinkage

cracks; added straw can help and adds slight tensile strength. About 10 percent water is the right consistency for forming adobes, while rammed earth is better at 7 percent. Stabilization uses either asphalt (about 4 percent) or cement (not more than 6 percent) to slow water absorption and surface erosion of blocks. The compressive strength of adobes ranges from 300 to 600 psi, strong enough for arches and carving. Rammed earth is considerably stronger.

Construction with adobes is wonderfully flexible. Just about any item can be embedded (from tiles to mailboxes); existing trees are often simply flowed around. The material seems to evoke artistic improvisation (Figure 6.10).

To shelter a freestanding landscape wall, an Asian- or Spanish-style tile coping projecting beyond the wall face is best. Concrete caps, placed like plaster on the top of the wall, actually accelerate erosion of the softer wall below. A waterproof foundation is also advisable. Traditionally, though, permanence in earth construction is achieved using the technique that makes Taos Pueblo the oldest continuously inhabited structure in North America: a new skin of mud plaster every couple of years.

One interesting variation on adobe is on-site firing, invented by Iranian-born architect Nader Khalili. By placing simple oil-fired burners inside a domed adobe house (or, for landscape walls, under ceramic-

Figure 6.10 Adobe is one of the most flexible materials to work with, and inspires site-specific construction that celebrates existing features like this tree. (*Photo:* Kim Sorvig.)

fiber blankets), the whole structure is fired and glazed. Khalili has also experimented with self-hardening sandbag walls, and other resource-efficient building methods.

Adobe is *both* the most expensive building material (if made commercially and trucked to the site) and the cheapest—if done by hand on-site. One study showed that for 1.5 gallons of gasoline, a dozen standard bricks can be fired and transported—or ninety adobes can be made using an on-site machine. Each adobe has the same volume as a dozen common bricks, and is ninety times as energy efficient. Hand-pressed adobes require so little fuel energy that they hardly register on the embodied energy scale.

Unstabilized earth-built structures also self-recycle: as long as they are maintained and used, they are lasting and solid, but once abandoned, they slowly return to the earth.

Earth building does pose one sustainability problem: the sandy loam soils that work best for adobe may also be the best agricultural soils an arid region has to offer. Stabilized adobe takes soil out of agricultural use for much longer, similar to fired bricks. Ideally, only poor soils from the building's footprint should be used for earth building.[14]

Find and Reuse Off-site Salvage

When materials are not available on-site, nearby sources are worth finding. Municipal greenwaste is one example (p. 112). Any salvage that slows the endless stream of waste going to landfills is worthwhile. Metal, wood, glass, brick, and concrete are often recycled, yet are also *reusable* landscape materials.[15] If they can be sourced locally, such materials can be reconfigured in artful landscapes *without* resource-intensive industrial recycling.

Stone

Reused stone may be particularly applicable for public projects: public-works departments often stockpile granite curbing and other used stone elements. Salvaged stone was used evocatively at Parque da Cidade in Oporto, Portugal (Figure 6.12). Sidonio Pardal, the park landscape architect, reused salvaged

granite to construct retaining walls and other structures, including faux ruins. One such "ruin" overlooks
the park's lake, resembling the remains of some fabu-
lous palace; in it are irrigation controls for the park.
Many other structures, in a variety of styles, could
be constructed with salvaged stone. Not all designers
approve of "fake" features, although reused materials
lend themselves to fantasy. The presence of salvaged,
durable stone can lend a remarkable sense of history
and place to new landscape work.

Timber

The challenge in using salvaged materials is not simply to make do with secondhand resources but to create visually powerful design and compelling places.
Landscape architect Marjorie Pitz accomplished this
when she constructed The Sacred Circle, a temporary
(1998) AIDS memorial, in Loring Park, Minneapolis

MN. Her budget was only $2,500. "My project in-
volved significant structure, which made the jury won-
der if it would be possible to pull it off with such a
limited budget," notes Pitz. "The use of salvaged materials made it feasible."

The Sacred Circle consisted of twelve "tree trunks"
made of salvaged utility poles, donated by the local
utility after removal from another Pitz project site.
Pitz's concept was to wrap the poles with saplings to
symbolize AIDS victims cut down in their prime, but
she was reluctant to cut trees of value to anyone. She
was able to locate, through her network of colleagues,
a farm outside Minneapolis on which willows were
being removed to restore native prairie. The property
owner had lost a cousin to AIDS and was happy to see
the saplings salvaged. Finding the poles and saplings
required a certain amount of scouting, compared to
the more usual route of obtaining materials through
a salvage dealer.

Figure 6.11   Reuse of stone can be monumental (see Parque de la Cidade, Oporto, p. 275, and Malinalco, p. 267) or
small-scale. At Millennium Park's Lurie Garden in Chicago, stone countertop scrap gives textured detail to walkways,
recalling similar uses of broken tile in traditional gardens. (*Project:* Terry Guen Design Assoc. *Photo:* Ryan Mikulenka.)

Crushed Glass

Crushed glass, or cullet, is a versatile recycled material. It can replace sand or gravel in many applications; its inherent beauty suits it to many decorative purposes. Even high-end projects, such as Los Angeles County Museum and Mandalay Bay Hotel in Las Vegas, have used recycled glass in their landscapes.[16]

Cullet is used in concrete, asphalt, and other paving mixes; as an ingredient in tiles and similar remanufactured products (p. 281); and as a fill material to replace aggregate. Glass for all landscape uses is tumbled to smooth away sharp edges.

"Glasphalt," replacing aggregate and sand with crushed glass, has been used in pedestrian and bike paths, parking areas, and even roads—up to 10 percent glass without instability or cracking. Cullet cannot be used without other aggregates because it is not as strong as crushed rock.[17] New York City, through a joint venture between its departments of sanitation and transportation, has made a commitment to using glasphalt in all repaving projects.

A glasphalt bike/pedestrian path leads to the top of the artificial hill at Danehy Park, a former landfill. (See p. 96.) Merle Ukeles's project combined community involvement, recycled materials, and artistic intent, recalling sacred Indian mounds. Twenty-two tons of glass were mostly collected by schoolchildren and community groups; a Washington manufacturer donated ten tons of scrap stained glass, normally considered unrecyclable, and a New York mirror manufacturer donated surplus. Because the state of Massachusetts had never used glasphalt, it requested testing at New York City's glasphalt plant.[18]

One caveat in specifying glass for paving is a small potential for contamination—not from the glass itself but from lead off wine bottles. Producers are required to test periodically for contamination; in properly handled cullet, lead should not be a problem. Test projects in King County WA have not detected appreciable lead leaching.[19]

Coarse recycled cullet is used as fill material. For drainage trenches, Glass Aggregate Corporation makes a cullet product called Redpak. It consists of cylindrical geotextile sacks filled with glass, placed end to end in a trench, which is then backfilled. The concept is similar to French drains (Principle 4) or reservoirs used under porous paving (Principle 5). Geotextile sacks filled with crushed glass are also used for erosion control.

Using glass in trenches and sacks nullifies its inherent beauty. It is an attractive replacement for gravel in walkways and garden borders, used at Seattle's Jardin Encore recycling exhibit. (See Figures 6.14 and 6.19.) Intriguing and semitransparent, cullet comes in green, amber, and clear; more exotic blues and reds are sometimes available. For walkways, the King County (WA) Commission for Marketing Recyclable Materials rec-

Figure 6.12 A "recycled folly" in Parque da Cidade, made of stone salvaged around the city of Oporto, Portugal. Many salvaged materials are becoming expensive because of demand for their weathered appearance. (*Project:* Sidonio Pardal. *Photo:* Lynn Miller.)

ommends screened glass, one-quarter to one-sixteenth inch, a consistency somewhat like coarse sand.

Reused Tires

Worn-out rubber tires are familiar decorative elements in vernacular landscapes, used as planters or to define a rural driveway. The classic tire swing attacks the recycling problem one tire at a time, while entertaining children of all ages; variations reshape a tire into a horse, goose or other animal. A few artists have mastered tires as a sculptural material. The Belgian artist Wim Delvoye carves intact car tires into intricate lacework wreaths, and twists cycle tires into improbable DNA-like loops. Ji Yong-Ho, from Seoul, South Korea, cuts and layers pieces of tire to create life-size animals, humans, and mythical hybrids (below). These intricate sculptures aren't immediately identifiable as recycled rubber at all.

Increasingly, whole scrap tires are finding pragmatic

Figure 6.13   In the hands of a master, recycled tires over stainless steel frames create astonishing textured animals like *Rhinoceros 1* (2009; 450 × 150 × 180 cm, stainless steel, used tires). (*Project and Photo:* Ji Yong-Ho [yonghoji.com/].)

Figure 6.14   At the Northwest Flower and Garden Show, Jardin Encore is primarily made of recycled materials, including glass, wood, and iron. A new exhibit each year promotes recycling in the landscape. (*Project:* King County Commission for Marketing Recycled Materials. *Photo:* David McDonald.)

and functional landscape uses, such as stream-bank and slope stabilization, check dams, and marine construction, and, filled with soil and plastered, as walls. (Tires should be cleaned thoroughly before reuse to remove any surface contaminants. For crumb rubber, see below.) These uses may slightly deflate the monstrous national glut of scrap tires, which increases by 280 million each year.[20]

Scrap tires, laid flat and buried into a slope, can create low garden terraces. Up to several feet high they can be built without reinforcement.

The Oklahoma Department of Environmental Quality, concerned about stream-bank erosion and more than 3 million waste tires in 200 illegal dumps, is promoting a single solution to both problems: armoring stream banks with tires. This approach not only reuses waste, but is also lower in cost and simpler to build than riprap or concrete bank stabilization. Tires for such projects are locally obtained from gas stations, tire dealers, and junk yards, minimizing transport. At least eighteen projects have been built, varying from 300 to 4,750 feet in length, protecting roads, bridges, and oil pipelines threatened by collapsing stream banks.

Overall, about 500,000 waste tires have been used in these projects.[21] Two to ten rows of car or truck tires are used, depending on bank height. Cost is low, typically $20 to $30 per linear foot. For one dem-

onstration project near Weatherford OK, 1,800 feet of stream bank was stabilized with ten rows of tires for $70,000—about $39 per foot—far less than the estimated $550,000 for regrading and riprap. Installation requires little skilled labor or machinery; in Oklahoma, it is typically done at no cost by work-release prison inmates. Where inmate labor is not available, such projects could conceivably be installed by community volunteers.

Bank construction is quite straightforward. Rows of tires are placed along the water line lying flat; tires ascending the bank are placed upright. Cables tie each row together, anchored into the ground using dead-

Figure 6.15   Tires and broken concrete achieve unexpected elegance as terraces at the Institute for Regenerative Studies. (*Project and Photo:* John Lyle.)

men (buried logs) at fifty-foot intervals and at least fifty feet back from the bank. Little or no stream-bank grading is required. After installation, silt settles inside the tires, further anchoring them. Over time, most are completely buried, forming a new and more stable bank. Native Black Locust is planted in these banks for its fast-growing fibrous root system.

In Pima County AZ, Stuart Hoenig, professor of agricultural and biosystems engineering at the University of Arizona, along with engineer Joshua Minyard, directed construction of a check dam made of 2,000 passenger-car tires. Five layers of tires were placed on their sides, held together by plastic bands, reinforced by quarry rock between each layer, and anchored to the arroyo sides like a conventional concrete structure. Funded by the state and approved by the Army Corps of Engineers and Arizona Department of Water Quality, the project shows institutional acceptance of "alternative" technology. Construction costs, including labor from the county probation service, totaled only $6,000. A year after installation, vegetation had begun to grow in the arroyo for the first time in years, and a road upstream no longer washed out as previously.[22]

Tires are available baled, stacked like straw bales for construction. Sliced sideways like bagels, tires have been laid under lawns to retain water. They can also be reused as flotation materials for docks, marinas, and wetland boardwalks. Topper Industries of Battle Ground WA uses discarded tires this way and finds them cheaper than other floats. According to Topper, nothing leaches from tires; they are biologically inert, making them ideal as floats in sensitive wetlands.[23]

Other interesting products made from scrap tires are turning up on the landscape market. In New South Wales, Australia, Tyredrain Australia has patented a system for drainage channels from half sections of recycled tires, much cheaper than concrete channels. Tyredrain is seeking to license the idea in other countries. In Fort Dodge IA, Dodger Enterprises promotes whole, cut, and shredded tires for varied landscape uses. One-inch tire chips spread on bare soil can control wind erosion and hold moisture and heat for seed germination. Dodger also offers cut-out sidewall rings to protect bare slopes. On slopes of 3:1 or less, the rings are simply laid next to each other. On steeper

Figure 6.16   Check dams reuse waste tires to stabilize an arroyo in Arizona. Tires in the trench form a footing for the dam at the upper level. (*Project and Photo:* Stuart Hoenig and Joshua Minyard.)

Figure 6.17   Strapped in place, tires form a strong, flexible structure that traps sediment and eventually supports plants. Some systems incorporate live staking. (*Project and Photo:* Stuart Hoenig and Joshua Minyard.)

slopes they can be tied together as a blanket. Grass grows through and between them.[24]

None of these tire structures is particularly beautiful, at least until completely overgrown (though Ji Yong-Ho's work proves they could be). Nor will they please believers in pristine landscapes. However, they show one environmental problem solving another. This mimics natural systems in a very fundamental way—one organism's waste is another's resource.

Specify Remanufactured Materials

Recycled materials specifically for landscapes are widely available today. What distinguishes them from products discussed above is energy to recycle the material, rather than reuse it. (This distinction frequently blurs.) The EPA's Comprehensive Procurement Guideline database has information on a range of recycled landscape materials a large agency might specify, though there are many more on the residential market.[25] Recycled content is found in glass-brick pavers; asphalt, rubber, and rubber-asphalt pavers and patching materials; lumber; used brick; reclaimed stone; plastic lumber; tile; resilient flooring; exterior paint and lacquer thinner; and tire structures. Much outdoor furniture is made of recycled plastic, as is the entire Invisible Structures line of soil retention and alternative paving materials.

Like any newly introduced material, recycled products are subject to market whims. For "plastic lumber," an industry database[26] listed thirty-three manufacturers as of 2016, and it is universally available, even from large home-improvement chains. By comparison, in 1992, when I wrote an early *LAM* article concerning plastic lumber,[27] there were fewer than half a dozen brands. By contrast, strawboard, a chipboard substitute made from agricultural wastes, once seemed promising, but by 2005, of eighteen startups reported by *EBN*, eleven had failed.[28] Among the causes, according to one insider, were enthusiastic expectations of easy marketing because the concept was sustainable.[29]

Plastic Lumber

Plastic lumber—a wood substitute from recycled milk jugs—has become a familiar landscape feature, most commonly as plastic benches and picnic tables. Despite texturing and coloring, plastic lumber lacks the beauty of real wood, but it has distinct advantages.

Plastic lumber is biologically inert—it does not give off toxins, in contrast to preservative-treated woods. This recommends it for use in such sensitive landscapes as wetlands. In wetland boardwalks and overlooks, recycled plastic may be especially appropriate, and environmental permitting agencies are increasingly favoring such uses. (Some plastic lumber, however, is PVC; see concerns, below.)

The fact that plastic can last virtually forever has been a major environmental problem. Plastic lumber turns this into an advantage. It does not rot, splinter, peel, or suffer insect damage. It never needs painting, will not bow or warp with age (though intense heat may cause sagging), and requires minimal maintenance—advantages that offset its initial cost, higher than that of wood. It is very durable, provided it is kept from high heat and is UV-stabilized (ultraviolet light degrades most plastics outdoors).

Plastic lumber provides new, productive uses for some of the immense quantities of throwaway plastic—and saves trees from being cut for lumber. Despite plastic lumber's advantages, its use was hampered for years by lack of reliable data on its strength, shear properties, and other performance criteria. That changed in 1997 when the American Society for Testing and Materials (ASTM) approved a number of testing methods to ensure uniform standards for plastic lumber.[30]

Three main types of plastic lumber are available, in hollow (light-load), solid (moderate), and structural forms:

Single-resin plastic lumber uses a single postconsumer plastic. Other factors being equal, single-plastic lumber provides consistency. (See Table 6.2.) High-density polyethylene (HDPE) is common, and has the advantage of being readily recycled. An increasing amount of PVC-based lumber is on the market. Although it is cheaper that HDPE, and rigid enough to use snap-fittings, PVC remains a material of concern.

Commingled plastic lumber is made with two or more plastics and is generally cheaper. It is potentially variable in physical properties, and difficult to recycle.

Composite plastic lumber is manufactured by mixing

sawdust, wood fiber, bamboo fiber, or fiberglass with plastic; one version, now defunct, recycled carpet scrap. Composites are stiffer than pure plastic lumber, with rougher textures. Structural plastic lumber is usually a fiberglass composite. Composites with more than 50 percent wood or organic fibers are sometimes termed "biocomposites." In rare cases, composites may absorb moisture or suffer insect damage. Composites are not recyclable with current technologies.[31]

Plastic lumber does have some disadvantages. The first is cost: on average, two to three times that of pine lumber. (Life-cycle maintenance costs more than offset this;[32] timber scarcity also affects wood pricing. See p. 18.) Second, plastic lumber is considerably heavier than wood; supports must be designed accordingly. Third, plastic lumber contracts and expands much more than wood, may deform slightly in hot weather, and melts in wildfires; burning PVC releases toxins. Finally, most plastic lumber is much more flexible than wood. In applications like boardwalks, supports for plastic boards must be spaced closer together than wood to minimize sagging. For use as beams and other structural elements, research strength and deflection carefully. Flexibility can be turned to advantage, and many suppliers feature images of sweeping curved decks and inventive patterning.

Plastic lumber was originally considered nonstructural, but most types have proven to have some load-bearing capacity. For decks overlooking the Upper Charles River outside Boston, however, landscape architects Carol R. Johnson Associates (CRJA) specified supporting piers of recycled plastic lumber to avoid leaching into wetlands along the river. Bruce Leish of CRJA notes that the designers did not use plastic lumber for beams or joists for fear it would flex too much, but the plastic piers have caused no problems. In 2010, Struxure, a patented mix of recycled plastics, was introduced by Axion Structural Innovations. The material is available as railroad ties (up to thirty-two feet long), pilings, beams and posts, and tongue-and-groove boardwalks, and has been the main structural material in several bridges carrying trains, heavy trucks, and in one test an MI tank weighing seventy tons. Judging by Axion's website, producing this "recycled structural composite" requires multiple recycled plastic feedstocks, carefully sorted and mixed;

compression of the molded material; and inspection that includes x-raying. The resulting strength should meet and exceed any landscape requirement.[33] Like Invisible Structures and Cali Bamboo (below), Axion is one of a number of companies whose mission starts from reducing material waste.

Working with plastic lumber is generally similar to working with wood: it can be sawed, drilled, and fastened with staples or nails.[34] Expansion can loosen nails, so nuts and bolts or screws are recommended. Unlike wood, most plastic lumber cannot be glued.

Plastic lumber is the most common use of recycled plastic in the landscape, but not the only use. Many grassed paving systems (see p. 254) are recycled plastic. The entire Invisible Structures (Aurora CO) line of landscape products is recycled plastic. A relatively

Figure 6.18   Recycled plastic lumber piers support decks along the Upper Charles River near Boston. Metal "pinned foundations" cause almost no site disruption and can be removed or adjusted easily. (*Project and Photo:* Carol R. Johnson and Associates.)

unusual recycled plastic is "plasphalt," combined like glasphalt as a paving material. It is frequently used in India and the Middle East, and seems to prolong asphalt life in hot, arid, or extremely rainy climates.[35]

Recycled Glass Tile

In addition to minimally processed cullet, glass can be refired in tiles and pavers. Stoneware Tile Company (Richmond IN) manufactures colorful pavers with 70 percent recycled glass content. New Design (Seattle WA) makes recycled glass tiles with a rugged, weathered look. Syndesis (Los Angeles CA) manufactures tile from glass in combination with other waste products such as sawdust and metal shavings. Such decorative products are becoming available at specialty stores.

Garden ornaments may also be crafted from recycled glass. These include decorative garden lanterns, manufactured by New Design. Glass block is available from recycled glass in standard shapes and sizes. Finally, limited-production art glass ornaments are hand-blown from recycled material in some small shops. To the artist's hand and eye, glass—new or recycled—remains an inspiration.

Figure 6.19 Glass fish swim in elegant recycled tile, part of the annual recycled garden exhibit staged by King County WA. (*Project:* King County Commission for Marketing Recycled Materials. *Photo:* David McDonald.)

Crumb Rubber

Discarded tires can be used whole or with minimal processing, as described above. Recycling rubber entails more intensive processing. Many discarded rubber products are ground into "crumb" rubber, resembling coarse sand in texture, then remanufactured.

Crumb rubber has found a number of landscape uses, primarily for surfacing. "Rubberized asphalt" (p. 369) mixes crumb rubber with asphalt; although more expensive than conventional asphalt, it is durable and elastic, reducing road maintenance and noise. Several companies process crumb rubber into resilient surfaces for athletic, safety, and playground use. These greatly reduce injury from falls in high-risk play areas, but are fairly expensive. Loose rubber "mulch," reconstituted mats or tiles, and poured-in-place resilient materials are available, in varied colors, with flexible rubber edging to contain it on-site.

Loose crumb rubber is also proving its worth as a trail-surfacing material. Polk City FL ground 10,000 scrap tires to surface the forty-nine-mile Withlacoochee State Trail—the first time Rails-to-Trails Conservancy used crumb rubber for this purpose. In Georgia, a sloping hundred-yard trail at Tallulah Gorge State Park was paved with ground tires donated by the manufacturer, Phoenix Recycled Products, to see how it would withstand heavy usage. The trail, which is wheelchair accessible, is resisting erosion. Georgia's Spalding County has ground scrap tires for a pedestrian trail at Airport Road Park; elderly users in particular like the trail because it is smooth and easy on their feet. The country received a $100,000 waste reduction grant from the state for this experimental project.[36]

Ground tires have also been used as a replacement for gravel in some drainage designs, and as fill.

Other Recycled Materials

Plastics, glass, and rubber are the most common and visible recycled materials in landscape use today. Some other manufactured products are not as easily recognized. Steel and aluminum are regularly recycled in large quantities, but there do not appear to be landscape-*specific* recycled metal products; without a labeling system like that for plastics, it can be hard to tell. Metals are particularly good for recycling in at least one sense: the recycled material is closely equivalent to virgin metal, not the case with many plastics, for instance.

Concrete is crushed and recycled as aggregate and for other uses, keeping this bulky and slow-to-degrade material out of landfills. Asphalt is also recycled; it is unique in that the recycling machinery comes to the asphalt. These large machines mill the surface off an existing road, reheat and mix the asphalt, and lay it down as new paving. It is unclear how energy efficient this process is, but it clearly makes good use of another material that not long ago was discarded after a short service life.

Recycle at the Job Site

Every construction job generates scrap material. Even when using salvaged and recycled products, cutting, fitting, and finishing leave scrap: cutoff boards, whole overestimated items, sawdust, surplus concrete and mortar. Construction machinery produces used blades and spent oils. Construction workers drink from disposable aluminum cans and Styrofoam cups, and buy lunch-wagon meals variously wrapped.

Setting up simple job-site waste sorting is an effective first step for recycling construction materials. On small residential jobs, this may take little more than some bins—just a couple more than for home use. For large jobs, one or more Dumpsters, possibly with internal partitions, may be required. Be sure to locate these in the staging area, where they can be hauled out without site damage at the end of the project.

Properly sorted construction leftovers can be taken to municipal recycling centers in some regions, but others prohibit this. Some commercial recyclers will buy construction salvage. A growing number of communities have special construction recycling programs. Many include a site set aside for *exchanging* construction salvage: those who have usable excess leave it; those who can use materials take them. An alternative to a physical exchange site is a newspaper or Web listing system: those who have materials list them, and others list what materials they need. Civic-minded newspapers, sometimes in cooperation with local governments, businesses, or social service organizations, donate space for these free listings. Habitat for Humanity runs ReStore outlets in many cities; donated construction leftovers are sold at half price.

Starting a construction recycling program takes time and has up-front expenses. One approach to funding such a program is analyzing costs *avoided* by keeping construction materials out of landfills. Even a relatively small exchange program can keep a ton or more a week out of the local dump. Encouraging reuse and avoiding waste are goals appropriate to public-private partnerships. Contractors benefit by reducing their landfill fees; the community benefits by not paying for constant expansion of landfills.

Evaluate Environmental Costs When Choosing Suppliers

Making sustainable choices among sources for similar materials is a big assignment and can be confusing. Concise rules continue to evolve. Some of the more official guidelines and materials certification criteria are covered in detail by Calkins, and *EBN* reports on the frequent controversies and changes that accompany certification. Meanwhile, here are several approaches worth trying.

Evaluate the *distance* between supplier and end user, and the number of intermediate deliveries involved. Does your wood come from California or Brazil? Is it sawed where it is felled, at your supplier, or transported to Michigan or Michoacán for processing?

Evaluate the mode of transport. Are logs floated to the sawmill or trucked (or flown whole to Japan)? If the supply chain has several links, evaluate each. Differences between diesel and gasoline trucks, or between relatively fuel-efficient ships and less-efficient air or land modes, can be significant. Finding out what transportation a supplier uses is not easy, but is information worth seeking.

Evaluate CO_2 production and carbon sequestration. One rule of thumb: for every billion Btu of energy consumed, one-eighth of a pound of CO_2 is released. This applies best to electrical power; avail-

ability and accuracy of data for specific practices and materials continue to improve slowly.

Evaluate embodied energy, a concept discussed in more detail in Principle 7. Like CO_2 figures, what is currently available is limited but useful, likely to be updated and improved by ongoing research.

Evaluate toxicity of materials over their life cycle. In most cases this cannot yet be done quantitatively, but should at least be considered in a reasoned way.

Evaluate each source. Many manufacturers and suppliers are just as green as you are; at the other extreme, many still resist all environmental responsibility. Ask about factory safeguards and mitigation, and about energy awareness. Favor those suppliers who will at least make an honest attempt to discuss these issues, and who are taking appropriate steps to reduce their environmental impacts. This kind of personal relationship-building is critically important if market forces are to drive sustainability and climate-focused construction past official obstructionism.

Use Sustainably Harvested Renewables

Wood is America's renewable resource, the slogan reads. Clearly, wood is the only structural material that is grown, rather than mined. Like recycling, using renewables is a very popular concept and in general worthy of support. But it, too, has limits that must be respected.

The primary limit is the *rate or speed* of renewal. *Given time*, forests can and do renew themselves. Historically, the entire US East Coast was logged by colonists, farmed, then abandoned as small family farms became uneconomical. Today's forests are evidence of renewability—and required a hundred years or more to reach their current size. For forests as well as people, time is the great healer.

If demand for wood is too great and too impatient, the rate of harvesting outstrips regrowth. Quick harvesting limits the size of wood a forest can produce: where old-growth forests once yielded huge beams, forestry today hurries to harvest two-by-twelves. With hasty harvesting, or where destructive methods are used, forest health declines, along with lumber quality. Eventually there comes a point of no return, meaning that at least in that location, the living ability of re-newal is lost. Push a renewable resource too far, and it faces at least local extinction.

In an unlogged forest, dead timber is recycled into soil by insects, fungi, microbes, and periodic fires. This complex natural composting determines how much new growth the forest can produce. Removing timber removes soil-renewing materials; too much removal without some replacement depletes forest soil, like any other. Perhaps the most striking example is tropi-cal rainforest: so much organic material is embodied in living trees, and so little stored in the soil, that carting away timber often leaves a brick-like, near-sterile soil called laterite. If forest is to renew itself on such soil, it will be over millennia, if at all.

For these reasons, the fact that wood is renewable does not give license for unlimited use—contrary to marketing of timber as *infinitely* renewable. Renewabil-ity fits into the Reduce, Reuse, Recycle equation as a form of recycling. As long as reduced use and sal-vage are the first-choice strategies, using renewables is a valuable concept.

Three major ways of managing forest resources for long-term sustainability affect today's market. These are salvaged wood, sustainable harvesting certification, and substituting waste for wood.

Salvage Wood Where Possible

Although mangled framing lumber still is landfilled with other bulldozed waste, salvaging wood during de-molition is becoming more common. Wood from the 1940s or before is particularly valued; harvested from healthier, older trees, it is often denser and stronger than any new lumber sold today. The wood salvage business mostly markets "antique" wood to high-end custom homes, at prices beyond reach for landscape use.

Salvage for landscape use is complicated by several factors. Outdoor timbers suffer from rot, termites, and other insects; they may also be hard to extract from concrete footings. Nonetheless, naturally decay-resistant landscape woods (tropical hardwoods and redwood, in particular, threatened by past overuse) should be salvaged where at all feasible. Similarly, pre-servative-treated lumber can be reused with care and

should be salvaged because there is no environmentally responsible way to dispose of it (see p. 298).

Specify Sustainably Harvested and Processed Wood

As this book's first edition was being published, a ma-jor step toward sustainably harvested wood was an-nounced. The world's largest lumber retailer, Home Depot, phased out all wood products from old-growth forests and required sources to be certified as sustainably managed. Environmental groups such as the Rainforest Action Network, as well as Home Depot's own staff, predicted the move would com-pel the rest of the market, including contractor sales, to follow, which has in fact happened.[37] Home De-pot did not expect its prices or availability to be di-rectly affected by certification. Since 2000, demand has changed lumber pricing so much that measuring the cost, if any, of certification is difficult.

Several organizations certify sustainable lumber. Certification takes into account basic issues of harvest rate and forest health, as well as whether previously untouched forests are cut, or whether clear-cutting is used. Carefully managed methods like "shelter-wood cutting," which selectively takes trees to main-tain health, size, and diversity of the whole forest, are usually required for certification. The use of waste-re-ducing sawmill tools, such as thinner blades and more efficient chippers, is often a consideration; the US Forest service estimates that such techniques reduce wood waste by 33 percent.[38]

Specifiers must become familiar with different cer-tification groups and their criteria. Like the various seal-of-approval systems that have emerged for con-sumer goods and health foods since the 1970s, wood certification is likely to produce both reputable and superficial claims of sustainability. For this very valu-able system to work, informed specifiers must support reputable certifying groups.

One particular conflict over wood certification is worth noting. The foremost sustainable wood certi-fication process is the Forest Stewardship Council's program (FSC). Competing with it is the Sustainable Forestry Initiative (SFI), established by the Ameri-can Forest and Paper Association. There are two ma-jor differences. FSC requires independent third-party verification that forest practices meet the standards, while SFI allows producers to self-certify.[39] In addition, FSC has a "chain-of-custody" approach, so that *products* made with wood from certified forests can also be certified. The SFI approach stops at forest certification. Many US governmental agencies, as well as other specifiers, have adopted FSC standards.[40]

Wood certifiers also work with the US government to curb illegal logging, as well as forced labor in the timber industry. In 2008, Congress amended the Lacey Act, originally about animal poaching, to ban illegally harvested wood imports. Both FSC and SFI, along with many other groups, support this ban because illegal imports drive down US wood product prices. In 2013, FSC initiated cooperation with the US Forest Service's Forest Products Lab to use forensic testing to uncover illegal wood materials. Under Lacey, purchasers who *should know* that a product is illegal can face penalties; only importers have been sued to date, but legal experts counsel that designers and contractors should have a clear policy and procedure ensuring a reasonable effort is made to avoid illegal supplies. Not only imports are involved; at least one high-profile case involved timber stolen from a US national forest. Forced labor, or more bluntly slavery, is an issue in some countries; it too does happen in the United States, particularly abuses against immigrants, whose visa uncertainties can be abused by unscrupulous companies.[41] The State Department offers a tool to identify product types and countries likely to involve illegal practices.

Substitutes for Wood

Straw, paper, and waste wood can substitute for new lumber. Plastic lumber is an example; composites incorporate straw or wood waste. Straw bales are occasionally used in stuccoed landscape walls, substituting for masonry. Wallboards manufactured from straw, primarily for interior use, appeared promising, but as noted above have simply never taken off.

Waste from straw, paper, wood, and woody materials like nut shells has often been nearly triple the comparable year's lumber production, with wheat and rice straw alone equaling the total tonnage of lumber produced.[42] Clearly, if all these wastes could substitute for wood, lumber production could cease for nearly three years without being missed. Just as clearly, these substitutes cannot really replace *all* uses of lumber. Besides, these wastes are in demand for ethanol, compost, and other products. So-called waste materials, however, offer significant opportunities to slow timber use and protect the renewability of forests.

One example of a thoughtful waste-for-timber substitution is plastic lumber production by the AERT company (Junction TX). AERT's product is a composite of recycled PET plastic with juniper fibers, a by-product of pressing scented oil from juniper wood. AERT manages lands from which juniper is harvested for eventual reforestation by more valuable hardwood species.[43]

Another unusual waste-based material that can be used outdoors is PaperStone. Stone-like panels, made from recycled paper fibers and a cashew nut shell liquid (CNSL) binder, have been used as countertops, as outdoor cladding on Starbucks buildings, and for skateboard ramps, where they have proven very durable. In 2006, the company changed from a part-CNSL formula that included some coal- and corn-based phenols, to 100 percent CNSL.[44]

Although bamboo is not a waste product, it is one of the most quickly renewable wood substitutes. In 2010, Cali Bamboo launched "Lumboo," a glulam

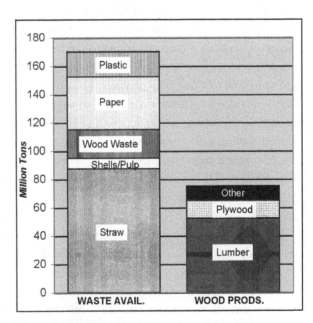

Figure 6.20 Wood products and possible substitutes annual tonnage. (Based on data from P. Fisk.)

bamboo product in sizes similar to dimensional lumber (but smaller because bamboo is so strong). In addition to being strong and renewable, bamboo is high in silica; centuries of construction use in Asia show it to be resistant to termites and rot. Lumboo was aimed at the framing market, but had to be predrilled because it is so dense. Unfortunately, the product was discontinued before its landscape potential could be tested. The company still offers bamboo plywood, as well as an unusually dense and strong plastic composite decking reinforced with bamboo fibers.[45]

Use Nonrenewable Materials Sparingly

Many construction materials are nonrenewable, meaning they are in limited supply and cannot be replenished, as opposed to recycled, after exploitation. Some nonrenewables are relatively harmless in use, like stone; others have additional problems of energy, water, or carbon footprint, and should be used in moderation; others are toxic, in which case avoidance may be appropriate.

Concrete

Concrete is second only to water as most-consumed product on Earth. Global annual use is 1.6 billion tons of cement (requiring 2.4 billion tons of limestone and something on the order of 6.6 trillion Btu of energy, most of it currently from coal, to produce). For concrete, add to this 10 billion tons of aggregate and sand, and a billion tons of water. The cement industry worldwide generates 5 percent of all human-caused CO_2 emissions. Different processes for making cement vary in energy use; older "wet" process can use 52 percent more than the most energy-efficient methods.[46] A 2012 industry report stated that its average carbon footprint had decreased 13 percent in a decade.

Several approaches to reducing concrete's impact are in progress. One is substitution of materials like fly ash (a by-product of coal burning) for part of the cement. So long as these materials, which may contain mercury and other contaminants, are encased in concrete, they appear to be safe, and produce a stronger, more waterproof concrete, though slower to cure.[47]

Civilizations as early as the Minoans appear to have added aluminosilicates called "pozzolans" (which includes fly ash) to their concrete. Roman concrete, which apparently used salt water in the mix, used less limestone, treated at far lower temperatures than Portland cement requires. Examples have endured 2,000 years, as opposed to modern concrete's life expectancy of 30–50 years. Roman concrete has been suggested as a sustainable material, but cures so slowly that modern workers don't consider it viable.[48]

Ordinary Portland cement (OPC) in the United States contains 5 percent unprocessed limestone; a European mix called Portland limestone cement (PLC) contains up to 35 percent limestone. A 2014 Athena Sustainable Materials Institute report found most environmental performance, including energy use, improved about 12 percent for PLC over OPC.[49]

Substitute aggregates, including recycled concrete and other masonry, glass, and recycled plastic, have been used; these may reduce the concrete's weight, as well as avoiding use of virgin gravels. Much of the impact of aggregate is energy for trucking; for a given volume of concrete, this can add 25 percent to the energy consumed for cement itself.[50] Sand, which many take for granted, is scarce enough that illegal mining threatens beaches, rivers, and marine environments, and has even been the cause of murderous "sand wars" in India. Abundant desert sand is unusable in construction because it is too wind-smoothed.[51]

Producers of concrete block have injected CO_2 into the mix in the molding process, sequestering a relatively small amount of carbon and making the blocks stronger, thus requiring about 10 percent less cement. The process, called CarbonCure, has the advantage of being easily retrofitted to conventional production lines.[52]

The equipment used to mix and place concrete strongly affects the material's environmental performance and cost. Ready-mix, as the name implies, is mixed at a plant; from plant to site cannot be longer than ninety minutes or 300 mixer-truck revolutions.[53] A new, high-tech type of truck carries the raw dry materials, in separate bins, plus water to the site; computer-controlled conveyors combine the mix with high accuracy, in precisely the amount needed. Conventional delivery *requires* estimating high (since running short is not an option), leading to waste. The newer method is called volumetric mixing, while the truck itself is called a mobile concrete batch mixer. Many models are available, mounted on truck, trailer, or skids. Some are as small as two cubic yards, potentially ideal for smaller landscape jobs; larger models range to twelve yards or more. One company promoting such machines for their environmental benefits is Habitat Verde, an environmentally focused construction company.

Besides avoiding wasted concrete—important because cement is high in embodied energy and is used in massive quantities—the volumetric concrete delivery method has other sustainability-related advantages.[54] Conventional cement trucks must be loaded at the ready-mix plant less than ninety minutes before each project; this limits how far the project can be from the plant, and requires driving back and forth. It also means that site crews usually wait for the truck or trucks to arrive. A large volumetric truck can be fully loaded the night before so as to arrive early at the site. If the company has several small jobs lined up, the same truck can do them in sequence without ever returning to the yard, a significant savings in fuel.

At the other end of the spectrum, concrete can be mixed by two people working a tarp. Tarps with handles, such as the Rapid Mixer from Seattle-based Brightwork Innovations, are simple and cheap; two people can mix an eighty-pound bag of concrete in ninety seconds. This is ideal for small jobs, but is fast enough to mix and pour many bags before the first starts to set. Although mostly for DIY use, this method uses no fuel, folds for reuse, and could be ideal for small-scale landscape construction or maintenance.

Concrete equipment must be washed before waste concrete has set. Concrete is almost as caustic as Drano and often contains toxic metals; in quantity, it is hazardous to workers, wildlife, soils, and water. Best management practices requiring concrete washout containers are part of the National Pollutant Discharge Elimination System (NPDES) and have become part of permit requirements. Containers may be simple small plastic-lined boxes, on-site straw-bale and plastic arrangements, or metal containers like flattened Dump-

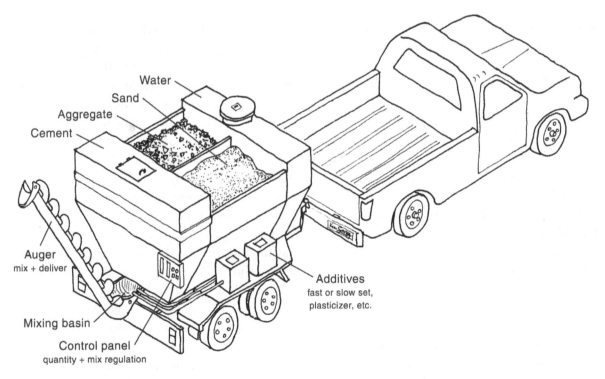

Figure 6.21 Diagram of volumetric concrete mixer, trailer mounted. Precision mixing avoids most waste. Some models can print out a receipt for the exact volume used. (*Diagram:* Kim Sorvig, based on information online from Nurock and Omega.)

sters. Some systems sieve sand and gravel out for reuse; water may be reused to wash more equipment, treated in wastewater facilities, or allowed to settle and evaporate. Solidified waste concrete should be recycled as aggregate.[55] The more accurate actual quantities can be, the less waste and washout are entailed.

Asphalt

Occurring in geological deposits, or as a by-product of crude oil refining, asphalt is a nonrenewable material widely used for paving and waterproofing. Although asphalt is mostly specified by engineers, landscape professionals should be aware of three strategies that save material as well as energy: warm-mix, thinlay surfacing, and on-site recycling. Reducing the quantity of paving should still be the first priority.

Conventional "hot-mix" asphalt is mixed at 300°F–350°F. Warm-mix is between 15 and 100 degrees cooler. This uses significantly less energy and produces fewer fumes. Warm-mix stays workable much longer than hot-mix, significantly increasing the distance it can be transported before use. It can also be placed when weather is too cold for hot-mix. The percentage of work done with warm-mix has risen quickly; as of 2013 it was 30 percent of the asphalt paving market.

Thinlay surfacing is a repair technique. At five-eighths of an inch thick, it uses significantly reduced quantities of asphalt and is quick to place. It is thus favored for projects where disruption of traffic must be minimized. By fixing rough surfaces, it reduces fuel consumption by cars.

On-site recycling involves grinding off the existing damaged surface, heating it, adding material if necessary, and placing it as a new surface. This is typically done with large machines, but might be possible for certain landscape-related jobs. Warm-mix techniques have helped make on-site recycling of asphalt more common.[56]

Reducing Use of Other Nonrenewables

Stone has been called "the original green material," but is still nonrenewable. Because of its weight, sourcing stone from long distances (including other continents, conventionally) has significant energy impacts. Good design can reduce quantities, as well as avoid some waste. In addition, stone can be reused and then recy-

cled, possibly several times, cutting it into successively smaller units, and ultimately crushing it for aggregate. The impacts of aggregate mining can be significant, so reducing quantities is a step toward sustainability.

Clay brick involves significant energy in firing. The Brick Industry Association estimates that about 235 million bricks are used in landscape projects nationally. Design for paving (open basket-weave, for instance) and freestanding walls (serpentine single-width) can halve the number of bricks used. Brick is reusable and recyclable. Consolidation of the industry, from 3,000 plants around 1950 to 200 in 2010, has resulted in longer transport; increased transportation, made cheap by fossil-fuel subsidies, almost certainly negates the "efficiency" of centralized production.

Avoid Toxic Materials

Some materials must be handled correctly, and others used sparingly if at all, to avoid costly hazards to human health and the environment.

An important addition to Nelischer's guidelines (p. 264) is whether a material is hazardous, and if so under what circumstances. Toxic materials can threaten construction workers, as well as anyone using the finished landscape. Hazards to the larger environment are not always visible on-site. In many instances, contractors or designers can act directly to reduce toxic exposure. In other cases, the combined influence of environmental professionals and other industries is required to affect pervasive or hidden hazards.

Toxic and hazardous materials affect landscape construction differently from effects in buildings. Radon is a good example. It is an indoor hazard, but a normal outdoor condition.[57] If trapped in unventilated buildings (or mines, where it was first noticed), concentration makes radon hazardous. Such variation does not justify dismissing concern about materials that are only hazardous in high concentrations, however. "Even too much water will kill you" is a posture that seldom promotes rational debate, let alone sustainability. It is critically important to know *at what point* a substance becomes toxic, and whether its toxicity is cumulative. If either is unknown, err on the side of caution.[58]

Responsible professionals must analyze how and where a material will be used, as well as how it is produced, transported, disposed of, or recycled. A few landscape materials (below) are so hazardous that their use is truly unsustainable. More frequently, toxicity is one important consideration among many in comparing material life cycles. (See Table 6.1.)

Anticipate Hazards from Prior Land Uses

Sites never developed for modern use seldom hold hazardous materials. In rare cases, site geology may produce hazards. An example is serpentine, a rock toxic to plants and humans. At Potrero Heights, a hillside housing development in San Francisco, prominent soil-filled retaining walls are a response to serpentine bedrock. Initial plans calling for terraced grading were abandoned on discovering serpentine, which releases toxins when excavated. Such hazards, however, are uncommon.

On brownfields and similar sites, toxic materials may be present before landscape construction ever begins. Recognizing hazardous materials in the field requires a great deal of experience. The following sections can help with basic knowledge, but clearly not with real-world identification. If contamination is suspected, hire a consultant.

Demolition or remodeling of structures may release hazardous materials. These can include not only landscape-specific materials (below), but also lead paint or asbestos from old buildings, or polychlorinated biphenyls (PCBs) from abandoned utility transformers. Lead used in flashing is found in old roofing waste and in antique garden-wall copings. Building demolition is messy; interior materials may well become part of the landscape. Thus, some materials that play no part in normal landscape construction can be site hazards.

If there has been *dumping* on the site, be alert for an even greater range of hazards. Illegal dumping is common, often affecting remote sites with no history of previous use—sites that may look pristine at first glance—as well as urban lots. It is very difficult to predict what might be in these dumps. Often it is merely household trash (which can still contain many toxics) that some ignoramus refused to take to a landfill (or there was no landfill). Some illegal dumping is deliberate criminal disposal of industrial or medical hazardous waste, dumped to avoid regulation, and could be truly deadly. Owners of farms and small businesses,

ignorant of hazards, used to dispose of wastes on-site. Public awareness has decreased this kind of dumping, but it still goes on. Pesticides, oils, solvents, old vehicles, and batteries may have been buried in such private dumps, sometimes in quantity. Neither illegal nor small-user dump sites are usually documented, unlike larger industrial sites.

If the site has ever been used industrially, be on the lookout. Soil and water can be contaminated by pollutants settling out of air around a factory, by leaching from stockpiles, or by tanks leaking, as well as by deliberate on-site disposal. Industrial pollution frequently spreads to neighboring sites; air and water pollutants can move long distances. Fortunately, public records usually indicate types of past land use at industrial sites, which can help predict hazards.

The following industrial operations are common sources of heavy metals, some of the more dangerous soil contaminants:

- electroplating (cadmium, chromium, nickel)
- battery production or use (cadmium, lead, nickel, zinc)
- paints and painting (cadmium, chromium)
- mining (arsenic, copper, nickel)
- metal production and products (chromium, copper, lead, mercury, zinc in brass and for galvanization)
- pesticides and preservatives (arsenic, copper, mercury)
- rubber production (zinc)
- petroleum and coal (arsenic)
- plastics (cadmium)
- fire brick (chromium)
- fly ash (copper)
- fertilizers (copper).

A number of manufacturing catalysts may leave traces of mercury. Nickel and lead traces can be carried and deposited by rain or air, far from their industrial sources.[59] A wide variety of industrial and household products may leave organochlorides and volatile organic compounds (VOCs). Some agricultural chemicals are very persistent, including DDT (banned in 1973, but still used against much-feared insects like tussock moth); arsenic or cyanide pesticides were often used in old orchards.

While actual remediation of hazardous sites is a task for specialists (see p. 89), landscape architects and contractors need to know what "red flags" to watch for. Removing found contaminants can add thousands of dollars to a project and subjects workers to hazards. *Failure* to remove such pollutants can harm workers and end users, leaving owner, designer, and builder open to lawsuits. It is far cheaper and smarter to investigate the possibility of existing hazards before work begins. Some basic methods:

- Check available records, such as land title, historical zoning maps, and other legal documents, for clues to land use over the past century. Watch for industrial uses, as well as agricultural ones.
- Carefully inspect the site for signs of dumping. On previously undeveloped sites, refuse is usually aboveground. If previous use seems likely to have generated hazardous wastes, look for ground disturbance or peculiar vegetation patterns. Try to imagine a convenient and accessible dump site, and how (or whether) people might have tried to hide it.
- Field-testing kits are available for early warning of hazards. For example, Labware Safety Supply lists kits to detect lead, PCBs, or chlorine in soils; other kits reveal liquid toxics. One test (in a kit of six to ten) costs about five dollars, a small price if it avoids a serious problem. Advertised as requiring no special training, they indicate in five to ten minutes whether hazards are above or below a safety standard, usually by an unmistakable color change. No substitute for specialist analysis, such tests can give a quick reading of potential hazards.
- If *anything* indicates serious contamination, get advice from specialists in hazardous waste mitigation. Trying to remove wastes yourself can subject you and your client to red tape and costs at least, and prosecution at worst.
- If you work in areas where many contaminated sites are found, investigate whether you or your client can be insured against unforeseen costs and liabilities related to cleanup.

Lest anyone think that these "engineering" matters are too complex for landscape architects, consider the Boston firm whose principals are Nina Brown, Clarissa Rowe, and Alison Richardson. They have developed, almost accidentally, a specialty in design for contaminated sites. In urban areas, it is hardly necessary to seek out such projects: many sites, especially those left to the public as open space, are blessed with fruits of industry and illegal dumping. Brown, Richardson + Rowe has uncovered buried car-battery dumps, extensive engine-oil spills, and, on one project, the threat of the biological warfare agent anthrax. Taking it all in stride, the three partners often interpret site history as part of their designs. (They usually collaborate with environmental specialists; see p. 89.)

Be Aware of Direct Hazards from Construction

The list of products, including building materials, suspected of causing health problems for people is a long one. Most research done on such toxicity, however, refers to *indoor* air quality.[60] Many chemicals, including some naturally occurring ones, are hazardous when trapped within walls and concentrated; adequate ventilation is the main user precaution. Since landscapes are by definition open-air places, hazardous chemicals are quickly diluted outdoors, greatly reducing *direct* risk to users.

Use of toxic materials in landscapes, however, raises different questions than the same materials used indoors. In the early days of environmental awareness, a popular slogan decreed that "dilution is the solution to pollution." This has proved shortsighted. The very openness that lets toxic chemicals dilute into air also means that they are free to move beyond the site. Some biodegrade, but others accumulate in ever-increasing quantities in air, water, or soil. Increased levels of global pollution parallel increasing allergies, respiratory diseases, and other chronic conditions, as well as resistant microorganisms and climate change.[61] The *outdoor* use of chemicals known to be hazardous *indoors* may contribute to regional pollution levels even if they do not pose immediate threats to users.

Some individuals suffer from Multiple Chemical Sensitivity (MCS), believed to be severe allergic reaction to chronic pollution. Very small quantities of chemicals, or materials not affecting most other people, cause mild to severe symptoms in MCS sufferers. Design for MCS has produced many advances in knowledge about "healthy building materials." Lists of such materials are available from a number of books

Table 6.1

Organic and heavy-metal chemicals common in building materials.

Chemical (synonym)	Found In
VOCs	
1,1,1-trichloroethane (methyl chloroform)	Solvent in paints and degreasers
1,2-dichlorobenzene (ortho-dichlorobenzene)	Solvent; fumigants and insecticides; dyes; metal polishes
4-PC (4-phenylcyclohexene)	Solvent; penetrating agent
Acetone	Solvent; lacquers; inks; adhesives; tool cleanup
Acrolein	Herbicides; used in polyurethane and polyester production
Acrylonitrile (vinyl cyanide)	Paints; adhesives; dyes; pesticides; used in plastic production; mixed with wood pulp as "synthetic soil"
Benzene	Very common in production of synthetic chemicals, especially plastics
Carbon tetrachloride (perchloromethane)	Metal degreasers; fumigants; rubber solvent; banned in household-use products
Ethylbenzene (phenylethane)	Solvent in resins; used in styrene production
Formaldehyde (oxymethylene)	Glues, and thus in wood composites, plywoods, and glulams; plastic resins; dyes; preservatives; fertilizers; urea-formaldehyde is least stable, longest outgassing, and cheapest form
Isophorone	Solvent, especially for polyvinyl and other resins; pesticides; specialized lacquers
Methyl ethyl ketone	Solvent in lacquers, paints, adhesives, inks, thinners, cleaners; peroxide of MEK is fiberglass hardener
Methyl isobutyl ketone	Solvent in paints, paint removers, lacquers, adhesives, cleaners; acrylic and vinyl coatings
Methylene chloride (dichloromethane)	Paint removers; degreasers; foams (blowing agent); used in plastic production
Naphthalene (tar camphor)	Dyes; fungicides; moth and animal repellents; cutting fluids and lubricants; coal tar; resins
Phthalate esters	Soft plastics, as plasticizer; hardener for resins; dyes; insecticides (examples: DEHP; phthalic anhydride)
Styrene	Used in production of plastics, synthetic rubber and latex (for adhesives and paints); polystyrene glazing, and Styrofoam
Tetrachloroethane (perchloroethylene)	Degreasers for metals; paint removers; varnishes; insecticides; herbicides; used in production of other chemicals
Toluene (methylbenzene)	Solvent; paints, coatings, plastics, plastic adhesives, cleaners, fuels
Trichloroethylene	Degreasers; paints; fumigants
Vinyl chloride	Used in plastics production, especially PVC; adhesives
Xylene (dimethylbenzene)	Solvent; paints, lacquers, resins, rubber cements, fuels
HEAVY METALS	
Antimony	Lead batteries; bearings; solder; pigments in paints, dyes, stains; metal alloys
Cadmium	Pigments; metal coatings; brazing rods; ceramic glazes; NiCad batteries; electrical parts
Chromium	Pigments for glass and paints; metal and plastic plating; alloys
Lead	Old paints; solder; batteries
Mercury	Mercury-vapor lamps; batteries; electrical controls; mirror plating
Nickel	Alloys; welding; electroplating; batteries

Sources: List from HOK, *Sustainable Design Guide*. Synonyms and "found in" data based on Hawley's *Chemical Dictionary*.

and on the Web; one book even includes sample specifications organized by CSI division.

Relatively few *outdoor* construction materials cause symptoms even for people with MCS. Large areas of hot asphalt are a concern. Pre-emergent herbicides or broad-spectrum insecticides sprayed around foundations and under unit pavers can affect indoor air quality.[62] Problem materials for MCS indoors may be fine outdoors; conversely, some MCS-safe materials are not weatherproof. Nonetheless, MCS deserves consideration in landscape construction and maintenance.

In 2006, the Architectural and Transportation Barriers Compliance Board, which oversees the Americans with Disabilities Act's demands on design, weighed in on green building—negatively. The Board attacked greenroofs because possible leaks or inevitable leaf drop *could* increase indoor molds, and because "plants can emit volatile fumes and pollen"; they consider brownfield redevelopment inappropriate for children or the elderly, essentially dismissing the ability to clean up any site; and they even blame indoor plants, not only for attracting bugs, but for the use of Raid! This is single-focus special-interest advocacy gone far afield indeed.[63] Green building's general reduction of pollution (including greenhouse gases that directly raise pollen levels) clearly outweighs these localized complaints, even for people with disabilities, let alone for the whole planet.

Many landscape materials are in direct soil contact, or unprotected from weather. Either situation may leach toxic materials into soil; taken up by plants, these could enter the food chain. Because of such risks, some outdoor materials may need to be *more* completely nontoxic than their indoor counterparts, just as brick exposed to weather needs to be more durable than interior grades.

Minimize Invisible Hazards Off-site

In addition to on-site hazards, some materials cause environmental problems during either manufacturing or disposal. Even materials completely nontoxic in use may present serious problems at the beginning or end of their life cycle. For genuine sustainability, these invisible issues cannot be ignored. In fact, for most common *landscape* materials, direct toxicity to users appears

to be minor compared to hazards of extraction, manufacturing, and disposal.

Suppliers of basic building materials, like the rest of society, have changed in response to environmental concerns. Many are sincerely committed to reducing environmental impact of their products. Others have improved their records only under threat of regulation. Overall, most basic US industries have made significant improvements in efficiency and pollution control within the past few decades. These improvements have been offset, and even overwhelmed, by increased consumption of goods and depletion of resources due to population pressures. (Humanity has used more raw resources since 1950 than in all prior history, and the trend continues to increase.)[64]

Not even the most conscientious manufacturers can prevent all toxic releases. Spills and accidents during transportation of hazardous materials can release toxics, as can natural disasters, sabotage, and human error. Facilities that *release* little or no pollution to the environment may still expose their own workers to serious hazards. Landscape professionals share a responsibility with other citizens to ensure that foreseeable pollution problems are prevented and that unforeseen problems are kept to a minimum.

Resource extraction is a related off-site issue. Timber and stone, for instance, are nontoxic materials, but conventional forestry and mining practices have caused widespread environmental damage. Transportation of materials causes pollution. As older mines and wells are exhausted, the search for new sources conflicts more frequently with spreading residential areas and parks in particular.

These general production processes, which are very much taken for granted by society, have serious environmental costs.

Impacts of General Production Processes

The following processes contribute to environmental costs of most construction products.

Electrical generation is a major source of CO_2, about one and one-half pounds per kilowatt-hour (from coal). According to the US Office of Energy Efficiency and Renewable Energy, converting a *single* light bulb from 60W incandescent to LED saves forty-eight watts of energy.[65] Over its lifetime the efficient bulb eliminates more than three-fourths of a *ton* of CO_2, fourteen pounds of SO_2, and other pollutants. If the electricity source is nuclear, the same bulb change eliminates generation of twenty-one grams (nearly three-fourths of an ounce) of plutonium, of which one-third of a *micro*gram is said to be enough to kill a person.[66]

Fuel combustion (industrial and vehicular) produces volatile organic compounds (VOCs), sulfur and nitrogen compounds ("Sox and Nox"), CO_2, and carbon monoxide. Diesels produce particulates. Fuel mining has its own impacts.

Petroleum production generates toxic and nontoxic drilling sediments, and air pollutants. Petroleum fuels are burned to drill and maintain wells. Oil spills, flaring of gas wells, poorly designed pipelines, and access roads seriously disrupt habitat. Drilling and fracking may disrupt groundwater. The industry is a poster child for externalization of costs—making the public pay costs of business, both direct (such as road upgrades to support heavy trucks) and indirect (costs of pollution or spills by bankrupt operators). The American Lung Association has estimated that covering the actual health costs of petroleum products would add $1.00 per gallon of gas; war spending to maintain access to Middle Eastern oil, at $30–$50 billion annually, would add $.50 per gallon; other social costs have been estimated at $5.00 or higher.[67] Tax dollars subsidize these costs, individuals pay in lost health or property value, and still the industry insists on tax breaks and exemptions from regulations like the Clean Air Act. Without even caring about the environment or climate change, these costs are reason enough to justify the switch to renewable energy.

Mining can elevate soil erosion rates (see Figure 6.22) up to 2,000 times what occurs in stable forested land. Some kinds of mine tailings give off toxic leachates, poisoning or clogging waterways. Physical site disruption, especially by pit mining, is difficult if not impossible to restore fully.

Logging elevates normal forest erosion rates by up to 500 times. Reduction of forest areas decreases global ability to process CO_2. Burning of slash and waste produces air pollutants. Overharvesting decreases biodiversity; even commercial productivity suffers from monoculture "reforestation."

Construction itself elevates normal erosion rates by up to 2,000 times, causing roughly the same degree of added soil and water problems as mining.

Disposal of materials can release toxic leachates (landfills) and fumes (incinerators). Bulky or nondegradable materials consume landfill space, increasingly at a premium.

In part because of these general impacts, and also because materials and manufacturing methods vary widely, it is important to consider the entire product life cycle when deciding on building materials or construction methods.

Use and Advocate Life-cycle Analysis (LCA)

Life-cycle analysis (LCA) takes into account the entire sequence of material production, use, and disposal or reuse. (See Figure 7.16.) At each life-cycle stage, energy consumption, toxicity, resource depletion, potential for misuse, and other factors are accounted

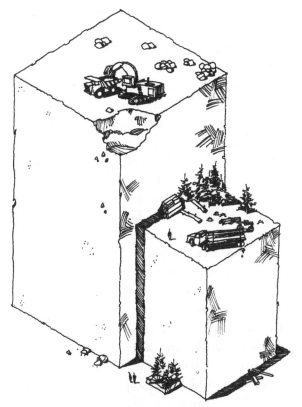

Figure 6.22 Erosion from healthy forests averages 0.0375 ton (seventy-five pounds) per acre per year. Logging raises this 500 times, while mining and construction raise it 2,000 times. (*Illust.*: Craig Farnsworth.)

for. Comparisons are made between whole life cycles, rather than between materials at the point of use. Examples include the Center for Resourceful Building Technology's *Guide to Resource Efficient Building Elements*, the AIA's *Environmental Resource Guide*, and a checklist for materials selection developed by *EBN*. Each offers guidelines for determining whether a product is in tune with sustainability over its life cycle.

Pliny Fisk points out that many LCA approaches are manufacturer-specific and suffer from limited data. While he supports the overall idea of "cradle-to-cradle" analysis, his own research is based on national statistical databases that make it possible to look at the life cycle of all materials of a specific kind, not just products from a few manufacturers. A study using national data was published in the 1980s by Stein and others. Still often cited, its data were collected in the late 1960s. Fisk's work, called BaselineGreen and GreenBalance, offers a method of computing up-to-date, detailed, and nationally averaged information.[68] With the advent of Big Data, it ought to be reasonable to expect such comprehensive accounting, regularly and automatically updated, of the actual costs of materials.

Although LCA (which in the broad sense includes Fisk's work) is probably the best basis for materials selection, there are difficulties applying *existing* LCA studies to landscape construction. Most existing research has focused on life cycles related to *buildings*. Basic materials are used differently in landscape applications; their life cycles may not be comparable to the same material used as a building component. In trying to make LCA information accessible to architects, many authors have also focused on building "assemblies" such as structural insulated panels or complete framing systems. These are seldom relevant to landscape construction.

Landscape-specific studies of materials, covering their whole life cycles as used outdoors, remain needed. Although much greater attention to these issues has been paid in landscape publications since 2000, full-scale original studies of this type remain rare. Studies of architectural materials sometimes include basic materials, but not necessarily in easily accessed form. Some basic information about toxicity and energy of landscape-specific materials is posted online (see p. xxv) in hopes that wider availability of this information will encourage landscape professionals and researchers to develop life-cycle studies of *landscape* materials in greater depth.

Construction and maintenance materials are being evaluated as part of governmental "environmentally preferable purchasing" (EPP) programs. "Bio-based" products, such as oils, alternative fuels, and paints, are often encouraged by EPP standards, and used in landscape maintenance (see p. 380).

Know General Toxicity Issues by Material Type

Publications on toxicity are mostly organized by technical names of chemical ingredients. It is possible to look up DEHP or 1,1,1-trichloroethane, but not to find out what each is used in; nor have I found any central site to look up "plastic pipe" or "oil-based paint" and get information on their chemical ingredients. This section gives an overview of toxicity and hazard issues specific to landscape materials, and a list of materials under names more recognizable to design and construction professionals.

This section *summarizes* hazards and concerns associated with basic landscape materials. Many minor hazards, important for particular sites or clients, are not noted. Detail on forty-nine common materials (the first edition's appendix) is now online (see p. xxv). That information is organized *by material*, and notes main ingredients or emissions associated with each. Situations when a material may pose special risks (such as accidental fires or improper disposal) are also noted.

For some materials, and for most chemical ingredients, Safety Data Sheets (SDS) from suppliers provide more detail than most landscape professionals will need. For any construction material, identify main ingredients that pose hazards, and then read the SDS for each ingredient. Several websites make SDS information available; federally sponsored ones are at risk of disappearance.

Published information indicates that most landscape construction materials, in the forms to which end users are exposed, are *relatively* nontoxic to humans. Their toxic effects on regional environments are not well understood. All construction materials require proper use and disposal, and continued improvement in handling and emission control by manufacturers. Alternative materials with fewer toxic effects are becoming increasingly available for many types of products.

Of the common landscape materials reviewed, only two (PVC and wood preservatives, below) are of such environmental concern that serious calls have been made to ban them outright. Controversy over these materials is discussed in the next section, along with a scandal concerning toxic materials relabeled as fertilizers.

Coatings, adhesives, and solvents expose users to hazardous fumes during application and curing. These volatile organic compounds (VOCs) have been reduced considerably in recent formulas, but still can harm both the user and the broader environment. More than 50 percent of all US use of paints and coatings is for construction work.[69] Some types of specialized outdoor paints (pavement marking or survey "flagging" paints) have unusual formulas, for example to allow use during freezing weather. Such proprietary formulas are often secret, concealing possible dangers.

Postconsumer disposal, accidental fires, and spills present problems for many plastics, coatings, preservatives, adhesives, and solvents. Improper and illegal disposal is one facet; officially approved disposal has also been criticized, especially incineration and waste-as-fuel in cement kilns and other industrial facilities.

Many plastics, coatings and preservatives, adhesives, and solvents, as well as a few metals and fertilizers, have toxic chemical ingredients, precursors, or by-products. Factory mitigation processes control many of these risks adequately, or are making progress toward doing so. Product specifiers have many opportunities to influence suppliers toward safer production and complete disclosure of product and production risks.

Be Aware of Landscape Plastics

Many types of plastics have landscape uses, either in construction or in landscape furniture and furnishings. An unscientific survey of catalogs, home cen-

ters, and garden stores produced Table 6.2, a list of landscape objects, by the type of plastic from which they are made. Many plastic landscape products are not marked with any information to allow identification of component materials.

Avoid Three Controversial Materials

PVC and conventional wood preservatives are toxic enough that reputable organizations, both industry and environmental groups, have called for phasing them out of general use.[70] Such calls, and controversy around them, have increased since this book's first edition. The US PVC industry has responded defensively, often heatedly so. By contrast, wood-preservative manufacturers have taken initiative to develop less-toxic products, with varied results.

A third controversial landscape material is fertilizer. As detailed below, the Associated Press has reported heavy metals, toxic chemicals, and radioactive waste being relabeled as fertilizer—without any actual processing, and no regulation.

Landscape professionals, as major users of PVC, preserved wood, and fertilizers, have a responsibility to know the hazards associated with these materials, and to make informed decisions about using them. Yet many practitioners remain ignorant of these issues, or have been unable to locate and learn to use safer alternatives that are available.[71]

Further detail on these materials is cited in the "online appendix." See p. xxv.

Polyvinyl Chloride (PVC and CPVC)

Evaluating PVC and CPVC is difficult. Many environmentalists regard them as the most dangerous plastics produced. Industry-funded studies and industry marketing materials claim that PVC is perfectly safe, but the director of Ball State's Land Design Institute cautions, "Cast a wary eye toward research funded directly or indirectly by the PVC industry."[72]

PVC is made from the "monomer" vinyl chloride, linked to form the polymer *poly*vinyl chloride. CPVC, also known as PVDC, is PVC made more heat-stable by adding extra chlorine. Many stabilizers and plasticizers are mixed into PVC, often 60 percent of the material by weight, resulting in products ranging from rigid pipe to rubber-like flexibility. They include pollutants like cadmium, lead, tin, and phthalates, and in many ways are more problematic than PVC itself. Unplasticized PVC (uPVC), from which pipe is usually made, has moderate life-cycle impacts, primarily in manufacture and disposal.[73]

Globally, some 50 million metric tons of PVC are produced annually, of which 50–75 percent is used in construction. The main landscape uses are pipe, fencing, and insulation on electrical wire, though some shade cloth and many other incidental products are also PVC; see Table 6.2. Production is growing, especially in the less-regulated Third World, where lead stabilizer is still used in 60–90 percent of output (US PVC no longer uses lead routinely). Greenpeace alleges that when DDT, PCBs, CFCs, and other deadly chemicals made from chloride (organochlorides) were banned in the 1970s, the industry hyped PVC to ensure a market for chlorine, 30 percent of which now goes to PVC manufacture.

PVC remains very popular despite its dangers, for several reasons. The primary reason is familiarity; it is required by many local building codes, despite preferable alternatives. Tensile strength is high, keeping PVC pipes from bursting under pressure. It is easily joined by glue fittings (the glue is toxic, and heat-joined systems like polypropylene leak less). It is relatively cheap in today's economy (although energy intensive to produce, and thus susceptible to energy-cost increases).

End-use issues: Chlorine compounds and additives including lead have been reported to leach from PVC pipe into water supply, especially when the water is chlorinated. The state of California requires labeling of all "vinyl" garden hoses (vinyl is essentially PVC with plasticizers) as follows: "This product contains chemicals known to cause cancer and birth defects or reproductive harm. Do Not Drink From This Hose." PVC is banned for food containers, and health-care giant Kaiser Permanente bans PVC from its hospitals.

End users can also be affected by gases if PVC accidentally burns or smolders, as when wiring insulated with PVC overheats. PVC in the World Trade Center caused a dioxin cloud that hung over Manhattan after 9/11. Designers of tunnels, ships, and other enclosed public spaces routinely specify non-PVC-coated wiring because of the danger of toxic smoke.

The Institute of Horticultural Research (Wellesborne UK) has documented that DBP, an additive used in PVC greenhouse glazing strips, kills or injures plants at low airborne concentrations. The institute documents such damage to greenhouse crops since the 1930s. Outdoor landscape plants are less likely to be damaged.

Production issues: Despite industry improvements, PVC and CPVC still risk release of dioxins and other highly toxic chemicals during manufacture and transport. Many common additives are neurotoxins or carcinogens; several common plasticizers are banned outright in Europe. Vinyl chloride is a known carcinogen; incomplete polymerization can leave leachable traces of this monomer in PVC. Liquid vinyl chloride is the glue used by PVC installers, such as irrigation contractors; other workers with vinyl chloride have shown extremely elevated risk for liver cancer. The US EPA's National Toxicology Program rates liquid vinyl chloride as "ultrahazardous"; a 2005 Bush-era emergency law banned its transport through Washington DC.

PVC's main ingredient, chlorine, is hazardous; production requires intensive use of electricity.

Factors that reduce/offset risks: Strictly regulated manufacture has reduced production risks, but cannot affect disposal or accidental hazards. There is no question that PVC has great practical and commercial value, but there is serious doubt that the risks are worth it. "The environmental community generally wants to see a phase-out or banning of [organochloride compounds, including PVC and its ingredients] except for essential uses."[74] Many national and municipal governments, plus a significant number of multinational corporations, have restricted use of PVC and mandated alternatives. In 2007, the USGBC released a report recommending avoidance of PVC but not an outright ban; this reflects the fact that PVC is really many different mixes, and that in some of its applications (including pipe) it is not environmentally worse than replacement materials.[75]

Renewability/recyclability: PVC recycling varies by country; European manufacturers have led a strong initiative, but in the United States almost none is recycled. The variety of additives in #3 PVC pose real challenges: older recyclables contained additives now banned, and waste PVC with different additives often

Table 6.2
Plastics used for landscape products—an unscientific survey.

	♻ 2: HDPE	♻ 3: PVC[a]	♻ 4: LLDPE	♻ 5: PP	♻ 7: Other[b]
IRRIGATION	watering cans supply pipes (incl. pressurized) hose reel carts and hose pots flexible downspouts	garden hoses drip tube ("spaghetti") supply pipes drainage pipes extendable downspouts	drip tube ("spaghetti") laser soaker hose nonpressurized pipe		irrigation heads (ABS)
FURNITURE	floating lounge chairs picnic tables	"wicker" furniture arbor with benches "leather" upholstery umbrella fabric closed-cell foam floats and pool lounges		outdoor furniture	"bentwood" rocker (resin) "wicker" furniture (resin) "cast-iron" furniture (resin) outdoor upholstery (acrylic)
HORT. USES	planters bins planter with trellis fake terra-cotta pots nursery pots artificial turf turf reinforcers	trellises arbors lattice lawn edging root barriers artificial turf		fake terra-cotta pots nursery pots	fake terra-cotta pots (foam resin) propagation trays ("polymer") planters (resin) arbors (resin) planters (fiberglass)
STORAGE	bins			boxes and bags	storage sheds (resin)
WORK CLOTHES	hard hats	work gloves rain and chemical-spray clothing work boots			
CONSTRUCTION SUPPLIES	"landscape plastic," clear and black sheets tarps most plastic lumber duct tape powder-coated metal some geotextiles	coated metal cable, wire, and screen tarps flagging and barricade ribbon some plastic lumber some geotextiles some adhesives		construction fence tarps	
ELECTRIC		light fixtures electrical conduit junction boxes, etc. electrical tape			
GREENHOUSES		corrugated clear panels glazing strips			greenhouse windows (polycarbonate) clear greenhouse fabric (polyethylene reinforcers with nylon mesh)
OTHER	basketball backboards chain-link privacy slats composting bins powder-coated chain-link fence and posts some signage	inflatable pools pool covers pool toys some pond liners dock structures fencing pickets, rails, posts, gates vinyl-coated chain-link fence vinyl grill covers some signage		doormats, "jute"-look and other mailboxes	in-lawn alligator and other ornaments (resin)

[a] Use of the ♻ 3 symbol allows PVC to be sorted from other plastics. The symbol does not mean that PVC is feasibly recyclable. For environmental problems with PVC, see p. XXX.

[b] The only landscape use found for PET (♻ 1, polyethylene terephthalate) and PS (♻ 6, polystyrene) was in pots for nursery growing. Polyethylene has many forms; only PET, HDPE (High Density), and LLDPE (Linear Low Density) have recycle numbers, above. PEX (cross-linked polyethylene) is stronger than PE and occasionally used in pipes. Others seldom if ever found in landscape use are UHMWPE and HMWPE (Ultra-High and High Molecular Weight), VLDPE (Very Low Density), and MDPE (Medium Density).

will not combine. If recycled at all, PVC is "down-cycled to manufacture inferior products such as garden benches and sound barriers along highways."[76] Much of this small amount of recycling is shipped to developing countries, where worker and environmental protection is weaker than in the United States. In many ways, PVC garden furniture may prove to be the landscape industry's overseas sweatshop scandal.

Burning PVC, both in trash-to-energy schemes and backyard disposal, releases chlorine compounds, dioxins, furans, and heavy metals. PVC in waste has been said to account for half of the chlorine in incineration fumes, and in many countries it is the main source of lead and cadmium in air pollution. Chlorine-based chemicals (organochlorides, chlorofluorocarbons, PCBs, DDT, dioxin, and others) are strongly implicated in cancer, reproductive disorders, species loss, and ozone depletion. When PVC is incinerated, these sorts of residues can remain in ash; stabilizing these residues requires adding inert materials, often exceeding the bulk of the original PVC.

Alternatives: Several other plastics are less toxic in manufacture and easier to recycle or dispose of than PVC. Various forms of polyethylene (PE) are suitable for pipes, furniture, plastic lumber, and other common products. ABS plastic is considered a slightly less environmentally damaging material, but not a general PVC replacement. Traditional materials like metal and clay, although less convenient and with energy and cost disadvantages, may need to be reconsidered for drainage pipes.

Landscape use of HDPE has been tested by Seattle Parks Department, EDAW (Fort Collins CO office), and Cahill Associates. In general, polyethylene is comparable to PVC in materials cost, but not as widely available. Installation can cost twice that of PVC, because contractors are unfamiliar with fuse-welding of PE (which actually produces less leak-prone water lines). Like other "learning-curve" costs, this should not be an excuse: the more PE is used, the more labor costs will fall. Some PE products, like catch basins and inlets, require redesign to achieve PVC's structural strength. PE, however, is more resilient, more UV resistant, and less likely to fail with age or extreme cold than PVC.[77]

Wood Preservatives

The wood-preservative industry has been in a state of rapid change.[78] This is due to several factors: a partial ban on CCA preservative (chromated copper arsenic), industry-standard until 2004, followed by limiting ACC (acid copper chromate) to commercial projects in 2007;[79] introduction of alternatives with varied performance; and economic battles as producers scramble to grab market share.

Wood preservation is a knotty problem: it can dramatically prolong life of renewable woods, but usually introduces serious pollutants. As Alex Wilson, editor of *EBN*, notes, there is no getting around the fact that "preservatives are designed to kill. [Preventing wood decay requires] finding the right balance between toxicity to the problem organism and safety to us and the environment."[80] Finding that balance has become even more complex since CCA was removed from much of the market for environmental reasons. As with PVC, preservatives pose relatively minor *user* health hazards, but serious manufacturing, contractor/installer, and disposal problems.

Annual US production of treated woods is about 8.4 billion board feet (20 million cubic meters), just over 20 percent of total softwood production in both volume and cost. How much is used in landscapes is uncertain, but outdoor uses far outnumber interior ones. Some 60 billion board feet (140 million cubic meters) of CCA-treated wood installed since the 1970s are now reaching the end of their service life. (Yes, even treated wood eventually breaks down.) Because "there is no environmentally sound way to dispose of [CCA] treated wood,"[81] this huge waste volume poses major—and growing—disposal problems.

Main types of treated wood are discussed in this section; only four can be expected to work reasonably well in fully exposed, wet, or ground-contact situations. Be certain whether termites are a risk; even preservatives that kill other insects may not stop termites.

Oil-based preservatives: Pentachlorophenol ("penta") and creosote still each account for about 10 percent of US treated wood. Penta combines two toxic chemicals (chlorine and phenol); creosote and its parent material, coal tar, are also toxic. Their use is limited by smell and difficulty sealing or painting over them;

they are most common on utility poles, railroad ties, and fenceposts, sometimes reused in ornamental landscapes. In general, they are best avoided.

Water-based copper preservatives: CCA and its arsenic-free relative, ACC (acid copper chromate), were industry standards. Both raised concern about human health (via skin contact), leaching into soil and water, and disposal. In 2004 the EPA banned CCA for high public-contact uses like playgrounds and decks; it is still used for foundation sills, pilings, piers, guardrails, sound-wall posts, and fenceposts, and it is almost universal for wood installed in salt water. ACC is discontinued; the EPA proposed reviving it, but retreated under public pressure in January 2007.

These bans have spurred a quest for kinder, gentler copper formulations. The two most common "second-generation" products are ACQ (alkaline copper quat, "quat" being quaternary ammonia) and copper azole. These are environmentally preferable to CCA, containing neither arsenic nor chromium. High hopes, as of this book's first edition, have been tempered by problems. The new preservatives contain higher percentages of copper, not as well bonded to the wood (fixed by chromium in CCA/ACC)—more copper to leach, and more likely to do so. A 2007 study found that both ACQ- and copper azole–treated wood was susceptible to brown rot fungus in both ground-contact and above-grade uses.[82]

Copper, the main fungus and insect killer in these formulas, is highly toxic to aquatic life and plants and causes human health problems. "Fixing" copper-based preservatives in pressure-treated wood is essential to performance and safety. At 70°F, fixing takes about three days; at 50°F, nearly two weeks; near freezing, it may not occur at all. Because wood is often shipped "wet" immediately after treatment, check how, where, and at what temperature it was stored at the sales yard. Use extra caution working with water-soaked pressure-treated wood.

ACQ and copper azole are more corrosive to metal fasteners than CCA, despite improvements by reformulation. Galvanized or stainless-steel fasteners are required.

The new copper preservatives are not usually guaranteed for ground-contact use, suggesting that manufacturers do not expect them to perform well in this situation—marketing claims notwithstanding. They appear to be safer for end users, but problems in manufacturing, installation, and disposal remain. The AIA concluded that the most serious environmental hazard of CCA was potential spills during transportation or production; the newer formulas still involve some hazardous ingredients, posing risks to treatment workers and anyone sawing or drilling copper-treated wood. Incineration puts preservative chemicals into the air; ash from this process concentrates toxic substances and greatly increases their leachability.

Of particular concern to landscape professionals is chipping waste wood for mulch. In theory, treated lumber is kept separate; in practice, it is hard to sort treated from untreated wood when weathered. Discarded after long service and chipped, wood leaches more easily than whole new treated boards. Wood mulch containing less than 0.1 percent copper-treated wood can leach enough to violate safety standards. Nearly 6 percent of wood construction waste is treated; the potential for contaminating mulch is great.

As with PVC, a main ingredient in mainstream wood preservatives is produced by a powerful industry, in this case copper. Industry preference for copper-based preservatives limits research and marketing for other types, while the EPA's current industry-friendliness contributes to "copper's hegemony," according to *EBN*'s Tristan Roberts.

"Micronized" copper is very finely ground and suspended in water rather than more toxic carriers. Manufacturers claim that using as little as half the copper of conventional formulas is effective because of better adherence to the wood, and that leaching is reduced 90 percent or more. Fastener corrosion is also reportedly less problematic.[83]

Chemically modified wood is infused with chemicals at moderate temperatures (about 200°F or 100°C). "Acetylization" uses vinegar; "furfurylation" uses plant-based alcohol. This changes the wood's molecular structure. These processes appear, as of 2017, to offer the best hope of exterior wood preservation with nontoxic materials. Handling, disposal, and combustion of these products is the same as for untreated wood, and leaching is reportedly minor; fastener corrosion is possible. Dimensional stability is improved, and water absorption decreased. An acetylated wood,

Accoya, was US code certified for ground contact uses in 2016; its main drawback is that sustainably harvested wood from New Zealand is shipped to Holland for treatment, and then to distributors worldwide.[84] Kebony, a furfurylated wood, is a Norwegian product using local wood, but is also shipped internationally for distribution. It is not for ground contact, but has a twenty-five-year warranty aboveground.[85] Both these products could substantially improve their energy footprint by decentralized manufacturing.

Thermally modified wood: Treated at high temperatures (about 480°F or 250°C), sugars in wood are converted to forms that decay organisms can't grow on or eat. Treated wood is said to be more dimensionally stable, but apparently somewhat brittle. Like chemical modification, thermal treatment involves no toxins. Two US-made products typify the difficult trade-offs common to sustainable products: PureWood is ground-contact approved, but requires 50–60 hours of fuel-consuming heat; Cambia wood is treated for 14–16 hours, but is for aboveground use only.[86]

Borate preservatives: Boron is relatively safe for humans, provides good control of both fungi and insects, and is long tested. Unfortunately, it is very water-soluble; attempts to make it suitable for outdoor use do not appear to have borne fruit as of 2017.

Silicate preservatives: Sodium silicate is inexpensive and abundant, presents few hazards in manufacture, use, or disposal, and has long been used as a preservative, although not for exterior wood. A silicate preservative called TimberSIL raised hopes in 2004; surrounding wood cells with glassy silicate, it kept water, insects, and fungi out *structurally* rather than by poison. However, there were production problems; an EPA investigation for making pesticide claims about a nontoxic product (allegedly urged by competitors); and marketing problems, topped off by poor performance in New Orleans dampness and New England cold. In early 2016, the company was bought as a "distressed asset," and though the new owners hope to bring TimberSIL back, a year later it is apparently not being manufactured.[87]

One innovative product is Pango Wrap from Stego Industries, a "cool new 2014 product" according to *EBN*.[88] This dual-purpose polyolefin sheet repels termites and acts as a vapor barrier. Although vapor is not usually a landscape structure issue, wrapping ground-contact posts in this material might reduce the need for preservatives, or enhance their performance. Material data indicate a proprietary mix of copper and carbon black; the Safety Data Sheet indicates it is stable and nonreactive.

So-called *organic* preservatives (meaning carbon based, not wholesome and healthy) are agricultural pesticides in solvents for wood treatment. The solvents give off VOCs (volatile pollutants). Because the agricultural chemicals are already EPA registered, their adaptations as wood preservatives can slip through regulatory loopholes. In any case, none appear to be intended for ground-contact use.

Finally, futuristic *nanotechnology* uses beads of preservative so tiny (one hundred nanometers, or about four-millionths of an inch) that they pass through microscopic pores in wood cells. This can put preservative where it cannot leach—possibly *increasing* disposal problems. Despite rapid expansion and commercialization, the National Academy of Sciences warns that nanotech's characteristics and hazards are still poorly understood.[89] In preservatives, nanomaterials are new and few. Preservatives claiming nano-ingredients appear to be surface-applied, probably susceptible to abrasion. They rely on unusual properties, such as electrical charge or hydrophilic molecules, so their performance, even if excellent, is bound to be different from more conventional preservatives.

Alternatives to Preserved Wood

Some woods naturally resist decay and insects. Tropical hardwoods (teak, ipe, etc.) should be used only if Forest Stewardship Council certified, and with careful consideration of transportation energy. Domestic softwoods (cypress, redwood, northern white and western red cedars, and yellow pine) are moderately resistant, but supplies, especially of most-resistant old-growth, are limited or gone. Most such woods are now obtained through salvage—including underwater salvage from an estimated 45,000 reservoirs worldwide.[90] Several species (Black Locust, Honey Locust, and Osage Orange) are very resistant, but too small to provide dimensional lumber. Laminating these woods is possible; exterior-grade products might result.

A second alternative to preserved wood is plastic lumber (p. 279). Although essentially rot and insect proof, most 100 percent plastic "lumber" is unsuitable for structural use. Wood-plastic composites incorporate wood fibers and can be used structurally in some cases; new products like Struxure (p. 280) offer structural strength but are costly for landscape purposes. Plastic wood has already become widespread for decking, a major substitution for treated wood.

Recommendations: There is no one-size-fits-all way to extend outdoor life of lumber. The following are options, roughly in priority order:

- Design to *avoid* wood in wet or soil-contact locations. Local stone footings, and sometimes concrete or steel, are substitutes. Question whether a permanent structure is necessary; other design solutions could meet functional and aesthetic demands.

- Evaluate whether protection is required from fungus, insects, or both, and whether wood will be soaked or buried. Less-toxic protection against specific threats may be easier than blanket protection.

- Consider resistant woods, with sustainable harvest certification, or salvaged.

- Consider plastic and composite lumber if not limited by structural requirements.

- If treated wood cannot be avoided, use the least-toxic type suitable for the purpose. Because disposal is a major problem, durability and life cycle interact significantly with toxicity issues.

- Ensure that any treated wood is installed with care. This includes skin and breathing protection for workers and proper job-site cleanup. Strictly follow manufacturer instructions for fasteners and for treatment of field-cut surfaces.

- For many treated woods, sealing with paint, stain, or varnish will improve resistance and longevity, and reduce user health risks, if any.

When disassembling any wood structure, make a serious attempt to separate treated from untreated wood. *Reuse* treated wood to avoid disposal. Verify what happens to wood wastes locally before dumping treated wood. Landfills vary widely in the United States; many dumps are not constructed to isolate heavy metal leachates such as those from treated lumber waste.

Toxics as "Fertilizer"

In 1997, the mayor of the small town of Quincy WA led an investigation for local farmers. Cattle had sickened; crop yields were declining. The farmers discovered that toxic waste was being repackaged and sold to them *as fertilizer*. *Seattle Times* reporter Duff Wilson pursued the investigation, finding examples of this practice nationwide. Wilson later documented the scandal in a book, *Fateful Harvest*. An Oklahoma uranium-processor licenses its radioactive waste as a liquid fertilizer. Pulp mills in Washington spread lead-laced waste on livestock grazing land. Two Oregon steel mills put a powdered waste into silos under federal hazardous waste permits and take *the exact same material* out of the silo for sale as fertilizer. While most industrialized nations regulate fertilizers, the United States does not. State governments do so inconsistently, leniently, and with little testing or enforcement.

Findings by Wilson and the Washington-based nonprofit Environmental Working Group show that over 600 toxic-waste-producing companies in 44 US states were involved in this shady but legal practice. These included smelters, chemical companies, mining, cement, waste incinerators (some handling medical wastes), wood-product firms, and other heavy industries. Over 450 firms in 38 states received the waste; some were fertilizer manufacturers, while others were farms. Between 1990 and 1995, some 270 million tons of wastes were shipped, some directly to farms, the rest relabeled as fertilizer, usually with minimal processing. The repackaged wastes contained cadmium, lead, arsenic, radioactive materials, and dioxins.

Thanks to the *Seattle Times* report, there was a flurry of activity in 2001 that culminated in 2002 with slightly stricter EPA regulations for a narrow portion of the problem: zinc waste recycled as zinc fertilizer. Since then, the issue seems to have been swept under a rug. Contaminants in fertilizers are still not regulated or tested federally, nor tracked, nor revealed on product labeling. The EPA considers fertilizers under its "land disposal" rules, as if farm fields were equivalent to landfills. The American Association of Plant Food Control Officers has attempted to set consistent state standards. Unfortunately, its rules accept heavy metals in fertilizers at levels that *average* 469 percent of levels allowed by the state of Washington, for example.[91]

Ironically, the scandal originates from the Resource Conservation and Recovery Act of 1976. Intended to encourage recycling, this law failed to distinguish between harmless recyclable "waste" and toxic by-products. This is no simple matter. Some industrial waste products, such as unbleached paper slurry, may actually provide beneficial plant nutrients without toxic contamination. But merely by stating that a material is a "product," it immediately becomes exempt from hazardous-material regulations. In a few cases, toxic materials have even been labeled as "organic" when sold as fertilizer.[92]

The EPA's official position, current as of July 2017, is uncritical: "EPA's longstanding policy encourages the beneficial reuse and recycling of industrial wastes. This includes hazardous wastes, when such wastes can be used as safe and effective substitutes for virgin raw materials. . . . The Agency believes that some wastes can be used beneficially in fertilizers when properly manufactured and applied." The policy includes a 1988 loophole for "fertilizer made from one specific type of hazardous waste . . . generated during steel manufacturing," and makes no mention of the practice of simply relabeling wastes without any testing or processing.[93]

The extent of selling toxic materials to the unwitting public remains murky. The practice is certainly unethical; at the very least labeling should be required. Industrial toxic waste likely has higher concentrations of harmful materials than treated sewage sludge (see p. 115)—yet it is biosolids that have been subject to public outcry, while repackaged industrial waste goes unchallenged.

As users of considerable quantities of fertilizer, landscape professionals would be well advised to keep abreast of this issue and to lobby for truth in packaging (at least) for all fertilizers. Those who *apply* fertilizers are at most risk from toxic exposure. If concentrated toxic materials are in fact being passed off, without any quality controls, as fertilizers, it is in the landscape industry's self-interest, not to mention the interest of environmental and public health, to demand that the practice be stopped.

Fertilizer, with potential effects on the food chain, has been the major concern. The Resource Conservation and Recovery Act's advocacy of recycling, however, has also allowed toxic waste to be incorporated in building materials such as asphalt, cement, glass, roofing materials, and noise barriers, as well as in combustible fuels. Some may be legitimate, but most require no permit or, at most, a rather informal permit from the regional EPA office. Landscape construction uses virtually all of these products, and contaminants in them affect the landscape. This abuse of the concept of recycling is something that landscape professionals need to expose and oppose.

Prioritize Hazard-reduction Efforts

Not all hazards are created equal, and landscape professionals should choose thoughtfully among potential efforts to lessen environmental impact of materials they use. In other words, choose your battles, since you cannot fight all of them.

- Focus on proper *disposal, salvage, and recycling* of construction materials, *reducing fuel use*, and *influencing manufacturers* toward nontoxic processes and accident prevention. Relatively few outdoor materials are directly hazardous to end users; end-use issues are probably *not* the area in which professional attention can produce greatest results.

- One end use on which landscape professionals can have significant influence is pesticides. These are toxic materials purposely used. As such, deliberate adoption of Integrated Pest Management and prioritization of the least-toxic pest controls (Principle 10) is well worth the effort.

- Reuse materials creatively, and create jobs and markets by doing so.

- Support technical and social efforts to reuse and recycle construction materials. Fairly small changes in disposal and recycling of construction materials could produce real results. Be sure, however, that zeal to recycle doesn't obscure the need to keep toxic by-products like chipped treated wood out of the mix.

- Analyze and reduce transportation, equipment use, and other fuel consumption (Principle 7). Fuel use, rather than materials hazards, probably contributes most to environmental impact of landscape materials.

- An increasing number of manufacturers have recognized the social and economic value of nontoxic processes and materials. Landscape professionals should support those whose claims can be documented.
- Select FSC-certified sustainable wood whenever possible.
- For plastics, give preference to manufacturers who use mostly recycled plastic, and who label each product (better still, each distinct piece of a product) with the recycle symbol and plastic-type number, and whose products are "designed for disassembly" where appropriate.
- Use the product with the fewest known end-use effects on human health and environment. Use products with known hazards only where no practicable alternative exists. Even minor effects may be cumulative or may interact with other pollutants. Sometimes, comparisons will lead to the conclusion that product A is no worse than B in impact.
- Avoid PVC and conventional wood preservatives wherever they are not absolutely essential. Consider "modified wood," but do your homework on each type and brand, on its regional suitability, and on any specialized carpentry or fasteners required.
- Work to ensure that landscape products, including fertilizers and "downcycled" materials, do not become a clandestine "sink" for toxic wastes.
- Information about architectural materials and indoor air quality, although more readily available than landscape-specific data, should be used cautiously as a guide to outdoor conditions.

Again, I recommend Calkins's *Materials* as an authoritative, accessible source on *landscape* products and their environmental impacts. Eventually, software will incorporate materials information to allow what-if comparisons of site-design options, but this will never be as easy as for building components.

Looking through 2016 issues of *LAM*, I am struck (almost fifty years since *Design with Nature*) by a disturbing disconnect: while most *LAM articles* include some sustainability concerns, the *material suppliers* who advertise in *LAM* seldom do. Out of 144 ads of all sizes, only 4 explicitly mentioned any synonym for "environmental" or "sustainable"—that's 3 percent. Even adding implicit references (energy efficient, local, recycled), only 16 percent used any aspect of sustainability as a selling point. Worse, the percentage is lower (12 percent) if only the influential full-page or double-page ads are considered. Does this mean the profession's providers don't get it, don't care, or assume every landscape product is automatically green? Despite hard work and many gains, sustainable purchasing for landscapes has a long way to go.

Subtopics and Search Terms for Principle 6: Consider Origin and Fate of Materials

Note: Subtopics are also useful search terms; add "innovation" or "controversy" to search terms as appropriate.

Materials
Search terms: landscaping materials || landscape construction materials

Materials selection
Search terms: "material selection"

Materials: on-site
Search terms: materials + "on-site"

Materials: recycled
Search terms: material + (recycled OR reused OR remanufactured)

Sustainable wood
Search terms: sustainable wood || bamboo construction || certified wood products || sustainable forestry

Construction waste management
Search terms: construction waste management || construction waste reduction

Hazard identification
Search terms: hazards identification || toxic materials identification

Materials: nontoxic or alternative
Search terms: chemical sensitivity || building materials + nontoxic OR alternative OR healthy

Life-cycle analysis
Search terms: life-cycle analysis || life-cycle assessment || life-cycle costing

Resource List:

Links to information sources related to this chapter are posted at http://islandpress.org/sustainable-landscape-construction

Principle 7:
Know the Costs of Energy over Time

The law of conservation of energy tells us we can't get something for nothing, but we refuse to believe it.
—Isaac Asimov, 1988

Energy is the core of life, central to doing, living, building. Since the first "energy crisis" of the late 1970s, design and construction professionals have been keenly aware of energy issues: energy-saving lights and appliances, efficiency standards for heating and cooling, and the seesawing costs of fuel. Energy efficiency can sell a property, and inefficient use of energy can sink a construction business. Construction "represents a huge, relatively long-duration energy investment";[1] currently, this investment is mostly gambled, rather than managed.

Architecture 2030, the group that has put designers into the forefront of the attempt to reverse global warming (see p. 20), estimates that nearly 50 percent of *all* energy used goes into constructing, operating, maintaining, and decommissioning buildings.[2] This and similar estimates worldwide have given architects the impetus to tackle climate change through professional efforts. Yet despite energy's increasing importance in *building* design and construction, it is still rare to find energy conservation principles systematically applied to *landscape* construction. Sadly, this remains nearly as true in 2017 as it was in 2000.

The role that *landscape* construction plays in existing energy estimates is unclear, since landscape work is sometimes but not always reported as part of architectural statistics. If landscape construction consumes even *one-fortieth* of what building construction does, however, this would be 1.25 percent of the US total—comparable to some estimates of energy used in constructing highways (1.64 percent) or single-family residences (1.19 percent).[3] It is well beyond the scope of this book to attempt accurate estimates of

Discussed in This Chapter

How energy affects landscape construction.
Making energy-conscious decisions about landscapes.
Energy for *constructing* landscapes versus energy for *using* them.
Energy generation and its landscape impacts.
Energy, greenhouse gases, and pollutants.
Embodied energy analysis.
Life-cycle costing.

total landscape-industry energy use. Landscape construction clearly consumes enough, however, to make energy analysis and conservation worthwhile.

Embodied energy and embodied carbon are often considered near-interchangeable measures of the impacts of human activities and material use. Landscapes, unlike most buildings, both emit and sequester carbon; soil and vegetation uptake of carbon can offset emissions from fuel consumption and other sources. Landscape practices can also partially prevent emissions resulting from clearance and soil loss.

In the evolution of knowledge about energy in construction, landscape professionals have real opportunities both to benefit and to contribute. Methods and tools for energy and emissions estimating have improved, are more accessible, and are still evolving—but, as is all too common, landscape aspects are largely overlooked. Software can calculate energy and carbon impacts of *buildings*, but do so in ways that make non-structural and outdoor calculations nearly impossible.

Construction, design, and planning professionals need to *help develop* practical methods and reliable standards for landscape energy evaluation. Nearly every day, fuel prices, oil wars, fracking damage, pipeline and train explosions, and climate change underline the urgency of rethinking how energy is managed.

Understand How Landscape Energy Use Is Different

There are significant differences between *building* construction and *landscape* construction, differences that have important environmental consequences. Energy use, too, differs between indoor and outdoor construction: types and total amounts used, as well as where and when. Most generation of energy either occurs outdoors, or requires large areas of landscape disturbance to extract fuel, or both. To understand why landscape professionals need to concern themselves with energy issues, it is essential to understand these differences.

Know the Types of Energy in Construction

Because energy plays so many roles in life, it is not surprising that the word has multiple definitions. Only two or three definitions are specifically important in talking about energy in construction.

It takes energy to produce construction materials, to install them, and to operate the site or structure once completed. The clearest terms for these types of energy are the following:

Operating energy (also called end-use energy) refers to power used in day-to-day functioning of a completed project. A common example is energy for heating and cooling buildings. In landscapes, examples of operating energy include electricity for irrigation valves and controllers, or gas for grills and heat lamps.

Fuel energy (sometimes called inherent or specific energy) is the energy that a material can give off when burned as fuel or food.[4] It is different from embodied energy (below), and applies only to materials that have practical value as fuel. For example, a one-pound piece of pine lumber might produce 2,600 Btu (British thermal units) when burned;[5] embodied energy

(for felling and sawing) would be about 2,776 Btu for the unprocessed board; planing, drying, and glue-laminating it could bring the embodied energy to as much as 6,788 Btu per pound.[6]

Fuel energy, and efficiency of transforming it into useful work, is a factor in computing both operating and embodied energy. Fuel efficiency for construction machinery is one area in which landscape contractors can directly affect both their operating costs and their environmental impacts.

Embodied energy refers to energy used to *produce* materials. Energy is required to mine or extract raw materials, to refine and combine them, to shape them, and, in complex products, to assemble the parts. Between each step, the material may be transported, at an energy cost. Transport from factory to construction site also uses energy. Embodied energy sums up all these energy inputs, usually in terms of energy per pound (or other unit) of material. Energy costs of disposing or recycling the material are important, but sometimes neglected, in embodied energy. For a whole construction *project*, embodied energy totals all energy inputs for materials, processes, and waste.

Embodied energy has a number of synonyms: embedded energy, process energy (which emphasizes factory processes and often excludes transportation), and energy intensity. Energy intensity emphasizes the relative level of energy required to produce a unit (weight, volume, size, etc.) of material. The same term, unfortunately, is used by the US Department of Energy and others to mean the amount of energy used to produce a *dollar's worth* of product.[7] Although this energy-per-dollar idea has its own uses, it should never be confused with energy-per-*material* figures. Architects have also used "energy intensity" to mean per-square-foot *operating* energy of buildings.[8] Because of these confusions, "embodied energy" seems the most consistent term for energy in materials production.

Differentiate Energy in Buildings versus Landscapes

In buildings, large amounts of energy are used for *operation*; 60 percent of the running costs of the building can readily be saved through efficiency in heating and cooling.[9] There is a trade-off, however: improved operating efficiency usually requires up-front investment in better construction and materials. Low-cost developments, for example, skimp on insulation to keep sale prices low; increased heating and cooling bills are the result. For poorly insulated houses, operating energy costs are so high that total energy to *produce* the structure is only about nine times the energy to *operate* the building for a year. By comparison, a house built to today's best efficiency standards can be operated for nearly eighteen years for the energy price of its materials; one year of operation equates to less than 6 percent of the energy embodied in construction.[10] Unfortunately, "spec building" means that the developer's interests (low up-front investment to maximize profit) conflict with the end user's interests (better, alternative construction to minimize life-cycle operating costs). Utility companies also have a major conflict of interest, since they profit from increased use of energy, and lose captive audience if households or businesses go off-grid. Last, but not least, the Jevons Paradox (see p. 6) means that efficiency gains may be offset by increased consumption. A 2013 report showed US residential energy use had grown by 2 percent even though heating had become 21 percent more efficient; larger houses, a 56 percent increase in air-conditioning use, and 18 percent more appliances and electronics ate up the improvement.[11]

In *building* construction, investing extra in the *embodied* energy of materials, such as insulation or double-pane glass, gives large savings in *operating* energy. (Transportation energy to get people and goods to and from buildings dwarfs most operating energy use; thus, siting of buildings—a landscape-related issue—strongly affects overall use of building-related energy.)

In constructed *landscapes*, the relationship between operating and embodied energy is quite different.

The major operating energy costs of buildings are either absent or greatly reduced in landscapes. Mechanical heating and cooling are rarely used outdoors, and insulation is not a consideration. As a result, if embodied energy is compared to operating energy, the *ratio* is much larger for landscapes than for buildings.[12] Thus, better landscape construction, at a higher cost in embodied energy, is unlikely to yield as dramatic a savings in *operating* energy for landscapes as the 60 percent quoted above for efficient buildings.

Some types of operating energy are certainly part of today's landscapes. Outdoor lighting, like its indoor equivalent, has been greatly improved for energy efficiency, and LED lighting promises even greater efficiency. This environmentally important subject is discussed in Principle 8. Irrigation controllers and valves (see p. 217) have been redesigned for energy efficiency and water conservation.

Other "outdoor appliances" also use energy: gas grills, heated pools and poolside conveniences, gate openers, and fountain equipment, to name a few. When purchasing or specifying such landscape items, energy efficiency seldom seems to be a client concern. Outdoor appliances are viewed as luxuries, and there is a peculiar human tendency *not* to expect efficiency from luxury items. Nonetheless, a few manufacturers are starting to design outdoor appliances to use less energy in operation. Energy consumption figures for such items, however, are still scarce.

The machines used in maintaining landscapes, such as lawnmowers, chipper shredders, and chainsaws, can be considered as operating energy costs. Because they are similar to construction equipment, however, their energy requirements are discussed in the section below on machinery and energy.

Save Energy in the Landscape

Any net energy savings is significant in sustainability, and where possible, the energy consumed in using landscapes should be minimized. However, the amount that can be saved by reducing landscape *operating* energy is limited. Much greater potential energy savings can be accomplished in three areas:

Site design strongly influences operating energy efficiency of *buildings*. Shade or windbreak plantings, solar orientation, rainwater management, and many other well-known techniques use landscape as part of green buildings, taking advantage of environmental services (see Principle 11). These design approaches are not detailed in this book, but relate directly to many techniques and materials of sustainable construction.

Site design is also increasingly involved with impacts of *generating* energy, and alternative methods and locations for doing so. A "landscape perspective" is badly needed in most decision making about energy systems. In addition, as on-site energy generation becomes more common, site design will have to evolve to accommodate it.

Carefully planned *machinery* use, both on-site and for transportation, can result in significant energy savings. Total machine fuel energy use on any project is strongly affected by choices: between local suppliers and distant ones; among options for bringing workers to the site; and between heavy or light equipment and hand tools. "Alternative" energy for landscape construction and maintenance tools is increasingly a real choice in 2017. Energy consumption estimates and guidelines for making such choices are given in the following section.

Significant savings are possible by analyzing *landscape materials' embodied energy and life cycles*. Each of these topics is discussed in a section of this chapter, which concludes with specific energy-saving suggestions for landscape construction.

Manage Energy for Machines, Tools, and Labor

Landscape construction makes use of a wide range of tools, from very heavy equipment to simple hand tools. Some, like dibbles or planting-sticks, have been in use since prehistoric times; others, such as bulldozers and laser levels, have come into existence only in the last few decades, a mere second in the long day of human existence on this planet.

In thinking about how energy is invested in landscape work, it is important to recognize that the *tools* of landscape construction also differ from those for building construction. Neither set of tools is better; they are simply suited to different jobs. Site work today relies on large motorized machines; building construction uses different, and in general fewer, heavy machines (except when constructing very large structures). A vast array of hand power tools is used in building construction; many are too specialized or too easily damaged by weather to be used regularly outdoors. Landscape construction frequently uses simple hand tools; many sites are remote from power supplies; variability of terrain, site size, access, and other outdoor conditions often requires the great adaptability of hand work. The differences between these two tool sets, especially in their balance of powered and nonpowered tools, means that the energy economics of landscape construction cannot be optimized by an approach based solely on architectural work.

A simple comparison shows the impact that choice of landscape equipment can have on energy consumption. A modern scraper (or earthmover) can move twenty cubic yards of soil a distance of 200 yards in less than two minutes. The same task would take a full day for eight workers using picks, shovels, and the kind of backpack baskets still common in the Third World. The machine, with a 450-hp engine, would have used 0.9 gallon of diesel fuel, or about 7,560 Btu. The eight laborers would use about 20,000 Btu to accomplish the work.[13] The fact that the machine's direct energy cost is less than that for human labor, however, can be misleading: indirect costs and problems change the equation significantly.

In industrialized countries, speed of work is highly valued; artificially cheap fuel prices and high labor costs disguise true energy costs. There is no question that the machine is faster—almost 240 times faster. But for sustainability, other considerations compete with convenience, speed, and monetary cost. In the earthmoving example, diesel is a nonrenewable source of energy that produces pollution. Oil exploration, drilling, refining, and transportation create pollution and cost energy to produce energy—adding at least 3 to 20 percent to the amount directly used. The workers' food is readily renewable and all their waste is biodegradable.[14] In addition, the scraper is composed of many tons of steel and other energy-intensive materials. Its size and weight damage the soil and limit its use to large unobstructed sites.

Few if any industrialized societies would willingly move back to manual labor for all tasks. This is not the only way, however, to cut energy costs. Choosing the most appropriate sources of energy and types and sizes of machinery, as well as prioritizing hand labor where it is effective, offers significant energy savings and site protection (see pp. 75–80).

Try Alternatives in Generating Energy

Energy for tools used in construction, manufacturing, and homes is *generated* in a variety of ways, each with implications for sustainability and for the landscapes in which people live and work. The most common sources of construction power are gasoline and diesel, plus "grid" electricity generated from coal, natural gas, hydro, and nuclear plants. Portable gas-powered generators are also common at job sites, along with gas or electric and recently, cordless air compressors.

Solar (photovoltaic, or PV) and wind-generated electricity have recently been the fastest-growing sector of the energy industry. The PV industry provided one of every fifty new US jobs in 2016, growing seventeen times as fast as the national employment rate.[15] Between 2008 and 2011, solar and wind more than doubled its share of the US market, while renewables pulled ahead of nuclear as an energy source.[16] Photovoltaics reached 40 percent efficiency and the cost per kilowatt-hour dropped to about twelve cents, equivalent to consumer prices for utility-produced electricity in some areas.[17] Market forces, as much as or more than idealism, are making "alternative energy" viable competitors to conventional fossil-fueled utilities. This affects not only how landscape workers and landscape users get their energy, but also how the landscape will change to accommodate these new generating systems (see the following section).

In addition to utility-scale and rooftop PV and wind generation, mobile solar generators are commercially available. In 2009, one such model won BuildingGreen's Top-10 Green Building Products awards; one year later, *EBN* listed five manufacturers of trailer-mounted units, rated from 1W to 240W output with varied heavy-duty batteries; at $8,000 to $80,000, prices are relatively comparable to gasoline units of the same size.[18]

PV-powered machinery can have a powerful impact on how people work—for the better. The Sun Horse solar tractor, pictured here, has made FreeEnergySystems founder Tom Lopez think differently about energy and his work schedule. "People always want to know, does it run long enough to work," says Lopez. In fact, most tractor-type equipment on farms is idle 90 percent or more of the time, he says, and rethinking how to benefit from that is more important than how long a charge lasts. "Small farmers don't want to plant huge fields all at once—they need to spread both the work and the yield." Solar tools are a reminder to work steadily in manageable doses. Giant corporate

Figure 7.1   The Sun Horse tractor generates its own power with a PV-panel canopy. When not in use, it is often parked near the 12V pump at rear, right, powering irrigation during the night. Both 12V and 110V outlets can power other tools in the field. (*Product:* FreePowerSystems. *Photo:* Tom Lopez.)

farms couldn't use the technology—another problem with monocropping, Lopez notes.

Novel generation methods continue to emerge, many of them landscape specific, and excellent subjects for interpretive landscape designs. John Deere released a Micro Hydroelectric Generator in 2008, essentially a turbine powered by water flowing through irrigation pipes.[19] Electricity can be generated from tides, from waves, and even from the chemical differences between salt water and fresh water in estuaries, using a "mixing entropy battery."[20] In Holland, a unique solar hot water system originally designed to reduce pavement maintenance is heating residences; a lattice of water-filled pipes embedded in a 200-yard section of road and a small parking area heats seventy housing units in a four-story building, via underground storage and a heat pump.[21]

Know the Landscape Impacts of Energy Production

The production of energy by whatever method almost always has impacts on the landscape, and those impacts are frequently overlooked. The air pollution resulting from fossil-fuel use (and burning of firewood), as well as the radioactive hazards of nuclear energy, are important and widely reported. However, operation of these extractive industries clears significant areas of vegetation and, in some cases, removes volumes of soil (as mining "overburden"), as well as clearing and regrading access roads, pipelines, or rail spurs. As discussed in "Landscapes Against Climate Change," vegetation and soil removal and compaction result in large-scale CO_2 emissions. Landscape professionals who become knowledgeable about these issues can work to protect the source of their livelihood, as well as ecosystem services in general.

A coal production technique called "mountaintop removal" excavates so much soil that whole valleys are filled with the waste, almost always impacting water bodies as well as topography. Even if there were such a thing as "clean coal" beyond the marketing strategy of a moribund industry, mountaintop removal would make a mockery of the concept. Mine tailings for uranium, often touted as carbon-neutral, not only destroy soil and vegetation but also have contaminated water and soil in many communities in the United States and abroad, and disposal of such waste is difficult and controversial. These landscape impacts (as opposed to impacts from using these fuels) are too often left out of comparisons among conventional and alternative fuels.

To produce crude oil and "natural" gas, fracking has become common. Liquid under high pressure is injected into a well to fracture the rock, releasing more oil or gas; "sand" (which is not simply a natural product) is introduced to hold the cracks open, and proprietary chemicals are added to improve flow and for other reasons. Concerns have focused on atmospheric and subsurface issues, especially groundwater contamination (hundreds of known endocrine disruptors are among the chemicals known to be used in fracking "mud") and induced earthquakes. However, Penn State landscape architecture professor Neil Korostoff notes that landscape *surface* issues are often equally critical: depletion of water used for residences and agriculture, as well as surface disposal of toxic drilling waste in pits, which in some states are not even lined. "Land surface impacts should involve landscape architects," says Korostoff, "but we're not asked to participate."

Pipelines to collect and transport oil and gas to market also have major landscape impacts. Charlie Yuill, head of the West Virginia University landscape architecture and environmental design program, says that pipelines and access roads impact probably five times as much acreage as actual well-drilling "pads"; pipelines run straight up and down slopes, and are often cleared with herbicides, drastically increasing erosion. Such linear features also cause intense habitat fragmentation.[22] So-called natural gas (an industry euphemism for methane) is clean-burning compared to other fossil fuels, but CO_2 emissions from drilling, fracking, and pipeline leaks make claims that it is a sustainable fuel extremely dubious. It may, however, be our best bet as a transition fuel while changing over to renewable energy.

For electricity, power generation has widely varied impacts. Coal-burning plants have the greatest greenhouse gas (GHG) and pollutant impact. Hydroelectric drowns valleys that often were agricultural or residential settings as well as habitat for wildlife. Nuclear power, often touted as GHG-free, is in fact not: besides emissions due to removal of vegetation and soil during mining, processing uranium ore releases significant greenhouse gases, and emissions increase as available ore quality worsens.[23]

The electrical distribution grid loses a high percentage of energy during transmission (not actually lost, but turned to heat), and each time it is stepped up or down by a transformer. The grid also has serious, and often ignored, landscape impacts. Transmission lines are routed through undeveloped areas (for shortest-distance routing and because of public opposition), ignoring topography in favor of straight-line distance savings; such routing is almost guaranteed to produce maximum land damage. Conversely, existing grid locations can actually limit possibilities for solar or wind "farms," making it costly or impossible to deliver the energy.[24] The grid is vulnerable to terrorism, vandalism, and extreme weather, and diagnosing, locating, and accessing damage is complex. By contrast, sabotage or weather damage of one distributed on-site generation system (rooftop solar or wind, for example) would not touch other installations. On-site systems are known for surviving hurricanes when all utility power goes down. If an on-site generator mal-

Figure 7.2   PV panels cover 170 acres at Davis-Monthan Air Force Base, Tucson AZ, the largest Department of Defense solar installation. The US military is transitioning to alternative energy far faster than are US politicians. Siting a huge "energy farm" next to a dense user community is the only time such vast centralized features make sense—and in most places, it would likely be opposed by the adjacent residents. (US Air Force photo: 1st Lt. Sarah Ruckriegle.)

functions, its location is easy to pinpoint, and, being on or near a building, no special access road is usually required. The grid works against many of this book's principles—use of local resources, site protection, reduced paving, and management to decrease runoff, among others. The national grid, an engineering marvel from a bygone period when home alternatives for electricity were primitive at best, today is preserved because utilities have so much invested in the infrastructure, and can make so much money from customers who essentially rent, rather than buy, power.

Centralizing solar or wind generation in utility-scale "farms" negates the inherent advantages of distributed on-site power. Huge areas covered with PV panels or concentrating mirrors have impacts, not yet well quantified, on habitat, vegetation, and soil. Industrial-sized windmills kill some birds and apparently even more bats; a voluntary 2015 industry plan has failed to curtail bat deaths.[25] Giant industrial windmills, if they do fail, do so spectacularly and dangerously[26] compared to smaller on-site wind power. I have not seen a definitive study, but any efficiency of scale gained by centralizing power production is likely canceled out by transmission and transformer losses, by maintenance trip distances, and by the fact that the grid does not incorporate any storage. On-site wind and solar normally have battery storage, making power available at night and during cloudy or windless days.

Distributed on-site power generation has by far the most potential in fighting climate change, as well as in making households energy independent. Even before these technologies became cheap enough to compete with grid electricity pricing, many people were adopting them. This fact poses some challenges in landscape design.

Learn to Design for Alternative Power

"Alternative" power generation links elegantly to landscape design. Unlike large utility networks that intrude on site-specific design, solar, wind, and even small-scale hydro generators are small landscape elements that can and must integrate into individual sites. Alternative generation uses site conditions—sun, wind, water—that landscape professionals already know how to analyze and work with. Few landscape architects will ever design a power plant, but many have been involved in site-scale energy generation.

Analysis of site suitability, and proper siting, is essential for alternative power. Photovoltaic panels vary

Figure 7.3   This "wind farm" in California is typical of the remote locations where such facilities are being sited, defeating the main advantage of wind (or solar) power, which is on-site, near-the-source generation. (*Photo:* Winchell Joshua, US Fish and Wildlife Service [public domain], via Wikimedia Commons.)

in tolerance for shading; wind turbines vary in the minimum wind speed at which they can generate, and the maximum their blades or bearings can withstand. They also require clearance and are usually mounted on towers, although building-mounted wind turbines are common. Site analysis also determines whether a specific system is cost-effective: for example, in most regions, the cost of running new utility wires any significant distance is greater than that of buying and installing alternative generators. With photovoltaics, for instance, this break-even distance is between 200 and 900 yards.[27]

Geothermal heat and electricity is as yet uncommon in most places. Underground storage of energy as heat or in some cases ice (called TES, or thermal energy storage) can balance day-and-night or seasonal

fluctuations; though often located in basements, buried versions of this idea could impact large areas of landscape, especially during construction.

A number of innovative projects have placed PV panels over parking, providing welcome shade beneath; on brownfields; and, in at least one case, over a stormwater detention basin. Such siting avoids one recent concern: on houses, PV panels can complicate firefighting.[28] "Floatovoltaics," originating in space-challenged Japan, are PV panels anchored on reservoirs; their effect on aquatic life is not well understood, but for artificial reservoirs they may be promising. Floating PV can reduce evaporation from reservoirs, while cooling the panels, thus raising their efficiency.[29] One study estimated that by siting PV only on already-developed areas, California could meet its energy needs

Figure 7.4 The SUDI photovoltaic sunshade is a stand-alone charger for electric vehicles. This is one of the most beautiful designs based on a widespread and almost obvious concept—PV-over-Parking. The curved shades are a deep transparent blue. (*Product:* French partners RCP Design Global; Fondation Océan Vital; Groupe Hervé; and Solutions Composites. *Photo:* Tatmouss, via Wikimedia Commons.)

five times over.[30] Such siting also avoids the problems of grid delivery from remote desert locations.

Perhaps the most unexpected PV development is the "solar road," which substitutes PV units for pavement. What is claimed to be the world's first such road, a kilometer-long test, was installed in 2016 at Tourouvre-au-Perche, France. The location is not unusually sunny, so if the test works—providing electricity for streetlights for a town of 3,400—it will indicate a system usable in many environments. A Dutch bike path, as well as early tests in parking lots, has also been constructed with a PV surface. As existing linear connectors between structures, these roads and paths both generate and distribute energy. These European

developments have been in the works for a decade; questions about surface texture, durability, obscuring of transparency, and weathering have been raised, and rigorously tested.[31]

An American company is pushing the concept of the PV road far beyond simple electricity generation. The proposal is to create hexagonal units combining PV, built-in LEDs, and pressure sensors. In theory, such a surface could be self-lighting at night; could warn of large animals and pedestrians crossing; and could be programmed like a computer screen to display lane markings and even sports-field boundaries as needed. A further proposal is to add snow-melting capacity for northern climates. A frenetic promotional

Figure 7.5 Large modular PV panels are placed for a bike and walking path that generates energy in Holland. (*Product and Photo:* SolaRoad Netherlands [courtesy photo].)

video,[32] which is heavy on artistic renderings and presents no hard data on how much energy would be generated, used, and stored by each panel, has made many Internet commentators rudely skeptical; their concerns need to be addressed. If such a system *can* be developed, it would certainly impact landscape and civil engineering in major ways. Stay tuned.

Detailed thought must be given to each component in relation to the whole system. Wind and hydro are turbine generators, their output a function of speed. Wear on moving parts, and noise, must be considered. Solar panels have no moving parts, but take up more space, and their output rating is different (see below). For all systems, output, storage capacity of batteries, and "loads" using energy must be carefully matched. Most alternative generators produce direct current (DC); alternating current (AC) requires an "inverter."

Controllers to protect generators and batteries from voltage extremes are frequently needed.

Most alternative generators work only part-time: when the sun is bright or wind is strong. (One interesting, if expensive, development is Bluenergy's wind turbine with solar cells embedded in its surfaces, generating whenever there is *either* sunshine or wind.) Storage batteries stash power for "off" times. Unlike car batteries, designed for high power for a short cranking period, storage batteries must supply power in small doses over long periods. "Deep-cycle" batteries can be fully discharged repeatedly and still recharge; nontoxic ones, based on salt water and other materials, are in development.[33] The battery "bank" must be sized for expected load. Most batteries contain pollutant chemicals; careful manufacturing, use, and recycling is essential. Tesla's entry into the battery market, us-

Figure 7.6 Small and thin—but tough—Wattway PV panels install over existing pavement. These were used for France's first solar roadway, at Tourouvre-au-Perche. (*Product:* Colas. *Photo:* © COLAS—Joachim Bertrand [courtesy photo].)

ing less-toxic lithium-ion technology, is widely seen as a game-changer for alternative power. (While fossil-fuel apologists have used falsely labeled imagery to argue that "lithium mines" are worse than tar sands or fracking, most lithium today is produced by pumping brine into solar evaporation ponds, a process so much cheaper than historical lithium pit mining that it drove such operations out of business. It has also been asserted that there is not enough lithium to meet the compulsive demands of electronics buyers, yet lithium is the twenty-fifth most abundant element on Earth, and abundant in seawater.[34]

As recently as 1954, Bell Labs scientists were overjoyed to get 6 percent efficiency from newly developed solar cells; their one-kilowatt panel cost more than one million dollars. In 2007, an experimental cell broke 40 percent efficiency; by 2017, a *commercial* cell from this manufacturer, Spectrolab, was rated at 29.5 percent.[35] PV continues to evolve, with "roofing" (tile, metal, or shingle) available from many sources; thin see-through films applied to windows, harvesting power and screening the interior; and flexible, even rollable films that, though still low-efficiency, have promise as portable chargers for landscape tools and

other devices. Organic films have been experimentally "grown" without toxic chemicals, about 11 percent efficient. Rising efficiency and falling cost make solar power not just a reality, but a serious economic threat to fossil fuels.

In 2000, there were two major types of PV materials: cells and films. In 2017, Wikipedia lists twenty-six types, each with links to detailed articles. The most common are still crystalline cells, usually about three inches round or square, soldered together in series and sandwiched under glass into a "panel" or "module." Thin-film, the other main type, also has subtypes; the best known is "amorphous silicone," common in solar calculators and watches, identifiable by long stripes rather than distinct cells. Efficiency is one-half to two-thirds that of cells. Groups of panels, of either type, are "arrays."

Each panel is rated in watts of electrical output, under Standard Test Conditions (STC wattage).[36] Actual operating conditions can be very different. Cloudy weather or shading decreases PV output. Most panels also lose about 0.5 percent efficiency for each degree Celsius hotter than 25°C (77°F). Cooler operating temperatures *increase* efficiency, somewhat offsetting

Figure 7.7   The Solaris PV umbrella is another elegant, multifunctional design that integrates solar electricity into objects of similar form. Catching the sun with a raised surface yields shade below and energy capture above. (*Proposal and Rendering:* Jose Vicent, Andre Castro, and Elizabeth Remelgado.)

shorter winter daylight hours. At least one manufacturer, SolarWall, has designed a combination PV and solar-thermal panel; by capturing heat for use in the building, the thermal part of the panel keeps the PV part cooler, and total energy (electrical and heat) is increased 50 to 300 percent.[37]

Location of panels is critical. Crystalline panels must be completely unshaded, and protected from vandalism; thin-film panels are less susceptible to either. (One California dreamer was caught stealing roadside call-box PV panels to heat his hot tub!) Large, flat panels are susceptible to wind and must be securely mounted; some mountings incorporate sun-tracking mechanisms, increasing efficiency, though arguably not enough to justify the extra cost. Measurement of available solar energy on-site is essential; sun direction and intensity, as well as shadowing, change throughout each day and season by season. The Solmetric SunEye is a digital tool that both measures and predictively models solar potential; though not cheap, at about $2,200, it is a worthwhile investment for anyone doing solar installations (including path lights and streetlights), and data from it could be used to match plantings to light conditions.

Photovoltaic generation is already widely used for outdoor lighting (see Principle 8) and other landscape-specific power. For truly remote sites, PV offers immediate savings; for others, initial cost is offset by reliability and near-zero operating costs. At Cholla Campground, a US Forest Service (USFS) facility near Phoenix AZ, landscape architect Kim Vander Hoek and her colleagues saved an estimated $435,000 in up-front costs by using solar power for everything: lights, water pumping and purification, even a power hookup for the campground host's motor home. Public-sector landscape architects dealing with remote, protected sites are in the forefront of solar landscape design. Albuquerque's Colleen Friends, responsible for a Parks and Recreation project that chose solar lighting and irrigation, puts it succinctly: "Without photovoltaics Tramway Trail wouldn't have been lighted."

PV systems are completely silent, nonpolluting, and highly reliable. (Federal transportation agencies are converting safety signals, including runway lights, to solar power.) PV has a long lifespan (at least twenty to thirty years); periodic cleaning of panels and checking of batteries is the only routine maintenance.

No power technology is without problems. The clear glass or plastic components take energy to manufacture; cheap plastic panels such as those used on the very cheapest stand-alone path lights have degraded in ultraviolet light in some regions. "Doping" cells (sensitizing them to light) uses hazardous chemicals, as do batteries; both are contained, and careful recycling lowers risks. Poor performance in PV systems is usually linked to incorrect site analysis, design, or installation, or excessive client expectations. All of these concerns are well within the purview of any landscape architect.

Technical assistance and supplies are available from a growing number of solar consultants and manufacturers. The Solar Energy Industries Association lists nearly 400 members nationwide. The Photovoltaic Design Assistance Center offers a clearly written handbook with step-by-step worksheets on designing custom systems. Real Goods Trading Company offers components from many manufacturers, design assistance, and its *Alternative Energy Sourcebook*. Many states, as well as the federal government, have offered tax credits and other support for buyers of PV systems as well as on-site wind generators. These are under regular attack by utilities and fossil interests, which have also begun proposing extreme bureaucratic hurdles for solar installers, under the guise of "consumer protection." Utilities also try to argue that PV users cheat grid users by not buying grid energy!

Evaluate Tools and Their Energy Sources

Each way of generating energy starts a chain of events leading to its final use by a tool or machine. Some of these chains are long: coal burned at a power plant heats steam, is converted into electricity and transmitted through utility wires, then runs an electric motor to compress air that powers actual tools. Other chains are very short. Internal combustion engines, for instance, convert fuel energy directly into mechanical energy. Each time energy is converted from one form to another (solar to electric, combustion to mechanical, etc.) there are losses, because no conversion is completely efficient.

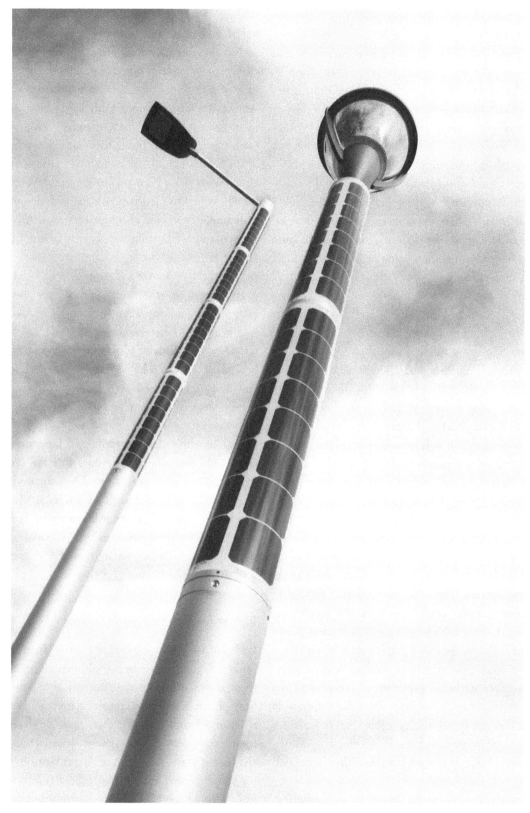

Figure 7.8 Solar panels and streetlights are usually elevated; here the structural Soluxio solar light post also functions as a panel. By rotating the cylindrical pole, the PV cells can be oriented for maximum solar input, avoiding the all-too-common flat panels stuck at awkward angles on top of the luminaire. (*Product and Photo:* FlexSol Solutions.)

Figure 7.9 Solar electricity for lights and other uses saved hundreds of thousands of dollars in utility installation at Cholla Campground, near Phoenix. Operating costs are near zero. (*Project:* USFS. *Photo:* Kim Vander Hoek.)

For in-depth analysis, all forms of energy should ideally be measured by a common yardstick, one that allows for conversion losses. Howard Odum and his associates quantify the energy value of solar radiation or of nuclear-generated electricity in terms of "fossil-fuel equivalents." Although Odum's conclusions about "alternative" energy sources seem dated, anyone interested in a thorough introduction to energy costs and their effects on society and the environment would do well to start with his book *Energy Basis for Man and Nature*, a classic since 1976. Odum's methods are particularly useful in putting day-to-day energy use into long-term policy perspective.

In thinking about energy and sustainability, what matters most is resource depletion and pollution from energy production and use. In many ways, this simplifies evaluation of energy consumption by specific tools.

Specific details of efficiency that affect tool *design* (for example, what percentage of the energy theoretically available from exploding gasoline actually reaches a tractor's tires) are less important for the tool user than the *total amount of fuel consumed* while the tool is in use. It is this total amount that affects the environment directly—and which most directly affects the pocketbook. This total use is what construction professionals need to reduce.[38]

The tables in the following sections give *rough* energy usage rates for machines and tools of many kinds. To interpret these rates, the source or type of energy must be considered. The following assumptions underlie these tables:

Gas, diesel, and gas/oil engines consume fuel directly. Energy use for the machine or tool is based on fuel used per hour, converted for ease of comparison to one of the standard units of energy, the Btu. (To convert to the metric unit, the joule, multiply Btu by 1,055.)

Electrical tools running from utility power are part of a system that, as a national average, *loses 60 percent of energy generated*, due to transmission loss. At the beginning of this energy chain, fuel is burned to produce 2.5 times as much electricity as ever reaches the user. This does not mean that electrical tools are necessarily inefficient. It does mean that, in comparing effects on the environment, electrical tools must be evaluated in terms of energy *generated*, rather than energy used "at the plug." The tables below give an at-the-plug figure for each tool, followed by the same figure multiplied by 2.5 to include transmission losses. Cordless battery-powered tools suffer the same problem if they are charged from grid power; with solar chargers on the market, and wind-powered chargers a possibility, batteries avoid transmission losses and in effect gain efficiency.

When an on-site generator is used, its total fuel use is a better gauge of environmental impact than measuring the electricity used by tools connected to it. A 10,000W generator running a 700W drill is consuming fuel based on generator capacity, not on the attached tool; it also consumes fuel while the tool is idle. Thus, for sustainability, it is important to evaluate the number of hours of fuel consumption *by the generator*, rather than trying to add up use by all the individual tools.

Air tools should also be evaluated by fuel usage *of the compressor*. Gas-powered or tankless compressors run constantly. Electric compressors with tanks run only when tank pressure drops, which is efficient but more difficult to estimate; based on experience, assess how many minutes per hour the compressor motor actually runs. Thus, tables include only compressors, not specific air tools.

Alternative power sources, such as solar and wind, are essentially "free," because no fuel is used or pollution generated. (Like any power-generating equipment, resources are used in *building* PV panels or windmills; these "second-order" resources are not usually considered in tool energy analysis, but will eventually need to be. Some "clean" power sources incorporate toxic materials, but so does fossil-fuel infrastructure. This is a difficult trade-off that needs deeper recognition, not abuse by partisans out to make a predetermined point.)

If installed on a site as the first step in construction, permanent solar or wind generators can provide construction power. Since this book's first edition, *portable* solar power for contractor use has become a real, though still little-known, option. In 2000 such systems were essentially homemade; one contractor had developed a way to recharge 12V cordless tools from a solar panel on his truck. *EBN* editors advised anyone modifying tools for this purpose to wait until the warranty ran out![39] Many cordless tool lines offer chargers that plug into a cigarette lighter or 12V outlet in a vehicle; with a solar trickle charger for the vehicle battery, such a system might serve for contractors.

PV has potential for landscape *maintenance* equipment, such as solar-powered trash compactors (p. 379).

Fuel cells have been long predicted, but slow to arrive. They are about 40 percent efficient, up to 80 percent if "waste" heat produces steam or hot water (compared to central power plants, at less than 30 percent). General Motors unveiled a prototype pickup-mounted fuel cell in August 2001.[40] From 2002 through 2006, DaimlerChrysler produced fuel-cell-powered public buses for the European Fuel Cell Bus Project; thirty-six buses were tested under real-world conditions in ten European cities, plus Beijing and Perth, Australia.[41] Toyota's Mirai and Hyundai's Tucson fuel-cell cars sold a few hundred between them in 2016; lack of hydrogen fueling stations is a major drawback.[42]

"Micro fuel cells" have been under development by computer giants like Toshiba and NEC. Prototypes operated a laptop for several hours on fuel cartridges as small as one ounce (roughly thirty cubic centimeters). If they are ever commercially viable, either regular or micro fuel cells could provide tool power for remote sites, with no point-of-use pollution. At present, they remain too expensive to market. Nor have

"micro-turbines," generating electricity from natural gas, become widely affordable. Rising oil prices could soon affect both.[43]

Energy Use: Heavy and Self-propelled Machinery

Usually adapted from agricultural and engineering machinery, landscape equipment looks tiny compared to truly *heavy* equipment. Mining-industry trucks, for example, may weigh 200 *tons* empty and carry 300 tons; there are 3,500-horsepower excavators that move 60 tons at a scoop.[44] Nonetheless, thousands of smaller landscape construction machines do add up. Their combined energy usage, as well as their effect on the soil (see Table 1.1), makes them important targets for energy efficiency and appropriate use.

Some rough estimates of energy use by various types and sizes of machinery are given in tables below, along with data that can be used for doing your own estimates. These are *rough* estimating tools only, and do not reflect specific performance of specific models. More accurate information, by brand name and under specific work conditions, is available, but these rough averages may be of equal value for several reasons. Fuel consumption varies with condition and age of equipment. Engines operate most efficiently at optimal RPM and full loads—but in the field, these conditions cannot be maintained constantly. Fuel consumption also varies with soil hardness, surface conditions affecting traction, outdoor temperature, and elevation. Thus an average figure may be more useful than detailed specifics in *planning* for energy efficiency across a whole job.

To estimate energy consumption, it is necessary to know how much energy is burned up with each gallon of fuel, and how many gallons are used to run a given machine for a time or distance. The following tables give rule-of-thumb figures.[45]

Fuel-usage factors, based on Nichols and Day's respected reference *Moving the Earth*, are given in *gallons* used per horsepower per hour in (Table 7.2). Based on Table 7.1, these are converted to *Btu* per horsepower per hour, which makes comparison between different engine types easier.

To use these figures, multiply the number in the table by the machine's horsepower to determine gallons of fuel or Btu consumed per hour.[46] For example, a 30 hp gas-powered tractor would use 30 × 10,000 Btu for each hour of operation, or 300,000 Btu. Hours of machine work required for particular jobs is given in standard estimating references like Means or Spons. If the Means book says that the task you are estimating requires a small tractor for nine hours, total energy use for that task would be 2.7 million Btu.

These figures are for ordinary machinery and average conditions. For extremely well-maintained equipment and light work, *subtract* 25 percent for diesel and 13 percent for gasoline (including two stroke). For poorly maintained machinery and difficult conditions, *add* up to 75 percent for diesel and 25 percent for gasoline. If manufacturer's data for a specific machine are available, Nichols and Day recommend using 80 percent of rated full-load fuel consumption. Such information must be converted first from *pounds* to gallons, which manufacturers use for unknown reasons, then to Btu.[47]

Table 7.3 gives *rough* energy estimates for various types of machinery, based on fuel consumption factors in Table 7.2. Machines listed were selected as representative of *types*—not specific models—used in landscape construction. The listing is not comprehensive, and tends toward *smaller* machines of each type. (Larger machines, less common in landscape work, may be estimated if horsepower and fuel type are known, using the method just described.) For each listing, horsepower, weight, and capacity figures are derived from real machines; closely similar models were averaged. Fuel usage, in Btu, was then estimated using Table 7.2.

These figures are intended *only* for project planning and general strategizing about machine use. Like most figures in this chapter, they will seem inaccurate to manufacturers and engineers used to very precise, model-specific fuel consumption estimates. These figures should certainly not be confused with thorough documentation of specific machines under specific conditions. Rule-of-thumb generalizations like the Nichols and Day factors used here are what allow *job estimators* and *field users* to make better decisions. Rough as they are, the estimates in Table 7.3 are a first step in an important process: gathering *and refining* information to help construction practice change in response to sustainability concerns.

Table 7.1
Fuel type and energy.

Fuel Type	Energy Produced in Use (Btu/gallon)	Weight per Volume (lb./gallon)[a]
Diesel	140,000	7
Gasoline	125,000	6
Two-stroke gas-oil mix[b]	125,000	6

[a]Machinery manufacturers and engineers usually chart fuel usage in pounds per hour of operation. Use these factors to convert pounds to gallons.
[b]The figure for gasoline is given as a round number, since the usual gas-oil mix (50:1) is primarily gasoline.

Table 7.2
Average fuel and energy consumption per horsepower-hour.

Fuel Type	Gal./hp-hr.	Btu/hp-hr.
Diesel	0.06	8,400
Gasoline	0.08	10,000
Two-stroke gas-oil mix	0.09	11,250

Example of Machinery Evaluation

The example of the scraper and the workers, given at the beginning of this section, shows one form of comparative thinking about energy options. Another example might be: excavating a particular job requires 4 hours with a mini skid-steer loader, and 2.25 hours with a standard-sized skid steer. The smaller machine is 16 hp and gas powered, while the larger is a 60 hp diesel.

Table 7.3 lists the mini machine at 160,000 Btu per hour of operation, the larger 60 hp model at 504,000 Btu/hr. Thus, although the larger machine is nearly twice as fast, it uses 1,134,000 Btu for the whole job, almost twice the mini machine's 640,000. Other factors affect such decisions: if tight access slows the larger machine, its total fuel/energy consumption will be still higher. If the mini machine is at another job fifteen miles away, while the larger machine is two miles away in the contractor's yard, the advantage may go to the larger machine. Furthermore, energy consid-

Table 7.3

Energy consumption estimates for heavy landscape machines.

Machine Type	Capacity or Rating	Operating Weight (lb.)	hp average for machine type	Fuel D = diesel G = gasoline G/O = gas/oil mix	Estimated Btu/hr.
Tractors and "Tool Carriers"					
Tractor, compact (range: 16–40 hp)	8 cu. ft., 1,400 lb. bucket	4,000	30	D	252,000
Lawn tractor (range: 10–20 hp)	Lt. duty only	635	13	G	130,000
Backhoe loader	5,000 lb. lift	14,000	75	D	630,000
Backhoe loader	7,500 lb. lift	22,600	100	D	840,000
Wheel loader	0.85 cu. yd.	10,000	40	D	336,000
Wheel loader	2.0 cu. yd.	15,000	90	D	756,000
Wheel loader	5.0 cu. yd.	51,000	250	D	2,100,000
Dozer	0.75 cu. yd.	8,710	40	D	336,000
Dozer	1.4 cu. yd.	13,500	70	D	588,000
Dozer	4.0 cu. yd.	27,000	120	D	1,008,000
Mini skid steer (stand-behind)	750 lb., 3.85 cu. ft.	1,350	16	G	160,000
Skid-steer loader	880 lb. lift	3,100	30	D	252,000
Skid-steer loader	1,750 lb. lift	6,200	60	D	504,000
Site dumper	2,500 lb. haul	1,200	13	D	109,200
Mini excavator (track)	0.03 cu. yd.	1,700	8	D	67,200
Mini excavator (track)	1.5 cu. yd.	3,600	23	D	193,200
Mini backhoe (wheeled, not self-propelled)	0.04 cu. yd.	1,300	8	G	80,000
Road grader (small)	10 ft. blade	11,000	35	D	294,000
Road grader (medium)	12 ft. blade	28,000	125	D	1,050,000
Compactor (double drum)	50 in. wide	5,400	33	D	277,200
Compactor (rubber tires)	50 in. wide	9,300	45	D	378,000
Asphalt road reclaimer	Full lane × 15 ft.	32,000	350	D	2,940,000
Trucks					
Pickup (small/import) (avg. 22 mpg, or 5,700 Btu/mi.)	½ ton	4,400	142	G	1,420,000
Pickup (full size) (avg. 13 mpg, or 9,600 Btu/mi.)	¾ or 1 ton	6,400	270	G	2,700,000
Dump truck, flatbed, etc. (avg. 8–11 mpg, or 12,750–17,500 Btu/mi.)	2 or 2½ ton	30,000	350	D	2,940,000
Specialized Machinery					
Chain trencher	36 in. deep cut	720	11	G	110,000
Chain trencher	60 in. deep cut	4,000	32	D	268,800
Wood chipper (portable)	Home use	140	5	G/O	56,250
Wood chipper (mobile)	Lt. coml. use	1,200	20	G	200,000
Wood chipper (mobile)	Hvy. coml. use	7,500	116	D	974,490
Stump cutter/grinder	Small	1,060	25	D	210,000
Brush mower	26 in. blade, cuts 1.5 in. stems	230	8	G	80,000
Curb-laying slipform or extruder	Asphalt or concrete	2,700	20	D	168,000
Motorized wheelbarrow/rough-terrain forklift	1,500 lb.	560	8	G	80,000

erations could be overridden by an imperative need to avoid soil compaction, so that only the smaller machine would be appropriate.

Monetary costs will frequently appear *totally unrelated* to energy-based comparisons. This is a symptom of a society that underprices fuel energy and overvalues speed. The decision to sacrifice some money savings to save energy is an ethical choice, and no one would argue that it is easy. Without considering energy, however, decisions about sustainability become complete guesswork. These figures are a first step toward informed decisions.

The Special Role of Mini Machinery

For landscape construction around valued existing features, small machinery makes great sense. Mini machines are second only to hand labor in minimizing damage and maximizing flexibility. Compared to their heavy relatives, mini machines:

- require far less clearing for access (see Figure 10.2)
- use less fuel (though efficiency per unit of work varies)
- may produce less pollution (again, compare case by case)
- are lighter to transport, saving fuel
- are manufactured from smaller quantities of material
- may exert less ground pressure than a person walking (Table 1.1)
- do tasks beyond human strength or endurance, without "overkill."

Size, weight, fuel efficiency, and maneuverability are criteria for choosing among machines for site work; contact manufacturers for this information. Intelligent tool-design choices are also important, like the decision that self-propulsion isn't a requirement for all backhoes (Figure 7.15). Machines that have a wide range of attachments (see Figure 7.11) sacrifice some mechanical efficiency, but often are more resource efficient overall than ultra-specialized machines.

Several mini machines are illustrated below, embodying some or all of these criteria. Mini machines have proliferated for purchase or rental, with dozens of attachments. In 2000, Ramrod appeared to be the only mini loader; today Boxer, Bobcat, Vermeer, Ditch Witch, and even Cat offer mini equipment (though each firm's idea of "mini" is different). Especially suited for constrained sites, "mini track loaders" (walk-behind tractors with rubber tracks) are about 36 inches wide and (without attachments) less than 70 inches long. Another maneuverability strategy is articulated steering, available on small equipment such as the Avant Tecno line. While these innovations are valuable to sustainable firms, it is still notable that none of the marketing material includes even rough fuel-usage estimates; neither do recent brochures from John Deere or from DR (mowers, powerwagons, chippers, etc.). Far from even nodding to sustainability, DR's advertising extols "busting through entire stands" of brush and small trees.

Several companies market all-electric machinery. These are quiet and pollutant free at the point of use. (Grid power to charge the vehicle has pollutant costs, of course.) Most are tractor-like, or powered carts, generally under 15 horsepower (but with the high torque typical of electric motors); attachments are similar to those for gas tractors. Running a full workday on a charge is common; recharge times vary. A few have AC inverters into which corded tools can be plugged in the field. At least one, the Sun Horse, is a small tractor roofed by a solar panel; a tiller-like walk-behind solar machine was the company's first product.

Energy Use: Small Power Equipment

In 2000, Jim Elmer of Tanaka America/ISM characterized the two-stroke engine industry as being "where cars were twenty years ago," that is, largely unconcerned about fuel consumption or emissions.[48] For most models available in 2000, Elmer noted, "you produce less pollution driving your car 2,500 miles than running your chainsaw for an hour." With approximately 10 million small engines sold per year, both fuel use and pollution were significant.

Beginning in 2000, both the US EPA and California's Air Resources Board (CARB) initiated requirements for two-stroke landscape equipment. By 2005 hand gas-powered tools produced 70 percent less emissions than similarly rated 1990 models and in

Figure 7.10 Some "heavy equipment" isn't. The small Bobcat excavator is about seven feet tall by three feet wide. Compared to the larger excavator shown, weight and fuel use are about 10 percent. (*Photo:* Kim Sorvig.)

Figure 7.11 This mini skid steer, from Ramrod, fits where larger machines can't, and has an unusually wide range of attachments. Size generally corresponds to decreased fuel use and ground pressure. (*Photo:* Ramrod Equipment.)

Figure 7.12 "Site dumpers" can be an efficient compromise between hand labor and full-size tractors. (*Photo:* Kim Sorvig.)

Figure 7.13 Motorized wheelbarrows, like this Honda PowerWagon or the newer Power Carrier, can do heavy work with decreased site impact, as in Sweet Brook's restoration. (*Project:* NY DEP. *Photo:* Dean Cavallaro.)

Figure 7.14 Articulated steering, as well as small size, means this roller can work around existing site features instead of obliterating them. (*Photo:* Kim Sorvig.)

Figure 7.15 Not all machines need to be self-propelled. Trencherman backhoes, by NorthStar, are towed to work; the bucket levers the machine around the site. As of 2017, such machines were found online or at auction; Northern apparently discontinued the model, one of the risks of innovative and sustainable design in a culture that doesn't see the point. (*Photo:* Northern Tool and Equipment, manufacturer of NorthStar machinery.)

many cases used 30 percent less fuel. Redesign eliminated much of the lubricating oil that passed through the engine unburned, improving both efficiency and emissions by about 20 percent.

Despite the improvements, a 2006 mower still emitted ninety-three times the smog-forming compounds per gallon of fuel as a 2006 car, according to CARB.[49] In 2008, further reductions were required, taking effect in 2011: 35 percent less exhaust emissions, a 45 percent decrease in fuel evaporation, and, for larger machines, catalytic converters. The Outdoor Power Equipment Institute (OPEI) supported these rules, and lobbied the EPA to use them nationwide, not just in California. Industry, led by Briggs and Stratton, attacked the regulations, especially the required catalytic converters, partly by claiming the converters posed a fire risk.[50] CARB estimated that these regulations would add 18 percent to the cost of a walk-behind mower.[51]

Many small-tool manufacturers resist discussing efficiency. They feel they have been unfairly targeted, and have not received credit or publicity for improvements that have been made. Energy efficiency of small power tools is especially difficult to rate, for several reasons. For handheld tools like chainsaws, both throttle speed and workload vary widely during a

single use. Others, like lawnmowers, run at relatively constant speed. Additionally, although power ratings for gas and electric are both in horsepower, different rating systems are used, with electric motors rated conservatively, and gas engines rated "as high as honestly possible."[52] In addition, "misfueling" of tools, especially "legacy tools" designed for non-ethanol mixes, is widespread; a 2017 survey[53] showed 63 percent of Americans believed that any gas-station fuel was fine for any outdoor tool. Misfueling decreases efficiency and increases emissions.

Given these difficulties and the changing market, the following table of estimates (Table 7.4) should be used judiciously. It is based on an average figure for two-stroke fuel consumption per horsepower per hour (Table 7.2). For the time being, a conservative estimate is appropriate to sustainability concerns, since many tools currently in use are older models.

Electric tools are listed below in their own table (Table 7.5). Energy-consumption estimates will have more meaning among tools of the same type (electric or gas) than between types, though these rough figures may still have some value for basic planning. The table does *not* include cordless battery-powered tools, which have become increasingly popular, powerful (up to 60V systems for a few tools, with 28V becoming fairly common), and long-lasting.[54] As one anonymous construction pro posted, "When battery-powered tools finally became *usable*, we all pledged our firstborns to whatever god made that possible and we never looked back." Cordless mowers, leaf blowers, string trimmers, power wheelbarrows, small tillers, chainsaws, snow blowers, and polesaws are readily available, along with miter saws, circular saws, reciprocating saws, drills, nailers, and other construction tools. Battery tools are rated in different terms than corded, but either type of electric tool is close to the same energy efficiency (assuming the ultimate source of electricity is the grid; solar chargers change the equation significantly).[55]

Air compressors, powered by either gas or electricity and used to power other tools in turn, are also listed separately (Table 7.6). According to Dave Moorman of Ingersoll-Rand tool company, a basic rule of thumb for *portable* air compressors is that they require about 1 hp to produce 4 cubic feet per minute (cfm) of air. The Compressed Air and Gas Institute gives a much wider range, but this includes large stationary industrial compressors.[56] Efficiency varies considerably with altitude, which directly affects ambient air pressure.

A few gas-powered electrical generators, their rated output, and fuel consumption based on horsepower are given in Table 7.7.

Finally, for landscape maintenance, energy use can be estimated per acre (Table 7.8), based on work by Helen Whiffen, agricultural energy specialist with the University of Florida. Although these figures were based on Florida conditions, they can serve as a model for information that should be public knowledge in every region.[57]

Energy Use: Hand Tools and Labor

Unlike many industries, landscape construction still relies on human labor, often the most efficient way to get landscape jobs done. Hand labor is economical for landscape work where limited access, awkward terrain, irregular materials, or artistic care are involved.

As a round figure, an adult male human's base energy use is about 300 Btu per hour, or on the order of 2,500 Btu for a working day.[58] As shown above, only a few of the smallest electric motors will run for an hour on less than 500 Btu of energy, while almost all petroleum-fueled machines use 10,000 Btu per hour or more. Virtually all machine energy produces pollution and comes from nonrenewable resources. Human (and draft-animal) energy is derived from agricultural

Table 7.4
Energy consumption estimates for small gas-powered landscape tools.

Machine Type	Capacity or Rating	Operating Weight (lb.)	hp average for tool type	Fuel	Estimated Btu/hr.
Tractor, compact (range: 16–40 hp)	8 cu. ft., 1,400 lb. bucket	4,000	30	D	252,000
Compact stump grinder	Small full duty	180	9	G	90,000
Horticultural sprayer, trailer type	55 gal., 500 psi, 3 gpm	130 empty	3.5	G	35,000
Lawn aerator	26 in. wide	200 + ballast	4	G	40,000
Lawn edger	Heavy duty	65	3	G	30,000
Pressure washer	3 gpm, cold water	74–130	5.5	G	55,000
Rototiller	26 in. wide, 8 in. deep	200	8	G	80,000
Lawnmower	30 in. cut	40	7.5	G	75,000
Sod cutter	18 in. wide	325	5.5	G	55,000
Sprayer, backpack	3 gal. tank	30	5	G	50,000
Auger, 1-person	12 in. max. bit	19	2	G/O	22,500
Auger, 1-person	10 in. max. bit	26	3	G/O	33,750
Auger, 2-person	10 in. max. bit	53	3.8	G/O	42,750
Blower, backpack	405 cfm, 195 mph	28	2.8	G/O	31,500
Blower/shredder, handheld	130 mph	12–18	1.2	G/O	13,500
Chainsaw	12 in.	11	2.2	G/O	24,750
Chainsaw	24 in.	16	3.1	G/O	34,900
Cutoff saw, handheld	12 in. blade	26 + blade	3.5	G/O	39,380
Cutoff saw, handheld	14 in. blade	32 + blade	4.8	G/O	54,000
Hedge trimmer	17 in.	11	1.2	G/O	13,500
Lawn edger	Lightweight	13	0.9	G/O	10,130
Line trimmer	Lightweight	8.5	1.05	G/O	11,820
Power pruner (chain type)	10 in.	18	0.9	G/O	10,130
Rototiller, mini	12 in. wide, 10 in. deep	20	2.0	G/O	23,630

products, which are among the most quickly renewable resources; wastes are easily biodegradable. In addition, a 180-pound man wearing size-ten shoes puts about 2 pounds per square inch (psi) pressure on the soil. When a self-propelled machine has a "ground pressure" of less than 5 psi, manufacturers start advertising the fact.

Thus, although energy comparisons between human and machine are more thought provoking than scientific, any work done by hand provides clear sustainability payoffs. Some hand tools amplify muscle power. Investing in such machines literally leverages human efforts, often producing better projects, paying off in reputation and financially too. An example is the Tree Toad, a hand-powered tree spade for transplanting nursery stock. Digging blades are driven into soil with a slide hammer (a tube with handles, used to drive steel fenceposts); the tree is lifted with a built-in jack; a long-handled handcart moves the lifted tree "in the earliest wet Spring, even in areas that no other machinery can access."[59] The smallest model handles trees up to 1.5″ in diameter with a 16″ root ball, weighing

up to 750 lb.; the largest model, intended for towing, moves 3.25″ diameter, 32″ root balls weighing up to 2,000 lb. Costing less than one-tenth of most powered transplanters, Tree Toad uses human power to real advantage in landscape work.

Virtually every landscape professional uses computing on the job. It is easy to forget the energy implications of these near-universal tools. A 2008 report noted that servers and data storage—thus *not* including non-networked personal or business computers—used 180 billion kilowatt-hours in 2007, with the figure expected to double every four years. In 2017, computer energy usage is estimated to exceed fuel usage for the entire air-transportation industry; others have stated that computers use more than the non-IT energy budgets of most nations.[60]

A final note on human energy use: "Thinking," says energy expert Vaclav Smil, "is an enormous energy bargain." Not only does brain activity require only about 5 percent of the base energy expenditure of staying alive, but that energy use stays the same whether zoning out or thinking furiously.[61] In energy

Table 7.5

Energy consumption estimates for electric landscape tools.

Tool Type	Capacity or Rating	Operating Weight (lb.)	hp or Watts[a]	Current[b]	Estimated Btu/hr.[c]	
Chainsaw	12 in. bar	7	1,600 W	AC	(5,470)	13,675
Lawnmower	30 in. cut	25	6 hp	AC	(16,000)	40,000
Chop saw (stand mounted)	14 in.	35	1,800 W	AC	(5,660)	14,150
Disc grinder	4.5 in.	5	780 W	AC	(2,450)	6,125
Horticultural sprayer, trailer type	15 gal., 40 psi, 1.4 gpm	53 empty	180 W	DC	(570)	1,425
Power pruner (chain type)	8 in.	12	1.25 hp	AC	(3,190)	7,980
Submersible pump	90 gph, 2 ft. head	1	5 W	AC	(16)	39
Submersible pump	180 gph, 20 ft. head	10	130 W	AC	(410)	1,025
Submersible pump	300 gph, 15 ft. head	6	220 W	AC	(690)	1,725
Submersible pump	520 gph, 15 ft. head	7	300 W	AC	(945)	2,360
Submersible pump	2,750 gph, 15 ft. head	10	700 W	AC	(2,200)	5,500
Winch	550 lb.	90	0.5 hp	AC	(1,275)	3,190
Winch	2,000 lb.	14	0.6 hp	DC	(1,530)	3,825
Winch	1,900 lb.	230	1.5 hp	AC	(3,825)	9,560

[a]Energy consumption for electric tools is based on watts where known, or horsepower if wattage is unavailable.

[b]All are 120V AC or 12V DC.

[c]Electric tools show two estimates, both converted to Btu/hr. The first, in parentheses, is usage by the tool "at the plug" without transmission losses. The second factors in 60 percent loss between generating plant and user; that is, 2.5 times as much energy is generated as is used at the plug. If using an on-site generator or photovoltaics, see "Evaluate Tools and Their Energy Sources" (**above**).

Table 7.6

Energy consumption estimates for portable air compressors.

Compressor Type	Capacity or Rating	Operating Weight (lb.)	Air Flow (cfm at 90 psi)	hp	Fuel	Est. Btu/Hr
Two-stage shop model	30 gal.	440	18	11	G	110,000
Twin tank wheeled	20 gal.	167	6.5	5	AC	(12,750)[a] 31,875
Twin tank wheeled	10 gal.	235	18	9	G	90,000
Twin tank wheeled	8 gal.	139	10	5.5	G	55,000
Single tank	3 gal.	25	2.9	1.5	AC	(3,825)[a] 9,560
Tankless	Light duty	15	1.8	0.75	AC	(1,915)[a] 4,790

[a] See the note on electrical ratings in Table 7.5.

Table 7.7

Energy consumption estimates for portable electric generators.

Electrical Output		Engine Fuel Estimates		
Watts max.	Amps	hp	Fuel	Est. Btu/hr.
1,000	7.5	2.5	G	312,500
2,700	20	5	G	625,000
4,400	35	8	G	1,000,000
10,000	80	16	G	2,000,000
12,000	110	20	G	2,500,000

terms, it costs nothing to think things through carefully—yet the result can be massive savings in both labor and equipment. Think about it!

Energy Use: Transportation

Transportation touches all aspects of construction efficiency. Materials, machinery, and workers are transported to and from the site. Energy use for all these movements is a significant part of the energy cost of the whole job.

Fuel to move materials and run machines gets more attention, but worker commutes should not be forgotten. Tractor-trailers are much more efficient per ton of material moved than passenger cars or small trucks. Although many older trucks guzzle diesel at a rate of 6 mpg, "for a compact car to get the equivalent mileage based on a fuel consumption *per ton mile*, the compact car would have to get almost 500 miles per gallon."[62] Passenger cars use a couple tons of machine to haul a hundred-and-some pounds of passenger—a classic example of using more power than the job requires. Large trucks running empty, however, still get 6–10 mpg while hauling only their driver, a situation that responsible companies avoid if at all possible. (Someone should start an Uber-like app for shared local haulage.)

Most researchers agree that one of the most important steps a construction professional can take to reduce environmental impact is to cut down transportation and fuel costs. Choice of transport can have a hundredfold impact on energy in transporting materials, as Table 7.9 makes clear.

Transportation of *workers* is a significant part of the total energy used by the landscape professions. Job sites tend to be far from either the firm's offices or the workers' homes.

Compare these numbers with those for heavy site machinery (Table 7.3), small gas-powered tools (Table 7.4), or embodied energy of materials (see p. 331). The average energy consumption for one hour's use of the large machines listed is about 95,000 Btu. A crew member who drives alone to the site in a car getting 20 mpg uses the same amount of fuel *every fifteen miles*. Those fifteen miles are equivalent in energy terms to 4,500 square feet of 1/8-inch aluminum sheet, or 5 tons of aggregate. Average for an hour's use of a gas-powered hand tool is around 12,000 Btu. The same employee uses that by driving two miles.

Notice also that getting the employee with the 20 mpg car to take one rider lowers the energy per passenger mile more than getting him or her to drive (still

Table 7.8

Energy use in landscape maintenance.

Maintenance Type	Energy Use per Unit	Energy Use per Acre	Annual Energy Use
Mowing, gas mower	86,650 Btu/hr.	125,000 Btu per mowing	1.25–2.5 million Btu per acre per year
Mowing, electric mower	40,000 Btu/hr.	60,000 Btu per mowing	600,000 to 1.2 million Btu per acre per year
Irrigation (municipal water)	18 Btu/gal.	N/A	16 million Btu per acre per year
Fertilizer (for lawns)	2,700 Btu/lb.	N/A	2.16–7.2 million Btu per acre per year
Pesticide (for lawns)	N/A	0.625–2.5 million Btu per application	N/A
Trees (water + fertilizer + pesticide)	N/A	N/A	0.5–1.0 million Btu per tree per year

Source: Based on Helen H. Whiffen, "Landscape Maintenance Takes Energy: Use It Wisely," Energy Efficiency and Environmental News (University of Florida Extension), Feb 1993. Unit conversions by Sorvig. Items marked N/A were not noted by Whiffen.

Table 7.9

Transportation energy consumption per ton of material per mile.

	Btu/Ton/Mile	
	Low	High
Boat	350	540
Train	680	820
Truck	2,340	6,140
Plane	37,000	?

alone) in a new car getting 35 mpg. Carpooling incentives can be a construction company's most effective energy-saving tool.

With construction sites frequently located on the suburban fringe, miles add up rapidly—twenty or thirty miles each way is not at all uncommon. At such distances a six-person crew, each in a 20 mpg car, racks up 2.25 million Btu per day; that equals 11.25 million Btu per five-day workweek. That energy would power three pieces of heavy equipment all week, assuming the average noted above. It would also be enough energy to produce 5 tons of common brick, or 500 pounds of steel. (This is without factoring in energy costs of vehicle maintenance or highway infrastructure, which Odum estimated at an additional 75 percent of fuel energy.)[63] Similarly, commuting to an office building, built to high efficiency standards, routinely uses twice as much energy as operating the building.[64]

As a society, Americans tend to overlook transportation costs—a difficult habit to change, even for one-self. No matter how well-intentioned, a professional

cannot truly stake a reputation on "green building" while commuting many miles daily in a single-occupant four-wheel-drive pickup. Transportation alternatives are hard to find, especially in newer cities and the West, but are every bit as important as green practices adopted at the site.

Much of the energy embodied in materials comes from transportation. For example, brick used 350 miles from the factory uses as much energy in transportation as was used to produce the bricks.[65] Obviously, ignoring transportation energy distorts decisions like "Is brick appropriate as a material at this site?" For this reason, one of the most consistent sustainability recommendations is to specify local materials.

Many specifiers already choose suppliers in part based on transportation distances, but international

Table 7.10

Transportation energy consumption per passenger mile.

Miles per Gallon→	20	25	30	35
↓ Number in Vehicle		Btu per Passenger per Mile		
1	6,250	5,000	4,000	3,500
2	3,125	2,500	2,000	1,750
3	2,000	1,700	1,350	1,175
4	1,550	1,250	1,000	875

Source: Howard T. Odum and Elizabeth C. Odum, Energy Basis for Man and Nature (New York: McGraw-Hill, 1976).
Note: Gasoline vehicles. Fuel only. To allow for all energy used to make travel possible, (e.g., road construction, gas stations, etc.), multiply these figures by 175 percent.

sourcing is still common. Monetary costs of shipping, plus unstable fuel prices and "fuel surcharges," are incentives to choose local products. Owners of large trucks can calculate fuel savings for various improved technologies at www.epa.gov/smartway.

Carpooling involves quite different incentives, requiring "green" businesses to put their money where their principles are. Fuel costs for getting to the job site are commonly borne by workers; thus the company gains nothing if an employee saves fuel. Having all employees report to the main office and then go to the site in company vehicles is not always efficient routing.

Mapping software may help. By entering employee home locations and project sites just once, such software can easily compute travel distances. "Logistics" programs save major transportation companies billions of dollars, hours, and fuel gallons by computing efficient routing. The same programs could provide decision-making support about suppliers as well. As of 2017, there are hundreds of logistics programs, most geared toward freight; fleet management software often combines logistics with vehicle repair recordkeeping.

Save Energy and Money with Machinery and Tool Guidelines

The following suggestions, although not ironclad, are a starting point for saving energy by careful planning about machinery:

• Plan! Conventional contractors may get by with seat-of-the-pants fuel-usage decisions; no one concerned with green building can afford such guesswork. Gasoline at four dollars per gallon makes planning a survival skill; unpredictable fuel prices are even more risky than high ones.
• Cut job travel miles and fuel costs by any means possible. Company-sponsored carpooling is one option. Regular tune-ups of company vehicles should be standard practice. One famous design-build architecture company, Jersey Devil, moves onto the site in Airstream trailers for the duration. Choose your own methods, but decrease work-related transportation.

• Use hand labor where it is reasonable to do so. Take pride in handwork's quality, eco-friendliness, and health benefits, rather than focusing only on speed and ease of power equipment.
• Use the *most efficient* tool for the job. If that tool is engine powered, balance low fuel consumption with speed.
• Use the *lightest* machinery that will do the job. Manufacturers and tool rental companies are offering more and more mini machinery.
• When buying or renting power tools large or small, insist on information about fuel consumption per hour, pollutant emissions, and ground pressure. Give your business to companies that provide this information willingly. Use the information in planning.
• Look for innovative ways of generating energy—solar and wind particularly, and battery tools—for mobile construction crews.

Embodied Energy—Why Do We Care?[66]

Embodied energy, as discussed at the beginning of this chapter, is the total energy used to produce something—either a single material, a complex product, or a whole project. It is a critical factor in understanding, achieving, or evaluating sustainability. In addition, being able to present energy and materials choices rationally is increasingly important in persuading clients, regulatory agencies, and the public that specific construction plans are well justified.

A general diagram of energy inputs adding up to embodied energy is shown in Figure 7.16. For some materials, inputs shown may be repeated or skipped. A simple "raw" material like landscape boulders or sand might only involve energy from extraction, transportation, and placement. Embodied energy of steel or aluminum bars would involve extraction, smelting ore, shaping the bars, plus transportation (during processing as well as from factory to site). If further manufactured into tubular fencing, energy used in making tubes and assembling fence panels would be added, as would energy to erect the fence on-site.

Embodied energy is usually expressed in terms of *energy per unit* of product, just as cost estimates are based on cost-per-unit or cost-per-quantity figures.

Energy is most commonly stated in Btu or in joules (the metric/scientific standard); calories and watts are also used as energy units. Thus the embodied energy of builder's sand might be in Btu/ton or in kilojoules/cubic meter; for metal ingots, in kilocalories/pound; and for fencing, in Btu per linear foot or per panel of fence. Conversion tables can be found under "measurements" in dictionaries or *Architectural Graphic Standards*; excellent shareware such as Master Converter is also available, and online converters are a click away.

Know the Embodied Energy of Landscape Materials

The most recent of perhaps ten major studies of embodied energy for construction materials was developed by the Sustainable Energy Research Team at the University of Bath. (Many others have been commissioned for in-house use, but not published.)[67] The Bath study, which includes over 200 construction materials, is available online from a group appropriately named Circular Ecology. None of these studies focused specifically on *landscape* construction materials.

Tables of embodied energy values specific to common landscape materials were included in the first and second editions of this book, along with an essay, "Limits of Embodied Energy Methods Today." Compiled by averaging the half-dozen studies then available, these tables are now dated. However, unlike most other tools for energy estimation, they include "raw" materials as used in landscape work, as opposed to "wall systems" or "floor assemblies" for architectural analysis. For anyone wishing to use the landscape-specific figures, they will be posted online with other sustainability analysis tools (see "Visit and Contribute to the Website," p. xxv). You can also access them in Wiley's 2007 *Landscape Architectural Graphic Standards*, p. 1044, where they were reprinted, without attribution.

Online calculators and databases from Athena Sustainable Materials Institute or the Building Energy Efficiency Standard (BEES) are excellent for buildings; for landscapes, not so much. BEES includes almost no site materials, while Athena keeps such materials "behind the scenes," used to calculate complex assemblies, but inaccessible to users. I would say that the Bath study is the current source most likely to be helpful for landscape purposes. No matter what source is used, interpretation and comparison of these statistics requires care. Be sure you:

- Read whatever information each study offers concerning its sources, methods, and limitations. A study that does not discuss these issues is hard to use or compare with other results, and potentially misleading.
- Use life-cycle costing (LCC, below) to account for the effects of time.
- Base final materials decisions on broad guidelines (end of this chapter) and good judgment, not just energy figures.

Benefit from Embodied Energy Analysis

In concept, embodied energy is straightforward. Embodied energy analysis has many potential benefits for designers and builders, though only part of this potential is currently feasible. In theory, embodied energy figures can be used to compare environmental impacts of widely differing materials and designs, revealing trade-offs that do not show up in economic or engineering analysis.

Embodied energy is far more *objective* than price as a measure of comparative product value. Accurate value comparisons in construction are critical to everyone—client, designer, and contractor—yet market prices are frequently misleading indicators of value, especially environmental value. Distorting effects of local and international markets, artificial price subsidies (favoring fossil fuels), inflation, and buyer psychology can be set aside in energy analysis. (See adobe, p. 268, as an example.) Once underlying or intrinsic value is established by energy analysis, financial value can be better understood, too. "Energy accounting" will one day be the most accurate way to predict business expenses, profits, and losses, as essential a tool for contractors and designers as monetary cost estimating is today. (I have suggested that the calorie or kilojoule become the standard unit of *currency*, and embodied energy the basis for pricing that would adjust to supply and demand.)

Energy is a common denominator in all manufacturing and construction, making complex apples-and-oranges decisions much easier. If you need to compare

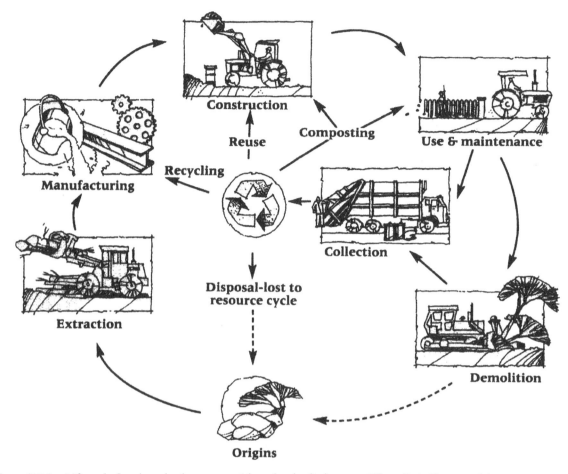

Construction

Reuse   **Composting**

Use & maintenance

Recycling

Manufacturing

Collection

Disposal-lost to resource cycle

Extraction

Demolition

Origins

Figure 7.16   Life-cycle flowchart: landscape materials and embodied energy. (*Illust.*: Craig Farnsworth.)

the environmental impact of two functionally equivalent designs—say, a cast-in-place concrete wall built with gas-powered machines versus a wood fence made with air-powered hand tools—energy analysis is the most meaningful measure available. Questions like "steel studs versus wood framing" get a new and important perspective from knowing that steel is relatively high in embodied energy per pound, and that wood is relatively low. (Strength, durability, and recyclability must also be factored in.)

Fuel burning to produce energy is a major source of pollution, so embodied energy is a rough-and-ready *indicator* for materials that pollute. For example, about 55 kg of CO_2 is released for every gigajoule (billion joules) of energy produced by burning natural gas (a relatively clean fuel).[68] Thus, if 1 megajoule (million joules) of natural-gas-generated energy is required to produce a ton of some material, its embodied energy (1 MJ/ton) also represents 0.055 kg of

CO_2 emissions (about 0.125 lb.) per ton. Fuels vary in how much pollution they release, and not all pollution is accounted for in fuel consumption. As a general rule, higher embodied energy means higher pollution during production.

Operating energy efficiency has been regulated since the 1970s, making dramatic changes in building design and contracting. Landscapes, using little operating energy, have largely been ignored. As energy efficiency in *all* aspects of construction becomes more critical, *embodied* energy standards will probably affect landscape materials and construction. New Zealand, for instance, studied the feasibility of embodied energy standards as part of national code (rejecting it as not *yet* practical).[69] Similarly, in 1993 the US government considered a "Btu tax" (a.k.a. carbon tax); the measure was not politically acceptable, but similar initiatives are likely to succeed as both energy costs and global temperatures continue to rise. Citizens' Climate

Table 7.11

Carbon dioxide emissions by fuel type—use to compare fuel impacts.

CO_2-emitting Material	For Each Unit Material Used	CO_2-emitted		For each Million Btu Energy Produced from CO_2-emitting Material	CO_2-emitted	
		Pounds	Kilograms		Pounds	Kilograms
Heating/Cooking						
Propane	gallon	12.70	5.76	Propane	139.05	63.07
Butane	gallon	14.80	6.71	Butane	143.20	64.95
Butane-propane mix	gallon	13.70	6.21	Butane-propane mix	141.12	64.01
Home heating and diesel fuel (distillate)	gallon	22.40	10.16	Home heating and diesel fuel (distillate)	161.30	73.16
Kerosene	gallon	21.50	9.75	Kerosene	159.40	72.30
Coal (all types)	short ton	4,631.50	2,100.82	Coal (all types)	210.20	95.35
Natural gas	thousand cu. ft.	117.10	53.12	Natural gas	117.00	53.07
Gasoline	gallon	19.60	8.89	Gasoline	157.20	71.30
Residual heating fuel (businesses only)	gallon	26.00	11.79	Residual heating fuel (businesses only)	173.70	78.79
Transportation						
Jet fuel	gallon	21.10	9.57	Jet fuel	156.30	70.90
Aviation gas	gallon	18.40	8.35	Aviation gas	152.60	69.20
Industrial and Other						
Flared natural gas	thousand cu. ft.	120.70	54.75	Flared natural gas	120.60	54.70
Petroleum coke	gallon	32.40	14.70	Petroleum coke	225.10	102.10
Other petroleum and miscellaneous	gallon	22.09	10.02	Other petroleum and miscellaneous	160.10	72.62
Municipal solid waste	short ton	5,771.00	2,617.68	Municipal solid waste	91.90	41.69
Tire-derived fuel	short ton	6,160.00	2,794.13	Tire-derived fuel	189.54	85.97
Waste oil	barrel	924.0	419.12	Waste oil	210.00	95.25
Waxes	gallon	21.11	9.57	Waxes	160.10	72.62
Coal by Type						
Anthracite	short ton	5,685.00	2,578.68	Anthracite	228.60	103.70
Bituminous	short ton	4,931.30	2,236.80	Bituminous	205.70	93.30
Sub-bituminous	short ton	3,715.90	1,685.51	Sub-bituminous	214.30	97.20
Lignite	short ton	2,791.60	1,266.25	Lignite	215.40	97.70
Coke	short ton	6,239.68	2,830.27	Coke	251.60	114.12
Other Energy						
Geothermal (average all generation)		N/A	N/A	Geothermal (average all generation)	16.99	7.71
Nonfuel Uses						
Asphalt and road oil	gallon	26.34	11.95			
Lubricants	gallon	23.62	10.72			
Petrochemicals	gallon	24.74	11.22			
Naphtha solvents	gallon	20.05	9.10			

Source: Based on US Energy Information Administration estimates, www.eia.gov/environment/emissions/co2_vol_mass.php.

Note: To convert CO_2 to carbon equivalents, multiply by 12/44.

Lobby's well-developed proposal for a carbon tax is a good example.

Energy Accounting and Sustainability

Energy accounting is as complex as economics—no more and no less. There is one major difference, however. Most modern societies monitor money and trade; in industrial societies, this monitoring is itself a huge industry. By contrast, accurate and detailed monitoring of energy has not yet become a priority, and tools, methods, and institutions for this task are far from fully developed. As a result, available statistics on embodied energy are sometimes confusing and hard to compare. Is this an unavoidable limitation?

Energy accounting today *is* rather complex and inexact. Critics argue that this will always be the case. These limitations would be overcome if energy statistics were collected with the same diligence that monetary and trade statistics are. Technology to collect energy data exists, at least in basic form. The ability to predict, plan, and make decisions would quickly and dramatically improve, for businesses, for individuals, and for society. Accuracy would increase, and "voodoo economics" would decline. The fact that vested interests actively prefer voodoo complicates matters.

Construction Influence on the Energy Future

Why consider this issue in a book on construction? Like any technological advance, energy analysis will only develop if there is a demand for it. That demand will come from those most directly affected by energy costs—those whose livelihoods make them energy power-users. As Architecture 2030 has publicized, construction and design decisions affect nearly half the world's energy use. Our professions cannot single-handedly create demand for accurate energy estimating and tracking—but our influence will be significant.

The Athena Sustainable Materials Institute, a major embodied energy research organization, states bluntly: "Building construction, renovation and operation consume more of the Earth's resources than any other human activity. This generates millions of tonnes of greenhouse gases, toxic air emissions, water pollutants, and solid wastes. No other sector has a greater impact on the global environment or faces a greater obligation to improve its environmental performance."[70]

Landscape designers and planners should choose materials at least partly on embodied energy considerations. Landscape contractors will need new skills to implement energy-conscious designs; they will have to understand embodied energy when proposing substitutions for specified materials. In order to stay competitive in a sustainable economy, contractors will also need to manage energy efficiently. Although it is an unfamiliar concept to most landscape professionals today, embodied energy is an idea whose time is coming soon—some would say, should have come long ago—and for which there is good reason to be prepared.

Embodied Energy Estimating Example

An example of how embodied energy statistics might be used is shown in Table 7.12 and described below. EE numbers used in this example are from my posted tables (see p. xxv).

You have decided to build a 5-foot-high garden wall, using either handmade adobe or straw-bale construction, with identical footings in either case.

Calculate the volume of the wall. Note that standard straw bales are 4 inches thicker than adobe blocks, so the bale wall's volume is larger. Assume a wall length of 100 feet.

Convert volume to weight, multiplying density by volume for each material. Density figures are available from many standard references in print and online, including the tables in previous editions of this book, posted at Island Press's website.

Unstabilized adobe (listed as packed Earth) has embodied energy of 172 Btu/lb.; baled straw is 103 Btu/lb. Multiply these by the total weight for each material. It appears that the bale wall, being much lighter per volume, uses less than 2 percent of the energy required for adobe.

Straw-bale construction, however, requires stuccoing. For stucco, calculate a volume, convert to weight, and compute embodied energy.

Stucco requires metal wire or lath. This material is listed by area, and can be looked up in online tables, showing 52,100 Btu/sq. ft. Multiply the area of wire used by this amount.

Adding stucco and lath to straw bale shows that adobe uses less than 15 percent of the energy for straw bale.

The analysis could go further. Steel reinforcing is optional in straw-bale construction, adding much embodied energy; you might decide on bamboo stakes as reinforcement.

The above assumes that the adobe blocks were made by hand on-site. If they were transported, you would need to look in Table 7.9, where trucking is shown to use an average of about 4,000 Btu per ton per mile. The wall weighs about 28.5 tons. If the supplier is 20 miles from the project, this adds 2.28 million Btu to energy for adobe. The total, even allowing for breakage during transport, is still only about 18 percent of the energy for stuccoed straw bale, even without calculating transportation for the bales.

However, if someone insists on stuccoing the adobe . . .

This example shows how similar energy estimation is to money estimation; it also shows that job- and site-specific inclusions or exclusions make a great difference in which material is most energy efficient. Factors like durability, distance to source, and so on must also be taken into account.

Not Energy Alone

Analysis of energy requirements is a strong baseline for comparing construction materials and methods. Though potentially far more realistic than price comparison, it must still be used in combination with other factors. These include:

Strength in proportion to weight or cross-section shows how much of a material is required to accomplish a structural function; a tiny amount of a high-energy material may be more energy effective than a large amount of a low-energy material.

Durability and service life tell how long a material can perform its function before being replaced or recycled and, thus, how often energy investment must be repeated.

Resource scarcity and renewability: glass is high energy, but sand to make it is more abundant than petroleum to make clear plastics. Neither is renewable.

Reusability and recyclability: reusing a material in its ex-

isting form requires only transportation and installation energy for the second use. For some materials, re*manufacturing* saves a high proportion of new production energy; aluminum can be recycled for as little as 5 percent of the energy needed to refine new ore.[71] Not all materials are equally recyclable. Some materials are themselves recyclable, but fasteners or adhesives interfere with reuse or recycling.

Toxicity: in addition to air and water pollution generated by energy use, some materials are inherently toxic or require toxic chemicals in production. See Principle 6.

Other design considerations: materials that degrade under ultraviolet light are unsuitable for exposed outdoor use, no matter how energy efficient they may be. Another example is steel: energy efficient for uses requiring strength, it can be corroded by some soils, affecting its suitability for in-ground fittings. To overcome this, steel may be coated—but the energy cost of doing so must be accounted for.

Although it is beyond the scope of this book to give comprehensive information on each of these factors, it is clear that they must be considered in materials selection and energy analysis. A promising approach to this type of multifactor analysis is usually known as life-cycle analysis, or LCA, which is discussed on p. 293. Despite decades of LCA information for general construction, there do not yet appear to be any *landscape-specific* LCA studies.

A simpler method called life-cycle *costing* (LCC), which can address core life-cycle issues without the extensive expertise required for LCA, is discussed in the following section.

Use Life-cycle Costing to Justify Sustainable Design

Life-cycle costing (LCC) is a *relatively* simple tool for apples-to-apples comparisons of long-term planning options. It was first developed for financial comparisons such as return on investment (ROI), but can easily be used for energy cost-benefit comparison (sometimes called eROI) as well. Unlike its similarly named cousin, life-cycle *analysis* (LCA), it does *not* deal with resource scarcity, pollution issues, or in any detail with recyclability. Nonetheless, LCC is a respected technique, and ready to use today, while LCA and embodied energy analysis are still evolving, and beyond most designers' expertise (or patience). For this reason, LCC is worth mentioning here.

Architects use LCC routinely; a rather complex explanation of the process is included in *Architectural Graphic Standards*.[72] Landscape professionals who use LCC will certainly reduce long-term costs passed on to their clients, a necessary step toward sustainability.

Use LCC for Better Comparative Costing

Life-cycle costing is particularly useful when comparing two or more proposed options, for example, two trucks for a landscape firm. Suppose one model costs $10,000, needs $750 maintenance once a year, and gets 20 mpg, while the other costs $12,000, requires

an average of $500 service every other year, and gets 30 mpg. Driving each truck 10,000 miles annually,[73] by the end of five years the first truck costs $16,250, and the second $14,915. Shortening the life cycle to two years before trade-in, the first model costs only $12,500, the second $13,166. The short life cycle, however, dramatically increases the cost *per year* for either truck. Cost per year over five years is $3,250 and $2,983 for the first and second truck, respectively; over two years, annual cost shoots up to $6,250 and $6,583. This is why designing for long-term durability is an important aspect of sustainability, and why the "disposable building/landscape" approach is so wasteful.

This example shows clearly how "sticker price" alone gives misleading comparisons. The person or firm who bought the first truck, or who traded in either truck early, would have to work a lot harder

Table 7.12
Worked example of simple embodied energy comparison.

Wall Volume				
Length	100	ft.		
Height	5	ft.		
Std. Width	(in feet)	× 500 sq. ft. =		
Adobe (14 in.)	1.2	600 cu. ft.		
Straw (18 in.)	1.5	750 cu. ft.		
Convert to Weight				
	lb./cu. ft.	× volume	Total	
Adobe	95	600	57,000	lb.
Straw	8	750	1,125	lb.
Basic Embodied Energy				
	Btu/lb.	× weight	Total	
Adobe	172	57,000	9,804,000	Btu/100 lin. ft.
Straw	103	1,125	115,875	Btu/100 lin. ft.
Reqd. for Straw Only				
1/2 in. Stucco	1,150	sq. ft. surface	46	cu. ft. stucco
	145	lb./cu. ft.	6,670	lb. stucco
	860	Btu/lb.	5,736,200	Btu for stucco
Wire lath	1,150	sq. ft. surface		
	52,100	Btu/sq. ft.	59,915,000	Btu for wire
Total Embodied Energy				
Adobe	9,804,000	Btu/100 lin. ft.		
Straw	65,767,075	Btu/100 lin. ft.		

to make a profit. The example *included operating costs and specified duration*; this is simple life-cycle costing, which gives much more accurate and useful information about the two trucks. Life-cycle costs *change* with length of service and amount of use; in general, the more use achieved for the same cost, the more sustainable the investment is.

Conventionally, many design and construction professionals have concerned themselves only with "sticker price" of projects. After all, it is this up-front cost that professionals must convince the client to pay; profits or fees are based directly on this price. For governmental and some commercial clients, the sticker price ("capital cost") cannot, by law or policy, be mingled with any "operating" costs. This fact explains much of the negligent maintenance that threatens infrastructure across the United States.

Sustainability requires broadening this perspective. If cheap to build means expensive to maintain, up-front profits are ultimately at the expense of society and the environment. The "cheap" truck burns more fuel and causes more pollution the longer it is on the road; trading it in after two years makes it appear cheaper, but actually doubles its annual cost. Whether looking at vehicles, buildings, or landscapes, simple sticker-price estimates encourage waste and short-sightedness. LCC is a tool for designing more sustainably and responsibly.

Learn Basic LCC

Over a project's useful life, costs occur in five major forms.[74] For LCC, these are referred to as Capital, Maintenance, Fuel, Replacement, and Salvage. Using the first letter as an abbreviation for each, the life-cycle cost of a project, system, or piece of equipment can be written as LCC = C + M + F + R − S.

These costs can be in terms of money, or of energy, but not mixed in the same computation. Capital costs in dollars and maintenance costs in energy would not produce a useful total, for example.

Capital costs include materials and construction work, as well as design and engineering services. Most designers and contractors are highly experienced in estimating capital costs. Conventional bid estimates include *only* capital costs, and lack the other four factors.

Maintenance costs include all anticipated *annual* operating expenses, such as routine inspection, seasonal start-up and shutdown, and minor parts changed routinely each year. ("Replacement" refers to major items replaced only a few times over the life cycle.)

Although *fuel* cost could be included in maintenance, it is better listed separately. In monetary analysis, the rate of inflation is often greater for fuel prices than for other goods. In energy analysis, it can be valuable to know how much goes directly to fuel.

Replacement represents overhauls that are not annual—for example, new photovoltaic-system storage batteries every eighth year of a thirty-year lifespan.

Salvage (or resale) is conventionally subtracted from costs; 20 percent of the original cost is a common salvage estimate. For environmental purposes, salvage can be either a reduced cost (when materials are reused or recycled) or an additional cost (when disposal is required). Dump fees, for example, would be added to the life-cycle cost; for more accuracy, an estimate of the total cost to society for disposal would be added.

Besides these cost amounts, it is necessary to know the predicted *useful life* of the project or equipment being evaluated. The *frequency* of maintenance and replacement tasks must be known, as well as fuel-consumption rates. These figures are usually obtained from manufacturers, or estimated based on professional experience.

When comparing several options, use the *longest* life cycle. For example, alternative power sources for a remote site might be a generator (rebuild or replace every seven years), a windmill (fifteen years between rebuilds), and photovoltaic panels (thirty years before replacement). All three should be analyzed over the thirty-year period, including costs of rebuilding the generator four times and the windmill once.

Try Energy LCC Analysis

For an *energy* LCC analysis, all that is necessary is to add up energy costs for C, M, F, and R, and allow for S. Unlike the simpler forms of embodied energy study, which stop once the project is built and do not consider long-term energy costs, LCC energy analysis reveals differences in durability, operating energy, and maintenance.

From an environmental perspective, the "salvage" factor is especially important. The costs of waste disposal and/or environmental cleanup are poorly accounted for in conventional financial analysis. LCC using energy units has potential to show real costs to society that are otherwise obscured.

Estimate with Monetary LCC

Economic analysis also has value for sustainable construction. Financial cost data are readily available, which cannot yet be said for energy data. Even very environmentally aware landowners and professionals must know the financial costs of proposed work; sometimes cost is the deciding factor in approving sustainable proposals. Money savings can reflect environmental savings, although usually with considerable distortion. LCC using dollar amounts is far preferable to simple capital cost or "sticker-price" analysis, as explained above.

The essential formula (LCC = C + M + F + R − S) is the same, whether plugging in dollars or Btu. For either approach, you must know costs of capital, maintenance, and so on. There is one major difference, however, called "present value," which applies only to money.

Present value is a conventional (or, bluntly, fictional) financial concept based on the idea that money in hand today is worth more than money promised later, because it can be invested. That is, if you have $100 today, in one year you will have $105 if interest is at 5 percent. If someone promises to pay you $100 in a year, you will have only $100. The promised money is thus considered to be worth 5 percent less; its "present value" would be about $95.

Unless you don't care about interest, all figures used in monetary LCC must be adjusted to present value. The standard formulas, called "present-worth factors," are briefly summarized here. Detailed explanations and tables are found in economics texts, on financial-planning websites, and built into computer spreadsheets.[75]

To establish present value, it is necessary to know two things. One is *when* the cost will be paid—at the beginning; annually; or in a specific year of the life cycle, for example, the ninth year of twenty.

The second item is a percentage called the "discount factor." The discount rate is the *expected interest rate* paid on investments, minus the *predicted* inflation rate.[76] For example, if money invested today would earn an annual 7 percent, with annual inflation predicted at 4 percent, the discount rate would be 3 percent. For some products, especially fuel, price inflation is more rapid than average. Thus, general inflation might be 4 percent, while fuel-price inflation could be 6 percent. If investments were still paying 7 percent, the discount rate for fuel costs would be 1 percent instead of 3 percent. The federal government and many banks publish projections of interest and inflation. (Remember that these are at best expert guesses, and at worst pure fiction.)

Given the dollar amounts for each cost, its timing, and a guess at the discount rate, you are ready to prepare a monetary LCC estimate. A blank form for trying such a calculation is online.

The capital cost C is always treated as a single expense, paid all at once in the first year of the life cycle. Because it is paid in the first year, it is *already* at present value. Even if capital costs will be financed by an interest-bearing loan, finance charges and interest are *not* included as capital.

All other costs are converted to present value, using one of two formulas.

Costs that *occur regularly every year* (usually maintenance and fuel) are given a present value as follows. If the discount rate is D, and the number of years in the life cycle is L, then $[1 - (1 + D)^{-L}]/D$ multiplied by the *annual* cost gives the present value. For example, to give present value of annual payments over 15 years at a discount rate of 2 percent, compute $[1 - (1 + .02)^{-15}]/.02$, equaling 12.849. This is called a "uniform present-worth (UPW) factor," referring to uniform payments over the whole life cycle. The UPW factor is multiplied by the dollar amount of the payment. In this example, if the annual payment is $400, the present value of payments over the whole period is 12.849 × 400, or $5,139.60.

Costs that *occur only a few times during the life cycle* (such as replacement and salvage) are computed by a different formula, called "single present worth." If the discount rate is represented again by D, and Y stands for the year when the cost occurs (counted from today), then the single present-worth (SPW) factor is $1/(1 + D)^Y$. Thus, the factor for a single expense paid 8 years from now, assuming a discount rate of 2 percent, would be $1/(1 + .02)^8$, or 0.853. If the actual payment in year eight would be $400, its present value would be 400 times 0.853, or $341.20. If a cost recurs *every* 8 years, the calculation uses single costs occurring in years 8, 16, 24, and so on. Thus, the present value of the same $400 replacement in year 16 is $1/(1 + .02)^{16}$ (SPW factor 0.728, present value $291.38). Note that this is less than the present value of the payment in year 8, because more time has elapsed, during which interest "losses" continue.

A simple spreadsheet to do these calculations is online (see p. xxv). It can be used for LCC energy analysis by ignoring the present-worth factors altogether, making sure to convert all energy costs into the same system of units. There are also dozens of similar worksheets (490,000, to be precise) to be found all over the Web, along with instructions on use and theory.

Apply Guidelines for Landscape Energy Conservation

- *Transportation energy* is probably where landscape professionals can make the most difference.
- Cut *shipping energy* costs by specifying local materials as first preference, then regional products. Use products from distant suppliers sparingly—much like non-native plants, for special accents rather than the whole landscape.
- Cut *worker-transportation energy* costs however possible. Make carpooling a company policy, with incentives. Track worker distances from home to each project; assign workers to short-commute projects where possible and make flexible arrangements for workers when their home is near their current job site.

- Choose the *right machine, tool, or hand labor* for each task with energy consumption in mind. See detailed suggestions on pp. 317–328.
- Improve your ability to *analyze energy* as part of materials selection and design, using embodied energy analysis, life-cycle costing, life-cycle analysis, or other big-picture methods.
- Remember that saving energy is an *ethical choice*, not just a financial one. It will sometimes pay off in immediate dollars, but sometimes will not.

Subtopics and Search Terms for Principle 7: Know the Costs of Energy over Time

Note: Subtopics are also useful search terms; add "innovation" or "controversy" to search terms as appropriate.

Energy
Search terms: energy OR power OR fuel || renewable energy || electricity || energy efficiency || energy conservation

Energy: site design
Search terms: energy + (site OR landscape) + (design OR planning)

Machinery
Search terms: (machinery OR tools) + (lightweight OR efficient OR low-impact OR "low ground pressure" OR "non polluting")

Embodied energy
Search terms: embodied energy || embedded energy || process energy

Solar energy
Search terms: solar energy || solar power || solar electricity || solar OR photovoltaic

Resource List:

Links to information sources related to this chapter are posted at http://islandpress.org/sustainable-landscape-construction

Principle 8:
Celebrate Light, Respect Darkness

At night make me one with the darkness; in the morning make me one with the light.
—Wendell Berry, 1980

Landscape lighting is a source of great pleasure, extending use of outdoor space into nighttime hours. Outdoor lighting, however, can be either well designed, or excessive and inappropriate. Extravagant lighting can be wonderful for temporary effects, but as a permanent landscape feature it wastes resources and causes direct damage to living things.

Lighting is one of the largest single uses of electricity in the United States, consuming just under 10 percent of all residential electricity, and 11 percent of commercial use.[1] Saving energy by more-efficient lighting has been a major priority of most environmental groups. By relamping older lighting with energy-efficient bulbs available today, enough energy could be saved to equal all the oil imported by the United States.[2] This immense energy savings could be accomplished without sacrificing existing levels of lighting at all. Further savings can appropriately be achieved by toning down or eliminating excessive lighting, but the Jevons Paradox applies: as the acting director of the International Dark-Sky Association points out, "One thing that's been true throughout history is that, as lighting tech gets cheaper, we use more of it."[3]

Since the first edition of this book, the lighting industry has changed significantly, and many of these changes affect landscape lighting directly. Dark-sky initiatives have become a major force in shaping outdoor lighting products and practices. Effects of artificial lighting on ecosystems and species, and human health, have received serious study. LED lighting, which had made its expensive and faintly illuminating US debut in 1999, has practically taken over new lighting, dramatically changing design possibilities,

> ## Discussed in This Chapter
>
> Lighting terms.
> When to limit or eliminate lighting.
> Efficiency in design and performance of lighting fixtures.
> Controllers and timers.
> Low-voltage lighting.
> Fiber-optic lighting.
> Solar landscape lighting.

and is widely being retrofitted. Solar power has become more efficient, and solar outdoor lighting, once an oxymoron, is reliable, competitively priced, and widely installed.

Landscape lighting, although a fairly small portion of the total, remains one of the fastest-*growing* sectors of the lighting industry. Because the landscape lighting industry is still developing, designers, contractors, and manufacturers have a real opportunity to ensure that efficiency and appropriate design become standard. Without such a standard, rapid growth of landscape lighting will contribute unnecessarily to national energy consumption.

Respect the Need for Darkness

The impulse to fight back the night is an ancient, almost unconscious human urge, as old as the discovery of fire. Yet although night held primitive dangers and still holds modern ones, it also offers mystery, and is

Talk Lighting—a Brief Glossary

Designing sustainably with light is much easier if basic terms are clear.

Lighting products:

Lamp—an artificial light source; laypeople call these "bulbs."

Luminaire—what laypeople call a fixture, holding a lamp/bulb.

Standard—a pole for a luminaire.

Measuring light:

Wattage—describes energy use. When all bulbs were incandescent, "60-watt" was used to mean a specific brightness. New lamp types vary in efficiency, so watts no longer simply parallel brightness.

Light—strange and wonderful stuff, wave-like one minute, separate energy packets (quanta) the next. Not surprisingly, even practical measurements for lighting design require special terms. Asking the following questions may help sort out the terminology.

Light is energy, but do you want to measure its total energy, or only what is visible? Ultraviolet light, for instance, isn't visible to humans, but its energy heats solar houses, sunburns people, is visible to other species, and affects some light pollution studies.

- Light's total energy is referred to as **radiation**, **radiance**, **radiant flux**, and so on. Measuring it is called **radiometry**; units used are **watts** (English) or **joules** (metric)—the same units used to measure electrical energy that powers a light source.
- Visible light includes only those wavelengths to which the human eye can respond. Such measurements are called **photometric**, or sometimes **photoptic**. Photometric measurements involve a second question:

*When dealing with visible light, are you measuring light **production**, light **moving through air**, or light **striking an object**?*

- Light production is called **luminance**. (**Luminosity** is glow-in-the-dark light from phosphorus.) Light production is measured in **candelas**, a rather arbitrary unit based on a standard candle.[4]
- Light moving or flowing through air is called **luminous flux**. It is measured in **lumens**—one lumen is one candela's worth of light in motion. You can't actually see this until it strikes an object. Directional light flow is called **luminous intensity**.
- Light striking an object becomes visible; it is then called **illuminance** or **illumination**. To measure this "lighting level," ask another question.

in fact biologically necessary to most species. It is important not to forget the *value* of darkness when current lighting technology makes it so easy to exorcise ancient fears.

Excessive lighting was once viewed as an offbeat concept, of concern only to hard-core environmentalists. But that view has changed. As the president of Lumec, a major lighting manufacturer based in Quebec, wrote in the company's newsletter, "What started as a concern among a select group of specialists is now regarded as one of the most fundamental forces changing this industry. The goal of preserving darker

How big an area is receiving the light, and how far is it from the light source? There are two standard measures of illumination, one English, one metric/scientific. They work the same way, but with different units.

Start with a one-candela light source. Place a one-foot-square surface one foot from the light, and the resulting light level is one **foot-candle**. Place a one-meter-square surface one meter from the light, and the light level there is one **lux**.[5] The one-candela source in both systems produces one lumen. A foot-candle is one lumen per square foot. A lux is one lumen per square meter. Thus, they convert by simple math: one foot-candle is 10.764 lux; one lux is 0.093 foot-candle—ten-to-one for quick conversions.

How much lighting bang is available for the energy buck? There are two measures for this, as well.

- **Efficacy** is how well electrical energy is converted to light by a particular technology. It is measured in **lumens per watt**, sometimes expressed as a percentage (a certain lamp has 20 percent efficacy).
- **Efficiency**, to lighting professionals, means how much light comes out of a luminaire, available for illuminating things. Efficiency is affected by the initial lamp efficacy, by reflectors, lenses, diffusers, beam spread, and distance from the fixture to the object being lit.

Color temperature and "spectral de-rating":

Color temperature—a precise color measurement of light. Daylight at noon has a color temperature of 5500 K; a 40-watt incandescent bulb, about 2680 K. The K stands for degrees Kelvin, the temperature scale starting at absolute zero. A theoretical "black body" heated to a Kelvin temperature glows a specific color; to describe that color, that temperature is used.

Spectral de-rating—lamp efficacy (energy efficiency) *discounted* for strongly colored light, which does not produce as good visibility as near-white light. Low-pressure sodium lamps, for example, produce a monochrome yellow light that makes the eye work 38 percent harder than light from a daylight-color lamp. Some experts therefore "de-rate" LP sodium lamps by 38 percent. A 90 lumens-per-watt lamp, de-rated 38 percent, would be equivalent to only 55 lumens per watt.

Light pollution:

Astronomical light pollution—light obstructing night visibility or telescopes.

Ecological light pollution—light that confuses, disrupts, or harms biological and ecosystem functions.

Light trespass—light that violates property boundaries and irritates neighbors.

---

skies calls for a redefinition of what 'quality lighting' is. The days of 'more is better' are behind us."[6]

Excessive lighting causes problems in two related ways: when it obscures the heavens and washes out the stars; and when it disrupts the day/night rhythms of plant, animal, or human life. Current thinking classifies concerns about visibility separately from species effects: "astronomical light pollution" and "ecological light pollution," respectively. It is important to remember that both can result from overuse or misuse

of landscape lighting. Other light sources contribute, but outdoor lighting plays an unusually significant role.

As David Crawford, founder and executive director of the Tucson-based International Dark-Sky Association (IDA), has said in thousands of lectures around the country, light that spills over where it is unwanted is *absolute* waste. "We waste $2 billion a year to light the sky, to light the bottoms of airplanes and birds," as he puts it. "Dark sky design is simply good lighting design." In fact, he notes that energy savings, even before LEDs, were high enough to pay off design, fixtures, and installation of many dark-sky retrofits in six to twenty-four months.

Celebrate Night-sky Visibility

As recently as 2000, concern about excess lighting was primarily astronomical and aesthetic. Researchers found that city lights dimmed their telescopes; laypeople lamented the inability to see the Milky Way or, in some locations, any stars at all. Areas like the American Southwest, where spectacular skies are major attractions, were concerned about lighting's impact on their tourist economies.

A related issue is the limitation of visibility by pollutant haze, something that affects many national parks and scenic areas. Most of this haze comes from factories and coal-fired utility plants, often several states distant from the parks they affect. All the techniques that reduce energy consumption and pollutant output, mentioned throughout this book, thus have potential effects on restoring visibility. Landscape professionals should be actively pursuing such reductions, even though it bucks political trends.

In 2001, the first worldwide atlas of the sky at night was published.[7] It includes graphics of night lighting on each continent as seen from space, and some telling statistics. Night skies are so constantly lit that more than 40 percent of Americans never use the part of the eye adapted for night vision (rod vision). Two-thirds of the country is too bright for the Milky Way to be seen; half the country's youth have never seen that awe-inspiring sight at all.[8]

Photographic studies, carried out by the National Park Service's Dark Sky Team in some of the world's most remote parks and wilderness areas, show that artificial light from over a hundred miles away is prominently visible even in these protected areas. This not only mars the wilderness experience for humans, but in many cases is bright enough to alter ecological dynamics (see below).[9]

"Astronomical light pollution" is caused by lights directed upward, or light that bounces upward from reflective or light-colored surfaces, including sidewalks and roofs. Serious though it is, "up-lighting" is rela-

tively easy to correct. "Cutoff" lighting fixtures that block light above the horizontal are the primary tools (see below). Eliminating this light is relatively painless, because most of it is truly waste.

"Ecological light pollution" is quite a different matter. It can be caused by lights completely shielded skyward, and its effects depend on subtle variations in light color, timing, and intensity. While astronomical and aesthetic lighting issues are well enough understood that IDA is publishing a model dark-sky ordinance (see below), research on ecological impacts of lighting is still relatively new.

Protect Health and Ecosystems from Excess Light

Most animals and plants have seasonal or daily "circadian" rhythms, regulated by patterns of darkness and light. *Natural* light's effects on plants, animals, and humans have been extensively studied for a century or more. Although it has long been suspected that excessive artificial lighting could disrupt these patterns and cause serious harm, hard research has only recently begun to emerge.

It is becoming increasingly clear that many species of animals and plants are strongly affected by artificial lighting. Because landscape professionals are in a position to do something very directly about lighting levels outdoors, it is important to have a basic understanding of these issues—and to know when to consult a specialist.

As far as effects on the human animal, artificial night lighting is increasingly of concern. Recent studies indicate that exposure to night light—or, to put it the other way, lack of sufficient hours of real darkness—is strongly implicated in extreme increases of breast cancer in the industrialized world.[10] Israeli researchers, between 2005 and 2011, used an ingenious combination of night satellite imagery, municipal GPS and GIS, and health records to correlate street-lighting levels and breast cancer spatially.[11] Overly bright nights are also suspect in other human cancers.[12] Other effects were established earlier: children who sleep with constant night-lights are nearly 30 percent more likely to develop nearsightedness; the brighter the light, the greater the chances of myopia.[13] All-night lighting exposure can cause sleeplessness and may contribute to well-known stresses affecting night-shift workers. The bluish light of phone and computer displays has also been shown to play a major role in insomnia, which affects at least 32 million Americans.[14]

Many doctors are researching health and lighting; one is R. G. Stevens of the University of Connecticut Health Center. Stevens makes a critically important distinction between task lighting and light for the "biological clock": "Electric lighting in the built environment is generally more than sufficient for visual performance, but may be inappropriate for normal neuroendocrine rhythms in humans; e.g., insufficient during the day and too much at night. Lighting standards and engineering stress visual performance, whereas circadian function is not currently emphasized."[15] Such findings will likely change lighting design radically, both outdoors and in.

In 2010, IDA published concerns specific to LED lighting outdoors. Some LEDs, especially early products designed to be "pure" white, have a strong intensity peak in the blue part of the spectrum. Blue light is known to increase nighttime "glow" as well as glare, but more important, it damages the retina if intense enough, and decreases melatonin production (a factor in the cancer studies, above), contributing to insomnia. These issues also apply to wildlife, though few detailed studies have been undertaken.[16] The American Medical Association issued a 2016 report that confirmed the concerns raised by IDA.[17] Manufacturers have been working to make LEDs in the "warm white" spectrum, partly because people prefer the aesthetics. One challenge has been that, at least in early designs, LEDs with the blue spike were more efficient than others. This issue, and the use of varied "color temperatures" to mimic the naturally varied colors of light at different times of day, are the focus of much research.

Another important reason to decrease light pollution is that it apparently increases smog. A 2010 study found that night lighting interfered (as sunlight does) with normal air-cleansing reactions that normally occur at night, increasing smog by as much as 5 percent. Dark-sky efforts can be effective at preventing this impact.[18]

From the landscape perspective, lighting's effects on trees, shrubs, and perennials is important. Day length at least partly controls when plants bloom or leaf out. Growing under constant street lamps, trees could be "confused" into shedding leaves too late in fall, risking damage from early frost; they might bud too early, making them vulnerable to late-winter storms. Very little research has ever been done on this topic. Some research indicates that overlighted trees fail to show fall coloration. Saplings have been shown to hold their leaves too long in the fall, but mature trees are less sensitive; the question of early budding never appears to have been addressed.[19] Thus, while little is proven, many observant professionals believe that at least some landscape plants are stressed by artificial lighting. Research to prove this should be an important priority. Any stress on landscape plantings may result directly in loss of plants, and indirectly in wasteful resource use. Documentation is at an early stage, but the effect of lighting on plants—both wild and horticultural— is clearly a sustainability issue, especially given other deforestation concerns related to climate change (see "Landscapes Against Climate Change," p. 20).

Researching light's effects on large woody plants is not easy, because isolating mature trees in laboratory conditions is very awkward. One possible approach, adopted from the light/cancer study noted above, would be to use GIS and GPS information to relate documented light levels to records of tree health.[20] Many municipalities have street-tree surveys that record species, locations, and health. Street lighting is tracked on the same cities' utility maps. Ambient light pollution can be tracked from satellite data. By *correlating* these data sources on a single map, it should be relatively straightforward to gain some hard data about night lighting and plants.

An important 2016 paper by researchers at the University of Exeter lays out (among other information) core research needs about artificial lighting and vegetation:

- Light is not uniform; how do variation in intensity, color, time of day and season, and duration of exposure change lighting's impacts?
- Plants seldom grow in isolation; how do effects on individuals add up to impacts on populations, communities, or ecosystems?
- Light's effects on insect, bird, and mammal behavior are better documented than those on plants;

what indirect impacts on plants result from effects on pollinators, herbivores, and pathogens?

- Stress from lighting occurs in context: how does it interact with other stressors, such as invasive species, chemical pollution, habitat fragmentation, and climate change?

The Exeter researchers and others have begun to answer some of these questions. Various common outdoor light sources have been characterized in terms of intensity and color; it has been shown that photoperiod (seasonal changes due to light levels) occurs at very low intensities of blue and red light, while photosynthesis requires red and infrared wavelengths in much higher intensities. Long suspected, it has now been documented that artificial lighting delays seasonal leaf-drop in some species and especially in younger trees. A list of species ranked by vulnerability to excess light is available. Ecosystem and contextual studies remain rare, and likely to require long-term monitoring. Progress, however, is being made in understanding vegetation-specific impacts of night lighting alongside effects on animals.[21]

Landscape architects have the opportunity to contribute to this field research. The built environment is to some degree a controlled environment for research on trees. As part of the long-term performance monitoring recommended in Principle 11, it would not be difficult to gather data toward answering the above research questions.

Neither plants nor humans seem likely to go extinct from overlighting, but for a significant number of animal species this is a real danger. Sea turtles are the best known. Turtles lay eggs in beach-sand nests, and hatchlings emerge at night. They rely on illumination from the ocean (which always reflects light more brightly at night than the land) to guide them back to the water. Artificial lighting on the land side of the beach will mislead hatchlings, which follow light onto roads and into built-up areas. "A single light left on near a sea turtle nesting beach can misdirect and kill hundreds of hatchlings," according to a Florida Bureau of Protected Species pamphlet. Because sea turtles are already endangered by hunting and egg gathering, many coastal communities restrict beach-front lighting during nesting season. The list of light sources that are deadly to hatchling turtles includes almost every type of landscape light: the same pamphlet cites "porch, pool, street, stairway, walkway, parking lot, security, . . . commercial signs, . . . and even bug-zappers," as well as spillover from interior lighting. An increasing number of luminaires and lamps are designed specifically to avoid endangering turtles (see below).

Moths are another species known for self-destructive attraction to light. Although not as dramatic as sea turtles, moths are pollinators. Extinction of large and unusual species like the turtle would be a tragedy, but lowly moths may be more important: a pollinator lost causes extinction of pollinated plants and creatures dependent on the plants for food or habitat.

Research collected in an excellent 2006 book by Travis Longcore and Catherine Rich shows that many more species are affected by artificial lighting than previously considered, even by ecologists and conservationists. Species now known to be affected (usually negatively) by artificial light include turtles, moths, frogs, salamanders, crows, songbirds, most migratory birds, fish, spiders, seals, many rodents, zooplankton, and a wide range of insects.[22] Longcore and Rich include one chapter on plants, among several on animals.

How lighting affects species varies widely. Light color matters to some species but not others—for example, red and yellow light affects sea turtles less than white. Timing can be critical—if a light appears just after sundown, when foraging creatures are active but winding down, they may graze longer, exposing themselves to predators. Rate and degree of *lighting change* may be important—frogs and fish have long been hunted by blinding them with sudden light, from which they take hours to recover.

A few species benefit from extra lighting, such as some bats that can hunt insects attracted to streetlights. As Longcore and Rich point out, however, extra light is "beneficial for those species that can exploit it, but not for their prey." Much of the so-called Balance of Nature is maintained by preferences for light or darkness—species that would otherwise compete take "shifts" based on light levels or moon phases. Artificial lighting is more and more recognized as affecting not just individual species, but species *interrelationships* critical to ecosystem health.

Lighting can induce activity—from hunting to mating—and can affect individual animals' judgment about locating nests or selecting mates. Some species are attracted by light; others are repelled. Animals that use light to orient themselves may increase activity; animals that navigate in the dark may become disoriented.

Birds in particular are often trapped by lighting—a famous photo shows hundreds of them circling within the temporary World Trade Center memorial's spotlights.[23] According to Toronto-based FLAP (Fatal Light Awareness Program), hundreds of thousands of birds have been killed in a single night because of unusual lighting (lighthouses and tall buildings are common culprits). FLAP estimates that 100 million birds are killed each year, with low-flying songbirds especially hard hit. (In 2012, a Canadian judge ruled that a building owner was liable for the light pollution that caused numerous bird deaths.)[24]

The bottom line for designers is that lighting needs to be integrated with site-specific ecological conditions on every sustainability-driven project. Longcore and Rich advocate light monitoring for all environmental-impact assessments (which often ignore nocturnal species) and development plans. As noted above, this is actually an opportunity for landscape professionals, including the possibility of getting grants to help fund project performance monitoring.

Even the way light is measured has effects on other species. The common unit of measure, "lux," expresses how the *human* eye perceives brightness. This is obviously useful for human lighting design. But other species see different wavelengths than humans do and respond differently to intensity and color as well. Insects, for example, respond far more to ultraviolet than to "visible" light. For evaluating potential impact on plants and animals, field records must show the full spectrum, direction, and timing of light. For some species, a very small amount of light pollution disrupts important behaviors. Some reptiles, for example, are affected by *one one-hundredth* of one lux;[25] even subdued path lights put out 8 lux. Raising *regional* ambient light levels by 0.01 lux takes thousands of lights, but

occurs cumulatively even from great distances, as Park Service studies (above) show.

A 2009 study has expanded the concept of light pollution to include daytime polarized light. Reflected off dark polished surfaces—smoked glass facades, black granite gravestones, even photovoltaic panels—polarized light confuses animals and insects in many of the same ways as excess night lighting.[26]

Thus, although "cutoff" fixtures are almost off-the-shelf solutions to *astronomical* light pollution, they may or may not improve *ecological* light pollution. "Tuning" LEDs to specific wavelengths can prevent some ecological impacts of lighting. It is increasingly evident that human demands for night visibility must be balanced with the pressing need—for animals, plants, and humans—to maintain dark nights.

A new specialty may be emerging: a hybrid of landscape design, lighting technology, and ecosystem/wildlife management, focused on sustainable lighting design. Such a blend of expertise, by a team or a single specialist, is needed when attempting regional regulation or site-specific solutions, discussed in the next section.

Keep the Night Dark

In October 2006, the International Dark-Sky Association (IDA) and IESNA (the Illuminating Engineering Society of North America) announced a model Dark-Sky Ordinance; the most recent version was released in 2011, and is available free through the website of either organization. The ordinance, according to IDA's Pete Strasser, will help communities avoid well-intentioned but poorly written regulations, and achieve better and fairer enforcement.

The model ordinance defines terms for clear communication between community and industry, and specifies how to measure acceptable light levels. It establishes a standard way of classifying luminaires according to light output, direction, and potential for glare or uplight. Five activity-appropriate lighting levels will define a zoning tool; methods to establish a special performance-review process will also be included. The model will likely accept urban lighting expectations, even where those have ecological implications. Although no code can please everyone, the IDA-IESNA model ordinance should be a long step in the right direction. Well-designed lighting adds value and beauty, but for sustainable landscape making, it is critical to balance these against medical, ecological, and aesthetic reasons for keeping the night dark.[27]

Over two hundred US jurisdictions already have dark-sky laws. These have significantly changed the design of outdoor lighting products and installations. For example, uplighting, a design effect that lights objects from below, is prohibited or limited in many areas today.

Most manufacturers of outdoor lighting now have at least some cutoff models among their luminaires. Definitions of "cutoff" have varied somewhat, but those used by the manufacturer Lumec are clear enough to be generally applicable. A "full cutoff" model emits no light above a horizontal plane passing through the bottom of the fixture. "Cutoff" models allow no more than 2.5 percent of their light output to escape above this horizontal, and "semicutoff" luminaires direct no more than 5 percent above that line.

Cutoff models are designed in different ways. Placing the light source in a glass-bottomed box is simplest. If a rounded or "sag" lens is used to direct or focus light, however, some light escapes upward from the rounded sides. Considerable cutoff can be achieved by making the top part of a glass globe reflective. This method is popular, creating cutoff luminaires that look, outwardly, like traditional streetlamps or modernist spheres.

Strong cutoff design tends to produce narrower downward illumination patterns as well. This creates a dilemma: narrower spreads require closer pole spacing; closer spacings may increase upward reflectance off light-colored horizontal surfaces. Streetlight studies by Lumec compared semi-cutoff fixtures, whose broader downward light spread allows wide pole spacing, with full-cutoff fixtures that require closer spacing. Semi-cutoff designs produced nearly 40 percent less upward-*reflected* light (bouncing from the sidewalk), more than offsetting the 5 percent direct uplighting that defines them as semi-cutoff.[28] Overall power consumption and maintenance were reduced using fewer, more widely spaced fixtures. While this

research was limited to a few models, it shows that *indirect* uplighting must be factored into dark-sky and light-trespass analysis. LEDs, which emit a narrowly focused beam, offer improved control of the direction and spread of light, assuming designers recognize the importance of doing so.

Mounting height, spacing, surface reflectivity, and other design factors interact in complex ways with product performance. Manufacturers list efficacy (lumens per watt of energy), service life, and beam spread for their products. Even given this information, most landscape professionals will want specialist assistance. The International Dark-Sky Association's website is one good resource. It certifies lighting products for dark-sky purposes, though ecological appropriateness is harder to certify. Links help find experienced lighting designers or illuminating engineers (see organizations in the resources).

Options for Limiting Outdoor Light Pollution

- Where "dark sky" (astronomical light pollution) is the only concern, use cutoff fixtures, remembering to evaluate reflected uplight, and unit height and spacing, to limit total uplighting.
- Evaluate reflectiveness (albedo) of surfaces that will be lighted. High albedo is often desirable to reduce heat-island effects (see p. 260). At night, the same high-albedo surface may reflect undesirable uplighting. Because high albedo can help achieve night visibility with less lighting, a coordinated design may resolve this apparent conflict quite successfully. Alternatively, a neutral surface color might avoid both heat absorption and uplight reflectance.
- Near observatories, consider monochromatic lamp types, like low-pressure sodium; their single-color output can be filtered out by telescopes, but is ugly and fairly ineffective at improving ordinary vision. LEDs can be tailored to specific colors too.
- Remember that even lighting that perfectly solves dark-sky problems may still cause serious *ecological* light pollution or light trespass. Solutions to ecological lighting pollution will be compromises, involving priorities among diverse demands: human, animal, and plant health; visibility; and commercial advertising or "curb-appeal" lighting.

- Simple light-trespass problems can often be solved using glare shields, similar to cutoff fixtures, but blocking light in specific horizontal directions. Directional screening is also a tool against wild-life impacts. Louvered fixtures are one effective way to control lighting direction, and are often recommended for wildlife-related design.
- Consider LED lighting (see below) for its extremely tight beam width (within three degrees) and focus. Tiny beams placed very close to illuminated objects may substitute for larger fixtures that light whole areas wastefully. Effects of multiple nearly invisible light sources may be highly aesthetic, too.
- For people, wildlife, and perhaps plants, *timing* and *duration* of night lighting can be critical. Timers, photosensors, and motion detectors correctly used can keep lights off except when truly necessary. For certain species, possibly including humans, a gradual change in illumination is less harmful than a sudden one; dimmers can ease essential lights on and off progressively.
- Lighting color may be critical in ecological impact. Turtles will not respond to red light, which still provides visibility for humans. Filtering reduces lamp efficacy, however—the same energy is used, but visible output is less. LEDs produce colored light without filtering, and one properly designed fixture could change color seasonally or at different times of night. Fiber-optic lights (see below) can also change color without relamping.

As with almost all sustainable design, the above options may enhance or conflict with other considerations, such as strict energy efficiency. There may be situations where increasing energy use reduces ecological impacts of lighting. Such conflicts are not just between sustainable and unsustainable demands, but between different aspects of sustainability. A positive approach recognizes that sustainable design requires greater-than-usual creativity.

Use Lighting Efficiently

In addition to issues of light pollution, lighting consumes energy and has implications for material use, recycling, and toxicity. All these concerns should be evaluated in sustainability-driven projects. For each project, varying concerns are likely to be prioritized somewhat site-specifically. This balance, rather than narrow optimization of one factor, such as energy savings, best characterizes sustainable design.

Older lighting installations waste up to 90 percent of the energy they consume.[29] Fortunately, great strides in lighting technology have been made in the past decade. If new efficient lamps were universally used, most electrical inefficiency and waste would be eliminated. Some newer bulbs are designed to work in existing fittings; in other cases, decreased operating energy requires replacing old fittings. The change generally pays for itself quickly.

From an environmental standpoint, lighting is an entirely artificial choice. Unlike protecting food crops from pests, or obtaining water from natural systems, permanent outdoor lighting is not a basic survival need. Thus it is particularly important to use lighting judiciously and to know exactly what it is intended to accomplish. Only then can technology be matched efficiently to need.

Design for Accurate and Appropriate Light Levels

Lights in the landscape need to put light where it is wanted, as bright as needed, when it is needed, and no more. This is accomplished in several ways.

Appropriate illumination levels must be established first. The Illuminating Engineering Society (IES) establishes recommended levels for various settings and activities, widely published in references like *TimeSaver* or *Graphic Standards*. Be sure to use the most current version, since LEDs particularly are rapidly changing these standards. IES updated its *Lighting Handbook* in 2011; AASHTO and Federal Highway Administration standards have also seen updates between 2012 and 2016. The ratio of illumination level to energy use is not one for one, but is an important indicator of potential energy savings.

One noticeable feature of IES levels is that light-colored surfaces can cut lighting by as much as two-thirds.[30] Light-surfaced steps require 200 lux; dark surfaced, the same steps would need 500 lux. Contrast with surroundings also makes an object easier to illuminate: bright-surfaced risers against dark treads might be visible with only 50 lux. Dark horizontal surfaces decrease upward reflection.

IDA's David Crawford points out that laypeople equate glare with light. "Take away the glare, you actually improve visibility—but people think there's no light." This fundamental difficulty in preventing wasted lighting can only be overcome by public awareness and by setting rational, situation-specific standards.

The levels set by the IES are based rationally on the human eye's ability to distinguish important objects or actions under given light levels; like so many engineering calculations, they err on the side of excess. Light levels, however, are sometimes set by much less justifiable means. Fast-food and all-night businesses, for instance, use very bright lighting for "curb appeal." Levels well beyond any functional need are used to attract drivers' attention and lure them to the business by giving the appearance of warmth and safety. Light as advertising takes many other forms, none of them candidates for sustainability.

Light levels on a surface are set not only by lamp choice, but also by distance and angle from lamp to surface, and overlap with any other light source. Carefully use manufacturers' specifications, including photometric charts showing light distribution, for maximum effective lighting from minimum energy. This clearly relates to issues of light pollution (see above), but "light trespass" can be a separate issue. It is increasingly a source of conflict between neighbors as development becomes denser. Because a single light may be visible from many directions, shielding all the neighbors can be quite complicated—more so even than preventing skyward light pollution.

The higher the light source is placed, the wider the area it can illuminate (beam spread being equal). This has been considered "efficient" and has resulted in highway intersections lit from fifty-foot poles or taller. This approach to lighting, however, should be thought of as lighting dead air. Lower, closely spaced, lights often produce better visibility with little light trespass, pollution, glare, or energy waste. "Standard" twenty-foot parking lot poles light about fifteen feet of air before reaching cars or pedestrians. Louvered bollards or wall lights better illuminate the area in which cars and people actually move and are widely recom-

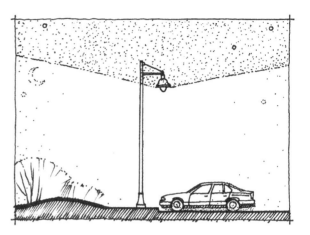

Figure 8.1a–c High, non-cutoff lighting (a) is cheap (few fixtures), but wasteful and light polluting. Cutoff lighting (b) still lights dead air; bounced uplight remains an issue. Louvered lighting (c) puts light where it is most effective and least polluting. (*Illust.:* Craig Farnsworth, based on beachtobay.org/. The website is no longer valid as of 2017, but similar information can be found from the Dark Sky Association and sea turtle conservation organizations.)

mended for wildlife-friendly lighting. LEDs and fiber-optics can also be set into pavement, walls, and even site furniture, providing way-finding with minimal area illumination.

Question "Safety" as Grounds for Overlighting

Overlighting is also done on the recommendation of lawyers, who treat bright-as-day illumination as a liability defense; overly bright regulations are often passed as emotional response to a publicized crime. However, IDA's David Crawford bluntly says, "There is no correlation between night lighting and safety." Landscape professionals are often pressured to overilluminate areas for "safety." IDA is a good source of strong, professional counterarguments. Recent thought among highway engineers leans toward "adaptive" lighting closely linked to actual use rather than blanket specifications.

Once IES or IDA-IESNA standards are met, extra lighting serves no purpose. Area lighting that allows people to recognize hazards can be quite dim. Proper *aim* is more important than extreme brightness for security lighting, best designed to reveal suspicious behavior rather than show detail. In fact, excessively bright light can actually blind the "good guys" while the "bad guys" disappear into dense shadow. As a deterrent, a motion-triggered bright light is more effective than a constant one. A lawyerly preference for brilliantly (not just adequately) lit property is no excuse for wasted energy and severe light pollution.

Crawford points out, only half jokingly, that historically the more night lighting is used, the *higher* crime rates become. During the year that New York City switched to full-cutoff streetlights, the crime rate fell. Crawford's theory relates to research showing that animals are stressed by excess lighting (see above). Humans, too, evolved with regular night/day cycles. "If we turn night into day," says Crawford, "we're stressing the human system. Stress probably increases both crime, and worrying about crime."[31]

Use Sensors and Controllers to Avoid Wasted Light

Like any electrical device, landscape lighting can be controlled by "intelligent" switches, such as timers and

Figure 8.2 Cutoff reflectors to prevent light pollution have become the norm for street and road lighting. Landscape-specific fixtures with or without cutoff design should be located with care to avoid glare and spillover. (*Photo:* Kim Lighting / Kevin Willmorth.)

Figure 8.3 End-emitting fiber-optics in Epcot's sidewalk create a moving, color-shifting bed of stars. Attracting more attention than the floodlights, they use far less energy. (*Photo:* Kim Sorvig.)

sensors. Home path-light systems are typically controlled by photocells or clocks or both. These save energy by limiting the amount of time lighting is on. They can, of course, be abused, turning lights on mindlessly when there is no need, like irrigation in a rainstorm. Carefully used, they contribute to lighting efficiency. "Smart home" technology, which is becoming common for interior controls, can be used to turn landscape lighting (and irrigation) on and off, or to start and end more complex programmed cycles—but only if planned and implemented for such tasks.

Motion sensors are common in security lighting and can control other types of light. They save significant amounts of energy, because the light comes on only if an intruder or visitor is detected. They decrease annoyance and light pollution from constant lights. Detectors must be carefully located and adjusted when used outdoors, or false alarms result. In landscape settings, vegetation that grows into the sensor's line of sight may require trimming; windblown branches trigger sensors. The sensor does not need to be located on the light fixture. Placing the detector remotely requires a little more wire, but often results in greater effectiveness and more flexible adjustment. Wireless links between sensor and light are becoming available.

As noted above, gradual dawn- or dusk-like changes in artificial illumination may be desirable for human health or ecological reasons. Dimmers and programmed controllers can accomplish such sequences, paired with LED mimicry of "warmth" and "coolness" of natural light at different times of day. Lumileds's Luxeon line of LEDs is specifically tailored to maximize photosynthesis in greenhouses (which usually look pink under these lights); the company claims savings of 75 percent energy and 90 percent water, while increasing crop growth rates.[32]

Try Low-voltage Lighting for Flexibility

The preceding sections discuss efficiency strategies that can be used with any type of lamp, old or new. Almost all new lamps available today are significantly more efficient in converting electricity to light than a decade ago. Several specific types of lighting may save additional energy by putting small amounts of light exactly where wanted.

In strict theory, low-voltage (12V or 24V) wiring is *less* efficient than 110V "line voltage" supplied by utilities; higher voltage loses less during transmission, which is why power companies transmit electricity over very high voltage cables. Low-voltage lamps, however, were among the earliest to achieve higher light output per watt; in this they compare favorably with line-voltage lamps. Low-voltage lamps also of-

fer two advantages that *indirectly* affect efficiency: size and safety.

A lighting fixture, or luminaire, consists of three main parts: a lamp, a reflector to focus the light, and a mounting system. In most older luminaires, the reflector was the "shade," part of the mounting system. In newer lamps, especially low-voltage systems, the tiny glass bulb contains both lamp and reflector, built-in. Even before LEDs, this miniaturization produced a wide variety of special-purpose "self-reflectorized" lamps, from very narrow spots to very wide floods, many still in use. Putting the reflector in the lamp has also made it possible to design smaller and simpler mounting systems. These in turn are easily located, aimed, and concealed at the precise spot where light is needed. LEDs take this micro-lighting to new levels.

From a sustainability perspective, miniaturization has several effects. It has significantly reduced the amount of material required to make either the bulb or the fitting. (It has also made the reflector disposable; unless lamps are recycled effectively, a small amount of reflector material goes to waste with each bulb; fluorescents contain mercury and must be carefully recycled.)[33] Miniaturization has also revolutionized lighting *design*, under the motto of "see the light, not the lamp." Precision lighting has generated much excitement for its subtle and dramatic effects. Thoughtfully used, it *can* decrease resource consumption.

The second advantage of low voltage is safety. This may not seem like an environmental issue, but in fact it has an important effect on precision lighting. Twelve-volt power's only real danger to humans is a painful but harmless shock. As a result, 12V wire can be run anywhere, even underwater, without conduit or other safety protection. Running small wire instead of rigid conduit considerably reduces material use and allows complete flexibility in placing 12V lighting fixtures. Although 110V lamps and fixtures have also miniaturized in the past decade, the need for conduit works against flexible placement, while 12V wiring enhances the advantages of miniature bulbs.

Flexibility and precision have changed the approach of landscape lighting contractors in another important way: because the lights are so precise, the best way to achieve an effect is to experiment in the field. Trial-and-error placement of different lights gives far better results than just drawing a paper plan, according to Jan Moyer, author of *The Landscape Lighting Book*[34] and former head of the Landscape Lighting Institute. This in turn encourages site-specific sensitivity, which, as noted throughout this book, is one of the keys to sustainable landscapes.

Low-voltage systems usually rely on a transformer, which steps the power down from household current to 12V DC. At the lower voltage, issues like circuit overload and voltage drop become more critical than with line voltage. The size of the transformer must be matched carefully to total lighting load; the length of wiring runs must also be well planned. Voltage drop at the distant end of a wire can be enough to hurt lamp performance and life noticeably. Since both efficiency and service life are sustainability issues, it is important to pay close attention to system design. Some designers, used to the simple assumptions of line-voltage systems, consider the need to design the whole low-voltage system a drawback. Others find it an interesting and rewarding challenge, with benefits far outweighing the extra planning work.

Don't Overlook Fiber-optic Lighting

Although primarily known for its special effects, fiber-optic landscape lighting may have environmental benefits, too. A single lamp, albeit a fairly strong one, can send its light through dozens of optical fibers spread throughout a landscape. The light may be emitted only from the end of the fiber, or all along it in "side-emitting" types, which resemble neon. The latter are the most common fiber-optics in landscape, used primarily to line path edges or other features with colored light. End-emitting fibers can be used much like spotlights, or can produce remarkable twinkling dots of light when drilled through any material.

Fiber-optics can be energy efficient because they are in fact a single light with greatly extended "lenses." They are even safer than low-voltage lights, because all the power is at the light source. The fibers themselves carry no current at all, only light. The idea of precision lighting as a sustainability benefit, noted above concerning low-voltage lighting, also applies to fiber-optics.

The magical ability to change color instantly is a fiber-optic feature that designers and artists enjoy. It might also have uses, however, in situations like the sea-turtle dilemma (above). A fiber-optic system could provide human safety by outlining paths, yet during turtle hatching season its color and intensity could be changed without relamping to decrease its hypnotic attraction to the animals.

Fiber-optics are a good example of the choices involved in sustainable design and construction. Originally adopted for the delight it provokes, fiber-optic landscape lighting might seem frivolous in view of environmental worries. With careful evaluation and creativity, it may actually serve sustainable goals in ways that have not yet been considered. While not every new technology can be sustainably used, it is important not to become rigid or dismissive about the possibilities.

Use Solar Lighting

Lighting the night with power from the sun has gone from paradox to reality in recent years. Development of solar lights is closely related to advances in LED and low-voltage lamps. Increased efficiency of lamps, batteries, and PV cells has reduced the required size of PV surface to manageable dimensions.

For lighting, solar fixtures accentuate the characteristics of low voltage: flexibility, economy, and the need for comprehensive evaluation of the whole system during design. Some package-system solar lights appear to avoid the need for system planning. Package solar lighting, however, varies widely; some types, like solar path lights, have until very recently been weak performers; many underperforming models remain, unfortunately, on the market. Custom PV systems, which take site conditions and user needs into very specific account, have a high success rate and can power almost anything (see p. 308). In offering a "package" system, whether for lighting, irrigation, or other purposes, PV manufacturers attempt to offer universality and convenience transcending site specifics. Package PV systems may work extremely well in one geographic area or for a particular application, and pose problems in another.

Solar Street Lighting

Lighting, especially of an area that must be fully lit all night, is probably the most difficult test of a solar-powered system. Yet this challenge has produced hundreds of mainstream products, along with some of the most exuberant creativity in twenty-first-century design.

Solar street lights combine high-efficiency lamps (usually LEDs), a pole, a PV panel, and a battery system. Insulated battery cases are available with some models to improve battery life. The PV panel often acts as a photocell, automatically turning on the lamp when it ceases to receive sunlight. Controllers are often built in to prevent high and low voltage, voltage backflow, and other problems. Such products typically cost $2,000 to $6,000 per light; by comparison, the first cost of a high-pressure sodium street light averages $1,300. However, supply wires and footings for the conventional unit easily brings the cost to $4,000 or more. Grid electricity typically adds $5,000 or more over a twenty-five-year useful life. A solar unit has the same lifespan, no electrical bills, and no wiring.[35] Krinner Ground Screws, a German variation on the auger foundation (see p. 74), is being marketed specifically for solar lights by Ground Connection. The screws install with a motorized auger attachment in most soils, without excavation. As with solar path lights, freedom from wires means flexible location.

The most prevalent designs remain boxy, with the PV panel either integrated into the top of the box or mounted on its own arm so the angle can be adjusted for maximum solar exposure. These have all the aesthetic appeal of tin cans on sticks, and look to be cobbled together out of the manufacturers' existing products. Fortunately, there are some extremely creative designs that take advantage of solar technology, many using biomimicry; a few are illustrated in this section.

Professional-quality solar luminaires tend to be rugged. Solar-powered street lamps for the Miami community of Sorbet were the only electrical items working for nearly three weeks after Hurricane Andrew. Residents complained that power should have been reconnected to their homes first!

At Cholla Campground (See Figure 7.9), integration of site, structure, and technology made solar power viable. Restroom facilities were designed with skylights, which cut artificial lighting needs in half. Solar electricity was used not only to power interior and exterior lights on these facilities, but also to operate motion sensors and timers to conserve energy. Solar power success often demands planning ahead

Figure 8.4 Flat, boxy streetlights solve "the design problem" in an engineering sense; they dominate the solar streetlight market today, with dozens of manufacturers offering near-identical products. They miss the exuberantly creative design possibilities that are starting to emerge. (*Illust.*: Kim Sorvig.)

for conservation, designing creatively, and reeducating builders as well as users.

Technological advances are changing how solar streetlights work, as well as their energy consumption. First Light Technologies, for example, uses proprietary software to make its products "learn" local conditions, adjusting both PV and lamp to maximize output. According to the company's brochure, this allows its bollard and street lights to reserve energy enough to function for fourteen days without recharge. Another electronic innovation is motion sensing, used (as in interiors) to turn lighting on only when needed. Several companies make hybrid-power lights that combine PV with electricity generated from wind, rain-driven micro-turbines, or even vibration caused by pedestrians.

Solar LED lighting for billboards and other signage is no longer a novelty. Solar is widespread for highway and airport warning signs, valued for reliability as well as off-grid installation.

Solar Garden Lighting

Solar path lights have featured prominently in mail-order catalogs and garden centers since the 1990s. These small lights, available in pagoda, coach-light, or wall-mounted designs, look like low-voltage landscape lights, but contain a solar cell and battery. In theory, each light is totally independent and self-contained and can be placed anywhere without wiring of any sort. Even more than transformer-powered low voltage, solar path lights promise flexible, movable placement, and user safety.

Despite the elegance of the concept, professional landscape architects and lighting designers have avoided these lights—until recently. Older models had extremely low illumination levels (equivalent to 20W to 40W incandescents), intended only to mark path edges. Operating time per night was limited and in cloudy weather or winter could be almost nothing; high/low settings on some models allowed a choice between brightness and operating time. Some early, cheaply made models suffered from mismatched battery and PV-cell capacity, nonreplaceable batteries and bulbs, or fragile UV-degradable plastic fittings. Others discharged on suppliers' shelves and failed to recharge when installed. Professionals who wanted solar lighting generally recommended regular PV panels powering standard low-voltage layouts.

Stand-alone solar path lights, however, have come a long way since then and are likely to improve further. Better thin-film PV efficiency and LEDs have improved performance, as has software to manage the energy/light juggling act. Dappled or cloud-filtered light is enough to run many modern PV products. Professional metal solar path lights giving 50 to 200 lumens cost from $20 to $300 each. These light outputs are well within the range of most landscape uses; run time has improved, and variety among solar models has caught up with conventional low-voltage and 110V products. Flexible placement remains an advantage, with a dark side: since the PV is built in, an optimal location for *charging* may not be where night light is most needed. Home-center models in plastic today cost as little as ninety-five cents per light in multi-light kits, some having only a single LED per unit; not surprisingly, these perform so poorly that they are treated as disposable, negating any sustainable value.

Although the old performance problems are not completely banished, with careful layout, solar path lights today are realistic, quality alternatives for landscape lighting.

Solar Security Lighting

Motion-sensitive prowler lights, which require a brief blast of intense light, are far easier to power with a small PV system than is all-night lighting. Many manufacturers offer such lights, very similar to line-voltage models in operation but requiring no household power or wiring. Prices are up to twice the cost of line-voltage models, but there are no operating expenses. The use of a capacitor instead of a battery (see below) appears well suited to security light design.

Capacitor Solar LEDs

One very interesting development in solar lighting involves substitution of "ultra-capacitors" for conventional batteries. This concept is used in a range of small landscape lights manufactured in Korea and distributed by SolaRight Lighting, which offers path lights and roadway guide/flasher lights cast in solid polycarbonate "bricks."[36] Capacitors (once called "condensers") are battery-like but solid-state, very low maintenance, and made without common battery pollutants like lead, nickel, cadmium, or lithium. They operate well in extreme temperatures and recharge quicker than batteries. Adapted for relatively low-output lighting like path lights, capacitors store PV energy enough to provide light all night. Capacitors for higher-wattage solar lighting have yet to be developed, but could be extremely useful.

Evaluate Lamp Performance

Informed decisions about landscape lighting require some awkward comparisons. Power use and efficacy are critical in deciding which lighting is most appropriate and sustainable for a specific setting—yet comparisons are seldom apples to apples. Before the improvements of the past few years, it was often enough to compare lamp wattage. Today more than ever, different lighting models operate on different voltages, have different service lives, and achieve efficacies that vary dramatically. A 25W PAR-36 lamp (one modernized low-voltage type) produces as much light as a 100W incandescent; yet it can be operated for one-quarter the energy cost.

"Efficacy" is lamp output in lumens per watt. Incandescent bulbs generally have lowest efficacy (8 to 20 lumens per watt). Halogens produce 12 to 24 lumens per watt. These numbers have improved somewhat since 2000, but the big increases have been in LED efficacy. As of 2014, Osram claimed the most efficient LED in the world, at 215 lumens per watt.[37] Although inappropriate for many nonindustrial settings, HID (high-intensity discharge) lamps (sodium, metal halide, and mercury vapor) are highly energy-efficient lamp types, when performing at their peak. Surprisingly, these industrial lamps have efficacy ranges so wide that at the lowest, they are little better than halogens.[38]

In 2000, compact fluorescent lamps (CFLs) looked to be *the* environmental lamp. In 2017, as *EBN*'s Brent Ehrlich notes, "CFLs have gone the way of Edison's incandescent bulb," while its LED replacement "syncs with your cell phone so you can change its color to match your mood or circadian rhythm."[39] CFLs are being phased out. Disposal of mercury in CFLs, plus the far greater efficacy that LEDs have developed, killed this once-bright technology. California's Title 24 building efficiency standards, effective in 2006, classify all fluorescent lamps as hazardous waste, which cannot be disposed of in household trash due to mercury.[40] (LEDs, ground to powder before placing in landfill conditions, leach some chemicals, but at levels still below federal standards.)[41] California's mandatory levels of lamp efficacy have boosted LED adoption.

The useful life of common landscape lamps varies from 600 hours to more than 10,000; LEDs can last 100,000. Luminaires vary even more widely. Some early manufacturers of outdoor lighting simply exported their interior models; corrosion from soil chemistry, temperature extremes, ultraviolet light, and other ground-level hazards soon sent them back to the drawing board. Except for the cheapest plastic fixtures, quality has improved, but service life still varies.

Because so many variables are involved, lighting evaluation is a very good candidate for life-cycle costing (p. 335). LCC makes it much easier to evaluate lighting's complex combination of energy inputs, efficiency, and durability.

Join the LED Lighting Revolution

The first edition of this book predicted that multiple-LED lights would become an important part of the lighting world—the crystal ball was understating things that day.

LEDs (light-emitting diodes) are semiconductors that light up. They were originally used only as signal indicators on control panels and came in any color you wanted as long as it was red or green. But by 2000, amber and white LEDs were beginning to be clustered for light output and were commercially available, if only as expensive flashlights. Thus my prediction: "If experience shows these new bulbs to be as good as they sound, they will make many new designs possible—including, perhaps, the elusive standalone solar path light." I wish I'd bought stock. By 2007, LEDs were available in almost any color, with efficacies of 25 to 40 lumens per watt, and it took only ten years to reach 200-plus lumens per watt. The effective output is sometimes enhanced by mounting the LED "backward" to shine into a parabolic reflector.[42] LEDs' tiny size (4 millimeters or ⅛-inch diameter), solidity, narrow beam width, and longevity have motivated huge changes in lighting, indoors and out. Savings from not having to replace a "bulb" for 100,000 hours are enough to motivate the switch, especially for businesses and in locations like atrium ceilings that are hard to access. LEDs have proven valuable for temporary job-site lighting. They require no electrician to install, can be moved as needed, and are solid-state and thus hard to damage.

LEDs have a few disadvantages. They do not burn out suddenly but give progressively less light, while still consuming the same amount of energy. In newer LEDs, this loss has been decreased. Service life for LEDs is usually listed in the form "75 percent lumen maintenance after 60,000 hours." This indicates that the light will lose no more than 25 percent of its brightness by the end of that period (also called "lumen depreciation"). Each emitter requires a heat sink, usually an aluminum extrusion with fins for air circulation, or its own heat degrades its performance; this increases resource costs and complicates recycling. LEDs are RoHS compliant (Restriction of Hazardous Substances, a standard adopted by the European Union in 2003) and can be recycled, usually with other electronics.

Colors of LEDs are extremely "pure." To simulate daylight or incandescent, several colors must be mixed. (Mixing red, green, and blue, as in theatrical lighting, can produce any color; this has been used in building-sized color display screens. Images 40 meters tall—130 feet—were produced in this way at the 2006 Asian Games in Doha, Qatar. Color-tuned lighting can also benefit wildlife behavior and human health, while the bluish cast of early LEDs raised concerns about impacts on sleep.) Because LED emitters are grouped in arrays for lighting use, they tend to give multiple shadows; diffusers and lenses can correct this but reduce efficiency somewhat.

Design with LEDs

Early adopters of LED landscape lighting nearly had to design each light from scratch. The flexibility to do that is still possible today, but those who don't wish to invest that kind of effort can choose from thousands of off-the-shelf models.

An early LED (but not solar) streetlight design, "CityWing," won an iF Design Award in 2006. Achieving area coverage with narrow-beam LEDs was a challenge. Once that was solved, the durability and energy efficiency of LED area lighting has made it ubiquitous, as well as leading to a wide variety of designs.

LEDs, photovoltaics, and aesthetics also intersected in the winning entry for New York City's 2004 City Lights design competition. Thomas Phifer and Partners Design used an arched tube nearly eight feet long, filled with LEDs, as the light fixture, braced on the top of its pole by a graceful triangular cable support. Photovoltaic film on top of the luminaire would collect power and store it, potentially a very large energy input if this design is used widely throughout the city.[43] The City Lights design is one of the standard offerings available from city government, and as of 2017 it was being installed in the Flatiron District. It is not clear whether the PV proposal remained part of the design.

The color temperature of LEDs, especially in white

Figure 8.5   "CityWing" LED streetlight by Philips (Holland). This early award-winning design is part of a wave of design innovations made possible by these tiny light sources. (*Photo:* Image from Royal Philips Electronics.)

light, is quite different from any other light source (see "Talk Lighting—a Brief Glossary," p. 342). White LEDs tend to be "cool"—and some people, clients and designers alike, may find the results take getting used to. Clanton and Associates, lighting specialists in Boulder CO, recommends field-testing any LED light at night to get a feel for its illumination and color properties.

LEDs actually offer completely new ways of thinking about lighting design, and conventional preconceptions about design of "lights" may be a hindrance. They can fit into standard categories of luminaires—spotlights, streetlights, and so on—but there is great potential for using them in entirely new ways. Translucent planters that glow at night, linear strips of blue

Figure 8.6   Tree-like supports and leaf-shaped collector/lamp housings are functionally well suited for street lighting designs and demonstrate the value of naturalistic design, or biomimicry. (*Product:* Qnuru, designed by Santa Fe blacksmith Tom Joyce. *Photo:* Noribachi Corp., current distributor of Qnuru and other designs.)

light inset in plaza pavement, radiant tire swings, or invisibly lit freestanding clear panels are a few examples that simply could not have been produced a decade ago.

There has been an explosion of LED products in garden catalogs—self-contained floating lamps, realistic cattails that light after dark, and even a set of "solar powered gnomes." Many incorporate solar power, and most are far smaller than anyone would expect a lamp to be. Although some are beyond the fringe of either sustainability or design aesthetics, LEDs are clearly opening new possibilities. One huge example of these possibilities is the Italian Light Sculpture Festival at Xuanwu Lake Park in Nanjing, China, where whole baroque buildings are interpreted using multicolor LEDs on wire frames.

Figure 8.7   The "Clover" streetlight, with irregular "trunk" poles and round lamps encircling the "stem," contrast with Paris architecture. (*Product and Photo:* Matthew Lehanneur.)

In theory, an LED can be installed without any "fixture" at all, a tiny light-generating spot on almost any surface. Since they are solid-state, they are almost completely weather- and vandal-proof. Individual battery-powered LEDs can, with some ingenuity, be wedged into a space as small as a mortar joint or a crack in tree bark, and aimed to illuminate small features throughout a landscape rather than whole areas. Some 2017 site furniture and parcourse exercise equipment is designed with thin lines of light on edges, plus overhead lighting in some cases. The effect could provide excellent visibility for way-finding, without any awareness of the space being "lighted." "Invisible lighting," as this might be called, meshes quite well with concerns about reintroducing the experience of darkness, while still providing enough light to entice people out into the night landscape.

LEDs could be deployed directly on trees, where their accurate aiming capabilities could create dramatic branch-lighting effects. This has potential to

Figure 8.8 Newfound freedom in lighting design is enlivening social spaces, like South 24th Street in Omaha NE, an American Planning Association "Great Street." (*Project:* © RDG Planning and Design. *Photo:* IRIS22 Production.)

Figure 8.9 Illuminated "tire swings" at the popular "Lawn on D" in Boston are an example of a design that would have been impossible without LEDs, solar power, and imagination. (*Project:* Sasaki. *Photo:* Courtesy of The Lawn on D, Massachusetts Convention Center Authority.)

Figure 8.10   The "Moon" bollard/path light is another innovative design facilitated by creative use of LEDs. (*Product:* Platek [Italy]. *Photo:* Courtesy platek.eu.)

solve a lingering problem with conventional lighting: manufacturers still tout uplighting of trees for dramatic effect, despite dark-sky and ecological problems. Manufacturers who continue to push uplighting are likely to find their products outlawed in an increasing number of jurisdictions, and they would be wise to begin developing dramatic alternatives, for which LEDs appear to have great promise.

The "fixtureless" approach to lighting means the designer is dealing with the technical aspects of each light and of wiring (or, in some cases, battery-powered stick-on mountings), rather than purchasing off-the-shelf luminaires. This is clearly not a challenge every designer will want to take on. In 2017, both this and the option of ready-made designs are available in huge numbers. Most of the illustrations of solar lighting involve LEDs; most designs could be converted to 110V, although the advantages of solar reduce any motivation to do so.

OLEDs—the Future of Lighting—Again?

OLEDs, or organic light-emitting diodes, are very thin sheets of carbon-based film between electrical conductors. The entire sheet gives off light when electricity is applied. OLEDs are widely used for phone screens and, to a lesser extent (because of cost), for TVs. The sheets can be transparent, and some types are flexible and can even be rolled. OLEDs do not contain the metals that LEDs do, nor do they require heat sinks. A good place to learn about the technology and watch for product news is www.oled-info.com.

OLEDs are just starting to be used for lighting, similar to the history of LEDs. As of 2016, efficacy was between 20 and 40 lumens per watt (lpw). Illumination is even and directionless, coming from the whole sheet; OLEDs can be color-tuned, like LEDs. Interior lighting takes advantage of the paper-like look of the material; self-lit origami ought to be pos-

Figure 8.11 Agent Studio's OLED shelter/seat/curb-lighting concept. Three wide blue-lit OLED bands edge the shelter and seat, then continue down the curb. (*Proposal and Image:* Rojkind Arquitectos.)

Figure 8.12 OLEDs illuminate whole surfaces, offering entirely new outdoor lighting possibilities, such as this design proposal. (*Proposal and Image:* Arq. H. Suarez, systemdesignstudio.com.)

sible. Displays at the Milan Design Week and in Japan have used thousands of small sheets; the Japan display was in the form of 5,000 programmable light-up tulips, each petal a small cupped OLED.

Other than such demonstrations, landscape applications of OLED lighting are still scarce. Agent Studio (Mexico City) has recently developed a prototype outdoor bench/shelter/information booth. Essentially a large folded transparent sheet that forms a roofed bench, its edges are lined with OLED strips that continue along the curb. The product was designed with Konica-Minolta, a major OLED supplier, so it may get some real-world exposure.

This is a technology to watch. It seems reasonably sustainable, avoids toxic materials, is durable and lightweight, and has reasonable light efficacy that may improve as LEDs have. It is also one of those rare materials that expands design into completely different ways of thinking.

Subtopics and Search Terms for Principle 8: Celebrate Light, Respect Darkness

Note: Subtopics are also useful search terms; add "innovation" or "controversy" to search terms as appropriate.

Lighting
Search terms: lighting efficiency || lighting technology || energy conservation lighting || landscape lighting

Light pollution
Search terms: astronomical light pollution || ecological light pollution || light pollution || artificial night lighting

Solar lighting
Search terms: solar lights || solar powered lighting || solar landscape lighting

Resource List:

Links to information sources related to this chapter are posted at http://islandpress.org/sustainable-landscape-construction

Principle 9:
Quietly Defend Silence

The day will come when man will have to fight merciless noise as the worst enemy of his health.
—*Robert Koch, 1880*

Gardens have traditionally been retreats where silence could be sought and savored. This feature of traditional landscapes is being eroded by the spread of technology and the increase in human population.

Is noise a sustainability issue? One research group concludes that "the most pervasive pollutant in America is noise."[1] Noise has physiological and psychological effects on living things; constant noise is unhealthy. If human lives are to be sustainable not only in basic physical needs but also psychologically, noise reduction becomes an issue much like energy consumption or toxicity.

Today there is almost nowhere on Earth where mechanical noises are truly absent. One professional "sound tracker," George Hempton, travels the world recording and studying noise; he finds it even in the most remote locations, always on the increase. In the mid-1980s, for example, he knew more than twenty places in Washington State where he could catch at least fifteen minutes of natural sounds with no motors, jets, radios, or foghorns; by 1999, there were only three.[2] Besides mechanized and broadcast noise, crowd noise and cell-phone conversations are pervasive.[3]

Discussed in This Chapter

Landscape sound barrier myths and facts.
New and developing outdoor noise control
  options.
Policy approaches to noise pollution.

Like the darkness of nighttime skies, silence is something worth respecting. Despite technology, darkness and silence cannot be *created*; light and noise can only be masked or excluded. In landscapes, truly excluding either is difficult, since to wall off the landscape is to make it something other than a landscape.

Understand Noise Terminology

In order to influence design and planning discussions about noise pollution, landscape professionals need to have a basic vocabulary about sound and how it is measured. Fortunately, terms to describe outdoor noise are fairly straightforward.[4]

Sound has two major qualities: frequency or pitch, and intensity or loudness. *Pitch* is measured in vibrations per second or hertz (1 Hz = 1 vibration, wave, or cycle per second). Musical or tonal sound involves a single frequency; for example, "middle C" is about 260 Hz. Multiplying a frequency by an integer gives its "overtones" or "harmonics"; for example, overtones of C-260 would include 520 Hz ($\times$ 2) and 1,040 Hz ($\times$ 4). Noise, which some avant-garde composers have tried to define as unappreciated sound, may be better described as a random mix of frequencies; their lack of mathematical relationship may be what makes them annoying.

The human ear can normally respond to frequencies between about 16 and 23,000 Hz. The majority of what humans hear, however, is in the range from 500 to 3,000 Hz. (The lowest note on a piano is about 27 Hz, the highest about 4,200; a piccolo, the highest-sounding orchestral instrument, can reach 4,500 Hz.)

Loudness is related to the amount of energy in sound waves. What humans register as loudness, however, is not identical to the level of sound energy measured by technical instruments. Variations in physical sensitivity of the ear as well as psychological factors influence how loud a sound seems to a particular person. It is the *perception* of sound that is most important in dealing with noise problems. Insisting that a noise problem is fixed because technical metering says so is seldom a successful approach.

As a unit of measurement for loudness, the decibel (dB) is the one most used in design, planning, and engineering. Breathing quietly produces about 10 dB; conversation, about 60; yelling, 80. Prolonged exposure to 85 dB or so can cause hearing loss, 120 or above causes pain, while at the upper limit of human tolerance, 150 dB can instantly burst the eardrums. ("Boom-car" stereo systems produce 140 dB or more.)[5] Louder sounds can even cause death.

The decibel scale is *logarithmic*, meaning that every 10 decibels represents a *doubling* of loudness (20 decibels is twice as loud as 10, but 90 decibels is also twice as loud as 80). For this reason, decibels cannot simply be added together. For example, if one car on a road produces 60 dB, two cars do not produce 120, but only 63.

Because the human ear is more sensitive to some frequencies than others (500–3,000 Hz, as noted above), sound engineers have developed a "weighted" decibel scale that simulates human hearing, called the "A-weighted response." Measurements that use this system are noted as dB(A), still read as "decibels." This weighted system causes two problems for sustainability-oriented landscape professionals.

First, the A-weighted decibel is explicitly tailored to *human* ears. Thus, dB(A) measurements are a poor indicator of noise responses in nonhuman species. For example, dogs hear from 65 to 45,000 Hz; noise too high-pitched to register on the dB(A) scale could still drive dogs crazy. Similarly, "bioacoustic" studies of noise effects on wildlife need more information than is provided by the A-weighted system. Among land animals, hearing ranges from 16 Hz (elephants) to 91,000 (mice); most birds have relatively narrow hear-

ing ranges, while aquatic species, like porpoises and whales, have very wide ranges reaching up to 150,000 Hz.[6] Just as light pollution outside the human visible range can disrupt animal and plant life cycles, noise beyond human hearing can have serious effects on nonhuman species.

The second problem with the dB(A) system is that it downplays sounds that are pitched *below* 500 Hz. Much of the annoying noise produced by trucks, trains, and planes is low-pitched enough to be missed by dB(A) measurements. Measuring traffic noise on the A-weighted scale may thus be misleading. Low-pitched noise is also the most difficult to screen with physical barriers; when barrier performance is rated with before-and-after dB(A) measurements, reductions in higher pitch may be impressive, but low-pitched noise problems may still exist.

Two other noise-measurement methods can be important when evaluating noise barriers. These are NRC (noise reduction coefficient) and STC (sound transmission class). An NRC value of 0 means that a panel reflects all the noise hitting it; a value of 1 means the panel absorbs all noise that hits it.[7] The STC indicates "transmission loss"—the amount of sound, in decibels, that is lost when passing through a panel. The higher the STC number, the better the panel insulates against transmitted sound. Combining NRC with STC is often the best way to gauge performance of sound-walls. Technically, such measures are frequency-specific; a material might reduce a high pitch by 50 percent and a low one by only 2 percent. Acoustic tests often show noise reduction or loss for each of a dozen frequencies, in graph form rather than as a single rating.

Many other terms are used to discuss acoustics and sound physics. Most apply only to acoustics of indoor spaces or are far more technical than necessary for outdoor noise pollution work.

Be Aware of Damage Caused by Noise

Noise is frequently treated as if it were merely a matter of personal likes and dislikes, but research shows clearly that the detrimental effects of noise are quite real. Many technical volumes have been devoted to effects of noise on health and on communities.

Continual exposure to 85 decibels (the level of a food blender, a noisy factory, or a small plane 1,000 feet overhead) creates a serious threat of hearing loss for most people.[8] Complaints about noise are to be expected when the volume reaches about 30 decibels; by 40 to 45 decibels legal action is common, and in many countries anything above this level is legally unacceptable.[9]

Worldwide, over 120 million people suffer from hearing loss due to noise exposure.[10] In the United States, 100 million people are exposed to significant traffic noise and 30 million workers to hazardous noise levels. Among the most affected are the two labor sectors in which *landscape workers* are categorized: construction and agriculture. More than half of all construction workers have noise-related hearing problems; 75 percent of agricultural workers do.

Because noise exposure is hard to monitor, there is disagreement about what its human health effects are. The United States lags far behind the rest of the world in studying noise pollution, in large part because the Reagan administration "defunded" the EPA's Office of Noise Abatement and Control.[11] Scientific studies, however, have linked excessive noise to the following: high blood pressure and heart rate; labored breathing; general stress and irritability; fatigue; susceptibility to colds; reduced sex drive; changes in brain chemistry; damage to fetus; and decreased learning ability. Borrowing a concept from smoking regulations, "secondhand noise" is becoming a serious topic of discussion among environmental health professionals.

Research about negative effects of noise on endangered species is a slowly emerging field, called "bioacoustics." Migratory birds are a particular concern.[12] Mass beachings of whales have also been linked (controversially) to navy use of very loud, low-frequency sounds for echolocation and other military purposes.[13]

Comprehensive 2004 and 2011 reviews of research about noise and wildlife showed "substantial changes in foraging and anti-predator behavior, reproductive success, density, and community structure in response to noise."[14] Early research focused on aircraft noise and little on roadway noise, with noise reported subjectively, not measured by instruments; recent work has become more rigorous. Many species avoid roads at least during nesting or other specific periods; road

noise interacts with other factors, such as light pollution, roadkill mortality, or the physical barrier of the road and adjacent structures. At least one study played recorded roadway noise in roadless habitat and found that animals abandoned habitat near the noise.[15] (Some roadside conditions, such as mowed grass or water collecting in ditches, attract wildlife.)[16]

Theoretically, noise has potential to interfere with animal life in many ways. Almost all vertebrate animals use hearing to navigate, find prey or avoid predators, and, in many species, communicate. Birds rely on songs to communicate, to distinguish among species and maintain habitat ranges, and to discover and attract mates. Even reptiles and invertebrates avoid some sounds and move toward others. As in humans, there is a strong likelihood that noise causes physiological effects, stress, and hearing loss in animals.

Despite the complexity of documenting environmental noise, it is becoming increasingly clear that beyond certain thresholds, noise can truly be "toxic" to living beings, including humans.

Don't Rely on Noise "Barriers" in Most Landscapes

There is a great deal of mythology about the ability of landscapes to *stop* noise. Various methods often proposed as noise stoppers, such as walls, berms, and plantings, are largely ineffective in that role. In a landscape setting, the only real remedy for noise is distance—a significant factor in the "get away from it all" roots of suburban sprawl and in the failure of suburbs to maintain promised quietude as new development moves closer. Sound levels decrease by about six decibels for every doubling of distance between source and hearer.[17] Although constructed barriers can affect noise, the general inability to screen landscape noise contributes directly to excessive consumption of space for residences—clearly a sustainability issue.

Walls

Conventional noise walls *reflect* specific noises, such as highway traffic, away from specific places. They are large and massive: usually at least eight feet tall and often twenty; twice as long as the distance from the noise source to the spot being protected; and of material thick and/or dense enough to provide about four pounds of material per square foot of wall surface.[18] Walls are most commonly concrete, sometimes with surface designs but often brutally minimalist; they are also made of wood or brick, and less commonly of metal, glass, or plastics, as well as compressed composites that can be decoratively molded. Such walls can decrease noise levels by five to ten decibels (rarely fifteen)—barely enough to bring air-conditioning equipment at fifteen feet (sixty decibels) down to the acceptable range. Larger reductions are prohibitively expensive.[19] Even "typical" noise walls cost between $1 million and $2 million per linear mile.[20] A one-foot-thick, twenty-foot-tall wall consumes nearly 8,000 tons of concrete per mile. The weight of such walls can prohibit their use on bridges.

Besides costs, walls have many drawbacks. They can make the noise *worse* somewhere else, especially if the noise source is in a reflector-shaped valley. Parallel walls on opposite sides of a road can result in neither side getting relief unless very widely separated (at least ten lanes), and can concentrate noise on the road.[21] Second or higher stories in houses behind noise walls often derive no benefit at all. Walls often physically separate communities and disrupt cross-traffic routes. These factors can lead to perceptions—often justified—that only one part of a community benefits at the expense of others; given that the placement of major roads is itself an environmental justice issue, noise wall proposals can be hotly contested. In some situations, walls may increase risks for drivers, either by making the road featureless and boring, or by increasing severity of accidents.

Depending on their compass orientation, tall walls can cast permanent shadows over the very landscapes they are intended to protect. Walls also act as windbreaks, which may be desirable, but can exclude cooling breezes and may also cause snowdrifts. Wind turbulence produced by the wall is often a problem on its own, and additionally, turbulence "warps" sound waves, diminishing or obliterating the effectiveness of the noise barrier.[22] Walls, unless carefully coordinated with wildlife crossings, can dramatically increase the barrier effect that highways have on animals.

Noise walls are frequently set on top of earth berms (see below). This increases effectiveness, but requires sufficiently wide property for the berm to be constructed. A six-foot berm topped by a ten-foot wall tends to *appear* less massive than a sixteen-foot wall. This strategy, however, does nothing to decrease the length of shadows thrown by the wall.

Because tires are a significant source of traffic noise, along residential streets low but massive stone or masonry walls may do some good. Using clear sound-reflecting material for the top one-third of a wall can dramatically decrease the claustrophobic effect, letting lighting into the adjacent space and allowing views outward.

All in all, performance of reflective noise barriers, evaluated against their economic, social, and resource costs, is extremely poor. Like many urban features, they are in demand primarily because they allow high-profit land-use density. The first US noise walls were built in California in 1968, and over 1,300 linear miles of barrier had been built by 2000, at costs exceeding $500 million. The concrete industry, in particular, considers noise walls a growth industry and lobbies hard for these structures. Many municipalities have made noise walls a prerequisite for zoning permission—not for roads, which are seldom denied permission, but for developments near roads.

Randomizing the wall's top edge or surface or both may disperse sound more fully. The results have been mixed. For example, a T-shaped wall top one yard wide can substitute for adding a yard in height.

If noise walls are unavoidable, they should at least be designed for visual interest. Probably the most spectacular example of an artistic noise barrier is along Pima Expressway in Scottsdale AZ, where giant southwestern-themed motifs—lizards, cacti, native pottery patterns—were designed into cast concrete walls, a collaboration of landscape architect Jeff Engelmann, artist Carolyn Braaksma, and architect Andrea Foreman. Rubber-molded designs and textures were layered onto formwork for the panels, then stripped, relayered in new combinations, and reused. This not only created almost infinite variations on the cast designs, but also applied the principle of materials reuse to this very large project. The use of 3D printing now enhances possibilities for custom mold-making and wall forms.

Figure 9.1 If noise walls are unavoidable, at least make them astonishing and creative (Pima Expressway, Scottsdale AZ). (*Photo:* Kim Sorvig.)

At least one wall manufacturer, Zeller International, has filed patents on a wall system made of recycled scrap or even some forms of toxic waste, bonded with proprietary resins. Zeller's Eco-Wall reflects inventive thinking: Eco-Walls are envisioned as solar collectors, storage panels for heat or water, or supports for photovoltaics or telecommunications infrastructure. Although these uses add value to the walls, the basic concept of the noise wall is badly flawed, and the Eco-Wall concept might be better applied to other types of construction.

Berms

Correctly sized and shaped, earth berms and other grading can deflect or redirect some noise, with or without a noise wall on top. Putting a roadway in a cut rather than on fill can prevent part of the road noise from spreading directly outward. Low-pitched noises like truck or train rumblings, however, are actually transmitted through the earth itself. Living in an underground or bermed house, as I do, or in a basement, people can sometimes hear trains a mile or more away, transmitted at low frequency through the soil, while higher sounds immediately outside are damped.

The main limitation on berms is the amount of space required for their footprint. This in turn is limited by the steepest angle at which soil will hold a slope, the angle of repose. Greenwall techniques (p. 140) are frequently used to produce steep berms for noise protection. Btec techniques of woven willow, geogrid, and soil have been used by Weavewall Ltd. for steep, shrub-covered berms.

According to the FHWA, berms provide one to three decibels *more* sound reduction than a wall of similar height. This is due partly to mass and partly to the vegetated berm surface, which absorbs and dissipates sound. Improved performance is also due, however, to the extra *width* of the berm creating a longer distance between noise source and hearers. Thus greenwalls, which are vegetated but thin, should be expected to perform better than ordinary walls because of vegetation, but not as well as much thicker berms.

Vegetation as Sound Barrier

Tree plantings as noise barriers are an article of faith with many landscape professionals and their clients. In fact, to cut noise significantly in terms of actual decibels, a band of planting at least 100 feet wide is required. These plantings must include both dense shrubs and trees; trees alone are ineffective. Even in these widths and with appropriate species, a tree barrier can reduce sound by only about three to five decibels per hundred feet width.[23] Any effect from a smaller planted barrier is primarily an out-of-sight, out-of-mind phenomenon—valuable in its own way, but not actually decreasing physical noise.

Sasaki, in its 2011 Wilmington Waterfront Park, was able to screen Port of Los Angeles noise from neighborhoods with a 400-foot-wide park, which was calculated to replace a 20-foot-tall noise wall. Except with the luxury of so much space, planting and berms join conventional walls in the category of relatively ineffective noise mitigation.

There are, however, several viable noise-control options for landscape professionals: noise-absorbing panels; noise-reducing pavement; screening the *perception* of noise; and lobbying for policies that prevent or decrease noise *at its source*. Each has its limits and its strengths; none will deal with all forms of noise. These options are discussed in the following sections.

Try Noise-absorbing Materials

Interior noise control relies heavily on acoustic tile and other materials that absorb or deaden noise. Few of these indoor materials will survive outdoors, nor are they manufactured in sizes or configurations that would be easy to use in the landscape.

A growing number of sound-absorbing blankets and panels, however, can be used outdoors. Blankets are usually quilted fabric plus fiberglass of varied thicknesses; they can be wrapped around some types of machinery, or hung on fences or other supports. They have the advantage of being easily cut to shape.

For a number of years, the Canadian government has required barriers that primarily absorb noise, instead of reflecting it. The Canadian requirements are specific: an NRC rating of 0.7 (70 percent absorption, minimum) and STC level of 30 (loss of 30 dB in transmission). Durisol, a Canadian manufacturer, makes wall panels that meet these criteria from wood particles bound with cement.[24]

Several brands of "mass loaded" sound-absorbing material are now available. These are flexible black plastic sheets, usually about one-eighth of an inch thick, that pack one pound into a square foot, or 96 pounds per cubic foot (for comparison, cement powder weighs 94 lb./cu. ft.). One brand, Acoustiblok, reduces noise by 85 percent (STC of 28), and more if layered into interior walls. Layered between extremely heavy-duty cloth and mounted in steel frames, the company's All Weather Sound Panels measure 4 × 8

feet by 2.5 inches thick, are resistant to oils, chemicals, and pollutants, and are washable and UV resistant. The most recent product in this line is Acoustifence, a green mass-loaded material with grommets for hanging on chain-link or nailing to wood fences or masonry walls. A final touch is Acoustifence-Landscape, a line of nonacoustic material printed with life-size photos of brick, stone, wood, and vegetated walls.[25] These have grommets to match the acoustic sheets, and can also be used as stand-alone disguises for ordinary fencing—sometimes with surreal results.

Mass-loading takes vinyl and incorporates dense materials; in some cases, these include lead, barium, and asbestos. (Acoustiblok is free of these, according to the manufacturer.) This may be a case where the advantages of vinyl outweigh the concerns, especially when maximum sound absorption in minimum thickness is critical. Some mass-loaded vinyl has fire-rated surfacing, but in a major fire is likely to give off toxic smoke. This is of less concern outdoors than indoors, but still serious. One nonvinyl alternative, for moderate sound insulation, is rubber sheeting made from recycled tires; an example is Audimute.

Most blankets and panels can be installed either permanently or as temporary noise screens (for example, around construction sites). They have been used both to screen point sources of outdoor noise, such as generators or HVAC equipment, and as linear barriers along transportation routes. They can be mounted to existing surfaces, hung on cables, or mounted to posts. Thus, they take far less footprint space than any conventional noise wall and achieve significantly greater noise reductions.

One other strategy for noise-absorbing walls is to use Helmholtz resonator cavities within the wall. These cavities are like honeycomb with small holes toward the noise, where sound enters. Changing the size of the cavity "tunes" the wall to absorb specific frequencies; multiple cavity sizes in one wall could in theory absorb all the frequencies of road noise (see next section). A 2003 patent[26] was issued for this concept, but to date there does not appear to be a commercial product.

Landscape art absorbs noise at Amsterdam's Schiphol Airport, one of the world's busiest. The eighty-acre Buitenschot Land Art Park has three-meter-tall

Figure 9.2 Noise walls can incorporate more than concrete, avoiding problems of shadowing and monotony. They are still not terribly effective against noise. (*Project:* Oslo, Norway; designer unknown. *Photo:* Kim Sorvig.)

ridges and furrows, set at GPS-precise angles to the flight path. Artist Paul de Kort designed the land art, inspired by plowed fields (which themselves measurably reduce noise) and sound-wave patterns. Working with Dutch landscape architects H+N+S, de Kort created a design that incorporates bike paths and other park amenities—and cuts airplane noise in half. This intriguing approach is very specific to its situation, but might work for ground-level sources, with modification.[27]

It is important to recall that the overall goal is less outdoor noise, not more and better barriers. Even noise-absorbing barriers can be socially divisive, block cross-connections, and cause microclimate problems. The availability of outdoor absorptive panels should not be used to excuse vehicle and building designs that "dump" noise into the outdoor commons.

Modify Pavement to Reduce Road Noise

Highway noise results from several distinct sources: engine noise; exhaust noise, especially from truck stacks; aerodynamic whistle; acceleration and braking; and tire whine. Each requires a different approach to noise control or reduction, most of them outside the direct influence of landscape professionals. This section deals with a road-construction material that reduces tire whine: rubberized paving.

Various mixes of rubber with binders have been tried for surfacing roads, often motivated by the need to recycle rubber. In Japan, recycled-rubber chunks as aggregate were bonded with polymers to create a porous and flexible pavement. The mix has been tested on roads by the Public Works Research Institute of Japan. At last report, the material was being improved for skid resistance and lower flammability.[28] In the Japanese studies, car-tire noise was reduced by fifteen decibels and truck-tire noise by eight decibels. (Remember that a ten-decibel difference *halves* the noise.)

Significant use or testing of "rubber asphalt" has occurred in some eight US states, with Arizona the leading exponent. Consisting of 15–18 percent crumb rubber in hot asphalt with additives, the mix needs to be stirred or agitated to prevent separation, and should not be kept hot longer than about eight hours; it is unknown whether cool-mix asphalt methods can incorporate rubber. According to the Rubber Paving Association, the Arizona mix, invented in the 1960s, can produce a 50–85 percent reduction in tire noise (comparable to the Japanese findings expressed in decibels). It also recycles about 500 used tires per lane-mile; rubber asphalt is the biggest single use of used tires in the United States. Although pound for pound it costs 40–85 percent more than conventional asphalt, it can be applied thinner and lasts longer, so that there are life-cycle cost savings. On some roads, re*surfacing* with rubberized asphalt can be an alternative to reconstructing the road, with major savings in materials and costs.

In the Netherlands and in India, experiments have tested recycled plastic for pavement; the Dutch concept appears to be a precast, hollow rectangular section with space for utilities; in India, recycled plastic replaces 15 percent of the asphalt in some 5,000 kilometers of roads built since 2004. In Texas, plastic pins have been used to keep asphalt from moving and cracking. Plastic may have similar pavement noise reduction effects as rubber; in India, it slightly reduces cost while improving the stability and strength of the mix.[29]

Make Noise Invisible

Decreasing the psychological *perception* of noise is usually the main or only realistic course for landscape design and construction. Once noise is present, no amount of outdoor construction at the receiving end can eliminate it. Although few people actually see sounds,[30] "making noise invisible" is one important tactic in landscape control of nuisance sound.

It has been shown repeatedly that a noise whose source is unseen is less annoying than noise from visible sources. Thus, coming back to walls, berms, and plantings, for most situations a *visual* barrier does nearly as much good for making landscapes *feel* quiet as a massive barrier intended to stop sound. Well-known urban "vest pocket parks," for example New York's Paley Park, rely on this as well as on the masking effects of water noise. Visual barriers generally need to be only as high as the user's eye level. A solid wall to about five feet, topped with trellis or open grille, can increase the sense of privacy and calm without blocking sun or breeze.

A related factor in noise perception is that sounds over which people feel some control are less bothersome than sounds to which they are exposed involuntarily. The noise of cars from urban streets is as loud, in decibels, as that of a plane in a flight path overhead[31]—but the plane, over which people feel no possibility of control, is more likely to attract complaints. (Similarly, my iPhone amplifier is music, while the neighbor's is noise.) This suggests that noise levels that result from community-based decisions might be less upsetting to people than those imposed on them by building first and asking questions later.

Fight Noise with Noise

A related, relatively reliable way of dealing with noise outdoors is to add other noises. These can distract from or mask objectionable noise. Like other psychological methods, masking does little to reduce physical risks like hearing loss from noise exposure. Adding noise can at least make the experience more pleasant.

Harmonious or desirable noises close at hand, like a fountain in an urban garden, can mask louder noises farther away. It is possible, though relatively uncommon, to plant or construct landscape features specifically for the sounds they produce—aspens for the shimmering rustle of their leaves, or sculptures that chime or whistle musically. Designing and building such elements could be a specialty for landscape pro-

fessionals, if not directly related to sustainability, at least as a service to mitigate one of the major effects of the unsustainable environments in which many people live.

A high-tech option with intriguing possibilities has recently become available, though apparently little tested in outdoor use. This is the so-called white-noise generator. White noise is sound containing all audible wavelengths, so named by comparison to white light, which contains all colors.

The simplest white-noise generators emit a constant low hissing or crackling that seems to fade into the background, taking some louder and more annoying noises with it. In this sense, it acts much like a fountain, offering a sound that masks other sounds without calling attention to itself. Straightforward white-noise sources like this have been available for some time.

More recently, *interactive* white-noise generators have been developed. These "listen" to ambient noises and immediately generate sounds exactly "opposite" or "complementary" to each new noise. The result is that ambient noise plus generated noise add up to all wavelengths, that is, they combine to create white noise. This strategy is called "active noise control" (ANC) and has been the subject of research since the 1930s.

ANC is the concept behind noise-canceling headphones. Headphones completely enclose the ear; canceling noise outdoors is much more complicated. The "opposite" noise must be carefully aligned with its target in both time and space. Outdoor noise sources are multiple, often moving, and the spaces in which they resonate are complex. Despite several tests of outdoor noise cancellation possibilities (most of them in Japan and Korea),[32] it has proven very difficult to apply ANC to complex outdoor noise.

ANC still has potential applications that affect landscapes, however. Some large trucks use noise-canceling equipment on their exhaust stacks, and the concept has been proposed for cars. Engine noise, aerodynamic whine, and even braking and tire noise are produced in fixed locations on a given vehicle and are fairly constant acoustically. Noise-canceling devices specific to each of these could be effective if installed *on each vehicle*. This seems unlikely unless public pressure against noise increases; noise-canceling car mufflers have been designed, but abandoned for the usual reason: because they would increase manufacturing costs.[33]

Like physical barriers, noise machines would not exist in an ideal world. Until and unless policy and technology turn down the volume of civilization's many noise sources, technical fixes may be worth investigating.

Push for Quieter Landscape Tools

Even among construction power tools, many landscape machines are known for noisiness. Gas-powered leaf blowers, once voted the worst invention ever created,[34] put out 110 decibels, just below the pain threshold. Two-stroke engines on many other lawn and garden gadgets, from lawnmowers to tillers, can also be disproportionately loud. Targeted for their contribution to air pollution (p. 323), such engines have been redesigned significantly since about 2000; in 2015 the Outdoor Power Equipment Institute (OPEI, an industry lobbying organization) stated that contemporary tools produced 85 percent less noise than 1970's models.[35] Landscape professionals should vote with their dollars, creating incentives for manufacturers whose machines cause less pollution, including noise pollution.

Cordless electric yard tools (powered by rechargeable batteries) are becoming more widely available (see Principle 7), and are generally quieter than gas-powered equivalents. Better yet, nonpowered hand tools are quietest of all and can become a trademark for quality construction and maintenance firms.

Protect "Soundscapes" Through Planning

What does the dearth of effective noise-stopping techniques mean for landscape professionals? Because we cannot wall noise out of our landscapes, we have a stake in quieting it at its source.

Architectural and engineering systems often vent their noise to the outdoors, protecting people inside at the expense of any person or creature in the landscape. This avoids the cost of truly effective sound insulation, but its consequences are not sustainable. This is not merely an abstract wish or theory. Commercial products are available to quiet noise from buildings, factories, chimneys, and exhaust stacks. Landscape professionals should prod any design team they work with to make full use of at-the-source noise-prevention methods.

Traffic noise increases with speed, at about 10 dB per 30 mph increase.[36] Traffic-calming measures (p. 240) are often aimed at noise reduction as well as safety. In addition to reducing aerodynamic, tire, and engine noise by reducing speed, well-designed traffic calming can smooth the flow of traffic, resulting in less braking and accelerating noise.

For a decade, the National Park Service (NPS) has been struggling to manage noise in some of the nation's most beloved landscapes. Grand Canyon National Park hears over 140,000 sightseeing flyovers, usually at low altitude, every year. Snowmobiles and Jet Skis were banned from many parks because of noise (as well as other environmental impacts, especially on wildlife).[37] Park maintenance itself contributes to noise with leaf blowers, chainsaws, and generators. Natural resource specialist Wes Henry, of the NPS's Washington DC office, wrote one of the first parks "soundscape" management policies in 1999; today many parks have one.[38]

On a day-to-day level, many communities have noise ordinances. These are difficult to enforce against individual moving sources of noise, such as cars or motorcycles, yet most ordinances are aimed at these kinds of sources. (Another target, boom-boxes, are almost extinct, and music from phones is mostly, though unfortunately not universally, enjoyed via earbuds.) Better ordinances and enforcement might target long-term repeat sources, such as HVAC machinery and other architectural service equipment, as well as industrial plants and public roads, and to require noise-reduction equipment *on* moving sources.

Noise, until perhaps a decade ago, was legally classified as a "nuisance," not a serious environmental problem. This attitude has slowly begun to change. Recent pro-business, anti-regulatory federal administrations have created a situation where federal noise laws exist but are unfunded for enforcement, yet state and local authorities are forbidden to pass legislation stricter than federal statutes.

With at-the-source noise control products available at reasonable cost, community standards could reasonably require that noises stay under a maximum level, and they might also require that noises cease at certain times, such as nights and weekends. New York City, for example, undertook a 2005 revision of its noise laws with neighborhood-by-neighborhood crackdowns called Operation Silent Night. Noise, like pollution, is a classic example of the democratic belief that one person's freedom ends where it impacts other people.

The impact of noise, especially highway noise, on communities is well-known, and mostly unsustainable. Noise is the number-one complaint by citizens about their community, and their main reason for leaving if they do;[39] in New York City, it tops the list of calls to a municipal hotline, with 1,000 noise complaints per day.[40] William Morrish, former director of the University of Minnesota's Design Center for the American Urban Landscape, puts the case for road-noise control succinctly. Speaking of a traffic-calmed, truck-free landscaped interstate in St. Paul MN, he says, "It costs more than a standard highway, but it's going to be cheaper than bailing out a failing neighborhood."[41]

Awareness is growing that noise is harmful to human health (and probably that of other species), as well as being a factor in psychological well-being.

Blocking noise after it leaves its source, however, has high costs, both monetary and environmental. For these reasons, decreasing noise *by eliminating or quieting its sources* should be an issue for sustainability. Proposing to *require* noise control certainly meets with social and technical challenges. Nonetheless, as a profession, we need to be advocates for silence.

Subtopics and Search Terms for Principle 9: Quietly Defend Silence

Note: Subtopics are also useful search terms; add "innovation" or "controversy" to search terms as appropriate.

Acoustics
Search terms: acoustics || outdoor acoustics

Noise
Search terms: noise science || noise definition

Noise control
Search terms: noise (control OR mitigation OR suppression OR abatement) || damping || sound insulation

Resource List:

Links to information sources related to this chapter are posted at http://islandpress.org/sustainable-landscape-construction

Principle 10:
Maintain to Sustain

Ask rice fields and gardens for the truth; learn from hedges and walls.
—*Zen Master Dogen, AD 1250*

Landscapes are living things. In one important sense, they are never finished. Growth, natural succession, weathering, change of use or ownership or neighbors—all keep landscapes evolving. Except in successfully restored native landscapes, the best of which maintain themselves (though not in a steady state), maintenance is not optional. Maintenance is the way an evolving landscape keeps pace with evolving human demands.

Most landscape professionals, and many landowners, are well aware that sustainability and careful maintenance go hand in hand. Yet the specialist structure of professional relationships often means that maintenance, construction, and design occur in totally separate compartments. At best, a conscientious maintenance contractor tries to guess the designer's intent or the builder's methods and work accordingly. At worst, maintenance is always *somebody else's problem*, deferred until decay and disrepair take over. The landscape is then ripped up and rebuilt, and the cycle starts over. This is unsatisfying to everyone involved and wastes resources that could be more sustainably used.

Maintaining a landscape consists, basically, of three interlaced goals:

- keeping the living part of the landscape healthy
- keeping the inanimate, constructed parts repaired
- and balancing the first two goals against human uses of the space.

Clearly, these goals are sometimes in conflict. Healthy vegetation can overrun the site, burying hardscape and making human access, let alone use, im-

Summarized in This Chapter

Designing for maintainable spaces.
Maintenance machinery, efficiency, fuel, and pollution.
Reducing pesticide use by good planning.
Sustainable use of fertilizers.
Conserving and using on-site resources.
Establishing and maintaining native plants.
Estimating the long-term costs and benefits of maintenance.
Coordinating design, construction, and maintenance.

possible. Repairing constructed elements, painting, repointing masonry, or fixing pipes or wiring can cause chemical and physical damage to vegetation and inconvenience to users. Excessive or unplanned use can damage either plants or hardscape in ways that cannot be repaired without stopping those uses. The human factor also includes the financial balancing act between ideals of perfect maintenance (often based on grounds-keeping practices of the rich and famous) and expenses that real owners can realistically afford.

Despite this complexity, landscape maintenance gets far less respect from society than it deserves: many people view grounds-maintenance professionals as one step up from unskilled labor. It is true that some *basic* landscape maintenance tasks are simple and can be done at a default level by unskilled people, and that as low-status work, it often goes to immigrants (who often have skills that Americans have lost) and the poor. Coordinating tasks and people so that their work favors the environment, however, is by no means simple. Anyone who can successfully juggle the above three goals is the equal of any other professional and should be valued as such.

It has been a theme of this book that sustainable landscapes are most likely to result from coordination among designers, contractors, and clients. This chapter offers an *overview* of how maintenance fits into a coordinated approach, with the focus on practices with the clearest *environmental* costs and benefits. A number of these practices overlap with sustainable techniques begun during construction or even design.

This is *not* a complete coverage of all the issues of landscape maintenance, nor of published sources on the topic. Rather, it concentrates on ways in which maintenance practices can contribute to sustainability (or hinder it), and how better coordination and planning can increase the value of good maintenance.

Know the Resource Costs of Conventional Landscape Maintenance

Conventional maintenance of landscapes uses many resources, particularly petroleum-based fuels, fertilizers, and pesticides. Comprehensive maintenance-specific figures for landscape costs do not appear to be tracked or updated regularly, but some indicators are worth considering.

The most recent (2005) estimate of total US lawn area (residential and institutional), made by NASA, is about 63,000 square miles (40 million acres), which is nearly 2 percent of the continental United States and roughly the size of Texas. It makes turfgrass the *largest irrigated crop* in the United States, by a factor of three. Other estimates have placed the total over 70,000 square miles.[1] Another way to get a sense of the scale of lawns is that the Interstate Highway System has nearly 9 million lane-miles (as of 2014), and averages eight acres of right-of-way lawn maintenance per lane-mile, totaling 72 million acres.

Monetary costs vary by region; older research indicated that maintaining an acre cost $500 for agencies and businesses using salaried staff,[2] and that homeowners spent nearly $400 on gardening supplies per household, of which a high percentage was for mainte-

nance. In 2006, landscape supplies were a $35 billion industry.[3] In neither study is it possible to determine how much of this cost went for fuel, pesticides, or other specifics.

Owen Dell, a Santa Barbara CA landscape architect-contractor, estimates comparative maintenance costs for a "conventional" garden and a sustainable one in California, as of 2004. Dell does not define "sustainable" or "conventional," but clearly includes water conservation, soil-health maintenance, and Integrated Pest Management in the former. The sustainable garden requires one-third the maintenance labor, one-fifth the pesticides, and about one-fourth the water of the conventional design. It also avoids dump fees and removal or replacement of unhealthy plants. Over a twenty-year lifespan, maintenance costs for the sustainable garden are about 37 percent of those for the conventional one. Maintenance is 86 percent of the design and construction cost of the conventional garden, and only 62 percent for the sustainable design.[4] (In a separate estimate, Dell notes that doing design and construction right the first time ends up costing about 57 percent of doing it cheaply and without professional input.)

Mowing turf is perhaps the simplest item to estimate for fuel costs, yet even that varies widely. Gas-powered mowing with home equipment averages about 125,000 Btu per acre (Table 7.8). Many of those acres are mowed ten to twenty times per year. Per acre, annual gas mowing consumes 1.25–2.5 million Btu; electric mowing, roughly half that.[5]

The same source estimates an annual 16 million Btu per acre for irrigation where water is supplied by municipal mains. About 2 million Btu per acre is used annually for conservatively fertilized turf, up to 7 million for some types. For pesticides, 1 million Btu per acre per application is conservative; 2.5 million is common. These figures include embodied energy of materials, and fuel energy to apply them.

The annual cost in energy for all these basic conventional maintenance tasks can be added up. Conservatively, assume each acre is mowed only ten times per year, and sprayed for weeds only twice. As shown in the table below, average energy to maintain *one acre* conventionally lies between 21 and 30 million Btu per year.

For the nation, the total energy is phenomenal—between 840 and 1,200 *trillion* Btu each year, based on 40 million acres (some estimates indicate 30 million acres). Even though this is not a particularly accurate estimate, it gives a sense of the huge energy investments involved in conventional landscape maintenance.

The fact that lawns sequester carbon, like any other vegetation, is often used to defend them.[6] The NASA study showed that lawns sequestered more carbon in the soil if artificial fertilizer was reduced and clippings were left on the ground, and estimated the total effective sequestration (after discounting for emissions from maintenance operations) at 16.7 million metric tons. Nationally, lawn maintenance is responsible for about 9 million metric tons of carbon; this is about 0.1 percent of total US emissions of 6,870 tons.[7]

Plan for Maintainable Spaces

Horticulturists say the most common ailment of landscape plants is Lawnmower Disease. While this may not be scientifically accurate, maintenance machinery commonly inflicts serious damage on the very plants it is intended to serve. Physical wounds allow bacteria, fungi, viruses, and insects to get past plants' first line of defense, which is bark. It is unclear how much plant disease starts in this way, but the percentage is likely quite high. Snow blowers and leaf blowers join mowers in assaulting the bark of trees. Maintenance equipment, like construction equipment, can also stress plants by compacting soil and contributing to air pollution or soil contamination.

Landscape architects and landowners are quick to blame the maintenance contractor for all forms of Lawnmower Disease, and in some cases, contractor carelessness *is* responsible. But equally often, landscape design or construction is also at fault. Maintenance machinery, and even hand maintenance, requires room to work and access to each task, and these are often forgotten in the design process.

People need room to work; average dimensions for these requirements are well-known. Maintenance also uses many machines and vehicles. Like vehicles for transportation, they need specific amounts of space in which to maneuver. No competent designer would think of laying out an office or kitchen without checking human dimensions, or a street or loading dock without checking turning radii of vehicles. Yet in laying out landscapes, it is common to create spaces that cannot accommodate the machines to maintain them.

Not all, or even most, maintenance *requires* machinery. However, when it is reasonable to expect that some machinery *will* be used, it is shortsighted not to design for that machinery. Lawns, for example, should not have narrow extensions or acute angles where even a hand mower is awkward to use. Grass immediately under trees should be left unmowed for several inches out from the trunk (and can be removed by hand weeding if desired); a bed of mulch or plantings is another option for protecting trunks from machinery, and removes grass, which some feel competes with tree roots. Structures that require regular painting should have a space around them in which no critically important plants are located. Space should be designed to pile

Table 10.1
Annual energy to maintain one acre of lawn (computed from Table 7.8).

	One Acre, One Time	Frequency per Year	Annual Total
Mowing	0.125 million Btu	10–20	1.25–2.5 million Btu
Irrigation	N/A		16 million Btu
Fertilization	N/A		2–7 million Btu
Pesticides	0.625–2.5 million Btu	2 or more	2–5 million Btu
EST. ANNUAL TOTAL for one acre	21.25–30.5 million Btu		
EST. US TOTAL based on 40 million acres	850–1,220 **trillion** Btu		

shoveled or plowed snow where meltwater helps plantings. The concept is obvious, the possible examples almost infinite—all the more remarkable that this important issue is so often overlooked or ignored.

Part of the problem may be that detailed information on landscape maintenance machinery is not easily available to designers. Exact dimensions for specific models are provided by manufacturers, but are seldom appropriate for design use. The designer needs rule-of-thumb averages, of the sort presented for cars and trucks in the *Graphic Standards* or *Timesaver Standards* series. These standard design sources typically do not even have an index entry for ordinary maintenance.

Dimensions of garden tools are given, but only as storage-planning items, and no commercial maintenance equipment is shown. *Landscape Architectural Graphic Standards* (Wiley, 2007), which devotes nine pages to the average sizes of humans from infant to adult, doesn't even have an entry under "Tools" or "Machines"; the "Equipment" entries are *not* graphic. The landscape volume of *Timesaver* does give one turning radius (thirty-six inches) for a generic "garden tractor." By comparison, it devotes about a dozen full pages to operating-space requirements for cars and trucks of all sizes, and a quarter-page to the turning radius of the Zamboni ice machine! This reflects the odd priori-

Figure 10.1 Design versus maintenance. To prune and remove trash, this worker had to cross the fence on his ladder; no other access was possible. (*Photo:* Kim Sorvig.)

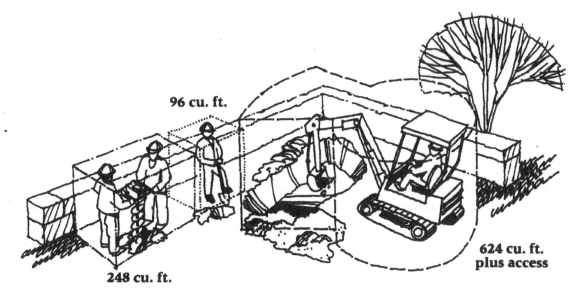

Figure 10.2   Comparative space requirements for machine and hand digging. The more powerful the tool, the greater the required clearance. On wooded sites, these spaces have to be cleared. (*Illust.:* Craig Farnsworth.)

ties and compartmentalization of conventional design training. Even with the proliferation of manufacturer information (and accurate, insertable CAD models) on the Web, there does not appear to be a single concise reference on this topic—and there should be.

Besides allowing space for maintenance, other aspects of design can make a difference in sustainability. Grouping plants together by their water requirements not only approximates natural plant associations and saves water, but also prevents over- and underwatering, which are major stresses leading to disease. Designing clear transitions between the neatest and the most naturalistic areas encourages users to accept the design, and discourages unwanted mowing and pruning of the naturalistic areas. Proper plant selection, focusing on native plants, can also decrease susceptibility to pests and diseases, resulting in decreased maintenance while increasing value to wildlife. The toxic chemical treatments used as a last resort when plants become seriously ill can also be avoided if stress and damage are reduced. Planning for durable materials, rather than the false economy of low purchase price, is another aspect of design with dramatic implications for maintenance.

In many landscapes, such as corporate headquarters, it is appropriate *to interpret maintenance processes* to staff and public. Try botanic-garden-type signage explaining why and how maintenance creates the visible

Figure 10.3   Neither wind nor rain . . . but this sycamore stopped the US mail. Growth and change are inevitable landscape forces that design and maintenance must work with, not against. (*Photo:* Kim Sorvig.)

landscape, and the relationships between that landscape and natural history. These and other interpretive devices can raise appreciation for the maintenance staff's work and enhance the company's commitment to sustainability.

Expect Change

Many people think of maintenance as "upkeep," keeping things the same. It is more accurate, especially in landscapes, to think of maintenance as *responding to change*. Plant growth and weathering are powerful forces in all landscapes and cannot be stopped (despite products advertised as "conquering" or "taming" these forces).

People also create change in landscapes, and it is almost as useless to resist these changes as to try to stop the tide from rising. Even well-designed and well-built landscapes change in response to user desires, which change over time or with new ownership.

If a design doesn't accommodate user desires, construction and planting may be trampled as users impose their wishes. To designers, builders, or maintenance workers, this often seems unreasonable, selfish, and uncaring—and in fact it often is. But unless the entire user population can be educated (preferably in advance) to respect the original design, there is nothing to do but change it.

Figure 10.4 "Desire lines" occur at the point pedestrians see their destination. These lines can be counteracted by visual screening (barriers seldom work)—or they can be opportunities to link design to real use patterns. (*Photo:* Kim Sorvig.)

Use Appropriate Machinery and Fuels

Guidelines for appropriate construction machinery (see pp. 75 and 320) also apply to maintenance equipment. The tendency to use the biggest machine available is even less suitable in maintenance. Heavy construction equipment causes soil compaction and vegetation loss, but on construction sites major changes are expected, and much damage can be remedied as the job is completed. Maintenance, however, takes place in a landscape that people want to keep as it is. The difference is like scratching a woodworking project at the rough-cut stage, or scratching it after sanding and oiling. Minor damage to a *finished* landscape may be worse than major changes made during construction. For this reason, using the lightest possible machinery may be even more important to main-

tenance work than it is in construction. Maintenance tools in general are smaller and lighter than their construction equivalents; for sustainability, use the smallest and lightest tool that can do the job. Pressure to speed up the work by using larger machinery should be evaluated very carefully, using life-cycle costing to reveal whether time savings are worth the trade-offs. Principle 7 offers information on the energy costs of various machines and on life-cycle costing.

Many small machines are powered by two-stroke engines. In general, these produce more pollution per horsepower or per unit of fuel than larger engines. This is because they are less efficient, and their combustion of fuel less complete. Although each individual machine may contribute only a small amount of pollution, small engines are very numerous. For example, home lawnmowers alone number an estimated

40 million in the United States, consuming "several hundred million gallons" of gas-oil mix per year.[8] Add the many other gas-powered consumer lawn and garden machines, plus professional equipment, and it becomes clear that fuel savings can have an important impact on resource use and pollution. As noted on p. 371, small landscape-maintenance machinery includes many egregious noise polluters.

Very recently, significant increases have occurred in two-stroke engine efficiency and cleanness (p. 323). Conscientious (and dollar-conscious) power-tool users will switch to the newer engines sooner rather than later, both because of the 70 percent decrease in pollution and to take financial advantage of the 30 percent increase in fuel efficiency. The landscape industry could benefit from *sponsoring* further research into cleaner fuel options for small equipment. For example, natural gas conversion is widespread for warehouse machines (used indoors, where exhaust is lethal) and is becoming more common for transportation. Bio-based fuels (below) are often cleaner at the point of use than petro-based equivalents. The feasibility of converting small engines may be limited by the size of fuel tank required, but could still be investigated. Creative thinking about tools used in other industries but not widely in landscape work (for example, compressed air) might yield insights as well. The design of the tool itself can be a sustainability issue. On one mower that I had the misfortune of using, the engine required twenty ounces of oil but had capacity for fifty-six. The oil level could not be seen except on the dipstick because the filler tube was long and bent. There was no practical way to avoid overfilling, which led to spillage, waste of oil and fuel, fouling of the engine, and finally scrapping of the machine. Bad design is clearly a sustainability issue, especially with fuel-consuming machines.[9]

Walk-behind powered equipment can be particularly appropriate for maintenance use. One example is the Muck-Truck, a quarter-ton, six-cubic-yard walk-behind dumper. At twenty-eight inches wide, it can pass through any standard door to access rear or courtyard landscapes. Accessories include a sidewalk-width snowplow; dolly-like flatbed; trailer hitch; low-ground-pressure tires, and a loading ramp to allow unloading into a dumpster.

Landscape maintenance tools are increasingly available in electric models, both plug-in and cordless. Corded equipment offers the "unlimited" supply of utility power, but tangled cords and the danger of 115V shock are drawbacks. Cordless equipment solves these problems. (See p. 325.) Operating time and recharge speed are improving; battery power has increased from the once-standard 18V to 40V, 56V, and even 60V equipment. Solar job-site generators are portable enough to take anywhere to recharge equipment (p. 309). Solar equipment specifically for fleet vehicles is becoming available.

An innovative solar trash compactor by Seahorse Power increases bin capacity from 40 to 300 pounds (750 percent) by compression; collection trips and fuel use should be reduced 85 percent. In 2017, with the "Internet of things" invading the world, even items like trash bins can call your cell phone with alerts about damage or to schedule emptying. (My people will call your people and we'll talk trash.)

Many landscape maintenance tasks can actually be done *better* with hand tools. High-quality results, low environmental impact, and the pleasure of quiet, unmotorized work make hand labor an attractive option. Despite social pressures to mechanize every possible task, landscape maintenance remains one of the most appropriate places for craftspeople working with hand tools.

A range of "mesh shovels" is available from http://seymourmidwest.com/en/toolite-pbn-sh. Flat shovels, spades, and a snow shovel are perforated with roughly half-inch holes. They are designed to make digging in wet conditions easier, and can also be used for sifting certain construction or agricultural materials.

Landscape tools, whether power or hand, can be major vectors for invasive species if not kept clean, from gypsy-moth egg masses on tools left outdoors, to weed seeds on tires. Spreading pest problems on construction equipment is a complicated problem, but keeping tools clean between sites is a simple part of the solution.[10]

Vehicle choice for getting to and from the site also has an impact. For conventional cars and trucks, switching to bio-based fuels and lubricants (see below) may cut emissions and costs. At least one landscape maintenance company (Terra Nova, of Santa

Cruz CA: video and images at www.terranovaland-scaping.com) sends its employees out on bicycles with equipment trailers. This takes advantage of the fact that maintenance work tends to concentrate in neighborhoods, where distances can be short. Owner Ken Foster credits cost savings from bike transport as a factor in profitability over nearly thirty years in business.

Vehicles not dependent on fossil fuels are rapidly becoming commercial. Tesla has 500,000 preorders for electric cars and expects to fulfill 80,000 of those in 2017;[11] and on April 13, 2017, Elon Musk announced an electric pickup by the end of 2019, and an electric *semi* truck to launch in October 2017.[12] Especially for those investing in new fleets, electric trucks charged by sun or wind are poised to change the game both environmentally and economically. There will likely be disinformation against these vehicles from the fossil lobby, but the momentum of this change is growing, and likely to have real impact on landscape businesses as well as society in general, soon.

Evaluate Bio-based Maintenance Products with Care

Petroleum is ultimately a plant-based material and can in many cases be replaced with products based on renewable plant crops. The idea is not new: Rudolf Diesel, introducing his new engine at the Paris Exhibition in 1909, ran it on vegetable oil.[13] The concept of a "bio-economy" that would substitute plant-based fuels and plastics for fossil-based ones, reducing pollution while creating agricultural jobs, has been promoted, subsidized, and mandated widely and, at first glance, seems promising. However, since the previous edition, serious concerns have been raised about this approach. As with so many policies, the impact on *land* seems to have been overlooked in touting bio-based products. This does not mean they are flatly to be rejected, but a better understanding that includes a landscape perspective is critical.

The concerns center on the need for more cropland to produce raw materials for biofuels.[14] Projected global demand for bio-based products would require 180 million hectares (445 million acres, or 695,000 square miles). Already, this land demand has caused an increase in forest clearance, especially in the trop-

ics. In addition, existing farmland is being converted from food production to biofuel crops, and from local smallholdings to consolidated corporate farming. Increasingly, the rush by the European Union and the United States to mandate biofuels looks like a misguided attempt to preserve current rates of fuel consumption, slightly lowering emissions, while enriching agribusiness. Taking land conversion into account and using life-cycle costing, even the emissions benefits of bio-based products are less than stellar. Some studies report decreased performance using biofuels, though this may be due to using them in engines primarily designed for petroleum fuels. As such, it is hard to give more than a cautious recommendation, with case-by-case evaluation, to these products.

An exceptionally wide range of commercial bio-based products is available, and a great number of these are relevant to landscape maintenance:

- fuels, including biodiesel, and fuel additives
- engine oils (automotive and two-stroke), as well as hydraulic, brake, power-steering, and transmission oils
- cleaners and solvents, including concrete-surface cleaners, oil- and pesticide-spill cleaners, paint and varnish removers, graffiti removers, and vehicle-washing soaps
- form release agents for concrete and asphalt
- paints, stains, and inks
- dust control sprays
- adhesives and sealers.

Balanced against the concerns noted above, most bio-based products are less toxic at the point of use than conventional petro-based equivalents. If grown without heavy pesticide use, their production is cleaner and less risky than, for example, fracking for oil and gas. Many, particularly bio-based paints and solvents (cleaners), are lower in polluting and toxic volatile components (VOCs). Most are also biodegradable. Since they are crop based, there can be potential for production at or near the point of use, potentially decreasing both transportation fuel costs and environmental-justice impacts.

Bio-based fuels and oils avoid many of the emissions problems associated with petroleum products. Federal studies of biodiesel, for example, showed that it produced 90 percent fewer toxic emissions than conventional fuel, and 78 percent less CO_2. Similarly, when bio-based oils are burned in two-stroke engines, there are fewer emissions. These facts cannot be ignored, but must be balanced with land-conversion problems, especially the release of CO_2 when forests are cleared.

Cost and availability of bio-based products vary. In many cases, they are competitive with or less costly than petro-based equivalents; others are more expensive to purchase, but achieve significant total-cost or life-cycle savings. As an example, the Federal Proving Ground at Aberdeen MD changed its paint procurement policies to favor bio-based and other alternatives.[15] The Aberdeen Proving Ground is essentially a small town of 15,000–18,000, with an estimated 40 million square feet of surfaces to be painted. The alternative paints proved to be less expensive than conventional, with direct savings of over $6,300 per year. Because the new paints are not hazardous materials, disposal was $25,000 cheaper, and tracking of inventory was not required, saving another $17,000. For many users, the decreased costs of environmental compliance are the most compelling reasons for using bio-based products.

Availability of such products is likely to increase, especially because many federal agencies are including them in environmentally preferable purchasing (EPP) specifications. The European Union changed policy in 2015 from *mandating* biofuels products to *limiting* them to 7 percent of total fuel use. US EPP programs still guide an increasing number of governmental purchases in both maintenance and construction. Landscape professionals who contract with governmental agencies may get incentives or be required to use such products. In many cases, EPP standards can help in evaluating maintenance products, even on nongovernmental projects. But be aware that existing evaluations seem to ignore both the land issues and eROI—energy return on investment. Buying local, or at least domestic, products is a partial answer.

Apply Integrated Pest Management

The dangers of pesticides were among the first environmental issues to be documented, notably by Rachel Carson in *Silent Spring*. In 1995, despite forty years of concern and awareness among consumers, government, and industry, Americans still spread 68 million pounds of pesticides on landscapes and gardens yearly;[16] in 2005 "organic maintenance" was being reported as a "hot landscaping trend."[17] In fact, ten times as much pesticide per acre is typically applied to landscapes as to farm fields.[18] The toxicity and persistence of pesticides today has been reined in since the 1950s; many products are very specifically targeted to pest species. Nonetheless, pesticide use remains an automatic, unthinking response to landscape problems for many users, rather than a last resort. It is sobering to recall that, in the San Francisco Bay Area at least, gardening has been shown to be the *largest* single source of pollutants.[19] Along with habitat loss, grounds maintenance operations and chemicals are suspected in the 2013 decline of butterfly species in Florida, according to the US Fish and Wildlife Service.[20]

Besides their toxic effects, a large percentage of pesticides are produced from nonrenewable resources, and many have significant embodied energy. Energy use in *applying* pesticides is also a sustainability issue.

There is little need to duplicate in this book the many detailed sources of information on how to reduce volume and toxicity of pesticide use. Most pesticides are (or ought to be) specific to region, species (both the plant to be protected and the species to be killed), and weather conditions at the time of application. Encyclopedic information of that type would be foolish to include in this book. What is important to point out is that these issues are not just homeowner problems, as many books imply. Maintenance professionals are, in many cases, guilty of overusing pesticides and encouraging clients to do likewise. The landscape most likely to be pesticide free is one in which designer, contractor, and owner have worked together to plan for landscape health. Healthy landscapes can fight off a high proportion of pests that would wreak havoc in a landscape under stress. In fact, arborists describe disease not just as host plus pathogen, but including the effects of environmental stress, often worsened by poor planting and maintenance.

At the design stage, it can be valuable to "zone" the landscape according to the likelihood of exposure to pesticides, and the hazards posed. For example, on a school playground, any pesticide applied to playing areas is very likely to come in contact with children, who are especially susceptible. In such an area, only low-hazard products should ever be used. Islands in the school's parking lot, which are tough to maintain and where children can be kept from playing, might be acceptable zones for stronger pesticides under some circumstances.[21] Skimpy planters or sidewalk "graves" and other unfriendly hardscape all lead to unhealthy plants that must be coddled along by using pesticides (see p. 159), as does inadequate irrigation. Similarly, mishandling plant stock, overamending soil, and burying waste in planting pits are construction misdeeds that complicate maintenance.

The maintenance contractor, or the owner who gardens, is the third link in this chain. Ideally, this person needs to be part of early design reviews to spot maintenance issues that require redesign. The American tendency to build (and landscape) on speculation, before a real owner is in the picture, complicates this and many other forms of planning for sustainability. Especially where owner involvement is not possible, the designer should prepare a maintenance calendar as part of contract documents (see p. 288 and Figure 10.7). Maintenance plans, in fact, should be part of every professionally created landscape. For lawns, mowing height, timing, and even reel-versus-power mowers must fit the grass species and coordinate with water availability and fertilizer use, or the lawn will need higher maintenance.

Use Integrated Pest Management (IPM)

Even well-maintained landscapes sometimes suffer from pests and diseases. IPM relies on biological controls (such as predator insects or scent traps) and nontoxic chemicals like diatomaceous earth,[22] plus carefully targeted pesticides as a last resort. Chemicals are usually applied with ultra-low-volume sprayers or other methods that minimize waste and drift.

Some pesticides are marketed as "reduced toxicity." In general, this means less toxicity *to humans*, but some of these products are still broad-spectrum poisons, highly toxic to nontarget species. Wherever possible, use pesticides *targeted to the problem species only*, and always evaluate toxicity to other species, not just to hu-

mans and pets. One highly targeted and nontoxic tool is the steam weed-killer; several brands are available, as well as instructions to make your own. Though labor-intensive and requiring good plant identification skills, this could aid maintenance for clients with chemical sensitivities, for example.

A number of tree species are threatened (or have gone extinct) because of lethal "cooperation" between boring insects and sap-infecting fungi, including Dutch Elm Disease, Chestnut Blight, Oak Wilt, and Piñon Beetle. These, and Emerald Ash Borer (which damages trees without a related fungus), are sometimes treated by "micro-injection" of pesticides. A history of failed *macro*-injection, as well as overly flashy advertising for micro-injection, have convinced some owners (and maintenance personnel) that all injection is bogus. However, micro-injection, done by inserting syringe-like cartridges through one-eighth-inch holes at the base of the tree, is a legitimate, if often last-ditch, technique. Because no spraying is involved, environmental risks are reduced; micro-injection is considered appropriate in Integrated Pest Management.[23]

If pesticides are used, there are end-of-life issues with the containers. In some areas, recycling services for agricultural pesticide containers exist, primarily for farmers. (See www.interstateagplastics.com for an example.) Landscape users should look for such programs.

Accurate timing is important in IPM. A nontoxic soap spray may kill larval insects, while the same species at maturity shrugs off the same or stronger chemicals. Rather than using high-strength or high-tech solutions to bring ailing plants back from near death, IPM treats problems when they are small. This requires more field knowledge and observation by maintenance workers and better ability to schedule treatments precisely. These are skills that sustainability-minded maintenance contractors must be willing to learn.

Some of these skills can be computer-aided. Even in 1998, Bob Boufford, author of *The Gardener's Computer Companion*, recognized online weather data for decision making; today apps are ubiquitous, and some interface with irrigation and maintenance software. Certain combinations of temperature, humidity, day length, and precipitation trigger predictable responses from plants, insects, or diseases: germination, blooming, insect attacks, or spread of fungi. Once the convergence of conditions is identified, optimum times for specific maintenance tasks can be scheduled automatically. On-site sensors for actual conditions, plus predictive evapotranspiration and weather data, can especially aid the professional maintenance of multiple properties. Many irrigation systems come with similar capabilities and might be tapped to send messages to the person in charge of pest control. One interesting product is the solar-powered, wireless Edyn Garden Sensor (www.edyn.com): it tracks not only soil moisture but also humidity, soil nutrients, and light levels. These are sent to a smartphone app, which can be a stand-alone decision-making tool or can control an in-line hose valve, creating simple automatic irrigation possibilities. The app will even recommend plant species for conditions the sensor detects; these appear to be focused on vegetable gardening, but do include some landscape plants. Although Edyn is a homeowner product, similar multisensors seem likely for professional maintenance too.

Use Fertilizers Sustainably

Highly refined artificial fertilizers are sometimes likened to addictive drugs, as opposed to foods. There are several concerns that apply during initial site work and during maintenance: that fertilizers are overused, encouraging weak and weedy species to replace hardy natives (p. 71); that artificial fertilizers involve hazardous chemicals and nonrenewable resources in production (Principle 6); and that artificial fertilizers have considerable energy costs (Principle 7). In addition, high fertilizer use (artificial or organic) can promote extra growth of immature vegetative material. This not only increases leaf litter or grass-clipping volume, but can also make fast-growing plants more susceptible to stress from drought and seasonal fluctuations.[24] Immature growth is also less likely to produce flowers.

Except for overfertilization, these problems can be avoided by using organic fertilizers, manures, and composts. Many organic products are available commercially (p. 110). Their use helps solve problems that occur when these organic materials are considered as "waste." Using compost decreases the need for additional fertilizer, both because the compost contains nutrients and because it helps the soil structure retain nutrients and make them available to plants.

Transportation to the site is a potential energy concern with any fertilizer, although sources of organic fertilizer are often more or less local. Artificial fertilizers are often transported huge distances. For example, superphosphate fertilizer used in the American Midwest most likely originates in mines at least as far away as Wyoming or Tennessee, and possibly as distant as Morocco or the Pacific Islands.[25]

As with pest management, fertilization requirements are site and species specific. Soil and/or foliar analysis (showing what nutrients have actually been taken up by a specific plant) are essential tools, as is knowledge of local conditions.

Don't Waste On-site Resources

Organic fertilizers with *no* transportation cost are frequently available on-site, and often wasted. Yard waste is raw material for compost. Decomposition of dead vegetation (composting) is how plant communities recycle nutrients. In fact, natural communities survive almost entirely by using and reusing on-site nutrients, plus water and sunshine. Out of horticultural habit these materials are *removed*, breaking this cycle and depriving the site of nutrients. This loss of available nutrients is one main reason why imported fertilizers are ever required. The energy costs alone for removing and replacing on-site nutrients make this practice unsustainable. In addition, it takes up landfill space unnecessarily. Simply as an attitude, it devalues resources into "waste."

Compost is one of the most valuable assets for maintaining healthy landscapes. Its ability to improve soil structure, water-holding capacity, and nutrient content has made it worth mentioning in almost every chapter of this book. Any compostable material can also be used to produce biogas for energy generation. The value of compost for landscape maintenance is too high, however, to recommend using it routinely to produce power. The jury remains out on compost tea; many professionals swear by it for maintaining soil health, while others rate it ineffective and expensive.

Except as a foliar spray (for which there are alternatives), solid compost works well and is simpler to produce or buy, and to apply.

Lawn clippings can be left on the lawn to compost by using a "mulching mower" that shreds grass finely and spreads it while mowing. This is also known as "grasscycling." For clients who find this objectionable, or if using a push mower to save fuel, clippings can be gathered and composted in a bin or pile for reapplication. Leaves can also be composted, with or without preshredding. Amounts can be significant: lawns in California have been found to produce 300–400 pounds of clippings per thousand square feet, or eight tons per acre, annually.[26] Clippings with many weed seeds should be pile composted; clippings from pesticide-heavy lawns should be avoided (preferably by avoiding pesticides). In arid climates, use a rotating drum composter to retain as much moisture as possible, or try worm composting.

Pruned branches are another overlooked resource. They decompose very slowly if left whole, but can be chipped to make mulch or compost. Some diseased wood, especially from fungal infections, should not be composted and spread near living trees, because fungal spores may persist. The regional Extension Service or university horticulture department can usually offer local advice on which diseases survive composting, and which plants those diseases affect. They can also advise whether termites may be an issue in recycling logs and branches. Prunings are a prime source of biochar (see "Materials and Energy for Soil Amendment," p. 110); the charring process should eliminate pests and diseases.

Chippers are available in a wide range of sizes. They consume energy, but certainly less than hauling away wood and importing nutrients to replace it. Home shredders cannot handle large branches and logs; maintenance pros and arborists have larger equipment. Many communities also collect yard waste, chip it, and offer it as mulch; this reintroduces transportation energy into the equation. Logs can simply be stacked to provide habitat for many types of wildlife, including butterflies and local bee species. After rotting a few years, logs can be broken up by hand for composting and replaced with a new habitat stack.

Composting can be done in piles, bins, or rotating containers; for large institutions, auger-aerated, semi-automated units are available. All types require space that landscape designers should include in site plans. Keeping compost accessible to the kitchen is not always easy to reconcile with people's desire to hide this utilitarian function. John Lyle's attitude on the subject—that seeing such processes is part of environmental education—is worth reminding clients about. Composting in piles is the messiest method, and has contributed to the negative image to some extent; bins and drums are much tidier, and their surfaces can be decorated if desired.

Septic tanks and municipal sewage systems that do not produce composted biosolids (p. 115) also waste valuable organic resources. An alternative is the composting toilet, which produces sterile compost on-site. This compost is less likely than municipal biosolids to contain heavy metals and pollutants. Although a composting toilet is not strictly part of the landscape, it produces an on-site resource valuable enough to be considered for sustainable maintenance planning.

It is still uncommon for Americans to think of sewage as a resource, preferring to put it out of sight and mind—with high environmental and financial costs. Conventional sewage systems require infrastructure, maintenance, energy, and up to 30 percent of a community's residential water supply.[27] Septic tanks return flush water to the site through the leach field, but solids accumulated in the tank are simply pumped and trucked to sewage treatment plants. In either case, the compostable resource is wasted, and a large energy and resource cost is paid for the privilege of wasting it.

Composting toilets were used in traditional communities in Japan and Europe long before they were produced commercially. Half a dozen manufacturers offer various models in the United States today. Modern composting toilets are normally odorless and clean when properly maintained; small solar fans and pumps may be used to keep the composting process active and to vent any smells. Compost is easily removed every few months for use. A few units separate urine from solids, since each has different value as fertilizer, and combining the two creates undesirable anaerobic conditions.

Composting has been linked in modern people's minds to rural outhouses and brush piles. As energy costs and plant health have become better understood, on-site composting has come to figure prominently in sustainability strategies. In areas with poor or very dry soils, residents import food in quantity and produce the very materials that could improve soil productivity and offset carbon emissions from soil disturbance—but usually pay to dispose of their potential compost, all the while paying to import commercial "soil amendments." Landscape professionals interested in sustainability need to work with on-site composting systems, and help clients get over any ick-factor.

No matter how good the recycling and composting effort, actual waste is a real issue. Every firm or individual doing landscape work must take responsibility for appropriate site cleanup. Avoid contaminating water bodies or large volumes of soil with concrete, paint, or other leftover products.

Consider Alternatives to Mowing

One emerging practice, on scattered landscapes in the United States, Canada, Australia, New Zealand, and Europe, is the use of grazing animals to keep vegetation trimmed. Grazing controls grasses and nonwoody plants and has been used around high-end residential communities such as Sea Ranch in California. This is actually a very old landscape practice; Olmsted and other nineteenth-century park designers used sheep to "mow" Central Park and the White House grounds. The practice is reemerging with awareness of the contribution of air-polluting mowers to global warming.

Browsing is a similar concept, using goats that prefer young *woody* plants. Because they will not eat most herbaceous plants, browsers can keep meadows from being overtaken by successional shrubs and trees. They can also be important for fire management (see p. 127), removing and "composting" small trees and shrubs and leaving larger ones, producing an open forest less susceptible to intense fires. Both grazing and browsing should be applied more broadly.[28]

Adapt to Using Native Plants

Using native plants has maintenance implications, too. Many people believe native plants can produce that modern fantasy, the No-Maintenance Garden. Sometimes they have been told as much by overzealous advocates. Often, it is merely wishful thinking from people tired of maintenance-*intensive* landscapes, the same impulse that leads to artificial turf.

Overall, regionally adapted and native plants do require *less* maintenance than exotics. They need as much care, however, as any other planting while getting established, usually the first one to two years. Watering is almost always required at first, as well as physical protection from native browsing animals, who are of course well adapted to eat them. Once established,

Figure 10.5 Sheep and goats are a nonpolluting alternative to lawnmowers at Sea Ranch on the California coast. (*Project:* Lawrence Halprin. *Photo:* Russ Beatty.)

natives need a *different kind* of maintenance, requiring adjustments from the people who care for them.

Because many natives will be completely weaned from irrigation after establishment, it is wasteful to install *permanent* sprinklers in native landscapes. This means that watering during the initial period is done with temporary systems or by hand. To those used to fully automated irrigation, hand watering a few natives for a couple of years may well seem like more maintenance than is required for a conventional garden. Hand watering may also be required in periods of extreme drought. A few sensors and timers (such as Edyn, above) are designed to work with garden hoses; they offer possibilities for partially automating temporary watering.

Pruning, another major maintenance job, is also different for native plants. Far fewer natives are as forgiving as their horticultural cousins of shearing or pollarding (also called lopping; see Figure 10.6). In fact, being tolerant of abuse is one criterion for a commercially successful horticultural plant: consider the species that survive being sold through large home-store chains. Even when a native species is tolerant of hard clipping, the style of most native-plant landscapes makes geometric topiary trimming look out of place. Natives are usually pruned naturalistically, which requires the eye and patience of a Japanese garden master. Properly done, such pruning is almost unnoticeable. This can disappoint people used to the showy results of European-style pruning. They may feel that they have spent hours (or paid someone to spend hours) of cautious snipping with little to show for it.

Landscape architect Jon Coe often specifies that his plantings should "prune themselves": only dead wood is to be removed, and only if really necessary. "How did magnolias," this son of a horticulturist muses, "survive 200 million years without us to prune out all that 'disease-attracting' dead wood? Do our planted trees live longer?" Especially with native plants, Coe's words are worth pondering.

These are problems of client education. The resource-conservation and habitat value of native plantings is clear, and although their beauty may be subtle, open minds learn to appreciate it. For the maintenance contractor, knowing how to take care of natives can be a profitable and fulfilling specialty. People who have seen their native landscapes butchered by careless conventional techniques are very loyal to the professional who can do the job right.

Manage Large Public Landscapes Holistically, Too

Environmentally minded gardeners have practiced organic maintenance for years. But can a large commercial property in the heart of a major city pull the plug on manufactured chemicals for fertilizer and pest control? Yes—if property managers support green maintenance and a skilled team makes it happen.

Battery Park City (BPC) in Manhattan—thirty-six acres used intensively every day—is maintained entirely without pesticides or synthetic fertilizers. Or-

Figure 10.6 Lopping is an example of maintenance that damages vegetation and disfigures designed landscapes. Originally a rural woodlot technique for growing poles ("pollarding"), it is unfortunately considered stylish in a few places. (*Photo:* Kim Sorvig.)

ganic maintenance on this scale in such a dense urban location required new tools and approaches, according to landscape architect James Urban.[29] Searching the Internet for "organic landscape (or lawn) maintenance" reveals a rapidly increasing number of public spaces where the concept has been implemented.

Maintaining a healthy "soil food web" in an urban landscape is not as simple as doing a few tests and adding something to the soil. Organic maintenance must be started with design and construction. Healthy soil requires good drainage as well as suitable organic levels; soil mixes, amendments, and drainage systems must be correctly designed. BPC, like many urban facilities, used manufactured soil, giving the designers control of the entire soil profile from subgrade to mulch level. At BPC, soil that is almost entirely sand is favored for even drainage and stability. Sand accepts organic material well, as part of the initial mix or added during maintenance.

A principal organic tool in keeping soil biology balanced is compost to feed the soil food web. In nature, organic matter is self-replacing; in the urban environment, much of this organic matter is removed. Purchasing specialty compost only when necessary, BPC makes most of its compost in a 2,000-square-foot facility, processing all greenwaste from the site (including park restaurants) plus manure from nearby police-horse stables.[30] The compost is tested for biological activity. Finished compost is spread one to two inches deep on plant beds once a year.

To further refine the balance of soil organisms, BPC maintains a bank of compost tea brewers (p. 113). This material gives excellent results in balancing soil microbiology, but is no silver bullet of organic maintenance. Compost tea "is the cream on top of an organic program," says BPC's director of horticulture, but does not work as well without good soils and an on-site composting program.[31] Especially for large-scale urban organic maintenance, coordinated care on a site designed for such practices is essential.

Evaluate Life-cycle Costs of Maintenance Options

The same cost-cutting pressures that made the 1990s the Downsizing Decade have spread deferred main-

tenance throughout the land. Those who think that maintenance is expensive, however, should consider the cost of neglect.

Landscapes built and then neglected waste resources and have little place in a sustainable future. To understand how wasteful lack of maintenance is, or to convey the idea to a client, use life-cycle costing (LCC, p. 335). This technique takes into account the costs of maintenance work, but also shows the savings that result. Reasonable maintenance is almost always cheaper in energy costs than replacement; frequently (though not always) it costs less money, too. LCC will also reveal when a landscape is so dilapidated that its maintenance is truly too expensive to justify. Maintenance work cannot be evaluated accurately by up-front costs alone. Using LCC, long-term costs and benefits are clearly seen and options easily compared. LCC is an essential tool for profitability and marketing, and takes on even more importance in pursuing resource efficiency and sustainability. It is also a path toward more respect for maintenance work; for many people, maintenance is an obligation for tidiness, imposed by the homeowners' association or public opinion. Seeing it as cost saving and environmentally important can be eye-opening.

Use Innovative Funding

Many large institutions are required to treat capital funding as completely separate from operations budget. This causes difficulty in coordinating maintenance with design, an especially important concern with sustainable projects. Although some of this policy is enforced by the Infernal Revenue Service, there are ways to ensure that maintenance and operational upgrades can be funded.

Tax Increment Districts (see p. 204) create an ongoing fund for improvements by reinvesting increased *revenue* that results from the improvements. At Harvard University, the Green Campus Loan Fund "inverts" this idea and keeps it in-house: the revolving fund pays for improvements such as smart irrigation controllers or switching to LEDs, and is repaid from *cost savings*. A similar approach could be used when sustainable innovations or native plantings require dedicated maintenance, but produce quantifiable savings.

Although not exclusively about funding, the concept of a performance-based green construction contract can improve results while reducing client costs. The EPA's Denver office, a leased build-to-suit structure, set LEED and Energy Star goals that had to be met and maintained, or lease payments would be reduced until the goals were achieved. The result was that the developer exceeded the performance requirements, and the tenants had less risk of costly performance failures.[32] Carefully written construction contracts must always clearly assign responsibility for meeting certification and other performance goals if there are monetary penalties for failing to do so. Landscape maintenance contracts based on specific performance could also carry reduced-payment penalties—or positive incentives.

Coordinate Design, Construction, and Maintenance

Perhaps the most important idea of all, going beyond specifics that vary from site to site, is coordination. This has been a theme throughout the book and bears repeating.

The most forward-thinking landscape designers prepare site-specific maintenance plans for their clients.[33] Increasingly, firms have experience in this aspect of landscape work; pioneers include Andropogon Associates (Philadelphia), Carol R. Johnson Associates (CRJA, Cambridge MA), Louise Schiller Associates (Princeton NJ), OLM Inc. (Atlanta), and Site Design and Management Systems (SDMS, Lansing MI).

These firms unanimously emphasize two key elements of such plans. One is making maintenance an issue in the very first design stages, not an afterthought. The other is building relationships with and educating the owner, maintenance staff, or contractors. Start talking maintenance with the owner while the plan is still on paper. With maintenance craftspeople, walking the site provides valuable "field education" that is usually two-way. Because job turnover is high in the maintenance industry, this education is an ongoing process. Frequent site inspections by the designer are essential and need to be negotiated up-front as a retainer or hourly payment.

The plan schedules landscape tasks: pruning some species in spring and others in fall, replacing pond filters every five years, repointing brickwork every twenty. But it goes beyond just scheduling. A good plan needs to:

- Establish standards for maintenance—how much, what kind, and with what results, including the expected "look."
- Quantify the amount of work required—square feet of lawn or mulch, numbers of lights or sprinklers, linear feet of paths or hedges or fence. These figures, readily available from quantity takeoffs prepared as construction documents, help in-house staff plan their work, or keep contractor bids equivalent.
- Prioritize tasks so that shortages (staff, budget, or resources like water) can be dealt with. If possible, estimate how long deferred maintenance can go without irreversible losses.
- Set procedures for bidding out maintenance or set staffing levels for in-house work.
- Reward performance, especially incentives for contracted maintenance. Set about 25 percent of the contractor's monthly payment as performance bonus dependent on meeting quality standards. This requires extremely clear performance specifications, but is very effective in rewarding conscientious work and avoiding carelessness.
- Provide for plan review every few years to adapt to changes in site use, climate, watering regulations, and so forth.

Some large clients, such as parks departments, may have their own standard plan, keyed to public events or financial deadlines as much as to seasonal changes. Maintenance plans may cover staff training, recommend specific products and machinery, or simply act as a reminder when to do specific tasks.

The designer may write the plan, or may hire a horticulturist or maintenance contractor to write it based on as-built drawings. The owner can do all or part of the maintenance, pass the plan to a contractor, or, in some cases, hire a branch of the designer's firm to do the work. For developments like subdivisions or business parks that are given homogenous landscapes, copies of the maintenance plan should be given (and

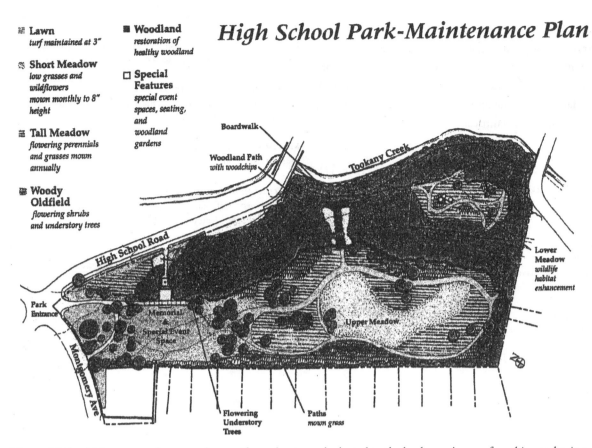

High School Park-Maintenance Plan

Lawn
turf maintained at 3"

Short Meadow
low grasses and wildflowers mown monthly to 8" height

Tall Meadow
flowering perennials and grasses mown annually

Woody Oldfield
flowering shrubs and understory trees

Woodland
restoration of healthy woodland

Special Features
special event spaces, seating, and woodland gardens

Boardwalk

Woodland Path *with woodchips*

Tookany Creek

Lower Meadow *wildlife habitat enhancement*

High School Road

Park Entrance

Montgomery Ave.

Memorial & Special Event Space

Upper Meadow

Flowering Understory Trees

Paths *mown grass*

Figure 10.7 Maintenance plans must be specific to the site and adapted to the landowner's way of working and using the place. This example graphically links tasks to specific areas of the landscape. (*Project:* Cheltenham Township PA with Friends of High School Park. *Graphic:* Andropogon Associates.)

explained) to each tenant or buyer, as well as to the developer. Ideally, the plan should be recorded by the county clerk as a legal document, not to make it binding but to ensure that it is passed on at each property sale. Such a system not only improves long-term landscape health but also increases the likelihood of realizing the designer's vision as the landscape matures.

Not every designer is competent to produce a maintenance plan. This can encourage teamwork. Having a maintenance contractor on retainer as a consultant to a design firm is unusual, but is an excellent way of producing maintainable designs. Despite conventional separation of trades, the ideal team for producing long-term sustainable landscapes includes an ecologist, a designer, a construction contractor, and a maintenance expert, at a minimum. Some design-build firms actually have such a team in-house; a consulting arrangement suits other firms better.

GPS and GIS systems (see p. 53) can improve maintenance by producing and storing detailed yet cost-effective real-world plans. GPS can easily locate construction or repairs as they occur—a must for irrigation, for example, which once buried becomes invisible. Drones make some aspects of data collection easier and more affordable, but may not be appropriate for recording some as-built details. GIS can convert GPS or other field measurements into clear diagrams and maps showing actual conditions, not just idealized intentions, and link to photos and annotated documentation. If data entry is done with foresight, GIS can also produce task-specific maps from a master file—accurate location maps, for example, of all shrubs of one species, all trees for January pruning, or streetlights due for relamping. In many cases, these can be displayed on a smartphone or tablet for field use.

Landscapes that do not age gracefully fall short of sustainability, no matter how environmentally sound their original design or construction. Landscapes, more than any other human construction, are about growth, change, and time. There is only one irreplaceable maintenance tool—an experienced person devoted to the place and the work. Maintenance, the task of adapting to time and change, cannot be neglected in the sustainable landscape.

Subtopics and Search Terms for Principle 10: Maintain to Sustain

Note: Subtopics are also useful search terms; add "innovation" or "controversy" to search terms as appropriate.

Maintenance
Search terms: maintenance || landscape maintenance || outdoor maintenance

Maintenance: energy use
Search terms: maintenance + energy (use OR efficiency)

Bio-based products
Search terms: "bio-based" with type of product, e.g., paint || non-food crops || ethanol || land conversion for fuel crops

Maintenance: organic and IPM
Search terms: maintenance + (organic OR IPM) || "integrated pest management" || pesticide-free

Maintenance: on-site waste
Search terms: composting || "on-site materials"

Maintenance: landscape
Search terms: (horticulture OR landscape OR garden) maintenance || plant care || arboriculture || tree surgery

Maintenance: computers and coordination
Search terms: landscape + maintenance + computers

Resource List:

Links to information sources related to this chapter are posted at http://islandpress.org/sustainable-landscape-construction

Principle 11:
Demonstrate Performance, Learn from Failure

I would rather have questions that can't be answered than answers that can't be questioned.
—*Richard Feynman, atomic physicist (1918–1988)*

It is easy to forget how young contemporary green building is. Many green *methods* are as old as vernacular construction, dating back millennia. But the current movement is often dated to the first Earth Day, in 1970, and to experimentation in response to the 1973 "oil crisis." Formation of the AIA's Committee on the Environment in 1989, and the launch of LEED in 1998, are other benchmarks. Depending on which of these dates is used, the movement is no more than forty-four years old, and in the United States, attempts to set *standards* began only twenty years ago. The pattern is typical: as a young discipline or industry grows, competing definitions of success, failure, and quality come to the fore, gradually resolving into agreed standards. Almost every type of product or service has its own certification and set of standards, sometimes more than one.

Along with standards and certification comes a shadow: failure, actual or perceived. Asking what failure means in a sustainable project is not a trivial question, and mirrors the complexity of standards of success. In many ways, green building represents a *shift* in standards, away from practices acceptable a few decades ago but now considered inadequate, even dangerous.

It is difficult to get landscape professionals to discuss failure because, like other design and contracting professionals, they are perpetually liable for their work in many states. Some governmental clients can sue over defects that appear years after signing off on the project, unlike private entities, who must sue within a statutory time limit.[1] Suits for personal injury allegedly caused by faulty construction can also consume time,

> **Discussed in This Chapter:**
>
> Certification programs.
> Clarifying monitoring, certification, and standards.
> Measure and mismeasure.
> Landscape forensics.
> Learning from failure.

money, and reputation. Understandably, designers and contractors are reluctant to have anything published that might be used as evidence in future lawsuits. But because learning from mistakes is essential to any profession, and even more when new standards are evolving, failure to discuss failures means failure to learn.

This is not the place for an extended history of green certification, but sustainability standards for *landscapes* differ from those for *buildings* (a theme that runs throughout this book), and are increasingly influential. This relatively short chapter, new in 2017, looks at how landscape certification works; at some of the difficulties inherent in certifying anything; and at the special challenges of a "seal of approval" for landscape projects. It offers an overview of how success and failure are defined for sustainable landscape planning, design, and construction, and what it means to monitor or document performance. Because of the general reluctance to discuss *specific* failures, this chapter uses neither firm or project names nor identifiable photos. One of the main current challenges for landscape professionals working toward sustainability is to find ways to share lessons learned, not only when they are positive but also where failure is involved. To paraphrase Winston Churchill, an industry that ignores its failures cannot truly succeed.

Anatomy of a Certification System

The Good Housekeeping Seal of Approval is an old and familiar example of product certification, and its history is instructive. The seal was first awarded in 1909, growing out of *Good Housekeeping* magazine's righteous campaign against adulteration of food products. The seal was also part of *GH's* advertising policy. Advertising was not accepted for products that failed testing or advertised deceptively, and the seal was a marketing device presented in ads and on packaging. The seal carried a warranty worth up to $2,000 if the product proved defective. Testing and warranty underwent many changes, some enforced by the government, which in the 1930s found the *GH* testing lab's methods not rigorous enough. The Hearst empire, which owned the magazine and for which the seal was a valuable asset, fought against governmental involvement in food and advertising standards, even though the goal of pure food was common to both. Socially, the idea of a Seal of Approval became a tongue-in-cheek reference to fifties-style conformism. Through all these changes, the Good Housekeeping Seal is still in use, and today there is a *Green* GH Seal as well.[2]

All these stages, including opposition to governmental standards, are typical in the evolution of product certification. Starting from a crusading attempt to take on a health and safety issue; setting what at first are often in-house and idiosyncratic standards; winning acceptance by turning standards into marketable incentives; playing defense (against competitors, affected industries, and governmental agencies—sometimes all at once); and evolving with time and experience: except for the simplest and most fact-based standards, this trajectory of development is characteristic.

Standards and certification are far from just marketing ploys. Interchangeable parts—often described as the key to the industrial revolution—are standards that permit predictable and reliable mass production. Similarly, the standardized sizes of shipping containers make maritime and land shipping far more feasible than when each shipment required different handling. Lack of standard fire hydrant connections made it impossible for firefighters from nearby cities to aid Baltimore in the Great Baltimore Fire of 1904.[3] Retrofitting the United States to metric standards would be immensely complex and expensive, but *not* adopting the metric system has hampered business and scientific exchanges. Proprietary standards (like those for computers or phones) initially let suppliers profit from the fact that users can't go elsewhere; ultimately, incompatibility becomes limiting enough to motivate standards. Standards that become inflexible can bottle up innovation until new products become "disruptive," which is not necessarily the most sustainable path to technological change. No one could make "disruptive technology" the fawning term of praise that it is today if they undertook any form of life-cycle costing, which would have to consider the waste and inefficiency caused by deliberately avoiding "backward compatibility."

Green Certification

Green certification is a huge trend today: with little effort, you can find a program to green-certify avocados or coffee; cut flowers; Galápagos tourism or Slovenian agricultural products; existing buildings or printers. Some companies, like Nike, have private programs; some programs allow a company to certify itself, in effect. Some programs are pass/fail, while others have rankings or ratings, like LEED and SITES.

Green *construction* certification can cover raw materials, including horticultural products; manufactured items; whole buildings; and, most recently, sites (with or without a building) and entire neighborhoods. *Environmental Building News* estimates that there are some 100 construction-specific programs in the United States alone, and over 600 worldwide.[4] *EBN* has, over the years, devoted countless articles to covering developments, controversies, and even lawsuits over LEED, Green Globes, Forest Stewardship Council, and other certification and ratings systems. An *EBN* special, costing subscribers $50 (and worth it), sorts out and compares different schemes.

Programs aimed at greener buildings and landscapes are numerous, with widely differing goals.

Figure 11.1   A simple Internet search for "green certification programs" retrieves thousands of results, including this display of major logos. (Trademarks remain property of their respective owners.)

Some, like EnergyStar, are governmental; others start from trade, industry, or research roots. A significant number are underhanded attempts to avoid meeting strict standards by substituting cheaper or easier rubber stamps. Many focus exclusively on energy performance (of appliances, buildings, etc.). Others incorporate "constructability," which emphasizes mechanical design and durability.[5] Only a few focus primarily on landscapes.

Standards and Certification

Standards are agreed-upon guidelines. By agreement, they may be either enforceable or purposely unenforceable.

The main requirement of a set of standards is that it sets *measurable* criteria. (The National Institute of Standards and Technology is responsible—not coincidentally—for establishing official weights and measures used in the United States, as well as product standards.) More accurately measurable criteria usually result in more meaningful standards. Industry-sponsored standards are often deliberately vague, while third-party or scientific standards have unequivocal criteria. However, for landscape standards, the inherent variability of materials and regional conditions often makes establishing measurable criteria difficult.

A robust certification system requires the convergence of many factors:

- The item(s) to be certified must be fairly *common*: a standard for a product so new that only five people own one is pointless.
- The item(s) must be *standardizable*. This is a problem with buildings and, even more so, with landscapes.

- The standard or certification must have *practical value* for the *developer* of the guidelines, the *producer* of certified items, and the *user or consumer*. These values frequently conflict.
- Standards and certification must be based on respected *authority*, for content and implementation. If stakes are high enough, there may be competing authorities and administrators, and occasionally, attempts to make unqualified individuals appear to be experts, usually for hire.
- Compliance must be *straightforward* enough that producers won't reject the extra effort involved.
- *Confirming* compliance must be feasible. This is much easier for products that can be sent to UL labs, for example, than for buildings or landscapes, especially since compliance may have to be monitored over time.
- There must be a possibility of *revoking* certification. Again, this is different for production-line items than for buildings or landscapes. Voluntary and self-validated certifications are not, in my opinion, "robust"; they often serve a good purpose, as the voluntary LEED program has done, but without teeth, they can become meaningless or even deceptive.

Certification versus Performance

It is important to distinguish between certification and performance monitoring, even though there is overlap. Either type may be voluntary or enforced (contractually, or by code).

Certification is simpler, and says "This project is *good enough* according to this authority"; it is often an award made before the product or project actually goes into use; and it often is a one-time process that grants permanent status. Meeting the criteria for certification may require verified documentation, self-reporting, or merely the subjective judgment of the certifier. Documentation may require actual testing of installed components; a checklist stating that certain components were installed; or the use of components with their own certifications. Certified status is often displayed, typically on a permanent plaque.

Monitored performance, although it can be one-time, is most valuable when it is ongoing, either continuous or regularly repeated. It records, tests, or calculates what the product or project *actually does*: saves water, removes toxins or adds nutrients, or increases value (as calculated from rent of a green property compared with others, for instance).

Monitored performance may be required for renewing certification. In some systems, performance results must be posted at intervals; in others, a digital "dashboard" or display communicates performance levels in real time—far more common for structural performance than for landscapes. Real-time displays may be for public education and to demonstrate general sustainability concepts; they are also used to influence user behavior, or to manage operation, flagging waste or leaks so that system users or managers respond to the problem, and optimizing systems for specific purposes.

Though carefully designed and administered certification schemes have great value, many of the problems associated with misleading green claims are associated more with certification than with monitoring. Some programs have turned out merely to be fronts for utility companies that wish to promote their brand of fuel or power as greener than others; some have had criteria that "allowed one strong category [of environmental performance] to make up for others" and have had to be revamped.[6] By contrast, monitored performance, especially in landscapes, can be difficult and expensive to accomplish, and it does not give a thumbs-up-or-down outcome even when excellent information is gathered.

Landscape Certification Programs

The main green building certification programs all include criteria that relate to landscapes. The two systems that affect US landscape professionals most are LEED and SITES. This section takes a deliberately brief look at both. It notes competitors, concerns about these programs, and legislation and lawsuits that have targeted LEED.

This book will not teach you to use either LEED or SITES. The basic user's manual for LEED v4 includes sixty-six pages just to *list* the available credits, and those who deal with getting projects certified take full-fledged courses to understand it. Think of this, rather, as a strategic guide to the impacts these programs have on *landscape* practice.

LEED, Its Critics, and Its Competitors

LEED (Leadership in Energy and Environmental Design) is a voluntary point-based certification system developed by the US Green Building Council (USGBC) and primarily focused on architectural and mechanical systems. Its first public release[7] occurred just five months before the first edition of this book; LEED v4 became fully effective in 2017. In addition to developing a half-dozen specialized rating systems, such as one for Existing Buildings Operation and Maintenance and one for Neighborhood Development, LEED also inspired and then swallowed the Sustainable Sites Initiative, now known simply as SITES. LEED has become a de facto US national standard for green architecture and development, and it is used in 140 countries, according to USGBC. SITES, as a stand-alone rating system, is administered by the same entity as LEED, and SITES criteria can provide points in LEED itself. Though building focused, LEED is important to landscape work in its own right, and as part of SITES history.

LEED criteria are either "prerequisites," which are nonnegotiable requirements, or "credits," for which a building or neighborhood can earn points (sometimes more than one point per credit), totaling 110 possible points in LEED v4.[8] These credits are grouped into seven categories: Location & Transportation; Sustainable Sites; Water Efficiency; Energy & Atmosphere; Materials & Resources; Indoor Environmental Quality; Innovation; and Regional Priority (credits specific to the geographic location of the project). Criteria for each credit are often based on external standards such as ASHRAE, ASTM, and others.[9]

With enough credits, buildings can be certified—

and marketed—as LEED Certified (40–49 points), Silver (50–59), Gold (60–79), or Platinum (80+). Designers can also become LEED Certified Professionals. Some 200,000 have done so—a tenfold increase since 2007.[10]

A substantial percentage of LEED credits are actually for landscape strategies that affect development. For New Construction, LEED v4 grants up to 30 points out of 110 for landscape-specific tactics like heat-island reduction and rainwater management. It also has landscape *prerequisites*: limiting pollution and waste from construction, reducing irrigation usage, and recycling. For Operations & Maintenance, 25 of 110 points relate to landscape, while for Neighborhood Development, 67 points and 9 prerequisites can be attained by landscape methods. This has a downside, however: some developers consider landscape credits to be fuzzy, low-hanging fruit, easy credits that avoid the need to earn harder ones.

Many governmental agencies and private clients have made LEED part of contracting or regulatory processes—something for which the original voluntary LEED was never intended. Competing for contracts now often requires LEED certification for design team members; cities, counties, and federal agencies require LEED-compliant buildings. Language from LEED has been inserted as boilerplate in local codes, almost always a risky approach. A few cities, such as Portland OR, have modified LEED to fit local conditions. LEED itself has been modified in recognition of the fact that it now serves as a model ordinance.

LEED is credited by many people with almost single-handedly catapulting green building into the mainstream. It has certainly attracted many builders, designers, and clients. Credits set concrete standards for claiming that a building is green and are, in theory at least, straightforward to achieve. The complexity and paperwork involved have been a constant bone of contention, along with the cost of registration. Lack of regional adaptability, an early and well-founded complaint, is at least partly addressed in v4 by including region-specific points.

In 2005 a competitor to LEED was introduced, called Green Globes (GG).[11] It uses a 1,000-point, seven-category system. A designer (even one with no training in sustainability) is supposed to be able to enter project specifics online; a sustainability assessment is produced by the computer. Such a report is free, and designers could complete the report for various design options to see how each impacted sustainability—if they had the time and patience. Initially only self-assessment was available, but paid third-party certification was later offered. Points may be eliminated as not applicable to a project; this avoids penalties for failing to achieve the impossible, but may reward opting out of hard points. Even GG's author admitted that its detailed point criteria were "kind of a black box," unavailable for public review.

The GG system was developed with primary support and funding from timber and home-building trade associations, through an organization confusingly named the Green Building Initiative. The timber industry prefers GG because it accepts any "certified wood" program, especially the industry-funded Sustainable Forestry Initiative (SFI), while LEED accepts only stringent Forest Stewardship Council (FSC) certification. GG is widely considered to be cheaper, but also less stringent, than LEED, and its marketing relies heavily on criticizing LEED. The Earth Island Institute, together with Sierra Club and Greenpeace, have a project called Greenwash Action (www.stopgreenwash.org/)—the website is under redevelopment but expected to be up by the time this book is in print); it flatly calls Green Globes and the Sustainable Forestry Initiative "greenwash standards" designed to water down certification while appearing to support it, and while lobbying against use of the genuine systems. The American National Standards Institute (ANSI) started a program to certify rating systems and to accredit the organizations that develop such systems, explicitly to deter greenwash. Such "meta-certification," backed by respected organizations like ANSI, ISO (the International Organization for Standardization), and the nongovernmental UL (formerly Underwriters Laboratories), has been effective in creating trustworthy customer knowledge for other industries.[12]

A variety of other green general-construction rating systems are in use in the United States, but LEED is clearly the leading contender. Competitors include BREEAM, originally British and nearly ten years older than LEED; the Living Building Challenge, considerably stricter than LEED in aiming toward "net-zero" projects; and an approval system inspired by William

McDonough's cradle-to-cradle concept. Google and UL have made some inroads on green product assessment as well.

LEED has also been deliberately attacked and undermined on several fronts. Various limits or outright bans on using LEED for public contracting or as a basis for local codes have been instituted, thanks to industry lobbying, in Maine, Alabama, Mississippi, Georgia, and Ohio, while pressure to ban LEED, to legitimize industry-preferred competitors, or both, has been brought to bear on Congress, the General Services Administration, and the military.[13] One research article from the University of Colorado claims that workers on green projects are less safe; the argument is that workers spend more *time* on green projects, thus risks are higher. The same would apply to custom-crafted buildings. Although the lead researcher appears to be experienced, the arguments seem stretched, and response has been skeptical.[14] In 2010, LEED was targeted by a class-action suit alleging fraud and antitrust violations, claiming that energy-efficiency testing by LEED was merely intended to monopolize the market. The suit was dismissed with prejudice in 2011.[15] At least two lawsuits have attacked state and local codes based on green rating systems, arguing that federal energy-efficiency standards preempted those codes. Oddly, federal courts gave opposite rulings in Albuquerque NM and the state of Washington.[16]

Market incentive systems like LEED are inherently temporary. As green building becomes more widespread, the marketing value of a Gold or Platinum seal decreases. Eventually what is now cutting-edge will become baseline, expected by every client. Like a great many valuable tools, LEED must ultimately succeed by making itself unnecessary.

SITES—the Sustainable Sites Initiative

Dissatisfaction with early LEED's marginal attention to site issues led the ASLA, the Lady Bird Johnson Wildflower Center at the University of Texas, and the United States Botanic Garden to develop the Sustainable Sites Initiative, later shortened simply to SITES. A pilot program attracted 175 landscape projects, 65 percent of which were on brownfields. Shortly after the pilot project closed, a yearlong lawsuit over trademark rights put SITES in limbo. Reminiscent of the

unfortunate patenting of CU-Soil, the University of Texas's attempt to trademark SITES was intended to avoid multiple ownership by licensing SITES to the other two partners at no cost; the US Botanic Garden accepted, while ASLA refused. Not the green building movement's finest hour, this impasse was resolved by SITES being acquired by the US Green Building Council, becoming one more program administered by its spinoff, GBCI (Green Business Certification Inc.). Standards for sustainable site development are also included in ASHRAE's Standard 189 (which sets minimum requirements for code compliance, not just for landscape issues but a complete and enforceable building code, which itself complies with international green standards); and in the Living Building/Community/Product suite of challenges from the Cascadia Green Building Council and its International Living Future Institute, based in Seattle WA and Portland OR. The Living Community Challenge is admirably rigorous, pushing communities to be entirely net-positive for water and energy and requiring appropriate land locations for all development. In fact, all the Challenge criteria are mandatory. To date, only six communities have implemented the Challenge, with another forty "considering."[17]

First released in 2009 and later updated to v2, SITES maintains LEED's point-based approach to environmental evaluation. Two hundred points are possible under the current version, all of them landscape specific; eighteen prerequisites are required. SITES's high-level categories are Site Context; Pre-design Assessment and Planning; Site Design—Water; Site Design—Soil and Vegetation; Site Design—Materials Selection; Site Design—Human Health and Well-being; Construction; Operations and Maintenance; Education and Performance Monitoring; and Innovation or Exemplary Performance.[18]

While SITES makes it possible for projects without any buildings to achieve sustainability ratings, and significantly expands the number of landscape-specific credits, it still suffers from two characteristics inherited from LEED: being voluntary and point based. In addition, there are questions about why landscapes need certification: most landscapes are considered, in the market, as adjuncts to a building; for public open spaces, marketing is more or less irrelevant. SITES may lend credibility to public-space funding and grant requests, but it seems unlikely to have as much impact on private landscape developments as LEED has had on buildings.

SITES also has problems indicative of general dilemmas in green certification. Initially, in an attempt to be evidence based, SITES criteria could be established only on the basis of peer-reviewed scientific journals, a limit later relaxed. This downplayed or excluded much *practitioner* experience, a major repository of site-performance knowledge. Rigorous landscape research under controlled conditions is simply uncommon, and studies by soil scientists, biologists, or even engineers don't have the focus, scope, or landscape perspective to underpin best practices or applied designs. Social and academic expectations trivialize site practice, and relying on "verifiable" studies therefore eliminates most of what is actually known about the interaction of built environments and unaltered ecosystems.[19]

As Carol Franklin, one of Andropogon's founders, observed, point-based ratings have many inherent problems when applied to complex open systems like landscapes. Points can be gained by implementing a single technique, alone, that flatly does not work except in combination with other factors. Ferguson's research on detention basins located without reference to existing geomorphology is a prime example. More generally, in landscapes, as distinct from buildings, connectivity is critical yet is exceptionally hard to rate meaningfully across the range of landscape types and regions.

Better Measures

It is often said that what can't be measured can't be managed. The dark side of that cliché is that using the *wrong* metric can contribute to project problems and even failure. The focus on energy efficiency may be such a mismeasurement, according to the Jevons Paradox (see p. 6): efficiency makes usage cheaper, thus encouraging people to consume more. The amount of recycled content in a product doesn't accurately indicate its embodied energy or carbon footprint if transportation energy isn't represented. The gross domestic product (GDP) is a mismeasure (and pushes world economies far toward unsustainability) because every financial transaction is counted as positive; as Robert F. Kennedy pointed out, the GDP considers new construction necessitated by *arson* to be a positive economic impact.[20] Many forms of greenwashing involve *deliberately* using the wrong measure—emphasizing that a product is CFC-free when all products are required to be, or claiming that electric hand-dryers are the greenest because they don't produce litter at the point of use.

Many metrics for landscape performance have been suggested; some overlap with building performance, while others do not.

- *Efficiency* is a common way of comparing options, but misleading (see Jevons Paradox, p. 6).
- *Conservation* (using less) requires a baseline, and "50 percent less than conventional" may still be far from sustainable.
- *Triple bottom line* is promising, though complex, and based on efficiency, conservation, or other basic measures.
- Resource *"footprints"* (carbon, energy, water, etc.) are useful, but hard to compare or combine.

The SITES rating system is primarily based on what is perhaps the most effective yardstick for sustainability goals: ecosystem services (ES). By focusing on what ecosystems provide to humanity, this approach has several advantages. Unlike the above metrics, which focus on human consumption, ES looks at the productiveness of the more-than-human world. Looking primarily at human activity introduces a blind spot and is negative, being about costs and things that humans should *avoid* doing. ES links human economics to the positive activity of the planet and all species, and makes the positive assumption that, in many cases, human actions can restore or improve the level of service a site can provide. The basic equation of ES, in the form of "if soil didn't filter water, we would be paying $X to do it," is what this book terms a "landscape perspective," and as such appropriate and adaptable as a metric for site performance.

Monitoring, Metering, and Data Logging

One-time certification may predict actual performance over time—or not. Testing the output of a machine fresh from the factory does not give actual data about its output in five years. This applies with special

Ecosystem Services
Based on the United Nations' Millennial Ecosystem Assessment (MEA).
Note: The MEA list leaves out geological resources (as nonliving), but these are also provided by the planet and part of an ecosystem; I have added them in parentheses.

Supporting Services
These are services without which the ecosystem would not exist, nor provide any services. These are the "infrastructure" of ecosystems, the basis of all services to humans.
- Primary productivity; plant production of nutrients through photosynthesis
- Soil formation
- Nutrient recycling

Provisioning Services
- Food, wild or cultivated, animal or botanical, including spices
- Raw materials: fiber crops, leather, lumber, organic matter, fodder; (stone, cement, metals)
- Genetic resources: ability to selectively breed plants and livestock
- Water and water transportation
- Medicines derived from organisms; research, test, and assay organisms
- Energy: all biomass fuels, including fossil; wind, solar, and hydroelectric power; wave and tide action; (uranium)
- Ornamental resources: including fashion, decoration, pets, worship, souvenirs like feathers, shells, ornamental plants

Regulating Services
- Climate regulation including carbon and carbon sequestration
- Decomposition and detoxification of wastes
- Air and water purification
- Regulation of pests and diseases (and of cyclical events such as wildfire)

Cultural Services
- Nature as symbol or motif in the arts
- Nature as metaphor for spiritual and historical concepts
- Recreation, active and passive, including tourism
- Science and education; nature as laboratory or museum
- Therapies based on interaction with nature and living things

force to living landscapes and to the dynamics of growth and weathering. To get a clear picture of performance throughout a life cycle, *ongoing* measurements are required.

Ongoing data gathering has developed rapidly in the past several decades. For most of the past century, the only metering devices in daily life were simple: water or electric meters, speedometers, thermometers.

These measured a single condition or quantity by direct contact with the object or process or flow; data could only be read at the device. Monitoring, for most people, meant repeatedly observing something—the growth of a tree or spread of erosion—by eye or with a camera, perhaps by air photography.

Modern "data loggers" have utterly transformed this situation, yet are not common in landscape use, despite many calls for "better documentation of performance." Data loggers rely on improvements in computer, battery, sensor, and communication technology within the past twenty years at most. Originally developed for research and industrial monitoring, data loggers are increasingly used to monitor building performance and environmental conditions.[21] They also offer a realistic way of understanding and documenting the performance of built and managed landscapes.

Data loggers have three main components: a body, with computation, display, clock, and memory capacities; sensors; and some way of connecting to a computer. The simplest are single-channel (sensing a single condition, often with the sensor built in) with a light-duty case and USB connectivity. These can cost as little as $25, while more complex multichannel units run to $1,000 or more. Upgrades include an outdoor or even underwater body; multiple channels; wireless sensors; and real-time streaming via Bluetooth or the cloud, sometimes with a monthly fee. All are intended to work unattended and have batteries expected to last at least a year, sometimes much longer.

Uses are limited only by the available sensors. Some loggers have interchangeable sensors or are reprogrammable. Sensors can capture any aspect of weather; water flow, pH, and clarity; soil conditions; light intensity; moisture, including moisture in wood or other materials; temperature; room occupancy; and many other types of data. Some companies can offer rapid customization of sensors to specific tasks. Data logging has tracked tagged animals, including fish, sharks, and whales, while measuring habitat conditions along their migration routes; collected before-and-after data on air quality or dampness in remodeled homes; helped design stormwater systems and then monitor them; and gathered evidence in construction litigation. Rates of soil erosion or changes in pH and nutrients; correlations between soil moisture and relative humidity; indicators of water quality; systemic pesticide uptake of trees and their transpiration rates; and deflection or structural soundness of hardscape are just a few of the types of landscape data that will likely be gathered in the near future.

Once the data are on a computer, software is required to graph or visualize it. Software is often included with the logger, but not always; the trend seems to be toward open-source code. The inclusion of a system clock greatly increases the value of the data, because different channels (say, solar intensity and soil moisture) can be graphed in synchronization, revealing cause-and-effect relationships.

In purchasing and using data loggers, it is important to be clear about what data are needed, how accurate it must be, and how frequently it is to be sampled and for how long. Careful decisions can bring costs down and improve results. Companies like Omnisense and Onset Computer Corporation offer a wide range of equipment and have extensive information online, from basics to advanced applications.

Data loggers put a wealth of information in reach for landscape performance monitoring. Visual data from drones (see p. 55), especially if time-stamped, can further enhance the ability to track and measure processes in the landscape. Even at $1,000 or more for a multisensor setup, the investment is within reach of many landscape firms, especially since loggers can be reused and are usually deployed for a limited time on a given project. Better and more complete data ought to mean better designs, better ability to back up claims of sustainability and evolve better performance, and fewer failures.

For data logging and mapping on an extreme budget, see Public Lab, in the section on drone surveying (Principle I).

Landscape Forensics and Learning (or Not) from Failure

If you spend any amount of time Web surfing, you have probably come across "fail videos": dozens of YouTube posts titled "Top Ten Architecture Fails" or "Greatest Engineering Fails of All Time." They contain grainy footage of buildings falling apart or falling over, some purposeful (the infamous Pruitt-Igoe demolition is popular), some without anyone's help (the thirteen-story Lotus Riverside apartments in Shanghai). Bridges that don't meet in the middle are a favorite, along with heavy equipment and giant loaded trucks toppling, crashing into buildings, or rolling down slopes. There is a subgenre of stairs and escalators ending at blank walls and (to offset them, I suppose) doors that open on a three-story drop.

Figure 11.2   A real "landscape fail"—crane and mower hedge trimming—fortunately without injury. (*Project:* subject insisted on anonymity. *Photo:* Bart Dinger, Hamilton NZ.)

You won't find any comparable glut of "landscape fails." You'll see a few utility poles in the middle of traffic lanes, or obscenely pruned bushes in garish color combinations, obvious failures of design. There are a few gardeners doing "World's Dumbest Home Video" stunts. (The best one I've seen is a big guy trying to shear a tall hedge by swinging a running chainsaw on a rope.) But functional failures, equivalent to the toppled building or the misaligned bridge, are almost nonexistent. The only large-scale park landscape to make one YouTube list of "Top Ten Design Fails" was New York City's Chelsea Waterside Park—and that only because some kids' fountain structures were considered too phallic.

There could be many reasons for the absence of landscape laughs. Our real failures are things like bad drainage that turns a lawn into pudding, or a clogged bioswale, and they just aren't photogenic—or funny. One collapsed retaining wall in Milwaukee made it onto the playlists, probably because matters ended up in court. Routine questions like "Why Did My Tree Turn Orange and Die?" don't have much video potential either. Or perhaps landscape problems are too small-scale, and the equipment we use not heavy enough, to seem entertaining. Conventional landscapes are so often afterthoughts ("parsley around the pig," as my Plants & Design professors at Penn liked

to say); maybe people don't think any problem that occurs in the backyard could be worth much of a fuss, let alone slow-mo and titling.

It's not just on video, however, that landscape failures get no respect. An Internet search for the phrase "landscape failure" returns a paltry 1,800 hits, and a high percentage of them are not literally about landscapes, nor about any kind of construction failure. The most common topic on these sites is horticultural, the death of individual plantings, equated with landscape failure. Most are generic; perhaps one in a hundred is about a specific project or site that failed.

But in fact, landscapes do fail, and the failures cause damage and cost money. Landscape professionals have always had private discussions and gripe sessions about this, but apparently we have undersold our importance once again. It appears that the new emphasis on performance and ecosystem services is starting to bring those discussions out in public and in print.

Landscape Forensics

At the 2014 ASLA annual meeting in Denver, a panel discussion called "Landscape Forensics" raised the question "Why do natural-systems-based designs sometimes fail?" The panelists[22] had many years of experience with design and construction, and some had acted as forensic consultants to identify the causes of landscape project problems. A substantial audience heard carefully thought-out observations on a topic rarely discussed directly.

In late 2016, three issues of *LAM* carried four stories that discussed failures. One was about risk management in general; one was about difficulties in specifying stabilized decomposed granite, laying out the "forensic" process that overcame failed test panels and public skepticism about the material. One was a research notice concerning the fact that biofiltration successfully removes metals from stormwater but may fail to remove, and can actually concentrate, phosphorus and nitrogen. The last covered a project involving substantial modeling of water management; one of the models simulated a worst-case *failure* of site management.[23] If we are to learn as a profession, these are important discussions, and the practitioners, authors, and *LAM* itself are to be commended for publishing them.

An important implied question is whether "natural-systems-based," ecological, or sustainable landscape projects are *more susceptible* to failure than conventional landscapes. This question should be kept in mind as the profession takes on the task of measuring, monitoring, and documenting performance of landscapes intended to be sustainable.

The following section summarizes comments on why sustainable landscape projects fail, from a variety of sources including my own experience. The majority of the section is based directly on observations from the Denver panel (see note 22). As noted at the beginning of this chapter, liability concerns make many designers and contractors reluctant to have a failure attributed to them and described in print. (This is not unique to our profession: in 2008, the American Society of Civil Engineers was accused, by engineers, of skewing investigations of Hurricane Katrina and the World Trade Center to protect colleagues.)[24] I am therefore naming neither firms, projects, nor individual sources in this section; the intent is to look at lessons learned, not to point fingers.

Why "Sustainable Landscapes" Fail

The failure of any design or construction project is a unique convergence of problems, but general patterns are also discernible. Any landscape is a complex system of systems, and failure can happen at virtually any point. Most professionals have encountered some or all of these: unexpected soil erosion; drainage problems; flooding; stunted or dead plantings; clogged filtration features; inadequately porous paving; invasive-plant growth; damage by wildlife or species that don't play well with humans; windbreaks that cause turbulence; or damage during maintenance. Such issues arise in conventional landscapes too, but when sustainable functioning and performance are major expectations, failure takes on new significance.

Biological systems are generally resilient, within limits. The root cause of many landscape failures is insufficient human thought, planning, or skill, though "circumstances beyond our control" certainly occur. From my discussions with other professionals, I would say that the roots of landscape performance problems fall under several general headings:

Lack of Contextual Knowledge

- Not doing your McHargian homework on existing conditions
- Assuming that knowledge from one region is valid in another
- Misinterpreting or failing to understand site data (e.g., researching soil types but not realizing that one was a shrink-swell soil; seeing poor plant growth and wasting fertilizer when the cause is poor drainage)

Off-site or Contextual Change

- Upstream development, including positive restoration, that changes streamflow
- Economic changes—new owner or agency, budget shortfall, rising water bills
- Use or policy changes—increase in sports-field demand; permitting of picnics where previously not allowed; anti-environmentalism and climate denial, impacting funding or maintenance
- Not recognizing that landscapes are open, interconnected systems
- Changing climate and severity or frequency of weather

Poor Design

- "Aspirational thinking" (doing site makeovers instead of working with opportunities and constraints)
- Cut-and-paste details, developed in one region and reused elsewhere
- Lack of ecological, biological, or horticultural knowledge for plant selection
- Skimping on space or materials—for example, street-tree root volumes
- Untested products, materials, or methods
- Expecting indoor materials to perform in outdoor exposures
- Design concepts, materials, or both that require extreme maintenance to fend off disintegration
- "Hand off the plans and run"

Poor Installation

- Outdated methods and standards
- Equipment damage; ignoring site protection
- Ill-conceived change orders for material and plant substitution
- Shortcutting of essential working methods
- Failure or discontinuation of a needed product
- Manipulating, or driving on, wet soils
- Pressure for speed and cost cutting, especially at project's end
- "Plant it and punt"

Poor or Lacking Maintenance

- Design intent and as-built knowledge not communicated to maintenance staff
- Treating all maintenance tasks as unskilled
- Applying conventional "mow and blow" to native and diverse plantings
- Over- or underuse of irrigation or fertilization
- Treating soil biology as a one-time concern, or ignoring it

Several sources noted that the "vast majority" of failures occur at the end of a project. Often the architecture has gone over budget and been delayed, and the landscape contractor is expected to make up for it.

Even without cost overruns, landscape installation is usually the last phase of work, and thus the last thing standing between the client and a certificate of occupancy. The end of a project is also the point of transition from contractor responsibility to owner; lack of clear communication can leave new plantings without any maintenance for weeks. The nursery or contractor is usually responsible for establishing the plantings; overwatering, in order (supposedly) to ensure establishment, often happens during this phase.

Soil-related failures are quite common, possibly because the soil system is mostly invisible beneath our feet, possibly below paving. Compaction of subsoil by heavy equipment has ruined the subsurface drainage on many larger projects; many contractors don't know to loosen subsoil immediately before placing topsoil or manufactured soil for the final grade. Topsoil stockpiling is a recommended practice, but many urban sites don't have enough room to do it properly.

Soil at construction sites often loses organic material; a 1 percent loss of organic carbon in soil increases runoff by 60,000 gallons per acre (in addition to runoff from impervious surfaces); a 1 percent increase in carbon increases moisture retention by a similar amount. The USDA estimates that many soils have lost *60 percent* of their original organic matter, so this problem can be severe. Within a site, sudden storm runoff may pond and drop sediment; unless this deposit is remixed with regular soil, it will form a "lens" of very different soil properties that can affect drainage and nutrition. Another potential soil failure is the temptation to assume that reasonably healthy existing topsoil is always right for any use. Heavily used parks, for example, need a hard-wearing manufactured soil that is at least one-third sand, plus compost and site soil. The weight of soil for plantings over structures, like greenroofs and wildlife crossing bridges, can be a critical factor, yet many specifiers and suppliers understate the weight, which can lead to failures. Designers, on the other hand, may have a realistic estimate of weight, and skimp on depth to avoid the issue.

Usually, several conditions come together to create a problem. One example is a public landscape in a coastal city that was carefully given dune-like soil and topography, with correctly chosen plants to approximate the dune vegetation community. Yet the plants started to die. The reason was that, considering dunes to be a "harsh environment," the designer had specified irrigation—which was killing the plants. Turning off the irrigation saved the vegetation, but wasted the cost of the watering system.

This raises a point about native species, regardless of opinions about the validity of designing with them. Native plants grow as part of a community, seldom in isolation or pure stands. As designers, many of us tend to "put the natives on a pedestal" by planting them as specimens. Root interconnections, variety of beneficial insects, and other interconnections are lost; the plantings may not die, but may fail to thrive.

PRECONDITIONS FOR FAILURE
Behind the evident mistakes in planning, design, installation, and maintenance lie some hidden factors. These can be categorized as attitudes and mismeasurements.

Attitudes

Professional firms vary widely in their approach to being professionals, from deep pride in workmanship to fast-buck haste. Sloppy, hasty, or irresponsible attitudes can contribute to failure, but many firms are successful precisely because they avoid them. Almost all firms bump up against these attitudes from other professions as well as their own.

The design and construction world is increasingly specialized, to the extent that people work in "silos" that make communication outside their area of responsibility difficult. "We are multidisciplinary, but not interdisciplinary," as one interviewee put it. This applies not only to the designer who hands off to the contractor and moves on, but also to limited communication among team members and across phases of work. Especially for sustainable design, coordination and an integrated approach are critical, since many sustainable methods and goals are unfamiliar and must be clearly shared among all team members.

Conversely, twenty-first-century instant global communication encourages adoption of far-flung ideas without time for analysis. Starting with landlines and faxes, each technological innovation has brought with it an *expectation* of increased speed—decisions are expected to happen as quickly as commu-

nication. There is no technical reason why we have to decide instantly: it's an attitude, and not a contributor to sustainability. "As a group, landscape professionals are prone to latch onto whatever comes along," one source commented, "and there's a good deal of snake oil out there." Especially where ecosystem services are the goal, good ideas implemented without sufficient knowledge can spell failure.

Paradoxically, what can be called the culture of the profession tends to preserve status quo ideas by default. Universities, whose landscape architecture curricula are overloaded because students need exposure to so many disciplines, are slow to add anything new. Sustainable approaches are often shoehorned into existing courses rather than given systematic treatment. Both in coursework and for licensing, there is a legitimate need for a standardized *minimum* competency requirement, but this undeniably leads to an attitude of "don't fail, but if you do, fail just like everyone else." One interviewee calls this "the Disease of Best Practice," which stifles innovation. Creosote and lead paint, it is worth noting, were once best practices. Legal judgments and insurance often rest on "standards of care" that are based on general consensus, and thus tend toward a cautious common denominator. Where maintenance staff is concerned, clients or agencies may refuse to accept training in sustainable methods; training costs money, has to be repeated because of high employee turnover, changes established practices, and may appear to increase the agency's liability.

As with any "culture," the landscape professions are affected by outside forces as well. For example, the IRS and federal law require that capital funding be kept strictly separate from operational budgets. There is logic to this, but it works better for assets like buildings, where the asset isn't growing and changing, and maintenance is reasonably predictable. Where very specific maintenance is essential to the health of vegetation and soils, the fact that the construction contract can't really include binding commitments about upkeep is a serious complication, and a common cause of failures.

Another external pressure that can contribute indirectly to failure is the competitive attitude taken by engineers and architects toward landscape architectural licensing. It is sadly common for the local AIA and ASCE chapters to work actively to prevent, minimize, or "sunset" licensure laws for landscape architects. The legal authority to (for example) stamp drainage plans varies from state to state, despite this skill being taught in most landscape architecture programs and tested in national and state licensing exams. The landscape perspective on drainage, which considers soil types, soil biotechnical engineering, and water harvesting in far more depth than many engineers are willing to discuss, is thus lost. Avoidable failures happen (though at least one can then blame the engineer or architect with a sigh of relief).

Mismeasurements

If it is true that what isn't measured can't be managed, then mismeasurement leads to mismanagement. While most professionals are careful to avoid simple mismeasurement (like arithmetic mistakes or using the wrong density in a materials estimate), there are times when the wrong yardstick altogether is used. Such mistakes are harder to see, but potentially have more impact, than simple misreading of the ruler.

A prime example is the assumption, by clients and professionals alike, that the "100-year storm" can't happen more frequently. The Upper Mississippi has actually had seven 100- to 500-year storms in the past 12 years. The x-year storm concept is valid, but only as a *probability* of occurrence. Many of us are uncomfortable with interpreting statistics and oversimplify what they mean. A second problem with the assumption that an x-year flood is consistently predictable is that historical data are the basis for such statistics—and those data have been changing fast over the past few decades. Storms are generally more severe, dropping more water faster, often on drought-hardened soils. Today's 100-year storm isn't what it was a century ago.

Faced with the challenge of climate change and the goals of sustainability, landscape-making is becoming far more reliant on hard data and statistical evidence than before. This is outside what, for many designers, is our comfort zone, that happy math-free country. Ensuring the survival of any garden in the face of less-predictable weather and shifting hardiness zones forces the landscape professional toward the hard sciences. But measured data and performance are here to stay, aggravating though that sometimes feels. In this transition, what we measure and how we measure it are critical, yet often unfamiliar, tasks. Unsurprisingly, we get them wrong at times.

A frequent barrier to getting good information is convenience and habit. During the early 1980s, the National Urban Runoff Program made some of the first attempts to study pollution in runoff, in part by monitoring chemical levels in constructed "NURP ponds." Monitoring, however, stopped during winter in regions where the ponds froze. It was discovered, more or less by accident, that phosphorus levels, acceptable during the three seasons when monitoring occurred, spiked in the first thaw of spring. Ice, by creating anaerobic conditions, had released hidden phosphorus, which a convenient monitoring schedule had masked. Similarly, road salt impacts on soils and plants sometimes go unanticipated because field conditions are checked in summer, and designs are done in a warm office.

Many landscape architects have noted, with sadness, that they got into the profession because they loved the outdoors, and they now spend their career in an office. Along with the fact that those offices tend to be in urban locations (including small town centers), this introduces a disconnect into our knowledge of the environment. Tropical beachfronts and resorts, notes one source who has worked on such projects, are usually remote from cities; although these sites have prominent wet and dry seasons, even the local professionals almost never visit during the rainy season. If deep contextual information is essential for sustainable design, such blind spots create real vulnerabilities, which standardized, conventional projects may, paradoxically, avoid.

Inaccuracy from convenience and habit extends right down to nitty-gritty detail tasks, such as the following:

- Street lighting levels are often measured on the ground because measuring at eye level is more difficult; yet the eye-level experience is arguably more important, and less likely to lead to overillumination.
- The nutrient composition of commercial compost tea, including "effective microorganisms," is tested where the materials are produced but tends to change during bottling and transport.

- Horticultural habit specifies seed mixes in terms of percentage by weight, but this means that species with very small seeds can be drastically overrepresented: 25 percent by weight of a tiny seed can be 50 or 75 percent of the number of seedlings, leading that species to dominate where it was expected to coexist.

- Viewshed analysis, until recently, was done (if at all) with two people and some tall flags. This way of measuring can be useful, but is labor-intensive and limited and can be manipulated deceptively. Using this method and carefully selected viewpoints, a mining or manufacturing proposal can be "proved" to have no visual impact, while modern computerized topographic methods systematically reveal all points from which a project can be seen, a far better basis for decisions.

In each of these examples, measurements done at considerable cost *cloud* the ability to understand complex landscapes and complex design criteria.

Is Greener Riskier?

For the four principals interviewed for *LAM*'s 2016 article "Life and Limb,"[25] the difference between green and conventional design is not a major factor in professional liability or risk. A much larger worry, repeated in the interviews, is the tendency for clients, especially large or governmental ones, to demand that designers bear all the risk for everything. Events over which the designer could have had no possible control become grounds for lawsuits, years after the client approved the project. Yet there is a link to green design here: if the primary risk is client expectations, setting green expectations is harder than setting conventional ones.

A report titled "Sustainable Design Risk Management," available from the AIA Trust, discusses some risks associated specifically with green design and construction, and is worthwhile reading for any green design or construction professional.[26] It points out that green design is *in the process* of becoming the norm and, as such, is becoming the "standard of reasonable care" that determines whether professional actions are negligent. In effect, what everyone does in a profession becomes the legal standard. Because green building is new and evolving, the standard of care becomes ambiguous, increasing the risk—not of *actual* failure but

of losing a lawsuit. Similarly, when the ASLA and similar professional organizations include sustainability as part of their code of ethics, it becomes a "duty of care" and can be used as argument in litigation. These implicit and explicit standards can affect whether a risk is covered by insurance. Last but far from least, because green building has sometimes been overenthusiastically portrayed to the public as a sensational solution and cost-saving method, client expectations are excessive. Combined with complex work, complicated or unclear division of responsibility among client, designer, and contractor, and performance that is affected by unusually complex and local variables, client dissatisfaction is a worry. I have seen no statistics on client satisfaction for sustainable landscape projects; from green architecture, it appears that satisfaction is generally high, but if it is low, it is extremely low. The *LAM* interviewees certainly did note that communicating with clients to get buy-in and to avoid unreasonable expectations was critical to managing risk.

There have been a few lawsuits over failure to achieve LEED certification, and one enterprising firm was apparently offering a form of insurance that *guaranteed* getting one's desired LEED level! The AIA Trust's risk management report suggests avoiding contracts that make achievement of certification a condition. If that isn't possible, spell out very clearly who is responsible for attempting to get LEED certification, at which level, and whether that is the same individual or firm that would bear costs associated with not being certified in a timely way, at the desired level, or at all.

Sadly, sustainable contract work *is* currently somewhat more risky than conventional—not because the design or the built project is more vulnerable to actual failure, but because communication about contractual responsibilities is less clear-cut. This shouldn't, and isn't likely to, scare anyone away from sustainable design or construction, which as far as I can tell remains the right thing to do, a profitable business model, and not *dramatically* more risky than any other capitalist adventure.

Multifunctionality as a Performance Measure

The more accurately we try to *measure* performance, the more we must home in on a single issue, or at most a few. A performance car, for example, is measurably fast; fuel efficiency isn't directly factored into its rating. The performance of the new family car, however, generally combines cost, fuel efficiency, reliability, infrequent maintenance, comfort, and interior space. Some of these factors can't be quantified, and even those that are numerical cannot be combined mathematically (no single number actually represents 50 mpg + 115 cubic feet cargo room + 5 cup-holders). Rating such a car on a single function would be misleading, in much the same way that valuing a vehicle purchase solely on first cost is a great way to get a gas-guzzling, repair-prone lemon. The family car is expected to fulfill multiple functions; evaluating its performance is less exact, more subjective, and more complex than evaluating single-factor performance, like racing speed.

This raises issues about the current, important trend to expect measured sustainability performance from designed landscapes. Self-maintaining ecosystems are probably the most multifunctional systems on this planet, and sustainable built landscapes aim for similar diversity. Measuring multifunctional performance is not a simple matter of metering one variable, or even monitoring a half-dozen variables and averaging the results.

To continue the car example, it is possible to get a single rating—from *Consumer Reports* perhaps—that takes multiple performance issues into account. *CR* and others have come up with workable and transparent ways to test and rank consumer goods. These involve understanding which features are the basis for decisions about performance; recognizing that some features matter to some people and not others; devising tests of single features that can be ranked; and following clear procedures to combine single-feature scores, including subjective ones, into overall rankings that are comparable across that class of product. SITES is in some ways similar in approach: it was developed using features of landscapes whose performance can be measured and used for decision making, and it sums up the results of testing single-issue performance measures by using a fairly transparent system of points. By relating performance to ecosystem services where possible, a degree of comparability between single-issue scores becomes possible.

Landscape ecology has a number of ways of evaluating ecosystem health. As with a great deal of scientific ecology, these methods have gradually been expanding to take in aspects of the built environment, rather than only rating high-quality undisturbed ecosystems. The concept of ecosystem services is a specific bridge between ecosystem "performance" and human land use. The use of these measures is a big step toward being able to determine what performance goals are most important for a site; to decide which ones are most feasible; to evaluate to what extent goals are met once a project is complete and in use; and to glean comparable, replicable design, construction, and maintenance skills by learning concretely from success and from failure.

Sarah Lovell and Douglas Johnston introduce their very useful paper on landscape multifunctionality by stating that "too often, anthropogenic landscapes are manipulated to serve a single function, such as cropland for the production of food, or parks for recreation." The article goes on to discuss multifunctionality as a strategy for sustainable landscape planning and design. They view any increase in multifunctionality, even on very fragmented urban sites, as part of regional improvement of landscape performance. "If landscapes are to be designed with the intention of increasing performance," they note, "methods are needed to assess and monitor the success in meeting these goals." Among the methods discussed are comparative evaluations between landscapes, or of one landscape across time, and modeling of landscapes as complex systems. Following Aldo Leopold, however, they also believe that landscape performance may best be achieved by treating built landscapes as experiments, tweaked over time as actual data indicate how more functions can be achieved.[27]

It seems clear that as a profession, we are tackling an important and challenging goal when we ask for monitored and rated multifunctional performance. The complexity and interconnectedness of landscapes means that simple monitoring cannot easily reveal true performance for the holistic regional network into which all landscapes are linked. It is important that, even as we gain skill in measuring performance, we don't oversell our ability to repeat and control successful performance from project to project. That may win bids, and is likely to improve the results of our work on average; but guaranteeing performance, especially in complex systems, is very much two-sided and also occasionally results, as noted above, in disappointment and lawsuits.

Measurement of performance and evaluation of failure are a part of almost everything humans undertake. For much of its existence, landscape gardening (by whatever name) has assessed success and failure in limited terms—visual and stylistic criteria, usefulness in facilitating human ritual and play, and the health of many individual plantings as opposed to the health of the whole. Contemporary changes are exerting pressure for multifunctional landscape performance and, as a necessary tool, more rigorous and complicated measurements of outcome. There is urgency in this process, but we should not be surprised that the process is challenging and slow.

Subtopics and Search Terms for Principle II: Demonstrate Performance, Learn from Failure

Note: Subtopics are also useful search terms; add "innovation" or "controversy" to search terms as appropriate.

LEED and relatives
Search terms: *combine* green building, sustainable, ecological *with* rating, ranking, certification

Landscape performance
Search terms: landscape performance || site performance || site monitoring || data logger + outdoor

Landscape failure
Search terms: forensic landscape architecture || for comparison, forensic architect || construction law || expert witness + construction

Resource List:

Links to information sources related to this chapter are posted at http://islandpress.org/sustainable-landscape-construction

Sustaining Principles, Evolving Efforts

If you are thinking a year ahead, sow seed. If you are thinking ten years ahead, plant trees. If you are thinking one hundred years ahead, educate the people.

—Chinese proverb

In the landscape, beginnings and endings overlap. Healthy landscapes are ecosystems, and they survive by constant change. In a self-sustaining landscape, marsh becomes meadow becomes forest, then returns to meadow after fires, or even to marsh after floods. Individual plants and animals die, but the community—the landscape—lives on through a constant "recycling" process.

Sustainability is about fitting into this endless cycle. Many conventional landscapes, and an even higher proportion of buildings, are constructed in defiance of the cycle of growth and decay. The cumulative effect of thousands of sites treated this way is what one author has called a "revenge effect"[1]—*too much* success in disrupting the cycle, which spells decline or even death for the land. With current technology, it *is* possible to break the cycle temporarily, but the costs are enormous.

This book asks which approaches to landscape construction might reverse these destructive trends, or at least help to do so. In fact, there are *many* techniques in landscape work that contribute directly to ecosystem health, or decrease damage already done. Taking the hopeful position that humanity still has a chance to live in harmony with the great cycle of life, these techniques are called sustainable, regenerative, or environmentally responsible.

Sustainable landscape construction is not merely idealistic—it is available and feasible today. Sustainability has been increasingly in demand for over three decades, and projects are widespread. This book includes discussion of many real projects, constructed by real people on real budgets, which include sustainable goals and techniques. Increasing numbers of professionals are doing this work in nearly every region of North America. Other countries are well ahead of the United States in some areas of sustainable construction. Sustainable landscape construction may be a young profession, but it is no longer an orphan. A growing network of landscape professionals have adopted, tested, and adapted the methods described. A growing number of do-it-yourselfers are also involved.

Although some are experimental and all are evolving, sustainable landscape methods can and do compete successfully with conventional ones on almost any criteria—economic, functional, aesthetic. They are practical (sometimes with a learning curve), durable, and safe. Some are simply conventional methods done with extra craftsmanship, extra care in siting and scaling them to existing conditions, or extra planning and preparation. Others have been resurrected from tradition. Only a few are truly new, and even these have developed enough of a track record that they cannot be called untried.

Not only is landscape-making headed toward sustainability, but the landscape itself is gaining theoreticians' and politicians' respect as the measure or unit most appropriate for studying and planning sustainability. As geographer-planner Adrian Phillips states, "In policy terms the appeal of the idea of landscape is that it unifies rather than disaggregates the factors at work in our relationship with the environment."[2] Landscape is the appropriate scale and level of detail for an increasing number of social and environmental initiatives.

Sustainability in general appears to be a trend strengthened by adversity. State and local jurisdictions have pushed harder for sustainable goals during periods of federal resistance, and private investment has supported sustainable innovation. China, long resistant to lowering emissions, has joined with Canada and the European Union to helm the attempt to meet Paris climate accord goals despite the abdication of the United States; fourteen US states and what's left of Puerto Rico have formed the United States Climate Alliance with the same intent.[3] A substantial part of the US population, 50 million strong and a prime market for design, the so-called cultural creatives, rates environment and sustainability as a top priority today.[4] Many support the "Not-So-Big House" movement against the lot-line-hugging McMansion. All these trends are positive signs that sustainable design is not a passing fad.

Sustainable landscape methods were realistic in 2000, and in many ways the profession reached a "tipping-point" toward sustainability about that time.[5] The ultimate conclusion of this book still depends, seventeen years later, on further growth in our field. It remains up to committed individuals to apply green principles creatively and courageously. Thus, two questions remain, not about what is feasible today, but about influencing the future. These are just as important, if not more so, today as they were just before Y2K.

The first question is this: does present sustainable practice suggest any general themes to guide and expand the landscape professions of the future? Seven key ideas are briefly discussed below, linking together practical principles and techniques from earlier chapters that at first glance might not seem related. These themes or strategies are *not* essential to day-to-day work in sustainable landscape construction, though they may help. Their real value, I believe, will be for those professionals who can step back, even for a moment, and take a longer view, looking to chart a course *beyond* what can be done today.

The second question about the future of sustainable landscape construction is that of education, both professional and public. Unless new students in landscape architecture, construction and construction management, architecture, planning, and engineering are exposed to sustainable methods, they will simply perpetuate the conventional past. This chapter lists a number of specific, positive changes for professional

schools to consider. It also describes some built landscapes that educate the *public* about sustainability and natural process. In doing so, these projects argue the cause of sustainability and can also become environmental art.

This book describes a changing profession whose focus is also ever-changing. Appropriately enough, the conclusions of this book are beginnings, too.

Learning from the Landscape: Themes and Strategies

Bringing together in one place so many tested and specific methods of landscape work reveals several underlying strategies, from which the specific methods have grown. These themes concern broad ways of dealing with the landscape—in the strict sense where "dealing" means negotiating, exchanging, and interacting. Clearly this is no exhaustive list. Themes and strategies like these can guide future creativity and adaptation in our profession. They are also strengths that many landscape professionals *already* have, and can build on. In these areas, what our professions have learned from the landscape is in short supply—and growing demand—among related professions such as architecture and engineering. These themes offer a direction in which to lead.

Keywords

The themes that emerge from this book can be stated as seven keywords, each linked to the others. Although there are certainly others, recalling this abbreviated list may be useful:

- Decentralization
- Coordination
- Resilience
- Synergy
- Community
- Integration
- Vision

Decentralize Deal with Issues near Their Source

In researching successful projects and methods of sustaining the land, one theme emerges time and again:

work close to the source. Stormwater and erosion are best managed with many small structures near the top of the watershed, the "source" of the runoff. Porous paving infiltrates raindrops almost literally *where they fall*— simulating the age-old relationship between healthy soil and precipitation. To keep invasive plants and animals from overrunning native ecosystems, importation and quarantine restrictions *where they enter the country* are far more effective than trying to eradicate a pest that has spread across a whole continent. These examples have one thing in common: acting at the source, where the problem is smallest. This concept resonates with many ancient texts, among them the T'ao T'e Ching.[6]

"Close to the source" rephrases E. F. Schumacher's advice that small is beautiful. Small, in dealing with landscapes, also means decentralized. Any environmental service or problem that requires an infrastructure is likely to be more cost-effective if it is decentralized. For example, constructed wastewater wetlands can be built to serve one home, or a small cluster—a significant advantage over large conventional treatment plants and their extensive infrastructure. Reuse is preferable to remanufacturing, in part because centralized recycling requires collection and redistribution.

Similarly, solar electricity and wind generation have increasingly shown potential to *place the source near the use,* eliminating not only miles of infrastructure but also major losses in long-distance transmission. This principle, however, is widely ignored by people trying to produce solar or wind "farms" to transmit energy across a still-inefficient grid, an effort spurred by fear of actual energy independence that would free citizens from the yoke of utility monopoly.

Dealing with the "small" problems takes on another meaning in ecosystems. For many types of environmental event—floods, fires, storms, and so forth—it is reasonable to take preventive action against the "ten-year" event, the frequent, low-intensity occurrence. It is impractical, costly, and actually destructive to attempt to prevent the hundred-year event. This is an ethical choice that American society frequently gets backward: while it is ethically essential to devote all possible effort to rescuing *one* child who *has fallen* down a well, it is impractical and counterproductive to devote the same absolute commitment to making it im-

possible for *any* child ever to fall down *any* well. The insistence on total prevention of risk is one of the most anti-sustainable social forces at work in the landscape today. Interestingly, and sadly, it is one mistaken attitude that conservatives and liberals seem to share.

This, then, is the first theme that emerges from the many landscape techniques discussed in this book: wherever possible, respond to the land in small, site-specific ways coordinated across a region rather than centralized in a single regional facility.

Coordinate Efforts

Coordination itself is a theme of this book. It applies to the multidisciplinary team doing green design and building. It applies to the well-known slogan of thinking globally while acting locally. It applies to involving a whole community, analyzing a whole watershed, and studying energy flows throughout a system.

Coordination can be lost when no one cooperates or plans ahead, but it can also be lost when all planning is centralized. In modern society, both conditions are obstacles to environmentally sound development. Extreme individualism keeps people from participating in decisions, and fuels single-issue lobbying *against* the common good. At the other extreme, convenience for governmental or corporate decision makers can exclude citizens, while economies of scale (often false) justify centralization. Because it makes such a difference to sustainable projects, coordination and cooperation should be high on the landscape professional's list of guiding values.

Rely on Resilience Rather than Strength

Another theme is that living strength comes from flexibility, not rigidity.[7] This is most clear in Btec: roots and branches are individually weaker than steel or concrete, but woven together into the soil, they outperform and outlast most rigid engineering structures. They stabilize soil not by resisting water's attack but by dissipating the flow of energy. Each small branch may deflect a few drops, each root hair holds a few soil particles—but here small is beautiful *and strong.*

The difference between conventional and sustainable pest control also involves resilience. Biological control of pests and diseases relies on living organisms to neutralize infestations (ladybugs to combat aphids, for instance). Being alive, these controls have a resilience of behavior that no chemical can match. They are often specifically targeted to a single type of pest, a quality that pesticide manufacturers have worked hard, but with limited success, to mimic with modern chemistry. In many cases, biological control is resilient over time, too: an introduced ladybug population may regenerate itself next year, or anytime the aphid population explodes. No chemical control can do this.

"Organic" methods of soil fertilization also rely on the resilience and endurance of living organisms, instead of the strength of nonliving chemical inputs. It is not that chemicals are simply bad; the issue is that living organisms respond to their environment in ways more complex and interactive, more resilient, than any nonliving chemical reaction.

Almost by definition, successful landscape *maintenance* is about resilience. No matter how well built (or even overbuilt), unmaintained outdoor structures decay sooner or later. Maintained structures, however, can be sustained almost forever—Taos Pueblo, made of mud but replastered every other year, is arguably the oldest structure still in use in America, inhabited a thousand years. Maintenance is about accepting change and growth, and relying on resilience to accommodate change. Especially in landscapes, with their many living components, rigidly resisting change is not even an option.

Resilience also means knowing when not to resist. In particular, the attempts to completely stop all floods, fires, or storms, no matter what size, is a too-rigid approach. Control can work for smaller events, and these are both the majority and the norm; but real resilience is required to survive and accept the rare and overwhelmingly large events, which simply cannot be controlled.

Build for Synergy

In the landscape, multipurpose solutions *sustain*, while single-purpose solutions usually *consume*. Many of the projects and products highlighted in this book, as well as on SITES and Landscape Architecture Foundation websites, set out to solve a single problem and found

that several other functions could be met at the same time.

Natural wetlands are a clear example of diverse functions. Constructed wetlands for wastewater treatment almost automatically serve a second function as habitat. With minimal extra expense, they can also function as public parks. The same wetlands, correctly located, provide stormwater infiltration and flood control. Multiple functions make the facility easier to finance, reflecting increased social and ecological value.

Porous paving is another example of at least dual function: supporting traffic and infiltrating precipitation. By accomplishing two functions in a single space, porous paving preserves land for other purposes. Accomplishing more with less, whether space or resources, is clearly desirable for sustainability. Cellular supported paving around trees similarly stabilizes the surface while keeping planting soil loose.

Synergy also means creatively turning one technique into several by noticing similarities. Photovoltaic panels are usually large, flat surfaces of a relatively strong material. This has inspired people to use those surfaces as roof tiles, shade structures, windows, and even roads. Crossover concepts like this are worth exploring and may yield other regenerative, sustainable innovations.

"Multipurpose" also goes beyond human purposes. Landscape design and construction can and should accommodate species other than humans. Particularly in the case of plants, those species in turn provide environmental services that humans need, and offer joy to people privileged to interact with wildlife.

Work from Community

Advocates of sustainability often quote the Iroquois awareness that present decisions affect future generations. Similarly, individual decisions also affect the whole web of *community*. The theme of community-based action has appeared repeatedly in the most successful projects described in this book.

Watershed restoration, in particular, benefits from working with the whole human community (everyone who owns or uses land in the watershed) and with the whole biological community (all the species that use or live in the watershed). Similarly, site restoration is seldom about reinstating one species. Rather, it is about restarting a whole community, giving it time and protection to resume self-maintenance.

Community means having important conditions in common. The ultimate community is the bioregion or eco-region. Landscape-based boundaries for decision making simply work better than the arbitrary political lines—and social communities in fact reflect shared eco-regional concerns as much or more than political ones.

Community-based action takes practical form in projects driven *from the start* by public input. Simultaneously, information is gathered early in the development process for an understanding of the whole site, seen as a community in a regional context. These community inputs can seldom be replaced successfully either by the wishes of an individual expert, engineer, or owner or by analyzing only those site features that meet a *preconceived* development purpose. Truly regenerative, sustainable, and ecological design grows from roots in both human and biological communities.

Integrate Natural and Man-made

In the landscape, human presence and natural dynamics are best when integrated. Dividing the two puts humans and nature in separate jail cells. Integration is essential even in the "wilderness" preserved for scenic or scientific value—humans must fit in by obeying rules that favor the nonhuman. In the landscapes where humanity dominates, integration is also of great value. Here, it means including at least enough of nature to sustain human well-being.

In a practical sense, integration applies to landscape technology. BTEC, for instance, is a pragmatic integration of human technology (the "hard" components and systematic design) with natural dynamics (living plants and soil). Because humans cannot actually create life, a great many landscape technologies rely on integration between nonhuman organisms and human construction.

This integration is reflected visually in many of the best-loved landscapes of the world. Japanese gardens frequently mix artificially cut stones with naturally shaped ones, or place dry bamboo fencing against a living bamboo grove. Examples of this are less common in European traditions, but they do exist: Luis Barragán's seamless steps in Pedregal's natural rock outcrops, or Richard Haag's formal, hedged reflecting pool amid the Bloedel Reserve woods. This integrative form of design artistry and the superb craft required to build it deserve more study and recognition than they have received in recent Western history. Integration is not complete until it satisfies the eye and mind.

Envision Richer Forms

Many of the techniques described in this book require the ability to envision forms more complex than those of conventional engineering. Although simplicity is a valued goal in design, simplicity in sustainable landscapes comes more appropriately from integration than from geometric minimalism.

Even a slight increase in the complexity of form can result in major improvements in function. The honeycomb structure of porous concrete is slightly more complex than solid cement—yet the increase in function is significant. In wetlands, the convoluted form of the root zone functions far better than a simple mechanical filter, and the variable depths and edges within the basin function better than an engineered, rectangular tank of even depth. The root path trench is considerably more complex in form than a simple planting pit but dramatically increases the odds of tree survival.

Envisioning and building these more complex forms places new demands on everyone associated with landscape work. Dreaming up and drawing a complex form, especially a truly nature-like one, is more challenging than designing a simple geometric structure. Reading the plans and building the form challenges the contractor. Understanding why he or she should pay for it is not always simple for the client.

Agent-based modeling and "complexity theory," along with fractal geometry, are important new tools—still underutilized—for envisioning richer yet better-integrated landscapes. The design theorist's prejudice against "nature mimicry" remains a ball and chain that prevents many landscape professionals from taking a serious second look at naturalistic form and function.

In some ways, the will and ability to break free from oversimplified convention and to dream with greater richness is this book's largest theme. Each of the other themes is richer and more complex than its conventional counterpart: integration is richer than overspecialization, community is richer than isolationism, resilience is more complex than rigidity, and so on. Educating ourselves, our students, and the public to understand and appreciate the richness of sustainable landscapes is an immensely important goal.

Green Education in Design and Construction

Education and training are critical to any profession, both for maintaining its standards and for enriching its vision. Landscape architecture, landscape contracting, and horticulture are no exceptions. The curriculum of today very directly influences the practices of tomorrow. So do requirements for licensing and for continuing professional education.

To make sustainable and regenerative practice a reality, teaching and training need to be in line with environmental goals. This applies to specialized training in any landscape profession, or in the related professions of architecture, planning, and engineering. Anyone who has had any recent contact with these branches of education knows that sustainability is of growing interest to students—and teachers. In many cases, however, current course content and teaching methods are in conflict with the trends outlined in this book.

James Steele, in his book *Sustainable Architecture*, outlines changes in curriculum to encourage environmental knowledge and attitudes among architecture students.[8] Summarized and slightly expanded here, these suggestions apply equally to landscape architecture; most also apply to the training of contractors, engineers, and planners.

- Assign studio problems that involve real sites, real issues, and review by real clients (or realistic role-playing).
- Simulate in studio the collaborative team approach students will encounter in their jobs.
- Emphasize holistic context (both ecological and cultural) in lectures and assignments. "Pure-design" assignments should be reserved for specific teaching purposes.

- Broaden perspectives by basing class projects on "appropriate technology" or setting them in Third World situations, or in First World communities affected by the persistent issues of poverty, race, and environmental justice.
- Require the use of local materials, energy estimates, and recycling as part of solving any design assignment.
- Encourage students to challenge policy limits during design; discuss (but don't grade) how completed projects may conflict with existing policies.
- Foster the ability to think about places from multiple perspectives: diverse cultural meanings of the same place, as well as multiple functionality.
- Expect students to plan for maintenance and constant change, both deliberate and accidental.
- Walk the talk: encourage students and faculty to make their school and their own lives more sustainable.

These goals for education are quite similar to the 1992 Rio Earth Summit recommendations for change in the construction industry.[9]

From personal experience, four educational goals related to outdoor construction should be added to Steele's list:

- Emphasize site selection (regional) and siting (within the property) in all design assignments.
- Include regional and vernacular traditions of design-building in the main curriculum, not merely as electives.
- Include "constructability" as part of every design review. Offer design-build classes, in which students actually construct what they design, perhaps donating it for public use.
- Insist that students understand the climate-change implications of every design or construction project; use www.architecture2030.org as a fundamental course "reading." (Architecture2010 was a parallel effort to change architectural curricula; its goals remain relevant to landscape teaching even while tending to ignore landscapes.)

Many teachers have already arrived at similar ideas, and some schools have made considerable strides toward greener curriculum. (An example is Brian Dunbar, a Colorado State University professor who takes landscape and interior design students to an ecotourism resort in the Virgin Islands as an intensive workshop in sustainable development and technology.)[10] There is a great deal of inertia to overcome, however, and conventional thinking still re-creates itself in each graduating class. Design students still get the message, subtly or blatantly, that the most idiosyncratic and outrageous forms of creativity are always the best. Engineering and contracting students are still taught "no-nonsense" and numerical attitudes that dismiss important social and ecological values; they are also indoctrinated with great fear of both regulation and liability. Sadly, accepted wisdom is often perpetuated unthinkingly, by default rather than intent.

Professional registration exams currently are slowly and apparently reluctantly adding sustainability to their topics. To some extent this is understandable because the exam sets a *minimum* standard of competence. Changes in practice, education, and the law, however, are eventually reflected in the registration requirements. In time, exam questions must shift focus to examples greener than the tired old joist-sizes-for-decks or retaining-wall-footing problems. Similarly, as building codes become greener, this should be reflected in professional continuing education. A number of "alternative" courses do exist, but too often they *still* seem like voices crying in a wilderness.

Any change toward professional environmental awareness is, in effect, a step toward equalizing the influence of landscape compared with that of architecture. Professional registration laws today give architects and engineers (and the "hard" methods they represent) great power over site design—in some states, even registered landscape architects cannot seal a drainage plan, for example. This legislated inequality hinders landscape architects from instituting many sustainable site practices. Educating architects and engineers about sustainable alternatives, and lobbying for increased authority to sign drawings for such alternatives, needs to be an expanded part of the ASLA's agenda in particular.

Educators—and students—have a special opportunity to help sustainable landscape-making evolve. Many are already taking this initiative; many more are needed.

The public also needs to learn about sustainable landscapes as a professional activity. Although a landscape architect has finally hit the big time—played by Jude Law as a lead character in the 2006 movie *Breaking and Entering*—the character represents the most controversial type of landscape thinker, a deconstructivist who sees naturalistic design as "fraudulent advocacy" and "miniature gestures of appeasement."[11] As this book makes clear, that position has some validity, but is usually presented polemically and wildly overstated. Landscape professionals need to educate their public far more broadly.

Education Means Research, Too

Most institutions of higher education include research in their mission, and education about sustainability needs to do much more of this. Research and documentation about landscapes, however, is not just an abstract and theoretical subject: its subject is largely real-world projects and their real-time effects. This means that research needs serious involvement of landscape practitioners.

One of the most pressing needs in green building is performance documentation. Without documented before-and-after data, no project in the built environment can be evaluated properly, and few well-supported conclusions about the causes of its success or shortcomings can be drawn. Neither baseline nor post-occupancy data are *routinely* gathered for either conventional or cutting-edge projects; this is unfortunately true both of architecture and landscape work, although in 2017 there is at least some movement. Even if gathered, these data are seldom cataloged, compared, or compiled. The Landscape Performance Series, by the Landscape Architecture Foundation, is changing this with online case studies that include detailed analysis of environmental benefits; SITES is attempting something similar, though the data shown for certified projects online is often sketchy. In writing a book like this, the inability to locate concrete proof, or at least strong empirical evidence, of the effectiveness of landscape techniques is frustrating. This is common in new fields, but also symptomatic of a build it and forget it approach that is very specific to the design world.

Every "green" project—landscape, infrastructure, or building—for the coming decade or three needs to be treated as a science project as well as a pragmatic job. Much more than a one-time pass based on a set of points as with LEED or SITES (valuable in their own right), there needs to be a shared method of documenting baseline conditions and actual ongoing performance of *everything* we construct. With modern computing and communication this is no longer a visionary idea. LEED is creeping in this direction, to be fair, and for buildings, the idea of displaying performance in real time (live graphs of water or electricity usage, for instance) is almost trendy. Yet today, for far too many sustainability-driven projects, no one can show what the pre-construction soil erosion rate actually was, nor how much it actually increased or decreased as a result of design or construction techniques. Pre- and post-project erosion is an example of standard data items that should be collected in a standardized format and placed in a national spatially linked database. Many planning departments and zoning commissions already have and use all the equipment necessary to archive such information and make it easily available; the National Resources Conservation Service or the US Geological Survey could act as coordinating bodies, or take on the task as a centralized process. The availability of affordable data loggers and a huge range of sensors removes one of the last excuses for not collecting and sharing performance information.

Academic and practicing landscape architects, public and private sector, need to make such data a priority. Research on performance of sustainability techniques doesn't need to go on forever—just until there is clear evidence of what works, under what circumstances. (The advent of climate change adds both urgency and longevity to the need for performance data.) Best management practices for sustainable landscapes will never be as cut and dried as current engineering standards (and that is for the better); but they need to be far better grounded than today's methods in careful observation and measurement of actual performance.

Landscapes as Public Environmental Education

One often-overlooked power of the built landscape is to educate. Landscapes can tell the story—often eloquently—of a place and the people who use or used it. The story might focus on regional ecology, lost or displaced peoples, vernacular construction or planting or fuel traditions, or industrial and military archaeology.

Methods of storytelling in landscapes are varied, limited primarily by creativity. Interpretive signs and self-guided tours are simple and effective ways of narrating site history. Educational landscapes can go far beyond these basic methods, however.

This book describes several projects that show visitors something about ecological process. These were termed "eco-revelatory." Places of this sort have also been called "narrative landscapes" or "interpretive landscapes." Whatever they are called, and whatever methods of storytelling they use, such projects are an important tool for sustainability (along with many other purposes). They raise public awareness of landscape as a vital force in history and in contemporary life. Revealing and interpreting the landscape is a way of working against cultural tendencies that tempt people to ignore the landscape except when they are exploiting it.

Landscapes for schools, libraries, and museums are particularly suited as storytelling spaces. Gilbert AZ's Riparian Reserve (Figure 4.37), located next to the town library, is an example. Like a great number of constructed or restored wetlands, it has taken on functions traditionally associated with botanic gardens and nature centers.

Los Padillas Elementary School, in Albuquerque NM's South Valley, shows how a sustainable landscape can have double value as an educational facility. When an older sewage-treatment system failed odoriferously, Campbell Okuma Perkins Associates and Southwest Wetlands designed a constructed wetland on school grounds. With pathways, seating, and shelters around the wetland, the site fascinates schoolchildren and serves as an outdoor classroom for biology studies. The children of Los Padillas will grow up with fewer NIMBY and out-of-sight inhibitions than most of their peers, a direct result of familiarity with a sustainable landscape.

Jardin Encore (Figure 6.14) performs a similar service for recycling, making it familiar, beautiful, and fun. Every year, King County WA constructs a demonstration garden of recycled materials at the regional flower show. Like the grand prize recycled-products

Figure 12.1 Landscapes and education reflect each other perfectly. Students at Los Padillas Elementary School in Albuquerque NM are fascinated by the treatment wetland that serves their building—and learn about biology, ecology, and technology in lessons held outdoors. (*Project:* Campbell Okuma Perkins Associates and Southwest Wetlands. *Photo:* Kim Sorvig.)

house in the America Recycles Day contest (p. 263), these gardens educate by making recycling real and attractive.

Interpretive landscapes are needed that directly tell the story of sustainable place making. One of the best of these is Deneen Powell Atelier's Water Conservation Garden at Cuyamaca College, near San Diego. The story of how gardens are created, and how they can be more sustainable, gets a comprehensive and entertaining look. Serious information combines with magic and imagination, creating a connection that goes beyond either how-to demonstration gardens or fun-focused playgrounds.

Visiting places where remarkable things happened is a fascination for many people. At memorials, monuments, and historic sites, "being right there" creates a powerful experience that no distant book or museum can match. This same experience can be used to educate people about *natural history*, too, as evidenced by Riverwalk in Memphis TN.

Figure 12.2   DPA's Water Conservation Garden eloquently shows that San Diego is at the end of the California water-supply pipe. (*Project and Photo:* Deneen Powell Atelier.)

Riverwalk is a topographic model of the Lower Mississippi—and what a model! Built of concrete at one inch to the mile, it stretches the entire length of a previously deserted island in the great river itself. Riverwalk has transformed Mud Island from waste space into a major attraction. Water flows through the modeled meanders, past street maps of major cities inset into the concrete banks. Visitors, striding thirty "miles" at a step, get a clear and unforgettable sense of how the river works, enhanced by being able to look out onto the real river only yards away.

The redesign of Zion National Park goes one step further: the landscape itself was the focus of the project, around which even building design was organized. In fact, many functions of the visitor center were deliberately moved outdoors to immerse visitors in the landscape—and also save costs. Shuttle buses replaced private cars, again because of the impact on the landscape and on people's experience of this awesome place. Interpretive signage, which in most such parks

Figure 12.3   A giant purple pop-up head is a fantastic image for serious information—using non-potable water for irrigation (San Diego Water Conservation Garden). (*Project and Photo:* Deneen Powell Atelier.)

focuses exclusively on nature, points out the environmentally responsible and sustainable features of the park's human structures.

Public environmental knowledge and awareness are key factors in whether sustainability will ever be achieved. There is a built-in feedback loop: as more people are educated about sustainability, some percentage of them take action to make it happen, something increasingly crucial in the face of climate change. In designing and constructing sustainable landscapes, look for opportunities to tell site visitors what is going on. Whether it is a serious interpretive project or a whimsical use of recycled materials, the *story told* may be as important as the functions fulfilled.

Figure 12.4 (left) Landscapes can tell their own story eloquently. Riverwalk (Memphis TN) is a one-inch to one-mile topographic model of the entire Lower Mississippi, located on a sandbar in the river itself. (*Project:* Roy P. Farrover, FAIA. *Photo:* Kim Sorvig.)

Figure 12.5 (below) Zion National Park's majestic landscape drove the design of buildings, transportation, and interpretation—which includes information about how sustainable structures fit in. (*Project:* National Park Service, Denver Design Assistance Center. *Photo:* Kim Sorvig.)

Thinking One Hundred Years Ahead

In the last half of the twentieth century, Americans, along with much of the world's population, went from complacency about the environment to concern. Despite the usual tendency to shoot the messenger, the bad news was eventually turned into action: public outcry and changes in social expectations about how to treat the land. Landscape professionals played a significant role in that cycle of change, from speaking at the first Earth Day to getting environmental-impact assessment into standard practice. Ian McHarg's influence, in particular, stretched far beyond the garden wall and into the public hunger for environmental knowledge and connection that arose in the 1960s.

Today, a new or renewed cycle of change is under way. Many people feel alarm and despair over the state of planet Earth. As with any process of change, there is resistance and denial from entrenched interests, and understandable burnout among those who have lived with worry for too long. Yet simultaneously and in parallel, more and more people are taking action, if only because inaction is unbearable. Regulatory progress, despite attempts to roll it back, has reined in many sources of major pollution and brought conservation and restoration into common practice. Even the anti-regulators are forced to frame their cutbacks in green-wash terms, where a few decades ago, they could have plundered the planet without questions or opposition. This shows just how far sustainability, by any name, has become accepted as an ideal. In the next cycle, the action is in bringing change home, down to the details and difficult choices that affect the built environments where we live. In these actions, landscape professionals once again have important roles to play. Happily, students and young professionals are taking up this challenge in increasing numbers, along with many of their more established colleagues.

Documentable destruction has been so widespread that people have seriously questioned whether nature is dead or was merely a "construct," a nostalgic cultural superstition. But nature is not a thing; it is a dynamic process. If humans ignore it, nature will simply outlive us, bloodied but unbowed. Remembering that we are part of nature, and that it deserves care, respect, and in some places even privacy, is probably our last best hope for survival as a species. May the techniques and attitudes described in this book be part of realizing that fragile and essential hope.

Notes

Preface to the Third Edition

1. Based on the *2015 Green Building Economic Impact Study*, prepared by Booz Allen Hamilton for the US Green Building Council. Interpretation of growth relative to GOP and Democrat administrations is by the author.
2. Yes, this is normative language. There is room for discussion of specifics, but both the environmental and the political realities of 2017 demand norms that progressives stand for and act on, and overrule the idea that any "norm" is a violation of individual freedom.
3. The infamous disappearance of the caribou migration map under Bush/Cheney is an example.

Basic Principles: "Sustainability" in Context

1. Robert France, "The Promise and the Reality of Landscape Architecture in Sustaining Nature," Harvard Graduate School of Design newsletter (Spring–Summer 2003).
2. One of the latest instances of this persistent theme is Heidi Hohmann and Joern Langhorst, "Landscape Architecture: An Apocalyptic Manifesto," PDF downloadable from www.pub lic.iastate.edu/~isitdead.
3. Meg Calkins, "Green Building Practice Survey," *Landscape and Urban Planning* 73 (Oct 2005): 29.
4. Sonja Bisbee Wulff and Colorado Public Interest Research Group, "Vast Open Spaces Vanishing," *Fort Collins Coloradoan*, 28 Dec 1998, 1.
5. This definition is so widespread that its original author is hard to determine. It was used in the widely circulated report by the World Commission on Environment and Development, *Our Common Future*, ed. by Norway's prime minister, Gro H. Brundtland (Oxford: Oxford University Press, 1987). A similar but expanded definition is given in a review of sustainability concepts in John D. Peine, ed., *Ecosystem Management for Sustainability* (Boca Raton FL: Lewis, 1999), 3: "Sustainable development integrates economic, environmental and social values during planning; distributes benefits equitably across socioeconomic strata and gender upon implementation; and ensures that opportunities for continuing development remain undiminished to future generations." The ten published sets of sustainability principles reviewed (Peine's Tables 1–10) stress the dynamic, boundary-crossing, and semi-predictable qualities of living systems; the need for coordination and teamwork; and the value of open public involvement in sustainability decisions.
6. In "Nature/Culture/Words/Landscapes" (*Landscape Journal* 21, no. 2 [Jan 2002]: 1–14), I argue that Jackson used linguistic evidence very selectively to bolster his contention that landscape absolutely excludes any sort of wild, unconstructed place. His view is popular, but in my considered opinion, false, dangerous, and self-serving.
7. Robert L. Thayer Jr., "The Experience of Sustainable Design," *Landscape Journal* 8 (1989): 101. Quoted in Robert France's very useful article (above), "The Promise and the Re-

ality of Landscape Architecture in Sustaining Nature." The part of the CELA definition that may be questionable is the idea of increasing species diversity—valid for damaged sites, but potentially damaging if applied to healthy ones.
8. This recognition of human dependence on more-than-human causes can be viewed either scientifically or religiously. Saying that we can exist only because of nature's "services" is tantamount to saying that we exist by the grace of the divine. Unfortunately, there are too many literalists who react to any mention of nature as pagan and, on the other side, literalists who refuse to acknowledge the mystery that still surrounds all existence.
9. The principle was worked out by a group assembled by UNESCO and released in March 2005. A PDF of the report is available at http://unesdoc.unesco.org/images/0013 /001395/139578e.pdf.
10. "There is no doubt . . . that sustainability has been taken up as a rallying cry by two completely different factions and has entirely opposite meanings for each," according to James Steele, *Sustainable Architecture: Principles, Paradigms, and Case Studies* (New York: McGraw-Hill, 1997), 22. Steele calls the concept a contradiction in terms; his two factions are, loosely, green capitalists (the Earth as resources to manage) and green socialists (the Earth as the focus of social reform).
11. Tristan Roberts, "When It's Greener to Build," *EBN*, Oct 2007, 2.
12. BASMAA, *Grow It! The Less-Toxic Garden* (San Francisco: Bay Area Stormwater Management Agencies Association, 1997).
13. For thoughtful critique of the potential for authoritarianism in pursuit of ecological goals, see Randolph Hester, *Design for Ecological Democracy* (Cambridge MA: MIT Press, 2006). At the far extreme, an attempt to equate all ecologists with Nazism is analyzed in Kim Sorvig, "Natives and Nazis: An Imaginary Conspiracy in Ecological Design," *Landscape Journal* 13, no. 1 (1994): 58–61.
14. I was SO hoping, with poetic justice in mind, that the storm named Jose would decimate Mar-a-Lago!
15. *EBN* devoted almost the entire Nov 2013 issue to resilient design principles. Alex Wilson, founder of *EBN*, was the first to propose "passive survivability," in *EBN*, Dec 2005, 2; the magazine covered the topic in detail in the May 2006 issue.
16. To put things in perspective, recall that the Second Law of Thermodynamics guarantees that over the long term *nothing* is sustainable!
17. William Stanley Jevons, *The Coal Question*, 2nd ed. (London: Macmillan and Company, 1866), 123.
18. The concept also applies in agriculture; see Frank A. Ward and Manuel Pulido-Velazquez, "Water Conservation in Irrigation Can Increase Water Use," *Proceedings of the National Academy of Sciences* 105, no. 47 (Nov 2008): 18215–20.
19. A good source for contemporary understanding of the Jevons Paradox is J. Polimeni et al., *The Myth of Resource Efficiency: The Jevons Paradox*, rev. ed. (London: Earthscan, 2009). I've bor-

rowed their title for this section heading. In the foreword, Dr. Joseph A. Tainter, an anthropologist widely published on social complexity, social collapse, and energy issues, asserts that "voluntary restraint or any other *laissez-faire* approach" cannot solve the paradox. I respectfully submit that without a voluntary component, any imposed solution will ultimately fail.

20. See www.sinsofgreenwashing.org. There is some debate about alcoholic beverages and gluten; they can be contaminated by processing, or by cheap grain alcohol additions. If you prefer, think of this Sin as "no DDT used" but DDT is banned.

21. *The Course of Landscape Architecture* by Christophe Girot (London: Thames & Hudson, 2016). The comment about "instrumentalization" is from a *LAM* review of the book (Jan 2017, pp. 136–46) by Julia Czerniak; it's not clear whether she agrees with Girot on this point, since she objects to Girot's "exaggeration of the disparity between the concerns of ecology and those of design."

22. These evaluations are not intended to be equivalent to instrumented scientific measurement (such as energy inputs and outputs, for example), although they may be based on such studies.

23. Allyson Wendt, "Regional Real Estate Service to List Green Features," *EBN*, Nov 2006, 5; Tristan Roberts, "Appraising Green in Vancouver," *EBN*, May 2007, 4; Rachel Navaro, "New Green Training Program for Real Estate," *EBN*, Oct 2007, 5.

24. Tristan Roberts, "Higher Occupancy, Higher Lease Rates for Green Buildings," *EBN*, May 2008, 5; Nadav Malin, "Non-Green Office Buildings Sacrifice 8% in Rent Revenues," *EBN*, Dec 2010, 3.

25. Andrea Ward, "Preliminary Study Supports LEED Productivity Benefits," *EBN*, Jan 2011, 4; "Productivity and Green Buildings," *EBN*, Oct 2004, 1.

26. Nadav Malin, "Investing in the Environment: The Financial Industry's Approach to Green Building," *EBN*, Nov 2007, 1; Candace Pearson, "Retrofits a Better Bet Than Stocks and Bonds, Says Analysis," *EBN*, Jul 2013, 12. (The retrofits in question were to achieve green performance; as investments, they beat Wall Street's average by 28.6 percent.)

27. Interview in "Living Architecture Monitor" (Green Roofs for Healthy Cities newsletter), Winter 2016, 8–9.

28. Nadav Malin, "High Perceived Cost of Green Persists, Says Survey," *EBN*, Jan 2008, 2.

29. Candace Pearson, "Entry-Level Green Doesn't Cost Extra, U.K. Report Finds," *EBN*, Oct 2014, 14.

30. Allyson Wendt, "Study Finds Quick Payback for LEED Investments," *EBN*, Nov 2008 (news brief on a study by Moseley Architects, Richmond VA).

31. Malin, "Non-Green Office Buildings Sacrifice 8% in Rent Revenues."

32. *EBN* has covered increasing investor interest extensively, in Dec 2012, 3; Jan 2013, 3; Dec 2013, 3; and May 2014, 19. Not only individual projects but also real estate trusts, whose value depends on multiple properties, show higher returns when green. *EBN*, Jul 2015, 16.

33. *EBN*, "Productivity and Green Buildings," 11.

34. Meenakshi Rao et al., "Assessing the Relationship Among Urban Trees, Nitrogen Dioxide, and Respiratory Health," *En-*

vironmental Pollution 194 (Nov 2014): 96–104. Unfortunately, like most Elsevier publications, available only as pay-per-view.

35. Perry Hystad et al., "Residential Greenness and Birth Outcomes: Evaluating the Influence of Spatially Correlated Built-Environment Factors," *Environmental Health Perspectives* 122, no. 10 (Oct 2014); full text at https://ehp.niehs.nih .gov/1308049/.

36. J. F. Benson and M. H. Roe, eds., *Landscape and Sustainability* (London: Spon Press, 2000). Chapters 5–9 are specifically about the use of the landscape perspective as a basis for a variety of policy measures well outside of "landscape issues."

37. I owe this observation to Benoit Mandelbrot, the discoverer of fractals, who commented on it in a lecture in New Mexico, probably twenty years ago.

38. Unless otherwise noted, statistics and quotes in this section are from Meg Calkins, "LEEDing the Way: A Look at the Way Landscape Architects Are Using the LEED Green Building Rating System," *LAM*, May 2001, 36–44.

39. In fact, if they subscribe to Newt Gingrich's theories, any environmental limits on their right to develop constitutes a "taking" and gives them the right to sue whoever established that limit as a legal requirement. The US Supreme Court has repeatedly ruled otherwise, but this ideology of opportunism persists.

40. Erin Weaver, "Home Size, Appliance Glut Cancel Out Efficiency Gains," *EBN*, Apr 2013, 35; also Paula Melton, "Efficiency Gains Nullified by Appliances and Electronics," *EBN*, May 2012, 4. It is difficult to determine whether green residences are bloating equally to conventional homes (+30 percent since 2000), but for at least a part of the market, those who can afford luxury salve their consciences by including green features.

41. As McHarg himself growled to me twenty-plus years ago, "It's astonishing the bloody thing hasn't been superseded."

42. The terms "Permaculture" and "Xeriscape" have both been trademarked to ensure that they are not abused. Like all other trademarks referenced in this book, they remain the property of their respective owners. The success of trademarking landscape design approaches as a defensive strategy has been mixed, because most theories are recombinant, borrowing from and overlapping with others.

43. Allyson Wendt and Nadav Malin, "Integrated Design Meets the Real World," *EBN*, May 2010, 1.

44. Candace Pearson, "GSA Links High-Performance Outcomes to Integrated Design," *EBN*, Jul 2015, 13.

45. Sandra Mendler, ed., *The HOK Guidebook to Sustainable Design* (Washington DC: HOK Architects, 1998), iv–vi.

46. Ibid., iv.

47. In this regard, many architecture firms are either ahead of landscape ones, or simply more vocal about it. Arup, SOM, Gehry (whose focus is on complex structural coordination as much as, or more than, on sustainability), and many others recognize that if the built environment must change, the methods of envisioning and realizing require new teamwork.

48. One of the best sites for detailed information and research supporting these allegations is www.ejrc.cau.edu, the Environmental Justice Resource Center (EJRC) at Clark Atlanta University. It offers extensive links (many archived, others nonfunctional or dated) to hundreds of other sources. The information in this

section is primarily compiled from EJRC and a few of its main links. As of 2017, there appeared to be difficulties with links to EJRC from any other site, though directly entering the URL (above) still works to reach the archives.

49. Environmental justice applies to transportation facilities, many of which are risky and polluting. There is some evidence that EJ considerations have helped shape the Federal Highway Administration's recent shift toward "context-sensitive design" of roads, discussed on p. 240.

50. Dorceta Taylor, "The State of Diversity in Environmental Organizations," 2011 (original publication unclear). Available from www.diversegreen.org, but only by joining the group's mailing list. Taylor, a professor at the University of Michigan's School of Natural Resources and Environment, is also the author of two books noted in the resource list.

51. Kim Sorvig, "The Wilds of South Central," *LAM*, Apr 2002, reports on one of Hester and Edmiston's successful projects and on demographic research into cultural support for nature conservation.

52. Randolph T. Hester Jr., *Design for Ecological Democracy* (Cambridge MA: MIT Press, 2006), 6–7. The bibliography of this book lists extensive, landscape-specific resources on community participatory methods and environmental justice, including many important articles by Hester himself.

53. Reported in Jennifer Reut, "Open Invitation," *LAM*, Oct 2016, 66–74.

54. Jared Diamond, *Guns, Germs, and Steel: The Fates of Human Societies* (New York: Norton, 1997). Diamond's follow-up volume, *Collapse: How Societies Choose to Fail or Succeed* (New York: Viking, 2005), details how societies that fail to adapt to local ecological assets have collapsed. Both are required reading in my University of New Mexico seminar on sustainable landscapes.

55. See Adrian Wong, "How Correlated Are Crude Oil Prices to Finished Petroleum Products?," *Seeking Alpha*, 15 Feb 2015, http://seekingalpha.com/article/2918546-how-correlated -are-crude-oil-prices-to-finished-petroleum-products.

56. Rob Thayer made a particularly convincing presentation of these contextual threats at the Sustainable Landscapes Conference, Sacramento CA, Feb 2004.

57. For specifics, see the nonpartisan Natural Resources Defense Council's magazine *onEarth*, Spring 2003, esp. 10 and 34, and www.nrdc.org/bushrecord/.

58. Vinnee Tong, "Buying into Green Building," *Santa Fe New Mexican*, 8 Mar 2007, C-7. Cites "extra" cost for green features as up to 15 percent. This figure is more than double the more common figures (see next note) and appears to originate with building-industry conservatives.

59. H. M. Bernstein and M. A. Russo, "Green Multifamily and Single Family Homes: Growth in a Recovering Market" (McGraw-Hill Construction Research & Analytics, 2014), MHC_Analytics@McGraw-Hill.com. The authors, employees of MHC, were both LEED AP certified professionals.

60. "About Green Homes," 1 Jul 2016, www.usgbc.org/articles /benefits-green-homebuilding.

61. Earthtalk, "Do Buildings with Green Features Cost More?" *Santa Fe New Mexican*, 8 Mar 2007, C-7. Unlike industry reports, this one analyzes life-cycle savings, not just capital costs.

62. Brad Knickerbocker, "The Changing Face of America," *Christian Science Monitor*, 15 Oct 2006.

63. Gillian Flaccus, "Hispanics Take Strong Stands on Environment," Associated Press syndicated report, 13 Oct 2006. See related information in Sorvig, "Wilds of South Central."

64. See http://vertical-visions.com/nps.php, which discusses a fatal October 1999 protest against a National Park Service prohibition of "base jumping" (parachuting off cliffs).

65. Paula Melton, "Spurred by Chemical Industry, Ohio Moves Anti-LEED Bill Forward," *EBN*, Apr 2014, 14.

66. See *EBN* news briefs for May 2006, 2.

67. This matches well with the work of other researchers, particularly from Canada, who have found that in developed countries, construction, maintenance, and decommissioning of buildings uses over 40 percent of all annual energy. (The DOE statistics group energy by economic segment—residential, commercial, industrial, and transportation. Mazria's analysis recognizes that all segments use buildings, and regroups the statistics accordingly.)

68. Mazria's figures, quoted in *EBN*, Apr 2016, 1.

69. A 2007 UN report reached similar conclusions: United Nations Environment Programme, "Buildings and Climate Change: Status, Challenges, and Opportunities," available for download at www.unep.fr/shared/publications/pdf /DTIx0916xPA-BuildingsClimate.pdf.

70. Very similar goals, released in 1995 and targeted for achievement by 2003, were the National Building Goals, from the National Institute of Standards and Technology and the National Science and Technology Council. They aimed for a 50 percent reduction in operation and energy costs and in waste and pollution, along with a 50 percent increase in durability, across the construction industry. Available for download at http://fire.nist.gov/bfrlpubs/build95/PDF/b95068 .pdf. The official title is "National Construction Sector Goals," prepared by the Civil Engineering Research Foundation, Washington DC, July 1995, and issued under the identification number NIST-GCR-95-680.

71. See "Progress on 2030 Goals, Ten Years Later," *EBN*, Apr 2016, 4.

72. The first edition's source was "Study: Land Use Affects Weather," Associated Press syndicated report, 9 Dec 1998. The study's author, Roger Pielke, has a research group with many valuable publications related to land use and climate change. See http://cires.colorado.edu/research/research -groups/roger-pielke-sr-group.

73. Climate effects of land clearance (or landscape transformation, or land-use change) have been estimated by several expert groups. The estimates are listed in the citations that follow, in order from low to high. Some estimate CO_2 (or all greenhouse gases) released when land is cleared; others include direct warming and drying effects, such as exposure of soil to sunlight; and some summarize their findings in terms of the relative importance of fuel burning versus land clearing. The slow but extensive land changes wrought by prehistoric and early historical agriculture are also considered to have raised CO_2 levels, but these figure in only one discussion of the issue. Obviously, these estimates are not completely comparable, but all indicate that the relationship is significant.

15–20 percent: The lowest estimate comes from a 1997 World Meteorological Organization paper called "Common Questions About Climate Change," which states, "Land use changes are responsible for 15 to 20% of current carbon dioxide emissions." This useful document is downloadable (in English) at www.siame.gov.co/siame/documentos/documentacion/mdl/03_VF_Bibliografia/General%20CDM/Climate%20change.pdf. Pages are unnumbered; the statement quoted appears on the twelfth page (title page included).

23 percent: Cynthia Rosenzweig and Daniel Hillel, "Potential Impacts of Climate Change on Agriculture and Food Supply," *Consequences* (newsletter of the Global Change Research Information Office) 1, no. 2 (Summer 1995): agricultural emissions, 15 percent, plus land-use changes, 8 percent.

24 percent: Columbia University's CIESIN (Center for International Earth Science Information Network) and NASA's SEDAC (Socioeconomic Data and Applications Center) ascribe 24 percent of total greenhouse gas emissions to forestry practices and land-use change, including soil disturbance. See www.ciesin.columbia.edu/.

32 percent: The IPCC (Intergovernmental Panel on Climate Change) states that 2.5 Gt (gigatons, or million tons) of CO_2 are generated by landscape transformation, and 5.2 Gt by fuel combustion. This translates to 32 percent from land clearing and related changes. See www.ipcc.ch/.

50 percent or more: In an interview with Rebecca Lindsey of NASA's Earth Observatory (http://earthobservatory.nasa.gov/Study/DeepFreeze/, 17 May 2005), Gordon Bonan, a climate modeler for the National Center for Atmospheric Research in Boulder CO, stated, "Land cover change is as big an influence on regional and local climate and weather as doubled atmospheric carbon dioxide—perhaps even bigger." Bonan's findings agree with Pielke's, who he credits for "bringing people around to the importance" of landscape change as a factor in global climate change.

Tim Flannery, in *The Weather Makers* (New York: Atlantic Monthly Press, 2005), especially pp. 28 and 66, notes the likelihood that very early agriculture, from about 8,000 years ago to 1800 CE, when the Industrial Revolution took hold, increased global CO_2 levels from 160 parts per million (ppm) to 280. By comparison, the rise caused by industrialization is from 280 to 380 ppm, today's level. Clearing, burning, rice-paddy flooding, and other farming activities are thus believed to have created "The Long Summer," the unusually warm and stable period in which all agricultural humanity has lived for the past many millennia. If this is accurate, land clearance produced a 120-ppm increase prior to industrialization, and 15 to 32 percent of the 100-ppm increase since industrialization. This would mean that land use is responsible for **61 to 69 percent** of human-caused greenhouse gas increases.

74. The final report can be downloaded from www.eea.europa.eu/about-us/governance/scientific-committee/sc-opinions/opinions-on-scientific-issues/sc-opinion-on-greenhouse-gas/view. It was primarily concerned with conversion of land to produce biofuels; it is unclear whether land-conversion carbon emissions were included, but if not, this report would overstate the emissions benefit of using biofuels.

75. The report summary, and updates concerning lawsuits and investigations since its original 2007 release, are available from http://blog.ucsusa.org/tag/exxonclimatescandal#.WLRj000zUdU. It particularly links ExxonMobil money to "bought" science from the George C. Marshall Institute, the Annapolis Center for Science-Based Public Policy, the Committee for a Constructive Tomorrow, the Heartland Institute, and other climate-change deniers. This public disinformation campaign was in addition to over $60 million spent on lobbying politicians directly; one "expert" associated with it, Phil Cooney, went from an oil-trade association to the President's Council on Environmental Quality and then to ExxonMobil. Similar undermining tactics have been aimed against many specific sustainable technologies that threaten oil interests.

76. Wind and hydropower are nonfuel energy sources, driven by solar energy; nuclear power does not rely on combustion, and uranium is not a fuel in the conventional sense.

77. Paula Melton, "Our Buildings Are Killing Our Oceans," *EBN*, Apr 2016, 25.

78. For details, see www.grida.no/climate/ipcc/land_use/index.htm, "IPCC Special Report on Land Use, Land-Use Change, and Forestry." The mechanisms by which land clearance and deforestation affect climate are common knowledge; what is new is putting these effects together.

79. See Flannery, *Weather Makers*. Other CO_2-exchange mechanisms involve the oceans, oceanic plankton, and carbon-based rocks, such as limestone. These hold far larger *volumes* of carbon than do plants and soil, but it is the relative speed of the cycles of uptake and release that makes vegetation and soil the most important site of atmospheric CO_2 exchange. Fossil-fuel combustion is, of course, plant based.

80. Two identically titled books make a compelling case for the belief that soil management is the key to understanding any society's rise or fall: Edward Hyams's *Soil and Civilization* (New York: HarperCollins, 1976), and Milton Whitney's *Soil and Civilization* (New York: D. Van Nostrand Company, 1925). A third book with this title, by Elyne Mitchell, is an Australian work. Although out of print, it can be obtained electronically through http://soilandhealth.org/copyrighted-book/soil-and-civilization/.

81. "Clearance" does not need to be total to cause most of the warming effects noted. To be truly accurate, clearance should be discussed in percentage terms. One hundred percent clearance would mean bare soil. The baseline (0 percent clearance) is biomass, above- and below ground, that is equivalent to the region's most mature successional vegetation. Deliberate removal of 20 percent of this mass would be "20 percent clearance." If 100 percent clearance causes x amount of warming, 20 percent clearance probably causes similar effects at something like 20 percent intensity. There is probably a straightforward relationship between total biomass and the amount of carbon released by clearance, at least for a given forest or ecosystem type. These relationships cannot be quantified without further research, and are probably variable by region. Nonetheless, even one rule-of-thumb formula would greatly advance the ability to value vegetation cover for its effects on climate.

82. Alex Wilson and Rachel Navaro, "Driving to Green Buildings: The Transportation Energy Intensity of Buildings," *EBN*, Sep 2007.

83. Excerpt from Alex de Sherbinin, "A CIESIN Thematic Guide to Land-Use and Land-Cover Change (LUCC)," http://sedac.ciesin.columbia.edu/tg/guide_frame.jsp?rd=LU&ds=1,

joint project of CIESIN and the Land-Use and Land-Cover Change International Project Office, Louvain-la-Neuve, Belgium; see the website for further details.

84. Paul Hawken, *The Ecology of Commerce* (New York: Harper-Collins, 1993), 21.

85. Associated Press, "Housing Construction Booms; Industrial Output Flat in January," *Santa Fe New Mexican*, 18 Feb 1999.

86. For the full visual impact of forest clearance in the United States, see comparative maps in *Smithsonian*, Sep 1999, 22. For a global deforestation map, see www.greenpeace.org/international/campaigns/forests/our-disappearing-forests/.

87. "Lost to agriculture" is the United States Department of Agriculture (USDA) estimate; it is not specifically about clearing land that previously supported native vegetation communities. The 1.5 million-acre estimate is based on the US NRCS National Resources Inventory, which shows that in 1997, 98 million acres of US land had been developed, a 34 percent increase since 1982. Assuming the same rate each year (the rate is actually increasing), this would mean 1.6 million acres developed each year. The 500,000-acre estimate is based on new housing starts, commercial construction, and new roads statistics from various US agencies. These tend not to include accurate areas for landscape around the facilities.

88. Jessica Boehland, "California Builders Pay for Degrading Air Quality," *EBN*, Feb 2006, 3. See also the San Joaquin Valley Air Pollution Control District's website, www.valleyair.org.

89. A good place to start is Andrea Ward and Alex Wilson, "Design for Adaptation: Living in a Climate-Changing World," *EBN*, Sep 2009, 1, 8–15.

90. See Candace Pearson, "Analysis: Economy, Environment Merge to Speed Global Decline," *EBN*, Aug 2013, 18.

91. See "Projected CREAT Climate Scenarios," www.arcgis.com /home/item.html?id=a840e485bd5e495d8e72a32a9b3dc4a2.

92. Read (and sign) the document at https://lafoundation.org /news-events/2016-summit/new-landscape-declaration/.

93. Mahesh Ramanujam, "Staying Committed After the U.S. Withdrawal from the Paris Agreement," 1 Jun 2017, www .usgbc.org/articles/staying-committed-after-us-withdrawal -paris-agreement.

94. Statistics cited in Charles Lockwood, "Save the Shade," *Hemispheres Magazine* (United Airlines), Sep 2006, 60–63.

95. Wade Rawlins, "Scientists Test Trees in Fight vs. CO_2," *Raleigh (NC) News & Observer*, 28 Jul 2007.

96. Study by FPInnovations, a nonprofit research initiative of the Canadian timber industry; reported in Brent Ehrlich, "Engineering a Wood Revolution," *EBN*, Aug 2013, 1.

97. Earthtalk, "Which Trees Best Combat Global Warming?" *Environment*, 12 Feb 2007. See the research center's website, www.fs.fed.us/ne/syracuse/.

98. Paula Melton, "Biggest Trees Sequester the Most Carbon, Study Reveals," *EBN*, Mar 2014, 16.

99. Chris J. Hanley, "Carbon Trading Creates Questionable Deals," Associated Press syndicated report, 22 Oct 2006. For US state emissions totals and per-capita rankings, see www .eia.gov/environment/emissions/state/. To calculate your own CO_2 footprint, try the several online calculators—but be aware they assume you heat with oil or electricity (no solar, wood, etc.), drive a gas or diesel vehicle (sorry, Prius owners), and so on. Keep searching; there must be good ones out

there. The IPCC recently estimated that increasing the cost of gasoline by one dollar per gallon would fund stabilization of greenhouse gases by 2030; this cost has also been compared to about 3 percent of economic growth worldwide. Marc Kaufman, "Scientists Put Price Tag on Strategies to Combat Global Warming," *Washington Post*, 3 May 2007.

100. "First Look," *Consumer Reports*, Jan 2007, 7.

101. Lewis Ziska, weed ecologist, USDA Crop Systems and Global Change Laboratory, quoted in *Life* (author unknown), 25 Aug 2006.

102. Study by J. Dunne, NOAA, published in *Nature Climate Change*, cited in *EBN*, Apr 2013, 27.

103. Zhanqing Li et al., "Long-Term Impacts of Aerosols on the Vertical Development of Clouds and Precipitation," *Nature Geoscience* 4 (2011): 888–94; see also University of Maryland, U.S. Department of Energy's Brookhaven National Laboratory, and Pacific Northwest National Laboratory, "Rising Air Pollution Worsens Drought, Flooding UMD-Led Study Shows," www.bnl.gov/newsroom/news.php?a=111345, cited in *EBN*, Aug 2014, 4.

104. John Roach, "Summer Storms to Create New Ozone Holes as Earth Warms?," *National Geographic News*, 26 Jul 2012, http:// news.nationalgeographic.com/news/2012/07/120726 -storms-ozone-hole-global-warming-environment-science/.

105. Bettina Boxall, "West's Trees Dying Faster as Temperatures Rise," *Los Angeles Times*, 23 Jan 2009. This author also won a Pulitzer Prize for reporting on climate-induced increases in wildfire.

106. Dave Gram, "Climate Change Blamed for Fading Foliage," Associated Press, 21 Oct 2007. Online at www.washington post.com/wp-dyn/content/article/2007/10/20/AR2007 102000534_pf.html.

107. Marc Kaufman, "Katrina, Rita Caused Forestry Disaster," *Washington Post*, 16 Nov 2007.

108. J. "A Significant Upward Shift in Plant Species Optimum Elevation During the 20th Century," *Science* 320, no. 5884 (27 Jun 2008): 1768–71. Online at www.ncbi.nlm.nih.gov /pubmed/18583610.

109. Jessica Boehland, "USDA Resists Updating Plant Hardiness Zones to Reflect Warming Trend," *EBN*, Aug 2006, 4.

110. See http://planthardiness.ars.usda.gov/phzmweb/About WhatsNew.aspx. The Arbor Day Foundation has also updated its maps, available at www.arborday.org/media/zone changes.cfm.

111. See www.telegraph.co.uk/news/worldnews/asia/japan/26 60948/Kyoto-protocol-fails-to-save-the-Japanese-citys -famous-Zen-gardens.html.

112. Rachel Kaplan and Stephen Kaplan have explored this concept in several books, including *The Experience of Nature: A Psychological Perspective* (Cambridge: Cambridge University Press, 1989).

113. E. O. Wilson, *Biophilia* (Cambridge MA: Harvard University Press, 1986).

114. William Browning, Catherine Ryan, and Joseph Clancy, "14 Patterns of Biophilic Design," Terrapin Bright Green, www .terrapinbrightgreen.com/reports/14-patterns/, available free to download. The site also discusses economics of biophilic design.

115. Alex Wilson, "Biophilia in Practice: Buildings That Connect People with Nature," *EBN*, Jul 2006.

116. Robert L. Thayer Jr., "The Experience of Sustainable Landscapes," *Landscape Journal* 8, no. 2 (Fall 1989): 101–10.

117. Joan Nassauer, "Messy Ecosystems, Orderly Frames," *Landscape Journal* 14, no. 2 (Fall 1995): 161–70.

118. William MacElroy and Daniel Winterbottom, "Toward a New Garden," *Critiques of Built Works of Landscape Architecture*, LSU School of Landscape Architecture (Fall 1997): 10–14.

119. William Thompson, "Cleansing Art," *LAM*, Jan 1997, 70.

120. The Landschaftspark has been described in many publications; an interesting perspective is Hugh Bailey, "Decaying Factories Become Vital Tourist Attractions," *Connecticut Post*, 6 Dec 2014, www.ctpost.com/local/article/Decaying-factories-become-vital-tourist-5925249.php.

121. Participants in the Committee for Eco-Revelatory Design were Brenda Brown, Terry Harkness, Douglas Johnston, Beth Randall, and Robert Riley.

122. Peter Whoriskey, "Louisiana Erosion Project Calls for River Diversion," *Washington Post*, 2 May 2007, 5.

123. Cain Burdeau, Associated Press, "New Land in Eroding Louisiana Wetlands Provides Cause for Hope," *New Orleans Times-Picayune*, 1 Sep 2011, www.nola.com/environment/index.ssf/2011/09/new_land_in_eroding_louisiana.html.

124. Benoit Mandelbrot, *The Fractal Geometry of Nature*, updated ed. (New York: W. H. Freeman, 1983). Although many other books (and movies!) have built on Mandelbrot's work, this remains a classic explanation of a truly revolutionary new discipline. See esp. chapter 1, "Theme"; for a straightforward graphic that explains the concept of fractals, see the Koch snowflake illustrations on pp. 42–44.

125. J. W. Baish et al., "Fractal Characteristics of Tumor Vascular Architecture: Significance and Implications," *Microcirculation* 4 (1997): 395–402.

126. These studies continue to find health benefits from strictly visual contact with fractal forms. See Hystad et al., "Residential Greenness and Birth Outcomes," note 35 above.

127. For an overview of this research, see John P. Wiley Jr., "Help Is on the Way," *Smithsonian*, Jul 1999, 22–24.

128. "Wild" is another difficult term. Most places on Earth are in some way influenced by human management, politics, pollution, or preservation. In this sense, no place is pristine. This fact is not, in my view, an excuse for failing to preserve those places that are closest to being wild, those that are most nearly self-sustaining. It is not the romance of being untouched that makes these places important, but rather what they show about the dynamics of biodiversity and how they preserve diversity lost elsewhere. Further discussion in Kim Sorvig, "Nature/Culture/Words/Landscapes," *Landscape Journal* 21, no. 2 (2002): 1–14.

129. See www.ftc.gov/enforcement/rules/rulemaking-regulatory-reform-proceedings/green-guides. Green Guides are properly known as "Guides for the Use of Environmental Marketing Claims" (www.ftc.gov/policy/federal-register-notices/guides-use-environmental-marketing-claims-green-guides, 11 Oct 2012). The Guides do not mention landscapes, focusing on claims of nontoxicity or recycled content in products. Odds are the Trump administration will kill the Guides if they notice their existence.

130. George Hazelrigg, "Peeling Back the Surface," *LAM*, Apr 2006, 112.

131. For details, see Michael Leccese, "No Shrinking Columbine," *LAM*, Nov 2003, 84.

132. The exhibition catalog, by the same title, is available from Princeton Architectural Press.

133. Mary Beth Breckenridge, "Green and Gorgeous: Designers Help Environmentalism Go Upscale," *Akron (OH) Beacon*, 27 Nov 2005.

134. Meg Calkins, "Assignment: Eco-Friendly Campuses," *LAM*, Jul 2002, 38.

135. Mary Padua, "Touching the Good Earth," *LAM*, Jan 2006, 100.

136. André Viljoen, ed., *Continuous Productive Urban Landscapes: Designing Urban Agriculture for Sustainable Cities* (London: Architectural Press, 2005).

137. Calkins, "Assignment," 40.

138. Peggy Barlett and Geoffrey Chase, eds., *Sustainability on Campus: Stories and Strategies for Change* (Cambridge MA: MIT Press, 2004), p. 5. The book contains one chapter on a native-plant experiment; the other chapters range from integrating environmental lessons throughout the curriculum to organizing faculty and staff initiatives.

139. "A New Option for Afterlife," *EBN*, Mar 1999.

140. Edvard Munch, *Kunskabens Træ på godt og ondt*, p. T 2547A41. This work is an unpublished scrapbook that Munch made himself; parts of it were published in *Edvard Munch: Symbols and Images*, an exhibition catalog from the National Gallery, Washington DC, 1978. Thanks to Gerd Woll and Tor Edvin Dahl, of Oslo, for tracking down this quotation's real source.

141. Memorial Ecosystems, www.memorialecosystems.com/.

142. Although in theory land preservation could be accomplished while retaining conventional sealed-casket burials, the degree of land disturbance caused by this approach reduces the "fit" considerably. It would, however, reduce the pesticide and energy inputs currently required to maintain the barren mono-cultural landscapes found in most conventional cemeteries.

143. Information on greening the slopes comes from two sources: a syndicated article by the editors of *E* magazine, "Ski Resorts Try to Cut Damage They Do," 10 Dec 2001, and the website of the National Ski Areas Association, www.nsaa.org/.

144. National Ski Areas Association, *Sustainable Slopes Annual Report 2016*, www.nsaa.org/media/276021/SSAR2016.pdf.

145. K. Sorvig, "Renewing Zion," *LAM*, Nov 2001, 62.

146. Brian Skoloff, "Remodeling of Yosemite Pits Preservation Against Access," Associated Press, 14 Dec 2003. The criticisms, from a group called Friends of Yosemite Valley, are disputed by (among others) the National Parks Conservation Association.

147. See http://caselaw.findlaw.com/hi-supreme-court/1440543.html. The case was dismissed on December 6, 2002, by the Hawaii Supreme Court, to the immense relief of tourism promotion boards everywhere. The court ruled that the Sierra Club lacked standing (legal right to sue) because the club itself had no concrete interest that would be damaged by the tourism advertising—only the environment would be damaged! This argument has repeatedly been abused to make it impossible to sue to defend public lands. The case was appealed back and forth, the legislature in special session wrote a law tailored to the desires of a specific tourist transport company, and a (probably) final decision was rendered in 2009.

148. L. A. G. Moss, ed., *The Amenity Migrants: Seeking and Sustaining Mountains and Their Cultures* (Cambridge MA: CABI, 2006), 5.

149. Among them the Centers for Disease Control and Prevention and the Robert Wood Johnson Foundation. An overview report on the relationship between urban landscapes and obesity appeared in *USA Today* (Martha T. Moore, "Walk, Can't Walk," 23 Apr 2003).

150. See, for example, Nick Dephtereos, "Young Residents, New Businesses Flock to Old Neighborhoods," *EBN*, Jul 2014, 12.

Principle 1: Keep Healthy Sites Healthy

1. Conversely, Ian McHarg often compared *humans* to a planetary disease, noting how sprawling modern cities seen from on high look like mold growths.

2. Paul R. Ehrlich et al., "No Middle Way on the Environment," *Atlantic Monthly*, Dec 1997, 98–104. See especially p. 101, which lists environmental services and states, "These services operate on such a grand scale, and in such intricate and little-explored ways, that most of them could not be replaced by technology—even if no expense were spared, as Biosphere 2 showed."

3. Hard figures on this perennial subject are surprisingly rare. Federal courts have ruled that loss of a single mature tree reduced property value by 9 percent, and have ruled on tree-specific financial losses in other cases. The Urban Land Institute, in a study cosponsored by ASLA (but involving only architects and development experts in actual research), considers the perception that landscape adds to property value as believable but unproven due to lack of quantification. Developers interviewed for the study indicated a 5 percent increase in value for individual gardens and a 20 percent increase for public landscape amenities affecting the whole development (this increase equals six times the extra construction cost for the amenities). Presumably these figures relate to newly installed landscaping. Lloyd W. Bookout, Michael D. Beyard, and Steven W. Fader, *Value by Design: Landscape, Site Planning, and Amenities* (Washington DC: Urban Land Institute and American Society of Landscape Architects, 1994). Other anecdotal evidence tends to be in this range, though I have heard realtors state that mature landscapes can add 75 percent to the sale price of a home. Appraisers are more likely than developers to know values for mature landscapes, and a study of appraising formulas would probably be revealing. Some wonderfully varied estimates of the value of specific trees are shown in Table 3.1, p. 158.

4. Floyd Swink and Gerould Wilhelm, *Plants of the Chicago Region*, 4th ed. (Indianapolis: Indiana Academy of Science, 1994); supplanted by Gerould Wilhelm and Laura Rericha, *Flora of the Chicago Region: A Floristic and Ecological Synthesis* (Indianapolis: Indiana Academy of Science, 2017).

5. See http://universalfqa.org/. Free registration is required.

6. Thanks to Leslie Sauer for acquainting me with this approach to site health.

7. See chapter 1 of John D. Peine, *Ecosystem Management for Sustainability* (Boca Raton FL: CRC Press, 1998).

8. For an overview and links, see www.santafe.edu/.

9. James S. Russell, "Wetlands Dilemma," *Architectural Record*, Jan 1993, 36–39. The architect was Elide Albert.

10. Thanks to staff at Holman's surveying supply in Albuquerque (www.holmans.com/) for up-to-the-minute information, first on GPS and, for this edition, on drones.

11. GPS satellites also "rise and set" in the sky; at some times of day, this may affect surveying.

12. As early as the 2000 edition, we noted a static, non-GPS-linked form of LiDAR used for structural surveys and predicted, "Sustainable work may someday benefit from advanced tools that offer better understanding of the dynamics of each site." UAS bring this hope a long step closer.

13. David Bird and Dominique Chabot, "Can Drones Help Our Wildlife?," *Ontario Professional Surveyor*, Summer 2015, 8–11. Based on research posted at www.nrcresearchpress.com/journal/juvs, special virtual issue on wildlife of the *Journal of Unmanned Vehicle Systems*.

14. Daniel Tal, "More Than Toys," *LAM*, Mar 2017, 38–40.

15. Cost range is from Robert Galvin, "Drones Earn Their Place in Surveying," *Point of Beginning*, 1 Feb 2016, www.pobonline.com/articles/98067-drones-earn-their-place-in-surveying. Prices are likely to drop, as for most electronics, as more users adopt UAS. Galvin points out that a single conventional aerial photo flight can cost $10,000; thus, a UAS could pay for itself, based on purchase cost alone, after five projects.

16. For more on Public Lab, see Jennifer Reut, "Open Invitation," *LAM*, Oct 2016, 66–74.

17. Herb Schaal, FASLA, is a master of such methods; see K. Sorvig, "Drawing the Experience of Place," *LAM*, Oct 2005, 170–78.

18. Samira Jafari, "Google Earth Used to Show Effects of Mining," Associated Press syndicated report, 5 Nov 2006.

19. Microsoft's Virtual Earth, released in 2006, appears to have little if any presence in the design world.

20. The parent company, Placeways, was purchased in December 2016 by City Explained, http://communityviz.city-explained.com/.

21. The thread is at https://forums.autodesk.com/t5/autocad-forum/autodesk-software-for-landscape-architects/td-p/5625174; there is no guarantee that it will remain posted indefinitely.

22. Jonathan Lerner, "The Toolmaker," *LAM*, Apr 2017, 92–104.

23. The original design was by Tower Optical Company of Norwalk CT, which began making these iconic tourist-trap fixtures in 1932. The term "owl-ized" refers to the viewer looking like an owl's face.

24. Concerns about the aging grid work toward better records; fear of terrorism works against it.

25. For some utilities, it is desirable to have a wide legal easement to keep trespassers away, but the full width does not need to be clear-cut.

26. Stuart H. McDonald, "Prospect," *LAM*, Sep 1993, 120.

27. Formerly Edison Field.

28. "U.S. Tower Counts and Site Information Are Often Inaccurate and Purposely Misleading," *Wireless Estimator*, http://wirelessestimator.com/articles/2015/u-s-tower-counts-and-site-information-are-often-inaccurate-and-purposely-misleading/. See also Ben Campanelli, "Planning for Cellular Towers," *Planning Commissioners Journal* 28 (1997): 4.

29. An example is the cell-and-clock tower at Arroyo del Oso Golf Course in Albuquerque, where city council members attempted to require that cell towers be concealed.

30. Robert L. Thayer Jr., *Gray World, Green Heart* (New York: Wiley, 1994), 46.

31. Jon Frandsen, "System Uses Cable Instead of Towers," Gannet News Service, 22 Mar 1998.

32. John Schaeffer, ed., *Solar Living Sourcebook*, 9th ed. (Ukiah CA: Real Goods, 1996), 374–76, 546.

33. Knight Ridder News, "Devices Will Let Households Generate Power, Experts Say," *Santa Fe New Mexican*, 7 Jul 1999, A4.

34. Center for Watershed Protection, "Model Development Principles to Protect Our Streams, Lakes, and Wetlands" (Ellicott City MD: Center for Watershed Protection, 1998). The specific guideline, Principle 19, p. 15: allowable clearing distance. It is based on 1991 standards from the Maryland Department of Natural Resources.

35. Phillip J. Craul, *Urban Soil in Landscape Design* (New York: Wiley, 1992), 135–37.

36. Ibid., 109.

37. Ibid., 45. The original gives figures per gram of soil; converted by me.

38. William Thompson, "A Long Road to Freedom," *LAM*, Feb 1998, 50–55.

39. See note 3 above.

40. Ann Brenoff, "Locution, Locution, Locution," *Los Angeles Times*, 14 Jan 2007, discusses various effects of wording in real-estate listings.

41. R. J. Hauer, R. W. Miller, and D. M. Ouimet, "Street Tree Decline and Construction Damage," *Journal of Arboriculture* 20, no. 2 (1994): 94–97.

42. See I. R. Jones et al., "Detection of Large Woody Debris Accumulations in Old-Growth Forests Using Sonic Wave Collection," *Transactions of the Important Tree Scientists* 120, no. 2 (Mar 2002): 201–9, www.scq.ubc.ca/detection-of-large -woody-debris-accumulations-in-old-growth-forests-using -sonic-wave-collection/.

43. Washington Department of Fish and Wildlife, "Living with Wildlife: Snags—the Wildlife Tree," http://wdfw.wa.gov/liv ing/snags/snags.pdf. A useful reference, downloadable.

44. Craul, *Urban Soil*, 137.

45. Robert Adams Ivy Jr., *Fay Jones* (Washington DC: AIA Press, 1992), 35.

46. Donald Hoffmann, *Frank Lloyd Wright's Fallingwater: The House and Its History* (New York: Dover, 1985).

47. Information from a photocopied graph attributed to AASHTO; title and date unknown.

48. Lisa Cowan and David Cowan, "Review of Methods for Low Impact Restoration," paper presented at the ASLA 1997 Annual Meeting.

49. Karl Vick, "Closed-Door Deal Could Open Land in Montana," *Washington Post*, 5 Jul 2008. Through at least 2015, Plum Creek's dealings remained in the news, in part because the company merged with Weyerhaeuser.

50. Kathleen Corish, *Clearing and Grading Strategies for Urban Watersheds* (Washington DC: Metropolitan Washington Council of Governments, 1995). European laws protecting trees, forests, and special land types are also worth studying.

51. Alex Wilson, "Dewees Island: More Than Just a Green Development," *EBN*, Feb 1997, 5–7. Descriptions that follow are from this article.

Principle 2: Heal Injured Soils and Sites

1. The EPA defines brownfields as "abandoned, idled or underused industrial/commercial facilities where expansion or redevelopment is complicated by real or perceived environmental contamination," a typically politic definition. Quoted by Alex Wilson, editor of *EBN*; personal correspondence.

2. Full project descriptions are on the ASLA's website, by year; see www.asla.org/honorsawards.aspx. It is possible that other brownfields won awards but escaped my attention.

3. Sam Roberts, "Bloomberg Administration Is Developing Land Use Plan to Accommodate Future Populations," *New York Times*, 26 Nov 2006.

4. See www.epa.gov/brownfields. This is the home page for the EPA's Brownfields program, containing (at present) many sources of information on brownfields and the legal and financial aspects of cleanup.

5. Derek Caney, "Friday Morning Briefing: 'The Atmosphere Has Become Toxic,'" Reuters, 3 Mar 2017, www.reuters.com /article/us-newsnow-leaks-idUSKBN16A15O, accessed 5 Mar 2017.

6. Nathan Kensinger, "Surveying the NYC Toxic Sites Owned by the Trump Family," *Curbed NY*, 9 Feb 2017, http://ny .curbed.com/2017/2/9/14551480/new-york-superfund -epa-donald-trump-jared-kushner.

7. Historic restoration is primarily a concept from architectural preservation, and even for buildings, picking the date to re-create is not always simple. See Kim Sorvig, "Relocating History," 2004 proceedings of ALHFAM annual conference (Association of Living History and Farm Museums), from www.alhfam.org/.

8. Information on the Yuma restoration is primarily from K. Sorvig, "The Same River Twice," *Landscape Architecture* 99, no. 11 (2009): 42–53, and interview notes for that article. For other information sources, see the resource list.

9. Rural decline can create similar conditions and may benefit from similar efforts.

10. Linn's vision, never implemented in Newark, was expressed in *From Rubble to Restoration*, published by Earth Island Institute, www.earthisland.org/. This brief, out-of-print title is still relevant if a used copy can be found.

11. For one US example of this approach, as part of the United Nations' Man and the Biosphere Programme, see John D. Peine, ed., *Ecosystem Management for Sustainability* (Boca Raton FL: Lewis, 1999).

12. See www.alemanyfarm.org/history/. According to articles in this archive, SLUG's management billed the city for gardener hours spent campaigning for a mayoral candidate, and subsequently dissolved. Reportedly, most of the garden legacy of the group persists.

13. Philadelphia's active community-garden movement has been a driving force in many "greening" initiatives that link human needs and environmental restoration. The city has an Office of Sustainability; its current programs and visions are described in Jim Kenney, "Greenworks: A Vision for a Sustainable Philadelphia," https://beta.phila.gov/media/20161101174249 /2016-Greenworks-Vision_Office-of-Sustainability.pdf.

14. O. L. Gilbert, *The Ecology of Urban Habitats* (London: Chapman and Hall, 1989), 40.

15. "Activists Rescue New York's Community Gardens," *Washington Post*, 13 May 1999.

16. Peter Bareham, "A Brief History," *Landscape Design*, Apr 1986.

17. Michael Lancaster and Tom Turner, "The Sun Rises over Liverpool," *Landscape Design*, Apr 1984, 36.

18. Rodney Beaumont, "Focus on the Festivals," *Landscape Design*, Jul–Aug 1992, 18.

19. Jon E. Lewis, "How Green Is My Valley," *Landscape Design*, Jul–Aug 1992, 11.

20. Andrew Grant, "Life on Earth," *Landscape Design*, May 1993, 33.

21. Jane Porter, "The Earth Center," *Landscape Design*, Feb 1996, 12.

22. Grant, "Life on Earth," 33.

23. Michael Ezban, "The Trash Heap of History: How Rome's Ancient Landfill Can Inform Contemporary Reclamation Projects," *Places Journal*, May 2012, https://placesjournal.org/article/the-trash-heap-of-history/?gclid=COL0mOKHw9ICFYa4wAodY3MOwA.

24. Joakim Krook and Leenard Baas, "Getting Serious About Mining the Technosphere: A Review of Recent Landfill Mining and Urban Mining Research," *Journal of Cleaner Production* 55 (15 Sep 2013): 1–9.

25. Joseph M. Suflita et al., "The World's Largest Landfill," *Environmental Science and Technology* 26, no. 8 (Aug 1992): 1486–95.

26. Peter Harnik, Michael Taylor, and Ben Welle, "From Dumps to Destinations: The Conversion of Landfills to Parks," *Places: Forum for Design of the Public Realm* 18, no. 1 (2006): 85.

27. This was Massachusetts's first effluent reuse project, according to CDM, and important because of Cape Cod's limited freshwater resources. Strict monitoring protects the aquifer.

28. Wolfram Hoefer et al., "Unique Landfill Restoration Designs Increase Opportunities to Create Urban Open Space," *Environmental Practice* 18 (2016): 106–15. Available at https://cues.rutgers.edu/publications/Hoefer_et_al_2016.pdf.

29. A. D. Bradshaw, "Landfill Sites—Outstanding Opportunities for Amenity and Wildlife," paper presented at *Design Now for the Future: End-Use of Landfills*, Nov 1992. Bradshaw is a researcher at the University of Liverpool. Similar findings by M. C. Dobson and A. J. Moffat, in "The Potential for Woodland Establishment on Landfill Sites" (publisher and date unknown), resulted in rescinding a British directive against trees on capped landfills. Further supporting these findings, no problems have been reported from closed-landfill festival gardens that include trees.

30. William Young, "Creation of Coastal Scrubforest on Landfill," *Land and Water* 40, no. 1 (Jan–Feb 1996): 6.

31. James Corner Field Operations, "Fresh Kills Park: Lifescape, Staten Island New York, Draft Master Plan," prepared for the City of New York, Mar 2006.

32. Hoefer et al., "Unique Landfill Restoration Designs," 114.

33. See Mira Engler, *Designing America's Waste Landscapes* (Baltimore: Johns Hopkins University Press, 2004). Although greatly overstated, this book raises many points about US attitudes toward waste.

34. Kathleen Spain, "Get It Right at the Start," *Waste Age*, Feb 1993, 57.

35. For an interesting look at the lives of reforestation workers, see Hélène Cyr, *Handmade Forests: The Treeplanter's Experience* (Stony Creek CT: New Society Publishers, 1999).

36. See www.habitatnow.com/index.htm for information. Financial return on restoration often involves enrolling in the federal agricultural Conservation Reserve Program or similar programs. Revegetation against global warming may produce parallel opportunities for nonagricultural restoration.

37. See note 124 in "Basic Principles," concerning fractal geometry.

38. Both quotes are from Horst Schor, "Landform Grading: Building Nature's Slopes," *Pacific Coast Builder*, Jun 1980, 80–83.

39. Gullying is "damage" from a conventional perspective and can literally undermine vegetation trying to reestablish a foothold. In the longer view, however, gullying is nature's first step in restoring the landform to its proper, irregular shape. The flatter and steeper a slope, the more destructively gullying attacks, until erosion and deposition begin to come back into dynamic equilibrium—something that can take far too long for human purposes. See note 41 below on the diffusion model.

40. Horst Schor and Donald Gray, "Landform Grading and Slope Evolution," *Journal of Geotechnical Engineering* 121, no. 10 (Oct 1995): 729–34. Full text is available (for a fee) online at http://ascelibrary.org/doi/10.1061/%28ASCE%290733-9410%281995%29121%3A10%28729%29.

41. See D. B. Nash, "The Evolution of Abandoned, Wave-Cut Bluffs in Emmet County, Michigan," PhD diss., University of Michigan, 1977. This research supports the "diffusion model" of slope formation, which states that natural processes optimize slope forms so that materials removed upslope balance downslope deposition. The resulting slope cross-section is an S-curve; top and toe of the slope are both rounded. As Schor points out, this model strongly indicates that "a planar slope with constant inclination, typical of conventional grading practice, is not a stable, long-term equilibrium slope" (732).

42. Schor and Gray, "Landform Grading and Slope Evolution," 732.

43. John Haynes, "Stepped Slopes: An Effective Answer to Roadside Erosion," *Landscape Architect and Specifier News*, Feb 1990, 31.

44. Joseph A. Todd, *Some Experiences in Stepping Slopes* (Gatlinburg TN: FHWA Bureau of Public Roads, 1967).

45. William Comella (FHWA Regional Engineer, Arlington VA), interview, 28 Jul 1971.

46. Phillip J. Craul, *Urban Soil in Landscape Design* (New York: Wiley, 1992), 237.

47. Ibid., 237.

48. Ibid., 239.

49. See, for example, P. Newman and J. Kenworthy, *Sustainability and Cities: Overcoming Automobile Dependence* (Washington DC: Island Press, 1998).

50. William Thompson, "Banking on a River," *LAM*, Sep 1998, 50–55.

51. See www.cbf.org/.

52. Examples of this in the mega-ditches of Albuquerque have been documented by Paul Lusk, former city planner and professor of architecture and planning, University of New Mexico.

53. J. G. Bockheim, quoted in Craul, *Urban Soil*, 86.

54. For example, Leslie Sauer, *The Once and Future Forest* (Washington DC: Island Press, 1998), 154–57, discusses soil protec-

tion and restoration. This is an excellent source for details on forest protection and restoration.

55. Based primarily on Craul, *Urban Soil*, 290–91.

56. V. P. Claassen and R. J. Zasoski, *The Effect of Topsoil Reapplications on Vegetation Reestablishment* (Sacramento: California Department of Transportation, 1994).

57. Orus L. Bennet, "Land Reclamation," in *McGraw-Hill Encyclopedia of Environmental Science and Engineering*, ed. Sybil Parker and Robert Corbitt (New York: McGraw-Hill, 1993), 329.

58. For a complete description of this project, see Sauer, *Once and Future Forest*.

59. Richard Wolkomir, "Unearthing Secrets Locked Deep Inside Each Fistful of Soil," *Smithsonian*, Mar 1997, 74–84. Wolkomir interviews scientists at the Soil Tilth Laboratory, Iowa State University. One of the interviewees comments about the ripping out of native vegetative communities that "agriculture is a violent activity."

60. Data on performance are from www.agrobotics.com/ as of 2017.

61. Simon Leake, "Reuse of Site Soils," *Landscape Australia*, Aug 1995.

62. Gilbert, *Ecology of Urban Habitats*, 47–51.

63. Ezban, "Trash Heap of History"—see note 23 above.

64. Sauer, *Once and Future Forest*, 156.

65. Robert Nold, *Penstemons* (Portland OR: Timber Press, 1999), 24. Elsewhere he notes that penstemons occur in severe soils considered so useless for agriculture or development that they are often the locations of reservoirs "built to satisfy the unquenchable thirst of endless expanses of compulsively planted lush green lawns" (52).

66. Whitney Cranshaw, *Pests of the West* (Golden CO: Fulcrum Publishing, 1992), chapter 1. See also Sauer, *Once and Future Forest*, chapters 17 and 22.

67. Davidson, D. J., "Organic Growers Take Note: There Is Such a Thing as Organic Gypsum," 14 Aug 2014, www.eco-gem .com/organic-growers-take-note-thing-organic-gypsum/. The website www.eco-gem.com/ belongs to a supplier of gypsum; it has useful, if not entirely unbiased, information on usage and benefits.

68. The website www.bartlett.com has research publications and sales brochures concerning biochar.

69. S. Abiven, M. W. I. Schmidt, and J. Lehmann, "Biochar by Design," *Nature Geoscience* 7 (2014): 326–27.

70. Kyna Rubin, "Root Cause," *LAM*, Apr 2017, 40. The same organisms are important in phytoremediation and bioremediation (see pp. 124–126).

71. Donna Mitchell, *Compost Utilization by Departments of Transportation in the United States* (Gainesville: University of Florida, Department of Environmental Horticulture, 1997), 8.

72. Ibid., 9.

73. US EPA, www.epa.gov/recycle/composting-home. This appears to replace the EPA composting Fact Sheet, published Sep 2015, cited in the second edition.

74. "Breakthroughs," *Discover*, Jul 1994, 18.

75. Mitchell, *Compost*, 16.

76. Ibid., 14.

77. For information, go to www.compostingcouncil.org/index .cfm and look for the tab labeled "Programs: STA & ICAW" (the full name of the testing program is not spelled out on the home page).

78. A practical guide is Michael Phillips, *The Holistic Orchard* (White River Junction VT: Chelsea Green, 2011). Chapter 4, "Orchard Dynamics," puts microorganisms in perspective; pp. 137–41 are specific to effective, beneficial, or probiotic microorganisms and application methods including compost tea. Phillips's somewhat aw-shucks style disguises a wealth of knowledge worth consulting about most woody-plant cultivation.

79. This was developed at Battery Park City and is discussed in more detail in Principle 10.

80. Terry Logan, *Lead Contamination in the Garden Factsheet* (Columbus: Ohio State University Extension, n.d.). This source also recommends peat moss; local organic material is far preferable, and usually plentiful.

81. Bill Thompson, personal communication.

82. Associated Press, "Report: Toxic Chemicals Recycled into Fertilizers," *Santa Fe New Mexican*, 7 Jul 1997.

83. US EPA, *Biosolids Recycling: Beneficial Technology for a Better Environment* (Washington DC: National Center for Environmental Publications and Information, n.d.), ref: EPA 832-R-94-009. Legal standards are in part 503, Code of Federal Regulations.

84. Craul, *Urban Soil*, 197.

85. Anita Bahe, "Science and Policy: The Biological, Environmental, and Policy Implications of Organic Waste Reutilization in Urban Landscape Management," PhD diss., North Carolina State University, 1995.

86. Michael Leccese, "Fresh Fields," *LAM*, Dec 1996, 44.

87. The Center for Media and Democracy's "SourceWatch" is an example of such reaction. See www.sourcewatch.org/index .php/Biosolids. It primarily warns against use of biosolids in food production, the same position taken in this book. SourceWatch considers the term "biosolids" to be an "Orwellian PR euphemism" for sludge, which it depicts as inevitably and always toxic and the EPA standards as inadequate and corrupt. This type of reaction tends to demand zero risk, while industry—which biosolids have become—often downplays real risks. Using biosolids on non-food-producing soils seems a reasonable compromise unless there is serious contamination.

88. Mitchell, *Compost*, 18.

89. Ibid., 17.

90. Phillip Craul, "Designing Sustainable Soil," in *Opportunities in Sustainable Development: Strategies for the Chesapeake Bay Region*, ed. Margarita Hill (Washington DC: American Society of Landscape Architects, 1997), 49.

91. Ibid.

92. George Hazelrigg, "The Ultimate Spectacle," *LAM*, Dec 2006, 56–63.

93. Joe Alper, "Wicked Weed of the West," *Smithsonian*, Dec 2004, 33–36.

94. Federal Interagency Invasive Species Council, *Draft National Invasive Plant Management Strategy* (Washington DC: US Department of the Interior and US Department of Commerce, 1996). For a clear discussion of horticultural introductions that have caused ecological havoc, see Francis M. Harty, "Exotics and Their Ecological Ramifications," *Natural Areas Journal* 6, no. 4 (1986): 20–26.

95. For a pragmatic and thorough way to define and assess a species' invasiveness, see the criteria developed by the Califor-

nia Invasive Plant Council (http://cal-ipc.org/). Critics of the very idea of invasiveness are mostly postmodern theorists who insist that any plant that can adapt to a region is good and that "native" is an elitist term. They base this on analogy rather than science: by comparison to the racism that can be implicit in classifying people as native or not; and by the analogy between ecosystems and economic markets, in which (they seem to believe) pure competition is the only legitimate approach.

96. This information is from a presentation on invasives and landscape practice at the ASLA annual meeting in San Jose CA, 2002.

97. Seth Hettena, "Officials Work to Eradicate Water-Grubbing Shrub," Associated Press syndicated report, 15 Jun 2003.

98. Benjamin Everitt, "Chronology of the Spread of Tamarisk in the Central Rio Grande," *Wetlands*, Dec 1998, 658–68. Everitt's finding that tamarisk invaded only after water-level disruptions has been used by some activists as proof that the plant is harmless and should be left alone.

99. Statistics are from Alper, "Wicked Weed of the West." Cal-IPC's newsletter, *Noxious Times*, Fall 2004, 6–9, notes that "many studies have shown that exotic plants transpire more water than California's indigenous plants," and sets a financial benefit of eradicating invasives, for California's economy alone, at up to $11 billion.

100. All information on knapweed is from Alper, "Wicked Weed of the West."

101. An ASLA presentation at the San Jose annual meeting, 2002, showed a wide range of species for which these effects have been studied in detail. Because the same plant's effect may differ between regions, the best sources of such information are usually state and local invasive plant agencies.

102. Paul H. Gobster and R. Bruce Hull, eds., *Restoring Nature: Perspectives from the Social Sciences and Humanities* (Washington DC: Island Press, 2000). The "Chicago restoration controversy," as it is widely known, is reported in Gobster's introduction; he was a participant in the events. While Gobster's perspective is thoughtful and broad, some of the articles in this collection, notably coeditor Hull's, border on deconstructivist polemics. In his contribution, for example, Hull asserts that there is no real difference between the "different natures" found in parks or parking lots. Clearly, natural processes occur even in the most constructed environment; arguments like Hull's, however, tend to deny any *qualitative* value for diverse, coevolved, self-sustaining systems. Although less strident, the Chicago public was also convinced that there was no qualitative difference between their planted forests and the native vegetative communities of the region. "Nature" and "natural" are very slippery terms, and careless use of them obscures any hope of clear thought; see my article "Nature/Culture/Words/Landscapes" (see note 6 in "Basic Principles," above).

103. Some titles, cited by Gobster, included "Prairie People Compile Tree Hit-List!" and "Guru's Restoration Plans Read More Like Destruction."

104. A voluntary code of conduct for landscape architects was first proposed at a 2001 workshop organized by the botanic gardens in Missouri, Chicago, and Kew (London). "Linking Ecology and Horticulture to Prevent Plant Invasions," authors unknown. The code urged self-education, elimina-

tion of regionally invasive plants from designs, and lobbying of suppliers not to sell invasives. As noted earlier, ornamental horticulture bears a large responsibility for the historical introduction of many invasives; some in that industry still actively and aggressively resist attempts to stop spreading these plants.

105. From DR Trimmer/Country Home Products (800-446-8746). Like many equipment manufacturers, DR portrays its clients as beating back unruly nature, an attitude that itself is problematic.

106. For a discussion of the ways in which patterns change over time, known as the "shifting mosaic steady state," see Bryant N. Richards, *Sustainable Development in Forestry: An Ecological Perspective* (Vancouver: University of British Columbia, 1989).

107. Sauer, *Once and Future Forest*. See especially pp. 165–93 and 298–300.

108. Information on this project is from K. Sorvig, "35,000 Transplants," *Landscape Architecture* 101, no. 8 (2011): 72–83, and interview notes for that article.

109. J. Zickefoose, *Enjoying Bluebirds More* (Marietta OH: Bird Watcher's Digest Press, 1993); like many birders' books, this contains extensive lists of trees, shrubs, and vines that attract birds.

110. Presciently foreseen as early as 1984 by Edward Theurkauf, MLA, at the University of Pennsylvania.

111. Amy Adams, "Heavy Metal Garden," *Utne Reader*, May–Jun 1998, 86.

112. Len Hopper, *Landscape Architectural Graphic Standards* (New York: Wiley, 2007). Figures are given in the table on p. 803. Conversion from hectare to acre, and phytomethods as percentage of other methods, are by me.

113. "Tumbleweed Could Be Low-Tech Tool for Uranium Contamination Cleanup," Associated Press syndicated report, 10 Nov 2004; John Fialka, "Salute the Jimson," *Wall Street Journal*, 18 Jun 1992, A5; Elizabeth Weise, "Watercress Engineered to Detect Land Mines," *USA Today*, 3 Feb 2004, 4D. Experiments with salt-tolerant plants have been widespread since the "green revolution" of the 1970s.

114. See www.timbre-project.eu.

115. Steven Rock, "Possibilities and Limitations of Phytoremediation," in *The Standard Handbook of Hazardous Waste Treatment and Disposal*, ed. Harry Freeman (New York: McGraw-Hill, 1997), 6.

116. Thanks to Tawny Allen, who produced an exceptionally clear summary of technical differences among phytoremediation methods for my University of New Mexico sustainable landscapes seminar, 2005.

117. Philip Rea, "Plants May Clean Out Poisons at Toxic Sites," *Philadelphia Inquirer*, 12 Jun 1999. Rea is the primary researcher on this University of Pennsylvania project.

118. Brian Kamnikar, "Biomounds Pass Tests in Minnesota," *Soil and Groundwater Cleanup*, May 1996, 34–43.

119. "Munching Microbes Make a Meal Out of Toxic Substances," *Purdue News*, Apr 1997.

120. "Bioremediation of Environmental Contaminants," originally at http://gw2.cciw.ca/internet/bioremediation/whatis.html, appears to have been removed from the Web.

121. Paul Bradley, title unknown, *Environmental Science and Technology*, Jun 1999, reported by wire services, 19 Jun 1999. For a list

of this author's titles on similar subjects, see http://toxics .usgs.gov/bib/bib-Solvents-on-line.html.

122. "UWI" is the term preferred by firefighters and "Firewise" activists, occasionally flipped as "WUI"; the latter phrase is from Tom Wolf 's excellent *In Fire's Way: A Practical Guide to Life in the Wildfire Danger Zone* (Albuquerque: University of New Mexico Press, 2003).

123. This phrase is the subtitle of *The Wildfire Reader* (Washington DC: Island Press, 2006), which Wuerthner edited. The many contributors to this volume focus on fire as an ecological necessity and on the deep-seated problems of conventional forest management regarding fire. (It contains relatively little about managing *development* in forests but is essential reading for the background facts required to make sense of UWI issues.)

124. John MacDonald, "Researchers Say Fire Becomes Political Tool," Associated Press syndicated report, 20 Apr 2003. The timber industry has used fear of fire as a lever to allow more tree removal in national forests under the guise of "thinning." Timber money probably explains the heavy federal funding of thinning programs. These political concerns are detailed in both Wolf, *In Fire's Way*, and Wuerthner, *Wildfire Reader*. Wolf also notes that the current system rewards fire departments more for fighting fires than for any prevention work (pp. 22–23).

125. Ted Williams, "Burning Money," *Audubon*, Jan 2001, 34. President Bush called the San Diego fires "nature at her worst," but in fact, conditions for most recent wildfires are as much man-made as natural.

126. Kim Sorvig, "Will Wildfire Ravage Our Profession?" *LAM*, Dec 2001, 32; "Crying Fire in a Crowded Landscape," *LAM*, Mar 2004, 26.

127. Ventura County CA, which enforces harsh regulations and still suffers repeated destructive fires, was the basis for estimating clearance area and percentage. Since UWI clearing, by definition, occurs in the wilder parts of a county, it represents a significant reduction of the little uncleared land that remains in most regions. In many counties, 90+ percent of the forested or wooded areas that existed prior to about 1800 have long been cleared. Thus, the 3 percent figure may be misleading: annual clearance should really be reported in terms of a percentage of remaining forested land rather than as a percentage of the total area of the county.

128. Sorvig, "Crying Fire."

129. Quoted in Wolf, *In Fire's Way*, 36. The US Forest Service has ostracized Cohen for statements like this and is especially displeased that environmental groups have used Cohen's sensible and honest findings to combat timber-industry pressure politics. (See MacDonald, "Researchers Say Fire Becomes Political Tool.")

130. Jonathan Thompson, Thomas Spies, and Lisa Ganio, "Salvage Logging, Replanting Increased Biscuit Fire Severity," *Proceedings of the National Academy of Sciences*, 12 Jun 2007. This study found that fire intensity was 16 to 61 percent higher in areas salvage logged and replanted that suffered a second burn, compared to areas that were allowed to revegetate by themselves after one fire, and then suffered a second. The authors note that "the hypothesis that salvage logging, then replanting, reduces re-burn severity is not supported by these data."

131. Restoration goals must be based on sound ecological understanding of specific ecosystems. (The Bush administration's so-called healthy-forest initiative is purely bogus.) Interviewees for my articles cited above note that some environmental groups fear timber industry meddling so much that they insist that no management of any sort be allowed in burned public forests (reflecting the belief that nature must be untouched by human hands). This makes it impossible to undo the damage caused by a century of fire suppression and actually leads some of these groups to support clearance around every structure.

132. This paraphrases the title of Stephen F. Arno and Carl E. Fiedler's useful book *Mimicking Nature's Fire: Restoring Fire-Prone Forests in the West* (Washington DC: Island Press, 2005).

133. See www.firegel.com.

134. He made this point in his book-signing talk in Santa Fe NM, 27 Nov 2006.

Principle 3: Favor Living, Flexible Materials

1. Technically, there are exceptions. Some would count salt and a few other minerals as foods; in addition, fungi are often plant-like in form, but they belong to their own biological kingdom and are not capable of photosynthesis. Neither minerals nor mushrooms, however, is a major food, nor nutritious enough to rely on exclusively. Electricity can be produced without fuel from wind, water flow, or photovoltaics, all of which rely on solar energy (which causes the temperature differences that drive wind, and the evaporation that raises water to high elevations). Uranium is called a nuclear fuel, but fission is quite a different process than combustion; in "fuel cells" the fuel is hydrogen, and again, the reaction is quite different. In any case, the technological evolution that gave rise to all high-tech energy production could not have happened without many generations of activity based on fuel (and food) directly from plant sources.

2. Isaiah 40:6. The verses immediately following focus on the fragility and impermanence of human life, which result, in part, from being completely dependent for survival on things outside ourselves. The humility of such a lesson is at the core of sustainability, but even greenies persist in assuming that our own technology can free humans from reliance on the rest of the global ecosystem.

3. Billie Leff, Navin Ramankutty, and Jonathan A. Foley, "Geographic Distribution of Major Crops Across the World," *Global Biogeochemical Cycles* 18, no. 1 (Mar 2004).

4. This site is useful for a wide variety of climate change analysis tools. Click on Tools: www.fs.usda.gov/ccrc/.

5. Thomas A. M. Pugh et al., "Effectiveness of Green Infrastructure for Improvement of Air Quality in Urban Street Canyons," *Environmental Science and Technology* 46, no. 14 (2012): 7692–99.

6. Peter Aspinall et al., "The Urban Brain: Analysing Outdoor Physical Activity with Mobile EEG," *British Journal of Sports Medicine* 49, no. 4 (2015): 272–76.

7. Sarah Lozanova, "Green Spaces May Deter Crime, Urban Studies Reveal," *EBN*, Jan 2017, 11.

8. Tina Susman, "A Tree Grows (and Dies) in Brooklyn," *Los Angeles Times*, October 15, 2009. Online at http://tinasusman .typepad.com/tina_susman/page/5/. Similar tree vandalism

has been reported in other cities; apart from politics, different ethnic groups seem to have widely different feelings about urban trees.

9. Calling these plant-focused construction methods "bioengineering" butts up against the use of that term to mean genetic engineering; expanding to "soil bioengineering" does not dispel the problem. "Biotechnical erosion control" is a far more accurate term, but a mouthful; I suggest an alternate abbreviation, Btec.

10. Still useful, these guidelines are available from sites such as these: www.studioizzo.org/geoplus/2015/03/12/software-per-ambiente-e-paesaggio-software-for-environment-and-landscape/?lang=enwww.nrcs.usda.gov/Internet/FSE_PLANTMATERIALS/publications/idpmcpussbfglpa.pdf www.blm.gov/or/programs/nrst/files/Soil%20bioeng.pdf.

11. Donald Gray and Robbin Sotir, *Biotechnical and Soil Bioengineering Slope Stabilization* (New York: Wiley, 1996), 3.

12. Ann Riley, *Restoring Streams in Cities* (Washington DC: Island Press, 1998), discusses the history of these methods, including the Works Progress Administration and Civilian Conservation Corps.

13. Information is from www.landlifecompany.com/ as of 2017.

14. These points were culled from USDA Natural Resources Conservation Service, *Soil Bioengineering for Upland Slope Protection and Erosion Reduction* (Washington DC: Natural Resource Conservation Service, 1992), 18-1 through 18-8.

15. USDA, *Soil Bioengineering*, 18-5.

16. Caroline Chiquet, John W. Dover, and Paul Mitchell, "Birds and the Urban Environment: The Value of Green Walls," *Urban Ecosystems* 16, no. 3 (Sep 2013): 453–62.

17. Booklets are at www.jakob.co.uk/solutions/view/green-walls/.

18. The National Gallery, London, "Van Gogh Painting Brought to Life as 'Living Wall,'" www.nationalgallery.org.uk/van-gogh-painting-brought-to-life-as-living-wall, posted 26 May 2011.

19. "Cost–Benefit Analysis for Green Façades and Living Wall Systems," *Building and Environment* 70 (Dec 2013): 110–21. Price/area unit conversions are by me.

20. Gray and Sotir, *Biotechnical and Soil Bioengineering Slope Stabilization*, 149.

21. Ibid., 148.

22. USDA, *Soil Bioengineering*, 18-31, 18-32.

23. EKOL, the division of Tessenderlo that manufactured these walls, as well as site furniture, compost bins, and similar products, listed each item with the amount of recycled plastic it repurposed. Active in 2007, at http://ekol.mediabeheer.be/, EKOL was sold by Tessenderlo in 2010, and may have gone out of business.

24. See www.krismer.at/01/en_Sonderkonstruktionen_03.html. Krismer appears to be represented in the United Kingdom by a firm called Terraqua; it does not seem to be available in the United States.

25. It is almost impossible to resist making jokes about the anti-environmental president of the same name—but we won't go there.

26. Theodore Eisenman, "Raising the Bar on Greenroof Design," *LAM*, Nov 2006, 22.

27. Michael Hough, *City Form and Natural Process* (New York: Van Nostrand Reinhold, 1984).

28. Tom Liptan et al., *Integrating Stormwater into the Urban Fabric* (Portland OR: American Society of Landscape Architects, 1997), 89.

29. Eisenman, "Raising the Bar."

30. Ibid.

31. Ibid.

32. Underground or earth-bermed houses (such as the one in which I live, near Santa Fe) may have several feet of soil over the roof, maintaining a year-round baseline temperature of 54°F, easily solar heated in winter and cool in summer.

33. See www.lid-stormwater.net/greenroofs_cost.htm, a toolkit site developed by the US EPA.

34. Rick Scaffidi, "Beware the Published Costs of Stormwater BMPs: Dig a Little Deeper, Engineers!" *Living Architecture Monitor*, Winter 2016, 35.

35. Erin Weaver, "Green Roofs Improve Solar Panel Efficiency," *EBN*, Dec 2012, 3.

36. Candace Pearson, "'Blue Roof' Adds Stormwater Detention Alongside Green Roof in New York," *EBN*, Oct 2013, 14.

37. Both studies are cited in *Living Architecture Monitor*, Winter 2016, San Francisco on p. 26 and Portland on p. 30. Separating the private and public benefits is my interpretation of the Arup data.

38. Christopher Hawthorne, "Building Designers Add Pizazz to Views from Above," *Los Angeles Times*, 10 Nov 2006.

39. Alex Wilson and Mary Rickel Pelletier, "Using Roofs for More Than Keeping Dry," *EBN*, Nov 2001.

40. Questions about both hydrogels and wind erosion are raised in Wilson and Pelletier, "Using Roofs," ibid.

41. Jacklyn Johnson and John Newton, *Building Green: A Guide to Using Plants on Roofs, Walls, and Pavements* (London: London Ecology Unit, n.d.), 64.

42. See Linda McIntyre, "Greenroof Guru," *LAM*, Jan 2007, 64, which reviews Snodgrass's work.

43. 2016 GRHC Awards of Excellence were published in *Living Architecture Monitor*, Winter 2016; the Edgeland project is on pp. 20–21.

44. Theodore Eisenman, "Chicago's Green Crown," *LAM*, Nov 2004, 106.

45. Intensive greenroofs fall between thin-soiled extensive greenroofs and roof gardens, but they are closer kin to the former in intent, structure, and plant choices. Their deeper soil can retain more stormwater but is not suitable for trees.

46. Lisa Owens Viani, "Prairie from Ground to Sky," *LAM*, Dec 2006, 28.

47. A proposed repurposing of the abandoned Vallco Shopping Mall in Cupertino CA will, if it ever is built, have thirty acres of greenroof and be by far the biggest US greenroof; it was voted down in 2016 by citizens objecting to potential traffic and school congestion. The phrase "world's largest greenroof" has been trademarked by SubTropolis, a converted limestone mine that rents underground storage space; the management seem bent on thumbing their noses at genuine green building.

48. Lorraine Johnson, "The Green Fields of Ford," *LAM*, Jan 2004, 16.

49. Under section 319(h), Clean Water Act.

50. Theodore Eisenman, "Sedums over Baltimore," *LAM*, Aug 2004, 52.

51. In her contribution to *Landscape Architectural Graphic Standards*

(New York: Wiley, 2007), "Living Green Roofs and Land-scapes over Structures," p. 713, Susan Weiler of Olin Partnership prefers the term "landscape over structure" for roof gardens with soil deeper than eight inches. She states that greenroofs and landscape over structure should not be compared. I agree that comparison should not be adversarial, but all sustainability-oriented landscapes benefit from deliberate evaluation, some of it necessarily comparative.

52. The interview with Prof. Khire was part of www.wbez.org /shows/curious-city/a-green-roofs-checkin/62fa16e6-e97c -4e4e-a969-04c3d67be4a9. The MSU greenroof research team has a long research history on performance of green-roofs, much of it described at www.greenroof.hrt.msu.edu /staff/index.html. Khire is currently with the Energy and Environment Cluster at the University of North Carolina, Charlotte.

53. Jacklyn Johnson and John Newton, *Building Green: A Guide to Using Plants on Roofs, Walls, and Pavements* (London: London Ecology Unit, n.d.), 48. Over 10 million square feet of German greenroof are older than 1989, for example.

54. Ecover, *The Ecover Manual* (Oostmalle, Belgium: Ecover Publishing, 1992), 24.

55. For information on waste-treatment greenroofs, see www .wwuk.co.uk/grow.htm. GROW and GROW2 are modular wetlands, in effect, and can be installed on roofs or in other ways. Concept development for this product was under the auspices of the UK Engineering and Physical Sciences Research Council (www.epsrc.ac.uk), but the council's published findings appear to be archived beyond recall.

56. Miller's interview was part of *The Green Machine*'s Season 1, Episode 3. Transcript at www.pbs.org/e2/episodes/103 _the_green_machine_trailer.html; for video, go to YouTube and search for fbTE6FyFhX4. For the GRHC Top Ten, go to www.greenroofs.com/virtualsummit/2011/virtualsum mit2011-agenda.htm; then look in the list of videos for a link to *VS2011#2—2011 Top 10 List of Hot Trends in Greenroof & Greenwall Design* (on YouTube). Going directly to YouTube and searching for VS2011#2 brings up the same video.

57. Trying to encourage sustainability by skimping on other compliance is risky even with good intentions. "Streamlining regulation" has disguised Reaganite bad intentions against environmental and social laws.

58. Cutler is cited in an in-flight magazine, possibly itself a first for any landscape architect! Quote and statistics on urban forests are from Charles Lockwood, "Save the Shade," *Hemispheres Magazine* (United Airlines), Sep 2006, 60–63. The article is available online at http://selecttrees.com/outside_literature /Save_the_Shade.pdf.

59. Darryl Fears, "Americans Once Moved Away from Forests. Now Forests Are Moving Away from Americans," *Washington Post*, 22 Feb 2017, www.washingtonpost.com/news/energy -environment/wp/2017/02/22/americans-once-moved -away-from-forests-now-forests-are-moving-away-from-ameri cans/?utm_term=.1159768de6d4.

60. R. J. Hauer, R. W. Miller, and D. M. Ouimet, "Street Tree Decline and Construction Damage," *Journal of Arboriculture* 20, no. 2 (1994): 94–97.

61. The author and date of this study are not known.

62. Pimentel's study was published in *BioScience*; reported in John Yaukey, "Environment's Output Placed at $2.9 Trillion," *Fort Collins Coloradoan*, 14 Dec 1997.

63. The study is credited to Dr. Rowan Rowntree. It may be from E. Gregory McPherson et al., "Quantifying Urban Forest Structure, Function, and Value: The Chicago Urban Forest Climate Project," *Urban Ecosystems* 1, no. 1 (Mar 1997): 49–61, one of the one hundred or more publications Prof. Rowntree authored or coauthored. Download for a fee from Springer, or for free via ResearchGate; search Publications for the lead author's name. Rowntree, McPherson, and others at the US Forest Service Center for Urban Forest Research (www.fs.fed.us/psw/) have made numerous useful contributions to understanding this field.

64. Statistics are from Lockwood, "Save the Shade." The US Forest Service study is by the Center for Urban Forest Research.

65. Blanc's excellent lectures were compiled in Alan Blanc, *Landscape Construction and Detailing* (New York: McGraw-Hill, 1996).

66. Phillip J. Craul, *Urban Soil in Landscape Design* (New York: Wiley, 1992), 1.

67. Ibid., 122.

68. Silva Cell 2, introduced in 2015, replaced the discontinued Silva Cell as of October 1, 2017. DeepRoot's website supposedly has "all the information you need," but downloading anything requires you to register for the privilege of getting marketing e-mails.

69. Silva Cell is rectangular, 48 × 24 × 16 in. (1,200 × 600 × 400 mm); Strata Vault is 600 mm (about 24 in.) square by 404 mm (about 16 in.) deep; and Strata Cell is hexagonal, 510 mm (about 20 in.) across and 250 mm (10 in.) deep.

70. This section is an updated version of Kim Sorvig, "Soil Under Pressure," *LAM*, Jun 2001, 36.

71. CU-Soil is a registered trademark. Like all other trademarks referred to in this book, it remains the property of its developers. "Structural soil" is a generic term.

72. H. F. Arnold, "The Down and Dirty on Structural Soil," *LAM*, Aug 2001, Letters, 9–11. This letter responded to my "Soil Under Pressure." The article, focused on the CU-Soil patent and enforcement controversy, did not discuss Arnold's system. This gave the mistaken impression that neither the historical nor the horticultural aspects of Arnold's work were appreciated. Hopefully, that misapprehension can be laid to rest here. Arnold gives general concepts for site-adjusted soil mixes in his book *Trees in Urban Design* (New York: Van Nostrand Reinhold, 1992).

73. "Gap-graded soil," based on sieved angular sand, provides golf greens' smooth, consistent surfaces. Porous paving (aka "open-graded friction course") uses asphalt or cement to bond "no-fines" (single-size) aggregate to produce pavement with voids through which water drains easily. Structural soil is unbonded, and soil fills the voids.

74. Nina Bassuk, "Using CU-Structural Soil to Grow Trees Surrounded by Pavement," posted at the website of the Ecological Landscape Alliance, www.ecolandscaping.org/01/soil/using -cu-structural-soil-to-grow-trees-surrounded-by-pavement/.

75. Interestingly, soil mixes are essentially recipes, and recipes cannot be copyrighted because they are simply lists of common ingredients and known procedures. To patent a recipe, the ingredients, processes, or outcome must be *significantly* different than common practice. UHI's strategy, called a "defensive

patent," is not uncommon; Xeriscape was trademarked in a similarly unsuccessful attempt to enforce consistency. Given the near-infinite site-specific variations possible and necessary with almost any horticultural process, enforcing such patents is nearly impossible.

76. Nina Bassuk and Peter Trowbridge, "Soils, Urban and Disturbed," in *Landscape Architectural Graphic Standards*, ed. L. Hopper (New York: Wiley, 2007), 646–61.

77. Bruce Ferguson, personal communication. Ferguson is probably the greatest US expert on land-focused stormwater management and one of the few landscape architects to pursue "hard" research on such subjects.

78. My article (see note 70 above) apparently made UHI defensive. The text of that article, edited *without permission* to express Nina Bassuk's objections to my conclusions, was reprinted *under my name* (!), in *City Trees*, journal of the Society of Municipal Arborists, Nov 2003. The *City Trees* version is extremely misleading, contradictory to my researched findings, semi-incoherent, and intellectually dishonest. Anyone concerned with evaluating structural soils fairly will avoid the *City Trees* article.

79. So far as I can determine, none of these installations have been dug up or monitored with instrumented methods, but they do provide strong observational evidence.

80. A consummate gentleman, Craul names no names, to avoid embarrassing the designers.

81. The title of this section is a nod to that panel. See www.asla.org/uploadedFiles/CMS/Meetings_and_Events/2010_Annual_Meeting_Handouts/Sat-B1The%20Great%20Soil%20Debate_Structural%20Soils%20Under%20Pavement.pdf.

82. J. Urban, personal communication.

83. Here's the math. V_b is the baseline volume of soil at 100 percent soil efficiency. E is soil efficiency, as a decimal: the percentage of volume available as soil of a given method, mix, or system. P_b is base price, from suppliers, converted to price per cubic foot. V_b/E = actual required volume. P_b/E = price per effective cubic foot.

84. The guidelines are summarized from James Urban's contribution to Ramsey et al., *Architectural Graphic Standards*, 10th ed., 177–82.

85. I have seen recommendations for an establishment period as long as seven years for some regional species. Always get local expertise and aim to wean plants off human assistance gradually.

86. Wild accusations have been made that defining plants as natives and aliens is comparable to racism against "alien" humans; see Kim Sorvig, "Natives and Nazis: An Imaginary Conspiracy in Ecological Design," *Landscape Journal* 13, no. 1 (1994): 58–61.

87. See entries for *Abies magnifica* in Elbert Little, *Audubon Society Field Guide to North American Trees, Western Region* (New York: Knopf, 1980); and John Kricher, *Ecology of Western Forests* (Peterson Field Guides, New York: Houghton Mifflin, 1993).

88. Contact Western Polyacrylamide or the Colorado Forestry Department for studies on polymer use.

89. From the 1999 seed catalog of Wildseed Farms, www.wildseedfarms.com.

90. Ted Steinberg, *American Green: The Obsessive Quest for the Perfect Lawn* (New York: Norton, 2006), 7. Steinberg is also the author of the wonderful *Slide Mountain: Or, The Folly of Owning Nature* and several other books tracing our often comical social and legal attempts to corral the natural world.

91. The root cause of drought, along with other extreme weather, is probably the greenhouse effect and global climate change. Water-use restrictions such as those that have made artificial turf popular are being passed both by legislators who deny global warming and by those who recognize it. Evaluating the sustainability of local drought measures requires looking at their larger-scale and longer-term implications.

92. Jessica Boehland, "Which Grass Is Greener? Comparing Natural and Artificial Turf," *EBN*, Apr 2004. Unless otherwise noted, statistics in this section are from Boehland's article. I agree with her conclusion that *neither* conventional nor artificial turf is particularly sustainable.

93. Charles Vidair, "Safety Study of Artificial Turf Containing Crumb Rubber Infill Made from Recycled Tires" (Sacramento: California Department of Resources Recycling and Recovery, October 2010).

94. See www.actglobal.com/aviation-turf.php. The quote is from an earlier version of the website, but the current one states substantially the same thing, in more detail.

95. The speaker is Chris Reuther, a botanist and science writer at Philadelphia's Academy of Natural Sciences. The original source appears to be a 1999 article, title and publication unknown; Reuther was quoted in both *EBN* and *LAM* discussing artificial turf issues.

96. *Washington Post*, "1 Out of 8 Plant Species Faces Extinction, Survey Says," *Santa Fe New Mexican*, 8 Apr 1998, B-1.

Principle 4: Respect the Waters of Life

1. Russell Ash, *Incredible Comparisons* (London: Dorling Kindersley, 1996), 23.

2. Ambrose Bierce, *The Devil's Dictionary* (Cleveland OH: World Publishing Co., 1941). Bierce's definition of "lexicographer" is also worth noting in regard to footnotes generally: "A pestilent fellow who, under the pretense of recording some particular stage in the development of [an idea], does what he can to arrest its growth, stiffen its flexibility, and mechanize its methods."

3. Michael Jameson, *Xeric Landscaping with Florida Native Plants* (Miami: Association of Florida Native Nurseries, 1991).

4. Paul Simon, *Tapped Out: The Coming World Crisis in Water and What We Can Do About It* (New York: Welcome Rain Publishers, 1998).

5. L. D. Rotstayn and U. Lohmann, "Tropical Rainfall Trends and the Indirect Aerosol Effect," *Journal of Climate* 15 (Aug 2002): 2103–16. Rotstayn is a research scientist at Australia's Commonwealth Scientific and Industrial Research Organisation. His research shows that pollutants from industrial countries, especially sulfur dioxide from power plants, affect cloud and precipitation patterns thousands of miles away in the Sahel desert in Africa, and that the start of emissions controls in industrial countries correlates with the return of rains to the Sahel. PDF available at http://journals.ametsoc.org/doi/full/10.1175/1520-0442%282002%29015%3C2103%3ATRTATI%3E2.0.CO%3B2.

6. John Fleck, "Hotter & Drier," *Albuquerque Journal*, 24 Jun 2006, A1, gives a regional example of increased rainfall offset by decreased availability.

7. For an enlightening summary of cultural and religious stances about water, visit www.waterandculture.org/264_Water_Wisdom.

8. Harvey M. Rubenstein, *A Guide to Site Planning and Landscape Construction*, 4th ed. (New York: Wiley, 1996), 189.

9. Dawn Thilmany, Phil Watson, and Steve Davies, "The Economic Contribution of Colorado's Green Industry," *Colorado State University Extension Economic Development Report* EDR-04-01, Apr 2004, http://webdoc.agsci.colostate.edu/DARE/EDR/EDR04-01.pdf.

10. Stuart Echols and Eliza Pennypacker, "Art for Rain's Sake," *LAM*, Sep 2006, 24.

11. BASMAA, *Start at the Source* (San Francisco: Bay Area Stormwater Management Agencies Association, 1997), 7; italics added.

12. In 1998 dollars; certainly more today. Rocky Mountain Institute, Studio for Creative Inquiry, and Bruce Ferguson, *Nine Mile Run Briefing Book (draft)* (Snowmass CO: Rocky Mountain Institute, 1998), 20.

13. This is a much more readable paraphrase of the EPA's legal definition. See www.epa.gov/owow/wetlands/what/definitions.html.

14. Donald A. Hammer, *Creating Freshwater Wetlands*, 2nd ed. (Boca Raton FL: Lewis Publishers, 1997), 16.

15. John Berger, *Restoring the Earth: How Americans Are Working to Renew Our Damaged Environment* (New York: Knopf, 1985), 61. Constructing the marsh requires a wider strip of land than the revetment; cost of land may or may not be an issue in such projects, and it is not included in Berger's figures. In 1982 dollars, revetments cost $150 per linear foot, marsh $15–$25.

16. Hammer, *Creating Freshwater Wetlands*, 115.

17. Ibid., 12.

18. This list is based on Hammer, *Creating Freshwater Wetlands*, 139.

19. Ibid., 171. Further comments throughout, notably pp. 137, 258, and 311.

20. As noted below, it is unclear whether this can ever be accomplished fully.

21. See, for example, a global study, David Moreno-Mateos et al., "Structural and Functional Loss in Restored Wetland Ecosystems," *PLoS Biology* 10, no. 1 (2012): e1001247. This indicates that most "restoration" achieves, at best, about 75 percent of full function. It also notes that larger wetlands (> 100 hectares, or 250 acres), those in temperate-to-tropical regions, and those that involve strong water movement, e.g., tidal flows, recover more quickly than do small, disconnected, cold-climate wetlands without much water exchange.

22. Hammer, *Creating Freshwater Wetlands*, 23, 337.

23. Ibid., 337.

24. Required under the EPA's 2003 National Pollutant Discharge Elimination System (NPDES) Construction General Permit (CGP), *Federal Register* 68, no. 126 (1 Jul 2003): 39087. See www.epa.gov/npdes/stormwater-discharges-construction-activities. This law has teeth, making it an important site-protection tool, especially on local road and public-works projects, where conventional engineers have often felt revegetation was decorative and optional.

25. Procedural "streamlining" is a legitimate need, but has also been used as a smoke screen for removing regulations.

26. Mary Kentula et al., *An Approach to Improving Decision Making in Wetland Restoration and Creation* (Boca Raton FL: CRC Press, 1993), 17–19.

27. Lisa Owens Viani, "A Question of Mitigation," *LAM*, Aug 2006, 24.

28. Susan Galatowitsch and Arnold van der Valk, *Restoring Prairie Wetlands: An Ecological Approach* (Ames: Iowa State University Press, 1994), 150; see also the chart on p. 49 of the same work.

29. Hammer is a strong advocate of this approach, for example.

30. Kentula et al., *An Approach to Improving Decision Making*; see particularly pp. 17–19 and 111–12. See also Galatowitsch and van der Valk, *Restoring Prairie Wetlands*, especially chapters 1 and 3.

31. Hammer, *Creating Freshwater Wetlands*, 39.

32. Hammer (ibid., 194) is one of many who have reported this concern.

33. Polly El Aidi, "Innovations in Wetlands Trail Construction," *LAM*, Jul 1993, 120–22.

34. Ibid., 299.

35. Another list of invasive plants, not specific to wetlands, is found in appendix B of Leslie Sauer, *The Once and Future Forest* (Washington DC: Island Press, 1998); it pertains to deciduous forests of the eastern United States.

36. Hammer, *Creating Freshwater Wetlands*, 264, 318–23.

37. "Sligo Creek: Holistic Stream Restoration," *Watershed Protection Techniques* 1, no. 4 (1995): 192.

38. This is a major theme of Ann Riley, *Restoring Streams in Cities* (Washington DC: Island Press, 1998), especially pp. 30–31.

39. Bruce Ferguson, "The Failure of Detention and the Future of Stormwater Design," *LAM*, Dec 1991, 76–79. See also Ferguson's *Introduction to Stormwater* (New York: Wiley, 1998), 162–64.

40. Erich Smith, "Trees for Streams," Associated Press syndicated report, 10 Jan 1997.

41. Riley, *Restoring Streams in Cities*, 362.

42. Ibid., 31.

43. These included the Metropolitan Washington Council of Governments, the Maryland-National Capital Park and Planning Commission, and the Maryland Department of Environmental Protection.

44. A useful published (but unbuilt) example is Rocky Mountain Institute, Studio for Creative Inquiry, and Ferguson, *Nine Mile Run Briefing Book (draft)*.

45. Rosgen has attracted serious academic hostility, a conflict termed "the Rosgen Wars." At least one researcher discusses his activities as typical of "neoliberal" disregard for disinterested expert training, and privatization/commercialization of environmental expertise. Rebecca Lave, *Fields and Streams: Stream Restoration, Neoliberalism, and the Future of Environmental Science* (Athens: University of Georgia Press, 2012). I'm not in a position to evaluate Lave's claims, except that they sound suspiciously like sour grapes and an elaborate defense of academic privilege.

46. Wikipedia lists these under "Riverwalk," with links to each project, but without a general article on the topic. A half-dozen foreign riverwalks are also noted.

47. Kim Sorvig, "Return on Investment," *Landscape Architecture* 99, no. 4 (2009): 32–41. Article and interview notes.

48. In 2012, Design Studios West was acquired by Matrix Design Group (Colorado Springs CO). Records of DSW's projects online seem now to be scarce. The following, from a subcon-

sultant on the Estes Park project, notes the awards won by the project: www.wrightwater.com/assets/estesparkchannelmods.pdf.

49. Alex Wilson, "Rainwater Harvesting," *EBN*, May 1997, 1. It does not appear that any updated count has been made since, though harvesting is increasingly used.

50. Bill Mollison, *Permaculture: A Designers' Manual* (Tyalgum, NSW, Australia: Tagari Publications, 1988), especially chapter 7.

51. Sustainable Cities Institute, "Rainwater & Stormwater Harvesting," sustainablecitiesinstitute.org/topics/water-and-green-infrastructure/urban-forestry/rainwater-and-storm water-harvesting.

52. Bruce Ferguson, *Introduction to Stormwater* (New York: Wiley, 1998); see chapter 10. Example projects are the University of Arizona's Casa del Agua in Tucson and Arizona Public Service's Environmental Showcase Home in Phoenix.

53. Kenneth Brooks et al., *Hydrology and the Management of Watersheds* (Ames: Iowa State University Press, 1997).

54. Information about Colorado and Arizona are from a database of state legislation, including proposals not adopted, maintained by the National Conference of State Legislatures; see ncsl.org/research/environment-and-natural-resources/rain water-harvesting.aspx.

55. T. Sharpe, "State Scraps Plan to Harvest Rainwater," *Santa Fe New Mexican*, 16 Aug 2007, C-1. The design competition winner was Ken Smith's team.

56. For example, the all-rainwater Santa Fe Railyard Park design. Kim Sorvig, "Railyard Remake in Santa Fe: Supplanting the Usual with the Unusual?" *Competitions* 12, no. 3 (Fall 2002): 13. The proposal anticipated significantly more rainwater harvesting than could actually be implemented, a fairly common excess of optimism.

57. Echols and Pennypacker, "Art for Rain's Sake," 26.

58. Olwen C. Marlowe, *Outdoor Design: A Handbook for the Architect and Planner* (New York: Watson-Guptil, 1977), 102–4.

59. Ibid., 104.

60. Information on this project is from Kim Sorvig, "Drowning in the Desert," *Landscape Architecture* 100, no. 1 (2010): 26–37, and interview notes.

61. J. Bousselot, K. Badertscher, and M. Roll, "Sustainable Landscaping," 2005, Colorado State University Extension, publication 7.243, www.carbondalegov.org/vertical/sites/%7 BE239F6F5-CCA3-4F3A-8B27-95E8145FD79A%7D/up loads/Sustainable_Landscaping.pdf. In 2011, the CSU Extension updated Bousselot's work and removed her name, although it is substantially the same. The new version has the same title, listing J. E. Klett and A. Cummins as the authors.

62. See Virginia Scott Jenkins's book *The Lawn: A History of an American Obsession* (Washington DC: Smithsonian Institution, 1994). The British, of course, share responsibility for this cultural fixation; see Tom Fort, *The Grass Is Greener: Our Love Affair with the Lawn* (London: HarperCollins, 2000).

63. Estimated at between 7 billion and 11 billion acre-feet. See Amy Vickers, *Handbook of Water Use and Conservation* (Amherst MA: Waterplow Press, 2002).

64. Maude Barlow, "The Commodification of the World's Water," *Earth Island Journal*, 22 Mar 2002, page unknown.

65. US Geological Survey, quoted in Alex Wilson, "Water: Doing More with Less," *EBN*, Feb 2008, 1.

66. See http://waterfootprint.org/en/.

67. Michael McCormack et al., "Modeling Direct and Indirect Water Requirements of Construction," *Building Research & Information* (Australia), 35, no. 2 (2007):156–62.

68. Stephen Wiman, "Water Demand Hardening," *Our Water Quality* (column), *Santa Fe New Mexican*, Dec 6, 2015, E-1.

69. Steve Maxwell, "Historical Water Price Trends," *Journal of AWWA* (American Waterworks Association), Apr 2010, 24–28, especially the graphs on p. 26. Another estimate, from the Federal Energy Management Program, found that water costs rose between 23 and 400 percent "in the 1990s"; the FEMP website no longer includes this document.

70. Wesley Groesbeck and Jan Striefel, *The Resource Guide to Sustainable Landscapes and Gardens*, 2nd ed. (Salt Lake City UT: Environmental Resources, 1995), 39.

71. Quote from Tony Whelan, "Irrigation for a Growing World," 10 May 2006; this white paper is available at www.rainbird.com/. Rainbird might be accused of bias in this matter, but the observation that water-conservation ordinances harshly and exclusively target the horticultural industry have been made by many others. In Santa Fe NM, where I live, the only industry other than landscape horticulture that faces *any* mandatory restrictions is commercial car washes, and only after virtually all landscape use has been completely banned.

72. Ibid.

73. Joshua Siskin, "The Next Generation in Automatic Sprinklers," originally published in *Los Angeles Daily News*, 1 Oct 2005, recently posted to Siskin's site, http://thesmartergar dener.com/next-generation-of-sprinklers/.

74. Irrigation Efficiency Program contract application forms, 2008, plus online searches. By 2017, the program had been replaced with other forms of incentive.

75. Elizabeth Brabec et al., *Save Water, Save Maintenance, Save Money* (Washington DC: Anne Arundel County Department of Utilities, 1989), 5.

76. The National Xeriscape Council ceased to function some time ago, and the trademark reportedly passed to the University of Texas Extension.

77. Janet Reilly, "Drip Irrigation—a Tool for the Future," May 2005, online publication at http://landscapeonline.com/re search/article-a.php?number=5240. The author is the landscape drip marketing manager at Rain Bird Corporation.

78. Robert Kourik, "Drip Irrigation Hardware: Selection and Use," *LAM*, Mar 1993, 74–78.

79. From www.water.ca.gov/wateruseefficiency/landscape/, a useful site with answers to a variety of common irrigation questions (scroll down to FAQs), maintained by the California Department of Water Resources, Office of Water Use Efficiency.

80. Denny Schrock, "Water-Efficient Gardening and Landscaping," 7 Jun 2006, Department of Horticulture, University of Missouri, Columbia, http://extension.missouri.edu/p /G6912.

81. Undated informational flyer. BECC is now the Center for ReSource Conservation; its website is www.conservationcen ter.org/.

82. From the Sacramento-based Water Education Foundation's booklet "California Water Facts," n.d., watededfdn@aol.com, 916-444-6240.

83. These statistics are from WeatherTRAK, an ET control-ler that in 2003 was licensed for use in Toro products. Other controllers claim similar or greater reductions in waste.

84. The company states that these tablets are "rugged enough to use as a wheel chock if the truck starts to roll."

85. Originally based on Kourik, "Drip Irrigation Hardware" and "Drip Irrigation for Lawns," *LAM*, Mar 1994, this list has been slightly updated with information from current manufacturers' catalogs.

86. Kourik, " Drip Irrigation Hardware," 78.

87. Kourik, "Drip Irrigation for Lawns," 40.

88. The sound of these sprinklers is probably one of the few landscape components ever memorialized in a song: "(I Want to Be Your) Rainbird," by the a cappella group The Bobs, on *Shut Up and Sing!* (1993).

89. This intuitive method of setting shapes has been used by a number of designs, though usually without dynamic adjustment. Our second edition noted a prototype nozzle, developed in 2004 by Dr. Prasada Rao of California State University, that could be similarly adjusted. It does not appear to have become commercially available.

90. The name seems slightly absurd, since virtually all water uptake occurs through the roots except in a few rare plant species. These devices are sometimes called "deep watering" systems, which is perhaps more accurate.

91. Kourik, "Drip Irrigation for Lawns," 41. This is in stark contrast to perceptions of drip as complicated.

92. From embodied energy tables, now posted at http://island press.org/sustainable-landscape-construction.

93. Richard V. Sole and David Alonso, "Random Walks, Fractals and the Origins of Rainforest Diversity," Santa Fe Institute, 1998, Ref: 98-08-60, working paper; and Wim Hordijk, "A Measure of Landscapes," Santa Fe Institute, 1995, Ref: 95-05049, work-ing paper, are examples of such math research, primarily in ecology and molecular biology. A number of working papers are available on related topics at www.santafe.edu/. Use of the term "landscape" for such widely varying and nonphysical concepts as a "fitness landscape" (evolutionary theory) or "the political landscape" (journalism) make electronic information searches in our profession both difficult and entertaining.

94. These are available at www.irrigation.org/. The BMPs are ex-tremely general; for more tangible recommendations, see the practice guidelines that flesh out the BMPs. These documents are regularly updated.

95. See http://waterfootprint.org/en/. The Water Footprint Network Foundation was undergoing bankruptcy as of mid-2017. Its website remains, and the research alliance connected to the foundation appears likely to continue making WFN's calculators, tools, and publications available.

96. Robert Kourik, "Graywater for Residential Irrigation," *LAM*, Jan 1995, 30–33.

97. Barry Jeppesen and David Solley, *Domestic Greywater Reuse: Over-seas Practice and Its Applicability to Australia* (Melbourne: Urban Water Research Association of Australia, 1994).

98. Examples of suppliers of gray- and blackwater systems: Bio-Microbics, www.biomicrobics.com; Aqua2use, www.aqua2use .com; and Grayworks, www.grayworks.com.

99. See Kourik, "Graywater," and Groesbeck and Striefel, *Resource Guide*, 41–43.

100. Alma Siggins et al., "Effects of Long-Term Greywater Disposal on Soil: A Case Study," *Science of the Total Environment* (1 Jul 2016): 627–35, online as of 31 Mar 2016. doi:10 .1016/j.scitotenv.2016.03.084.

101. See, for example, Claudia Seiler and Thomas U. Berendonk, "Heavy Metal Driven Co-selection of Antibiotic Resistance in Soil and Water Bodies Impacted by Agriculture and Aqua-culture," *Frontiers in Microbiology* 3 (14 Dec 2012): 399.

102. Alex Wilson, "Rainwater Harvesting," *EBN*, May 1997, 12.

103. Alex Wilson, "On-Site Wastewater Treatment," *EBN*, Mar–Apr 1994, 18.

104. Estimate from Professor Brad Finney, Humboldt University Constructed Treatment Wetland System Performance data-base, personal correspondence.

105. The project won an ASLA award and was published in *LAM* but was never built.

106. Hammer, *Creating Freshwater Wetlands*, 312.

107. Rich Patterson, "From Wasteland to Wetland," *Public Risk*, Jan 1998, 29.

108. Mary Padua, "Teaching the River," *LAM*, Mar 2004, 100.

Principle 5: Pave Less

1. Total paved Roman roads, about 50,000 miles, www.britan nica.com/technology/Roman-road-system. Using stone slabs on cement underlayment, laid by hand, this is an astonish-ing achievement. (The Roman road system included another 200,000 miles of unpaved roads.) US figures, see following note. The "twice as much" is conservative, since Roman paved roads were usually twenty-four feet wide (two lanes, by cur-rent standards), though in remote provinces skimping on this standard was probably common. To be completely fair to the Romans, every mile of road should perhaps be tallied as two "lane miles." Even using this calculation, four years' worth of US paving would equal more than six *centuries* of Roman road construction. For diagrams of how Roman roads were con-structed, and other data, see www.crystalinks.com/romeroads .html. Dates of Roman road building are from www.history .com/news/history-lists/8-ways-roads-helped-rome-rule -the-ancient-world, which estimates 55,000 miles rather than 50,000, built from 312 BC into the fourth century AD.

2. From www.rita.dot.gov/bts/sites/rita.dot.gov.bts/files/publi cations/national_transportation_statistics/html/table_01 _06.html; statistics are from 1980, 1985, then annually from 1990 through 2014. The 25,500-mile average includes two years when lane-miles were reduced (1998 and 2011) for rea-sons unknown. If those two negative years are excluded, the average is over 30,000 lane-miles per year. The Federal High-way Administration estimated in 2012 that there were 1.4 million miles of *unpaved* roads in the United States, about seven times as many miles as unpaved Roman roads. (From http://mtri.org/unpaved/, a project using drones and other recent technology to assess remote roads.)

3. From www.earth-policy.org/Alerts/Alert12_data2.htm. If the standard space is 10 × 18 feet, this represents about 1.15 billion spaces. The International Parking Institute's website, www.parking.org/, listed 105.2 million in 1999, clearly a dif-ferent method of estimating.

4. Russell Ash, *Incredible Comparisons* (London: Dorling Kinders-ley, 1996), 26.

5. From the May 2016 catalog of HD Supply Construction & Industrial, Norcross GA; www.hdsupplysolutions.com; their source is not cited.

6. Bruce Ferguson (University of Georgia) estimates US paving, based on volumes of asphalt and concrete sold, at a quarter-million to half-million acres each year. This is a growth rate of 1.5 to 3 percent of our estimated total area—higher than the population growth rate!

7. Ben Kelley, *The Pavers and the Paved* (New York: Donald Brown, 1971).

8. Jonathan F. P. Rose, *The Well-Tempered City: What Modern Science, Ancient Civilizations, and Human Nature Teach Us About the Future of Urban Life* (New York: Harper Wave, 2016). Rose's bibliography is a great place to start for current integrative thinking about urban design.

9. Nadav Malin, "Walkable Neighborhoods Replace Suburbs as Preferred Real Estate," *EBN*, Oct 2012, 3.

10. Mark Childs, *Parking Spaces* (New York: McGraw-Hill, 1999), 195.

11. Candace Pearson, "Diesel Exhaust Throws Honeybees Off the Scent," *EBN*, Nov 2013, 18; American Cancer Society, "Diesel Exhaust and Cancer," www.cancer.org/cancer/cancer-causes/diesel-exhaust-and-cancer.html.

12. Ibid., 197.

13. Erin Weaver, "Rural Areas Feel Heat from Cities," *EBN*, Mar 2013, 5.

14. Tom Schueler, *Site Planning for Urban Stream Protection* (Ellicott City MD: Center for Watershed Protection, 1995), 148.

15. Ibid.

16. This was known as SAFE-TEA, a broad transportation act that includes clarification of accountability for "flexible" but well-reasoned designs. It was signed by President George W. Bush in 2005. The Context-Sensitive Design resource information website, www.contextsensitivesolutions.org/, confirms that "most legal experts agree that context-sensitive solutions will not cause the engineer [liability] problems as long as they are well reasoned and comprehensively documented." For the authoritative source on this subject, see Richard O. Jones (Federal Highway Administration Regional Counsel, Region 8), Transportation Research Board 2004 Distinguished Lectureship, "Context Sensitive Design: Will the Vision Overcome Liability Concerns?" available from the above website.

17. Erik Sherman, "Tales of Commuter Terror," *Computerworld*, 30 Oct 2000. Statistics from the Texas A&M Transportation Institute study of 1999, www.tti.tamu.edu/. ("We were waiting for the 2000 study, but the researchers got stuck in traffic," notes the writer wryly.)

18. The transit part of these cities was deliberately killed by auto interests, as fictionally depicted in the 1988 film *Who Framed Roger Rabbit?*

19. Cited in David Gram, "Paving Costs Skyrocket with Rising Oil Prices," Associated Press syndicated report, 16 Jun 2005. The article notes that the financial costs are due almost entirely to the high energy costs of paving. A version of this article, dated 3 Jul of the same year and citing a twenty-city average increase of 13 percent in 2004 alone, is online at www.washingtonpost.com/archive/politics/2005/07/03/rising-oil-prices-force-states-to-put-paving-projects-on-hold

/bf36f44d-11eb-4013-82b8-2217085a53b7/?utm_term=.fdf0178e320f.

20. Foundation for Pavement Preservation, "Pavement Preventive Maintenance Guidelines," update of 27 Mar 2001, 5, www.mdt.mt.gov/publications/docs/brochures/research/toolbox/FHWA/PavPrevMainGuides.pdf.

21. These policy suggestions are based on University of Georgia School of Environmental Design, *Land Development Provisions to Protect Georgia Water Quality*, ed. David Nichols (Athens: Georgia Department of Natural Resources, 1997).

22. *Impervious Surface Reduction Study* (Olympia WA: City of Olympia Public Works Department, 1995), final report, 84–85.

23. Center for Watershed Protection, *Model Development Principles to Protect Our Streams, Lakes, and Wetlands* (Ellicott City MD: Center for Watershed Protection, 1998), 76.

24. Richard S. Wilson, "Suburban Parking Requirements and the Shaping of Suburbia," *Journal of the American Planning Association* 61, no. 1 (1995): 29–42.

25. Center for Watershed Protection, *Model Development Principles*, 73.

26. Ibid., 75.

27. Richard Unterman, "Office Park Paradise," *LAM*, Aug 1998.

28. Like any other useful policy, it can be used as a smoke screen, where speedway standards are still the outcome and "public input" simply means "You had your say; now shut up."

29. K. Sorvig, "Paving of County Road 42 Without Storm-water Measures Gouges 8 Foot Deep by 100 Yard Gullies in Private Property." Unpublished white paper; to be posted with other supplemental materials for this book.

30. EPA regulations (NPDES Phase Two) require permanent soil stabilization for all projects larger than one acre; state and federal road projects in the same county routinely comply.

31. Technically, the "Green Bible" is titled *A Policy on Geometric Design of Highways and Streets*, 5th ed. (Washington DC: AASHTO, 2004). The problem of engineers insisting on *inflexible interpretations* of this book is so great that AASHTO also publishes "A Guide for Achieving Flexibility in Highway Design," a precursor to CSD. From https://bookstore.transportation.org/, or www.contextsensitivesolutions.org/, also the source for R. O. Jones, "Context Sensitive Design" (above). Jones explains the engineering community's overblown fear of liability: attempts to avoid lawsuits through rigid "standards" were a response to the historical loss of "sovereign immunity" for state officials in the 1950s. Limitations on design liability were not made law until the 1980s. Any engineer schooled in the intervening unprotected decades is likely to verge on paranoia about liability.

32. This and the following quote from R. A. White were found on his office's website (www.tlcnetwork.org/bobwhite.html), which has since been removed.

33. Emily Catacchio, "More Cyclists + Better Design = Safer Roadways," *EBN*, Feb 2011, 3.

34. Erin Weaver, "Pedestrians and Cyclists Are Good for Business," *EBN*, Jan 2013, 5. These results argue against complaints by businesses when pedestrianization of a street is proposed. Interestingly, supermarkets did not share the increased spending trend, probably because people tend to make single visits to stock up, which are awkward on a bike.

35. Drivers.com staff, "Traffic Calming and the Battle for the Roadway," 24 Dec 2009, www.drivers.com/article/122/.

While many motorists' associations treat traffic calming as a governmental conspiracy against their "rights," Drivers.com takes a very balanced view of the issues. Note that the full URL for the motorists' resource is www.drivers.com/*driving.php*; entering only www.drivers.com takes you to a site that offers software driver updates!

36. On traffic calming and scenic roads, see Christiana M. Briganti and Lester A. Hoel, "Design and Information Requirements for Travel and Tourism Needs on Scenic Byways—Final Report," VTRC95-R1 (Charlottesville: Virginia Transportation Research Council, Dec 1994), https://ntl.bts.gov/lib/36000/36900/36912/95-R1.pdf.

37. These acts, renewed periodically, have names like IS-TEA and TEA-21.

38. Robert B. Noland, "Traffic Fatalities and Injuries: The Effect of Changes in Infrastructure and Other Trends," *Accident Analysis and Prevention* 35, no. 4 (2003): 599–611. PDF online at www.sonic.net/~woodhull/trans/Noland_Hwy_Stds2.pdf. Originally presented at the 2001 annual meeting of the US Department of Transportation's Transportation Research Board.

39. Italics added. The study differentiates between controlled-access freeways, where some widening and straightening can improve safety, and other road types. On non-freeway roads, lanes wider than eleven feet encourage speeding and inattentiveness and result in more accidents and a higher percentage of accidents resulting in serious injury or death.

40. Federal Highway Administration Research and Technology, "Roadway Widths for Low-Traffic Volume Roads," FHWA-RD-94-023, Jul 1994, www.fhwa.dot.gov/publications/research/safety/humanfac/94023.cfm.

41. Alex Wilson, "Traffic Calming Ahead!" *EBN*, Mar 2003.

42. Daniel B. Wood, "American Cities Clearing Streets to Lure Residents Out of Their Cars," *Christian Science Monitor*, 25 May 2007.

43. This paranoiac view appears in T. Peter Ruane, "Zealots Would Stop Road Work," *Engineering News-Record*, 14 Jun 1999, 11. Ruane, president of ARTB, even considered urban sprawl to be "in the public interest," for obvious self-serving reasons.

44. Center for Watershed Protection, *Model Development Principles*, 33.

45. Crystal Atkins and Michael Coleman, "Influence of Traffic Calming on Emergency Response Times," *ITE Journal* (Aug 1997): 42–47.

46. A. Ann Sorensen and J. Dixon Esseks, "Living on the Edge: The Costs and Risks of Scatter Development," *American Farmland Trust Newsletter*, Mar 1998.

47. Wilson, "Traffic Calming Ahead!" Roundabouts only work where drivers are familiar with the rules, and many Americans are not.

48. See the Drivers.com website, note 35 above.

49. An official AASHTO "NCHRP Project 15-33 Status Report" was created, apparently in 2016 (https://design.transportation.org/wp-content/uploads/sites/21/2017/05/Overview-of-Creating-Complete-Corridors.pdf). This indicates that revisions to the 1991 guide began in 2000, and went through four or five major attempts before being submitted for "balloting" under the title *Creating Complete Roadway Corridors: The AASHTO Guide to Transportation Landscape Architecture and Environmental Design*. No part of that title appears in any subsequent AASHTO publications catalog that I can locate. The fact that new editions of guidelines on "inspection of safety hardware" and the like do appear would seem to indicate a reversion to conventional engineering attitudes among whomever the "balloting" parties were. In any case, these standards have been under development for exactly the amount of time that it has taken this book to go through three editions; authorship by engineering committee is clearly fraught. The unfortunate absence of a new standard makes the "NCHRP Project 15-33 Status Report" (a PowerPoint presentation) worth reviewing.

50. All references in this paragraph are from *EBN* reports: Jessica Boehland, "Dense Development Saves Energy," Sep 2005, 6; Allyson Wendt, "Report Finds Shorter Commutes in Portland," Nov 2007, 6; Candace Pearson, "The Poor Stay Poor in Sprawling Cities," Sep 2013, 19, referencing www.equality-of-opportunity.org/documents/; Alex Wilson and Rachel Navaro, "Driving to Green Buildings: The Transportation Energy Intensity of Buildings," Sep 2007, 1; and Paula Melton, "Study Says Urban Heat Islands Worsen Smog," Jul 2011, 5.

51. General information on road ecology is primarily from the website of the UC Davis Road Ecology Center, http://roadecology.ucdavis.edu/.

52. See James T. Carlton and Gregory M. Ruiz, "Vector Science and Integrated Vector Management in Bioinvasion Ecology," in *Invasive Alien Species: A New Synthesis*, ed. H. A. Mooney et al. (Washington DC: Island Press, 2005). It is well established that road construction, with soil disturbance and heavy equipment movements, is a major vector for invasive plant seeds.

53. Beginning with the 1997 transportation policy TEA-21, wildlife protection has been eligible for federal "intermodal" and context-sensitive funding.

54. From the executive summary of STPP's report by Patricia A. White and Michelle Ernst, "Second Nature: Improving Transportation Without Putting Nature Second," 22 Apr 2003, http://transact.org/wp-content/uploads/2014/04/Second_Nature.pdf.

55. See www.israel21c.org/waze-to-prevent-wildlife-from-becoming-roadkill/.

56. The same concept, using attacking forces to protect oneself, distinguishes "soft" martial arts, like aikido and tai chi, from "hard" ones, like karate and tae kwon do.

57. *Impervious Surface Reduction Study*, executive summary, 20.

58. Gary Cramer, "Naturally Secluded," *LAM*, Jan 2006.

59. BASMAA, *Start at the Source* (San Francisco: Bay Area Stormwater Management Agencies Association, 1997), 15; Bruce Ferguson was one of the consultants for this book.

60. The use of porous asphalt over a reservoir was first researched in the 1970s by Edmund Thelan and Fielding Howe of Philadelphia (the latter a practicing landscape architect). Firms such as Cahill and Associates, Resource Technologies, and Andropogon Associates were pioneers in its use.

61. Bruce Ferguson, *Porous Pavements* (Boca Raton FL: CRC Press, 2005), 499–500, cites five studies demonstrating 3-dB reduction.

62. John E. Paine, *Pervious Pavement Manual* (Orlando: Florida Concrete and Products Association, n.d.).

63. Porosity figures are from B. Ferguson, personal communication.

64. Grasspave[2] brochure from Invisible Structures.

65. *Impervious Surface Reduction Study*, 79–80.
66. James Sipes and Mack Roberts, "Grass Paving Systems," *LAM*, Jun 1994, 33.
67. "Henderson Field Demonstration Project Summary" (Olympia WA: City of Olympia, 1996), 13.
68. Sipes and Roberts, "Grass Paving Systems," 33.
69. "Henderson Field," 7–13.
70. Matthew Evans, Nina Bassuk, and Peter Trowbridge, "Sidewalk Design for Tree Survival," *LAM*, Mar 1990, 103.
71. Adam Arvidson, "A Green Demonstration," *LAM*, Sep 2006, 50.
72. Meg Calkins, "Cooling the Blacktop," *LAM*, Feb 2007, 54–61.
73. Hashem Akbari, US EPA, Climate Change Division, Lawrence Berkeley Laboratory, and US Department of Energy, *Cooling Our Communities: A Guidebook on Tree Planting and Light-Colored Surfacing* (Washington DC: Government Printing Office, 1992), US Lawrence Berkeley Laboratory report LBL-31587.
74. Childs, *Parking Spaces*, 196.
75. Information on these coatings comes from interviews with Deco Asphalt in California and Integrated Paving Concepts in Canada. Information on integral asphalt color is from interviews with Asphacolor (Madera CA). See resources for more information.
76. One study, funded by the asphalt industry and involving a very small sample of very small test sites, argued that surface-reflective paving did little to affect air temperatures, very likely an attack on the competition, concrete. See Candace Pearson, "More Questions Than Answers in Report on Reflective Pavements," *EBN*, Mar 2014, 19.
77. Jenny Anderson, "Willing to Lease Your Bridge," *New York Times*, 27 Aug 2008, C1.

Principle 6: Consider Origin and Fate of Materials
1. Quoted in William Thompson, "Is It Sustainable? Is It Art?," *LAM*, May 1992, 56–57.
2. Meg Calkins, *Materials for Sustainable Sites* (Hoboken NJ: Wiley, 2009), 24–27.
3. Kathleen Baughman, "The Use of Recycled Materials in the Landscape," unpublished, Washington State University, 1995, 16.
4. Reported in K. David Pijawka, "Dozens of Activities Mark Second Annual 'Arizona Recycles Day,'" *AZ Recycling Review*, Spring 1999, 16.
5. Maurice Nelischer, quoted in Thompson, "Is It Sustainable? Is It Art?"
6. See Table 7.9, p. 329, for these and other transportation energy rates.
7. Candace Pearson, "Waiting for Take-Back Programs for Building Materials," *EBN*, Nov 2013, 9.
8. Kevin Killough, "The Recycling Crisis," *Santa Fe (NM) Crosswinds Weekly*, 17 Apr 2003, 10–13. Statistics cited are from Killough's interviews with solid-waste management specialists throughout the United States.
9. Robert Weller, "Copper Snatchers Moving On to Aluminum," Associated Press syndicated report, 6 Jun 2006. The article notes that such thefts have been common on the East Coast for years but have spread, partly driven by demand from China.
10. US Environmental Protection Agency, Office of Resource Conservation and Recovery, "Advancing Sustainable Materials Management: Facts and Figures 2013," EPA530-R-15-002, Jun 2015, www.epa.gov/sites/production/files/2015-09/.../2013_advncng_smm_fs.pdf.
11. Even the formidable AIA *Environmental Resource Guide* (Joseph Demikin, ed. [New York: Wiley 1997]) misuses the term "renewable," making it a synonym for recyclable (p. 06118:2).
12. HOK Architects, *Sustainable Design Guide*, ed. Sandra Mendler (Washington DC: HOK Architects, 1998), iii. (This was the in-house edition; see above for Wiley's publication of this title.)
13. "Adobe" derives from Egyptian *al-tub* ("the brick"), showing how ancient this material is.
14. A large population building expansive adobe homes could threaten its own farmland, as appears to have happened in some areas of Egypt. Whether this should be blamed on adobe, overpopulation, or McMansion consumerism is debatable.
15. Baughman, "Recycled Materials," 19.
16. These projects were featured in an article in *Dwell* magazine, Apr 2002. The supplier/designer was the Glass Garden of Los Angeles, which has apparently gone out of business as of 2017.
17. Baughman, "Recycled Materials," 29.
18. Barbara Ryder, "Glass: Landscape Applications," *LAM*, Jun 1995, 28.
19. Baughman, "Recycled Materials," 29.
20. Ibid., 39.
21. "Waste Tire Problem Becomes Opportunity for Erosion Control," *Land and Water*, Mar 1998, 36.
22. "Recycled Tires Turn a Problem into a Solution," *Erosion Control*, Sep 1998, 18–21.
23. According to Pliny Fisk, tire surfaces pick up some pollutants from road contact, but these are removed by simple washing. Fisk notes that the EPA has tested the chemical content of tires because they are so common in playgrounds and has found them inert.
24. "Recycled Tires."
25. See www.epa.gov/smm/comprehensive-procurement-guideline-cpg-program. A good, though dated, introduction to the surprising breadth of recycled landscape materials is Wesley Groesbeck and Jan Striefel, *The Resource Guide to Sustainable Landscapes and Gardens*, 2nd ed. (Salt Lake City UT: Environmental Resources, 1995). It can still be found used on Amazon, and in libraries, and could be handy if the EPA disappears. Lists more than 2,000 products by CSI section.
26. See www.plasticsnews.com/rankings/plastic-lumber/search?count=600&CompanyName=&State=&Country=&Public=&Processes=.
27. Kim Sorvig, "Brave New Landscape," *LAM*, Jul 1992, 75–77.
28. Mark Piepkorn, "A Strawboard Manufacturing Update," *EBN*, May 2005, 8.
29. Andrea Johnson, "Turning Straw into Board Remains Daunting, but 'Do-able,'" *Farm & Ranch Guide*, 6 Sep 2001, www.farmandranchguide.com/news/turning-straw-into-board-remains-daunting-but-do-able/article_b5fa1f33-387a-5202-afbe-1276746208d2.html.
30. Alex Wilson, "Test Methods Approved for Plastic Lumber," *EBN*, Oct 1997, 4. (Includes contacts for further information.)
31. Daniel Winterbottom, "Plastic Lumber," *LAM*, Jan 1995, 34. Updated from Calkins, *Materials*.
32. Calkins, *Materials*, 394.

33. See Emily Bragonier, "Recycled Plastics Enter Structural Applications," *EBN*, Mar 2010, 8; other information is from www.axionintl.com.

34. New Mexico designer Buck Dant refers to it as "woodworking with pasta." It occasionally gums up power tool bits and blades temporarily.

35. Anil Srivastava and Ronald van Rooijen, "Bitumen Performance in Hot and Arid Climates," conference paper, *Innovative Road Rehabilitation and Recycling Technologies*, 24–26 Oct 2000, Amman, Jordan; online at www.e-asfalto.com/datoseuropa /Bitumen%20performance%20in%20hot%20and%20 arid%20climates.htm. See also http://earthuntouched.com /plastic-roads-revolutionary-idea/.

36. "Where the Rubber Meets the Trail," *Rails to Trails*, Winter 1999, 5.

37. *San Jose Mercury News*, "Old-Growth Forests Get a Break from Home Depot," *Santa Fe New Mexican*, 29 Aug 1999, D-1. The Rainforest Action Network, which was instrumental in persuading Home Depot to make this decision, notes that by 2000, six other major lumber suppliers had taken the same pledge. See www.ran.org/ran30_30_years_of_preserving_rainforests.

38. Daniel D. Chiras, *Environmental Science: Action for a Sustainable Future*, 4th ed. (Redwood City CA: Benjamin/Cummings, 1994), 203–9.

39. This insistence that all environmental standards be voluntary and self-policing typifies American policy, from certified lumber to LEED to refusal to ratify the Kyoto Protocol, or Paris climate accord.

40. The EPA's website, Sustainable Market Place (www.epa.gov /greenerproducts), provides information for governmental, private, and institutional purchasers, as well as manufacturers, about "EPP," which stands for environmentally preferable purchasing, and is governmentese for sustainable products. "Preferable" avoids endorsing any particular product, conforming to the demand for exclusively voluntary standards (see the previous note).

41. The following *EBN* articles provided information on illegal activity: Candace Pearson, "Forced Labor Common in Producing Bricks, Timber," Oct 2016, 17; Paula Melton, "The Lacey Act and the Building Industry: Sourcing Legal Wood," May 2016, 24; Paula Melton, "FSC to Use Forensics to Uncover Criminal Forestry Practices," Dec 2013, 14; and Michael Wilmeth, "Illegal Timber Trade Targeted by New Law," Oct 2008, 4.

42. Pliny Fisk, *Comparison of Available Wastes and Production of Wood Products* (Austin TX: Center for Maximum Potential Building Systems, 1993). This information is graphed from data by the US Department of Commerce, the Natural Resources Research Institute, the US EPA, and the Institute for Local Self-Reliance.

43. Information on AERT thanks to Pliny Fisk.

44. Nadav Malin and Mark Piepkorn, "PaperStone: Panels Made with Cashew-Nut-Hull Resin," *EBN*, Apr 2006, 10.

45. Tristan Roberts, "Bamboo Dimensional Lumber? Lumboo Is Here," *EBN*, Jun 2010, 8; current offerings at www.cali bamboo.com. Abandonment of the Lumboo trademark as of January 2017 is recorded at www.trademarkia.com/lum boo-85005211.html. From personal experience using bamboo plywood, Cali Bamboo is helpful and innovative, and the com-pany might work with designers to test bamboo dimensional products for landscape use.

46. Calkins, *Materials*, 103–5. Conversion of GJ/tonne to Btu/ ton by me.

47. Candace Pearson, "EPA Finds Coal Fly Ash Safe in Concrete and Gypsum Wallboard," *EBN*, Apr 2014, 19. This has been *EBN*'s position for some time.

48. Nicole Saldarriaga, "Roman Concrete: A Forgotten Stroke of Genius," *Classical Wisdom Weekly*, 15 Jul 2016, http://classical wisdom.com/roman-concrete-forgotten-stroke-genius/.

49. L. Bushi and J. Meil, "An Environmental Life Cycle Assessment of Portland-Limestone and Ordinary Portland Cements in Concrete," technical brief, Jan 2014, www.athenasmi.org /wp-content/uploads/2014/01/CAC_PLCvsOPC_Final _Technical_Brief.pdf.

50. Paula Melton, "Impact of Concrete Extends to Sand and Gravel Production," *EBN*, Nov 2013, 25.

51. Candace Pearson, "Sand, a Surprisingly Limited Resource," *EBN*, Dec 2016, 16.

52. Brent Ehrlich, "CarbonCure: Capturing Carbon in Concrete Blocks," *EBN*, Jul 2012, 6. The process does not seem to be adaptable for in-situ poured concrete.

53. "Buying Concrete—12 Tips to Determining Project Success," 26 Jan 2014, *On the House* (blog), http://onthehouse.com /buying-concrete-12-tips-determing-project-success/.

54. There have been objections from conventional ready-mix operators that volumetric trucks are classified as machinery or "plant" rather than as vehicles, and thus avoid weight limits and taxes; see, for example, Jim Taylor, "Volumetric Mixer Trucks Should Be Banned!," 18 Nov 2015, www.linkedin .com/pulse/volumetric-mixer-trucks-should-banned-jim-tay lor. IMHO, these objections don't weigh up against the waste, fuel, and time savings offered by this system, and can be corrected by revising tax codes, rather than banning the technology. It astonishes me how often laissez-faire ideology is abandoned when a threat to one's own commercial success is perceived.

55. US Environmental Protection Agency, Office of Water, "Stormwater Best Management Practice: Concrete Washout," EPA 833-F-11-006, Feb 2012, www3.epa.gov/npdes/pubs /concretewashout.pdf.

56. Audrey Copeland and Kent Hansen, "Innovation in Asphalt Pavements," *Civil + Structural Engineer*, Sep 2014, http://ce news.com/article/9874/innovation-in-asphalt-pavements. "Thinlay" techniques are discussed. The authors are employed by the National Asphalt Pavement Association.

57. The EPA's recommendation for maximum indoor concentration of radon, 4 picocuries, was set at the average amount of radon found naturally in outdoor air, an example of zero-risk application of the Precautionary Principle (see the next note). European standards allow slightly higher concentrations.

58. This concept is formally called the Precautionary Principle.

59. Phillip J. Craul, *Urban Soil in Landscape Design* (New York: Wiley, 1992). Based on Craul's Table 6.1, p. 186.

60. Indoor air or environmental quality is IAQ or IEQ to specialists.

61. Paula Baker, Erica Elliott, and John Banta, *Prescriptions for a Healthy House* (Santa Fe NM: InWord Publishers, 1998), xv–xvi.

62. Ibid., 55–59.

63. Kingsley Hammett, "When Building 'Green' Isn't Green Enough," *Designer/Builder*, Nov–Dec 2006, 27–28.

64. Mark Matrusek with Bill McKibben, "Live Better with Less: Our High-Powered Economy Is Based on Growth, So Why Is All Our Stuff Making Us Less and Less Happy?," *AARP The Magazine*, May–Jun 2007, 54–57.

65. US Department of Energy, Office of Energy Efficiency and Renewable Energy, "How Energy-Efficient Light Bulbs Compare with Traditional Incandescents," https://energy.gov/energysaver/how-energy-efficient-light-bulbs-compare-traditional-incandescents. Amory Lovins, Rocky Mountain Institute, for watts-to-toxins conversion rates.

66. A conservative estimate of plutonium toxicity, from www.physics.isu.edu/radinf/pluto.htm.

67. Alex Wilson, "Making Recycling Work," *EBN*, Feb 2005, 2. Subsidizing fossil fuels has the added effect of making virgin materials, especially plastics, so cheap that recycling (and alternative energy and transportation) falsely appears not to be economically viable.

68. Fisk's work is reported in many publications but is not as well-known or widely used as it should be. In the following citations, "ASES" refers to the American Solar Energy Society, www.ases.org/. Pliny Fisk III and Richard MacMath, "Carbon Dioxide Intensity Ratios: A Method of Evaluating the Upstream Global Warming Impact of Long-Life Building Materials," *ASES National Conference Proceedings*, 2000. Pliny Fisk III, Gail Vittori, and Roldolfo Ramina, "BaseLine Green and GreenBalance: A Step Beyond Sustainability in Building Performance," *ASES National Conference Proceedings*, 2000. Much of this literature is available at www.cmpbs.org/flash/download.htm.

69. US Environmental Protection Agency, Office of Research and Development, "Guide to Cleaner Technologies: Organic Coating Replacements," EPA/625/R-94/006, Sep 1994, and the more recent www.epa.gov/stationary-sources-air-pollution/architectural-coatings-national-volatile-organic-compounds-emission and www.epa.gov/stationary-sources-air-pollution/fact-sheets-architectural-coating-rule-volatile-organic-compounds.

70. On PVC, see AIA, *Environmental Resource Guide*, Mat-09652: 35–37. On wood preservatives, see Alex Wilson, "A Call for CCA Phase-Out," *EBN*, Mar 1997, 2, and other articles in *EBN*.

71. Meg Calkins, "To PVC or Not to PVC," *LAM*, Mar 2006.

72. John Motloch, quoted in Calkins, "To PVC or Not to PVC."

73. "The PVC Debate: A Fresh Look," *EBN*, Feb 2014, 1–11. Brent Ehrlich's article is an excellent source of detail.

74. AIA, *Environmental Resource Guide*, Mat-09652: 36. Additional information for the revised edition on PVC comes from Calkins, "To PVC or Not to PVC," and from Greenpeace International, "The Poison Plastic," 2 Jun 2003, www.greenpeace.org/international/en/campaigns/detox/polyvinyl-chloride/the-poison-plastic/.

75. Tristan Roberts, "USGBC Releases Final Report on PVC Avoidance," *EBN*, Mar 2007, 2.

76. The quoted example, from the Greenpeace website cited above, emphasizes how downcycling uses the landscape as a "sink" for materials that are not acceptable in other uses.

77. These findings are summarized from Calkins, "To PVC or Not to PVC."

78. Tristan Roberts, "Treated Wood in Transition: Less Toxic Options in Preserved and Protected Wood," *EBN*, Aug 2006. Roberts provides an excellent historical perspective on changes in the industry and *EBN*'s involvement in calls for improvement.

79. Tristan Roberts, "EPA Limits Wood Preservative ACC to Commercial Uses," *EBN*, Feb 2007, 4.

80. Alex Wilson, "Using Wood Outdoors," *LAM*, Sep 1999, quoted from manuscript.

81. Alex Wilson, "CCA Phase-Out," *EBN*, Jan–Feb 1993, 10; earlier research backing up the phase-out proposal.

82. Barry Goodell et al., "Brown-Rot Decay of ACQ and CA-B Treated Lumber," *Forest Products Journal* 57, no. 6 (Jun 2007), www.freepatentsonline.com/article/Forest-Products-Journal/166092797.html.

83. Tristan Roberts, "Smaller Copper Particles, Smaller Environmental Impact for Treated Wood," *EBN*, Feb 2008, 8. See also Calkins, *Materials*, 306.

84. Paula Melton, "Treated Wood for Ground Contact, Minus the Toxic Pesticides," *EBN*, Sep 2016, 18.

85. Information is from the company's US website, www.kebony.com/us.

86. *EBN*, Mar 2008, 10, and May 2008, 11, cover PureWood and Cambia wood, respectively.

87. Tristan Roberts, "New Owner of TimberSIL Hopes to Put Failures in the Past," *EBN*, Apr 2016, 24. This was the most recent of a series of articles going back to 2004. EBN (and I) had high hopes for this product; reporting on promising products inevitably entails a percentage of guessing wrong.

88. Brent Ehrlich, "Cool Products from the Latest Greenbuild Expo," *EBN*, Dec 2014, 2.

89. National Research Council, *A Research Strategy for Environmental, Health, and Safety Aspects of Engineered Nanomaterials* (Washington DC: National Academies Press, 2012). Online at www.nap.edu/catalog/13347/a-research-strategy-for-environmental-health-and-safety-aspects-of-engineered-nanomaterials.

90. *EBN*, Jul 2006, 11, and Apr 2005, 9, discuss this process, which reduces the need for terrestrial logging and often produces large logs of exceptional quality. Some methods disturb aquatic ecosystems; others, specifically designed to avoid this, have won environmental awards.

91. AAPFCO's rules on metals are found on its website, www.aapfco.org/. The Washington levels are noted in a report written by Erika Schreder, "Holding the Bag: How Toxic Waste in Fertilizer Fails Farmers and Gardeners," for the Washington Toxics Coalition, an activist group, available at https://48h57c2l31ua3c3fmq1ne58b-wpengine.netdna-ssl.com/wp-content/uploads/2016/09/holding-the-bag.pdf. The latter table shows levels found in fertilizers in the state.

92. Associated Press, "Report: Toxic Chemicals Recycled into Fertilizers," *Santa Fe New Mexican*, 7 Jul 1997, and other reports subsequently.

93. The source of these quotes is www.epa.gov/agriculture/agriculture-nutrient-management-and-fertilizer#Wastes. Unlike most EPA pages, this one has no link to any legally binding policy, nor to any guidelines about converting waste to fertilizer. It also acknowledges that some states have passed

regulations more stringent than the federal ones, which is disingenuous given that interstate commerce is often involved in these conversions.

Principle 7: Know the Costs of Energy over Time

1. Tracy Mumma, "Reducing the Embodied Energy of Buildings," *Home Energy*, Jan 1995, 19–22.

2. See "Landscapes Against Climate Change," p. 20, for further information on Architecture 2030. Statistics for other countries are similar, from 40 to nearly 50 percent. In the first edition, we noted that the American Institute of Architects estimated more than 30 percent of US energy went to buildings (American Institute of Architects, *Environmental Resource Guide*, ed. Joseph A. Demkin (loose-leaf, current through 1998; supplement ed., New York: Wiley, 1998) (AIA-ERG). The difference probably represents greater sophistication in Mazria's more recent statistical methods; the AIA has endorsed Architecture 2030.

3. R. G. Stein et al., *Handbook of Energy Use for Building Construction*, vol. DOE/CS/20220-1, *Energy Conservation* (Washington DC: US Department of Energy, 1980), 9–10. These statistics are based on conditions in the 1970s and are probably not exactly comparable to the AIA figures.

4. The term also applies to radioactive energy, and to explosive materials. For comparison of specific energy among different materials, see the Wikipedia entry on energy density (a close synonym).

5. Kenneth M. Swezey, *Formulas, Methods, Tips, and Data* (New York: Harper and Row, 1969), 595, 620; based on average density for different species of pine of 37.5 lb./cu. ft., and an average of 12.5 million Btu per cord (128 cu. ft.).

6. Both statistics are from AIA-ERG, closely comparable to Stein et al.

7. This use of the term is scattered throughout the several informative publications of the DOE's Office of Industrial Technology.

8. HOK Architects, *Sustainable Design Guide*, ed. Sandra Mendler (Washington DC: HOK Architects, 1998), 2.21, for example.

9. Mumma, "Reducing Embodied Energy," 19.

10. Ibid., 20. Costs are in energy terms, not in dollars paid for energy.

11. Erin Weaver, "Home Size, Appliance Glut Cancel Out Efficiency Gains," *EBN*, Apr 2013, 35.

12. A high embodied:operating energy ratio is also common in *buildings* in developing nations, where HVAC and appliances are not as large a factor. See Paula Melton, "EDGE: A Green Building Playbook for Developing Countries," *EBN*, Jun 2016. See also www.edgebuildings.com. EDGE is a project of the World Bank International Finance Corporation, offering software to help reduce resource intensity. Like so many attempts to standardize sustainability, the software assumes conventional building types and systems; for example, in the category "fuel used for water heating," users must choose among electric, LPG, natural gas, diesel, or none; a building with solar hot water equipment cannot be distinguished from a building that lacks hot water. EDGE also certifies buildings, but as the site notes, certification is about green assets (features of the building), and explicitly not about performance. This entry in the crowded field of green certification appears to be primarily aimed at financiers and investors. One useful aspect of EDGE is that it takes into account in which country or region the project is to be built; however, omissions like solar hot water versus no hot water undermine the attempt to represent developing countries, or, perhaps, push EDGE toward modeling only the buildings of the upper classes in such countries.

13. Work and time comparison from Erik Bruun and Buzzy Keith, *Heavy Equipment* (New York: Black Dog and Leventhal, 1997), 10. (Assume a full workday means eight hours in this context.) Horsepower of scraper from pp. 22–23 (a bulldozer or second scraper is often required to push the working scraper in hard soils; this doubles the energy consumption, but is not included here). Horsepower to gallons per hour from Herbert L. Nichols Jr. and David A. Day, *Moving the Earth: The Workbook of Excavation*, 4th ed. (New York: McGraw-Hill, 1998), 12.111. Gallons to Btu based on Table 7.1. Human energy expenditure per workday based on Richard C. Dorf, *The Energy Factbook* (New York: McGraw-Hill, 1981), 10, approximately 0.7 kW per worker per day, converted to 2,500 Btu; some sources give much higher energy use for human labor, which is very variable and, in a mechanical sense, inefficient.

14. The concept of ERoEI (energy return on energy invested, a.k.a. net energy) is useful for understanding both fuels and foods in terms of the energy used to produce them. Specifics, however, are hotly debated and are often distorted by pro-oil/anti-oil partisanship. Only the briefest overview is appropriate here. Petroleum products' ERoEI varies widely: difficulty of discovery, depth of well, distance to refinery, and so on, all affect it. Historically, however, the rate of return has fallen drastically: as recently as the 1940s, one barrel of crude invested in producing more crude returned 100 to 200 barrels. Today, even oil-industry estimates admit a 1:30 ratio, and many sources indicate that 1 barrel invested now produces only 5 to 7 barrels. Fracking, though expensive, increases ERoEI initially, but it appears that this applies only when fracturing is quite new and is releasing a lot of gas previously untapped; many fracked wells seem to go dry quite quickly. For some offshore or otherwise difficult wells, ERoEI can actually be negative. Transporting the crude to a refinery, and the refined products to consumers, is apparently not included consistently. The best "alternative" energy sources have ERoEI in single digits, but despite disinformation spread by the oil industry and conventional utilities, these ratios are positive, and renewability makes a serious difference, since the return declines only slowly over a long usable production life. As for food, "primitive" societies, because they grow food where it is used and recycle local organic wastes to do so, manage to squeeze just slightly more calories from their harvests than are used to grow those crops (ERoEI about 1.1). "Advanced" agribusiness, using petroleum-based fuels, fertilizers, and pesticides, and distributing food thousands of miles from where it is produced, gets less energy out of food than is embodied in its production (ten times less, by some estimates). Even using ERoEI, comparing human and animal energy to machine energy is seldom precise. It is clear, however, that human labor generally uses energy more sustainably: renewably, and without pollution. For more information, Wikipedia's entry is a good, detailed introduction. Howard Odum's many works are also a good source; he terms this issue "emergy."

15. The National Solar Jobs Census, conducted annually by The Solar Foundation since 2010; see www.thesolarfoundation.org/national/.

16. Erin Weaver, "Renewables Jump to 11% of U.S. Energy Production," *EBN*, May 2013, 19.

17. Joshua D. Rhodes, "When Will Rooftop Solar Be Cheaper Than the Grid?" *U.S. News & World Report*, 31 Mar 2016. The online article has animated maps showing where rooftop PV at different installed prices would outcompete the grid. As noted elsewhere, this economic threat is inciting backlash, some of it very underhanded, from conventional utility companies.

18. Brent Ehrlich, "Mobile Photovoltaic Power Generators," *EBN*, Feb 2010, 6.

19. The specific product no longer has any Web visibility in 2017; however, similar generators are being installed on municipal supply lines. See "Harnessing Hydropower from Urban Water Pipes," *Popular Science*, Jun 2015. Generation can occur only when water is flowing. Because both flow volume and pressure are relatively low in residential plumbing, output from in-line generators is usually limited. The concept appears to work better with the major and relatively constant flows of municipal and industrial water systems.

20. Fabio La Mantia et al., "Batteries for Efficient Energy Extraction from a Water Salinity Difference," *Nano Letters* 11, no. 4 (2011): 1810–13; see also Bob Yirka, "New Entropy Battery Pulls Energy from Difference in Salinity Between Fresh Water and Seawater," Phys.org, 25 Mar 2011, https://phys.org/news/2011-03-entropy-battery-energy-difference-salinity.html#.

21. Arthur Max, "Hot Pavement Tapped for Heat Among Solar-Power Innovations," Associated Press, 29 Dec 2007.

22. For more detail on oil and gas landscape impacts, see K. Sorvig, "Welcome to Frackville," *LAM*, Jun 2013, 75–91.

23. J. W. Storm van Leeuwen and Philip B. Smith, "Nuclear Power—the Energy Balance," Nuclear Power Insights, Chaam, Netherlands, Aug 2005. Online at www.stormsmith.nl. See also Frank Barnaby and James Kemp, eds., "Secure Energy? Civil Nuclear Power, Security, and Global Warming" (London: Oxford Research Group, 2004), http://oxfordresearchgroup.org.uk/sites/default/files/secureenergy.pdf.

24. Matthew L. Wald, "Wind Energy Bumps Into Power Grid's Limits" *New York Times*, 27 Aug 2008, A1.

25. Amy M. Amos, "Bat Killings by Wind Energy Turbines Continue: Industry Plan to Reduce Deadly Effects of Blades May Not Be Enough, Some Scientists Say," *Scientific American*, 7 Jun 2016. Turbine rotation kills bats directly and can also create such vacuums around the blades that bats die with lungs bleeding. Sonic patterns made by the blades can reportedly interfere with bat navigation as well. The industry plan involves stopping turbines at low wind speeds, when bats are most active, but wildlife biologists believe the stoppage must extend to slightly higher speeds. Industry claims their plan reduces bat deaths by 30 percent; scientific evidence indicates that 90 percent or more could be achieved without reducing energy output by even 1 percent.

26. Search online for "windmill fail videos" for dramatic footage.

27. Kim Sorvig, "Sun on the Water," *LAM*, Sep 1994.

28. Candace Pearson, "Solar-PV Safety Training Offered to Firefighters," *EBN*, Sep 2014, 18. Panels must be disconnected, or they will pose electrocution risks; they also obstruct some firefighting methods that require holes through roofs.

29. R. P. Siegel, "Will 'Floatovoltaics' Become the Next Big Thing?," GreenBiz.com, 24 Jun 2015, www.greenbiz.com/article/will-floatovoltaics-become-next-big-thing.

30. Rebecca R. Hernandez, Madison K. Hoffacker, and Christopher B. Field, "Efficient Use of Land to Meet Sustainable Energy Needs," *Nature Climate Change* 5 (2015): 353–58, www.nature.com/nclimate/journal/v5/n4/full/nclimate2556.html#contrib-auth.

31. French installation was reported in *The Guardian* (London); video at www.youtube.com/watch?v=9PoHXscWdGM. A *National Geographic* video discusses other European projects, interviewing engineers involved: www.youtube.com/watch?v=YQba3ENhlKA.

32. "Solar Freakin' Roadways!," www.youtube.com/watch?v=qlTA3rnpgzU.

33. "Energy storage without the toxic chemicals," in Brent Ehrlich, "Greenest of the Green Energy-Saving Products from Greenbuild," *EBN*, Jan 2016, 13, part of a Top-10 Green Building Products awards article.

34. For debunking of the "lithium mining is worse than tar sands" meme, see https://cleantechnica.com/2016/05/12/lithium-mining-vs-oil-sands-meme-thorough-response/, from an organization devoted solely to clean technologies in various industry and consumer sectors. Ranking as an element is from Wikipedia's entry on lithium, which includes extensive detail.

35. Tristan Roberts, "Solar Cell Breaks World Record," *EBN*, Jan 2007, 7.

36. The standard is 1,000 W/m² insolation at a cell temperature of 25°C (77°F).

37. According to the manufacturer's published analysis, at http://solarwall.com/en/products/pvthermal.php.

38. Professionals should also vote with their dollars for more efficiently designed machines.

39. Nadav Malin, "Battery Fanatic," *EBN*, Mar 1993, 4.

40. Associated Press, "General Motors Unveils New Stationary Generator," 8 Aug 2001.

41. See http://auto.ihs.com/news/2006/, "European Fuel Cell Bus Project Extended One Year" (search this site for "fuel cell"), and Joel Makower and Ron Pernick, "Clean Energy Markets," *Solar Today*, Sep 2002, 30.

42. Inside EVs (electric vehicles) website: http://insideevs.com/toyota-mirai-sales-in-u-s-hits-milestone-of-250-hyundai-tucson-fuel-cell-exceeds-100/.

43. The National Fuel Cell Research Center, University of California, Irvine, has a website that explains fuel cells from both technical and market perspectives, in clear language and diagrams. Start at www.nfcrc.uci.edu/3/FUEL_CELL_INFORMATION/FCexplained/index.aspx.

44. These are the 1997 record holders for largest truck and largest hydraulic excavator in the world, both built by Komatsu. Even these, picked because they resemble familiar equipment types, are far from the world's largest or heaviest equipment, since bucket-wheel excavators range up to nearly 15,000 tons, moving 10,000 or more cubic yards of soil per hour. Bruun and Keith, *Heavy Equipment*.

45. These are rough figures within what is actually a range of energy, influenced especially by temperature and elevation at the site. Diesel, for example, can produce between 132,000 and 152,000 Btu per gallon. For extremely detailed information on this topic, see John B. Haywood, *Internal Combustion Engine Fundamentals* (New York: McGraw-Hill, 1988). Eventually, evaluation will have to include biodiesel, ethanol, and other biofuels.

46. Properly speaking, the horsepower figure should be actual, tested horsepower. For *rough* estimating and comparison of different machine *types*, using the rated or theoretical horsepower is probably accurate enough; it is often the only figure available.

47. Machinery engineers seem to rate fuel usages in pounds. Nichols and Day, *Moving the Earth*, 12.110–12.111, gives the basic figures; conversion to Btu and to light/heavy percentages is mine.

48. Tanaka was one small-engine manufacturer that met stringent CARB emission standards from *before* the 2000 deadline. Others include Komatsu-Zenoah and Redmax.

49. Felicity Barringer, "Greener Way to Cut Grass Runs Afoul of Powerful Lobby," *New York Times*, 24 Apr 2006, A1. Information on the political machinations against the CARB effort are from this article. OPEI's statement of support for the regulations is posted on its website.

50. The senator who controlled the EPA's budget during this period was Kit Bond, a Republican from Missouri, where Briggs and Stratton has two lawnmower plants. (According to a *New York Times* editorial from 25 Apr 2006, "in 2003, Mr. Bond reached a deal with Senator Dianne Feinstein that allows California to enact its own clean air laws but blocks any other state from following its lead.") Fire safety was used, unsuccessfully, as a Detroit argument against catalytic converters on cars in the 1970s. A 2005 study by the EPA found that converters on mowers posed little increased fire risk (see http://epa.gov/). For a conservative Republican, Bond was remarkably willing to use taxpayer money to force the EPA and National Research Council to beat this dead horse, and he reportedly (in the *New York Times*, cited above) considered even further studies, one of them with a $650,000 price tag, to get the desired results. In 2010, however, Bond gave up his legislative seat and went into private business. Even the Republicans for Environmental Protection's 2006 Scorecard rated Bond's environmental voting record at minus two.

51. Michael Wilmeth, "New Rules Will Reduce Lawnmower Emissions," *EBN*, Oct 2008, 6.

52. Irwin Post, "Horsepower: Is Bigger Really Better?" *Independent Sawmill and Woodlot Management*, Apr 1999, 15–17.

53. OPEI survey, reported in "New Nationwide Poll Finds Increased Misfueling of Engines Despite Awareness of Ethanol in Gasoline," *Landscape and Irrigation*, "Daily News," 15 Mar 2017.

54. Alex Wilson, "Milwaukee Introduces Tools with Greener Batteries," *EBN*, Mar 2005, 11.

55. Glen D. Huey, "Corded or Cordless: Which Is More Green?," *Popular Woodworking Magazine*, 4 Mar 2008, www.popularwoodworking.com/woodworking-blogs/editors-blog/corded-or-cordless-which-is-more-green.

56. John P. Rollins and Compressed Air and Gas Institute, *Compressed Air and Gas Handbook*, 5th ed. (Englewood Cliffs NJ: Prentice Hall, 1989), 846, Table 13.31.

57. Helen H. Whiffen, "Landscape Maintenance Takes Energy: Use It Wisely," *Energy Efficiency and Environmental News* (University of Florida Extension), Feb 1993. This newsletter is viewable at http://edis.ifas.ufl.edu/.

58. Based on Dorf, *Energy Factbook*, 11. Human metabolism and energy output are notoriously variable. Other experts consider 300 Btu per hour an average for light labor, like desk jobs or driving a truck, and rate very heavy labor up to 1,500 Btu per hour.

59. Tree Toad products are available directly from www.treetoad.com/.

60. *PMI Network*, March 2008, "Power Trip," unattributed article; PMI is the Project Management Institute, www.pmi.org.

61. Vaclav Smil, *Energies: An Illustrated Guide to the Biosphere and Civilization* (Cambridge MA: MIT Press, 1999), 90.

62. The calculation is based on the tonnage hauled by an eighteen-wheeler, but similar ton-mile efficiency is achieved by some large construction trucks. From a very interesting and unusually objective website on all matters truck related: www.yondar.com/yondar/faq.htm. The website has been removed; contact for Yondar International: Ray Gompf, President and General Manager, 2889 Haughton Street, Ottawa, ON K2B 6Z4 Canada, 613-596-5173.

63. Howard T. Odum and Elizabeth C. Odum, *Energy Basis for Man and Nature* (New York: McGraw-Hill, 1976), 34, Figure 2-5.

64. Alex Wilson and Rachel Navaro, "Driving to Green Buildings: The Transportation Energy Intensity of Buildings," *EBN*, Sep 2007, 1, 11–18.

65. Based on Bill Lawson, *Building Materials, Energy, and the Environment* (Red Hill, Australia: Royal Australian Institute of Architects, 1996), Tables 1.2 (road transport) and 1.3 (brick embodied energy).

66. This section's heading is borrowed from one of the first articles on embodied energy in construction: Nadav Malin, "Embodied Energy—Just What Is It and Why Do We Care?" *EBN*, May–Jun 1993, 8–9.

67. Ibid., 9.

68. Lawson, *Building Materials*, 12, Table 1.1.

69. G. Baird et al., "Progress Toward the Specification of Embodied Energy Performance Criteria for New Zealand Buildings" (Ponrua NZ: Building Research Association of New Zealand, 1998).

70. ASMI's website, www.athenasmi.ca/; click heading "The Challenge."

71. Mumma, "Reducing Embodied Energy," 22.

72. 1994 edition (Wiley), 122–23.

73. Gas, observant reader, is exactly $1 per gallon; prehistoric.

74. Based on Hal Post and Vernon Risser, *Stand-alone Photovoltaic Systems: A Handbook of Recommended Design Practices* (Albuquerque NM: Sandia National Laboratory, 1991), Ref: SAND877023, revised, 59–64 and worksheet on B-57.

75. Although the two terms are used interchangeably, present *worth* seems to refer to the formulas or factors used to compute present *value*.

76. The acceptance of interest and inflation predictions as gospel makes present value a fiction—one that has excessive influence in free-market society.

Principle 8: Celebrate Light, Respect Darkness

1. John Schaeffer and Real Goods staff, *The Book of Light* (Ukiah CA: Real Goods, 1996), 4–11, discusses energy use and lighting. "Largest single use of electricity" varies by year and between residential, commercial, and industrial. For 2016, air-conditioning and refrigeration held the title in both residential and commercial sectors, with lighting in third place (residential, after water heating) and fifth place (commercial). Data are from www.eia.gov/energyexplained/index.cfm?page =electricity_use.

2. Schaeffer and Real Goods, *Book of Light*; the original source of this information appears to be Amory Lovins and the Rocky Mountain Institute.

3. Ucilia Wang, "How LEDs Are Going to Change the Way We Look at Cities," *Forbes*, 29 Sep 2014. Interesting paired photos before and after LEDs were installed in Los Angeles are in the online article, at www.forbes.com/sites/uciliawang/2014 /09/10/bright-lights-big-profits/#46d3c9be50ba.

4. If you really care, one candela is the light production of a standard whale-wax candle, 7/8 of an inch in diameter and weighing 1/6 of a pound; this determines the candle's density and how fast and bright it burns. Once whale-wax fell out of favor, candelas were redefined in terms of the electromagnetic spectrum (monochromatic radiation at 540 terahertz with an intensity of 1/683 watt per steradian)—but all that was a mathematical way of describing the output of the same old candle. Aren't you glad you asked?

5. The one unit square, one unit from the source point, also defines the steradian, or "solid angle," used for measuring directional intensity. The steradian is a cone or pyramid with its tip at the source point; its base is the one-by-one surface. The point is considered to be the center of a sphere with a one-unit radius, and the steradian is a wedge taken out of that sphere.

6. J. F. Simard, *Lumec Chronicles*, Spring 2001, 1 (editor's comments in manufacturer's newsletter).

7. P. Cinzano et al., *The First World Atlas of the Artificial Night Sky Brightness*, 13 Aug 2001, Royal Astronomical Society, available in high resolution from www.lightpollution.it/dmsp/.

8. Deborah Schoch, "Fading Glory," *Los Angeles Times*, 20 Oct 2003, D-1.

9. For information on NPS initiatives to protect night skies in the parks, visit www.nps.gov/subjects/nightskies/wilderness .htm.

10. R. G. Stevens and M. S. Rea, "Light in the Built Environment: Potential Role of Circadian Disruption in Endocrine Disruption and Breast Cancer," *Cancer Causes and Control* 12, no. 3 (Apr 2001): 279–87, www.ncbi.nlm.nih.gov/.

11. Several articles by Itai Kloog and colleagues have appeared in the journal *Chronobiology International*; see, for example, "Light at Night Co-distributes with Incident Breast But Not Lung Cancer in the Female Population of Israel," vol. 25, no. 1 (2008): 65–81, and "Does the Modern Urbanized Sleeping Habitat Post a Breast Cancer Risk?," vol. 28, no. 1 (2011): 76–80. Much of the content of this journal relates to light and lighting as they affect the biological clock. See also note 18 below.

12. S. Davis and D. K. Mirick, "Circadian Disruption, Shift Work and the Risk of Cancer: A Summary of the Evidence and Studies in Seattle," *Cancer Causes and Control* 17, no. 4 (May 2006): 539–45.

13. Richard A. Stone, "Infant Myopia and Night Lighting," *Nature*, 13 May 1999.

14. See www.cureresearch.com/i/insomnia/stats.htm; 2003 figures.

15. Stevens and Rea, "Light in the Built Environment." Software to adjust color temperature of computer and phone screens to mimic circadian cycles is available from f.lux at https://just getflux.com/ and is beginning to be built into smartphones.

16. International Dark-Sky Association, "Visibility, Environmental, and Astronomical Issues Associated with Blue-Rich White Outdoor Lighting," 4 May 2010. A five-page executive summary is titled "Seeing Blue." Both are available for download at www.darksky.org.

17. American Medical Association, Council on Science and Public Health, "Human and Environmental Effects of Light Emitting Diode (LED) Community Lighting," CSAPH Report 2-A-16. Link at www.darksky.org.

18. Harald Stark et al., "Nighttime Photochemistry: Nitrate Radical Destruction by Anthropogenic Light Sources," paper presented at the fall meeting of the American Geophysical Union, Dec 2010, www.researchgate.net/publication/252609588 _Nighttime_photochemistry_nitrate_radical_destruction_by _anthropogenic_light_sources.

19. Nina Bassuk, personal communication.

20. I. Kloog, B. Portnov, and A. Haim, "Light Pollution as a Risk Factor for Breast Cancer: A GIS-Assisted Case Study," 21 Jun 2005, conference paper, available at http://slideplayer.com /slide/8955928/.

21. For the Exeter research, see Jonathan Bennie et al., "Ecological Effects of Artificial Light at Night on Wild Plants," *Journal of Ecology* 104, no. 3 (2016): 611–20. For species vulnerability to light and other detail data, see William Chaney, "Does Night Lighting Harm Trees?," 2002, www.extension.purdue .edu/extmedia/fnr/fnr-faq-17.pdf, online only, from Purdue University, Department of Forestry and Natural Resources.

22. Catherine Rich and Travis Longcore, eds., *Ecological Consequences of Artificial Night Lighting* (Washington DC: Island Press, 2006).

23. WTC photo at www.flap.org/.

24. Erin Weaver, "Building Owners Responsible for Bird Deaths, Judge Rules," *EBN*, Apr 2013, 40. The ruling was based on including light as a pollutant. In the United States, we can't even get agreement that CO_2 is a pollutant!

25. Study reported in Ben Harder, "Light All Night: New Images Quantify a Nocturnal Pollutant," *Science News* 169, no. 11 (18 Mar 2006): 170.

26. Gábor Horváth et al., "Polarized Light Pollution: A New Kind of Ecological Photopollution," *Frontiers in Ecology and the Environment* 7, no. 6 (Aug 2009): 317–25.

27. Karen Peterson, "Night-Sky Law Needs to Be Tougher, Researchers Say," *Santa Fe New Mexican*, 8 Apr 1999, B-4. Exemptions, from prisons to ordinary billboards, are commonly pushed through by lobbyists.

28. J. F. Simard, *Lumec Chronicles* (manufacturer's newsletter), Spring 2001, 9. Lumec's report did not claim that semi-cutoff designs were always better at reducing reflection.

29. Based on the fact that new lamps *save* up to 90 percent; see the multi-LED bulb description in this chapter.

30. Charles W. Harris and Nicholas T. Dines, *Timesaver Standards for Landscape Architecture* (New York: McGraw-Hill, 1988), 54011–13.

31. All D. Crawford information is from his videotaped lecture at University of New Mexico, Albuquerque, n.d., Santa Fe Public Library collection.

32. See www.lumileds.com/horticulture/applications-with-leds/#greenhouses.

33. Alex Wilson, "Disposal of Fluorescent Lamps and Ballasts," *EBN*, Oct 1997, 1, 9–14.

34. Janet Lennox Moyer, *The Landscape Lighting Book* (New York: Wiley, 1992). This has a truly remarkable amount of detail on materials, operation, and design.

35. Figures are for 2017; footing, wiring, and electrical cost based on typical US pricing. Information is from a solar manufacturer with intent to persuade, but appears credible: www.engoplanet.com/single-post/2016/03/19/Solar-Street-Light-price-Why-cost-of-installing-solar-street-light-makes-sense.

36. The manufacturing branch, formerly SolarCap Infinity, was purchased by SolaRight in 2015. See www.businesswire.com/news/home/20150721005233/en/SolaRight-Lighting-LLC-Acquires-SolarCap-Infinity.

37. See www.osram.com/osram_com/press/press-releases/_trade_press/2014/osram-constructs-the-worlds-most-efficient-led-lamp/index.jsp.

38. Harris and Dines, *Timesaver*.

39. Part of discussion in Brent Ehrlich, "The Death and Rebirth of DC Power," *EBN*, Aug 2016, 8.

40. Tristan Roberts, "Full Line of Residential LED Lighting Arrives" (Product Review), *EBN*, Jul 2006.

41. Seong-Rin Lim et al., " Potential Environmental Impacts from the Metals in Incandescent, Compact Fluorescent Lamp (CFL), and Light-Emitting Diode (LED) Bulbs," *Environmental Science and Technology* 47, no. 2 (2013): 1040–47; online at http://pubs.acs.org/doi/pdf/10.1021/es302886m. See also Emily Catacchio, "LEDs Exceed California's Hazardous Waste Standards," *EBN*, Feb 2011, 5. The same test produced almost no violation of federal standards, which consider fewer metals.

42. This is a good example of the difference between efficacy and efficiency, as used in lighting. The efficacy of the LEDs (how much light they put out per watt of energy) remains the same, but the efficiency of the whole fixture (how much light comes out where it is useful) is increased by the reversed-reflector design. This design is also used in high-performance flashlights for emergency rescue personnel (Pelican Products, Torrance CA).

43. Described in an article posted at www.archlighting.com/. See also the lighting chapter in the New York City Department of Transportation's *Street Design Manual*, 2nd ed., www.nyc.gov/html/dot/html/pedestrians/streetdesignmanual.shtml.

Principle 9: Quietly Defend Silence

1. Eric Rosenberg and Ilene J. Busch-Vishniac, "Continued Investigation of Noise Reduction by a Random-Edge Noise Barrier," paper presented at the 133rd Acoustical Society of America Meeting, State College PA, 17 Jun 1997.

2. Associated Press, "Population Boom Makes for a Noisy Planet," *Santa Fe New Mexican*, 27 Jun 1999, A-1, A-3. Ironi-cally, the next item on the page with this article was a small ad headed "Hearing Loss? 24-hour recorded message."

3. Two documentary films have been made about sound and those who track it. *Soundtracker*, from Nick Sherman in 2010, follows George Hempton in the wild for a month. *In Pursuit of Silence*, a 2017 release by Patrick Shen, visually tours varied soundscapes. Both are available on DVD, with Shen's also downloadable.

4. Information on the description and measurement of noise is compiled from the following sources: Peter Yost, "Building Green, Quietly," *EBN*, Jan 2001, 1; www.lsu.edu/deafness/HearingRange.html (hearing ranges for humans and other species); http://hypertextbook.com/; and http://encarta.msn.com/. There is some variation in the range-of-hearing estimates, and there are varying conventions on exactly what pitch a musical instrument is tuned to.

5. Ron Chepesiuk, "Decibel Hell: The Effects of Living in a Noisy World," *Environmental Health Perspectives* 113, no. 1 (Jan 2005): A34–A41, PMC1253729 (see the following paragraph for an explanation of PMC archive numbers). Chepesiuk quotes Les Blomberg of Noise Pollution Clearinghouse as noting that even ordinary cars today have far bigger speakers than those used in concerts by the Beatles!

    An excellent source of information on noise pollution is *Environmental Health Perspectives, the peer-reviewed journal of the National Institute of Environmental Health Sciences*. This chapter relies on several *EHP* articles, cited as print publications plus an identifying "PMC number" for each article, as archived online by PubMed Central. These numbers take the format PMC9999999. To access the full text of archived *EHP* articles, enter www.ncbi.nlm.nih.gov/pmc/articles/ followed by the article's PMC number and a slash (/). A list of issues is at www.ncbi.nlm.nih.gov/pmc/journals/253/; scroll to a year, and select a monthly issue. The main website for *EHP* is https://ehp.niehs.nih.gov/; for the institute, www.niehs.nih.gov/.

6. See www.lsu.edu/deafness/HearingRange.html.

7. A "panel" refers here to a noise barrier of a specific material and a specific thickness. In some cases, the shape or design of the panel also influences NRC and STC ratings, for example, if the surface is rough or if there are openings through the panel.

8. Charles George Ramsey, Harold Reeve Sleeper, and John Ray Hoke Jr., *Architectural Graphic Standards*, 9th ed. (New York: Wiley, 1994), 59, tables.

9. Charles W. Harris and Nicholas T. Dines, *Timesaver Standards for Landscape Architecture* (New York: McGraw-Hill, 1988), 660–65, tables.

10. The January 2005 issue of *Environmental Health Perspectives* included several articles that inform this chapter (see note 5 above, on PMC numbers for online archive retrieval): Wolfgang Babisch, "Guest Editorial: Noise and Health," *Environmental Health Perspectives* 113, no. 1 (Jan 2005): A14–A15, PMC1253720; Erin E. Dooley, "EHPnet: Noise Pollution Clearinghouse," *Environmental Health Perspectives* 113, no. 1 (Jan 2005): A27, PMC1253724; Ron Chepesiuk, "Decibel Hell: The Effects of Living in a Noisy World," *Environmental Health Perspectives* 113, no. 1 (Jan 2005): A34–A41, PMC1253729;

Charles W. Schmidt, "Noise That Annoys: Regulating Unwanted Sound," *Environmental Health Perspectives* 113, no. 1 (Jan 2005): A42–A44, PMC1253730; John Manuel, "Clamoring for Quiet: New Ways to Mitigate Noise," *Environmental Health Perspectives* 113, no. 1 (Jan 2005): A46–A49, PMC1253731.

11. A discussion of the loss of the EPA noise program is at http://airportnoiselaw.org/epaonac3.html. The Airport Noise Law site, though awkwardly organized and incompletely indexed, still offers a wealth of information on noise legislation, activism, and other topics.

12. Some research on the subject of bioacoustics, related to endangered birds and legislation to protect them from excessive noise, has been done at the Transportation Noise Control Center, a research institute at the University of California, Davis.

13. For those interested in this topic, search the Web for LFAS (low-frequency active sonar).

14. Paul A. Kaseloo and Katherine O. Tyson, *Synthesis of Noise Effects on Wildlife Populations*, report HEP-06-016 (Washington DC: Federal Highway Administration, 2004), www.fhwa.dot.gov/ENVIRONMENT/noise/effects/intro.htm. See also Yost, "Building Green, Quietly." In 2011, a seventy-one-page annotated bibliography of research on noise and wildlife was authored by members of the National Park Service's Natural Sounds Program. Available by e-mail (not download); see www.nps.gov/subjects/sound/index.htm (a site useful for information about the National Park Service's work on noise pollution and soundscapes).

15. Ronald P. Larkin, "Human Noise and Wildlife," 1995, Illinois Natural History Survey, http://wwx.inhs.illinois.edu/resources/inhsreports/jan-feb95/human/.

16. Note that recording equipment and speakers are designed with human hearing in mind and in this sense may "filter" the original sounds. A recording might sound lifelike to humans and still be very different in the ranges perceived by animals.

17. Yost, "Building Green, Quietly." Remember that a ten-decibel reduction would indicate noise levels cut in half, and six decibels represents much more than 60 percent of that.

18. Harris and Dines, *Timesaver*, 660–63, and FHWA online information (see www.fhwa.dot.gov/, and click to the "environment/noise" section). Weight per surface area can be increased either by using denser materials or by using a thicker wall, or both. Some older sources indicate that as little as 1.3 pounds per square foot is sufficient for sound barriers, but this appears to be inaccurate according to current publications. The FHWA indicates that a wall that blocks line of sight to the road (usually about six to eight feet tall) offers 5 dB reduction; that for each additional meter (or yard) in height, about 1.5 dB additional reduction can be achieved; and that the maximum feasible reduction is 10 dB. This strongly suggests that a twenty-foot-tall wall is the maximum useful height, because by the height criteria just noted, it will achieve 10 dB reduction.

19. Harris and Dines, *Timesaver*, 660–63.

20. Rosenberg and Busch-Vishniac, "Continued Investigation of Noise Reduction."

21. FHWA online information (see www.fhwa.dot.gov/ and click to "environment/noise" section). The FHWA considers parallel walls to degrade each other's performance unless they are ten times as far apart as either wall's height. Noise walls are typically at least twelve feet tall, which is the equivalent of one traffic lane.

22. Some of the best research on this subject is by K. R. Fyfe of the University of Alberta, Canada. A. Muradali and K. R. Fyfe, "Accurate Barrier Modeling in the Presence of Atmospheric Effects," *Applied Acoustics* 56, no. 3 (Mar 1999): 157–82, https://doi.org/10.1016/S0003-682X(98)00023-1. Most design-engineering methods still ignore atmospheric decreases when estimating noise barrier effects. The FHWA's approach acknowledges the effects, but merely recommends that measurements of noise not be made when the wind is blowing!

23. Harris and Dines, *Timesaver*, 660–66.

24. Yost, "Building Green, Quietly."

25. I have to boast: our second edition commented as follows about Acoustiblok: "Available in a number of fabric colors, it seems likely that creative printing techniques could be used to expand visual design possibilities."

26. US Patent 20030006090 A1, Broadband noise-suppressing barrier.

27. Heather Hansman, "This Crazy Land Art Deflects Noise from Amsterdam's Airport," *Smithsonian*, 27 May 2015, www.smithsonianmag.com/innovation/crazy-land-art-deflects-noise-from-amsterdams-airport-180955398/.

28. S. Meiarashi, "Porous Elastic Road Surface as an Ultimate Highway Noise Measure," the 22nd World Road Congress, Oct 2003. Download from the Public Works Research Institute, www.pwri.go.jp/team/zairyou/pers_final.pdf.

29. Katie Valentine, "Netherlands Company Introduces Plastic Roads That Are More Durable, Climate Friendly Than Asphalt," ThinkProgress.org, 22 Jul 2015, https://thinkprogress.org/netherlands-company-introduces-plastic-roads-that-are-more-durable-climate-friendly-than-asphalt-ecb7c2a11a50; Yara Salem, "From Plastic to Pavement: Another Example of Creative Waste Management," *Sustainable Cities* (World Bank blog), 29 Sep 2014, http://blogs.worldbank.org/sustainablecities/plastic-pavement-another-example-creative-waste-management; Sagar Pokharel, "Utilization of Waste Plastics in Construction of Flexible Pavements (Re-use of Waste Plastics)," www.slideshare.net/sagar22account/utilization-of-plastics-in-flexible-pavement; Dykes Paving, "Texas Roads Made from Plastic," www.dykespaving.com/blog/texas-roads-made-from-plastic.

30. There is, however, a rare psychological gift called synesthesia in which people see specific colors simultaneously with hearing certain sounds. Does noise torment them like an allergy?

31. Ramsey, Sleeper, and Hoke, *Architectural Graphic Standards*, 59, table.

32. For an overview, see Won-Pyoung Kang, Hak-Ryong Moon, and You-Jin Lim, "Analysis on Technical Trends of Active Noise Cancellation for Reducing Road Traffic Noise," *Journal of Emerging Trends in Computing and Information Sciences* 5, no. 4 (Apr 2014): 286–91.

33. This information is from an excellent FAQ site about active noise control, http://chrisruckman.com/ancfaq.htm. It was last updated in 2007, so it is not completely current with emerging research, but it readably explains the concept and its

history. It *can* be downloaded, if you want to read a font that looks like it's from a dot-matrix printer; much easier to read on-screen. For book-length detail, fairly accessible to the layperson, see Colin H. Hansen, *Understanding Active Noise Cancellation* (Boca Raton FL: CRC Press, 2002).

34. Reported by Noise Free America on its website, www.noise free.org/, this distinction was the result of a national poll.

35. Outdoor Power Equipment Institute, "Leaf Blower Facts," http://opei.org/leaf-blower-facts/.

36. This statistic is from the website of IAC Acoustics, www.in dustrialacoustics.com/.

37. The Bush administration, predictably, pushed to rescind the ban.

38. Associated Press, "Park Service Officials Want to Get a Word In: 'Quiet,'" *Santa Fe New Mexican*, 3 Jul 1999, A-1, A-2.

39. Information from Noise Free America's home page, www .noisefree.org/.

40. John Fecht, "New York Mayor in Fight Against Noise Pollution," *City Mayors*, 10 Jun 2004.

41. Quoted in Phillip Langdon, "Noisy Highways," *Atlantic Monthly*, Aug 1997. Full text online at www.theatlantic.com /issues/97aug/langdon.htm.

Principle 10: Maintain to Sustain

1. C. Milesi et al., "A Strategy for Mapping and Modeling the Ecological Effects of US Lawns," conference paper, International Society for Photogrammetry and Remote Sensing, Tempe AZ, 14–16 Mar 2005. The other estimates are cited in Milesi.

2. Research by University of Wisconsin landscape architecture professor Darrel Morrison, reported in John Berger, *Restoring the Earth: How Americans Are Working to Renew Our Damaged Environment* (New York: Knopf, 1985), 124.

3. Gwendolyn Bounds, "Organic Lawn Care: It's Not for Wimps," *Wall Street Journal*, 7 Oct 2006, P5. Bounds's estimate of the total horticulture-care industry is $9 billion greater than a 1999 estimate used in this book's first edition.

4. Owen Dell and Melanie Yanke, *Recent Writings*, brochure published by Dell's County Landscape & Design, 2004, www .owendell.com/. Dell has been active in promoting a sustainability pledge among southern California landscape professionals. For a firm known for full implementation of fossil-free work methods, see www.terranovalandscaping.com /what-is-fossil-free-landscaping/.

5. Helen H. Whiffen, "Landscape Maintenance Takes Energy: Use It Wisely," *Energy Efficiency and Environmental News* (University of Florida Extension), Feb 1993. Still one of the best attempts to summarize landscape maintenance energy consumption—there should be more studies like this for each bioregion.

6. For example, the Outdoor Power Equipment Institute commissioned a study showing that lawns captured "four times more carbon from the air than is produced by the engine of today's typical lawnmower." Ranajit (Ron) Sahu, "Technical Assessment of the Carbon Sequestration Potential of Managed Turfgrass in the United States," http://opei.org /content/uploads/2014/02/TurfGrassSahu.pdf. OPEI and various turf promotion groups have quoted this report widely (http://opei.org/new-study-shows-responsibly-managed -lawns-reduce-carbon-footprint/). With due respect to a consultant who has done good work for environmental activist

associations as well as industry, OPEI's summary glosses over the obvious question of *how much* lawn area or mower operation time is compared to estimated sequestration to arrive at the "four times more" assertion. OPEI's article also uses bare soil as a basis for comparison (obscuring the fact that other vegetative cover may be far more effective than lawns at sequestration—see note 7 below). Dr. Sahu himself, quoted in the OPEI piece, calls well-maintained lawns only "a decent foot soldier in our quest to reduce our carbon footprint," suggesting that there are better weapons. Whether OPEI intended it or not, "X times more than an unspecified alternative" and "great because better than nothing" are both classic greenwash memes. A related document is http://opei.org/value -of-lawns-fact-sheet/, which in turn refers to a publication by CAST (Council for Agricultural Science and Technology), "Water Quality and Quantity Issues for Turfgrasses in Urban Landscapes." CAST is an agricultural lobbying organization and, while stating the goal of "science-based" policy, leans heavily toward emphasizing "innovation," including genetic engineering of crops, while downplaying concerns about turf and turf-care chemicals. All of these reports should be considered, as some of their assertions are at least partially valid, but should be analyzed with care and critical thinking.

7. US total for 2014, from US Environmental Protection Agency, "U.S. Greenhouse Gas Inventory Report: 1990–2014," www .epa.gov/ghgemissions/us-greenhouse-gas-inventory-report -1990-2014.

8. Wesley Groesbeck and Jan Striefel, *The Resource Guide to Sustainable Landscapes and Gardens*, 2nd ed. (Salt Lake City UT: Environmental Resources, 1995), 39.

9. Briggs and Stratton 6.5 OHV Intek. Its design also made it impossible to change the sparkplug without interference from an air-filter cover, a throttle cable, and the engine housing. Design flaws like these afflict most manufacturers occasionally; sustainability makes quality engineering imperative. Briggs and Stratton (as noted in Principle 7) has actively opposed pollution and efficiency regulations for two-stroke machines.

10. USDA Animal and Plant Health Inspection Service, publication 1329, n.d. For spreading gypsy moth, and potentially for other major pests, the USDA has the authority to level significant civil penalties.

11. Fred Lambert, "Tesla Model 3: Perfect Production Execution Means Around 80,000 Vehicles in 2017," *Electrek*, 27 Feb 2017, https://electrek.co/2017/02/27/tesla-model-3-per fect-execution-production-2017/.

12. Jethro Mullen, "Elon Musk: Tesla Will Reveal Semi-Truck 'Beast' Next Month," *CNN Tech*, 14 Sep 2017, http://money .cnn.com/2017/09/13/technology/tesla-semi-truck-octo ber-elon-musk/index.html.

13. Information in this section is primarily from the United Soybean Board, a major bio-based product marketing and research fund (www.unitedsoybean.org/). Other agricultural crops can also be used for bio-based products. The United Soybean website and publications cite a large number of federal studies (DOE and USDA, primarily) for statistics quoted here. For details, see the board's website, and its pamphlet *The Soy Products Guide: A Listing of Soy Industrial Products*.

14. See "Land Under Pressure: Global Impacts of the EU Bioeconomy," a thirty-six-page report by Friends of the Earth

Europe. It focuses on EU policies and economics but includes global information; the arguments apply to the United States as well. Available at www.foeeurope.org/sites/default/files /resource_use/2016/land-under-pressure-report-global-im pacts-eu-bioeconomy.pdf; appendices (called "annexes") are available through a link in the main document.

15. Information on the Aberdeen paint standards, and on Environmentally Preferable Purchasing programs, is from US EPA publication EPA742-R-99-005, "Painting the Town Green: Aberdeen Proving Ground's Paint Pilot Project." See www.epa .gov/sites/production/files/2015-05/documents/paint.pdf. The estimate of painted square footage is a rough one, based on 14 million square feet of building floor space, and assuming an average ten-foot wall height, painted inside and out. It is intended only to give a sense of scale to the overall savings quoted.

16. Groesbeck and Striefel, *Resource Guide*, 39.

17. Bounds, "Organic Lawn Care."

18. City of Boulder (CO) Environmental Affairs office pamphlet *Take Control with Integrated Pest Management*, Aug 2001. Pamphlet cites "Natural and Environmental Resources Report, Jan/ Feb 1995" as the source of the statistics quoted—author and publisher unknown.

19. BASMAA (Bay Area Stormwater Management Agencies Association), from its executive director, Geoff Brosseau. Similar results have been found for many other regions.

20. Candace Pearson, "Grounds Maintenance Implicated in Butterfly Extinctions," *EBN*, Aug 2013, 15. The US Fish and Wildlife Service's website refuses to display the original article as of April 2017; information extinction?

21. This concept, similar to Xeriscape zoning, was developed by Phil Boise, Ag Ecology Consulting, Gaviota CA, and published as a working paper by the National Foundation for IPM Education. Boise calls his system "PHAER Zones," for Pesticide Hazard and Exposure Reduction. More details may be available by doing an Internet search using this phrase.

22. Diatoms are tiny algae, whose beautiful silica-based skeletons are minutely sharp. These nonpoisonous shells, in what is called diatomaceous earth, are applied as pest deterrent around plants.

23. Arthur C. Costonis, "Tree Injection: Perspective, Macro-Injection/Micro-Injection," *Journal of Arboriculture* 7, no. 10 (Oct 1981): 275–77; Deborah G. McCullough et al., "Evaluation of Trunk Injections for Control of Emerald Ash Borer," publication of US Department of Agriculture, Forest Service, Northern Research Station, available online at www.nrs.fs.fed .us/pubs/jrnl/2005/nc_2005_mccullough_001.pdf; Daniel A. Herms et al., "Insecticide Options for Protecting Ash Trees from Emerald Ash Borer," North Central IPM Center Bulletin, 2nd ed.

24. See, for example, Janet Hartin, Dennis Pittenger, and J. Michael Henry, "Best Management Practices to Reduce Production of Organic Materials in Landscape Plantings," Jun 2001, California Integrated Waste Management Board publication 443-01-022, www.calrecycle.ca.gov/Publications/Documents /905/44301022.pdf.

25. Gessner G. Hawley, *The Condensed Chemical Dictionary*, 10th ed. (New York: Van Nostrand Reinhold, 1981), entry for Phosphate Rock, 809.

26. Janet Hartin and Ali Harivandi, "Reusing Turfgrass Clippings to Improve Turfgrass Health and Performance in Central and Northern California," Jun 2001, California Integrated Waste Management Board publication, www.calrecycle.ca.gov/Publi cations/Documents/Organics/44301021.pdf.

27. Groesbeck and Striefel, *Resource Guide*, 39.

28. Russell Beatty, "Prescribed Grazing," *LAM*, Mar 2005, 50.

29. James Urban, "Battery Park City's Invisible Landscape," *LAM*, Feb 2004.

30. The stables are reportedly to be moved, an example of the extra complexity involved in on-site or near-site sourcing of materials.

31. James Urban, "Organic Maintenance: Mainstream at Last?" *LAM*, Mar 2004.

32. Candace Pearson, "EPA Region 8 Building Fares Well Under Performance-Based Contract," *EBN*, Sep 2013, 18.

33. Information on current practice with maintenance plans is from interviews with Leslie Sauer of Andropogon or summarized from Jo Kellum, "The Legacy of Design," *LAM*, Sep 1999, 108. Kellum refers to the difficulty of maintenance coordination as being similar to herding cats.

Principle 11: Demonstrate Performance, Learn from Failure

1. Hinckley Allen Construction Newsletter, 31 Mar 2015. Hinckley Allen is a construction law firm with CT, RI, NH, NY, and PA offices. Peter J. Martin and Jared Cohane, "Fear and Loathing: The Specter of Perpetual Liability When Working for Municipal Owners," www.hinckleyallen.com /publications/fear-and-loathing-the-specter-of-perpetual -liability-when-working-for-municipal-owners/. Laws exempting the state from the statute of limitations are called "nullum tempus" statutes and vary by state. Design and construction professionals should determine whether their state has such a law. For a state-by-state review, see https://web .archive.org/web/20140108165345/http://web.uslaw.org /wp-content/uploads/2013/08/Nullum_Tempus_Com pendium_of_Law.pdf.

2. "The History of the Good Housekeeping Seal," www.good housekeeping.com/institute/about-the-institute/a16509 /good-housekeeping-seal-history/, with additional information from the Wikipedia entry on GH.

3. The story is described in detail at https://en.wikipedia.org /wiki/Great_Baltimore_Fire.

4. Cited in Stephanie Vierra, "Green Building Standards and Certification Systems," updated 9 Dec 2016, WBDG, www .wbdg.org/resources/green-building-standards-and-certifi cation-systems. WBDG is the Whole Building Design Guide (www.wbdg.org), a useful program of the National Institute of Building Sciences in Washington DC (www.nibs.org).

5. Studies of constructability (on video as well as in print) are available from the Construction Industry Institute, Austin TX, 512-232-2000, or http://construction-institute.org/.

6. See Alex Wilson, "Green Builder Programs Proliferating," *EBN* 4, no. 1 (1995): 6–7.

7. Release history: LEED 1.0, essentially a pilot, was released in 1998. An "expert charrette" (in which I took part) significantly revised the system for release as LEED 2.0 in March 2000. A further update, LEED 2.1, is primarily about streamlining the documentation process to overcome criticism that

the bureaucratic effort was too ponderous. The USGBC planned to revise the system every three years. LEED 3.0 was expected in 2003 but was delayed until 2007. Like Microsoft, USGBC inserted LEED 2009 between v3 and v4. LEED v4 was released in 2013; applications under LEED 2009 were accepted through 2016, with LEED v4 taking over in 2017.

8. Go to www.usgbc.org, website of the US Green Building Council, select Resources, and then search for checklists. Sandra Mendler and William Odell, *The HOK Guidebook to Sustainable Design* (New York: Wiley, 2000) discusses early LEED and is an excellent general reference.

9. ASHRAE = American Society of Heating, Refrigerating, and Air-Conditioning Engineers. ASTM = American Society for Testing and Materials.

10. See www.usgbc.org/articles/usgbc-statistics. Actual certification is now by GBCI, the Green Building Certification Institute, spun off from USGBC. The Certified Professional has split into LEED Green Associate and LEED Advanced Professional, and can be earned in one of five specialties. See https://new.usgbc.org/credentials.

11. Nadav Malin, "Green Globes Emerges to Challenge LEED," *EBN* 14, no. 3 (Mar 2005), online at www.buildinggreen.com/.

12. Candace Pearson and Paula Melton, "ANSI to Pilot Greenwash-Busting Eco-Label Program," *EBN*, Apr 2014, 18. Underwriters Laboratories was a nonprofit from its founding in 1894 through 2011, after which it became for-profit under the name UL (according to Wikipedia; the entry on UL has a useful long list of "similar organizations" for anyone deeply interested). UL Environment has offered green certification of low-emissions products (GreenGuard) and multiple-criterion sustainability (EcoLogo) since about 2011.

13. Jason Grant, "Greenwash Action: Defending Real Sustainability Standards," *Earth Island Journal*, Winter 2015, www.earthisland.org/journal/index.php/eij/article/greenwash_action/.

14. Bernard R. Fortunato III et al., "Identification of Safety Risks for High-Performance Sustainable Construction Projects," *Journal of Construction Engineering and Management* 138, no. 4 (Apr 2012): 499–508.

15. Shari Shapiro, "LEED Lawsuit Gets Dismissed, but Energy Efficiency Fight Goes On," GreenBiz.com, 19 Aug 2011, www.greenbiz.com/blog/2011/08/19/leed-lawsuit-gets-dismissed-energy-efficiency-fight-goes.

16. Shari Shapiro, "Decision in BIA v. Washington Does Not Clarify When Energy Efficient Codes Are Preempted by Federal Law," *Green Building Law* (blog), 13 Jul 2012, www.greenbuildinglawblog.com/articles/litigation/.

17. Details on these programs are not included for several reasons. SITES is part of the LEED behemoth and is the most widespread in the United States, at least. The text of ASHRAE, a large proportion of which is not relevant to landscapes, is only available by paying $128. The Living Challenge programs are hidden many layers deep (download basics from https://living-future.org/lcc/basics/), suggesting a need for a Living Website Challenge.

18. Excel "checklist" from www.asla.org/uploadedFiles/CMS/AboutJoin/Copy%20of%20SITESv2_Scorecard%20Summary.pdf.

19. Truth in advertising: Although I consulted on both the early landscape criteria in LEED and later on SITES, this book's earlier editions were among the titles considered insufficiently academic to include.

20. John de Graaf and David K. Batker, *What's the Economy For, Anyway? Why It's Time to Stop Chasing Growth and Start Pursuing Happiness* (New York: Bloomsbury Press, 2011). In addition to being the source concerning RFK's comments, this is a book of immense importance in trying to understand why the current world economy works so blindly against sustainability—and happiness.

21. "HOBO Data Loggers: Not Just for Researchers Anymore," *EBN*, Nov 2012, 7. HOBO is a brand of the Onset Computer Corporation.

22. Panelists were Tom Ryan, FASLA, Principal, Ryan Associates; Steven Apfelbaum, Principal Ecologist, Applied Ecological Services; Duke Bitsko, Director of Interdisciplinary Design, Chester Engineers; and Robert Pine, FASLA, Pine & Swallow Environmental. Each gave me a generous interview for this book. My summarizing and interpreting of their thoughts should not be blamed on them, however.

23. The four articles, all in 2016 issues of *LAM*, were "Life and Limb: Four Principals Talk About Risk Management" (Oct, p. 86); "The Right Path" (Nov, p. 48); "The Right Ingredients: Why Biofiltration Sometimes Fails" (Nov, p. 44); and "Weather-Smithing" (ASLA Professional Award, Research; Sep, p. 126).

24. Cain Burdeau, Associated Press, "Engineering Society Under Fire," *Santa Fe New Mexican*, 26 Mar 2008. Online under a slightly different title at http://newsok.com/article/3220872.

25. See note 15 above.

26. Available online at http://theaiatrust.com/filecabinet/Sustainability-risks-2013.pdf. The report is a white paper from insurer Victor O. Schinnerer & Company but not freely available from the company's website. It was written by Kristin Ballobin, 2008 Milton F. Lunch Research Fellow. *Please, oh please, let Milton's middle name be "Free"!*

27. S. T. Lovell and D. M. Johnston, "Designing Landscapes for Performance Based on Emerging Principles in Landscape Ecology," *Ecology and Society* 14, no. 1 (2009): 44, www.ecologyandsociety.org/vol14/iss1/art44/.

Sustaining Principles, Evolving Efforts

1. Edward Tenner, *Why Things Bite Back: Technology and the Revenge of Unintended Consequences* (New York: Vintage, 1996). Tenner is a former science and history editor at Princeton University Press. His lively account of technology proves you should be careful about what you wish for.

2. A. Phillips, "International Policies and Landscape Protection," in *Landscape and Sustainability*, ed. J. F. Benson and M. H. Roe (London: Spon Press, 2000). Other chapters in this book reinforce the concept that landscapes (often viewed bioregionally) are unifying constructs within which sustainable policies have the greatest chance at success.

3. Arthur Neslen and Karl Mathiesen, "China, EU, and Canada to Take Lead on Climate at Montreal Meeting," *Climate Home News*, 13 Sep 2017, www.climatechangenews.com/2017

/09/13/china-eu-canada-take-lead-climate/; Lisa Friedman and Brad Plumer, "U.S. Governors at U.N. Assembly: 'You Have Allies' on Climate Change," *New York Times*, 18 Sep 2017, www.nytimes.com/2017/09/18/climate/climate-change-unga-governors.html.

4. P. H. Ray and S. R. Anderson, *The Cultural Creatives: How 50 Million People Are Changing the World* (New York: Three Rivers Press, 2000). See also James Richards, "Placemaking for the Creative Class," *LAM*, Feb 2007, 32.

5. Malcolm Gladwell, *The Tipping Point: How Little Things Can Make a Big Difference* (New York: Back Bay Books, 2000).

6. Lao Tzu. *Tao Te Ching*, translated by Gia-fu Feng and Jane English. (New York: Vintage, 1997). "Deal with problems when they are small" is a central tenet of this Taoist classic.

7. This concept can be studied in detail through the "soft" martial arts, such as aikido; I have been teaching this discipline for many years and apply it frequently to ecological concepts as well.

8. James Steele, *Sustainable Architecture: Principles, Paradigms, and Case Studies* (New York: McGraw-Hill, 1997), 244.

9. For a summary, see Steele, *Sustainable Architecture*, chapter 1. Construction-specific recommendations were in section 4 of the original report.

10. Sonja Bisbee Wulff, "CSU Students Learn Sustainable Landscape Design at Tropical Resort," *Fort Collins Coloradoan*, 12 Jul 1999, A5.

11. For those deeply interested in the difficulties of defining or communicating about the nature/culture "split," see K. Sorvig, "Nature/Culture/Words/Landscapes," *Landscape Journal* 21, no. 2 (2002): 1–14. Clearer communication about these issues is ever more essential, even in the most pragmatic landscape or planning practice.

Index

Names of individuals, firms, and organizations are in **boldface**; projects and place-names are *italicized*.

Product tradenames are capitalized; please see note at copyright page. Where product and firm names appear to be identical, the most relevant format has been used.

Following a page number, "f" and "t" indicate figures and tables.